Lecture Notes in Artificial Intelligence   5773

Edited by R. Goebel, J. Siekmann, and W. Wahlster

Subseries of Lecture Notes in Computer Science

T0189931

Zsófia Ruttkay
Michael Kipp
Anton Nijholt
Hannes Högni Vilhjálmsson (Eds.)

Intelligent Virtual Agents

9th International Conference, IVA 2009
Amsterdam, The Netherlands, September 14-16, 2009
Proceedings

 Springer

Series Editors

Randy Goebel, University of Alberta, Edmonton, Canada
Jörg Siekmann, University of Saarland, Saarbrücken, Germany
Wolfgang Wahlster, DFKI and University of Saarland, Saarbrücken, Germany

Volume Editors

Zsófia Ruttkay
Anton Nijholt
University of Twente
Department of Computer Science
Human Media Interaction
P.O.Box 217, 7500AE Enschede, The Netherlands
E-mail: {zsofi, anijholt}@cs.utwente.nl

Michael Kipp
DFKI
Campus D3.2, Room +2.10, 66123 Saarbrücken, Germany
E-mail: kipp@dfki.de

Hannes Högni Vilhjálmsson
Reykjavik University
School of Computer Science
Center for Analysis and Design of Intelligent Agents
Kringlan 1, 103 Reykjavik, Iceland
E-mail: hannes@ru.is

Library of Congress Control Number: 2009933885

CR Subject Classification (1998): I.2.11, I.2, H.5, H.4, K.3-4

LNCS Sublibrary: SL 7 – Artificial Intelligence

ISSN   0302-9743
ISBN-10   3-642-04379-8 Springer Berlin Heidelberg New York
ISBN-13   978-3-642-04379-6 Springer Berlin Heidelberg New York

springer.com

© Springer-Verlag Berlin Heidelberg 2009
Printed in Germany

Typesetting: Camera-ready by author, data conversion by Scientific Publishing Services, Chennai, India
Printed on acid-free paper   SPIN: 12758661   06/3180   5 4 3 2 1 0

Preface

Welcome to the proceedings of the 9th International Conference on Intelligent Virtual Agents, held September 14–16, 2009 in Amsterdam, The Netherlands. Intelligent virtual agents (IVAs) are interactive characters that exhibit human-like qualities and communicate with humans or with each other using natural human modalities such as speech and gesture. They are capable of real-time perception, cognition and action, allowing them to participate in a dynamic physical and social environment.

IVA is an interdisciplinary annual conference and the main forum for presenting research on modeling, developing and evaluating IVAs with a focus on communicative abilities and social behavior. The development of IVAs requires expertise in multimodal interaction and several AI fields such as cognitive modeling, planning, vision and natural language processing. Computational models are typically based on experimental studies and theories of human–human and human–robot interaction; conversely, IVA technology may provide interesting lessons for these fields. The realization of engaging IVAs is a challenging task, so reusable modules and tools are of great value. The fields of application range from robot assistants, social simulation and tutoring to games and artistic exploration.

The enormous challenges and diversity of possible applications of IVAs have resulted in an established annual conference. It was started in 1998 as a workshop at the European Conference on Artificial Intelligence on Intelligent Virtual Environments in Brighton, UK, which was followed by a similar one in 1999 in Salford, Manchester. Then dedicated stand-alone IVA conferences took place in Madrid, Spain in 2001, Irsee, Germany in 2003, and Kos, Greece in 2005. Since 2006 IVA has become a full-fledged annual international event, which was first held in Marina del Rey, California, then Paris, France, in 2007, and Tokyo, Japan, in 2008. Since 2005 IVA has also hosted the Gathering of Animated Lifelike Agents (GALA), a festival to showcase state-of-the-art IVAs created by university students, academic or industrial research groups. This year, papers on selected GALA submissions are also included in the IVA proceedings. The current conference represents well the range of expertise, from different scientific and artistic disciplines, and the value of both theoretical and practical work needed to create IVAs which suspend our disbelief.

The special application theme of IVA 2009 was games. The game industry is the source of the world's largest selection of interactive characters. To date, the creation of these characters and their social behavior has largely relied on carefully hand-crafted techniques rather than automation. However, hand-crafted approaches are unlikely to scale to larger environments, grander stories, more players and a greater demand for realism. An ongoing and so far unfulfilled goal of the game industry is to imbue characters with more intelligence and self-determination. IVA 2009 was an opportunity to reveal, tackle and discuss the issues that relate to using IVAs in games, and aimed to strengthen links and the exchange of knowledge between academia and the game industry.

IVA 2009 received altogether 104 submissions. Out of the 72 long paper submissions, only 19 were accepted for the long papers track. Furthermore, there were 30 short papers presented in the single-track paper session and 35 demo and poster papers were on display. Finally, seven GALA papers document some of the work presented in the other categories.

IVA 2009 was locally organized by the Human Media Interaction Group of the University of Twente, and took place in NEMO, the National Science Museum in Amsterdam. We would like to thank the people who contributed to the high scientific quality of the event: the members of the Program Committee for their reviews and the members of the Senior Program Committee for their advice on preparing the event and evaluating the papers. We express our appreciation to Thomas Rist for his sincere selection of the best paper, and to Dirk Heylen for arranging the busy poster and demo session. Special thanks go to Patrick Gebhard, who was always available to assist with the submission and selection process. We acknowledge Jan Miksatko for administrating the conference website. We express our appreciation to the team of local organizers for taking care of the practical matters of the conference, and to the student volunteers for their assistance on the spot. Special thanks go to Lynn Packwood for keeping the financial issues under control. We are grateful for the support of our sponsors, which was essential for making the event happen.

Last but not least, these proceedings represent the scientific work by the participants and the invited speakers of IVA 2009. We thank all of them for their high-quality contributions. We hope that this volume will foster further research on IVAs, and we look forward to hearing of new work at future IVA conferences.

June 2009

Zsófia Ruttkay
Michael Kipp
Anton Nijholt
Hannes Högni Vilhjálmsson

Organization

Conference Chairs

Zsófia Ruttkay	University of Twente, The Netherlands
Michael Kipp	German Research Center for AI (DFKI), Germany
Anton Nijholt	University of Twente, The Netherlands
Hannes Högni Vilhjálmsson	Reykjavík University, Iceland

Senior Program Committee

Elisabeth André	University of Augsburg, Germany
Ruth Aylett	Heriot-Watt University, UK
Marc Cavazza	University of Teesside, UK
Jonathan Gratch	University of Southern California, USA
Stefan Kopp	Bielefeld University, Germany
Jean-Claude Martin	LIMSI-CNRS, France
Patrick Olivier	Newcastle University, UK
Catherine Pelachaud	CNRS, TELECOM-ParisTech, France
Helmut Prendinger	National Institute of Informatics, Japan

Best Paper Chair

Thomas Rist	FH Augsburg, Germany

Submissions Chair

Patrick Gebhard	DFKI, Germany

Poster and Demo Chair

Dirk Heylen	University of Twente, The Netherlands

GALA Chair

Phil Heslop	University of Newcastle, UK

Local Organization Chair

Betsy van Dijk   University of Twente, The Netherlands

Program Committee

Jan Allbeck
Angélica de Antonio
Norman Badler
Dana H. Ballard
Christian Becker-Asano
Kirsten Bergmann
Jonas Beskow
Timothy Bickmore
Marco De Boni
Tony Brooks
Stéphanie Buisine
Lola Cañamero
Phil Carlisle
Peter Cowling
Zhigang Deng
Stephane Donikian
Arjan Egges
Anton Eliens
Magy Seif El-Nasr
Attila Fazekas
Doron Friedman
Sylvie Gibet
Nuria Pelechano Gomez
Alexis Heloir
Dirk Heylen
Katherine Isbister
Toru Ishida
Mitsuru Ishizuka
Ralf Jung
Kostas Karpouzis
Patrick Kenny
Yasuhiko Kitamura
Tomoko Koda
Takanori Komatsu
Nicole Kraemer
Michael Kruppa

James Lester
Ben Lok
Sandy Louchart
Wenji Mao
Andrew Marriot
David Moffat
Louis-Philippe Morency
Hideyuki Nakanishi
Yukiko Nakano
Michael Neff
Toyoaki Nishida
Magalie Ochs
Ana Paiva
Igor Pandzic
Maja Pantic
Sylvie Pesty
Christopher Peters
Paolo Petta
Hannes Pirker
Paul Piwek
Rui Prada
Dennis Reidsma
Matthias Rehm
Mark Riedl
Martin Rumpler
John Shearer
Candy Sidner
Ulrike Spierling
Matthew Stone
Tapio Takala
Daniel Thalmann
Mariët Theune
Kris Thórisson
Rineke Verbrugge
Vinoba Vinayagamoorthy
Seiji Yamada

IVA Steering Committee

Ruth Aylett   Heriot-Watt University, UK
Jonathan Gratch   University of Southern California, USA
Stefan Kopp   Bielefeld University, Germany
Patrick Olivier   University of Newcastle upon Tyne, UK
Catherine Pelachaud   University of Paris 8, INRIA, France

Held in Cooperation with

The American Association of Artificial Intelligence (AAAI)
The European Association for Computer Graphics (EG)
The Association for Computing Machinery (ACM)
Special Interest Group on Artificial Intelligence (SIGART)
Special Interest Group on Computer-Human Interaction (SIGCHI)
Special Interest Group on Computer Graphics (SIGGRAPH)
Cluster of Excellence: Multimodal Computing and Interaction (M2CI)

Sponsored by

Netherlands Organisation for Scientific Research (NWO)
SenterNovem
ESF Research Network COST 2102: Cross-Modal Analysis of Verbal and
    Non-verbal Communication
The City of Amsterdam

Table of Contents

Gesture and Bodily Behavior

Evaluation

Facial Expression and Gaze

Culture, Affect and Empathy

Agents in Virtual Worlds and Games

Tools and Motion Capture

Speech and Dialogue

Posters

GALA Papers

Endowing Virtual Characters with Expressive Conversational Skills

Marilyn A. Walker

University of California, Santa Cruz, Ca. 95060, U.S.A.
mawalker@ucsc.edu

Keywords: Dialogue, Conversation, Personality, Affective Generation.

1 Introduction

When humans interact with one another, socially intelligent conversational behaviors arise from the interaction of a number of different factors: the conversants' personality, cultural knowledge, the ability to observe and reason about social relationships, and the ability to project and detect affective cues. For virtual agents to be socially intelligent, they must have an expressive conversational repertoire. Moreover, scientific progress in this area requires that these expressive capabilities be easily parameterized, to support experimentation, and that at least some of the factors mentioned above be used to control the parameters. In this talk, I describe our research on expressive spoken language generation, and discuss how our work aims for both psychological plausibility and realistic usability. To achieve psychological plausibility we build on theories and detailed studies of human language use, such as the Big Five theory of personality, and Brown and Levinsons theory of politeness [1,2,3]. To achieve realistic usability, we have developed both rule-based and trainable generation methods that can dynamically, and in real time, change an agents linguistic style by modifying the values of these theoretically motivated parameters. This will allow us to experiment with dynamically modifying an agent's linguistic style based on theories of audience design, entrainment and alignment.

We built the first generator based on B&L as part of the VIVA virtual theatre, an application for teaching English as a second language [1]. We recently extended these ideas in the PoLLy system [4], and evaluated human perceptions of the politeness variations that PoLLy can generate, and how these vary across cultures and discourse contexts, encoding relevant factors. See Table 1.

Our work on personality is embodied in PERSONAGE one of the first parameterizable generators based on the Big Five theory, which provides 67 different parameters, controlling utterance length and polarity, lexical, syntactic and pragmatic choice, and rhetorical structure. See Table 2. PERSONAGE's parameters are all motivated by previous corpus-based studies on the linguistic reflexes of personality. Our evaluation experiments show that humans recognize utterances as manifesting the personality that the agent intended.

Zs. Ruttkay et al. (Eds.): IVA 2009, LNAI 5773, pp. 1–2, 2009.

Table 1. Example outputs of POLLY for Politeness Strategies, with average ratings of human judges on politeness perceptions, on a scale from 1 to 5, with 1 = rude and 5 = over-polite, when the utterance was spoken to a Friend (**F**) or a Stranger (**S**)

Strategy	Possible Utterances	F	S
Direct	Chop the onions, Please chop the onions, You could chop the onions. You must chop the onions.	2.3	1.8
Approval	Could you please chop the onions. If you don't mind you can chop the onions.	3.3	2.8
Autonomy	Would it be possible for you to chop the onions. I'm sure you wouldn't mind chopping the onions. Could you possibly chop the onions for me. I know I'm asking you for a big favor but could you please chop the onions. I'm wondering whether it would be possible for you to chop the onions. Would you not like to chop the onions.	3.6	3.1
Indirect	The onions aren't chopped yet. The onions should have been chopped. Someone should have chopped the onions. Someone has not chopped the onions yet.	2.0	1.7

Table 2. Example outputs of PERSONAGE for Extraversion, Emotional Stability and Agreeableness Traits, with perceptual ratings of human judges, on a scale of 1 to 7, with 1 = very low (e.g. introvert) and 7 = very high (e.g. extravert)

Trait	Params	Utterance	Rating
Extraversion	low	Chimichurri Grill isn't as bad as the others.	1.00
	high	I am sure you would like Chimichurri Grill, you know. The food is kind of good, the food is tasty, it has nice servers, it's in Midtown West and it's a Latin American place. Its price is around 41 dollars, even if the atmosphere is poor.	6.33
Emotional stability	low	I am not sure! I mean, Ch-Chimichurri Grill is the only place I would recommend. It's a Latin American place. Err... its price is... it's damn ex-expensive, but it pr-pr-provides like, adequate food, though. It offers bad atmosphere, even if it features nice waiters.	4.00
	high	Let's see what we can find on Chimichurri Grill. Basically, it's the best.	6.00
Agreeableness	low	I mean, Chimichurri Grill isn't as bad as the others. Basically, the staff isn't nasty. Actually, its price is 41 dollars. It's damn costly.	2.00
	high	You want to know more about Chimichurri Grill? I guess you would like it buddy because this restaurant, which is in Midtown West, is a Latin American place with rather nice food and quite nice waiters, you know, okay?	5.75

References

1. Walker, M.A., Cahn, J.E., Whittaker, S.J.: Improvising linguistic style: Social and affective bases for agent personality. In: Proceedings of the 1st Conference on Autonomous Agents, AGENTS 1997, pp. 96–105 (1997)
2. Gupta, S., Walker, M.A., Romano, D.M.: How rude are you?: Evaluating politeness and affect in interaction. In: Proceedings of ACII, pp. 203–217 (2007)
3. Mairesse, F., Walker, M.A.: Trainable generation of Big-Five personality styles through data-driven parameter estimation. In: Proceedings of the 46th Annual Meeting of the Association for Computational Linguistics, ACL (2008)
4. Gupta, S., Walker, M.A., Romano, D.M.: Polly: A conversational system that uses a shared, representation to generate action and social language. In: IJCNLP 2008, The Third International Joint Conference on Natural Language Processing, pp. 203–217 (2008)

Intelligent Expression-Based Character Agent Systems

Steve DiPaola

Simon Fraser University Surrey
250 -13450 102 Avenue
Surrey, BC V3T 0A3 Canada
sdipaola@sfu.ca

1 Parameterized Approach

By using parameterization techniques which model artistic, living or cognitive systems it is becoming possible to create new types of behavior and expression character systems. These techniques are allowing virtual agent creators to incorporate models of expression, emotion, behavior and even human creativity into their work. Additionally, rather than simply using realism as a goal, is it becoming possible to computationally model knowledge from other expression-based sources including artists, musicians and designers, to go beyond communication to creative expression.

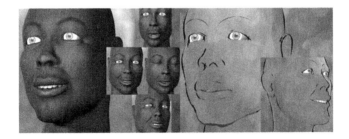

Fig. 1. iFace: parameterized systems for muscle, personality, expression and creative depiction

In this paper, a modular multi-dimensional parameter space for character agents is described as an underlying structure that allows for this knowledge-based approach, especially in the areas of faces[1], characters, personality[2], biological creatures (i.e. whales behaviors in a pod) and depiction as well as higher level constructs like creativity[3]. Once a parameterized knowledge space is created, it optionally possible to control the parameter space with artificial intelligence techniques [4].

The basis of this approach creates a low level set of parameters that are object-oriented, encapsulated and mathematically rigorous—aligned to the knowledge being gathered. These can be thought of as letters in a specialized alphabet, which form the basis for words and phrases (high-level components). These low-level dimensions (e.g. axes) create a large knowledge space that can be accessed through higher-level constructs, which are solely composed of the lower-level parameters often with logical,

Zs. Ruttkay et al. (Eds.): IVA 2009, LNAI 5773, pp. 3–4, 2009.

spatial and temporal attributes. For example, in our iFace facial agent system, low-level muscle parameters can be built up into a more semantic 'smile' parameter and 'smile' with other parameters and temporal considerations can be built up into 'joyousness'. We use this approach with facial agents to create expression, personality and creativity depiction types (figure 1).

Most computer-based communication and information systems, such as websites and applications are informational in nature. However, people use more socially-based techniques to convey their message – they rely on their passion for the subject, narrative techniques, flexible content depending on audience or audience feedback, eye contact, humor and voice modulation. Similarly, expressive character systems used by game and agent designers can introduce more engaging characters that can change expressions more intelligently, demonstrate personality traits and have expressive behavioral interactions with the user and other agents (e.g. whales).

We believe that hierarchical parameterization can provide a comprehensive and effective agent system via: (1) the use of higher-level parameters which apply lower level ones in combination and with constraints, and (2) defining time-based parameters that control actions. For example, we have used this method for: parameters that control how expressions group into behaviors, creating a personality type of a face agent; an artificial intelligence systems for 3D whales that exhibit natural behaviors in a whale pod; and genetic algorithms that work with facial type parameters for evolving faces in the game "The Sims" (figure 2A and 2B).

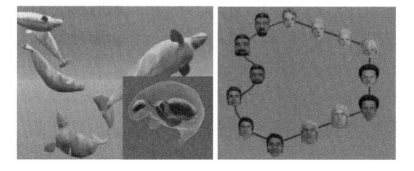

Fig. 2. Artificial intelligence: A) whale pod behavior, B) genetically evolved "The Sims" faces

References

1. Arya, A., DiPaola, S., Parush, A.: Perceptually Valid Facial Expressions for Character-based Applications. International Journal of Computer Games Technology 2009 (2009)
2. Arya, A., DiPaola, S.: Multi-Space Behavioral Model for Face-based Affective Social Agents. Journal of Image and Video Processing 2007, Article ID 48757 (2007)
3. DiPaola, S., Akai, C., Kraus, B.: Experiencing Belugas: Developing an Action Selection-Based Aquarium Interactive. Adaptive Behavior 15(1), 99–113 (2007)
4. DiPaola, S., Gabora, L.: Incorporating Characteristics of Human Creativity into an Evolutionary Art Algorithm. Genetic Prog. & Evolvable Machines 10(2), 97–110 (2009)

Past and Future Challenges in Creating Emotionally-Engaging Real-Time Digital Actors in Videogames

Casey Hudson

BioWare Edmonton, Alberta, Canada
http://www.bioware.com

Abstract. Evolving beyond their origins as a novel pastime, videogames have developed into a medium with tremendous power to entertain and engage players through emotionally powerful interaction. These emotional connections are often powered by the quality of the digital actors that inhabit game worlds and bring them to life. But as technologies for creating lifelike characters escalate, so do the challenges of the creation process. This discussion examines methods used by cutting-edge games to create deeply compelling digital actors, and explores future challenges and solutions that will help videogames unlock the full potential of emotionally engaging human interaction.

Zs. Ruttkay et al. (Eds.): IVA 2009, LNAI 5773, p. 5, 2009.
© Springer-Verlag Berlin Heidelberg 2009

Engagement vs. Deceit: Virtual Humans with Human Autobiographies

Timothy Bickmore, Daniel Schulman, and Langxuan Yin

Northeastern University College of Computer and Information Science,
360 Huntington Ave, WVH202, Boston, MA 02115
{bickmore,schulman,yinlx}@ccs.neu.edu

Abstract. We discuss the ethical and practical issues involved in developing virtual humans that relate personal, fictitious, human autobiographical stories ("back stories") to their users. We describe a virtual human exercise counselor that interacts with users daily to promote exercise, and the integration of a dynamic social storytelling engine used to maintain user engagement with the agent and retention in the intervention. A longitudinal randomized controlled experiment tested user attitudes towards the agent when it presented the stories in first person (as its own history) compared to third person (as happening to humans that it knew). Participants in the first person condition reported enjoying their interactions with the agent significantly more and completed more conversations with the agent, compared to participants in the third person condition, while ratings of agent dishonesty were not significantly different between the groups.

Keywords: Embodied Conversational Agent, Relational Agent, Longitudinal Study.

1 Introduction

One design issue faced by all developers of conversational virtual human agents that interact with users in non-entertainment domains is to what extent the agents should present themselves as actually being human. The decision as to *whether* the agents should be presented as humans at all is moot, since fidelity to human appearance and behavior is the overarching objective of this field of research. However, many researchers feel that they are somehow crossing an ethical boundary if their agents start discussing their childhood home or the fight they just had with their (presumably human) spouse. Just as Deckard in the movie *Blade Runner* was shocked when he learned that replicants (bioengineered anthropomorphic beings) were being created with autobiographical memories, many people seem to recoil at the thought of a computer being designed to actually present itself *as* human, without any fictional or "as if" framing. However, there has been no systematic exploration of this topic from an empirical perspective. How would users actually react to agents that present themselves with human autobiographical memories compared to the same agents that make no such pretense? Do users feel cheated and deceived, as many researchers contend, or do they take it in stride as part of their "suspension of disbelief"? Are there any

Zs. Ruttkay et al. (Eds.): IVA 2009, LNAI 5773, pp. 6–19, 2009.

user benefits to giving agents human personal histories? These are the research questions we sought to address in this work.

Aside from their ethical and intellectual merits, answers to these questions have practical ramifications as well. Many applications in healthcare, education, entertainment and other fields require designing voluntary-use interfaces for long-term use. Designing such systems requires novel approaches to maintaining user engagement over dozens, if not thousands, of interactions. Social chat by agents in these applications provides a mechanism for maintaining user engagement over arbitrary lengths of time, provided that the stories the agent tells are, in fact, entertaining and engaging. Within this context, first person stories may provide the additional engagement required to make a longitudinal application successful.

A number of empirical studies suggest that users actually want agents to be more like them, whether they are conscious of this desire or not. For example, in the Media Equation studies, Reeves and Nass demonstrated that users prefer agents that match them in personality (along the introversion/extroversion dimension) compared to agents that do not [1]. Van Vugt, et al, demonstrated that users prefer characters that match them in body shape [2]. Finally, Bickmore related anecdotes from study participants in which they stated their desire for the animated exercise coach they had worked with for the prior month to have a more human back story [3]. For example:

> *"I wish she could imitate a real person's life in her answers rather than sticking to the reality and saying things like she is limited to that box. Maybe this has something to do with trainees wanting to have role model to achieve their own physical fitness roles by taking the trainer as a role model. Or maybe it is just about having a richer conversation helping getting connected to the other person."*

1.1 Ethical Issues

Deception and its negative consequences have been widely studied in ethics [4, 5]. User trust in conversational agents that tell fictitious stories (as well as trust in their developers and marketers) can be greatly damaged if users actually thought the stories agents told were true and later discovered they were not. Widespread use of such deceptive agents could begin to erode generalized trust towards all agents, all technology or universally within a community.

This condemnation of deception extends into the human-computer interaction and agents research communities as well. For example, Fogg states that deception, used in the context of persuasive technology, is "almost always" unethical [6]. Shneiderman contends that computers must clearly relate their capabilities and limitations to users, rejecting any notion of anthropomorphization of the interface [7].

However, deception is rarely a black and white phenomenon. Even ethicists argue whether there are absolute truths, without which deception loses its meaning. Deception is both common in all societies and a necessary component of many professions [4]. One could argue that virtual humans or anthropomorphic robots of any kind represent a kind of deception. Perhaps the degree of deception lies solely in the degree to which such agents are presented without explicit messages or cues that they are not really human, regardless of the number of messages or cues they present to the contrary (e.g., anthropomorphic body, natural language, etc.).

Docents who provide historical re-enactments at living history museums provide a good analogy to the current issue. Good actors will go to great lengths to stay "in character" even in the face of in-depth questioning and explicit questions about their authenticity ("You're not *really* Abraham Lincoln, are you?"). However, the larger context of the museum is intended to provide the meta-message that this kind of deceit is not only tolerable, but done for the engagement and benefit of the visitors. Most virtual human researchers who are not working in entertainment-related domains similarly dismiss any accusations of deceit by saying that, obviously, users know they are only interacting with a computer.

Other researchers justify their deceit by saying that people engage in deceitful behaviour similar to the one they are modelling, therefore it must be acceptable for their agents to do the same thing. For example, Klein, in his work on artificial caring, argues that computers that exhibit empathy, sympathy and caring for users are no less authentic than people who express caring for others without really understanding their feelings, or pets who seem to respond in comforting ways to their owner's negative moods [8].

Finally, some researchers would argue that if their deceit is ultimately to the benefit of the user, then the ends justify the means, and it is sanctioned within a utilitarian ethical framework. For example, Bickmore justifies the possible deceit and manipulation effected by his health promotion agents by the fact that they result in users leading healthier lives [9].

1.2 Related Work

Bates, et al, conducted some of the earliest research into the development of virtual characters in the "Oz" project at CMU [10]. The explicit objective in this work was to create a "believable character", which is not "an honest or reliable character, but one that provides the illusion of life, and thus permits the audience's suspension of disbelief". Mateas argues that believability is not the same as realism, and that characters are artistic abstractions of people, which have been exaggerated in order to engage users [11]. He states that believable agents are "designed to strongly express a personality, not fool the viewer into thinking they are human." Unlike our work, the overarching goal of the Oz project was entertainment, and the work was always presented to users as such. This stance is continued in the majority of work in the growing field of interactive drama and narrative, in which systems are only used to present fictional autobiographies within the explicit framework of make believe.

In contrast, most researchers investigating human-agent interactions in non-entertainment domains carefully avoid giving their agents human back stories. Examples include the Reeves & Nass Media Equation studies [1], studies by Moon [12], Klein [8], and Bickmore [13]. For example, in the Moon study on reciprocal self-disclosure exchanges between a user and a computer, she explicitly states that the computer never referred to itself as "I" to avoid creating the impression that the computer regarded itself in human terms [12]. Self-disclosures for the computer were also scripted to avoid any hint of human back story:

> *"This computer has been configured to run at speeds up to 266 MHz. But 90% of computer users don't use applications that require these speeds. So this computer rarely gets used to its full potential. What has been your biggest disappointment in life?"*

There are a few exceptions, of course. The earliest, and most famous, being the ELIZA system, created intentionally to demonstrate how easy it is to trick people interacting with a computer into thinking they are interacting with a person [14]. This tradition has been continued in the development of many "chatterbots" and the institution of the Loebner prize [15]. Valerie, a robotic receptionist at CMU, was given a running human back story that was continuously updated [16]. However, there have been no experimental investigations into the impact of these back stories on users. We are also unaware of prior investigations in which users were even asked whether they felt they were being deceived by a conversational agent they had interacted with, regardless of how the agent presented itself.

Another related area of investigation is the use of autobiographical memory for virtual agents as a way of making them more adaptive and socially intelligent (e.g., [17]). However, these memories are typically not seeded with a fictitious past for the purpose of relating to a user in a task-oriented context.

1.3 An Empirical Investigation

In order to investigate reactions of actual users to agents that relate personal human ("first person") back stories, we conducted a randomized longitudinal experiment in which users conducted daily conversations with an agent that related such stories. In the remainder of this paper we describe the experimental framework in which the study was conducted, the narrative generation system that was used to produce the stories, and finally present findings from the experiment itself before concluding and discussing future work.

2 The Virtual Laboratory System

To answer the empirical questions about user reactions to autobiographical agents and how these change over time, we constructed a longitudinal experiment in the "Virtual Laboratory" system [18]. This system provides a framework for running longitudinal studies of ongoing interactions between humans and conversational virtual humans, in which a standing group of study participants interacts periodically with a computer agent that is remotely manipulated to effect different study conditions, with outcome measures also collected remotely. This architecture allows new experiments to be dynamically defined and immediately implemented in the continuously-running system without delays due to recruitment and system reconfiguration. In the current instantiation, 30 older adults interact daily with a virtual human who plays the role of an exercise counselor to promote walking behavior. Older adults were selected as the target population because of their particular need for physical activity and their lower levels of computer literacy [19].

Fig. 1. Virtual Laboratory Exercise Counselor Agent

The Virtual Laboratory has been running continuously over the last year, with a total of 36 study participants aged 55 or older conducting a total of over 3,500 conversations with the animated exercise counselor (Fig. 1). The subject pool has had 24 participants on average, with participants staying in the intervention between 18 and 308 days. Participants are on average 60 years old (range 55-75), 73% female, and 54% married.

Fig. 2 shows the virtual laboratory architecture. The client side of this architecture features a virtual agent, web browser, and user input windows (Fig. 1). The server features the following components: an agent database for storing all user data and information about previous user-agent interactions; a measures database for storing all experimental results (e.g., from questionnaires remotely administered to users); an experiment database that contains specifications for all experiments to be run; a dialogue engine that manages conversational interaction between the agent and a user; a web server that provides users with web content (e.g., multimedia educational material and study questionnaire forms); the dialogue engine parameters to instantiate for a particular user on a particular day; an experiment planner that schedules requested experiments; and an experiment evaluator that produces data files and web-based summaries of experimental results.

For the virtual laboratory, we have developed a new dialogue engine—RADIUS (relational agent dialogue system)—which subsumes both augmented transition network-based and task-decomposition-based models of dialogue. In contrast to more

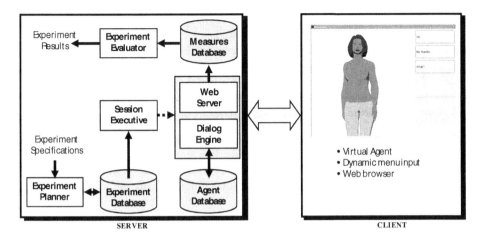

Fig. 2. Virtual Laboratory Architecture

complex systems, such as COLLAGEN, RADIUS models a recipe as a state machine, in which agent utterances are states, and user utterances are state transitions. A state transition may invoke a sub-task by specifying a goal, which will cause the dialogue engine to find an appropriate recipe and execute it, before continuing to the next state. In practice, this provides increased modularity and reuse with only a small increase in complexity for authors. Dialogue may still be written as state machines. However, when modifications are required in order to reuse a dialogue fragment, this may be implemented by providing additional recipes for those portions of dialogue.

3 Dynamic Social Story Generation

Providing social dialogue in daily conversations between a user and an agent over months or years requires a considerable number of narratives as the agent's background stories. While these could be manually scripted in their entirety, a less laborious alternative is to generate the stories at runtime with a narrative generation system.

3.1 Narrative Generation Technology

A number of interactive narrative generation systems have been developed over the last two decades, such as Façade [22], FearNot! [23], and those developed in the Oz project [10, 11]. These systems employ different levels of natural language generation to create dynamic content that is used to fabricate interactive experiences. Interactive narrative systems, however, are generally domain specific and depend on large scale domain knowledge. Furthermore, in many of these interactive narrative systems, such as Façade and FearNot!, users are allowed to make their contributions using unconstrained typed text input. Narratives generated in response to unconstrained input may fall significantly short of human generated narratives (e.g., lacking in coherence), resulting in loss of believability by the user.

A different approach to narrative generation exists in "Say Anything" [20, 21], which collaborates with users in constructing narratives by contributing sentences extracted from tens of thousands of weblogs. Although this approach creates unique narratives in almost every interaction, and studies have shown that users rate these narratives as being more coherent than ones generated randomly [21], these narratives still fall far short of human-generated stories and do not provide longitudinal coherence (subsequent stories that are logically consistent with earlier ones).

3.2 Our Approach to Agent Back Story Generation

We have developed a method for generating social narratives that avoids manually scripting every day's conversation while providing significant day-to-day variability and maintaining coherence throughout each story. Our approach is similar to Swanson and Gordon's [21], in that it involves run-time linking of pre-authored story fragments, but differs in several significant ways. We begin with a set of story fragments, each just one to three utterances in length that conveys a complete event or thought. We then manually tag particular words and phrases within each story fragment as mentioned and elaborated concepts, and then we create a link from every story A to story B, where story A has a mentioned or elaborated concept which is also an elaborated concept in story B, following the notions and methodologies from Cleary and Bareiss [22]. This process provides a set of links that point from one story fragment to another, based on common concepts. Finally, we annotate each link with a transition utterance. Fig. 3 is an example of an annotated story fragment, where the utterances between the <link> tags point to the other four story fragments. N12 and N13 are two other stories about more of the storyteller's high school life, and N22 and N23 are stories about sports games.

During a conversation with a user, the system randomly picks one of the story fragments and tells it to the user. Following this, the agent selects a linked fragment (at random if there are several), speaks the transition utterance associated with the link, and then begins telling the linked fragment. Between each story fragment and linking utterance the agent pauses and gives the user the choice to continue to the next utterance, or to repeat the previous one. Each conversation consists of two or three story fragments, and thus is composed of seven or eight utterances, including the linking utterances. An example of part of a storytelling interaction can be found in Fig. 4.

```
N7:
Mentioned: biking, hiking, walk, picnic, health
Elaborated: family, sports, exercise, outdoor activities
When my family was living in Falmouth, my parents always had us doing outdoor stuff.
So especially when it was nice out I would go biking or hiking or we just go for a walk
and have a picnic, things like that. And I think I really developed an appreciation for
exercise and being outdoors and just staying healthy and moving around all the time.
<link>
N12: And this made my high school life much more interesting.
N13: And this made my high school life much more interesting.
N22: Although I love sports, I don't watch sports games very much.
N23: Although I love sports, I don't watch sports games very much. I go to a few Red
Sox games though.
</link>
```

Fig. 3. Example Story Fragment Representation

1st-person	3rd-person
1. I'm not quite sure if I told you about this before.	1. I'm not quite sure if I told you about this before.
2. When my family was living in Falmouth, my parents always had us doing outdoor stuff.	2. When her family was living in Falmouth, her parents always had them doing outdoor stuff.
3. So especially when it was nice out I would go biking or hiking or we would just go for a walk and have a picnic, things like that.	3. So especially when it was nice out she would go biking or hiking or they would just go for a walk and have a picnic, things like that.
4. And I think I really developed an appreciation for exercise and being outdoors and just staying healthy and moving around all the time.	4. And I think she really developed an appreciation for exercise and being outdoors and just staying healthy and moving around all the time.

Fig. 4. Example Narrative Dialogue Showing the Same Story Fragments in 1ST-PERSON and 3RD-PERSON Conditions

In order to maintain global and longitudinal coherence, we developed an initial set of story fragments for the exercise advisor agent based on autobiographical stories told by a professional exercise trainer. The stories were verbally related to a member of our research staff, recorded, and transcribed. The transcript was then partitioned into fragments and annotated following the scheme above.

4   Longitudinal Evaluation Study

In order to compare the effects of the use of 1st-person and 3rd-person narrative dialogue by an agent, we conducted a brief longitudinal study using participants enrolled in the virtual laboratory system. The agent conducted daily conversations about exercise identical to those used in earlier studies with the system [18], with the addition of narrative dialogue generated using the social story generation system described above. Participants were randomized into one of two conditions: In the first (1ST-PERSON), the agent presented the narrative as its own life story, while in the second (3RD-PERSON) the agent presented the narrative as stories about a friend.

We expected that the use of 1st-person narrative would promote greater engagement with the agent due to a perception of self-disclosure by the agent, leading to more consistent usage of the system. However, we were also concerned that users would perceive the agent as dishonest when it presented a life story for itself that was not plausibly true for a computer character. Participants were administered daily questionnaires to assess their enjoyment of the stories, their engagement with the system, and their belief that the agent was dishonest.

Hypothesis 1: Participants in the 1st-person condition will use the system significantly more than those in the 3rd-person condition.

Hypothesis 2: Participants in the 1st-person condition will report greater enjoyment of the stories and greater engagement with the agent than those in the 3rd-person condition.

Hypothesis 3: Participants in the 1st-person condition will report greater perceived dishonesty by the agent than those in the 3rd-person condition.

4.1 Participants

A total of 26 participants (21 female, 5 male, aged 54-67, 80% Caucasian, 20% African American) took part in the study, all recruited via ads placed on craigslist.com. The sample was well-educated (92% had some college education), computer literate (12% self-identified as computer experts, the other 88% said they use computers regularly), and had positive attitudes towards computers overall (64% said they enjoyed working with computers). Fifteen had previously been interacting with the system at the start of the study, while 11 were newly recruited. All participants were compensated $1 per day for each day they completed a conversation with the agent. Exactly half of the participants were randomized into each arm of the study (1ST-PERSON and 3RD-PERSON). Participants were exposed to these study conditions for varying periods of time, ranging from 5 to 37 days (mean 28.8 days).

4.2 Measures

To assess system usage, we recorded whether or not each participant had a complete conversation with the agent each day. Following each complete conversation, after the agent walked off the screen, participants were given three single-item measures in randomized order, asking how much they (1) "enjoy the stories that the counselor tells", (2) "look forward to talking to the counselor", and (3) "feel that the counselor is dishonest". Each item was assessed on a 5-point rating scale ranging from "not at all" to "very much".

4.3 Narrative Dialogue

Narrative social dialogue was generated using the dynamic social story generation described above. In the first-person condition, the narratives were initially introduced as being part of the agent's own life story ("I'd like to tell you some stories about myself"). In the third-person condition, the narratives were introduced as being from the life story of a human friend of the agent with a similar role and occupation ("I'd like to tell you some stories about a friend of mine. She's an exercise counselor too.").

The differences between the first- and third- person variants of the dialogue were minimal, and consisted mainly of replacing pronouns. Fig. 4 shows an example of the narrative dialogue, in both variants.

4.4 Results

The 3 self-report items were analyzed by fitting linear mixed-effect regression models[1] to the data, while system usage was analyzed as a binary outcome with a logistic

---

[1] Linear mixed-effect regression is a generalization of ordinary linear regression, which adds random effects in order to account for clustered data, such as multiple measurements per subject in a longitudinal study. Similarly, logistic mixed-effect regression is a generalization of logistic regression, suitable for analyzing repeated binary measurements.

mixed-effect regression model. Analysis was performed using R 2.9.0, with the "nlme" and "lme4" packages [23].

For all outcomes, models were used which included fixed effects of study day and study condition. Initially, we considered models which included an additional fixed effect modeling the interaction of day and condition, thus allowing for a different rate of change in the outcomes between the two conditions. However, both inspection of the data and model selection procedures indicated that any interaction effects were minimal, most likely due to the short duration of the study. All models include random effects of intercept and study day. Table 1 shows the results of the analysis.

Table 1. Mixed-Effect Regression Estimates of Effects of Study Day and Condition on Outcomes

Condition 0 = 1ST-PERSON, 1=3RD-PERSON
* p < 0.5; ** p < 0.01; *** p <0.001

		Look Forward	Enjoy Stories	Dishonest	System Usage
Random Effects	Intercept	0.676 ***	1.127 ***	0.794 ***	1.477 ***
	Day	0.031 ***	0.038 ***	0.034 ***	0.012 ***
Fixed Effects	Intercept	4.410 *** (0.198)	3.384 *** (0.326)	1.688 *** (0.236)	3.207 *** (0.478)
	Day	-0.017 * (0.007)	-0.035 *** (0.009)	0.272 (0.326)	-0.046 *** (0.010)
	Condition	0.145 (0.281)	-1.059 * (0.461)	0.002 (0.008)	-1.148 * (0.560)

Enjoyment of the Stories. Participants in the 1ST-PERSON condition reported significantly greater enjoyment of the stories compared to those in the 3RD-PERSON group. There was also a significant effect of study day on the degree to which participants reported enjoying the stories; participants reported decreasing enjoyment of the stories over time (approximately 0.035 per day).

Engagement. There were no significant differences between conditions on degree to which participants said they "looked forward" to working with the agent. However, the average participant (both groups) reported significantly decreasing levels of engagement over time (approximately 0.017 per day).

Perceived Dishonesty. Participants, overall, did not perceive the agent as very dishonest. Average perceived dishonesty (both groups) following the first conversation was 1.69 (on a 1="not at all" to 5="very much" scale). There was no significant effect of study day or of study condition on this measure.

System Usage. Participants in the 1ST-PERSON condition had a significantly greater probability of talking to the agent on any given day, compared to those in the 3RD-PERSON group (Fig. 5). There was also a significant effect of study day on this measure; for the average participant, the probability of completing a session on any given day decreased over time.

Continuing vs. New Participants. The 11 participants who were newly recruited for this study did use the system significantly more compared to participants who had already been interacting with the system at the start of the study, p=.01. Including old vs. new participant as a covariate in the regression analysis does not change the significance status of any of the results above.

4.5 Discussion

As hypothesized, participants who interacted with an agent that used first-person stories reported greater enjoyment of the stories, and were more likely to use the system. Therefore, we can conclude that the first-person stories led to greater engagement with the system, at least during the short duration of time studied here. Both measures had significant decreases over time (in both conditions). This is likely due to increasing repetitiveness, as the agent had only a small set of story fragments to draw from in generating each day's story.

However, participants were not significantly more likely to report that they looked forward to working with the agent in the first-person condition. We consider two possible explanations: First, scores on this measure were all quite high (mean 4.22 on a 5-point scale), so ceiling effects may be hiding any difference caused by study conditions. Second, this result may indicate that our self-report measure of engagement does not reflect actual behavior; this raises methodological issues for future studies.

Participants were not significantly more likely to report that the agent was dishonest when it used first-person narrative, despite the fact that these stories could not possibly be true stories about a virtual character. This result suggests that users are willing to accept a fictional narrative that would be plausible for the character if the character were human.

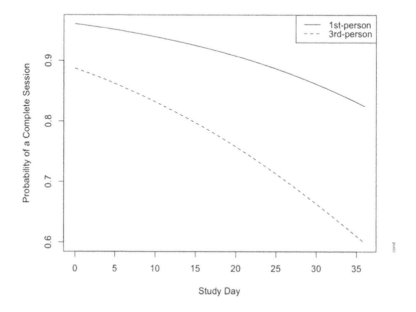

Fig. 5. Effects of Study Day and Condition on System Usage

Finally, we note that there were highly significant random effects of intercept and study day on all outcomes: there was a large amount of variability between participants both on outcomes at the start of the study, and on the rate of change over time. This suggests that there are predictors we have not examined, such as personality traits, which play an important role in these outcomes. This may represent a fruitful area of research in the future. Other limitations of the study include the small sample size, the recruitment methodology that resulted in a relatively well-educated and computer literate sample, the relatively short time span of the intervention, and the use of single-item questionnaires.

5 Conclusion

We believe this is the first systematic investigation into user reactions to human autobiographical stories told by a virtual human. We find that, rather than rejecting such an agent because of the perception of being deceived, the stories led to greater user engagement with the agent, and users did not rate the agent as being any less dishonest than an equivalent agent that did not relate the stories as its own history. Whether this behavior should be called deceitful is an open question.

Of course, participants in the study knew that they were interacting with a virtual human from the outset: they were told during enrollment that they would be interacting with a computer character; the agent is rendered using a cartoon rendering style (Fig. 1); and most participants had already experienced weeks or months of daily conversations with the agent that most report as repetitive and robot-like before beginning the study described above. How users would feel if one or more of the above cues regarding the agent's authenticity were removed also remains an open question.

These results are significant for designers of "serious" virtual humans that engage users in counseling, pedagogical or health care conversations over long periods of time. Maintaining user engagement with these systems is a pre-requisite for achieving any intervention outcomes, since users who stop using such a system or use it at a sub-optimal frequency do not receive the therapeutic and informational messages required to achieve the desired results. The autobiographical stories evaluated in our study perform what Jakobson defined as the "phatic" function of dialogue, to simply keep the communication channel open so that the primary functional messages can be conveyed [24].

In our ongoing work in this area we are developing virtual human-based health counseling interventions that span a year or more of daily conversations with a user. In addition to procedural dialogue content generation (e.g., based on weather data or sports scores) we see autobiographical conversational storytelling by the agent as one of the most important methods available for maintaining user engagement in the intervention over time. We plan to continue exploring ways in which such stories can be dynamically generated and integrated into the counseling conversation in a coherent and natural manner [25].

Acknowledgments. Thanks to Thomas Brown, Jenna Zaffini and the rest of the Relational Agents Group at Northeastern for their help, and to Jennifer Smith and Laura Pfeifer for their helpful comments on this paper. This work was supported by NSF CAREER IIS-0545932.

References

1. Reeves, B., Nass, C.: The Media Equation. Cambridge University Press, Cambridge (1996)
2. van Vugt, H., Konijn, E., Hoorn, J., Veldhuis, J.: Why Fat Interface Characters Are Better e-Health Advisors. In: Intelligent Virtual Agents (IVA), Marina Del Rey, CA, pp. 1–13 (2006)
3. Bickmore, T.: Relational Agents: Effecting Change through Human-Computer Relationships. PhD Thesis in Media Arts & Sciences. Massachusetts Institute of Technology, Cambridge, MA (2003)
4. Nyberg, D.: The varnished truth: truth telling and deceiving in ordinary life. University of Chicago Press, Chicago (1993)
5. Ford, C.: Lies! Lies!! Lies!!! The psychology of deceit. American Psychiatric Publishing, Washington (1999)
6. Fogg, B.J.: Persuasive Technology: Using Computers to Change What We Think and Do. Mogan Kaufmann, New York (2003)
7. Schneiderman, B.: Looking for the bright side of user interface agents. Interactions 2, 13–15 (1995)
8. Klein, J., Moon, Y., Picard, R.: This Computer Responds to User Frustration: Theory, Design, Results, and Implications. Interacting with Computers 14, 119–140 (2002)
9. Bickmore, T.: Ethical Issues in Using Relational Agents for Older Adults. In: AAAI Fall Symposium on Caring Machines: AI in Eldercare, Washington, DC (2005)
10. Bates, J.: The Role of Emotion in Believable Agents. Communications of the ACM 37, 122–125 (1994)
11. Mateas, M.: An oz-centric review of interactive drama and believable agents. In: Veloso, M.M., Wooldridge, M.J. (eds.) Artificial Intelligence Today. LNCS (LNAI), vol. 1600, pp. 297–328. Springer, Heidelberg (1999)
12. Moon, Y.: Intimate self-disclosure exchanges: Using computers to build reciprocal relationships with consumers. Harvard Business School report, Cambridge (1998)
13. Bickmore, T., Picard, R.: Establishing and Maintaining Long-Term Human-Computer Relationships. ACM Transactions on Computer Human Interaction 12, 293–327 (2005)
14. Weizenbaum, J.: Eliza - a computer program for the study of natural language communication between man and machine. Communications of the ACM 9, 36–45 (1966)
15. Loebner, H.: The Loebner Prize in Artificial Intelligence,
    http://www.loebner.net/Prizef/loebner-prize.html
16. Gockley, R., Bruce, A., Forlizzi, J., Michalowski, M., Mundell, A., Rosenthal, S., Sellner, B., Simmons, R., Snipes, K., Schultz, A.C., Wang, J.: Designing Robots for Long-Term Social Interaction. In: IEEE/RSJ International Conference on Intelligent Robots and Systems (2005)
17. Ho, W., Watson, S.: Autobiographic Knowledge for Believable Virtual Characters. Intelligent Virtual Agents, 383–394 (2006)
18. Bickmore, T., Schulman, D.: A Virtual Laboratory for Studying Long-term Relationships between Humans and Virtual Agents. In: Proceedings of Autonomous Agents and Multi-Agent Systems, Budapest, Hungary (2009)
19. Bickmore, T., Caruso, L., Clough-Gorr, K., Heeren, T.: It's just like you talk to a friend - Relational Agents for Older Adults. Interacting with Computers 17, 711–735 (2005)
20. Gordon, A., Cao, Q., Swanson, R.: Automated Story Capture From Internet Weblogs. In: Fourth International Conference on Knowledge Capture, Whistler, BC (2007)

21. Swanson, R., Gordon, A.: A Comparison of Retrieval Models for Open Domain Story Generation. In: AAAI 2009 Spring Symposium on Intelligent Narrative Technologies II, Stanford, CA (2009)
22. Cleary, C., Bareiss, R.: Practical Method for Automatically Generating Typed Links. In: Hypertext 1996, pp. 31–41 (1996)
23. R Core Development Team: R: A language and environment for statistical computing. R Foundation for Statistical Computing, Vienna, Austria (2009)
24. Jakobson, R.: Linguistics and Poetics. In: Sebeok, T.A. (ed.) Style in language, pp. 130–144. MIT Press, Cambridge (1960)
25. Jefferson, G.: Sequential aspects of storytelling in conversation. In: Schenkein, J. (ed.) Studies in the organization of conversational interaction, pp. 219–248. Academic Press, New York (1978)

A Socially-Aware Memory for Companion Agents

Mei Yii Lim[1], Ruth Aylett[1], Wan Ching Ho[2], Sibylle Enz[3],
and Patricia Vargas[1]

[1] School of Mathematical and Computer Sciences,
Heriot Watt University,
Edinburgh, EH14 4AS, Scotland
{myl,ruth}@macs.hw.ac.uk, p.a.vargas@hw.ac.uk
[2] Department of Computing Science,
University of Hertsfordshire, England, UK
w.c.ho@herts.ac.uk
[3] Otto-Friedrich-Universitaet Bamberg,
Kapuzinerstrasse 16,
D-96045 Bamberg, Germany
sibylle.enz@uni-bamberg.de

Abstract. Memory is a vital capability for intelligent social Companions. In this paper, we introduce a simple memory model that allows a Companion to maintain a long-term relationship with the user by remembering past experiences in order to personalise interaction. Additionally, we implemented a situational forgetting mechanism that gives the Companion the ability to protect the user's privacy by not disclosing sensitive data. Two test scenarios are used to demonstrate these abilities in our Companions.

1 Introduction

Memories are part of what makes up our personality, shapes our reactions to life situations and often influences our mood [1]. Besides giving us identity, memory is fundamental to intelligence. Learning and memory are the basis of our knowledge and abilities that allow us to consider the past, place us in the present and help us to predict the future. Additionally, memories help us to determine who and what are important to us. They allow us to behave in socially appropriate ways and hence maintain a long term relationship with our interaction partners. Since memory is such an important aspect of human intelligence and social life, we argue that in order to create intelligent artificial social Companions, memory is crucial. A 'human-like' memory in these Companions will help them to comprehend their world, focus their attention on important information relevant to the current interaction situation and to make predictions about it. These Companions will be able to act consistently and hence exhibit a 'personality', a reflection of 'self' that is important in social communication [2].

Zs. Ruttkay et al. (Eds.): IVA 2009, LNAI 5773, pp. 20–26, 2009.

In this paper, we discuss the important aspects of memory for intelligent artificial social Companions. Section 2 summarises aspects of the background in human memory research on remembering and forgetting. Section 3 discusses issues related to the memory of social Companions. Section 4 describes our initial memory prototype complete with example scenarios of personalisation and social awareness. Section 5 presents some conclusions and describes future work.

2 Remembering and Forgetting

It is yet unclear and controversial among scientists, how exactly memory works, but the following review introduces some of the ideas that are more widely agreed upon. Three fundamental stages in the formation of memory are encoding, storage and retrieval which take place on sensory, short-term and long-term levels [3]. Information from STM is stored in LTM through repeated exposure and generalisation (reconstruction).

Bartlett's work [4] emphasized the reconstructive view of LTM showing that memories are often reconstructed based upon world knowledge and schemata. He rejects the notion that memory representations consist of accurate traces that are consistent over long durations. Alba and Hasher [5] proposed a prototypical schema theory of memory, assuming the operation of four central encoding processes: "selection, abstraction, interpretation and integration". In addition, a fifth process, reconstruction, occurs when an individual attempts to reproduce a memory episode.

On the other hand, forgetting is useful to improve efficiency, scalability and adaptability of cognitive systems operating in dynamic task environments. Forgetting is also important to prevent stale information from interfering with fresh information and can be explained by decay theory, displacement, reconstruction process, interference and repression.

When it comes to recalling information from memory, contextual cues are crucial. Tulving and Psotska [6] have shown that the absence of a valid cue for recall causes forgetting (cued recall) and if contextual information is missing, memory recall fails. Bouton and colleagues [7] suggest that retrieval is most effective when a match exists between encoding and retrieval conditions. They add that a mismatch might occur with the passage of time due to the fluctuation of internal and external contextual cues, hence, reducing the likelihood of the target material being retrieved.

3 Artificial Social Companions and Memory

In recent years, artificial Companions have become increasingly popular especially as a form of entertainment and to assist the elderly in maintaining an acceptable standard of life. These Companions can include digital pets, such as the popular Tamagotchi, or robots, such as the PARO[1] and the Sony AIBO[2]. In

---

[1] http://www.parorobots.com/
[2] http://support.sony-europe.com/aibo/

this paper, the term "companion" refers to an artificial agent who is frequently in the company of the user. Up to date, the social, psychological and cognitive foundations and consequences of such technological artifacts entering our daily lives over an extended period are not well understood. Many scientists and philosophers [8, 9] discuss the potential ethical danger of these artifacts. In the field of robotics, a new discipline named Roboethics [10] has evolved as a result.

In the design of an artificial social Companion memory, important ethical issues have to be addressed alongside the aim of providing the companion with a memory that can maintain long term relationships. Significant questions would be 'what' the companion should remember, 'how' these data are processed and to 'whom' the information should be disclosed. One of the important aspects of memory modelling for an ethical Companion is forgetting [11], particularly motivated forgetting or repression [12] which allows the Companion to repress ('forget') sensitive information under specific circumstances to prevent harmful consequences to its relationship with the user. To maintain long-term relationships, it is important for the Companion to be adaptive so that its interaction with the user can be personalised.

4   Initial Prototype

4.1   The Architecture

Based on the reviews and discussions in the previous sections, we have developed an initial memory prototype for intelligent artificial social Companions. The prototype is built on top of FAtiMA [13], an emotional model for virtual agents that incorporates reactive and deliberative appraisal components responsible for agents' decision making. We take advantage of this functionality to help the agent determine the appropriateness of its behaviour. Additionally, FAtiMA includes an autobiographic memory [14] where previous events are stored as well as a knowledge base that stores information related to the interaction environment. This provides a basis for our Companion memory design, testing and development. However, FAtiMA memory does not distinguish between short-term and long-term storage and the existing memory is comparable to LTM. Additionally, FAtiMA stores all actions and events without any forgetting.

In order to create a more human-like memory, FAtiMA memory was restructured. Since we adopt an iterative prototyping approach, our initial memory model is very simple as shown in Figure 1. The autobiographic memory (AM) and knowledge base (KB) are considered as LTM and a STM is added. The KB in the LTM and the STM are comparable to the recently enhanced ACT-R components: the LTM-DM (declarative memory) and the LTM buffer (working memory) respectively [15]. However, the ACT-R theory does not include motivated forgetting mechanism and the model has not yet been used in human-agent interaction scenarios. Our STM acts as a buffer to actions and events before they are transferred to the AM and consists of a working memory that holds information related to current goal processing. This information includes properties of objects and people in the interaction and the Companion's internal representations of its evaluation of potential events that might take place. When a goal either succeeds or fails, the companion will update its knowledge base (LTM) with the new evaluation information from its working memory. The flow of information between these memory components can be seen in the dotted box component of Figure 1.

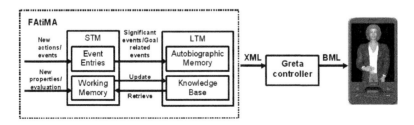

Fig. 1. Linking FAtiMA to Greta

(a) Memory Records

Details

ID	Subject	Action	Target	Parameters	Feeling	Evaluation	Time	Location
0	Greta	look-at	Greta	0	Neutral-0 0	0	6500	LivingRoom
1	Greta	look-at	Amy	0	Love-0.39999998	0	6500	LivingRoom
2	Greta	look-at	apple	0	Neutral-0 0	0	6500	LivingRoom

Working Memory

(b)

SpeechContext()		cake(eatable)	
EVENT(Greta,SpeechAct,Amy,greeting)			True
ProbBias(Amy,GreetBack,Greta)		Greta(isPerson)	
0.20000005			True

(c) Memory Events

Time	People	Location	Objects
(RT) 124059378 2472 (NT) 1453 (ES) 1	[Sarah, John]	LivingRoom	0

Details

ID	Subject	Action	Target	Parameters	Feeling	Evaluation
2	Sarah	look-at	Luke	0	Love-0 436	0
3	Sarah	look-at	Paulie	0	Love-0 47524	0

Fig. 2. (a)The Structure of Memory Records in Short Term Memory; (b)Working Memory and (c)Autobiographic Memory

The structure of STM memory records and the working memory are presented in Figure 2(a) and Figure 2(b) respectively. Instead of storing all actions and events taking place in the environment, only significant events (eg. events with emotional impact) and those related to goal processing (activation, success and failure) are transferred to the AM as shown in Figure 2(c). In addition, the AM stores general information about a particular episode of interaction such as time, location, participants and objects. For more information about the memory architecture, please refer to [16].

4.2   Testbed and Test Scenarios

In order to embed the memory into an interaction environment, the version of FAtiMA used has been connected to the Greta [17] agent. The components link is presented in Figure 1. Information from FAtiMA is sent to the Greta controller in XML format that is translated to the Greta understandable format, BML, so that actions can be performed and texts can be synthesised to speech accordingly. The user interacts with the system through a graphical user interface by choosing actions from a drop-down list.

Two scenarios have been devised to test our initial memory prototype, one relates to personalisation and the other addresses the user privacy issues [11]. In the first scenario, we aim to show how an agent, Greta, remembers its interactions and uses this information in later encounters with the user. The interaction involves the agent offering food to the user, Amy, and remembering her preference. Additionally, we included the notion of time which is currently represented as a property of the agent about the environment. Greta selects different actions based on the time of interaction - offering fruits in the morning and cake in the afternoon. The interaction takes place at different locations in Amy's house. Details of the scenario are presented below:

- Case 1: Location - Living Room; Time - Morning; Description - Greta will offer Amy fruits - either apple, banana or orange, one at a time and will stop offering when the user accepts one of the fruit
- Case 2: Location - Study Room; Time - Afternoon; Description - Greta will offer Amy cake
- Case 3: Location - Kitchen; Time - Morning; Description - Greta retrieves from its memory previous interactions and offers the fruit that Amy has accepted before

After each interaction in this scenario, Greta updates its knowledge base with new information from current processing. So, after case 1, suppose Amy rejected banana and accepted orange, it will have the information (probability that Amy accept banana is -0.392 and orange is 0.20000005) as shown in Figure 3(a) in its memory. During case 3, Greta retrieves this information into its working memory

Fig. 3. (a)Greta's evaluation of probabilities user accepting certain fruit; (b)Tagging of sensitive information

and it is this information that helps Greta to decide on what to offer the user next, hence personalising its interaction with the user.

In the second scenario, we aim to show how an agent, Sarah (using the same graphical representation as in Figure 1) tags its memory about information sensitive to a particular user and how it handles queries related to the information when being asked by the respective user. The interaction takes place in an office setting and three users are involved - John, Luke and Pauline. Details of the scenario are as below:

- Case 1: Location - Reception; Agents - Sarah and John; Description - John tells Sarah about him being drunk at a party and told Sarah that she should keep it secret from Luke, a good friend of his wife. Additionally, he also told Sarah that he is getting a new job and his existing boss Pauline should not know about this
- Case 2: Location - Common Room; Agents - Sarah, Luke and Pauline; Description - Luke and Pauline ask Sarah about John regarding the party and the new job. Sarah will hide the information since each piece of the information is sensitive to one of them - the party to Luke, and the new job to Pauline
- Case 3: Location - Pauline's office; Agents - Sarah and Pauline; Description - Pauline ask Sarah again about the related topics. This time Sarah will expose the information about John being drunk to Pauline but not about him getting a new job

When John tells Sarah his personal information and to whom this information is sensitive, Sarah tags its memory entry as shown in Figure 3(b). Later, when it is being asked about this information, it will retrieve its memory of the entry and will know to whom the information should or should not be disclosed.

5   Conclusion and Future Work

This paper demonstrates a simple artificial social Companion memory model that allows personalisation of interaction and takes ethical issues into consideration. The design of a full working memory model is still on-going, therefore an initial prototype of the memory model has been implemented and two case scenarios were used to show how the above issues are addressed. Future work includes a more detailed specification of the Companion memory model that addresses issues such as general forgetting, generalisation and retrieval. This would entail modification to the existing memory organisation as it currently only allows storage based on events and does not employ any ontological or hierarchical structure.

Acknowledgements

This work was partially supported by the European Commission (EC) and is currently funded by the EU FP7 ICT-215554 project LIREC (Living with Robots and Interactive Companions). The authors are solely responsible for the content of this publication. It does not represent the opinion of the EC, and the EC is not responsible for any use that might be made of data appearing therein.

References

[1] Carver, J.M.: Emotional memory management: Positive control over your memory. Burn Survivors Throughout the World Inc. (2005),
http://www.burnsurvivorsttw.org/articles/memory.html

[2] Dautenhahn, K.: The art of designing socially intelligent agents – science, fiction and the human in the loop. Applied Artificial Intelligence 12(7-8), 573–617 (1998)

[3] Atkinson, R., Shiffrin, R.: Human memory: A proposed system and its control processes. The Psychology of learning and motivation: Advances in Research and Theory 2 (1968)

[4] Barlett, F.C.: Remembering: A Study in Experimental and Social Psychology. Cambridge University Press, Cambridge (1932)

[5] Alba, J.W., Hasher, L.: Is memory schematic? Psychological Bulletin 93, 203–231 (1983)

[6] Tulving, E., Psotka, J.: Retroactive inhibition in free recall: inaccessibility of information available in the memory stores. Journal of Experimental Psychology 87, 116–124 (1971)

[7] Bouton, M.E., Nelson, J.B., Rosas, J.M.: Stimulus generalization, context change, and forgetting. Psychological Bulletin 125, 171–186 (2008)

[8] Sparrow, R.: Killer robots. Journal of Applied Science 24(1) (2006)

[9] Walters, M.L., Otero, N.R., Koay, K.L., Syrdal, D.S., Dautenhahn, K.: He knows when you are sleeping - privacy and the personal robot. Technical report (2007)

[10] Veruggio, G.: The birth of roboethics. In: ICRA 2005, IEEE International Conference on Robotics and Automation Workshop on Robo-Ethics (2005)

[11] Vargas, P.A., Ho, W.C., Mei Yii Lim, S.E., Fernaeus, Y., Aylett, R.: To forget or not to forget:towards a roboethical memory control. In: Killer Robots or Friendly Fridges: the Social Understanding of Artificial Intelligence, AISB 2009, Edinburgh, pp. 18–23 (2009)

[12] Freud, A.: The Ego and the Mechanisms of Defence. Hogarth Press and Institute of Psycho-Analysis, London (1937)

[13] Dias, J., Paiva, A.: Feeling and reasoning: A computational model for emotional agents. In: Bento, C., Cardoso, A., Dias, G. (eds.) EPIA 2005. LNCS (LNAI), vol. 3808, pp. 127–140. Springer, Heidelberg (2005)

[14] Ho, W.C., Dautenhahn, K., Nehaniv, C.L.: Computational memory architectures for autobiographic agents interacting in a complex virtual environment: A working model. Connection Science 20(1), 21–65 (2008)

[15] Schultheis, H., Lile, S., Barkowsky, T.: Extending act-r's memory capabilities. In: Proc. of EuroCogSci 2007, pp. 758–763 (2007)

[16] Ho, W.C., Lim, M.Y., Vargas, P.A., Enz, S., Dautenhahn, K., Aylett, R.: An initial memory model for virtual and robot companions supporting migration and long-term interaction. In: ROMAN 2009, IEEE International Symposium on Robot and Human Interactive Communication (to appear, 2009)

[17] de Rosis, F., Pelachaud, C., Poggi, I., Carofiglio, V., Carolis, N.D.: From Greta's mind to her face: Modeling the dynamics of affective states in a conversational embodied agent. Special Issue on Applications of Affective Computing in Human-Computer Interaction, The International Journal of Human-Computer Studies 59, 81–118 (2003)

A Model of Personality and Emotional Traits

Margaret McRorie[1], Ian Sneddon[1], Etienne de Sevin[2], Elisabetta Bevacqua[2], and Catherine Pelachaud[2]

[1] School of Psychology
Queen's University, Belfast
BT7 1NN, UK
[2] CNRS - Telecom ParisTech
37/39, rue Dareau
75014 Paris, France
{m.mcrorie,i.sneddon}@qub.ac.uk, {etienne.de-sevin,
elisabetta.bevacqua,catherine.pelachaud}@telecom-paristech.fr

Abstract. How do we construct credible personalities? The current SAL (Sensitive Artificial Listeners) characters were constructed intuitively and can be unconvincing. In addressing these issues, this paper considers a theory of personality and associated emotional traits, and discusses how behaviours associated with personality types in people may be adapted to develop characteristics of virtual agents. Our objective is to ensure that behavioural perceptions of a virtual agent credibly reflect the agent's 'actual' personality as prescribed.

Keywords: Personality traits, Eysenck, emotional traits, virtual agents.

1 Introduction

This paper proposes that the way in which personality dimensions affect various attributes of animated characters should reflect similar processes in the humans upon which they are modelled. Our work is part of the EU project SEMAINE, which aims to provide a multimodal system of conversational agents, or Sensitive Artificial Listeners (SAL). These virtual agents are designed to sustain realistic interaction with human users, despite having limited verbal skills.

We first present different theories of personality. Then in later sections, we explain how we kept a computationally appropriate level of complexity to model personality in virtual agents and how personality affects behaviours. Section 4 describes a model to build agents with different behaviour propensities. The four SAL characters are presented in the next section. We end this paper by introducing the SAL architecture where we detail how personality acts not only on the behaviour characteristic of the virtual agent but also on its communicative styles, in particular when being a listener.

1.1 Trait Models of Personality

Trait models of personality assume that traits influence behaviour, and that they are fundamental properties of an individual. The five-factor model [1] is a modern lexical

Zs. Ruttkay et al. (Eds.): IVA 2009, LNAI 5773, pp. 27–33, 2009.

approach, and posits five main personality dimensions – extraversion, neuroticism, openness to experience, agreeableness and conscientiousness.

In comparison, Eysenck [2] developed a model based on traits which he believed were heritable and had a probable biological foundation. Likely personality traits were identified from clinical and experimental literature, and the three main traits which met these criteria were extraversion-introversion, neuroticism-emotional stability, and psychoticism.

There is evidence of some form of theoretical integration between the two models. Eysenck's traits of extraversion and neuroticism are virtually identical to the similarly named dimensions of the 'Big Five', and psychoticism seems to correspond to agreeableness and conscientiousness combined – suggesting these traits may be components of psychoticism [3].

Extraversion and neuroticism have also been associated with the basic assumptions of Gray's [4] two-dimensional model of impulsivity and anxiety. Gray proposed that people differ in sensitivity of their Behavioural Approach System (BAS, responsible for impulsivity) or Behavioural Inhibition System (BIS, responsible for anxiety).

1.1.1 Biological Underpinnings of Eysenck's Three-Factor Model

Eysenck attempted to provide causal explanations based on individual differences in nervous system functioning. His biological theory suggests that as extraverts are less cortically aroused than introverts, they should need more external stimulation and be more comfortable under arousing conditions.

Highly neurotic individuals are predicted to show more autonomic nervous activity in stressful situations. Alternatively, M.W. Eysenck's Hypervigilance Theory argues that as 'highly anxious' people constantly look out for signs of threat, they will use many rapid eye movements, and attend selectively to threat-relevant stimuli [5].

Psychoticism is less well understood, however Eysenck suggested psychoticism is linked to male hormones (e.g. testosterone) which influence impulsivity.

1.2 Trait Emotionality

Neuroticism is primarily an emotional disposition – 'negative emotionality', or the propensity to experience negative emotions. Similarly, extraversion 'predisposes an individual towards positive emotion' [6]. These reliable and stable individual differences in the propensity to experience global positive and negative affect confirm the notion of trait emotionality [7], and also warrant consideration when defining characteristics of conversational agents.

2 Complexity/Adequacy

There is a continued debate in the literature as to which of the two main personality models is more theoretically appropriate. What *we* must consider is which dimensions best reflect the various attributes of a virtual agent. The diversity created by the trait models provides a comprehensive framework, however modelling personality as a reflection of complex multivariate solutions might be difficult if virtual agents need more easily controlled parameters [8].

Confining interpersonal behaviour to fewer dimensions would allow for more effective management, and Eysenck's three-dimensional model would arguably serve as an acceptable foundation. Its core dimensions of extraversion and neuroticism are undisputed and central to all major trait theories. Psychoticism is useful as it seems to reflect agreeableness and conscientiousness. Further benefits in adopting Eysenck's model are that its biological underpinnings could to some extent direct and justify specific response patterns of behaviour in developing characters of virtual agents.

3   Building Personality

Our objective is to provide a sound theoretical basis to generate behavioural characteristics which will allow an observer to infer a personality. Personality predicts specific behaviours. Individual personality types are deduced from the answers to questions about behaviours. We need to do the opposite, and generate consistent sets of behavioural attributes (an agent's visual cues etc) from a personality.

In doing so, it should be remembered that extraversion is not just linked with positive affect, but associated with a general level of activation and behavioural approach [9]; neuroticism similarly is related to behaviour avoidance. Both dimensions thus reflect differences in behaviour, affect and cognition [7].

4   Representing and Modelling Distinctive Characters

To model behaviour tendencies of virtual agents, we use the approach developed by [10] where an agent is defined by a *baseline* that captures the global behaviour tendency of the agent. The baseline is defined as a set of numeric parameters: the agent's modality preference and the agent's behaviour expressivity. The modality preference refers to the agent's degree of preference in using each available modality (face, head, gaze, gesture and torso) to communicate while the behaviour expressivity is represented by a set of 6 parameters that influence the quality of the agent's movements as was proposed by [11]: the frequency (OAC parameter), speed (TMP parameter), spatial volume (SPC parameter), energy (POW parameter), fluidity (FLD parameter), and repetitivity (REP parameter) of the non-verbal signals produced by the agent. These expressivity parameters are defined for each modality: one set of parameters for the head movements, another set for the facial expressions, and so on.

5   Definition of Characters

These are the principles. The challenge now is to map the connections and consider how we translate these stable traits into personality-dependent actions. We should thus be aware of the links between impressions of personality and verbal/nonverbal behaviour, i.e. which behaviours actually effect a viewer's perception of personality. The five major categories typically used to classify nonverbal behaviour are facial expressions, eye and visual behaviour (e.g. gaze), kinesics, paralanguage, and proxemics.

5.1 Defining Representative Behaviour of SAL Characters

The design of the characters draws on the above. The application consists of a system of Sensitive Artificial Listeners (SAL), designed to sustain an interaction with a human user via generation of nonverbal behaviour in real time. SAL characters represent four psychologically different affective/personality types, which try to draw the user into their own emotional state. Poppy is outgoing (extraverted) and optimistic; Spike is angry and argumentative; Prudence is pragmatic and practical; and Obadiah is gloomy and depressed. Figure 1 portrays the 4 SAL facial models.

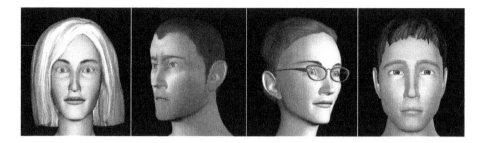

Fig. 1. The 4 SAL agents: Poppy, Spike, Prudence and Obadiah

Although the literature describing behaviours associated with particular human personalities is not couched in the same terms used to describe the agents, we can begin to use the human research to help us specify the design parameters for our characters. The definition of the 4 characters is work in progress. Let us concentrate on the behaviour characteristics of Poppy. The facial expressions of extraverts tend to be 'friendly', and the literature suggests that individuals are perceived as more sociable when smiling than with a neutral face [12]. We might further expect Poppy's facial appearance to be attractive (see Fig. 1). This relates to the 'what is beautiful is good' stereotype - positive personality attributions tend to be projected on to those possessing attractive faces [13]. Faces high in symmetry have similarly received significantly higher ratings of attractiveness, and facial symmetry is associated with personality attributes such as sociability, liveliness, and happiness [14].

Drawing on Eysenck's theory of extraversion and arousal, Poppy would be characterized as having high levels of general activation. For example, extraverts tend to demonstrate more body movements, and display greater levels of facial activity [15]. Studies have also shown that extraversion is associated with greater levels of gesturing, more frequent head nods, and general speed of movement [12]. During conversation, extraverts tend to position themselves closer to others, and direct facial posture and eye contact is more likely to be maintained [16].

Regarding language and paralanguage, extraverts tend to talk more loudly and more repetitively, with fewer pauses, shorter silences, and less hesitations [17]. Extraverts initiate more interactions, using more positive emotion words and informal style [18].

6 SAL Architecture

Our system analyses user's movements and voice to determine the agent's behaviour while listening to the user. The agent can perform non verbal signals (called *back-channels* [19]) to show how it is reacting to the user's speech, if it is listening, understanding, agreeing and so on. The system is divided into three modules [20]: the *agent definition*, the *backchannel planner* and the *backchannel realizer*.

Agent definition. The agent definition module contains the information that characterises a SAL agent: the baseline and the agent's *mental state*, which describes what the agent thinks about the user's speech.

In our system, we define the mental state as a set of communicative functions the agent wishes to transmit during an interaction. We consider twelve communicative functions, a subset chosen from the taxonomy proposed by Allwood et al. and Poggi [19, 21]. Each communicative function is associated with a set of behavioural signals that must be performed to convey the given function. The listener functions should vary during the interaction, since they depend on several factors like the content of the speaker's speech, the listener's own beliefs, the relationship between the two parties and so on. However, at present, for sake of simplicity, we link the agent's mental state to the emotional characteristics that differentiate the four SAL agents. For example, Spike, who is angry and argumentative, conveys negative communicative functions, in particular dislike, disagreement and lack of interest.

Backchannel Planner. The backchannel planner module decides when and how the agent must provide a backchannel signal. To determine when a backchannel is triggered, this module analyses the user's verbal and non verbal behaviour; researches have shown that backchannels are often emitted according to the speaker's behaviour [22, 23]. Then, the backchannel planner calculates all the possible signals and chooses the most appropriate one through an algorithm of action selection [24].

Backchannels can be potentially conflicting at the signal level. In this case, only one of these backchannels can be displayed and a backchannel selection is necessary to choose the most appropriate one relative to the context of the interaction. For example, personality has an influence on the backchannel selection by modulating the number of displayed backchannels (e.g. Poppy shows a lot of backchannels while Obadiah much less).

Backchannel realizer. The backchannel realizer instantiates the backchannel output from the action selection module into a set of signals. This step considers also the agent's definition: the baseline and the agent's mental state. For each communicative function the agent intends to transmit, the backchannel realizer determines the corresponding non verbal behaviours from the backchannel lexicon [25, 26] taking into account the agent's modality preference and its expressivity parameters. Finally, the resulting animation is played on a graphic window where the virtual agent is shown.

7 Conclusion

In this paper we have presented a model of personality and emotional traits for virtual agents. We have applied this model to SAL agents. The model we have adopted from the different theories of personality is the Eysenck's model. Four distinctive agents have been designed with a given personality each. For each of them, personality affects the agent's global behaviour quality as well as their backchannel productions (frequency and type of signals).

Acknowledgements

This research was supported by the STREP SEMAINE project. We are greatly thankful to Martine Delage for the facial models of the SAL agents.

References

1. McCrae, R.R., Costa, P.T.: Validation of the five-factor model of personality across instruments and observers. Journal of Personality and Social Psychology 52, 81–90 (1987)
2. Eysenck, H.J.: The Measurement of Personality. Medical and Technical Publishers, Lancaster (1976)
3. Goldberg, L.R.: The structure of phenotypic personality traits. American Psychologist 84, 26–34 (1993)
4. Gray, J.A.: The psychophysiological nature of introversion-extraversion: a modification of Eysenck's theory. In: Nebylitsen, V.D., Gray, J.A. (eds.) Biological Bases of Individual Behaviour, pp. 151–188. Academic Press, London (1972)
5. Eysenck, M.W., Byrne, A.: Anxiety and susceptibility to distraction. Personality and Individual Differences 13, 793–798 (1992)
6. Costa, P.T., McCrae, R.R.: Influence of extraversion and neuroticism on subjective well-being: happy and unhappy people. Journal of Personality and Social Psychology 38, 668–678 (1980)
7. Revelle, W., Scherer, K.R.: Personality and emotion. To appear in the Oxford Companion to the Affective Sciences. Oxford University Press, Oxford (in press)
8. Arya, A., Jefferies, L., Enns, J.T.: DiPaola: Facial actions as visual cues for personality. Computer Animation and Virtual Worlds 17, 1–12 (2006)
9. Rogers, G., Revelle, W.: Personality, mood, and the evaluation of affective and neutral word pairs. Journal of Personality and Social Psychology 74, 1592–1605 (1998)
10. Reisenzein, R., Weber, H.: Personality and emotion. In: Corr, P., Matthews, G. (eds.) Cambridge Handbook of Personality, Oxford University Press, Oxford (2008)
11. Hartmann, B., Mancini, M., Buisine, S., Pelachaud, C.: Design and evaluation of expressive gesture synthesis for embodied conversational agents. In: 3th International Joint Conference on Autonomous Agents and Multi-Agent Systems, Utretch (2005)
12. Borkenau, P., Liebler, A.: Trait inferences: Sources of validity at zero acquaintance. Journal of Personality and Social Psychology 62, 645–657 (1992)
13. Feingold, A.: Good-looking people are not what we think. Psychological Bulletin 111, 304–341 (1992)
14. Fink, N., Neave, N., Manning, J.T., Grammar, K.: Facial symmetry and the big-five personality factors. Personality and Individual Differences 39, 523–529 (2005)
15. La France, B., Heisel, A., Beatty, M.: Is there empirical evidence for a nonverbal profile of extraversion? A meta-analysis and critique of the literature. Communication Monographs 71, 28–48 (2004)

16. Farabee, D., Nelson, R., Spence, R.: Psychosocial profiles of criminal justice- and non-criminal justice-referred clients in treatment. Criminal Justice and Behaviour 20, 336–346 (1993)
17. Gill, A., Oberlander, J.: Taking care of the linguistic features of Extraversion. In: Proceedings of the 24th Annual Conference of the Cognitive Science Society, pp. 363–368 (2002)
18. McCroskey, J., Heisel, A., Richmond, V.: Eysenck's Big Three and communication traits: three correlational studies. Communication Monographs 68, 360–386 (2001)
19. Allwood, J., Nivre, J., Ahlsén, E.: On the semantics and pragmatics of linguistic feedback. Semantics 9(1) (1993)
20. Bevacqua, E., Mancini, M., Pelachaud, C.: A listening agent exhibiting variable behaviour. In: Prendinger, H., Lester, J.C., Ishizuka, M. (eds.) IVA 2008. LNCS (LNAI), vol. 5208, pp. 262–269. Springer, Heidelberg (2008)
21. Poggi, I.: Backchannel: from humans to embodied agents. In: Conversational Informatics for Supporting Social Intelligence and Interaction - Situational and Environmental Information Enforcing Involvement in Conversation workshop in AISB 2005, University of Hertfordshire, Hatfield (2005)
22. Ward, N., Tsukahara, W.: Prosodic features which cue back-channel responses in english and japanese. Journal of Pragmatics 23, 1177–1207 (2000)
23. Maatman, R.M., Gratch, J., Marsella, S.: Natural behaviour of a listening agent. In: 5th International Conference on Interactive Virtual Agents, Kos, Greece (2005)
24. de Sevin, E.: An Action Selection Architecture for Autonomous Virtual Humans in Persistent Worlds. PhD. Thesis. VRLab EPFL (2006)
25. Bevacqua, E., Heylen, D., Tellier, M., Pelachaud, C.: Facial feedback signals for ECAs. In: AISB 2007 Annual convention, workshop "Mindful Environments", Newcastle upon Tyne, UK, pp. 147–153 (2007)
26. Heylen, D., Bevacqua, E., Tellier, M., Pelachaud, C.: Searching for prototypical facial feedback signals. In: Pelachaud, C., Martin, J.-C., André, E., Chollet, G., Karpouzis, K., Pelé, D. (eds.) IVA 2007. LNCS (LNAI), vol. 4722, pp. 147–153. Springer, Heidelberg (2007)

BDI-Based Development of Virtual Characters with a Theory of Mind

Michal P. Sindlar, Mehdi M. Dastani, and John-Jules Ch. Meyer⋆

University of Utrecht
P.O. Box 80.089, 3508 TB Utrecht, The Netherlands
{michal,mehdi,jj}@cs.uu.nl

Abstract. Users expect characters in role-playing games to be proactive and social, but these characters fail to deliver in this respect due to limitations of traditional game AI programming approaches. BDI-based approaches are suited for development of proactive systems, such as NPCs in games. This paper argues that a BDI-based approach is also highly suited for developing social NPCs in a principled way.

1 Introduction

In a recent survey regarding the believability of non-player characters (NPCs) in popular role-playing games (RPGs) a questionnaire was distributed on several major game-related forums [1]. One of the aims of this survey was to determine whether what players expect from NPCs corresponds to what they encounter in practice. The results of the study showed significantly that avid gamers expect more from characters' proactiveness in comparison to what they find in the games they play, and that they believe that richer social behavior of NPCs would improve their gaming experience. This belief is supported by literature on virtual characters, which suggests that proactive and social behavior are among the key factors that determine characters' believability [2].

The behavior of NPCs in games is determined by the *game AI*, which is defined in [3] as "building algorithms that make game characters appear human or animal-like". Traditional approaches to game AI programming fall short if characters' behavior relies largely on their (unobservable) mental state, as is the case when characters are to have (long-term) goals and display social interaction. To remedy this problem game developers may embrace the Belief-Desire-Intention (BDI) model of practical reasoning [4], which is the paradigm of choice for developing rational autonomous agents. In this paper, it is argued and shown by means of examples in a BDI-based agent programming language that BDI-based approaches are not only suitable for developing proactive NPCs but also for developing virtual characters that are socially believable.

⋆ This research has been supported by the GATE project, funded by the Netherlands Organization for Scientific Research (NWO) and the Netherlands ICT Research and Innovation Authority (ICT Regie). The authors also express their thanks to Frank Dignum, for the stimulating discussions and valuable ideas pertaining to this work.

Zs. Ruttkay et al. (Eds.): IVA 2009, LNAI 5773, pp. 34–41, 2009.

The structure of this paper is as follows. In Sect. 2 the basic principles of BDI-based agent programming are introduced. Sect. 3 deals with implementing socially aware characters in the agent programming language 2APL, and presents an example in terms of an adaptation of the classic Sally/Anne false-belief test. In Sect. 4 this scenario is extended to simulating theory of mind by reinterpretation of behavioral rules, and Sect. 5 concludes the paper.

2   BDI-Based Agent Programming

Practical reasoning can be described as the process of figuring out which actions to take, and a particular philosophical view on how human beings perform practical reasoning is the BDI (Belief-Desire-Intention) model [4]. This model, based on folk-psychological concepts, reflects the assumption that human beings do not strive to fulfill multiple desires randomly, but commit to fulfilling some desire as long as this is considered a possibility and as long as the desire remains active. If the desire ceases to exist or is deemed unfulfillable, the agent ceases to pursue it. The BDI model thus describes rational agency, and has been adopted as a basis for architectures for developing resource-bounded autonomous agents. Such agents have components that in some way reflect the mental attitudes of Belief, Desire and Intention, which are balanced to achieve different types of behavior (for example by postulating different degrees of commitment [5]).

In the early '90s there have been attempts at formalizing BDI into logical characterizations of rational agency [5,6], which have given rise to a number of BDI-based agent programming languages, such as 2APL [7], JACK, Jadex and Jason [8]. These languages allow a programmer to use goals — a specific kind of desires — and beliefs as primary programming constructs, and provide a deliberation process that governs the selection of appropriate plans, which on the one hand are recipes the agent has at its disposal to achieve its goals, and on the other hand can be regarded as mental attitudes when selected by the agent. In the line of [6], plans which have been selected and are on the 'execution stack' are considered intentions.

The BDI model does not commit to a particular instantiation of the presumed mental states of practical reasoners. However, because the logical formalizations of the BDI model are by nature symbolic, the programming languages they have inspired tend to be focused on symbolic representations of goals (desires) and beliefs with a logical semantics. In the next section such an agent programming language is employed to illustrate the suitability of BDI-based approaches for developing social virtual characters.

3   Socially Aware Virtual Characters

In RPGs like the highly acclaimed game Oblivion [9] game developers attempt to create virtual societies in which NPCs do not only serve as mindless punching bags for the player's amusement, but appear to have lives of their own and pursue their own interests, which may or may not have something to do with the player's quest. Unfortunately, many of Oblivion's background characters do not appear to be *socially aware*, meaning that they do not react in a believable way to other characters in their environment. They interact with other NPCs by means of repetitive, superficial conversation, and sometimes exhibit queer behavior, like the storekeeper who doesn't flinch when the player vandalizes his store, but starts calling the guards the moment the player picks up an item.

3.1   A Social Scenario — The False-Belief Test

For characters to be regarded by players as socially aware they should take into account the presumed beliefs and goals of other characters when deciding upon their own actions. In developmental psychology the false-belief test [10] is used to measure social skills, and this test is here paraphrased to a computer-based setting. Imagine two characters, anne and sally, and two containers, basket and box. In this setting the location of an item, the marble, is either in(marble,basket), in(marble,box) or visible(marble). The characters have the ability to execute actions, which are transfer(marble,basket) and transfer(marble,box) to transfer the item into a container, and the self-explanatory enter(room) and leave(room) which modify present(anne) and present(sally).

The scenario unfolds as follows: initially both characters are present in the room, and the marble is visible. One of the characters then proceeds to transfer the marble into one of the containers, after which the other character leaves the room. While this character is gone, the character remaining in the room transfers the marble into the other container. Then the character which was not present enters into the room again. In the classical false-belief test a third party (typically a child) observes the scenario as it unfolds and is afterwards asked where the returning character will look for the marble [10]. The test measures the ability to attribute false beliefs to others, such that if Sally was present when Anne put the marble into the basket, but was out of the room when Anne transferred the marble into the box, the correct reply to the question would be that Sally will look in the basket (where she falsely, but justifiably, believes the marble to be) and not in the box (where the child itself knows the marble is).

3.2   Implementing the False-Belief Test

In the adaptation presented here it is assumed that a developer implements the AI of a third character, observer, which observes this scenario and can be queried by a presumed player regarding the location of the marble, as believed by observer itself, by anne or by sally. The observer should then give a response which is believable from the perspective of the player. Obviously, to give a sensible reply the observer should take into account the mental state (beliefs) of the other characters (anne and sally). If it did not and based itself on the state of affairs as itself believed them to be, it would make the error that is made by healthy children up to four years of age and 'mindblind' persons [11].

To implement this scenario the developer could opt for a separate representation of the belief state of each of the characters regarding the location of the marble, which is updated if a character perceives the transfer/2 action. Querying the observer would then simply involve a lookup into the *actual* mental state of the character, such that it appears that the observer has the 'right' (i.e. possibly false) beliefs about the character's beliefs.

This approach suffices for the scenario as presented, but does not hold if it is extended such that the observer too can leave the room. In this case a simple lookup into characters' actual belief state to fake observer's social awareness is not possible because the beliefs of the observer are also dependent on its presence in the room. A more principled solution would be to represent the beliefs of a character about the mental state of others in terms of its own beliefs, which are updated in accordance with perception. Ex. 1 shows such a principled implementation of the false-belief scenario in the 2APL agent programming language.

Example 1 (Implementation of the false-belief test scenario). observer.2apl

```
BeliefUpdates: // syntax: { precondition } Update { postcondition }
  { visible(marble) } In(marble,C)    { not visible(marble),in(marble,C) }
  { in(marble,C1)   } In(marble,C2)   { not in(marble,C1),in(marble,C2)  }
  { not present(Ag) } Present(Ag)     { present(Ag)                       }
  { present(Ag)     } NotPresent(Ag)  { not present(Ag)                   }
  { not bel(Ag,Fact)} Bel(Ag,Fact)    { bel(Ag,Fact)                      }
  { bel(Ag,Fact)    } NotBel(Ag,Fact) { not bel(Ag,Fact)                  }
Beliefs: // initial belief state (Prolog-style facts and rules)
  present(anne).    present(sally).    visible(marble).    eq(A,B) :- A = B.
PC-rules: // syntax: event or procedure call <- belief query | { plan }
  observation(Agent,leave(room))  <- present(Agent)     | { NotPresent(Agent) }
  observation(Agent,enter(room))  <- not present(Agent) | { Present(Agent)    }
  observation(Agent,transfer(marble,C1)) <- visible(marble) or in(marble,C2) |
    { In(marble,C1); B(findall(A,present(A),L)); updateBel(in(marble,C1),L) }
  updateBel(in(marble,C),AgentList) <- eq(AgentList,[Ag| Tail]) |
    { if B(bel(Ag,visible(marble))) then { NotBel(Ag,visible(marble)) }
    else if B(bel(Ag,in(marble,OldC))) then { NotBel(Ag,in(marble,OldC)) };
    Bel(Ag,in(marble,C)); updateBel(in(marble,C),Tail) }
```

The agent implemented in Ex. 1 perceives the actions performed by other agents (not restricted to anne or sally) in the form of perceptory events. If, for example, the agent anne performs the action transfer(marble,box) then this is perceived by the observing agent as percept observation(anne,transfer(marble,box)). An event-triggered PC-rule is then fired to update the beliefs of the observer itself, and its beliefs about others' beliefs. Table 1 shows a trace of the observer's beliefs evolving with the scenario. Lack of space forces us to skim over details of the code and the 2APL semantics, but see [7] for more information.

Table 1. Trace of percepts and observer's belief state, where for reasons of space conservation A=anne, S=sally, M=marble, Ba=basket, Bo=box, and pres=present

t	percept	beliefs of the observer after processing percept
0	—	pres(A). pres(S). visible(M).
1	S,transfer(M,Ba)	pres(A). pres(S). in(M,Ba). bel(A,in(M,Ba)). bel(S,in(M,Ba)).
2	S,leave(room)	pres(A). in(M,Ba). bel(A,in(M,Ba)). bel(S,in(M,Ba)).
3	A,transfer(M,Bo)	pres(A). in(M,Bo). bel(S,in(M,Ba)). bel(A,in(M,Bo)).
4	S,enter(room)	pres(A). pres(S). in(M,Bo). bel(S,in(M,Ba)). bel(A,in(M,Bo)).

4   Virtual Characters with a Theory of Mind

In order to make NPCs behave as if they are socially competent, they must appear to be aware of the mental states (beliefs, goals) of other characters and the ways in which these relate to their behavior. In other words, socially competent NPCs should appear to have a *theory of mind*. If these other characters are also NPCs, then one possibility to achieve this awareness is to look up their mental state in the game state and directly implement appropriate behavior. However, as addressed in Sect. 3.2, such an approach is not desirable if the NPC in question cannot always be expected to 'know' the mental state of other characters. Moreover, if these other characters are human players — whose mental state cannot be inspected at will — then this will not work at all!

In computer games it is feasible to make actions (by virtual and possibly also human-controlled characters) accessible for perception by NPCs. Perception of actions can serve as a basis for inferring agents' mental states (goals and beliefs), and this capacity to infer the unobservable from the observable is sometimes referred to as *mindreading* [12]. In Ex. 1 it was shown how an agent can be programmed to form beliefs about others' beliefs on grounds of observed actions.

4.1   Reinterpretation of Behavioral Rules

From characters' observed behavior it is not only possible to say something about their beliefs, but about their goals as well. The 2APL agent programming language offers an interesting opportunity in this respect, as it interprets declarative goal-based rules in order to generate goal-directed behavior. Such PG-rules have the form fact1 $<-$ fact2 | plan, and are interpreted as stating that "if the agent has the goal fact1, it should select plan given that it believes fact2".

In previous work we have shown that such rules can be reinterpreted in a (logically) abductive sense in order to explain observed behavior, stating that "if some agent is believed to have the rule fact1 $<-$ fact2 | plan and its observed behavior can be related to plan, then it *might* have the goal fact1 and belief fact2" [13]. Note that explanations of this sort need not be correct, but if the presumption that an agent has a particular rule is justified and the explanatory method is sound, then explanations given on grounds of this rule should be plausible and an agent that bases its own behavior on an incorrect (but plausible) explanation of another agent's behavior would not lose its believability.

Given that game developers currently resort to ad hoc measures in order to create NPCs that make believable mistakes [14,15] — an approach which is error-prone and detrimental to players' enjoyment in case of failure — the gains to be had by adopting a principled approach to developing characters that may show plausibly misguided behavior are large. Because declarative behavioral rules can be reinterpreted they need to be specified only once and can be used in different contexts, thus reducing programming effort and the possibility of errors. This feature adds to the appeal of BDI-based agent programming as a solution to developing believable virtual characters. Ex. 2 illustrates this, based on [13].

Example 2 (Reinterpreting PG-rules for explaining behavior). abduction.2apl

```
PG-rules: // syntax: goal <- belief | { plan }
  in(C,Obj) <- reachable(Obj) | { @env(transfer(Obj,C),_) }
PC-rules: // syntax: event or procedure call <- belief query | { plan }
  observation(Ag,Act) <- dislike(Ag) | { G = abduceGoal(Act) ; thwart(Ag,G) }
```

The agent in this example observes actions of other agents, and infers their goals if it dislikes them. Assuming it dislikes anne and can abduce explanations from its own PG-rules, the percept observation(anne,transfer(marble,box)) — generated if the 2APL external action @env(transfer(marble,box),_) is perceived — leads it to abduce that anne had the goal in(marble,box) such that it attempts to thwart this goal by means of some (unspecified) rule for 'thwarting' goals of others.

4.2 Related Work

To put this work into context a comparison is drawn with [16], which deals with implementing a death match bot in Quake II that anticipates opponents' behavior based on its own tactics. This approach can be considered agent-based as the bot is given perceptory information similar to that of the player, and selected behavior is the output of the rule-based SOAR decision-making engine. The results are highly satisfactory, as bots show improved and more enjoyable behavior and even learn new tactics by means of 'chunking'.

A drawback of this approach is that the SOAR architecture does not have mentalistic concepts as primary constructs and primarily operates on generic operators which are decomposed down to the level of (internal or external) primitive actions. The anticipatory process can simulate an opponent's behavior given some attributed perceptory input, and an anticipatory bot can base its own actions on the outcome of this process. Having mental concepts as primitives grants more flexibility, though, since it allows for checking whether goals coincide or conflict with one's own and taking appropriate action. Furthermore, the concepts of BDI correspond to how people generally explain their own behavior, facilitating knowledge elicitation and ease of NPC programming [17]. Another limitation of [16] is that only a single line of prediction is followed, whereas in [13,18] we have shown that often multiple different possible explanations for observed behavior exist, the relative plausibility of which may depend on contextual information (such as the role the observed agent is believed to enact).

5 Conclusion

Developing believable social NPCs requires a primary focus on characters' mental states. In principle, traditional AI programming techniques such as FSMs combined with scripting or decision trees can be used to implement behavior based on beliefs about other characters. However, the need for a principled model of characters' decision-making increases with the complexity of their personalities, such that a character which is to have (possibly conflicting) short- and long-term goals along in correspondence with beliefs about the mental states of other characters, is difficult to model using traditional methods.

The BDI model of practical reasoning presents such a principled model, and this paper shows in terms of the BDI-based agent programming language 2APL that it is also highly suitable for implementing socially aware characters. The separation of declarative rules from their interpretation allows for using rules to generate behavior, as well as to explain and/or predict the behavior of others. This decreases programming effort and chances of errors, and also introduces 'believable stupidity' into characters' behavior if the attributed mental state they base their own actions on is incorrect, yet plausible.

In future research we intend to formally characterize the process of inferring beliefs and goals from observed behavior, concentrating our efforts on a modal logical setting as well as the practice of agent-oriented programming.

References

1. Afonso, N., Prada, R.: Agents that relate: Improving the social believability of non-player characters in role-playing games. In: Stevens, S.M., Saldamarco, S.J. (eds.) ICEC 2008. LNCS, vol. 5309, pp. 34–45. Springer, Heidelberg (2008)
2. Loyall, A.B.: Believable Agents. PhD thesis, Carnegie Mellon University (1997)
3. Millington, I.: Artificial Intelligence for Games. Morgan Kaufmann, San Francisco (2006)
4. Bratman, M.: Intentions, Plans, and Practical Reason. Harvard University Press, Cambridge (1987)
5. Cohen, P.R., Levesque, H.J.: Intention is choice with commitment. Artificial Intelligence 42(2-3), 213–261 (1990)
6. Rao, A.S., Georgeff, M.P.: Modeling rational agents within a BDI-architecture. In: Proc. of the Second Int. Knowl. Repr. Conf (KR 1991), pp. 473–484 (1991)
7. Dastani, M.: 2APL: A practical agent programming language. Autonomous Agents and Multi-Agent Systems 16, 214–248 (2008)
8. Bordini, R., Dastani, M., Dix, J., El Fallah Seghrouchni, A. (eds.): Multi-Agent Programming: Languages, Platforms and Applications. Kluwer, Dordrecht (2005)
9. Bethesda Game Studios: The Elder Scrolls IV, Oblivion (2006)
10. Wimmer, H., Perner, J.: Belief about beliefs: Representation and constraining function of wrong beliefs in young children's understanding of deception. Cognition 13, 103–128 (1983)
11. Baron-Cohen, S.: Mindblindness: An Essay on Autism and Theory of Mind. MIT Press, Cambridge (1995)
12. Nichols, S., Stich, S.P.: Mindreading. Oxford University Press, Oxford (2003)
13. Sindlar, M.P., Dastani, M.M., Dignum, F.P.M., Meyer, J.-J.Ch.: Mental state abduction of BDI-based agents. In: Baldoni, M., Son, T.C., van Riemsdijk, M.B., Winikoff, M. (eds.) DALT 2008. LNCS, vol. 5397, pp. 161–178. Springer, Heidelberg (2009)

14. Lidén, L.: Artificial stupidity: The art of intentional mistakes. In: Rabin, S. (ed.) AI Game Programming Wisdom, pp. 41–48. Charles River Media (2002)
15. West, M.: Intelligent mistakes: How to incorporate stupidity into your AI code. Gamasutra (2009)
16. Laird, J.E.: It knows what you're going to do: Adding anticipation to a Quakebot. In: Proc. of the 5th International Joint Conference on Autonomous Agents (2001)
17. Norling, E.: Folk psychology for human modelling: Extending the BDI paradigm. In: Proceedings of AAMAS 2004, pp. 202–209 (2004)
18. Sindlar, M.P., Dastani, M.M., Dignum, F., Meyer, J.-J.Ch.: Explaining and predicting the behavior of BDI-based agents in role-playing games. In: Proceedings of DALT 2009 (2009)

How Do Place and Objects Combine?
"What-Where" Memory for Human-Like Agents

Cyril Brom[1], Tomáš Korenko[1], and Jiří Lukavský[2]

[1] Charles University, Faculty of Mathematics and Physics, Prague, Czech Republic
[2] Institute of Psychology, Academy of Sciences, Prague, Czech Republic

Abstract. Believable spatial behaviour is important for intelligent virtual agents acting in human-like environments, such as buildings or cities. Existing models of spatial cognition and memory for these agents are predominantly aimed at issues of navigation and learning of topology of the environment. The issue of representing information about possible objects' locations in a familiar environment, information that can evolve over long periods, has not been sufficiently studied. Here, we present a novel representation for "what-where" information: memory for locations of objects. We investigate how this representation is formed and how it evolves using a simplified model of a virtual character. The behaviour of the model is also compared with behaviour of real humans conducting an analogical task.

1 Introduction

Humans act in space. They furnish the space they live in with objects. Be it a van Gogh's painting or a pen, it pays to remember where ones' belongings are located. Intelligent virtual agents (IVAs) usually act in space as well. This demands them to have similar "what-where" information as humans do. In many today applications, IVAs read this information directly from the world map, which corresponds to complete environmental knowledge. While this approach may suffice for static words or dynamic but fully observable words, it results in unbelievable behaviour in dynamic words that are not fully observable. The latter kind of environments is increasingly employed by today applications. For instance, think of non-player characters (NPC) from a role-playing game (RPG), or virtual/robotic companions required to orient themselves in humans' houses. Here, a better approach is needed.

Why not to memorise all objects that an agent encountered? Assume we have a large, partially observable environment with objects that are passive but whose locations can be changed by external forces beyond the agent's capabilities. For instance, a pen can be moved by a fellow agent unbeknown to our agent. In this situation, we can expect multiple memory records of a position of each object based on the history of the object's moves. Where is the pen: at the working table or next to the TV? A simple list or a stack of memory records can not answer this.

How can we improve the performance? Consider objects that humans use. Humans have some organisation of the placement of their belongings; things are not placed randomly within their surroundings, instead, they are clustered purposefully according

Zs. Ruttkay et al. (Eds.): IVA 2009, LNAI 5773, pp. 42–48, 2009.

to their needs and cultural norms. Some objects appear regularly at some places (newspapers inside a mailbox). Other objects are almost never being relocated (a van Gogh's painting). Yet others are being relocated so often that it is not practical to remember their exact position. Consequently, when a human searches for an object, often, a sort of stimulus-response mechanism is employed. For a different object, several places are inspected in a specific order; sometimes, the whole house is scrutinised but starting at a specific place.

This brings us to the notion of *searching rules*, which are basically a sequence of places that should be inspected when searching for an object of a particular kind. Importantly, we mean by place any logically coherent space abstraction. These abstractions can differ in size and can be hierarchically nested; e.g. a bedside table, a place between this table and the bed, a corner of the living room, a living room, a house, etc. This corresponds to the way humans are supposed to cluster space [e.g. 7]. A "what-where" memory for IVAs acting in large, partially observable environments with movable objects should have the ability to develop searching rules.

In this paper, we present a model with this ability. To its advantage, it is quite simple. The model has been integrated with our agent with general memory capabilities [2] and investigated in scenarios mimicking a situation of a person moving into a new house. Specifically, we focused on the questions of how the initial representation is formed, how (and whether) searching rules emerge, and how the model relearns, measuring effectiveness of the model' behaviour. We also investigated behaviour of the model with different parameters, aiming to find a point of "optimality." Additionally, we conducted a simple experiment with human subjects that mimicked the agent's task using a simple Flash application, and evaluated the model qualitatively against the acquired human data.

The results allow us to conclude that the searching rules emerge easily and quickly and that they are qualitatively similar to searching rules developed by humans in their version of the task. The model also relearns well. Additionally, humans' data helped us to isolate one feature of human behaviour that cannot be explained by the notion of searching rules straightforwardly, but it can be added onto a top of the model easily. In overall, our opinion is that the model is now ready to use in real-world applications requiring plausible "what-where" memory.

The structure of the paper is as follows. Sec. 2 reviews related work. Sec. 3 details the memory model. Sec. 4 reviews and discusses the experiments.

2   Related Work

From the psychological perspective, the ability to locate objects is a faculty of spatial cognition, which is tightly connected to spatial memory. Spatial memory is conceived as a set of multiple interconnected systems rather than a monolithic block [4].

Recently, several general memory frameworks for IVAs were presented [2, 8, 9, 13, 14]; however, the degree to which they address any issue of spatial cognition is minimal. Fortunately, several works directly focussing on some aspects of spatial cognition for IVAs have emerged to increase believability of their spatial behaviour, including mapping, localisation, and navigation. Noser et al. developed IVAs learning topological structure of the environment and navigating using this structure [12]. In a psychologically more plausible manner, Thomas and Donikian [18] addressed similar issue. A mechanism for anticipating position of an object that can move itself, e.g. a sheep, was presented by Isla and Blumberg [10]. Unfortunately, neither of these works addressed sufficiently the issue of "what-where" memory for passive, but movable objects. Unlike these models, the mechanism of Strassner and Langer [15] directly aimed at representing both topological as well as "what-where" information and this information could gradually deteriorate when not refreshed. However, neither this model was designed to cope with objects that can be moved several times, lacking the ability to develop searching rules.

The field of gaming AI predominantly addresses believable and efficient pathfinding and automatic construction of space representation [e.g. 6, 16]. To our knowledge, the issue of "what-where" memory is not addressed. Finally, we are not aware of any work either from computational psychology or robotics that could suit our purpose directly. Robotics tend to focus on the issues of localisation and terrain mapping [e.g. 11], which are "low-level" from the perspective of IVAs, pointing to the significant difference between application domains. Even designers of robots with episodic memory systems [e.g. 5] do not seem to consider the "what-where" issue as a crucial one for their discipline. Psychological experiments investigating spatial abilities of humans are of considerable interest to the field of IVAs [see 4, 17 for reviews of some], but computational psychology tends to produce special-purpose models replicating data gained during laboratory tasks [e.g. 1]. It is hard to imagine a meaningful application in which an IVA could be engaged in such a task directly. Additionally, regarding "what-where" information, psychology tends to investigate what would be called in our context short-term representations of positions of static objects and their mental rotations, e.g. for the purposes of elucidating the allocentric—egocentric tension [reviewed in 4].

3 Model

The model we have developed is a simple associative network. It is composed of two kinds of nodes: *objects* and *places* (Fig. 1). Place nodes represent places with different levels of complexity and they are hierarchically nested. Object nodes have weighted links with place nodes; these stand for "what-where" information: a possible occurrence of a particular object at a particular place. Now, if an object is found by the agent, or comes to the agent's attention, the links to *all* the locations where it has been found are strengthened (e.g. the links from the glasses to a) the bedside table, b) to the bedroom, and c) to the whole house – see Fig. 1).

How could searching rules possibly emerge from this network? Note several things. (1) Links from an object node to nodes representing places at a similar level of complexity approximates the probability distribution of finding the object at given places. (2) Links to nodes representing more abstract places are strengthened more often than links to nodes of concrete places ("glasses are always in the house, but only sometimes at the bedside table"). Now, if queried for an object position, we can find the appropriate object node and past locations of the object's occurrence via the object—place links. Assuming that the pattern of the object's movement will be same in the future as it was in the past, we can arrange the place nodes in order of the strengths of the links leading to them (Point (1)). However, because of Point (2), before we do this, we need to scale the links' strengths by an inverse function of the complexity of places; otherwise, the abstract places will be always first in the list.

The fundamental assumption is that with an appropriate scaling function, the result will be a searching rule, i.e., a list with balanced ordering of concrete and abstract places where the object can be looked for. Concrete places should be first on the list provided that there are only a few concrete places where the object can be found. Otherwise, an abstract place should be first or very close to the beginning of the list. Particular places can be searched directly (e.g. the bedside table) while abstract places should be inspected (e.g. scrutinise the kitchen). The fact that this mechanism really produces believable searching rules is demonstrated in the next section.

An important question is how to deal with distances. The model ignores distances, conceiving the searching rules as verbal answers on the question: "Where do you think is an object X?" Our opinion is that in a middle-sized environment, e.g. in the ground-floor house used in our experiments, we can ignore distances letting the agent search for at most probable places, but distances become important in larger worlds, such as in multi-floor buildings or cities. How to take distances into account? One can take outputs of our model as inputs for an engine solving the *travelling salesman problem* (TSP) with *uncertainties*. Ideally, the engine should reflect how people solve the same problem. Surprisingly enough, it seems the TSP with uncertainties, as opposed to the classical TSP, has not been investigated in psychology until recently [19], and this work is not conclusive from the standpoint of IVAs. Thus, we assign the question of plausible penalisation of distant places as future work.

Formal definition. Formally, the network is a triple $<P, O, E>$.

P is the set of all *place nodes*, each of which is a quintuple $<p, up, down, level, size>$, where p is the node, *up* its super-location, *down* its sub-locations, *size* is a number of its sub-locations, and *level* is the level of abstraction. Abstractions are numbered from the bottom: *level* for a specific place is 1, and then the levels are enumerated by one towards the root of the hierarchy.

O is the set of all *object nodes*, i.e. the object records.

E is a set of weighted *edges*, each of which is $< x, found, missed >$, where $x \in P{\times}O$ is the edge, and *found* $\in \mathbf{N}$ is the number of times the object was found (and taken) or seen at the particular place, and *missed* $\in \mathbf{N}$ is the number of times the object was being searched for at the place but not found there.

In the present version of the model, we assume that P is specified in advance by a designer and fixed during the simulation (but see also Sec. 4).

Learning. When the model stores positional information about an object, it first checks whether the corresponding object node exists and creates a new one if needed. Then, the *found* variable of links between the object node and place nodes of *all* the places where the object was found are increased by 1 (e.g. the house, the bedroom, the bedside table). When the agent is looking for an object at a specific place and this object is not there, the *missed* variable is increased by 1. If the agent is searching in a location and the object is not in any of its sublocations, *missed* variables for this location and all the sublocations are increased by 1.

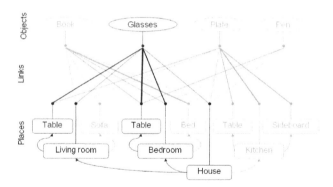

Fig. 1. Spatial memory. Some nodes from the experimental scenario are schematically depicted; the glasses' links are highlighted. The width of the links denotes the size of the *found* variable.

Rules formation. When the model is queried for an object position, *size-normalised trustfulness* (SNT) is computed for every place the object has an edge with as:

$$SNT = f\,(found,\,missed)\,/\,complexity\,(level,\,size) \tag{1}$$

The function f determines influence of the *found* and *missed* variables on the estimation of likelihood of finding the object at the given place and *complexity* is the scaling function. There are more options how to choose f and *complexity*. In our experiments, we have investigated how the model behaves with the following functions, where a, b, and c are parameters having been found during the trialling:

$$f = b.found - missed \tag{2}$$
$$complexity = level^{a} \tag{3}$$
$$complexity = size^{c} \tag{4}$$

The places are arranged in order of SNT. More specific places after their super-location are dropped from the rule. The sorted list presents a searching rule.

Notice that (3) completely disregards sizes of places, leading to assigning the same SNT to two rooms: one very small and another very large. Clearly, a human would prefer to inspect the latter room first. This motivates Eq. (4). Further discussion on how f can look like can be found in [3]. Note also that thanks to the equations above, the learning works in a Hebbian manner.

4   Implementation and Experiments

The model has been integrated with our generic agent with episodic memory abilities [2], becoming the agent's the long-term memory for positions of objects (LTSM). The agent also possesses a BDI-based *action selection*, an *emotion module*, an *attention filter* through which only some percepts can pass, a simple *short term memory* – an intermediate stage for object records that are to be later stored in the LTSM –, and an *autobiographic memory* with plausible timing of events and forgetting.

We investigated on a rigor basis the following questions: Do searching rules emerge? Does the time to emergence depend on the frequency of usage of an object?

Do the rules emerge quickly and is searching effective? How quickly the network relearns? Is there one optimal setting for all situations? Are the rules similar to those used by humans; are they believable? The methods and results are detailed in [3]. Here, we present a summary of the methods and discuss the main findings.

For testing the model, we have used a "new house" scenario, where we simulate the agent living for several weeks in a house with 6 rooms to which it just has moved. We defined five objects' classes modelling prototypical behaviour of five distinct kinds of objects, such as "90% class" (there is 90% chance that the object is located at a particular place, and 10% chance that it is located elsewhere; this applies e.g. for a can opener), or "3x30%" (there are 3 places in a same room in each of which the object can be located; 10% chance that it is elsewhere; e.g. glasses). Although we have a 3D implementation of the agent, for the experiments here, we use a 2D world. For validating our model against human data, we developed a simple Flash-based application in which we investigated behaviour of human subjects in a task similar to the task used in experiments with the model (however, note a limitation here: this application tested subjects' memory for time intervals of minutes, not weeks).

In a sum, the searching rules indeed emerged and the time to emergence depended on frequency of object's usage. Most searching rules emerged in less than 6 searches and the subsequent searching was nearly optimal. Additionally, in most cases, searching rules of the model were more effective than humans' behaviour. In general, the model driven by Eqs. (1), (2), and (4) performed better than the model driven by Eqs. (1), (2), and (3). The latter variant is not robust to changes of sizes of rooms.

Two problematic issues were revealed. First, we conducted many variants of the experiment and it was not possible to find one common parameter setting that would suit well for all the variants. The best common values found, that is $a = 9.6$, $b = <1, 15>$, produced behaviour that was worse (summing over all experiments) than average human behaviour by 56% and worse than the best distinct parameter settings by 89%. Especially, for the common parameter setting, there were problems with re-learning: the model took it long to forget over-learned places (e.g. after changing a PC to another room). Yet the model relearned well for distinct parameter settings, pointing to the necessity of extending the model with a mechanism deriving automatically parameters based on the context, and perhaps to use another kind of Hebbian rule to alleviate forgetting abilities of the model.

Second, qualitative comparison of searching rules of the model with those of humans revealed that humans behaved differently. However, we identified a simple cause: humans consistently used an additional heuristic to search at a place where the object was found last time. Only after the object was not found there, the subjects turned to their searching rules. When we added this heuristic to the model, the model's searching rules were qualitatively similar to those of humans.

5   Summary

The experiments we conducted showed that, in a middle-sized environment, searching rules emerge easily and the searching for objects is effective and comparable to the searching conducted by a human. However, there is a room for improvement concerning relearning. Our present work is organised around these points: a) testing the model in a larger environment, in particular in a city, b) improving forgetting, c) development of a mechanism that would learn space abstractions automatically. Should the model be used in a real application with a larger world, an engine solving travelling salesman problem with uncertainties should be added. The extended version of the paper detailing the experiments and supplementary videos are available [3].

Acknowledgement. This work was partially supported by the Program "Information Society" under project 1ET100300517, and by the Ministry of Education of the Czech Republic (Res. Project MSM0021620838).

References

1. ACT-R research group. Publications on Spatial Reasoning and Navigation (April 19, 2009),
   http://act-r.psy.cmu.edu/publications/index.php?subtopic=23
2. Brom, C., Pešková, K., Lukavský, J.: What does your actor remember? Towards characters with a full episodic memory. In: Cavazza, M., Donikian, S. (eds.) ICVS-VirtStory 2007. LNCS, vol. 4871, pp. 89–101. Springer, Heidelberg (2007)
3. Brom, C., Lukavský, J.: Tech. Rep. January 2009. Dept. of Software and Computer Sciences. Charles University in Prague (2009),
   http://artemis.ms.mff.cuni.cz//main/tiki-publications.php
4. Burgess, N.: Spatial memory: how egocentric and allocentric combine. Trends Cognitive Sciences 10(12), 551–557 (2006)
5. Dodd, W.: The design of procedural, semantic, and episodic memory systems for a cognitive robot. Master thesis. Vanderbilt University, Nashville, Tennessee (2005)
6. Hamm, D.: Navigation Mesh Generation: An Empirical Approach. In: AI Game Programming Wisdom, vol. 4, pp. 113–124. Charles River Media (2008)
7. Hirtle, S.C., Jonides, J.: Evidence of hierarchies in cognitive maps. Memory & Cognition 13(3), 208–217 (1985)
8. Ho, W., Dautenhahn, K., Nehaniv, C.: Computational Memory Architectures for Autobiographic Agents Interacting in a Complex Virtual Environment. Connection Science 20(1) (2008)
9. Ho, W., Dias, J., et al.: Agents that remember can tell stories: Integrating Autobiographic Memory into Emotional Agents. In: Proc. of AAMAS, ACM Press, New York (2007)
10. Isla, D., Blumberg, B.: Object Persistence for Synthetic Creatures. In: Proceedings of the International Joint Conference on Autonomous Agents and Multiagent Systems (2002)
11. Kuipers, B.: The Spatial Semantic Hierarchy. Artificial Intelligence 119, 191–233 (2000)
12. Noser, H., Renault, O., et al.: Navigation for Digital Actors based on Synthetic Vision, Memory and Learning. Computer Graphics 19(1), 7–19 (1995)
13. Nuxoll, A.: Enhancing Intelligent Agents with Episodic Memory. PhD thesis, The University of Michigan (2007)
14. Peters, C., O'Sullivan, C.: Synthetic Vision and Memory for Autonomous Virtual Humans. Computer Graphics Forum 21(4), 743–752 (2002)
15. Strassner, J., Langer, M.: Virtual humans with personalized perception and dynamic levels of knowledge. Comp. Anim. Virtual Worlds (16), 331–342 (2005)
16. Sturtevant, N.R., Buro, M.: Partial Pathfinding Using Map Abstraction and Refinement. In: Proceedings of AAAI, pp. 1392–1397 (2005)
17. Taylor, H. A., Rapp, D. N.: Updating Human Spatial Memory. In: Animal Spatial Cognition (2006) http://www.pigeon.psy.tufts.edu/asc/taylor/ (April 19, 2009)
18. Thomas, R., Donikian, S.: A spatial cognitive map and a human-like memory model dedicated to pedestrian navigation in virtual urban environments. In: Barkowsky, T., Knauff, M., Ligozat, G., Montello, D.R. (eds.) Spatial Cognition 2007. LNCS (LNAI), vol. 4387, pp. 421–438. Springer, Heidelberg (2007)
19. Wiener, J.M., Lafon, M., Berthoz, A.: Path planning under spatial uncertainty. Memory and cognition 36(3), 495–504 (2008)

EXSTASIS – An Extended Status Model for Social Interactions

Martin Rumpler

Fachhochschule Trier, University of Applied Sciences
Umwelt-Campus Birkenfeld
m.rumpler@umwelt-campus.de
http://www.umwelt-campus.de/ucb/index.php?id=mrumpler

Abstract. In this article we show how socio-psychological status theories can be formalized and used to control the expressive and communicative behavior of intelligent virtual agents. We describe EXSTASIS, a model that computes the status and action tendencies for all actors in a situation based on their status characteristics and behavior patterns. As a configurable software component EXSTASIS can be integrated in existing systems to extend the social capabilities of the virtual characters.

1 Introduction

Researchers and game developers want to build applications with intelligent virtual agents that are able to interact with each other and the human user(s) in a dynamic social environment. In the last two decades great efforts have been made to imbue characters with social and emotional intelligence. Computational models of affect play an important role at this because it is widely accepted that emotions and personality are key ingredients in creating believable and life-like characters [1,2]. Status in social interactions is a concept that has not been investigated thoroughly in this context despite the fact that status strongly influences the verbal and nonverbal behavior in such situations [3,4,5].

Social status usually refers to one's position or rank in society and depends largely on things like occupation, income, social class and so on. Status in social interactions or *group status* on the other hand refers to the standing of an actor relative to all other actors in a group during face-to-face interactions. Status in society is rather static, it changes only slowly if at all. Group status is rather dynamic and adapts constantly to the interaction partners and the social situation: "You may be low in social status, but play high, and vice versa. [...] Audiences enjoy a contrast between the status played and the social status." [6]. In this article we present a status model that describes how members of task groups use information about the status-value of characteristics they possess to form performance expectations for themselves and their co-actors. In turn, these performance expectations are used to compute action tendencies (e.g. likelihood of accepting or rejecting influence) which inform the selection of status-related behaviors.

Zs. Ruttkay et al. (Eds.): IVA 2009, LNAI 5773, pp. 49–55, 2009.

2   Status Characteristics Theory

Status Characteristics Theory is a branch of a larger program of research on expectation-states processes [7]. The theory offers the most comprehensive understanding of status generalization processes and is recognized for its logical structure, scope-restricted arguments, graphic interpretation, and confirmation status [8]. It's objective is to analyse situations in which people come together in a face-to-face setting for the purpose of accomplishing a shared goal and with the understanding that it is both necessary and appropriate to take others' behaviors and opinions into account in decisions related to that task. The theory argues that, under conditions of task performance and collective orientation of members, external status characteristics (e.g. educational level, physical attractiveness, occupational position etc.) function to affect behavior by acting through their effects on the expectations that individuals form for each other during interactions. A *performance expectation* is a generalized anticipation of one's own or another's capacity to make useful contributions to the group task. These underlying performance expectations become the basis for power and prestige (i.e. status) differences among group members.

The theory requires that a *status characteristic* consists of at least two states (e.g. high or low mathematical ability, male or female) that are differentially evaluated in terms of honor, esteem, or desirability. Furthermore, it is required that status characteristics are culturally associated with expectations for superior (or inferior) ability. If the status characteristic is *diffuse* (e.g. age or gender), the associated abilities are general and their range of application is not restricted to specific situations. If the status characteristic is *specific* (e.g. mathematical or reading ability), the associated ability is only relevant to a specified type of task situations. When a diffuse status characteristic differentiates members, as in a heterogeneous group, the cultural expectations associated with that characteristic become activated and become the basis of the expectations the members form for their own and each other's performance at the group task. Given that more than one status characteristic is relevant to the task the effects of each, weighted by its degree of relevance, are combined to form *aggregated expectations states* [9].

3   Status and Behavior

The impact of status characteristics on performance expectations has also been used to explain the empirical association between certain communicative behaviors and status in task groups such as length of initial eye contact, verbal response time, voice volume and tone, maintenance of gaze while talking rather than listening, touching, and interruptions [4]. It has been experimentally confirmed that the type and amount of these behaviors that an actor displays in relation to another is a direct function of his or her performance expectation advantage: A factual voice tone, fluent, rapid speech with few hesitations or stumbles, quick verbal reactions, a steady direct gaze with normal break-offs, and a straight but relaxed posture communicate high performance capacity. Low-task cues are a hesitant, uncertain voice tone, slow speech with frequent stumbles and hesitations, slow verbal reactions, a low level of direct eye contact, and a slumped but not too tense body posture [5]. Empirical evidence also shows that low status is associated with avoidance of assertive forms of speech, such as interrupting, and use of tentative or powerless speech, which include such linguistic features as disclaimers, hedges, politeness, and tag questions [10]. In this context, tag questions refer to declarative statements that are followed by a question concerning the statement, for example, "Gender can act as a diffuse status characteristic, *can't it?*" Hedges are adverbs or adverb phrases, such as *kind of, sort of,* and *maybe,* that weaken the strength of a statement. Disclaimers qualify and weaken statements by suggesting that the speaker is uncertain, for example, *I don't know but, I'm just guessing,* or *I'm no expert.* By identifying these behaviors as components of the observable power and prestige order in a group, and by assuming that these behaviors are probabilistic functions of the interactant's group status, we are thus able to select appropriate status behaviors for each virtual actor.

4   EXSTASIS

EXSTASIS (Extended Status Model for Social Interactions) computes the status and action tendencies for all actors in a situation based on their status characteristics and behavior patterns. It is based on a graph-theoretic formulation of the Status Characteristics Theory developed by Berger et al. [11] but extends the original model in several ways by allowing more than one instrumental characteristic [12], by integrating behavior patterns [12], by using new approaches to compute action tendencies [13] and by modeling different degrees of status characteristics [14,15]. EXSTASIS also introduces new concepts: modeling the strength of possession and relevance relations, modeling reoccuring and inconsistent patterns in status behaviors and an improved formula for calculating the path strength in status diagrams.

   In this section we give a concise description of the model. [16] provides further details about EXSTASIS and demonstrates its applicability by presenting a quiz show scenario, in which the computed status information is used to control the gaze behavior of two virtual characters as well as the course and style of their simulated conversation.

4.1   Modeling Social Interactions

EXSTASIS represents a group situation as an undirected graph which is referred to as the *status diagram* of the situation. Status diagrams consist of basic elements which are represented as nodes and relations between these elements which are represented as edges. The following elements can appear as nodes in a status diagram: task outcome states representing anticipated success and failure in the group task, diffuse and specific status characteristics and the different types of expectations associated with them (Sect. 2), behavior patterns that are linked to status typification states (abstract conceptions of typical high-status or low-status behaviors) and abstract task ability states (representing the ability of doing generally well or poorly at tasks). Three kinds of relations are represented as edges connecting these nodes: *possession* – actors may possess states of characteristics and behavior patterns, *relevance* – states of characteristics may be relevant to other characteristics or activated elements such as generalized expectation states and *dimensionality* – the positively and negatively evaluated states of the same characteristic or behavior pattern if possessed by actors in the situation, are dimensionally related to each other, signifying that these states are opposites of each other (e.g. high versus low mechanical ability).

4.2   Computing Performance Expectations

EXSTASIS computes the performance expectations for each actor in a given situation in a series of steps: (1) Determine all paths in a status diagram connecting an actor to the task outcome states. (2) Determine the sign of these paths as the algebraic product of the signs of the values of the edges on the path and the sign of the task outcome state. (3) Remove all paths that are not *effective*. A path is not effective if it is too long, if there exists a shorter subpath to the same task outcome state with the same sign or if there exists a path of equal length to the same task outcome state with the same sign but fewer dimensionality relations. (4) Combine paths in like-signed subsets where positive paths form the basis of positive expectations and negative paths form the basis for negative expectations. (5) Compute the *strength* of each path. In general, the shorter the path, the larger the magnitude of expectations. Formula 1 multiplies the weight $g(n)$ for a path of length n with the combined values for the strengths g' of possession and relevance relations and the significance g'' of status characteristics and behavior patterns s_i.

$$f'(n) = f'(s_1, s_2, \ldots, s_{n+1}) = g(n) \cdot \prod_{i=1}^{n} g'(rel(s_i, s_{i+1})) \cdot \prod_{i=2}^{n} g''(s_i) \qquad (1)$$

Two paths of length i and j in the same subset are then combined according to the following rule: $f(i \cup j) = f(i) + f(j) - f(i) \cdot f(j)$ which can be generalized to more than two paths as follows:

$$f(i_1 \cup i_2 \cup \ldots \cup i_n) = 1 - \prod_{k=1}^{n}(1 - f(i_k)) \qquad (2)$$

These rules reflect the assumption that there is a strong saturation effect in adding items of status information that have the same task significance as those that already exist [11]. When negative paths are combined, a minus sign is attached to the resulting value. The *aggregated performance expectation* e_x of an actor is the sum of the combined value of all positive and negative paths:

$$e_x = e_x^+ + e_x^- = f(i_1 \cup i_2 \cup \ldots \cup i_n) - f(j_1 \cup j_2 \cup \ldots \cup j_m) \qquad (3)$$

4.3   Computing Status and Action Tendencies

Given the aggregated performance expectations for each actor, the *expectation standing* of an actor is computed as follows for a group with size n:

$$s_i = \frac{1 + e_i}{\sum_{j=1}^{n}(1 + e_j)} \quad \text{for } i = 1, 2, \ldots, n \tag{4}$$

The behaviors of principal interest are power and prestige behaviors, i.e. behaviors having to do with the evolution and maintenance of task-effective group structures. The probability of an actor's staying with his own choice when faced with a disagreeing other actor, usually symbolized as $P(S)$, is the primary indicator of the power and prestige order [11]. EXSTASIS computes this so-called *stay-response probability* based on the expectation advantage between the two actors. In 5 the constant m represents the stay-response rate for interaction among status equals and the constant q represents the degree of collective orientation of the members of the group.

$$P(S) = m + q\,(e_p - e_o) \tag{5}$$

EXSTASIS also computes the *participation rate* for an actor, i.e. the probability $P(A_i)$ that a problem-solving attempt is initiated by this actor. In the simplest case this probability is identical to the group status of the actor. However, EXSTASIS also implements a more sophisticated model that differentiates between two categories of members: top-ranking members whose leadership is accepted as legitimate by the group; and all other members. Group leaders have per se higher participation rates because they guide and coordinate the group's discussion [13].

5   Related Work

So far only few attempts have been made to model and use status in social interactions. Hayes-Roth and her colleagues used status in a system called "While the Master's Away..." to model the interaction between a master and his servant [17]. Their work is based on theories about acting and drama [6] and not on socio-psychological status theories. The initial status and the status transitions are specified by the author. They do not use a formal status model to dynamically compute the status for the master and his servant in the scenario. In [18] a model of interpersonal attitude and posture generation is presented which uses the two dimensions affiliation and status to select appropriate interpersonal distances and body postures: close (high affiliation) versus distant (low affiliation) and space filling, relaxed (high status) versus shrinking and nervous (low status). The initial values for affiliation and status are selected by the user. Other researches have investigated the role of status in social navigation behaviors, i.e. avoidance of collisions and approach behaviors based on social roles and norms [19]. In [20] status is used to compute default interaction rates for socio-emotional and task-oriented behaviors based on the classification scheme provided by Bales [21].

None of these systems recomputes the status of the participants in a dynamic social environment based on new information (status characteristics) and social interactions (behavior patterns).

6 Summary and Conclusion

In this article we deliberately ignored all other aspects that can influence the verbal and nonverbal behavior in social interactions. The next step would be to investigate the correlation between status and affect because they influence the same aspects of human behavior: body postures, gestures, gaze behavior, manner of speaking etc. It has been shown that actors who like the other actor will emit fewer high status behaviors, and actors who dislike the other actor will emit more high status behaviors [22] and that influence rejection should be highest when one holds high relative expectations for self and dislikes the partner, and lowest when one holds low relative expectations and likes the partner [23].

There are at least two ways how status and affect could be integrated into an overall architecture: affective states could be treated as additional status information (apart from status characteristics and behavior patterns) or they could modify the way how status influences behavior. In the status theories this difference is denoted as *sentiment as constituent of expectations* versus *sentiment as mediator of expectations* [22]. The status information computed by EXSTASIS may be used similarly to inform affect computation and to regulate affect display.

References

1. Bates, J.: The role of emotion in believable agents. Communications of the ACM 37(7), 122–125 (1994)
2. Hayes-Roth, B.: What makes characters seem life-like. In: Prendinger, H., Ishizuka, M. (eds.) Life-Like Characters: Tools, Affective Functions, and Applications. Cognitive Technologies. Springer, Heidelberg (2004)
3. Ridgeway, C.L., Berger, J., Smith, L.: Nonverbal cues and status: an expectation states approach. American Journal of Sociology 90, 955–978 (1985)
4. Ridgeway, C.L., Berger, J.: Expectations, legitimation, and dominance behavior in task groups. American Sociological Review 51, 603–617 (1986)
5. Ridgeway, C.L.: Nonverbal behavior, dominance, and the basis of status in task groups. American Sociological Review 52, 683–694 (1987)
6. Johnstone, K.: IMPRO: Improvisation and the Theatre. Routledge, New York (1981)
7. Berger, J., Conner, T.L., Fişek, M.H.: Expectation States Theory: A Theoretical Research Program, Winthrop, Cambridge, MA (1974)
8. Walker, H.A.: A program for calculating P(S) in complex, asymmetric status structures. Current Research in Social Psychology (An Electronic Journal) 4(2) (1999), http://www.uiowa.edu/~grpproc/crisp/crisp.4.2.htm
9. Berger, J., Murray Webster, J., Ridgeway, C., Rosenholtz, S.J.: Status cues, expectations, and behavior. Advances in Group Processes 3, 1–22 (1986)
10. Carli, L.L.: Gender, status, and influence. Advances in Group Processes 8, 89–113 (1991)

11. Berger, J., Fişek, M.H., Norman, R.Z., Zelditch, M.J.: Status Characteristics and Social Interaction: An Expectation-States Approach. Elsevier, New York (1977)
12. Fişek, M.H., Berger, J., Norman, R.Z.: Participation in heterogeneous and homogeneous groups: A theoretical integration. American Journal of Sociology 97(1), 114–142 (1991)
13. Balkwell, J.W.: From expectations to behavior: An improved postulate for expectation states theory. American Sociological Review 56, 355–369 (1991)
14. Foddy, M., Smithson, M.: Relative ability, paths of relevance, and influence in task-oriented groups. Social Psychology Quarterly 59(2), 140–153 (1996)
15. Shelly, R.K.: Some developments in expectation states theory: Graduated expectations? Advances in Group Processes 15, 41–57 (1998)
16. Rumpler, M.: Statusbasierte Verhaltenssteuerung von virtuellen Charakteren. PhD thesis, Universität des Saarlandes (December 2007)
17. Hayes-Roth, B., van Gent, R., Huber, D.: Acting in character. In: Petta, P., Trappl, R. (eds.) Creating Personalities for Synthetic Actors. LNCS, vol. 1195, pp. 92–112. Springer, Heidelberg (1997)
18. Gillies, M., Ballin, D.: A model of interpersonal attitude and posture generation. In: Rist, T., Aylett, R.S., Ballin, D., Rickel, J. (eds.) IVA 2003. LNCS (LNAI), vol. 2792, pp. 88–92. Springer, Heidelberg (2003)
19. Rehm, M., André, E., Nischt, M.: Let's come together — social navigation behaviors of virtual and real humans. In: Maybury, M., Stock, O., Wahlster, W. (eds.) INTETAIN 2005. LNCS (LNAI), vol. 3814, pp. 124–133. Springer, Heidelberg (2005)
20. Guye-Vuillème, A.: Simulation of nonverbal social interaction and small groups dynamics in virtual environments. PhD thesis, École Polytechnique Fédérale de Lausanne (2004)
21. Bales, R.F.: Personality and Interpersonal Behavior. Holt, Rinehart & Winston, New York (1970)
22. Fişek, M.H., Berger, J.: Sentiment and task performance expectations. Advances in Group Processes 15, 23–39 (1998)
23. Webster Jr., M.: Working on status puzzles. In: Thye, S.R., Skvoretz, J. (eds.) Power and Status. Advances in Group Processes, vol. 20, pp. 173–215. Elsevier, New York (2003)

Authoring Behaviour for Characters in Games Reusing Abstracted Plan Traces*

Antonio A. Sánchez-Ruiz, David Llansó,
Marco Antonio Gómez-Martín, and Pedro A. González-Calero

Dep. Ingeniería del Software e Inteligencia Artificial
Universidad Complutense de Madrid, Spain
{antsanch,llanso,marcoa,pedro}@fdi.ucm.es

Abstract. Authoring the AI for non-player characters (NPCs) in modern video games is an increasingly complex task. Designers and programmers must collaborate to resolve a tension between believable agents with emergent behaviours and scripted story lines. Behaviour trees (BTs) have been proposed as an expressive mechanism that let designers create complex behaviours along the lines of the story they want to tell. However, BTs are still too complex for non-programmers. In this paper, we propose the use of plan traces to assist designers when building BTs. In order to make this approach feasible within state-of-the-art video game technology, we generate the planning domain through an extension of the component-based approach, a widely used technique for representing entities in commercial video games.

1   Introduction

According to the number of papers dedicated to the subject in the editions 3 and 4 of the AI Game Programming Wisdom [5,6], Behaviour Trees are the technology of choice for designing the AI of NPCs in the game industry. BTs are proposed as an evolution for hierarchical finite state machines (HFSM) intended to solve its scalability problems by emphasizing behaviour reuse.

BTs have been proposed as an expressive mechanism that let designers create complex behaviours along the lines of the story they want to tell, but at the same time, BTs appear as a too complex mechanism for non-programmers [1,2]. Commercial game development teams usually build some support tools in the form of graphical tree editors, where the designer can choose from a set of predefined composite nodes, conditions to be checked, and basic actions. Nevertheless, in practice, there is a tension between the freedom that the designers require to include their narrative in the game and the effort required from programmers to debug faulty AI authored by non-programmers. In this paper we propose the use of planning techniques to assist game designers when authoring the AI for NPCs.

A drawback for using declarative knowledge-intensive AI techniques in games is the additional effort required to model the domain. In this case, we require having a

* Supported by the Spanish Ministry of Science and Education (TIN2006-15140-C03-02 and TIN2006-15202-C03-03).

Zs. Ruttkay et al. (Eds.): IVA 2009, LNAI 5773, pp. 56–62, 2009.

```
<blueprint>
<entity type="goblin" ontType="Goblin" parentOnt="Monster">
  <components list="Take,MoveTo,TakeCover,MeleeAttack,LongRangeAttack,..."/>
  <attributes>
    <attrib name = "strength" value = "weak"/>
    <attrib name = "weapon-tech" value = "rudimentary,elaborate"/>
    <attrib name = "height" value = "short"/>
    ...
```

Fig. 1. Partial list of blueprints file

model of the actions that NPCs can do in the game world. In order to close this gap between academic and industrial game AI, we propose generating the planning domain through an extension of the component-based approach for representing entities, which is widely used in commercial video games.

The rest of the paper runs as follows. Next section briefly describes component-based game entities and BTs. Section 3 summarizes our proposal, how to support the authoring of BTs using planning and ontologies. Sections 4 and 5 provide the details and exemplify the approach. Last section reviews related work and concludes the paper.

2 Background

2.1 Components

During the last years, game developers tend to use a component-based approach to represent entities in the world rather than the classical approach based on a inheritance hierarchy [9,7]. From this point of view, each entity is just a collection of components, each one of them providing a concrete functionality, skill or ability. The definition of what an entity is and can do depends exclusively on the components it contains.

Usually, the different types of entities available in the game are described in a text file called *blueprint*, similar to the one shown in Figure 1. Each entity is a collection of components and their behaviours can be parametrized using attributes and values. For example, the figure defines a goblin entity that, among other things, can go through the environment and pick up objects. The attribute `strength` determines with objects the component `Take` can deal with, while the `height` predefines the kind of objects the `TakeCover` component should consider as protections.

2.2 Behaviour Trees

BTs [1,2] define an AI driven by goals, in which complex behaviours can be created combining simpler ones using a hierarchical approach. The inner nodes of the tree represent complex behaviours and leaves describe concrete actions. Besides, behaviours may be parametrized to promote their reusability in different contexts. In this way, each tree node is represented through: a behaviour (composite or a primitive action); bindings for its parameters; and a guard condition that controls, in runtime, whether

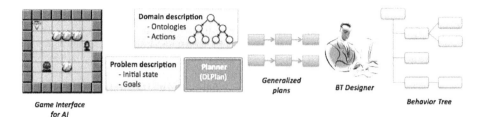

Fig. 2. Interactive process to create Behaviour Trees

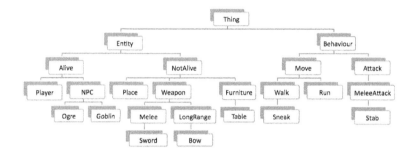

Fig. 3. Ontology that defines the domain vocabulary

this behaviour must be activated or not. Note that each instant there is only one active branch, going from the root to a leaf, of behaviours being executed. Finally, there are 3 commonly accepted composite nodes: sequences, static priority lists, and dynamic priority lists. Later, in Figure 5, we show an example of BT.

3   Planning with Ontologies to Support BT Creation

The creation of BTs is a difficult task that designers usually perform by means of a try-and-fail process. They must take into account the great amount of basic behaviours or primitives and the different ways available to combine them. The consequence is that the final quality of the BTs depends to a large extent upon the ability and experience of designers. We propose the use of AI planning techniques to automatically manage all those basic actions and its interactions.

Figure 2 summarizes our proposal to support the AI designer during the creation of BTs. By means of a graphical interface, that can be a simplified version of the game interface, the designer sets up a particular game scenario and some goals. Next, we automatically generate the equivalent symbolic description using the planning language, and by means of a planner, we compute all the possible plans that solve the problem. Then, designers can use that information to build more robust BTs. Actually, this is an interactive process in which designers propose different scenarios to the system and incrementally complete the BT.

We use a planner called DLPlan[1] that uses ontologies to describe the domain. Ontologies are an intuitive way to describe different components of a game (see Figure 3), making easier the interaction with the user. Besides, using such ontologies we can generalize the solutions and obtain not only specific plans for the current scenario but general strategies that can be reused in a broader set of situations. We will show an example in Section 5.

Finally, plans are integrated into the current BT by hand, i.e., the designer is the only person responsible of changing the BT to add new branches. It is important to remark that the planner works with a limited model of the game, while the designer can take into account many more factors (like story plot or special situations) in order to select behaviours, modify preconditions under certain circumstances and set the priority of each alternative. In this way, the designer is in complete control of the final result.

4 Generating the Planning Domain

To be able to use planning techniques, we need a symbolic representation of the world, in our case a domain ontology, as well as the actions that each type of entity can perform. However, this information is, at least partially, already in the C++ classes, which programmers have to implement in order to develop the game, and in the configuration files that define the different types of entities. Our goal is to extract that information to make it available for the planner.

First we need a base domain ontology that describes the basic vocabulary of the game genre and it is independent of the concrete game being developed. This ontology will be similar to the one in Figure 3 but without the leaves that correspond to the concrete types of entities in the game. Then, in order to populate the ontology with the specific entities, we use the information in the *blueprints* file. This file provides two special fields for each entity, *ontType* and *parentOnt*, that set the corresponding symbolic name for this entity in the ontology and the branch or branches in which it must be added. Once the entity has been added to the ontology, we can complete its description iterating over its components and asking them more details that must be injected into the ontology. As an example, we would add the description of the `Goblin` entity that appears in Figure 1 with symbols `canWalk`, `canTake`, `hasStrength.weak`, etc.

As regards the planning operators, we propose to extend the components such that they describe themselves at symbolic level. Note that most of the components are in fact in charge of the execution of one or more actions over the environment. In that sense, every component that represents a behaviour must be able to provide, through its programming interface, the planning action that describes it. As an example, Figure 4 shows the planning operator generated by the component `Take`.

5 Plan Generation and BT Authoring

With the propose of exemplifying our process of BT authoring using planning support, let us imagine that we have to develop a BT to control a greedy goblin that has entered

---

[1] Freely available at *http://sourceforge.net/projects/dlplan/*

```
TAKE(?who: alive, ?what: resource )
vars :  ?w, ?s
pre:  canTake(?who), nextTo(?who,?what), hasWeight(?what, ?w),
      hasStrength (?who, ?s ),  enoughStrength(?s , ?w)
post:  inInventory (?who, ?what)
```

Fig. 4. Example of planning operator for a basic behaviour

in a room to discover a diamond in the opposite corner. This goblin is a warrior well armed with a short sword, a small knife, a short bow and a sling. The room, in turn, contains some furniture: a table, two chairs and a bookcase. We assume the existence of a graphical interface to define these scenarios without having to deal with logical predicates but just setting items and units in the map and defining theirs attributes. This way, the scenario is automatically translated to the equivalent symbolic representation for the planer using the vocabulary in the ontology.

The goal for the new BT (and for the planner) is to lead the goblin to get the diamond. Let's start with the simplest situation, where there are no enemies near. Under these restrictions the planner shows only one possible plan, to walk until the diamond location and to take it:

```
1. WalkTo(goblin1,diamon1), Take(goblin1,diamon1)
```

Actually, using the abstraction capabilities of DLPlan, we are able to point out that this plan is applicable in several more scenarios, because the plan only requires *goblin1* to be an entity that can walk and take things and that it is alone in the room, and *diamon1* to be a small item. The generalization process followed by DLPlan to reach this conclusion is based on the ontological domain definition and it is described in [8].

Using this information, the designer builds the red branch, with dashed borders, of the BT shown in Figure 5. It is important to mention that plans generated using the planner are sequences of actions that correspond to the leaves of the BT. The definition of internal nodes in the tree to group basic actions and to represent different alternatives is responsibility of designers.

Next, the designer must complete this basic BT to make it useful in other scenarios as well, for example when there is an enemy in the room that has already detected the goblin. This time the planner computes several more possible plans:

```
1. ChargeAt(goblin1,sword1,enemy1), WalkTo(goblin1,diamon1),
   Take(goblin1,diamon1)
2. ChargeAt(goblin1,knife1,enemy1), WalkTo(goblin1,diamon1),
   Take(goblin1,diamon1)
3. TakeCover(goblin1,table1), LRAttack(goblin1,bow1,enemy1),
   WalkTo(goblin1,diamon1), Take(goblin1,diamon1)
4. TakeCover(goblin1,table1), LRAttack(goblin1,sling1,enemy1),
   WalkTo(goblin1,diamon1), Take(goblin1,diamon1)
5. TakeCover(goblin1,bookcase1), LRAttack(goblin1,bow1,enemy1),
   WalkTo(goblin1,diamon1), Take(goblin1,diamon1)
6. TakeCover(goblin1,bookcase1), LRAttack(goblin1,sling1,enemy1),
   WalkTo(goblin1,diamon1), Take(goblin1,diamon1)
```

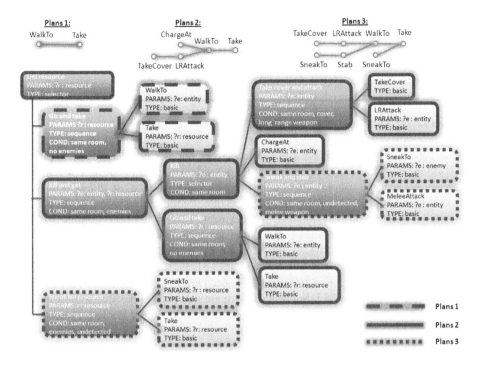

Fig. 5. Example of BT creation from different plans

It is important to mention that during the computation of these plans the planner has performed some interesting inferences using the domain knowledge. For example, the planner has used the table and the bookcase as possible covers and different weapons have been classified in melee or long range weapons. With those inferences, the six generated plans are in fact two different strategies parametrized with different values: charge against the enemy and then take the diamond; or look for a cover, attack the enemy from the distance and then take the diamond:

1. `ChargeAt(goblin1,sword1,enemy1)`, `WalkTo(goblin1,diamon1)`,
   `Take(goblin1,diamon1)`
2. `TakeCover(goblin1,table1)`, `LRAttack(goblin1,bow1,enemy1)`,
   `WalkTo(goblin1,diamon1)`, `Take(goblin1,diamon1)`

In these plans, *sword1* represents any melee weapon and *bow1* any long range weapon. The computation of the plans and the later generalization is performed behind the scenes, and so, the designer only sees the generalized strategies. Then, he has to complete the previous BT to incorporate the new possibilities. The resulting BT is built adding the orange branches, with continuous borders, shown in Figure 5. Basically, the previous branch is only applicable if there are no enemies in the room, and in other case the goblin has to kill the enemies first.

Finally, the designer wants to complete the BT with new branches that will be executed when there is an enemy in the room but he has not detected the goblin yet. This time, the planner computes several plans that can be summarized in three strategies: (1) take a cover, attack from the distance, go until the diamond and take it; (2) sneak until the enemy, stab him, go until the diamond and take it; and (3) sneak until the diamond and take it (without killing the enemy). The final BT is shown in Figure 5, and the green branches with dotted borders correspond to this last scenario.

6   Related Work and Conclusions

In this paper we describe an interactive process to support designers during the creation of BTs. We use planning to compute all the possible solutions to concrete scenarios, then generalize those solutions to obtain strategies and finally we use that information to build robust BTs. On the other hand, the use of ontologies provides an intuitive way to interact with the planner. Finally, in order to make this approach feasible within state-of-the-art video game technology, we generate the planning domain through an extension of the component-based approach commonly used to representing entities.

Related approaches have been described in [4,3]. Pizzi et al. [4] use a planner to compute every combination of actions to solve each level, and show them to the human designer like a comic, to let him check if there are any gaps in the storyline or in the design of the level. Another related work is the one described in [3] where the authors propose the use of planning to coordinate the behaviours for NPCs that are not main characters in the storyline of role games.

As future work we will study how to improve the interface between the planner and the BT authoring tool, and how to semi-automate the translation process between both representations. We are also interested in developing debugging tools in order to help the designer to understand the inferences that the planner does why the planner proposes some solutions and rejects others in particular scenarios.

References

1. Isla, D.: Handling complexity in the Halo 2 ai. In: Game Developers Conference (2005)
2. Isla, D.: Halo 3 - building a better battle. In: Game Developers Conference (2008)
3. Kelly, J.P., Botea, A., Koenig, S.: Offline Planning with Hierarchical Task Networks in Video Games. In: AIIDE (2008)
4. Pizzi, D., Cavazza, M., Whittaker, A., Lugrin, J.-L.: Automatic Generation of Game Level Solutions as Storyboards. In: AIIDE (2008)
5. Rabin, S. (ed.): AI Game Programming Wisdom 3. Charles River Media (2006)
6. Rabin, S. (ed.): AI Game Programming Wisdom 4. Charles River Media (2008)
7. Rene, B.: Game Programming Gems 5. In: chapter Component Based Object Management. Charles River Media (2005)
8. Sánchez-Ruiz, A.A., González-Calero, P.A., Díaz-Agudo, B.: Abstraction in Knowledge-Rich Models for Case-Based Planning. In: Proc. of Int. Conf. on Case-Based Reasoning (2009)
9. West, M.: Evolve your hiearchy. Game Developer 13(3), 51–54 (2006)

Modeling Peripersonal Action Space for Virtual Humans Using Touch and Proprioception

Nhung Nguyen and Ipke Wachsmuth

Faculty of Technology
Bielefeld University
33594 Bielefeld, Germany
{nnguyen,ipke}@techfak.uni-bielefeld.de

Abstract. We propose a computational model for building a tactile body schema for a virtual human. The learned body structure of the agent can enable it to acquire a perception of the space surrounding its body, namely its peripersonal space. The model uses tactile and proprioceptive informations and relies on an algorithm which was originally applied with visual and proprioceptive sensor data. In order to feed the model, we present work on obtaining the nessessary sensory data only from touch sensors and the motor system. Based on this, we explain the learning process for a tactile body schema. As there is not only a technical motivation for devising such a model but also an application of peripersonal action space, an interaction example with a conversational agent is described.

1 Introduction and Related Work

In order to carry out sophisticated and challenging interaction tasks in a spatial environment like a virtual world, one requisite is to perceive how far away objects in the peripersonal space are in relation to the protagonist's own body. The peripersonal action space is the space which immediately surrounds our body, in which we can reach, grasp and manipulate objects with our limbs without leaning forward. The ability of virtual humans to perceive and adapt to their peripersonal space enables them to manipulate and also to avoid objects while moving their limbs through this space. Additionally, it raises more interpersonal interaction possibilities with other agents and also with human partners.

Since virtual worlds are fast-changing and becoming more demanding, we go along with Magnenat-Thalmann and Thalmann who stated that it is important to enable virtual humans to have a realistic perception of the environment surrounding them, and to make them aware of it by building touch, vision and proprioception modeled on humans' perception [9]. Conde and Thalman [1] presented a model which emphasizes the role of a unified agent perception to establish a cognitive map of the virtual environment. This perception model integrates multiple virtual sensors and enables an autonomous virtual agent to predict object locations in an agent-centered vision space. In our definition we also consider the agent's peripersonal space as being centered on the agent, but spanned by its body. It enables the agent to predict object locations in reaching space.

Zs. Ruttkay et al. (Eds.): IVA 2009, LNAI 5773, pp. 63–75, 2009.

In humans the representation of peripersonal space is intimately connected to the representation of the body structure, namely the body schema [6]. The most comprehensive definition of the body schema, as a neural representation, which integrates sensor modalities, such as touch, vision and proprioception, was provided by Gallagher [3]. This integration or mapping across the different modalities is adaptive and explains phenomena like tool use as an integration of tools into the body schema [10]. Learning of body schema is very versatile. We can not only learn configurations of a body structure, but according to Holmes and Spence [6] it also supports learning of the space surrounding the body.

Learning a body schema can also be of great interest for developing advanced virtual characters in computer games. Especially games, which integrate user generated game content become more and more popular since they offer more diverse game courses. One example is the game Spore[1], where players are allowed to create characters and creatures according to their own imagination. The player can, for instance, add several legs, arms, wings and other body parts to the creature. Its locomotion changes with the added parts, but is predefined in the game. For these new kinds of games, where the body structure of the characters are built by the player, learning the kinematic functions of body structures could, in the future, lead to smoother and more lifelike movements and behaviour.

To our knowledge, work on learning reaching space for embodied agents has yet been done isolated from body schema acqusition ([7], [4]). So far, this topic has been dominated by robotics researchers in order to build adaptive body schemas. For example, Yoshikawa et al. [12] presented work on how a robot learns a body schema by mapping visual, proprioceptive and tactile sensor data using a cross-modal map. Fuke et al. [2] used the same modalities for learning a representation of a simulated face, using a self-organizing map. One crucial argument for an adaptive representation of the body structure are possible changes in the body configuration of humanoid robots. This method can replace laborious, manual adjustments. Although the topic is mainly treated by roboticists and has yet not been applied to virtual agents, we want to point out how learning a body schema can also further the design of virtual humans and characters.

In this paper we will show how to model a tactile body schema for a virtual agent and how this can be used to build a representation of its peripersonal action space. Both approaches, as far as we can see, have not been presented in previous works. Preconditions for the tactile body schema are our work on building touch sensors and motor abilities for a virtual agent. For learning a body schema, we base our computational model on the algorithm proposed by [5]. Unlike their approach, we will not use vision but will feed touch and joint information into the algorithm, in order to learn a tactile body schema, which therefore gets along without any visual information. Combining it with motor abilities, the virtual human is able to perceive its peripersonal space. This can also be regarded as a proof of concept which shows that the spatial representation of the body and peripersonal space, respectively, are not bound to visual information, since congenitally blind people are also able to perceive their peripersonal space. Therefore, everytime the agent perceives tactile stimuli on a certain body part (e.g. the left upper arm), coming from objects within his reaching space, the learned body representation

---

provides the spatial relation between the object and any other body part (e.g. the right hand). This enables the agent to carry out adequate movements, like avoiding or reaching an object, by taking the objects' spatial location into account.

The remainder of this paper is organized as follows. In the next section, we describe how virtual sensors were realized and prepared in order to feed our model of tactile body schema, described in Section 3. In Section 4 we present a demonstration scenario in which the tactile body schema can make an impact on peripersonal space. In Section 5 we briefly discuss how the properties of the model account for designing intelligent virtual humans on the one hand and virtual characters and creatures in computer games on the other hand. Finally, in Section 6 we give a brief conclusion and an outlook on future work concerning the interaction abilities of our virtual human Max.

2   Touch Perception and Proprioception for a Virtual Human

In this section we will first describe in general how a virtual sense of touch was realized for the virtual human Max [11]. In order to feed our computational model which we present in Section 3, we had to prepare the sensory data from the touch modality and complement it with sensory data from the motor modality. Therefore, in this section we specify which informations are extracted from the touch sensors and from the motor system to feed the model.

The touch receptors were developed and technically realized for Max's whole virtual body. These receptors allow for differentiating between different qualities of tactile stimulation. Findings from studies on the human tactile systems were incorporated to build an artificial sense of touch for Max, which is conceived not only for virtual but for artificial agents in general. In our work on modeling and realizing passive touch for Max's whole body, each tactile stimulation is associated with characteristics, namely, where on Max's body it was applied and what kind of tactile stimulation it was, e.g. stroking or tapping.

Max has a segmented body, i.e. his virtual graphical embodiment consists of several geometry parts. Around every geometry representing a limb of Max's body, 17 proximity geometries were added forming a "proximity aura" (see Figure 1, middle). This allows for predicting when an object in the VR environment is approaching Max's body. In humans, the somatosensory modality is represented in body-part-centered reference frames [6]. This aspect is also modeled by the virtual proximity auras and therefore they enable Max to identify the body part an object may be going to touch. Below the proximity aura, the surface of Max's body is covered with a virtual "skin". The virtual skin consists of flat quadrangle geometries varying in size, each representing a single skin receptor (see Figure 1, right). Altogether the virtual skin consists of more than 200 virtual skin receptors. The receptors are located on the body in neighborhoods, which are represented in a somatotopic map (similar to the map in the human brain).

This representation encodes the information which body limb a virtual skin receptor is attached to, and it allows to determine, in a fine-grained way, where Max is being touched. Depending on the location on the body, a tactile stimulation can thus be interpreted differently. Instead of different kinds of skin receptors as in the human skin, only one kind of virtual skin receptor is utilized for Max, for it is sufficient to discriminate

Fig. 1. Max's segmented body (left) with proximity geometries allowing for predicting touching of objects and identifying the touch receptor's corresponding limb (middle). Max's virtual body covered with over 200 virtual skin receptors (right).

between different tactile stimulations. Every object that is graphically represented in our VR environment can cause tactile stimuli on Max's virtual skin.

Any geometry's collision with a skin receptor is regarded as tactile stimulus. This also includes skin receptors colliding with each other which is crucial for identifying self-touch. Specific stimulation patterns arise from the temporal and local spatial changes connected to the stimulation. When a stimulus is, e.g., moving continuously over the skin, neighboring receptors are responding successively over time. This temporal information along with the spatial information about each triggering receptor, extracted from the somatotopic map, allows for classifying the stimulation as a continuous touch movement about the respective body parts. A central component, that fuses these stimulations of the receptors into a coherent touch sensation, forms our touch sensor.

So far, the classification of the different tactile stimulations depend on a somatotopic map, which was constructed manually. The skin receptor geometries are each assigned to a unique ID and are organized in 8-neighborhoods. That is, for each skin receptor ID, there exists an entry in the map, which contains the skin receptor IDs of the eight neighbors. Additionally, each skin receptor is assigned to a unique body limb, therefore the receptors' locations and distances are not centrally encoded, which reflects the already mentioned body-part-centered representation of the human touch modality. In the computational model described in Section 3, for each skin receptor, the touch sensor provides the assignment to the unique body limb and its position in the frame of reference (FOR) of that corresponding limb.

In addition to the artificial sense of touch, we need proprioceptive information about Max's body. In humans, proprioception is the sense of the orientations and positions of the limbs in space. It is important for perceiving motor control and body posture. We will refer to it, as commonly used in embodied agents, as the angle configuration of the joints in Max's body skeleton. The virtual agent's body has an underlying anthropomorphic kinematic skeleton which consists of 57 joints with 103 Degrees of Freedom (DOF) altogether [8]. Everytime Max is executing a movement, the joint angle informations of the involved joints are output. Synchronously with the tactile informations,

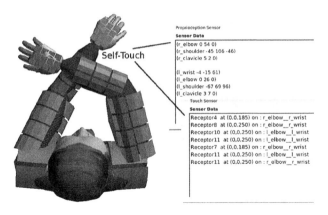

Fig. 2. Tactile body schema learning: For each random posture, sensory consequences are output by the sensory systems. The touch sensor provides an ID of the receptor, the limb it is attached to, and the position in the frame of reference (FOR) of the corresponding limb. Angle data for the involved joints are output by the motor system, representing the proprioceptive information.

the proprioceptive informations can be observed. In Figure 2 we can see the data for a sample posture, where Max is touching his own arm. In the next section we will explain how these input data can be integrated to form a body schema.

3 A Computational Model of Peripersonal Space Based on a Body Schema

In this section we present our model on how to learn a tactile body schema for our virtual human Max. The idea is to integrate tactile and proprioceptive information from his virtual body. In a first step, Max executes random motor actions resulting in random body postures. For each posture he perceives proprioceptive data from his joints and tactile stimuli when touching himself (see Fig. 2). The model integrates input data given by the touch sensors and joint angle data given by the proprioception sensors described in Section 2.

3.1 Tactile Body Schema for Peripersonal Space

The tactile body schema, learned by the virtual human, in our model depends on its sensory system and FOR transformations associated with the sensory input coming from the touch and proprioception sensors. For our purposes, that is, perceiving and acting in peripersonal space, a tactile body schema is sufficient. We do not need a precise representation of the physical properties of the body, rather we need the kinematic structure and functions of the body for controlling and predicting the sensory consequences and movements with regard to tactile stimulations coming from objects located within the reaching space.

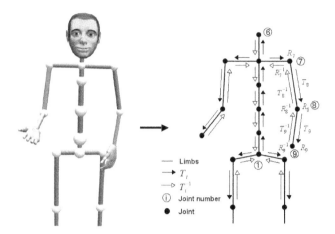

Fig. 3. Kinematic tree (right) representing Max's body skeleton (left). Following an edge in direction to the root node representing the hip joint (joint 1), a FOR transformation $\mathbf{T}_i$ and a rotation $\mathbf{R}_i$ associated to the respective joint i (numbers are free chosen) have to be carried out, in the other direction we use the inverse FOR transformation $\mathbf{T}_i^{-1}$ and rotation $\mathbf{R}_i^{-1}$. Example: The following composition transforms a FOR centered on joint 7 to a FOR centered on joint 6 (joint 5 is located between them): $\mathbf{R}_6^{-1} \circ \mathbf{T}_6^{-1} \circ \mathbf{T}_7 \circ \mathbf{R}_7$.

Given a proprioceptive input, together with input from a certain touch receptor to a corresponding particular posture, the body schema can predict proprioceptive sensor consequences for other touch receptors. This can be used to generate a movement, corresponding to the proprioceptive data. The following example makes its utilization more clear. Let us assume a virtual human accidentally touches an object located in its peripersonal space with its right upper arm. Note that there is no visual information. In order to "touch" the same object with the left hand, the agent needs to know how to move the left arm (see Section 4).

3.2   Learning a Tactile Body Schema

We follow Hersch et al. [5] by considering the body schema as a tree of rigid transformations. In our case this kinematic tree is prescribed by the skeleton of the virtual human Max. In this tree each node corresponds to a joint in Max's skeleton and each edge corresponds to a limb between two joints (see Figure 3). That means, the number of joints linked in their respective order with the number of limbs are represented in the kinematic tree, but not the joint orientation and position. In our model the touch receptors are attached to the limbs (see Section 2) and their position is represented in the limb's FOR. In the kinematic tree representation, the touch receptors can therefore be represented as located along the edges.

Following an edge from one joint to another is associated with a FOR transformation which transforms the FOR centered on one joint to the FOR centered on the other joint. Therefore, following any path linking one joint to another represents a kinematic chain. Max's skeleton prescribes the hierarchy of the FOR transformations. This determines

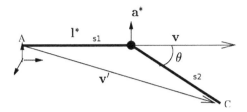

Fig. 4. Example of a single segment manipulator with A as the origin, C as the end effector, s1 as the proximal, and s2 the distal segment. A rigid transformation is here parameterized by vectors **l** (*joint position) and **a** (*rotation axis). Along with the known angle θ and given a vector **v** in the FOR of s2, and its transform **v'** in the FOR of s1, **l** and **a** can be adapted online (after [5], Fig.2).

whether a normal or inverse FOR transformation has to be carried out along a kinematic chain. Figure 3 shows the transformation hierarchy with the hip joint as root node in the kinematic tree representing Max's skeleton. The kinematic chains transform positions and orientations from the FOR centered on the different joints. Since the touch receptors are attached to the limbs, we can transform the position for one touch receptor, given in the FOR of the corresponding limb, into any other touch receptor position also given in the FOR of its corresponding limb.

So far, we use the number of joints and the hierarchy of Max's skeleton as prior knowledge about his body structure. However, what is not yet known is the position and orientation of these joints which also determine the limb lenghts. This is where the algorithm proposed by Hersch et al. [5] comes in. We can use the algorithm straightforward, since it provides a new and general approach in online adapting joint orientations and positions in joint manipulator transformations. Our challenge in using this algorithm is the adaptation to a case different from the one it was originally applied to. In our case we do not use visual and joint angle data but instead, replace all visual by tactile information in order to update all the rigid transformations along the generated kinematic chains. As far as we know, this case has not been presented before.

Here we will only sketch the key ideas of the algorithm and then describe how they can be adapted for our purposes. The algorithm deals with the problem of having a single segment manipulator as shown in Figure 4. A rigid transformation carried out by the manipulator is parameterized by unknown vectors **l** (the joint position) and **a** (the unit rotation axis) and a known rotation angle θ. The vectors **a** and **l** can be adapted, so that they match the rigid transformation. This is done by means of a given vector **v** in a FOR attached to the distal segment s2, and its given transform **v'** in a FOR attached to segment s1 and the rotation angle θ. A gradient descent on the squared distance between **v'** and its guessed transform vector **l**+**R**(**v**) is used in order to update the guesses of the vectors **a** and **l**.

Having sufficient examples of positions (values for **v**) given in the FOR of segment s2 and the corresponding positions (values for **v'**) given in the FOR of segment s1, it is possible to adapt the joint positions and orientations. For an adaptation of multisegmented manipulators the simulated transform vector **l**+**R**(**v**) was replaced by a transformation $\mathcal{T}(\mathbf{v})$, which contains the transformations along the kinematic chain of the multisegment manipulator. In our case the kinematic chains can be generated using the

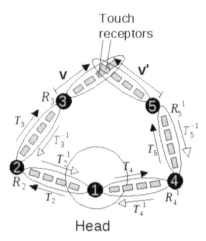

Fig. 5. Schema of Max touching himself (notation following Figure 3). The following composition transforms the position **v** (given in the FOR centered on joint 3) of a touch receptor into the FOR centered on joint 5: $\mathbf{R}_5^{-1} \circ \mathbf{T}_5^{-1} \circ \mathbf{R}_4^{-1} \circ \mathbf{T}_4^{-1} \circ \mathbf{T}_2 \circ \mathbf{R}_2 \circ \mathbf{T}_3 \circ \mathbf{R}_3$. Note that retracing the same chain in the opposite direction transforms the position of the other touch receptor **v'** (given in the FOR centered on joint 5) into the FOR centered on joint 3.

kinematic tree representing Max's body skeleton (see Figure 3). The rotation axes and translation vectors of joint i can then be updated by using the equations (1) and (2) (taken from [5]) with a small positive scalar ε, and rotation matrix $\mathbf{R}_i$ of axis $\mathbf{a}_i$ and angle θ_i for joint i.

$$\Delta \mathbf{l}_i = \varepsilon (\mathbf{v}'_n - \mathscr{T}(\mathbf{v}_n))^T \prod_{j=1}^{i-1} \mathbf{R}_j \tag{1}$$

$$\Delta \mathbf{a}_i = \varepsilon (\mathbf{v}'_n - \mathscr{T}(\mathbf{v}_n))^T ((\prod_{j=1}^{i-1} \mathbf{R}_j) \frac{\partial}{\partial \mathbf{a}_i} (\mathbf{R}_i (\mathbf{T}_{i+1} \circ \mathbf{R}_{i+1} ... \circ \mathbf{T}_n \circ \mathbf{R}_n (\mathbf{v_n})))) \tag{2}$$

In order to use the algorithm, we have to start with an onset body schema which is an initial guess of Max's target body schema. It is described on the one hand by known parameters and on the other hand by initially guessed parameters. The number of joints and their hierarchical order are determined by the kinematic tree of Max's body skeleton, described above. The parameters which are not known yet are the joint orientations and their positions, determining the body segment lenghts. Thus we choose the orientations randomly and assign the segment lengths with small values.

For modeling peripersonal space we start with learning the schema for Max's torso, which includes all nodes above the hip joint to the wrist joints. For a first approach we do not use the joints in the hands, since a sophisticated touch sensation for the hands and fingers (with over 30 receptors per hand) may not be nessessary for reaching space. We then have to choose random joint angle configurations for the torso. For each randomly chosen posture, the agent will carry out a motion which leads to the joint angle configuration and then stop. If skin receptors are touching each other during the motion, Max will immediately stop moving in order to avoid the case of passing through the virtual limbs. The originally assumed joint angle configuration will then be discarded, and instead, the current joint angle data is taken and the resulting sensor data is processed. The input for the algorithm are the positions of two touch receptors touching each other in the FOR of their corresponding limbs, both provided by the touch sensor (see Figure 5). Interestingly, both positions can take over the role of the input vectors **v** and **v'** for the Equations 1 and 2. This is also illustrated in the pseudo code for the tactile learning process in Algorithm 1. Additionally, the angle values of the joints involved in the current posture are input to the algorithm. It then takes the sensor data for updating its guesses of the joint orientations and positions of the involved kinematic chain.

Algorithm 1. Pseudo code: Tactile learning process

```
 1: repeat
 2:      for all torso joints do
 3:          choose random angle θ
 4:          set torsojoint of current body schema to θ
 5:      end for
 6:      if two touch receptors trigger then
 7:          pos_i ← position of touch receptor with ID i
 8:          pos_j ← position of touch receptor with ID j
 9:          joint_n ← joint of limb n where pos_i is attached to
10:          joint_m ← joint of limb m where pos_j is attached to
11:      end if
12:      Set Transformation T ← kinematic chain (startnode ← joint_m, endnode ← joint_n)
13:      pos_j = T ( pos_i )
14:      for  k = startnode to endnode  do
15:          update Δl_i
16:          update Δa_i
17:      end for
18:      if pos_j not transformed yet then
19:          Set T ← kinematic chain (startnode ← joint_n, endnode ← joint_m)
20:          pos_i = T ( pos_j )
21:          GOTO 14
22:      end if
23: until (pos_j - T(pos_i)) = 0
```

In the adaptation process the idea is to use the algorithm two times for each posture (see Algorithm 1, Line 18-22). In a first process the transformation of the position **v** of one touch receptor is transformed into the FOR of the other touch receptor (Line 13). This is used to update the current body schema (Line 14-16), in a second pass the angles of the postures stay the same, but the kinematic chain linking the two touch receptors is retraced to transform the position **v'** of the other touch receptor. Note that this "double-use" is only possible in the case of learning a tactile body schema.

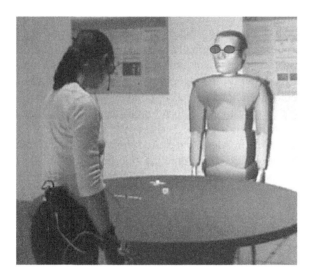

Fig. 6. Virtual agent Max with a human interaction partner standing around a table in a CAVE-like Virtual Reality environment. By means of his peripersonal space Max may perceive objects located on the table in front of him as near or far away from his body.

After completion the learned body schema expectedly contains the kinematic functions derived from the sensory input. This can be used to control Max's movements with regard to tactile stimuli.

4   Peripersonal Space in Interaction

Based on the work presented in Section 2, we devised the computational model in Section 3 for building a body-representation for the virtual humanoid Max. This model can enable him to acquire a perception of his peripersonal space, i.e. the space immediately surrounding his body and which he can reach with his limbs. In this section we outline an interaction example in which peripersonal space can be utilized by the virtual human Max. Previous works on peripersonal space and body schema acquisition may lack the application and interaction possibilities, since the agents are often regarded as technical platforms. However Max is an embodied conversational agent and is primarily intended for interaction with human or other virtual partners, hence the application of peripersonal space can be shown in an example. In this example Max is standing at a table. In an interaction scenario Max could interact in a CAVE-like environment with a human partner as shown in Figure 6.

In our test scenario, several objects are located on the table. Let's assume Max is (technically) "blindfolded". The interaction partner, aware of Max's inability to see, asks him to reach for an object near to his body. He then explores his peripersonal space with one hand. Depending on the object's location he might touch it with his hand but also with any other part of his arm, since it also has skin receptors. As soon as he touches it, the partner could ask him to carry out tasks, such as touching the object with the other hand or putting it as far from him as possible. The first task is supported by the tactile body schema which contains the kinematic transformations relating two touch receptors. This can be used to compute a movement to the respective position. The task of putting the object as far away as possible is an interesting aspect relating to peripersonal reaching space. It is conceivable that Max could also learn the kinematic function of leaning forward in order to extend his peripersonal space.

5   Discussion

Our model aims at learning a tactile body schema using touch and proprioception instead of vision and proprioception. Knowledge about the joint number and hierarchy of Max's body skeleton is given in advance. This approach is important to produce the effectiveness of the used algorithm. Hersch et al. [5] for example argue that the kinematic structure in humanoids usually does not evolve over lifetime, limbs grow, but new joints do not appear. We agree with this opinion, but do not regard it as a contribution to ongoing neuroscience research of body schema acquisition. In fact we consider it as a contribution to learning kinematic structures for the special requirements of intelligent virtual agents like Max. In robots it is not easy to realize a sophisticated skin and it takes much longer to learn a body schema, since random explorations cannot be executed very fast. Due to these circumstances, a "virtual" simulation model of the robot is usually employed to learn the schema and afterwards is transferred to the physical robot. We want to point out that methods from other research fields which already incorporate "virtual bodies" are of special interest for the design of virtual humans. In Section 1 we mentioned the applications for virtual creatures in computer games. Body structure learning would enable the players to design creatures even with more unusual kinematic structures, not comparable to humanoid ones. In these cases, the skeleton is also predefined by the designer, therefore methods which take this pre-knowledge for learning lend themselves for an immediate use in character animation in computer games.

6   Conclusion and Future Work

In this paper, we proposed a computational model for building a tactile body schema for the virtual humanoid Max, which can enable him to acquire a perception of his peripersonal space. The proposed computational model uses tactile and proprioceptive informations and relies on an algorithm, which was originally applied with visual and proprioceptive sensor data. In order to feed the model, we presented work on obtaining the nessessary sensory data from touch sensors and the motor system. Based on this, we described the learning process for a tactile body schema. The next step in our work will be to test the proposed model for its online learning features.

As Max is a conversational agent, a possible example for using peripersonal space in interaction was shown. Subsequently the described interaction scenario could be used to study further research questions. In future work we will investigate how spatial perspective models of two agents can be aligned. In a cooperative interaction task, two artificial agents, or an agent and a human partner, jointly have to solve a problem by moving or manipulating (virtual) physical objects. In the shared space between the partners, one agent can use his peripersonal space representation (the space immediately surrounding the body) and map it onto the interaction partner. This representation could then be augmented with visual information. Based on the interlocutor's position and orientation, the agent can now infer the spatial perspective of the partner, by aligning the mapped peripersonal space representation of his own with position and orientation parameters of the other. This perspective model can help the agent anticipate actions performed, or hindrances encountered, by his partner. For example, when the agent sees an object which he infers to be hidden from the perspective of the other, the agent can move the object so the partner can see it. In a further step, the agent can develop a representation of interpersonal action space, i.e. the space between the two partners where their individual peripersonal space representations meet or overlap. A challenge is to develop an analogical spatial representation suited for peripersonal and interpersonal action space and, further, to devise methods for a dynamical alignment of interpersonal space representation when one or both interlocutors change their positions or body orientations.

Acknowledgments

This research is carried out in the context of the Collaborative Research Center 673 "Alignment in Communication" granted by the Deutsche Forschungsgemeinschaft.

References

1. Conde, T., Thalmann, D.: An integrated perception for autonomous virtual agents: active and predictive perception. Journal of Visualization and Computer Animation 17(3-4), 457–468 (2006)
2. Fuke, S., Ogion, M., Asada, M.: Body image constructed from motor and tactile image constructed from motor and tactile images with visual information. International Journal of Humanoid Robotics (IJHR) 4(2), 347–364 (2007)
3. Gallagher, S.: How the body shapes the mind. Clarendon Press, Oxford (2005)
4. Goerick, C., Wersing, H., Mikhailova, I., Dunn, M.: Peripersonal space and object recognition for humanoids. In: Proceedings of the IEEE/RSJ International Conference on Humanoid Robots (Humanoids 2005), Tsukuba, Japan, pp. 387–392. IEEE Press, Los Alamitos (2005)
5. Hersch, M., Sauser, E., Billard, A.: Online learning of the body schema. International Journal of Humanoid Robotics 5(2), 161–181 (2008)
6. Holmes, N.P., Spence, C.: The body schema and multisensory representation(s) of peripersonal space. Cognitive Processing 5(2), 94–105 (2004)
7. Huang, Z., Eliëns, A., Visser, C.: "Is it within my reach?" – an agents perspective. In: Rist, T., Aylett, R.S., Ballin, D., Rickel, J. (eds.) IVA 2003. LNCS (LNAI), vol. 2792, pp. 150–158. Springer, Heidelberg (2003)
8. Kopp, S., Wachsmuth, I.: Synthesizing multimodal utterances for conversational agents. Comput. Animat. Virtual Worlds 15(1), 39–52 (2004)

 9. Magnenat-Thalmann, N., Thalmann, D.: Virtual humans: thirty years of research, what next? The Visual Computer 21(12) (2005)
10. Maravita, A., Iriki, A.: Tools for the body (schema). Trends in Cognitive Sciences 8(2), 79–86 (2004)
11. Nguyen, N., Wachsmuth, I., Kopp, S.: Touch perception and emotional appraisal for a virtual agent. In: Proceedings Workshop Emotion and Computing – Current Research and Future Impact, KI-2007, Osnabrück (2007)
12. Yoshikawa, Y., Yoshimura, M., Hosoda, K., Asada, M.: Visio-tactile binding through double-touching by a robot with an anthropomorphic tactile sensor. In: International Conference on Development and Learning, p. 126 (2005)

GNetIc – Using Bayesian Decision Networks for Iconic Gesture Generation

Kirsten Bergmann and Stefan Kopp

Sociable Agents Group, CITEC, Bielefeld University
P.O. Box 100 131, D-33615 Bielefeld, Germany
{kbergman,skopp}@techfak.uni-bielefeld.de

Abstract. Expressing spatial information with iconic gestures is abundant in human communication and requires to transform a referent representation into resembling gestural form. This task is challenging as the mapping is determined by the visuo-spatial features of the referent, the overall discourse context as well as concomitant speech, and its outcome varies considerably across different speakers. We present a framework, GNetIc, that combines data-driven with model-based techniques to model the generation of iconic gestures with Bayesian decision networks. Drawing on extensive empirical data, we discuss how this method allows for simulating speaker-specific vs. speaker-independent gesture production. Modeling results from a prototype implementation are presented and evaluated.

Keywords: Nonverbal Behavior, Gesture Generation, Inter-subjective Differences, Bayesian Decision Networks.

1 Introduction

The use of speech-accompanying iconic gestures is a ubiquitous characteristic of human-human communication, especially when spatial information is expressed. It is therefore desirable to endow virtual agents with similar gestural expressiveness and flexibility to improve the interaction between humans and machines. This is an ambitious objective, as de Ruiter [4, p. 30] recently put it: "The problem of generating an overt gesture from an abstract [...] representation is one of the great puzzles of human gesture, and has received little attention in the literature". The intricacy is due to the fact that iconic gestures, in contrast to language or other gesture types such as emblems, have no conventionalized form-meaning mapping. Apparently, iconic gestures communicate through iconicity, i.e., their physical form corresponds with object features such as shape or spatial properties. Empirical studies, however, reveal that similarity with the referent cannot fully account for all occurrences of iconic gesture use [10]. Recent findings actually indicate that a gesture's form is also influenced by specific contextual constraints and the use of more general gestural representation techniques such as shaping or drawing [9,2] .

In addition, human beings are all unique and inter-subjective differences in gesturing are quite obvious (cf. [6]). Consider for instance gesture frequency: While some people rarely make use of their hands while speaking, others gesture almost without

Zs. Ruttkay et al. (Eds.): IVA 2009, LNAI 5773, pp. 76–89, 2009.

interruption. Similarly, individual variation becomes apparent in preferences for particular representation techniques or the low-level choices of morphological features such as handshape [2]. See Figure 1 for some examples of how people perform different gestures that refer to the same entity, a u-shaped building. The speakers differ, first, in their use of representation techniques. While some speakers perform drawing gestures (the hands trace the outline the referent), others perform shaping gestures (the referent's shape is sculpted in the air). Second, gestures vary in their morphological features even when speakers use the same representation technique: Drawing gestures are performed either with both hands (P1 and P5) or with one hand (P8), while the shaping gestures are performed with differing handshapes (P7 and P15).

Fig. 1. Example gestures from different speakers, each referring to the same u-shaped building

Taken together, iconic gesture generation on the one hand generalizes across individuals to a certain degree, while on the other hand, inter-subjective differences also must be taken into consideration by an account of why people gesture the way they actually do. In previous work we developed an overall production architecture for multimodal utterances incorporating model-based techniques of generation as well as data-driven methods (Bayesian networks) [2]. In this paper we now present a complete model for the generation of iconic gestures combining both methods. We present GNetIc, a gesture net specialized for iconic gestures, which is a framework to support decision-making in the generation of iconic gestures. Individual as well as general networks are learned from annotated corpora and supplemented with rule-based decision making. Employed in an architecture for integrated speech and gesture generation, the system allows for a speaker-specific gesture production which is not only driven by iconicity, but also by the overall discourse context. In the following, we survey existing approaches to model gesture generation (Section 2) and present our integrated approach of iconic gesture generation (Section 3). We discuss how it accounts for both, general characteristics across speakers and idiosyncratic patterns of the individual speaker. In Section 4 we describe modeling results from a prototype implementation, and present an evaluation of the gesturing behavior generated with GNetIc in Section 5.

2   Related Work

Work on the generation of speech-accompanying iconic gestures and its simulation with virtual agents is still relatively sparse. The first systems investigating this challenge were lexicon-based approaches [3]. Relying on empirical results, these systems focus on the context-dependent coordination of gestures with concurrent speech, whereby gestures are drawn from a lexicon. Flexibility and generative power of gestures to express new content, therefore, is obviously very limited. A different attempt that is closely related to the generation of speech-accompanying gestures in a spatial domain is Huenerfauth's system [8] which translates English texts into American Sign Language (ASL) focussing on classifier predicates which are complex and descriptive types of ASL sentences. These classifier predicates have several similarities with iconic gestures accompanying speech. The system also relies on a library of prototypical templates for each type of classifier predicates in which missing parameters are filled in adaptation to the particular context. The NUMACK system [10] tries to overcome the limitations of lexicon-based gesture generation by considering patterns of human gesture composition. Based on empirical results, referent features are linked to morphological gesture features by an intermediate level called image description feature level (IDF). However, as shown empirically, iconic gesture use is not solely driven by similarity with the referent [10]. In contrast, in our approach we additionally consider the discourse context and also the use of different gestural representation techniques which are found to have an impact on gesture production in humans.

The research reviewed so far is devoted to build general models of gesture use, i.e., systematic inter-personal patterns of gesture use are incorporated exclusively. What is not considered in these systems is individual variation which is investigated by another line of relatively recent research. Ruttkay [15] aims at endowing virtual humans with unique style in order to appear typical for some social or ethnical group. Different styles are defined in a dictionary of meaning-to-gesture mappings with optional modifying parameters to specify the characteristics of a gesture. The focus of this work is a markup language to define different aspects of style which are handcrafted and model the behaviour of stereotypic groups instead of individuals. In a similar account Hartmann et al. [5] investigate the modification of gestures to carry a desired expressive content while retaining their original semantics. Bodily expressivity is defined with a small set of dimensions such as spatial/temporal extent, fluidity or power which are used to modify gestures. Similar to [15], the focus of this approach is a framework to individualize gesture style.

Another line of research uses data-driven methods to simulate individual speakers' gesturing behavior. Stone et al. [17] recombine motion captured pieces with new speech samples to recreate coherent multimodal utterances. Units of communicative performance are re-arranged while retaining temporal synchrony and communicative coordination that characterizes peoples spontaneous delivery. The range of possible utterances is naturally limited to what can be assembled out of the pre-recorded behavior. Neff et al. [13] aim at generating character-specific gesture style capturing the individual differences of human speakers. Based on statistical gesture profiles learned from annotated multimodal behavior, the system takes arbitrary texts as input and produces synchronized conversational gestures in the style of a particular speaker. The resulting gesture animations succeed in making a virtual character look more lively and natural and have empirically been shown to be consistent with a given performer's style. The approach does not need to account for the meaning-carrying functions of gestures, since the gestures focussed on are discourse gestures and beats.

In summary, previous research has either emphasized general patterns in the formation of iconic gestures, or concentrated on individual gesturing patterns. What we present in this paper is a modeling approach going beyond previous systems by accounting for both, systematic commonalities across speakers and idiosyncratic patterns of the current individual speaker.

3   The GNetIc Gesture Generation Approach

In this section we introduce the *Gesture Net for Iconic Gestures* GNetIc: We employ Bayesian decision networks, which allow us to tackle the challenge of considering both, general and individual patterns in gesture formulation. Decision networks[1] supplement standard Bayesian networks by decision nodes [7]. The formalism has been proven itself in the simulation of human behavior, e.g., Yu and Terzopoulos used decision networks to simulate social interactions between pedestrians in urban settings [19]. Decision networks are suited for our purpose since they provide a representation of a finite sequential decision problem, combining probabilistic and rule-based decision-making. Each decision to be made in the process of gesture generation, e.g., whether or not a speech-accompanying gesture will be planned or which representation technique will be used, is represented in the network either as a decision node or as a chance node with a specific probability distribution. All factors which potentially contribute to these choices (e.g., visuo-spatial referent features) are also inserted into the model.

Applied to our task, employing a probabilistic approach as it is available from Bayesian decision networks is advantageous for a number of reasons. First, networks can be learned either from the annotated data of single speakers or from a larger corpus containing data from several speakers. This allows for observing inter-subjective differences not only at the level of surface behavior, but also to detect differences in the underlying generation strategies. Second, a network can be easily extended by introducing further variables, either annotated in the corpus, or inferred from that data. Third, the same network can be used to calculate the likely consequences of causal node states (causal inference), as well as to diagnose the likely causes of a collection of dependent node values (diagnostic inference). In other words, either the gestural behavior of an agent can be generated, e.g., by propagating evidence about an object's properties. Or, given a particular gesture, the features of its referent object might be inferred. Further, the use of decision nodes allows to enrich the dependencies directly learned from the data by additional model-based rules. Finally, the approach provides the possibility to detect clusters of speakers who share particular interrelations between causal nodes and observable behavior, i.e., it enables us to determine and to distinguish between different forms of inter- and intrapersonal systematics in the production of iconic gestures.

3.1   Data Corpus

Building decision networks from empirical data requires an adequate comprehensively annotated corpus. To build such a corpus of multimodal behavior we conducted a study on spontaneous speech and gesture use in direction-giving and landmark descriptions (25 dialogs, ∼5000 gestures). An example transcript[2] to illustrate the kind of communicative behavior we are dealing with is given in Table 1.

---

[1] Decision networks are also known as influence diagrams.
[2] The verbal utterances are translated from German to English.

Table 1. Example transcript from the corpus

Router: If you found the city hall ...
           It looks like ...
           The outline is [u-shaped like this]$_{g1}$.
Follower: Mhm.
Router: And uhm it is quite symmetrical.
           Uh [two]$_{g2}$ trees are standing in front.

Gesture $g1$ Gesture $g2$

In the work report here, we concentrate on descriptions of four different landmarks from 5 dyads (292 gestures). We transcribed the spoken words and coded further information about the dialog context (see [9,2] for details). All coverbal gestures have been segmented and coded for their representation technique, and their gesture morphology in terms of handshape, hand position, palm and finger orientation, and movement features. In addition, all gestures used in the object descriptions have been coded for their referent and some of its spatio-geometrical properties. These object features are drawn from an imagistic representation we built from the VR stimulus of the study (e.g., houses, trees, streets). This hierarchical representation is called *Imagistic Description Trees* (IDT) [16], and is designed to cover all decisive visuo-spatial features of objects one finds in iconic gestures. Each node in an IDT contains an Imagistic Description (IMD) which holds a schema representing the shape of an object or object part.

Features extracted from this representation in order to capture the main characteristics of a gesture's referent are (1) whether an object can be decomposed into detailed subparts (whole-part relations), (2) whether it has any symmetrical axes, (3) its main axis (4), its position in the VR stimulus, and (5) its shape properties extracted on the basis of so called *multimodal concepts* (see [1]). In Table 2 the complete annotation scheme is summarized.

As reported in [2] individuals differ significantly in the surface level of their gestural behavior, i.e., in their gesture rate and their preferences for particular representation techniques or morphological gesture features. As concerns the question whether or not a gesture is produced for a particular object (part), gesture rates differ from a minimum of 2.34 to a maximum of 32.83 gestures per minute in our whole corpus (N=25). The mean gesture rate is 15.64 gestures per minute (SD=7.06). For the five dyads which are analyzed in detail here, the gesture rates vary between 12.5 to 25.0 gestures per minute.

Another example illustrating how speakers differ inter-subjectively concerns the question which hand(s) to use when referring to an entity. The general distribution of handedness in the five dyads is as follows: With 56.6% the majority of gestures is performed two-handed, while right-handed gestures occur in 28.6% of the cases and left-handed gestures in 14.8%.

3.2   Building Gesture Decision Networks

Bayesian networks can be built from the corpus data, both for the whole data corpus, or, for each individual speaker seperately. In either case, the structure of the Bayesian

Table 2. Coding scheme for gestures and their discourse context

	Variable	**Annotation Primitives**
Gesture	Representation Technique	indexing, placing, shaping, drawing, posturing
	Handedness	rh, lh, 2h
	Handshape	ASL handshapes, e.g. ASL-B, ASL-C
	Palm Orientation	up, down, left, right, towards, away
	Finger Orientation	up, down, left, right, towards, away
	Movement Direction	up, down, left, right, forward, backward
	Movement	linear, curved
Discourse Context	Information Structure	theme, rheme
	Information State	private, shared
	Communicative Goal	introduction, description, construct, position
Referent Features	Subparts	true, false
	Symmetry	mirror, round, none
	MainAxis	x-axis, y-axis, z-axis, none
	Position	3D vector
	ShapeProp	round2d, round3d, longish, etc.

network is learned using the Necessary Path Condition (NPC) algorithm. The NPC algorithm is a constraint-based structure learning algorithm that identifies the structure of the underlying graph by performing a set of statistical tests for pairwise independence between each pair of variables. That is, the independence of any pair of variables given any subset of other variables is tested. Once the structure of the network has been found, its maximum likelihood estimates of parameters are computed employing the EM (Estimation-Maximization) algorithm. The EM algorithm performs a number of iterations, each of which computes the logarithm of the probability of the case data given the current joint probability distribution. This quantity is known as the log-likelihood, and the EM-algorithm attempts to maximize this quantity iteratively.

The learning algorithm can be applied for the set of all variables in our data shown in the second column of Table 2. That way, influences of three types of variables manifest themselves in dependencies (edges) between the respective nodes, i.e., influences of (1) referent features, (2) discourse context, and (3) the previously performed gesture. We expect the latter to be influential in terms of self-priming which has been shown for various levels of linguistic representation, yet [14].

However, not all variables whose value assignment are indispensable for a complete gesture specification can be learned from the data. This is due to the large set of values some of the variables have. For example, values for palm and finger orientation are combined out of six basic values which can moreover be concatenated into a sequence to describe temporal variation in dynamic gestures. It is therefore indispensable

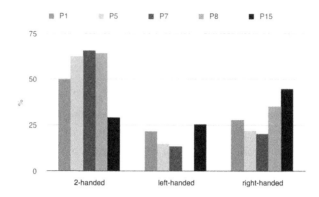

Fig. 2. Inter-subjective variability in gesture handedness across five speakers

to formulate additional rules and constraints in decision nodes of the network to specify these values adequately. This is especially expedient since each gestural representation technique has its own characteristics (cf. [12,18]) which are to be formalized as sets of feature combinations (at least partially) dependent on referent properties. Accordingly, a set of if-then rules is specified in each decision node of the network. For our current domain of application a set of 50-100 rules is defined in each node. The following examples illustrate the character of these rules:

```
if (and (Gesture="true", Handedness="rh",
Handshape="ASL-G", Technique="drawing",
ShapeProp="round2d"), "MR>MD>ML>MU").

if (and (Gesture="true", Handedness="lh",
Handshape="ASL-C"|"ASL-G"|"ASL-5", Technique="shaping",
Childnodes="0", MainAxis="z", ShapeProp="longish"), "PTR").
```

A resulting decision network learned from the data of one individual speaker (P5) and supplemented with decision nodes is shown in Figure 3. Each of the four chance nodes (drawn as ovals) of interest is connected to at least four predecessor nodes. Influences from the set of referent features are present for every variable, whereas the discourse context is especially decisive for the choices to be made early in the generation process ('Gesture (y/n)' and 'Technique'). In contrast to the chance nodes, the dependencies of the decision nodes (drawn as rectangles) are defined generally, i.e., they do not vary in the individual networks. Nevertheless, each decision node has chance nodes as predecessors so that these rule-based decisions are also dependent from chance variables whose (individual) values have been found previously. Furthermore, each decision node is informed from the set of referent features accounting for iconicity in the resulting gesture.

3.3 Gesture Formulation

The decision network described above can be used directly for gesture formulation. However, a few pre- and post-processing steps are additionally necessary to complete

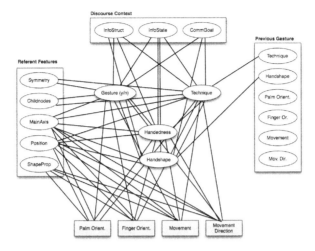

Fig. 3. GNetIc decision network for one particular speaker (P5)

the mapping from representations of imagistic semantics (IDT representation) and discourse context to an adequate speech-accompanying iconic gesture. Figure 4 gives a schematic overview of the formulation process. The gesture formulator has access to a structured blackboard since it is part of a greater speech and gesture generation architecture in which all modules operate concurrently and proactively on this blackboard. Details of this architecture are described elsewhere [2]. Information is accessed from that blackboard and results are written back to it.

The initial situation for gesture formulation is an IDT representation (kind of a 'mental image') of the object to be referred to. In a pre-processing step, this representation is analyzed to extract all features that are required as initial evidence for the network: (1) whether an object can be decomposed into subparts, (2) whether it has any symmetrical axes, (3) its main axis, (4) its position in the VR stimulus, and (5) its shape properties. Further information drawn upon by the decision network concerns the discourse context. It is provided by other modules in the overall generation process and can be accessed directly from the blackboard. All evidence available is then propagated through the network resulting in a posterior distribution of probabilities for the values in each chance node. We make the decision which value is filled in the feature matrix specifying the gesture morphology by selecting the maximum a posteriori distribution. Alternatively, sampling over the distribution of alternatives (probability matching) could be applied at this stage of decision-making to result in non-deterministic gesture specifications. This would, however, decrease the accuracy of simulation results compared to the human archetype modeled in the network.

To avoid gesture specifications with incompatible feature values, a post-processing of this intermediate result is necessary. Take the example of a posturing gesture referring to a round window: If the speaker whose gesturing behavior is simulated, strongly prefers the handshape ASL-B (flat hand), it is likely that this handshape is also inferred from the network in this case. However, since in posturing gestures the hands themselves

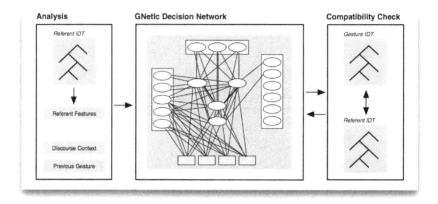

Fig. 4. Gesture Formulator in interaction with the blackboard

form a static configuration to stand as a model for the object itself, the handshape has to be reflective of the object's shape, i.e., the suggested flat handshape is inadequate for its referent. To reveal discrepancies like this one, each gesture feature matrix derived from the decision network is analyzed for its semantics: The morphological gesture features are transformed into an IDT representation according to form-meaning relations analyzed as described in [16]. This *gesture*-IDT is compared to the initial *referent*-IDT by means of formal graph unification. If a discrepancy is detected, the decision network is requested again with the additional constraint to either plan a gesture with a different technique or to return a feature matrix with a different handshape. The implementation of this post-processing is work in progess. It will be particularly important when extending our domain of application.

4   Modeling Results

A prototype of the previously described generation model has been realized[3]. In this prototype implementation a virtual agent explains the same virtual reality buildings that we already used in the previously described empirical study. Being equipped with proper knowledge sources, i.e., communicative plans, lexicon, grammar, propositional and imagistic knowledge about the world, the agent randomly picks a landmark and a certain spatial perspective towards it, and then creates his explanations autonomously. Currently, the system has the ability to simulate five different speakers by switching between the respective decision networks built as described above.

The resulting gesturing behavior for a particular referent in a respective discourse context varies in dependence of the decision network which is used for gesture formulation. In Figure 5, examples are given from five different simulations each of which based on exactly the same initial situation, i.e., all gestures are referring to the same

---

[3] We use the Hugin toolkit for Bayesian inference [11].

referent (a round window of a church) and are generated in exactly the same discourse context ('Landmark Construction', 'Rheme', 'Private'). The resulting nonverbal behavior varies significantly depending on the decision network underlying the simulation: For P7 no gesture is produced at all, whereas for P5 and P8 posturing gestures are produced which, however, differ in their low-level morphology. For P5 the handshape ASL-C is employed using both hands while in the simulation for P8 ASL-O is used with the right hand only. P1 and P15 both use drawing gestures which differentiate in their handedness.

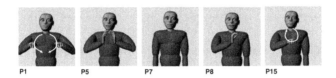

Fig. 5. Example gestures simulating different speakers, each of which produced for the same referent (a round window of a church) in the same initial situation

These differences in the surface behavior do not only result from differing conditional probability distributions. Rather, as shown in Figure 6, individual differences between speakers also come to differing network structures in GNetIc. Actually, the networks learned separately from the data of each of the five speakers reveal significantly different generation strategies. Take for instance P1: Here the production choices are made only dependent on the discourse context, i.e., neither referent features nor the previous gesture have an impact. At first glance, it seems implausible that fundamental choices in the planning of iconic gestures can be done without considering any aspects of the object. On closer inspection, however, P1 has a very strong preference for drawing gestures (46.9% vs. 15.3% in the whole corpus) which goes along with a high proportion of handshape ASL-G typically used for drawing gestures. Note, iconicity of drawing gestures mainly established by the movement trajectory determined in the decision nodes.

Another case which is remarkable is P5. In the data of this individual a large number of dependencies are found. Every single generation choice in this network has predecessor nodes from all three variable sets. In other words, every inference process relies on evidence from at least three variables of different type. In fact, the choice of handshape depends on evidence from six variables ('Childnodes', 'Technique', 'Position', 'Symmetry', 'Main Axis' and 'Previous Handshape'). In contrast, in P8 the same choice is only influenced by one predecessor node ('Technique'). Moreover, P5 is unique in the data in that variables linked to the previous gesture influence 'Technique' and 'Handshape'.

One conclusion is therefore that the GNetIc simulation approach beside being valuable for an adequate simulation of speaker-specific gestures (as evaluated in the next section), allows for gaining insights into iconic gesture production in humans.

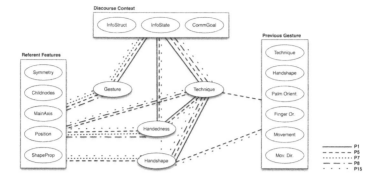

Fig. 6. Dependencies in the network for five different speakers

5   Evaluation

Whether the nonverbal behavior produced with GNetIc really is an adequate simulation of individual speakers is still to be shown. For this purpose we conducted an evaluation in which we measured the model's prediction accuracy by computing how often the models assessment agreed with the empirically observed gesturing behavior. First, to evaluate the decisions for those four variables we currently assess with GNetIc's chance nodes, we divide the corpus into training data (80%) and test data (20%) and use the training set for structure learning and parameter estimation of the decision networks. For the cases in each individual's test set we compare the gestures generated with a *general* decision network (learned from the whole data corpus) with gestures generated with the *individual* decision networks (learned from only this speaker's data).

Table 3. Evaluation results for the variables assessed with GNetIc's chance nodes with a specific probability distribution

Generation Choices	Chance Level Baseline	Accuracy (%)									
		P1		P5		P7		P8		P15	
		Ind.	Gen.	Ind.	Gen.	Ind.	Gen.	Ind.	Gen.	Ind.	Gen.
Gesture (y/n)	50.0	60.0	53.3	63.0	77.8	70.0	75.0	52.4	52.4	76.5	76.5
Technique	20.0	66.6	66.6	77.8	16.7	40.0	40.0	50.0	30.0	80.0	90.0
Handedness	33.3	66.6	50.0	66.6	61.1	66.6	73.3	70.0	60.0	60.0	90.0
Handshape	20.0	66.6	66.6	61.1	16.7	53.3	40.0	40.0	40.0	60.0	80.0

In total, we achieved a mean of 62.4% (SD=11.0) accuracy for generation with individual networks, while the mean for general networks is 57.8% (SD=22.0). See Table 3 for the detailed results of every individual speaker for each generation choice. Notably, all accuracy values clearly outperform the chance level baseline. The results show, by trend, that individual networks perform better than networks learned from non-speaker specific data. Particularly remarkable is the case of P5, for which the accuracy of both, technique and handshape decisions is considerably better with the individual network than with the general one.

Second, we validate the performance of the four local generation choices made in decision nodes of GNetIc. Note that decisions are made in a particular order, which has an impact on the validation results. If one of the earlier choices does not match the observed value in the test data, the following decisions typically cannot match the data either. Assume for instance that the predicted representation technique is 'indexing' although the representation technique in the test data is 'shaping'. The following choices concerning morphological gesture features are accordingly made under false premises. Results for these rule-based decisions therefore are validated locally, i.e., we take the test case data for previous decisions as a basis and evaluate the quality of our decision making rules directly. The detailed results are given in Table 4. Notably, we cannot employ the same measure for all four variables. Palm and finger orientation are compared by calculating the angle between the two orientation vectors. For instance, there is an angle of 90° between 'left' and 'up', and an angle of 45° between 'left' and 'left/up' . A maximal angle of 180° is present if the two vectors are opposing (e.g. 'left' and 'right') and can be considered the worst match. The mean deviation for palm orientation is 54.6° (SD = 16.1°) and the mean deviation for finger orientation is 37.4° (SD = 8.4°).

For the movement direction we distinguish between motions along the following three axes: (1) sagittal axis (forward, backward), (2) transversal axis (left, right), and (3) vertical axis (up, down). Each segment in the generated movement description is tested for co-occurrence with the annotated value, resulting in a accuracy measure between 0 (no agreement) and 1 (total agreement). For multi-segmented movements the mean accuracy is calculated, i.e., if a generated movement consists of two segments from which only one matches the annotation, the similarity is estimated with a value of 0.5. Evaluating GNetIc with this measure gives a mean similarity of .75 (SD = .09). For the movement type (linear or curved) we employed the standard measure of accuracy, i.e., we compared if the generated value exactly matches the annotated value. The mean accuracy for the movement type is 76.4% (SD=13.6).

Altogether, given the large range of potential values (or value combinations) for each of the variables, the results are quite satisfying. Moreover, generated gestures whose features do not fully coincide with our original data may still serve their purpose to

Table 4. Evaluation results of generation choices assessed in GNetIc's decision nodes

Generation Choices	P1	P5	P7	P8	P15
Palm Orientation	37.1°	61.9°	76.4°	57.1°	40.5°
Finger Orientation	29.0°	41.7°	41.9°	27.9°	46.6°
Movement	.69	.84	.84	.56	.89
Movement Direction	.82	.76	.82	.61	.76

communicate adequate semantic features of their referent–even in a speaker-specific way. A perception-based evaluation study is underway to investigate how the generated behavior is judged by human observers.

6   Conclusion

In this paper we have presented a novel approach to generating iconic gestures for virtual agents in an integrated model, combining probabilistic (data-based) and rule-based decision making. Going beyond previous systems, the generation with GNetIc is not only driven by iconicity, but also takes into account the current discourse context and the use of different gestural representation techniques. The results from a prototype implementation are promising so that we are confident that this approach is a step forward towards a comprehensive account of gesture generation. Nevertheless, we are aware that our modeling results also reveal deficiencies of the current model, which mark starting points for further refinements. For instance, some individuals tend to perform their gesturing behavior in a sloppier way, i.e., trajectories and hand orientation barely match the spatio-geometrical features of their referent. Further, we found that gesturing behavior varies over time such that gestures become more simplified in the course of the discourse. Finally, the application of the gesture formulator in the greater production architecture necessitates to decide between several variants of gesture morphology in combination with alternative results from the speech formulation processes. One particular feature of decision networks lends itself to this purpose, namely, the possibility to incorporate functions judging the utility of single decisions or collections of decisions. These extensibilities substantiate that Bayesian Decision Networks are an adequate formalism to successfully tackle the challenge of iconic gesture generation.

Acknowledgements

This research is partially supported by the Deutsche Forschungsgemeinschaft (DFG) in the Collaborative Research Center 673 "Alignment in Communication" and the Center of Excellence in "Cognitive Interaction Technology" (CITEC).

References

1. Bergmann, K., Kopp, S.: Multimodal content representation for speech and gesture production. In: Theune, M., van der Sluis, I., Bachvarova, Y., André, E. (eds.) Proceedings of the 2nd Workshop on Multimodal Output Generation, pp. 61–68 (2008)
2. Bergmann, K., Kopp, S.: Increasing expressiveness for virtual agents–Autonomous generation of speech and gesture in spatail description tasks. In: Decker, K., Sichman, J., Sierra, C., Castelfranchi, C. (eds.) Proceedings of the 8th International Conference on Autonomous Agents and Multiagent Systems, pp. 361–368 (2009)
3. Cassell, J., Stone, M., Yan, H.: Coordination and context-dependence in the generation of embodied conversation. In: Proceedings of the First International Conference on Natural Language Generation (2000)

4. de Ruiter, J.: Postcards from the mind: The relationship between speech, imagistic gesture, and thought. Gesture 7(1), 21–38 (2007)
5. Hartmann, B., Mancini, M., Pelachaud, C.: Implementing expressive gesture synthesis for embodied conversational agents. In: Gibet, S., Courty, N., Kamp, J.-F. (eds.) Gesture in Human-Computer Interaction and Simulation, pp. 45–55. Springer, Heidelberg (2006)
6. Hostetter, A., Alibali, M.: Raise your hand if you're spatial–Relations between verbal and spatial skills and gesture production. Gesture 7(1), 73–95 (2007)
7. Howard, R., Matheson, J.: Influence diagrams. Decision Analysis 2(3), 127–143 (2005)
8. Huenerfauth, M.: Spatial, temporal and semantic models for American Sign Language generation: Implications for gesture generation. Intern. Journal of Semantic Computing 2(1), 21–45 (2008)
9. Kopp, S., Bergmann, K., Wachsmuth, I.: Multimodal communication from multimodal thinking–Towards an integrated model of speech and gesture production. Intern. Journal of Semantic Computing 2(1), 115–136 (2008)
10. Kopp, S., Tepper, P., Ferriman, K., Striegnitz, K., Cassell, J.: Trading spaces: How humans and humanoids use speech and gesture to give directions. In: Nishida, T. (ed.) Conversational Informatics, pp. 133–160. John Wiley, New York (2007)
11. Madsen, A., Jensen, F., Kjærulff, U., Lang, M.: HUGIN–The tool for bayesian networks and influence diagrams. Intern. Journal of Artificial Intelligence Tools 14(3), 507–543 (2005)
12. Müller, C.: Redebegleitende Gesten: Kulturgeschichte–Theorie–Sprachvergleich. Berlin Verlag, Berlin (1998)
13. Neff, M., Kipp, M., Albrecht, I., Seidel, H.-P.: Gesture modeling and animation based on a probabilistic re-creation of speaker style. ACM Transactions on Graphics 27(1), 1–24 (2008)
14. Pickering, M., Garrod, S.: Toward a mechanistic psychology of dialogue. Behavioral and Brain Sciences 27, 169–226 (2004)
15. Ruttkay, Z.: Presenting in Style by Virtual Humans. In: Esposito, A., Faundez-Zanuy, M., Keller, E., Marinaro, M. (eds.) COST Action 2102. LNCS, vol. 4775, pp. 23–36. Springer, Heidelberg (2007)
16. Sowa, T., Wachsmuth, I.: A model for the representation and processing of shape in coverbal iconic gestures. In: Proc. KogWis 2005, pp. 183–188 (2005)
17. Stone, M., DeCarlo, D., Oh, I., Rodriguez, C., Stere, A., Lees, A., Bregler, C.: Speaking with hands: Creating animated conversational characters from recordings of human performance. In: Proceedings of SIGGRAPH 2004, pp. 506–513 (2004)
18. Streeck, J.: Depicting by gesture. Gesture 8(3), 285–301 (2008)
19. Yu, Q., Terzopoulos, D.: A decision network framework for the behavioral animation of virtual humans. In: Proceedings of SIGGRAPH 2007, pp. 119–128 (2007)

A Probabilistic Model of Motor Resonance for Embodied Gesture Perception

Amir Sadeghipour and Stefan Kopp

Sociable Agents Group, Cognitive Interaction Technology (CITEC),
Bielefeld University, P.O. 100131, D-33501 Bielefeld, Germany
{asadeghi,skopp}@techfak.uni-bielefeld.de

Abstract. Basic communication and coordination mechanisms of human social interaction are assumed to be mediated by perception-action links. These links ground the observation and understanding of others in one's own action generation system, as evidenced by immediate motor resonances to perceived behavior. We present a model to endow virtual embodied agents with similar properties of embodied perception. With a focus of hand-arm gesture, the model comprises hierarchical levels of motor representation (commands, programs, schemas) that are employed and start to resonate probabilistically to visual stimuli of a demonstrated movement. The model is described and evaluation results are provided.

1 Introduction and Background

In social interactions, we are continuously confronted with a variety of nonverbal behaviors, like hand-arm or facial gestures. The same holds true for intelligent virtual agents that are increasingly employed in interfaces where they are to engage in similar face-to-face interactions. Consequently, they are ultimately required to perceive and produce nonverbal behavior in a fast, robust, and "socially resonant" manner, i.e. based on an understanding of and entrainment with what the other intends, means, and how she behaves. In humans, this capability is supposed to be rooted in an embodied basis of communication and intersubjectivity. Many studies (e.g. [2,15,3]) have demonstrated that the motor and action (premotor) system become activated during the observation of bodily behavior. The resulting *motor resonance* is assumed to be due to perception-action links and to emerge at various levels of the hierarchical human perceptuomotor system, from kinematic features to motor commands to goals [11]. These resonances allow for imitating or mimicking the observed behavior, either overtly or covertly, and thus form a basis for understanding other embodied agents [22]. In addition they foster coordinating with others, e.g., in mimicry or alignment, in order to establish social resonance and rapport (see Fig. 1 for illustration).

As evidenced by brain imaging studies [18,16], an animated interlocutor with sufficiently natural appearance and motion can – to a certain extent – evoke in humans similar motor resonances. However, behavior perception and understanding on the part of the artificial interlocutor is usually treated as pattern classification focused on trajectory recognition rather than intention recognition.

Zs. Ruttkay et al. (Eds.): IVA 2009, LNAI 5773, pp. 90–103, 2009.
© Springer-Verlag Berlin Heidelberg 2009

Fig. 1. Interacting agents engaging in embodied perception and behavior matching

Many approaches employ probabilistic methods with convenient properties like graceful degradation, processing of uncertainty, or learning schemes. Calinon and Billard [6] apply Hidden Markov Models to recognize gestures after applying PCA and ICA in order to decorrelate, denoise and reduce the dimensionality of data. Further work [5] applies Gaussian mixture models to provide a more accurate modeling of uncertainty. However, the classification of movements is based on spatio-temporal feature correlations and does not aim at the abstraction into the intention or meaning of a gesture. Some recent approaches [21,20]) apply Bayesian inference to derive the goal of a movement, defined as a spatial configuration. Hierarchical probabilistic models were proposed [1] for temporally grouping motor primitives into sequences. However, co-speech gestures are meant to transfer information to the addressee and different, spatio-temporally uncorrelated movements can be employed for this inter-changeably. Thus more abstract levels are eventually necessary for capturing a gesture's intention. None of the techniques applied so far has attempted to tightly link perception and action in motor resonances, which should enable fast and incremental embodied gesture perception, across different levels of abstraction. In the effort to endow IVAs with increasing capabilities of social interactivity, we present a probabilistic approach to model the automatic emergence of motor resonances when embodied agents come to observe another agent's hand-arm gestures. In the following Section 2 we introduce the overall computational model, and we present an probabilistic approach to simulating motor resonance in Section 3. In Section 4 we present results of applying this model to real-world gesture data.

2   A Model for Embodied Gesture Perception

In previous work, we proposed an approach to learning motor acts of hand-arm gestures by imitation, built atop a model for procedural gesture animation [12,14]. It has been developed in a scenario with two virtual humans of identical embodiment, one demonstrator and one learner and imitator. In the present work, we extend this model in two ways to allow for resonance-based gesture perception. First, as motivated above, we add more abstract and less contextualized

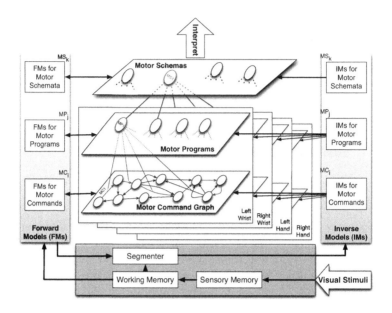

Fig. 2. Overall model for resonance-based embodied gesture perception

motor levels in order to work hierarchically from reception toward understanding. Second, we add a probabilistic method for how these hierarchical structures can be utilized for behavior perception by starting concurrently and incrementally to resonate when observing a gesture. Finally, the framework is connected to a marker-free 3D camera to enable embodied human-agent interaction (Sect. 4). Overall, the model consists of four modules (see Fig. 2): preprocessing, motor knowledge, forward models, and inverse models. We will describe them here briefly; details can be found in [12,14].

2.1   Preprocessing

The preprocessing module receives visual stimuli about the movement of relevant body parts of a demonstrator (positions and orientations of the wrist, fingers of both hands) and buffer them in chronological order in a *working memory*. A *segmenter* then decomposes the received movement of each body part into sub-movements, based on its kinematic features (velocity profile, direction changes). For example, the movements of a wrist in space are decomposed into spatio-temporal segments, called guiding strokes [13]. The movements of the fingers are decomposed into key postures of the hand. A guiding stroke represents a spatial movement segment in 3D space and, suitably parametrized, describes the movement trajectory and the performance speed. Since the focus in this paper is on intransitive actions, all parameters attributed to the segments refer to the morphological features of the movement, and they are not defined relative to an object. Such parametrized segments are atomic movement components (called submovements) of each body part and a sequence of them represents a gesture.

2.2 Motor Knowledge

A directed graph is used to store the motor knowledge about gestural movements as a sequence of its submovements. Edges of the graph stand for movement segments; nodes represent the intermediate states of the corresponding body part. That is, edges for the wrists' spatio-temporal movements are assigned the proper guiding strokes and each node represents a spatial position. In the case of hand and finger configuration, each node represents a keyframe (hand posture) and the edges indicate the transition (parametrized with a velocity profile) to reach the next hand posture. In that way, a movement becomes a sequence of edges, i.e. a path in the graph (see [4] for similar modeling approach). A novel gesture can be added as new path in the graphs and, if necessary, it may add new edges and nodes to the graph. When performing a gesture, the agent should follow the corresponding path in the graph and perform its edges sequentially. Therefore, each edge in the graph, independent from the related body part, represents a motor command (MC), and a path in the graph stands for a motor program (MP). Neurobiological studies showed that the human brain uses a similar principle of decomposing complex movements into simpler elements, called motor primitives, and generates them (in performing phase) in parallel and sequence [9,10]. Modeling internal motor representations of each body part separately is also consistent with the somatotopic organization found in motor cortex.

Due to the fact that MCs for each body part have their own features and parameterization, they are stored separately in specialized knowledge submodules, called motor command graph (MCG) and motor program graph (MPG), respectively. The MPG is a more compact representation of the MCG and clusters each motor sequence as a single node. In this way, the agent has an exact representation of the individual gestures in its own repertoire. However, in general, gestures are not limited to a specific performance but have some variable features. These are the parameters of the performance which, when varied, do not change the meaning and intention of the gesture but the way of performing it. Consequently, understanding a gesture can *not only* involve an exact motor simulation (direct matching), but also infernal of communicative meaning. For example, seeing a demonstrator waving should be recognized by an imitator as the act of waving, independent of the absolute spatial position of the wrist joint, the swinging frequency or to some degree the speed of the movement. Although different persons have different styles of waving, all those performances can be classified by an observer to the same meaning. And, when reciprocating, the observer likewise performs an individual way of doing it. Thus, embodied agents must be able to cluster numerous forms of a gestural movement into one schema, which ignores the variable features of the gesture, e.g. spatial position, number of repetitions, etc. Therefore, we define motor schemas (MS) as a generalized representation that groups different allowed performances (motor programs) of a gesture, possibly performed through many body parts, into a single cluster.

Analogously, a motor schema graph (MSG) consist of motor schemas as nodes. Such a generalization process is an important capability and can foster the understanding and imitation of behavior in two ways. First, it forwards the problem of inferring the goal of a gesture from the motor level to a more abstract, yet less complex level, namely schema interpretation. Second, an imitator can retain his own personal form of performing a gesture, while being able to relate other performances of the same gesture to the same schema.

2.3 Forward and Inverse Models

An agent may follow two routes to imitate an observed gesture. On the one hand, it can recognize a movement as familiar, i.e. approximately similar to an act in the own repertoire. In this case, the agent can perform an *active imitation*, activating the motor system during the perception process. One the other hand, when the model is not in the observer's repertoire, the agent perceives the new movement and analyze it afterwards, drawing upon the motor knowledge it has acquired before. In result, new motor knowledge about the novel movement is created, inserted into the internal motor representation, and can then be executed for imitation. This process is called *passive imitation* [7].

In our model, active and passive imitation are modeled with forward and inverse models, respectively. Forward models are predictors derived from the agent's motor knowledge in order to predict the continuation of a familiar gesture at each motor level. By comparing this prediction with the actual percepts at each time step, these models are to find the motor command, program or schema that most likely correspond to the observed behavior. If there is no sufficiently similar representation, the analyses switch from the forward models to inverse models, which receive their input from the segmenter and turn it into parametrized submovements. These submovements are used to augment the MCG, MPG or MSG, if necessary, with new nodes and edges. Performing the newly acquired act, then, accomplishes the modeling of *true imitation*.

3 Probabilistic Motor Resonances

The basic mechanism of perceiving a gesture (either for imitation or understanding) is to compare the predictions of the forward models, derived for possible candidate motor structures, with the observed movement of the other. This basic mechanism is employed at all three levels (by different kinds of forward models) and results in motor resonances that represent the agent's confidence about the correspondence between what it sees the other doing and what it "knows" from itself. Given the visual stimuli about moving relevant body parts of the other as the only evidence, we define this confidence in recognizing a certain motor candidate as the mean over time of its a posteriori probability given the evidences at each time step (cf. eq. 1). This can also be considered as a kind of *expectation value* of the respective motor candidate. We apply the prior feedback approach (see [17]) to accumulate the expectation up to each time step. This also enables the use of Bayesian networks to model how the motor levels interact in order to allow resonances to percolate bottom-up and top-down in between them, to find (possibly a variant of) a known gesture fast, effectively and robustly. Furthermore, in this way, the probabilities of motor candidates of different lengths are comparable. In the following we focus on the perception of hand position or trajectory; finger movements can be modeled analogously.

3.1 Level 1: Resonating Motor Commands

At this level, the spatial positions of a wrist at each time step t are our evidences and the motor commands in the MCG are the hypotheses. Since our approach should work incrementally and in real time, the more evidences we have the higher the recognition confidence should be. The probability of a hypothesis equals the resonance or expectation of the corresponding motor command c on basis of all perceived evidences ($\mathbf{o} = \{\mathbf{o}_{t_1}, \mathbf{o}_{t_2}, ...\}$) up to the current time step, T. Employing the Bayesian law, we have:

$$P_T(c \in H_c) = P_T(c|\mathbf{o}) := \frac{1}{T} \sum_{t=t_1}^{T} P(c|\mathbf{o}_t) = \frac{1}{T} \sum_{t=t_1}^{T} \alpha_c P_{T-1}(c) P(\mathbf{o}_t|c) \quad (1)$$

The term $P_{T-1}(c)$ is the a priori of the hypothesis c and indicates the previous knowledge about the probability of motor command c, which is equal to the expectation of c at the previous time step, $T-1$. In the case of $T = t_1$, the a priori will by default be the uniform distribution across all alternative motor commands outgoing from the same parent node. The likelihood term $P(\mathbf{o}_t|c)$ refers to the probability of passing the coordinate $\mathbf{o}_t = \{x_t, y_t, z_t\}$ with motor command c and, now, represents a probabilistic prediction of the forward model. In other words, it represents the probability of where the hand would be if the agent now performed the motor command c. We model this as a four dimensional Gaussian probability density function of $\{x, y, z, t\}$ (PDF, in short), which is formed for each possible next motor command, i.e., each possible continuing submovement of the wrist in space (see Fig. 3). Each likelihood reaches its maximum value if the observed performance exactly matches the own motor execution in both spatial and velocity features.

Let H_c be the set of currently active ("resonating") motor command hypotheses. The criterion to add a motor command into this set is as follows. As soon

Fig. 3. Visualization of the likelihood of motor command hypotheses, models as (4D) Gaussian density functions that change over time in accord with the motor command and its corresponding velocity

as the first evidence, $\mathbf{o}_{t_1}$, is perceived, its probability to represent a node of the MCG is computed with the aid of Gaussian densities centered at the 3D position of each node. Comparing with a predefined threshold yields the most likely candidate nodes for the starting point of a gesture (or not). All outgoing motor commands from these nodes are added to H_c. At the next time steps, the probability of each of these hypothesis is computed from the next evidence (eq. (1)). If the probability of a hypothesis is smaller than a predefined threshold, it will be omitted from H_c. Note that the resonance of each motor command varies with the duration of its execution: the longer the performance takes, the more evidences are used to update the expectation of that motor command. That is to say, the confidence of the imitator in the computed probability of each motor command increases.

3.2   Level 2: Resonating Motor Programs

The probability (or resonance) of a motor program p, which is represented as a path in the MCG and as a node in the MPG, depends on the probabilities of its components (motor commands) and thus, indirectly, on the evidences $\mathbf{o}_t$. We compute this probability, similar to motor commands, as an expectation of p considering all evidences until the current time step, T.

$$P_T(p \in H_p) = P_T(p|C, \mathbf{o}) := \frac{1}{T} \sum_{t=t_1}^{T} P(p|C, \mathbf{o}_t) =$$

$$\frac{1}{T} \sum_{t=t_1}^{T} \alpha_p P_{T-1}(p) \sum_{c \in H_c} P(\mathbf{o}_t|c) P_t(c|p) \tag{2}$$

The a priori term is equal to the expectation at the previous time step. The term $P_t(c|p)$ indicates the probability of performing the command c at time t, if the demonstrator were to perform the program p. This probability is time-dependent and is modeled using a PDF as a function of t and the motor commands c. The mean of the Gaussian moves through the motor commands of a motor program, as fast as the velocity of each motor command. Thus, this term along with $P(\mathbf{o}_t|c)$ together yield high resonance to the observation $\mathbf{o}_t$ of the right position at the right time step with respect to p.

The set of motor programs considered as hypotheses H_p is defined to contain all programs with at least on active motor command in H_c. Motor programs with too small expectations will be removed from the set. At each point in time, the computed expectation for each motor program refers to the confidence of the agent in recognizing that gesture for which, in contrast to the MCG, not only a submovement but the morphological properties of the whole gesture performance are considered. Note, however, that these probabilities are incrementally computed and adjusted from the evidence at hand, also during the perception while only parts of the gesture have been observed yet. That is, the agent does not need to specify the start and end point of gestures, but can even recognize gestures that are started at a later point of a trajectory, e.g., in the case of performing several gestures successively without moving the hand to rest position.

3.3   Level 3: Resonating Motor Schemata

The top level of motor knowledge consists of motor schemas, represented in MSG, which group different motor programs for different body parts into a single node. The expectancy (resonance) of each motor schema depends on the expectation values of active motor programs in all body part modules, and indirectly on the related motor commands and evidences about each body part. Figure 4 illustrates these causal influences between the graph nodes in a hierarchical Bayesian network.

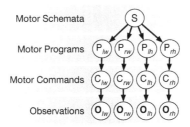

Fig. 4. Bayesian network of the relations between different levels of the motor hierarchy

The expectation of each schema s is computed as follows:

$$P_T(s \in H_s) = P_T(s|\mathbf{C}, \mathbf{P}, \mathbf{o}_{lw}, \mathbf{o}_{rw}, \mathbf{o}_{lf}, \mathbf{o}_{rf}) := \frac{1}{T} \sum_{t=t_1}^{T} P(s|\mathbf{C}, \mathbf{P}, \mathbf{o}_{lw}, \mathbf{o}_{rw}, \mathbf{o}_{lf}, \mathbf{o}_{rf})$$

$$= \frac{1}{T} \sum_{t=t_1}^{T} \alpha_s P_{T-1}(s) \prod_{i \in \{rw, lw, rh, lh\}} \sum_{p_i \in H_{p,i}} P(p_i|s) \sum_{c_i \in H_{s,i}} P(\mathbf{o}_{i,t}|c_i) P_t(c_i|p_i)$$

$$\tag{3}$$

The likelihood $P(p_i|s)$ is uniformly distributed among the $p_i \in s$, and 0 otherwise. Because of the OR relation among the associated motor programs ($p_i \in H_{p,i}$), the probability of a motor schema s is the sum of the probabilities of its possible performances. However, we may also consider schemes that are more tolerant to velocity, position or direction deviations than discrete paths in the MCG. For one thing, such allowed deviations should be set by the motor schema that has a view to the goal of the gesture and can differentiate between acceptable and unacceptable deviations context-sensitively. In addition, in this way we avoid rapid extension of the MCG and MCP, which are brought about by the inverse model analysis when expectations run too low.

But how to define what's a waving gesture and what's not? Or, in other words, how to define the invariants and variants in a motor schema? We allow four different possible variations in performing gestures, which we can map onto the model's structure in order to define parameters for the related motor schema: (i) velocity variability, (ii) position variability, (iii) repetition of a submovement, and (iv) left and right hand performance.

Velocity variability: Many hand-arm gestures can, within certain limits, be performed with different speed without altering the intention being the gesture, e.g., showing the victory sign or pointing somewhere. In order to recognize such variants as instances of the same gesture, the motor commands should deliver same expectations in all cases. One argument of the Gaussian likelihood $P(\mathbf{o}|c)$ for each motor command is time. Hence, its variance σ_t defines the tolerance of the motor command c to variations in performance speed. By increasing the value of this parameter of the likelihood model through the motor schema, we decrease the tolerance of the corresponding schema regarding the performance velocity during the perception process.

Position variability: The spatial position of a gesture often does not decisively affect its meaning. In order to avoid creating too many motor commands and programs for different performances of the same gesture, special prototype nodes in the MCG and MPG are created as the invariant structures of a motor schema, while leaving the variant features open. Each evidence position $\mathbf{o}$ is normalized to the corresponding position in this prototype as given by the distance between the start positions: $\Delta\mathbf{o} = \mathbf{o}_{template} - \mathbf{o}_{perceived}$. That is, when starting to perceive a gesture, all prototype nodes as well as the matching normal nodes in the MCG are considered as start point candidates.

Repetition of a submovement: Some gestures comprise repetitive parts, like waving or beat gestures, and the number of repetitions is often subject to considerable variation. Such repetitions correspond to cycles in the MCG that start and end at nodes which represent branching points for such a schema (one more cycle or continue otherwise). This can be handled straightforward, by splitting the PDFs that model the likelihoods $P(\mathbf{o}_t|c)$ and $P_t(c|p)$ into distributions that covers both expectations. The expectation of the corresponding motor schema then equals performing one of the alternatives, i.e., the sum of the expectations.

Left and right hand performance: A gesture should be recognizable as the same schema, regardless of the hand it is performed with. Since a motor schema comprises motor programs for both hands, it can specify how their probabilities affect the expectation of the schema. In the normal case (3), all body parts are assumed to have their own task during performance. Nevertheless, the way of combining different body parts is not always an AND relation $(\prod_{i \in \{rw,lw,rh,lh\}})$ but sometimes an OR relation, like in this case. Therefore, each motor schema specifies the way of combining the body parts depending on the gesture.

In order to be able to cover all aforementioned variations, each motor schema has following parameters: (1) the means and variances of the Gaussian PDFs of all comprised motor commands; (2) a flag to specify if the schema is a template for position variable gestures; (3) a set of all cycles in the graph; (4) flags indicating the causal relation (AND or OR) between body parts.

3.4 Horizontal and Vertical Integration

The described probabilistic model simulates the bottom-up emergence of motor resonances, where the expectations at each level induce expectations at higher levels. The other way around, higher levels should also affect and guide the perception process at lower levels. For instance, after recognizing a motor schema the agent should expect to perceive the remaining movements over the next time steps. That is, the expectation of a motor command should increase the expectation of subsequent motor commands from the same gesture. In our framework, this capability can be mediated via the higher levels: The computed expectation of a motor program determines the a priori knowledge in computing the expectation of next motor commands. To this end, we update the a priori of the future motor commands, $c \in p$, using the Bayesian rule $P(c|p) = \alpha P(p|c)P(c)$, where $P(c)$ indicates the *previous* a priori of c. Likewise, a "resonating" motor schema affects the expectation of its comprised motor programs. Overall, every time new evidence arrives, we not only percolate expectations about active hypotheses up, but also adjust the prior probabilities of current or future hypotheses top-down in a context-dependent way. To this end, the a priori probabilities are calculated both from default priors and expectations during the last time step, as well as new a priori knowledge coming from higher levels. This vertical interaction of motor levels occurs continuously; see Sect. 4 for a simulation of this.

Horizontal integration refers to how forward model-based perception and inverse model-based learning interact. Switching from the former to the latter is controlled by continuously comparing the current likelihoods with predefined rejection thresholds. That is, as long as the MCG can predict the observed movement, and as long as the MPG can predict the resonating motor commands, the agent remains in perception mode. Beyond the scope of this paper, we briefly mention that the other mode, i.e. acquiring motor structures that then can resonate to observed behavior, is a crucial problem for embodied agents. Our model comprises the inverse models (Fig. 2, right-hand side) to analyze a demonstrated behavior for new motor commands and programs, which are then inserted into the graphs and can be tested and refined in subsequent imitation games [12,13]. The learning of motor schemas likewise can only succeed in social contexts, where repeated demonstration-imitation interactions with informative feedback guide the learner in finding the schema boundaries. While these acquisition processes are subject of ongoing work, we note that the model presented here directly enables behavior generation (internally or overtly) and, thus, imitation. This can be mediated by each of the three levels. For example, when starting from the highest level, the agent chooses a motor schema and then selects those comprised programs or commands with the highest priors, which encode how often the agent has observed the corresponding performance for that motor schema. In other words, the imitator tends to act in the way observed (and imitated) most often. The schema-specific parameters for the motor commands indicate the velocity and position changes for movements. The agent takes the mean values of these parameters and simply executes the correspondingly set motor commands.

Horizontal integration also refers to how behavior perception and generation in an embodied agent come to interact because they both employ identical motor structures. One direct consequence is that the behavioral tendencies of the agent are affected by its perceptions. In our model, the a priori for each motor representation in MCG, MPG or MSG is defined by default, depending on the number of alternative hypotheses. However, during observing and perceiving a gesture as described above, the a priori probabilities that match the observation are increased as an effect of the top-down propagations. We do not reset these priors directly after perception to their default values, but let them decline following a sigmoidal descent towards the default values. As a result, when producing gestures the agent tends to favor those schemas, programs, and motor commands that have been perceived last (cf. [8]).

The other way around, our model also allows to simulate so-called "perceptual resonance" ([19]), which refers to the opposite effect of action on perception. Since we use the same a priori probabilities for both generation and perception processes, we can model this phenomenon by simply increasing the a priori probabilities of *generated* motor commands, programs and schemas temporarily. This will bias the agent's gesture perception toward the self-generated behavior, which has been suggested to be another mechanism for coordination in social interaction.

4   Results

We have implemented the proposed model for resonance-based gesture perception and evaluated it with real-world gesture data. In a setup with a 3D time-of-flight camera (SwissRanger[TM]SR3000[1]) and the marker-free tracking software iisu[2], the agent observes the hand movement of a user during several performances of three different gestures: waving, pointing upwards, and drawing a circle. These gestures are familiar to the agent and we report how the present motor structures resonate, i.e., how the confidences of the alternative hypotheses evolve *during* perceiving a gesture. All gestures have been started at the same position increasing the agent's uncertainty as to which gesture is performed. Figure 5 (top-left) shows the agent's MCG, which corresponds to the spatial arrangement of the corresponding motor commands. This MCG is generated during learning by the corresponding inverse model after segmentation. The overlaid dashed-line shows the trajectory of a demonstrated waving gesture. The other subfigures show how the expectancies, i.e., resonances, of different motor commands (top-right), motor programs (bottom-left), and motor schemas (bottom-right) evolve.

The motor commands in the MCG imply hypotheses about how familiar gestures would proceed. While perceiving the demonstrated gesture, new hypotheses are generated, old hypotheses are extended, and unlikely ones are omitted. At each time step, one hypothesis corresponds to the most expected movement

---

[1] http://www.mesa-imaging.ch
[2] http://www.softkinetic.net

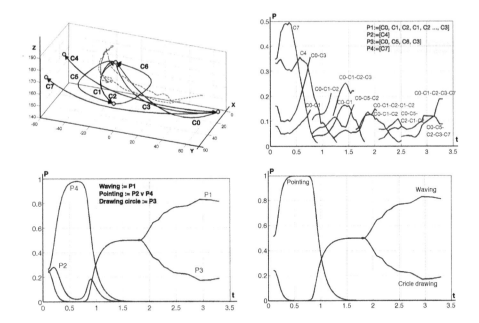

Fig. 5. Evaluation results: *top-left:* motor command graph with observed trajectory overlaid (dashed line); *top-right/bottom-left/bottom-right:* changing probabilities of the hypotheses currently entertained on the three motor levels (*commands/programs/schemas*)

segment. Depending on the number of hypotheses, the maximum expectation value changes over time and the winner threshold is adopted respectively. Figure 5 (top-right) shows a subset of the active motor commands hypotheses. The first winning hypothesis indicates that the observed movement starts similar to a pointing gesture, c_7. Therefore, the agent thinks that the user is going to point upwards (p_4). However, after one second the user starts to turn his hand to the right and, thus, the resonance of the motor commands c_1 and c_5 increases. Consequently, the other gestures (p_1 and p_3) attain higher expectancies but the agent still cannot be sure whether the user is going to draw a circle or wave to him. After about two seconds, the agent perceives a swinging movement, which is significantly similar to the waving gestures known to the agent. In result, the agent associate the whole movement to waving schema and, e.g., could start to perform a simultaneous imitation.

5   Conclusion

In this paper we have described a probabilistic model for simulating motor resonances and, thus, perception-action links in the processing of non-verbal behavior. Based on a hierarchy of graph-based representations of motor knowledge, our model enables an embodied agent to immediately start to "resonate" to familiar aspects of gestural behavior, from kinematic features of movement segments (modeled through motor commands) to complete movements (motor programs) to more general prototype representations (motor schemas) that cover possible variants in a gesture's performance. The hierarchical motor structures of the agent are employed to realize two proposed key components of embodied gesture perception, horizontal and vertical processing. The former refers to prediction-evaluation schemes to figure out on each level which command, program, or schema matches best an observed behavior; the latter refers to the bottom-up and top-down flow of activation, which affords concurrent and incremental abstraction and recognition of the perceived stimulus. The probabilistic model proposed here implements these fundamental processes in an integrated way. In this view, resonance of a particular motor unit is broken down to the expectancy of its effects (if it were executed) given the evidence at hand (what has been observed so far), given current activations of the connected motor structures. Resonance thereby results from a Bayesian inference, in which we take not only the conditional probabilities to change depending on what arrives bottom-up, but also adjust the priors continuously in accordance to predictions and biases that flow top-down. Evaluations with simulated and real-word data (gesture trajectories) showed this approach's potential for fast and incremental perception–two properties indispensable for smooth social interaction. Building upon the perceptual and motor representations employed in the agent architecture thus paves the way for engaging in social behavior in a more human-like way, including automatic coordination effects like motor mimicry, imitation, or alignment.

Acknowledgements. This research is supported by the Deutsche Forschungsgemeinschaft (DFG) in the Center of Excellence in "Cognitive Interaction Technology".

References

1. Amit, R., Mataric, M.: Learning movement sequences from demonstration. In: ICDL 2002: Proceedings of the 2nd International Conference on Development and Learning, pp. 203–208 (2002)
2. Brass, M., Bekkering, H., Prinz, W.: Movement observation affects movement execution in a simple response task. Acta Psychologica 106(1–2), 3–22 (2001)
3. Buccino, G., Binkofski, F., Fink, G.R., Fadiga, L., Fogassi, L., Gallese, V., Seitz, R.J., Zilles, K., Rizzolatti, G., Freund, H.-J.: Action observation activates premotor and parietal areas in a somatotopic manner: an fMRI study. European Journal of Neuroscience 13, 400–404 (2001)
4. Buchsbaum, D., Blumberg, B.: Imitation as a first step to social learning in synthetic characters: a graph-based approach. In: SCA 2005: Proceedings of the 2005 ACM SIGGRAPH/Eurographics symposium on Computer animation, New York, pp. 9–18 (2005)
5. Calinon, S., Billard, A.: Incremental learning of gestures by imitation in a humanoid robot. In: HRI 2007: Proceedings of the ACM/IEEE international conference on Human-robot interaction, pp. 255–262. ACM, New York (2007)

6. Calinon, S., Billard, A.: Learning of Gestures by Imitation in a Humanoid Robot, pp. 153–177. Cambridge University Press, Cambridge (2007)
7. Demiris, J., Hayes, G.R.: Imitation as a dual-route process featuring predictive and learning components: a biologically plausible computational model. In: Imitation in animals and artifacts, pp. 327–361. MIT Press, Cambridge (2002)
8. Dijksterhuis, A., Bargh, J.: The perception-behavior expressway: Automatic effects of social perception on social behavior. Advances in Experimental Social Psychology, vol. 33, pp. 1–40 (2001)
9. Flash, T., Hochner, B.: Motor primitives in vertebrates and invertebrates. Journal of Current Opinion in Neurobiololgy 15, 660–666 (2005)
10. Gutemberg, G.-F., Yiannis, A.: A language for human action. Computer 40(5), 42–51 (2007)
11. Hamilton, A., Grafton, S.: The motor hierarchy: From kinematics to goals and intentions. In: Attention and Performance 22. Oxford University Press, Oxford (2007)
12. Kopp, S., Graeser, O.: Imitation learning and response facilitation in embodied agents. In: Gratch, J., Young, M., Aylett, R.S., Ballin, D., Olivier, P. (eds.) IVA 2006. LNCS (LNAI), vol. 4133, pp. 28–41. Springer, Heidelberg (2006)
13. Kopp, S., Wachsmuth, I.: Synthesizing multimodal utterances for conversational agents. Journal of Computer Animation and Virtual Worlds 15(1), 39–52 (2004)
14. Kopp, S., Wachsmuth, I., Bonaiuto, J., Arbib, M.: Imitation in embodied communication – from monkey mirror neurons to artificial humans. In: Wachsmuth, I., Lenzen, M., Knoblich, G. (eds.) Embodied Communication in Humans and Machines, pp. 357–390. Oxford University Press, Oxford (2008)
15. Fadiga, G.P.L., Fogassi, L., Rizzolatti, G.: Motor facilitation during action observation: a magnetic stimulation study. Journal of Neurophysiology 73(6), 2608–2611 (1995)
16. Oztop, E., Chaminade, T., Franklin, D.: Human-humanoid interaction: is a humanoid robot perceived as a human? In: 2004 4th IEEE/RAS International Conference on Humanoid Robots, vol. 2, pp. 830–841 (2004)
17. Robert, C.P.: Prior feedback: A Bayesian approach to maximum likelihood estimation. Technical Report 91-49C (1991)
18. Schilbach, L., Wohlschlaeger, A.M., Kraemer, N.C., Newen, A., Shah, N.J., Fink, G.R., Vogeley, K.: Being with virtual others: Neural correlates of social interaction. Neuropsychologia 44(5), 718–730 (2006)
19. Schutz-Bosbach, S., Prinz, W.: Perceptual resonance: action-induced modulation of perception. Journal of Trends in Cognitive Sciences 11(8), 349–355 (2007)
20. Shon, A., Storz, J., Rao, R.: Towards a real-time bayesian imitation system for a humanoid robot. In: 2007 IEEE International Conference on Robotics and Automation, pp. 2847–2852 (2007)
21. Verma, R., Rao, D.: Goal-based imitation as probabilistic inference over graphical models. Advances in neural information processing systems (18), 1393–1400 (2006)
22. Wilson, M., Knoblich, G.: The case for motor involvement in perceiving conspecifics. Psychological Bulletin 131(3), 460–473 (2005)

A Groovy Virtual Drumming Agent

Axel Tidemann[1], Pinar Öztürk[1], and Yiannis Demiris[2]

[1] IDI, NTNU, Sem Sælands vei 7-9, 7491 Trondheim, Norway
`axel.tidemann@idi.ntnu.no`
[2] BioART, EEE, Imperial College, Exhibition Road, SW7 2BT London, UK

Abstract. This paper presents an architecture for an intelligent virtual agent that imitates human drumming behaviour. Through imitation, the agent models the user-specific variations that constitute the "groove" of the drummer. The architecture comprises a motor system that imitates arm movements of a human drummer, and a sound system that produces the sound of the human playing style. The presence of a sound system alleviates the need to use physical models that will create sound when a drum is struck, instead focusing on creating an imitative agent that booth looks and sounds similar to its teacher. Such a virtual agent can be used in a musical setting, where its visualization and sound system would allow it to be regarded as an artificial musician. The architecture is implemented using Echo State Networks, and relies on self-organization and a bottom-up approach when learning human drum patterns.

Keywords: Embodied cognitive modeling, Architectures for virtual agents, Artistic application.

1 Introduction

The research focus of this paper is to create a virtual drumming agent that plays drum patterns in an intelligent way. The intelligence lies within its ability to *model* and *imitate* drum patterns from human drummers. The agent learns drum patterns from human drummers, and is able to create new drum patterns that are similar but not identical. The sound system can be regarded as an intelligent drum machine in itself. Drum machines play patterns perfectly, however this flawless way of playing is also what makes it sound rigid and mechanical. Human drummers will always introduce small variations in both tempo and dynamics when they play; this is what makes the drummer sound *groovy*. The sound system models these variations to create a groovy drum machine; it can be used in a live setting on itself, however a visualization of the drumming agent would increase its appeal as an artificial *drummer*. For this reason, the system incorporates a motor system in addition to the sound system that is able to imitate arm movements of human drummers. The imitative drumming agent both sees and hears the teacher, and the architecture fuses these two modalities. The sound system is based on previous work on groovy drum machines [1], and the motor system is based on previous work on imitation of arm movements

Zs. Ruttkay et al. (Eds.): IVA 2009, LNAI 5773, pp. 104–117, 2009.

[2]. The research goal in this paper is to combine these two areas of research, to create an intelligent virtual drumming agent. The agent relies on the human cognitive function of imitation, and its implementation draws on biological inspiration, with self-organizing neural networks being an important feature. Both the sound system and the motor system are discussed in the paper, but due to space limitations the self-organization of the motor system is investigated in slightly more detail. Two important distinctions need to be clear: the sound system models user-specific variations, and is able to imitate them to create new groovy drum tracks. The motor system tries to *accurately* produce the arm movements that will yield the desired groovy drum track, i.e. it "remembers" the arm movement that produced the desired sound. Therefore, it is evaluated by how similar the produced arm movement is to the original trajectory.

2   Background

Learning motor skills by imitation has long been regarded as an important cognitive function, and has been studied extensively in developmental psychology [3,4]. The discovery of neurons firing both when performing and observing the same action (dubbed *mirror neurons* [5]) has been suggested as a neural implementation of the imitative capability [6], language [7] and mind reading [8]. In computer science, model-based learning is regarded as the most suitable approach to implement imitation of motor actions [6], an approach well-known in the control literature [9]. This approach pairs an inverse model (i.e. controller) with a forward model (i.e. a predictor), and has been used in architectures for imitation learning [10,11]. It has been argued that the cerebellum contains inverse/forward model pairings, and it is therefore a suitable approach for an architecture for motor control and learning in an imitative setting [12].

Modeling user-specific variations (i.e. "modeling virtuosity") in the cross-section of AI and music has been the focus of several studies (predominantly on piano music), where various techniques ranging from string kernels [13], first-order logic and clustering [14], Markov models [15] and case-based reasoning [16] have been used to model and subsequently generate music that sound like they were made by humans. The most sophisticated drum machines today (e.g. FXpansion BFD, Toontrack EZdrummer, DigiDesign Strike, Reason Drum Kits, Native Instruments Battery) are made in software, since they allow large sample libraries (some are in the gigabyte range) and fine-tuned control over various parameters to tweak the sound of the drums. However, there is no *intelligent* way to generate human-like drum tracks, apart from adding random noise with the intention that the noise can be perceived as "human". The approach in this paper is to *model* how human drummers play, and use these models to imitate the style of human drummers. With an ability to imitate arm movements, the groovy drum machine would become closer to a groovy artificial drummer, suitable to be part of a band in a live setting. The Haile robotic percussionist [17] has some similarities, but it is limited to playing with one arm (albeit in real-life, not only as a simulation). It replays and modifies drum patterns during interaction with other players, but it does not *learn* the patterns.

3   Architecture

The architecture presented in this paper is called "Software for Hierarchical Extraction and Imitation of drum patterns in a Learning Agent" (SHEILA), see figure 1. It combines techniques from imitation of drum patterns [1] as well as imitation of body movements [11,2,18]. The two subsystems that make up the architecture will now be described.

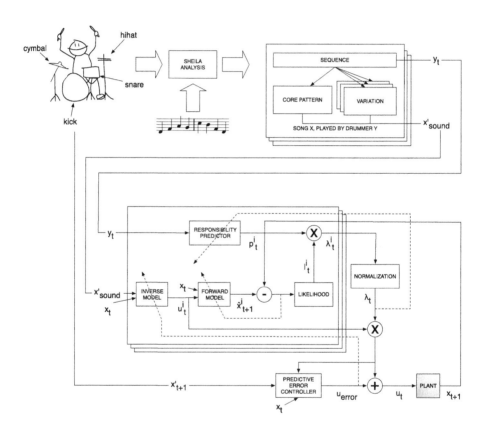

Fig. 1. The SHEILA architecture. On the top is the sound generative part, driving the motor part at the bottom.

3.1   Sound System

The sound generative part is on the top of figure 1. It consists of several Echo State Networks (ESNs) [19] that learn user-specific variations from human drummers. MIDI[1] recordings facilitate the analysis of drum patterns. The resulting drum patterns are analyzed in a hierarchical manner: first, the MIDI drum sequence is transformed into a string. Similar patterns are then found by looking for supermaximal repeats, a technique used to find sequences of genes [20]. The melody of the song is used to divide the song into different parts (in common music terms, these would constitute the verse/chorus/bridge of the song). The most commonly played pattern within a part is then regarded as a core pattern C_x, where a pattern has the length of one bar (i.e. 4 quarter notes). Patterns that differ are regarded as *large-scale variations* of the core pattern, i.e. $C_x V_y$. Similar patterns are grouped together. From the similar patterns, the *small-scale variations* are extracted. These consist of variations in tempo and dynamics that the drummer introduces when playing a certain pattern. These are found in the MIDI data by looking at two parameters: 1) the onset time, which says how much a beat was offset relative to the metronome, and 2) the velocity, which describes how hard a note was played.

Both the small- and large-scale variations are stored in ESNs, to exploit the memory capacity and fast training algorithm. The sequence of core patterns and variations are transformed into a bit matrix, where each row encodes a core pattern and its variation (if any), and stored in an ESN called ESN_{seq}, one for each melodic segment. The onset time and velocity are scaled to $[0, 1]$ and the resulting matrix is used to train ESNs that model the small-scale variations of a pattern. The ESN_{seq} thus gates the corresponding ESNs modeling the small-scale variations of a pattern, and the output is scaled back to the MIDI format. All these ESNs are self-generating networks, there is no input signal to drive them; the ESNs use the feedback connections from the output layer to reverberate around the desired state. To use the sound system as a groovy drum machine alone, the user must decide which core pattern should be played, and for how long. The system then lets the specified ESN_{seq} run for the desired length of time. The output of the ESN_{seq} then gates the output of the corresponding ESNs that represent the actual core pattern and the variations of the core pattern. The output of these ESNs are what creates the actual sound, the ESN_{seq} merely governs when large-scale variations are to be introduced.

3.2 Motor System

An important aspect of this research is the idea that in order to achieve a lifelike visualization, it is crucial to have an underlying motor architecture based on biological inspiration. For this reason, the research in this paper focuses more on the underlying principles that will yield a control architecture capable of generating arm movements similar to that of the teacher; the implementation of the visualization is simple compared to the effort that went into the control architecture. The research is performed more from an AI perspective than an approach with a focus on the animation of the agent. The latter approach could simply use the recorded motion tracking data to create the desired trajectories.

---

[1] Musical Instrument Digital Interface: a protocol for real-time communication between electronic instruments and computers.

The approach in this paper is to *learn* the arm movements that will generate the same trajectories; this is intrinsically linked to the research goal of creating an intelligent drumming agent. The motor part of SHEILA can be seen at the bottom of figure 1. The motor architecture consists of a number of paired inverse and forward models, and a responsibility predictor (explained below). It is inspired by Demiris' HAMMER [10] and Wolpert's MOSAIC [11] architectures, combining the best of both: the consistent inverse/forward ordering of HAMMER and the responsibility predictor of MOSAIC. The core of the architecture is the pairs of inverse and forward models. An inverse model is a controller that issues motor commands u_t^i based on the current state x_t and a desired state x_t'[2]. A forward model is a predictor, that predicts the next state $\hat{x}_{t+1}^i$ based on the current state x_t and the motor commands u_t^i from its paired inverse model. The inverse and forward model, along with the responsibility predictor are grouped together in a *module*. Each module learns and represents a different motor skill (or a set of skills). The motor control problem then comes down to the selection of the module(s) that best produces the desired movement. The responsibility predictor (RP) predicts p_t^i, signifying how suitable a module is to control the robot prior to movement, based on contextual information y_t. In [11] the following example is given: if the robot is to lift a cup, contextual information would be whether it is empty or full, so the proper inverse model can be chosen. The likelihood (l_t^i) is a model that expresses how well the forward model predicts the next state (see [18] for details), which is multiplied with p_t^i. The result is λ_t^i, representing how well the module is performing *and* a prediction of how suited the module is to control the robot. All the λ_t^i from the different modules are normalized into the final λ_t vector. The motor output u_t^i from each module is multiplied with its corresponding λ_t^i value, and all the motor commands are summed to form the final motor command u_t, see equation (1).

$$u_t = \sum_i \lambda_t^i u_t^i \tag{1}$$

λ_t thus enables switching of control between different modules. This also gates the learning of the models; modules that perform well will receive more of their error signal than modules with bad performance. This way, the motor system self-organizes the control of the robot. Figure 4 (which will be explained in the Results section) illustrates how the λ value of each module changes when playing different sound patterns; the motor system self-organizes what motor knowledge each module will capture.

The inverse models need good error signals in order to converge. This is supplied by the predictive error controller (PEC), which is inspired by the human cerebellum. Like the cerebellum, it is able to predict how well motor commands

---

[2] In this paper, the following notation is used: a desired state is indicated by a prime symbol, e.g. x'. An estimated state is noted by the hat symbol, e.g. $\hat{x}$. A superscripted i indicates that the signal comes from one of the modules, e.g. u^i, otherwise it is system-wide, for instance the desired state x' is the same for all modules. A subscripted t indicates time, so the current state at time t is x_t.

will achieve the goal of the movement, and make adjustments before the final motor commands are sent to the motor system. The inputs are thus the current state x_t, the desired state x'_{t+1} and the motor commands u_t sent from the motor system. It then uses a model to predict the outcome of the motor commands on the system, and if there are any discrepancies between the goal and the predicted outcome, it issues motor commands u_{error} that will correct the situation, which are added to u_t before sent to the robot. This approach was initially inspired by the universal feedback controller [21]; however it is only *reactive* because it issues corrective motor commands based on the performance of the system at the previous timestep. The PEC is *predictive*, and thus more able to issue good corrections to the final motor command. u_{error} is used to train the inverse models of the motor system. The forward models are trained on the actual next state x_{t+1}, whereas the RPs are trained on the final λ_t vector.

3.3   Combining Sound and Motor Systems

The sound generative part was previously used solely as a neural network-based drum machine [1], now it is the neural centre that drives the motor part of SHEILA; it provides both the context input to the motor system, as well as the desired state input. The sequence of core patterns and variations serve as context input y_t to the motor part. In previous work [2,18] y_t was defined by the designers of the experiment, now it is extracted from the low-level data recorded from the drummer, i.e. the context signal is *data driven*. The actual sound output is used as the desired state x'_{sound} to the motor system. In previous work, the desired state was the same as the desired state of the robot at the next timestep. Now, the inverse models receive the current state x_t of the robot and the desired *sound* x'_{sound} which is what the *effect* of moving the arm should sound like; i.e. a target state that is in a different coordinate system than that of the robot. This makes it harder for the inverse models to issue the correct motor commands u^i_t, since it must model the different coordinate systems used for the two input signals. The desired state of the robot x' is used as input to the PEC, which then is able to correct erroneous motor commands sent from the motor part of SHEILA. This can be thought of as a memory of what the resulting arm movement should look like.

It should be noted that a more realistic simulation of a drummer would include a physical simulation of the drums that the robot is hitting. In the current implementation, the imitation of sound is done regardless of the movement of the arms. The current simplification, however, made it possible to have special focus on the actual imitation of movement and sound, which allowed the creation of a virtual agent that will look and sound similar to the original drummer.

4   Experiment

The five drummers that participated in the experiment played drum patterns to a melody written by the first author. The drummers had to play specific drum

Fig. 2. (a) One of the patterns the drummers were told to play. (b) A drummer playing on the Roland TD-3 velocity sensitive drum kit, which was also captured using motion tracking.

patterns (see figure 2a), but were free to introduce variations that felt natural to them. The task of the imitative architecture was then to imitate both the sound and arm movements of the drummer. To achieve this, two experiments were conducted: 1) the training of the sound system and 2) the training of the motor system. These experiments will now be explained.

4.1   Experiment 1: Training the Sound System

MIDI was recorded using a Roland TD-3 velocity sensitive electronic drum kit, see figure 2b. The software for recording MIDI was Propellerhead Reason 3.0. After analyzing the melodic structure and finding the corresponding core patterns and the variation of core patterns, the ESNs of the sound system was trained. The size of the ESNs depended on the complexity of the recorded drum patterns. The high-level ESN_{seq} learned the sequence of core patterns and the variations, and the low-level ESNs learned to model the sequences of velocities and onset times. All the ESNs in the sound system were self-generative, i.e. they were not driven by an input signal. The ESNs were teacher-forced [19], using the reverberations of the hidden layer dynamics to generate the correct output. Since the complexity and size of the target matrices differed from each drummer, the size of the ESNs were not determined beforehand, but searched for by the system itself (described in detail in [1]). After training the sound system, it was set to imitate the same sequence that had been used for training. The output of the trained sound system served as input to the motor system.

4.2   Experiment 2: Training the Motor System

Movement data was gathered using a Pro Reflex 3D motion tracking system, which uses five infrared cameras to track fluorescent markers. The markers were put on the shoulders, arms and wrists of the drummer in the experiment. The song consisted of two alternating patterns with corresponding melody, i.e. verse/chorus/verse/chorus, lasting 98 seconds. The Pro Reflex sampling rate of 20Hz made the models predict 0.5 seconds into the future. The noisy motion data was the desired state x' used by the PEC. The elbow coordinates were normalized to the range $[-1, 1]$ for all three dimensions, with the shoulder as origin. The wrist coordinates were normalized to the same range with the elbow as origin. The robot was defined in the same way, to overcome the correspondence problem [22]. Neuroscientific data suggest that such a transformation of visual input from an external to an intrinsic coordinate frame occurs in the brain [23]. To simulate a robot with human-like arms, a four degree of freedom (DOF) model of a human arm was implemented [24]. The model has a three-dimensional spherical shoulder joint, and a one-dimensional revolute elbow joint. The entire simulated robot was described by 8DOF.

The inverse models had 30 input signals. 12 represented the current state x_t of the robot, corresponding to the 3D coordinates of the elbow and wrist of both arms. The remaining 18 inputs corresponded to the x'_{sound} signal, i.e. the velocity and onset time of the various elements of the drums, i.e. snare drum, kick drum, hihat and so on. There were 8 outputs in the range $[-1, 1]$ which made up the motor commands u_t^i to the robot. The forward model had 20 inputs, 12 stemming from x_t and 8 from u_t^i, and 12 outputs to predict the next state $\hat{x}_{t+1}^i$. The RPs had 14 input signals, coding the core pattern and variation to be played. The output was a prediction of the suitability of the module to control the robot, p_t^i, in the range $[0, 1]$. The motor system was tested with different sizes of the hidden layer of the ESNs. All networks of the motor system had spectral radius $\alpha = 0.9$ which determine the length of the internal memory (range $[0, 1]$, with increasing memory as α increases) and noise level $v = 0.2$ which adds 10% noise to the internal state of the network. The PEC implements the same model as the simulated robot, which enables it to make accurate predictions and therefore good error signals u_{error} for the inverse models, crucial for such a high-dimensional system to converge. The motor system started out with 10 modules in each experiment. For every second epoch the activity of the modules was examined: a module had to be at least 20% active (i.e. $\lambda > 0.2$) for at least 10% of the time, otherwise it was pruned. The check was done every other epoch to allow the system to stabilize before pruning again. There were three stopping criteria: 1) the performance error p_e had to be less than 1%, 2) the RP/λ error had to be less than 5%. If the output of the RPs correspond to the final λ value of a module, it correctly predicts how well suited the module is, indicating stability in the system, 3) the u_{error} had to be less than 50% of the total motor command, so that the inverse models control most of the robot.

5   Results

5.1   Experiment 1

In order to test the imitative quality of the sound system, the groovy drum machine was set to play back the same sequence that it was trained on. Performing the same statistical analysis on both the original and generated data sets reveals that the system is able to model and generate the learned drum patterns, see

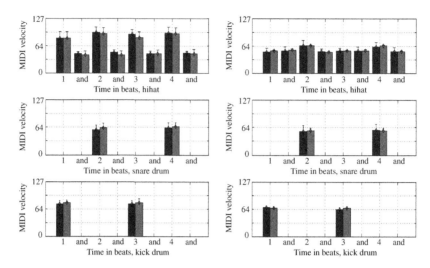

Fig. 3. An example of the imitative quality of the sound system; *two* different drummers are shown, one in each plot. The sound system was used to generate a drum sequence similar to that of the original training data. These similarities are shown in bars, they are all organized in pairs within each plot. The bar on the left of each pair (blue) shows the training data, and the bar on the right of each pair (red) shows the generated sequence. This similar pairs of bars shows how the sound system learned the same drum pattern as in figure 2a for each of the two drummers.

figure 3. More details about the imitative qualities of the sound system, including statistical analysis of the imitative performance of the system, can be found in [1].

5.2   Experiment 2

Note that the experiment reported in this paper focuses on *one* case of motion tracking, whereas the previous work on the sound system alone [1] featured several drummers. The motor system was tested with five different sizes of the hidden layer: 100, 250, 500, 750 and 1000 nodes. Each network configuration was run 20 times. The results from the experiments can be seen in table 1. The motor system distributed the movement knowledge across different modules, as can be seen in figure 4, which also shows the complexity of the context signal. Figure 5 shows how the system matches the target trajectory when imitating.

6   Discussion

Figure 3 shows how the sound system successfully models and imitates the playing style of different drummers. The sound system learns user-specific variations of drumming patterns, and stores the grooves in the hidden layer dynamics of the ESNs. The sound system is able to generate drum patterns that are similar to the training data, but not identical. The sound system then drives the motor

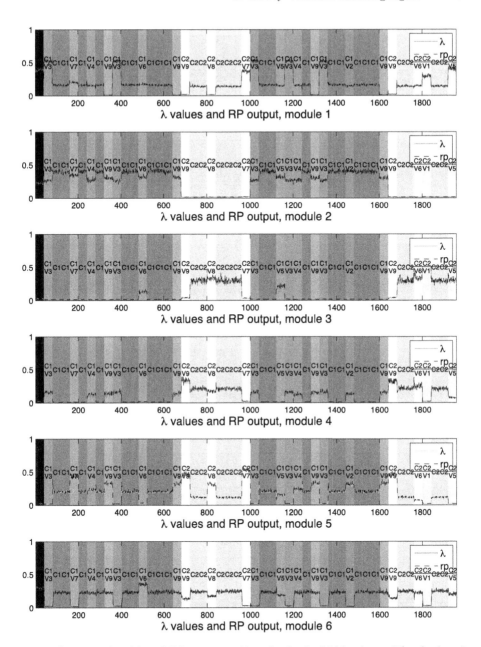

Fig. 4. An example of λ and RP output, 500 nodes in the hidden layer. The shades of gray in the background shows the boundaries of the context signal. The letters indicate which core pattern and corresponding variation the context signal was made up from, making it easier to see recurring context signals. The black column to the far left signify the count-in. In accordance with table 1, it allows for a visual inspection of how the system self-organizes the decomposition the control of the target movement into different modules, and how they collaborate when controlling the robot.

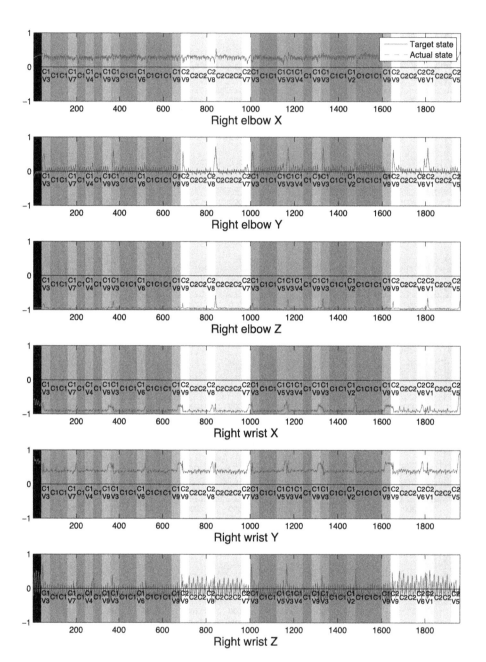

Fig. 5. Performance of the motor system. Note how the two lines depicting the actual state versus the desired state overlap. In the background the context signal is shown, as in figure 4 (same experiment). This shows the right arm; due to space limits the left arm is not shown. The left arm plots show a similar match between desired and actual state, a p_e around 0.03% is typical (see table 1).

Table 1. Results from the experiments of the motor system. The "Modules" column shows how many modules the system was using on average after training. "Rec. activ." is short for *recurrent activation* and tells to what extent the λ value of each module was recurring when the context signal was repeated. The recurring activation value was calculated as follows: for repeating context signals, the mean and standard deviation of λ was calculated for all modules. If the standard deviation was more than 5% of the mean during one part of the recurring context signal, it was counted as *not* being recurrent. Within those λ values within the 5% limit, only those that differed less than 1% from the mean counted towards the recurrent activation percentage. A high recurrent activation value indicates that modules specialized on certain parts of the movement, since modules had the same λ value (i.e. influence) over the robot during recurring context signals. "Perf. error" is short for *performance error* (p_e), representing how much the imitated trajectory differed from the desired trajectory. The u_{error} ratio indicates how much the PEC influenced the final motor command after training. "Conv. exp" is short for *converged experiments*, showing how many of the 20 experiments converged (if the experiment had not converged within 40 epochs, it was terminated).

Nodes	Modules (μ, σ)	Rec. activation (μ, σ)	Epochs (μ, σ)	Perf. error (p_e) (μ, σ)	u_{error} ratio (μ, σ)	Conv. exp.
100	4 ; 0	99.58% ; 0.83%	15 ; 0.82	0.0285% ; 0.0036%	49.72% ; 3.3%	20%
250	4.47 ; 0.70	98.57% ; 1.58%	14 ; 2.87	0.0273% ; 0.0037%	48.64% ; 1.05%	95%
500	5.20 ; 0.83	93.74% ; 4.21%	12 ; 1.81	0.0349% ; 0.0103%	47.47% ; 1.88%	100%
750	5.05 ; 0.87	91.39% ; 5.94%	12 ; 1.84	0.0341% ; 0.0104%	45.82% ; 1.88%	100%
1000	5.15 ; 0.81	88.46% ; 6.11%	12 ; 1.63	0.0358% ; 0.0091%	44.91% ; 1.84%	100%

system: the sound system produces a sequence of drum patterns similar to the original training data, which the motor system receives as a target state representing what the end result of the arm movement should be (i.e. the sound). Since the sound system has been thoroughly discussed in [1], the discussion will now focus on the motor system. The results show that the motor system produces the correct arm movements based on the produced sound patterns, see table 1 (the column for *performance error*) and figure 5. Since the research focus of this paper is to create an intelligent agent, there has been an emphasis on developing a motor architecture based on biological principles. Table 1 and figure 4 reveal that the motor system successfully distributes control of the movement to be imitated between the different modules. Table 1 indicates that the smaller networks (100 nodes) are the most efficient networks, when solutions are found (only 20% of the experiments converged). These networks have the highest recurrent activation value, meaning that the modules actively repeat their activation for repeating context signals. This is less for the biggest networks, which could indicate an excess in neural resources allows for modules to have overlapping motor knowledge.

The sound and motor systems are both based on biological principles of self-organization, implemented with neural networks, and are designed to be *intelligent* systems. The sound system drives the motor system, which is where the fusion of modalities happens - the motor system "hears" what the end result should be, and issues motor commands that will result in that particular sound. The motor system is able to transform a desired state in a different reference frame (i.e. sound) into actions that will lead to that sound; the sound system operates at a higher level than the motor system since it outputs *consequences* of arm movements. The fusion of modalities is therefore not limited to sound: the sound system could be replaced with any other centre that issues desired states in different reference frames from that of the motor system.

An agent that understands the link between sound and movement could also be used in the gaming industry. Current popular games such as Rock Band and Guitar Hero receive musical input from the player (typically through a guitar-like interface), but the avatar on the screen does not respond to this input. A possible use of the SHEILA architecture could be to generate a visualization of an avatar that would move in accordance with the performance of the player, for greater visual feedback when playing.

7   Future Work

For all experiments, the u_{error} ratio is relatively high on average (ranging from 44.91% to 49.72%). The architecture controls most of the motor output, but the PEC is crucial for the system to function well. However, this resembles how the brain works: high-level motor commands are sent from the dorsolateral frontal cortex to the posterior parietal and premotor areas, specifying the spatial characteristics of the desired movement. Details of the motor signals are defined in the motor circuits of the spinal cord [25]. Future work will show if the motor system of SHEILA works in a similar fashion.

SHEILA does not imitate drum tracks that are unknown to the system. However, it should be fairly trivial to implement this feature in the sound system. Based on the already learned models of drum patterns, the knowledge of similar drum patterns could be used to generalize to unknown patterns. Once this mechanism is in place for the sound system, the motor system would require some way of estimating the arm movement required for the novel drum patterns. A model that learned drum patterns and the corresponding trajectories of the arm could then be employed to create predictions of what trajectories would be the result of an unknown drum pattern, required for the PEC to function.

References

1. Tidemann, A., Demiris, Y.: Groovy neural networks. In: 18th European Conference on Artificial Intelligence, vol. 178, pp. 271–275. IOS press, Amsterdam (2008)
2. Tidemann, A., Öztürk, P.: Self-organizing multiple models for imitation: Teaching a robot to dance the YMCA. In: Okuno, H.G., Ali, M. (eds.) IEA/AIE 2007. LNCS (LNAI), vol. 4570, pp. 291–302. Springer, Heidelberg (2007)
3. Piaget, J.: Play, dreams and imitation in childhood. W. W. Norton, New York (1962)
4. Meltzoff, A.N., Moore, M.K.: Imitation of facial and manual gestures by human neonates. Science 198, 75–78 (1977)

5. Rizzolatti, G., Fadiga, L., Gallese, V., Fogassi, L.: Premotor cortex and the recognition of motor actions. Cognitive Brain Research 3, 131–141 (1996)
6. Schaal, S.: Is imitation learning the route to humanoid robots? Trends in Cognitive Sciences 3(6), 233–242 (1999)
7. Arbib, M.: The Mirror System, Imitation, and the Evolution of Language. In: Imitation in animals and artifacts, pp. 229–280. MIT Press, Cambridge (2002)
8. Gallese, V., Goldman, A.: Mirror neurons and the simulation theory of mind-reading. Trends in Cognitive Sciences 2(12) (1998)
9. Jordan, M.I., Rumelhart, D.E.: Forward models: Supervised learning with a distal teacher. Cognitive Science 16, 307–354 (1992)
10. Demiris, Y., Khadhouri, B.: Hierarchical attentive multiple models for execution and recognition of actions. Robotics and Autonomous Systems 54, 361–369 (2006)
11. Wolpert, D.M., Doya, K., Kawato, M.: A unifying computational framework for motor control and social interaction. Philosophical Transactions: Biological Sciences 358(1431), 593–602 (2003)
12. Wolpert, D.M., Miall, R.C., Kawato, M.: Internal models in the cerebellum. Trends in Cognitive Sciences 2(9) (1998)
13. Saunders, C., Hardoon, D.R., Shawe-Taylor, J., Widmer, G.: Using string kernels to identify famous performers from their playing style. In: Boulicaut, J.-F., Esposito, F., Giannotti, F., Pedreschi, D. (eds.) ECML 2004. LNCS (LNAI), vol. 3201, pp. 384–395. Springer, Heidelberg (2004)
14. Tobudic, A., Widmer, G.: Learning to play like the great pianists. In: Kaelbling, L.P., Saffiotti, A. (eds.) IJCAI, Professional Book Center, pp. 871–876 (2005)
15. Pachet, F.: Enhancing Individual Creativity with Interactive Musical Reflective Systems. Psychology Press (2006)
16. de Mantaras, R.L., Arcos, J.L.: AI and music from composition to expressive performance. AI Mag 23(3), 43–57 (2002)
17. Weinberg, G., Driscoll, S.: Robot-human interaction with an anthropomorphic percussionist. In: CHI 2006 Proceedings, April 2006, pp. 1229–1232 (2006)
18. Haruno, M., Wolpert, D.M., Kawato, M.: MOSAIC model for sensorimotor learning and control. Neural Comp 13(10), 2201–2220 (2001)
19. Jaeger, H., Haas, H.: Harnessing Nonlinearity: Predicting Chaotic Systems and Saving Energy in Wireless Communication. Science 304(5667), 78–80 (2004)
20. Gusfield, D.: Algorithms on strings, trees, and sequences: computer science and computational biology. Cambridge University Press, New York (1997)
21. Kawato, M.: Feedback-error-learning neural network for supervised motor learning. In: Eckmiller, R. (ed.) Advanced neural computers, pp. 365–372 (1990)
22. Nehaniv, C.L., Dautenhahn, K.: The Correspondence Problem. In: Imitation in Animals and Artifacts, pp. 41–63. MIT Press, Cambridge (2002)
23. Torres, E.B., Zipser, D.: Simultaneous control of hand displacements and rotations in orientation-matching experiments. J. Appl. Physiol. 96(5), 1978–1987 (2004)
24. Tolani, D., Badler, N.I.: Real-time inverse kinematics of the human arm. Presence 5(4), 393–401 (1996)
25. Kandel, E.R., Schwartz, J.H., Jessell, T.M.: Principles of neural science. McGraw-Hill, New York (2000)

Motion Synthesis Using Style-Editable Inverse Kinematics

Gengdai Liu, Zhigeng Pan, and Ling Li

State Key Lab of CAD&CG, Zhejiang University, Hangzhou, 310058, China
{liugengdai,zgpan,liling}@cad.zju.edu.cn

Abstract. In this paper, a new low-dimensional motion model that can parameterize human motion style is presented. Based on this model, a human motion synthesis approach by using constrainted optimization in a low-dimensional space is proposed. We define a new inverse kinematics solver in this low-dimensional space to generate the required motions meeting user-defined space constraints at key-frames. Our approach can also allow users to edit motion style explicitly by specifying the style parameter. The experimental results demonstrate the effectiveness of this approach which can be used for interactive motion editing.

Keywords: Human motion, Style, Constrained optimization, Inverse kinematics.

1 Introduction

Nowadays, synthesizing motions with various styles is still a challenge because motion style is hard to be defined quantitatively. But in general, it can be regarded as subtle variations on the basic motions. Motion style and content can be thought independent mutually and separatable. In this paper, motion style is expressed as a subspace, i.e. *style subsapce*, of the low-dimensional motion model we adapted.

Existing style-handling techniques such as interpolation and signal processing are hard to generate stylistic motions meeting user-defined constraints. In this paper, we construct a optimization framework that employs inverse kinematics in a low-dimensional space. Thanks to the style subspace that is well separated from motion contents, the synthesized motions can meet both user-defined constraints in visual space and style parameters in low-dimensional subspace. Basically, our approach can be devided into twon main steps as follows:

1. Learning motion models. Independent Feature Subspace Analysis (IFSA) is employed to train the motion capture data. The learnt motion model encapsulate the characteristics of motions, especially the motion styles.
2. Optimization with style-editable IK. Damped Least Square (DLS) based IK solver is adapted to solve constrained optimization problem in the low-dimensional space. To achieve this goal, we relate full-body configuration to low-dimensional parameters by combining a full-body Jacobian matrix and a projection matrix. In addition, the style subspace in the motion model is forced to be tuned to meet user defined style parameter. As a result, motion style is edited while the constrants are satisfied.

Zs. Ruttkay et al. (Eds.): IVA 2009, LNAI 5773, pp. 118–124, 2009.

2 Related Works

In recent years, more and more researchers found machine learning techniques are effective to synthesize stylistic character animation. Brand and Hertzmann [1] apply Hidden Markov Models to capture motion styles and reuse them to other motions. Urtasun et al [2] use Principal Component Analysis (PCA) to train large sets of loco-motion data and use PCA coefficients to synthesize new motions with different heights and speeds. Wang et al [3] present a parametric Gaussian mixture model to learn a probabilistic mapping from style variable to high-dimensional 3D human motion poses and synthesize real-time boxing motions. Shapiro et al [4] use Independent Component Analysis (ICA) to decompose a single motion into many components. All the research works above can produce good results, but user-defined constraints can not be satisfied.

The works on generating motions with constraints have been well done. Kovar et al [5] synthesize new motion sequencs by interpolating examples based on automated analysis and parameterization of motions in large datasets. Safonova et al [6] synthesize physically realistic motions in the PCA space using constrained optimization. Inverse kinematics is a common method to solve geometric constraints based motion synthesis. Other than traditional numerical IK solvers, example-based IK solver is another effective alternative. Grochow et al [7] and Rose et al [8] use non-linear PCA and Radial Basis Function interpolation respectively to implement example-based IK solver. Carvalho et al [9] present an interactive motion editing method using PCA motion model and IK. Tournier et al [10] use Principal Geodesic Analysis to resolve IK problem on a riemann manifold. Raunhardt et al [11] introduce a motion constraint operating in the latent space from a sparse motion database and integrated it into a Prioritized Inverse Kinematics framework. Our approach can also fall into this category, but we project all examples on a style-defined low-dimensional space and the style parameters are expressed explicitly.

3 Learning Motion Models

IFSA is a combination of Multidimensional ICA and invariant feature subspace [12]. In multidimensional ICA model, the components s_i are not assumed to be all mutually independent. Instead, these components can be divided into n-tuples and s_i in a given n-tuples can be dependent on each other, but dependencies among different n-tuples are not allowed. Invariant feature subspaces is supposed to represent features with some invariances. The value of the invariant of an invariant feature subspace is given by the square of the norm of the projection of the given data on the subspace.

In this paper, we take boxing motions including straight and hook as examples. We specify 27 different targets, ask the actor to hit these targets with hook and straight respectively and record these data. The motions in the motion dataset are composed of $C/2$ motion pairs ($C=54$ in our experiment). Each pair contains two motion clips where the actor hits a specified target with straight and hook respectively. Each motion $\mathbf{m}$ can be expressed as a high-dimensional vector: $[\boldsymbol{\theta}_{t_0}, \boldsymbol{\theta}_{t_1}, ...\boldsymbol{\theta}_{t_1}]^T$, $0 \le k \le 1$, where $\boldsymbol{\theta}_{t_k}$ is the character pose at normalized time t_k. We use the method in [9] to normalize all motion vectors. As a result, the actor hits those targets at the same normalized time. Since the dimensionality of motion vector is very high, PCA is adopted as a pre-processing step.

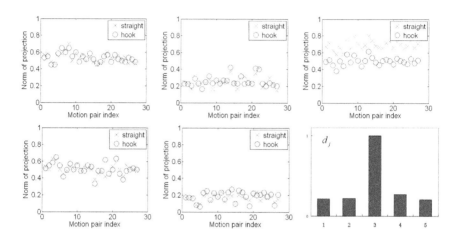

Fig. 1. Results of style extraction. Note that the dissimilarity between two motion groups on the third subspace is the largest (top-right). Therefore this subspace is defined as style subspace. The dissimilarity values on five subspaces are also computed and illustrated (bottom-right).

After data pre-processing, we learn the motion model using IFSA. Based on the principle of invariant feature subspace, the value of motion style can be measured by:

$$\phi_{cj} = \sum_{i=1}^{k} (\mathbf{b}_i^T \mathbf{u}_c)^2, i \in \mathcal{S}_j \tag{1}$$

where $\mathbf{b}_i$ is the basis vectors of leant feature subspaces, $\mathbf{u}_c$ is the PCA coefficient vector of the cth motion and k is the dimensionality of invariant subspaces. $\mathcal{S}_j$, $j=1,...J$ represents the set of the indices of the s_i belonging to the subspace of index j. It is obvious that independent feature subspace analysis is able to transform and reorganize basis vectors of PCA space to construct several mutually independent subspaces.

In order to find the style subspace, a metric is defined to describe the dissimilarity between corresponding subspaces of neutral motions and stylistic motions as:

$$d_j = (\frac{2}{C} \sum_{i=1}^{C/2} (\phi_{ij}^s - \phi_{ij}^h)^2)^{1/2} \tag{2}$$

where ϕ_{ij}^s and ϕ_{ij}^h represent the style value of straight and hook of the ith motion pair respectively. We define the style subspace j^s as one of these subspaces that make d_j

maximum [13]. The degree of style of hook motions can easily be changed by just tuning φ_{js}, the norm of projection of motion data on the style subspace.

Fig. 1 illustrates the norm of projection of our motions on five independent feature subspaces. Blue circles and red forks represent hook and straight motions respectively. The reason why we use IFSA to extract motion style is that it considers some high-order invariant features that describe the style more precisely.

The motion model based on independent feature subspace can be expressed as:

$$\mathbf{m}_i \approx \mathbf{m}_0 + \mathbf{P}\overline{\mathbf{A}}\mathbf{s}_i^J \tag{3}$$

where $\mathbf{m}_0$ is average motion vector. $\mathbf{P}$ is a PCA matrix and its columns are ei-gen-vectors of covariant matrix of means-subtracted motion data. $\overline{\mathbf{A}}$ is a square matrix that maps data from independent feature subspace to PCA space. $\mathbf{s}_i^J$ represents the projection of motion data on J independent feature subspaces. We can easily derive the pose vector at arbitrary normalized time t_k from equation (3):

$$\boldsymbol{\theta}_i(t_k) \approx \mathbf{m}_0(t_k) + \mathbf{P}_{t_k}\overline{\mathbf{A}}\mathbf{s}_i^J \tag{4}$$

4 Low-Dimensional Inverse Kinematics

Conventional IK solver can not handle motion style. We present a new IK solver by combining conventional IK and our motion model. It is well known that Jacobian pseudo inverse is a common iterative algorithm for IK. It can be described mathe-matically as follows [14]:

$$\Delta\boldsymbol{\theta} = J(\boldsymbol{\theta})^{\dagger\xi}\Delta\mathbf{x} + (\mathbf{I} - J^{\dagger}(\boldsymbol{\theta})J(\boldsymbol{\theta}))\varphi \tag{5}$$

where $\Delta\boldsymbol{\theta}$ and $\Delta\mathbf{x}$ are respectively the variation of joint angles and end-effector po-sitions at each step. $J^{\dagger}(\boldsymbol{\theta})$ and $J(\boldsymbol{\theta})^{\dagger\xi}$ is the pseudoinverse and damped pseudoinverse of Jacobian matrix in the visual space respectively. $\mathbf{I}$ is an indentity matrix and φ is an arbitrary vector. The Jacobian matrix in the low-dimensional space can be derived easily by chain rule:

$$J(\mathbf{s}) = \left(\frac{\partial\mathbf{x}_i}{\partial\mathbf{s}_j}\right)_{i,j} = \left(\frac{\partial\mathbf{x}_i}{\partial\boldsymbol{\theta}_n}\right)\cdot\left(\frac{\partial\boldsymbol{\theta}_n}{\partial\mathbf{s}_j}\right)_{t_k} = J(\boldsymbol{\theta})\cdot J_{P\overline{A}} \tag{6}$$

where $J(\boldsymbol{\theta})$ is the original Jacobian matrix in the visual space. $J_{P\overline{A}}$ is just $\mathbf{P}_{t_k}\overline{\mathbf{A}}$ since $\boldsymbol{\theta}$ is the linear combination of $\mathbf{s}$ as described in equation (4). Therefore, the new it-erative IK solver can be expressed as:

$$\Delta\mathbf{s} = J(\mathbf{s})^{\dagger\xi}\Delta\mathbf{x} + (\mathbf{I} - J^{\dagger}(\mathbf{s})J(\mathbf{s}))\varphi \tag{7}$$

The formal description of our algorithm is listed as follows:

Algorithm 1. Style-editable inverse kinematics

INPUT: the initial low-dimensional motion $\tilde{s}$ and constraint $\mathbf{x}$

OUTPUT: a new motion $\mathbf{m}$

1:   $\tilde{\mathbf{s}} := \mathbf{s}; \Delta \mathbf{s} := 0; J_{P\bar{A}} := \mathbf{P}_{t_k} \bar{\mathbf{A}}$

2:   **while** not converged **do**

3:      compute $\{J(\tilde{\boldsymbol{\theta}}_{t_k}), \Delta \mathbf{x}\}$

4:      $J(\tilde{\mathbf{s}}) := J(\boldsymbol{\theta}_{t_k}) \cdot J_{P\bar{A}}$

5:      compute $(\mathbf{I} - J^{\dagger}(\tilde{\mathbf{s}})J(\tilde{\mathbf{s}}))\varphi$

6:      $\Delta \tilde{\mathbf{s}} := J(\tilde{\mathbf{s}})^{\dagger \lambda} \Delta \mathbf{x} + (\mathbf{I} - J^{\dagger}(\tilde{\mathbf{s}})J(\tilde{\mathbf{s}}))\varphi$

7:      $\tilde{\mathbf{s}} := \tilde{\mathbf{s}} + \Delta \tilde{\mathbf{s}}$

8:      $\tilde{\mathbf{s}}^{js} := \mu \tilde{\mathbf{s}}^{js}$

9:      $\tilde{\boldsymbol{\theta}}_{t_k} := \mathbf{m}_0(t_k) + \mathbf{P}_{tk}\bar{\mathbf{A}}\tilde{\mathbf{s}}$

10: **end while**

11: $\mathbf{m} := \mathbf{m}_0 + \mathbf{P}\bar{\mathbf{A}}\tilde{\mathbf{s}}$

---

where $\tilde{\mathbf{s}}^{js} = \sum_{i=1}^{k} (\tilde{\mathbf{s}} \cdot \mathbf{e}_i^{js}) \mathbf{e}_i^{js}$, which is a vector whose nonzero components are projec-

tions of motion data on style subspace. $\mathbf{e}_i^{js}$ is the unit basis corresponding to the basis vector of the style subspace. The projection of average pose of all straight motions at key-frame on low-dimensional space is chosen as initial value for s. The step 8 is crucial for style editing. This step guarantees that the user-specified style can be recovered after each step. μ is obtained by:

$$\mu = [(\| \mathbf{s}^{js} \|^2 \pm \alpha d_{js}) / \| \tilde{\mathbf{s}}^{js} \|^2]^{1/2} \tag{12}$$

where $\alpha \in [0,1]$ is the style parameter that defines the proportion of hook style. d_{js} is the dissimilarity between straight and hook motions in the style subspace computed by equation (2).

    Our low-dimensional motion model is based on *motion space* but not *pose space*, Provided that a key pose is determined, this kind of motion model can give the whole continuous motions.

5 Experimental Results

In our experiment, we reduce dimensionality of original motion data to 15 by PCA, and learn five 3-D independent feature subspaces.

    Convergence condition of algorithm 1 is that the error $e = \|\mathbf{x}(\boldsymbol{\theta}) - \mathbf{g}\|$ is less than 1cm or maximum iteration number is greater than 1000. We record the error between the target and the end-effector at each step and illustrate the curves in Fig 2. Our algorithm can usually achieve convergence within 1000 steps even though step 8 is included.

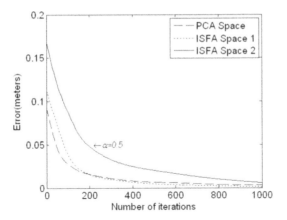

Fig. 2. Convergence performance of algorithm 1 (damping factor $\xi = 10$). Dashed curve is obtained in PCA space [9]. Solid curve and dotted curve are figured out respectively when the algorithm runs with and without style, i.e. step 8 is excluded and included. It is obvious that convergence speed decreases when step 8 is included. But with the increase of iteration number, the difference of error between them is not clear.

The Fig. 3 illustrates the motion sequences when $\alpha = 0.4$ (top left) and $\alpha = 0.8$ (bottom left) where the character hits the same target. The yellow point in this figure is the user-specified target. The magnitudes of arm swing in these two cases are quite different. The right picture in Fig. 3 illustrates the trajectories of right fists. There are more hook style in the motion with $\alpha = 0.8$. It is also obvious that the two motions are both continuous.

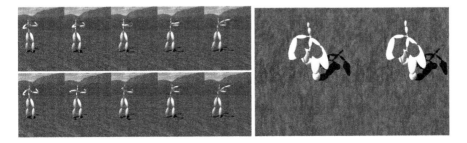

Fig. 3. Motion sequences of hitting a target with different hook styles

6   Conclusions

In this paper, a new low-dimensional motion model is proposed. Based on this model, a low-dimensional inverse kinematics solver is developed. Users can specify not only the style parameter for human motion, but also the constraints of end-effectors at key-frames. Our approach is well suitable for synthesize motions with high speed, such as sports motions. The subtle variations in space domain can be captured and used to tune the style. The experimental results demonstrate the effectiveness of this approach which can be used for interactive motion editing and synthesis.

Acknowledgment

This work is co-supported by Project 863 (grant no: 2006AA01Z303) and NSFC project (grant no: 60553080). Authors would like to thank Zhang Liang and Cheng Chen for their help with motion capture.

References

1. Brand, M., Hertzmann, A.: Style machines. In: ACM SIGGRAPH, pp. 183–192 (2000)
2. Urtasun, R., Glardon, P., Boulic, R., Thalmann, D., Fua, P.: Style based motion synthesis. Computer Graphics Forum 23, 1–14 (2004)
3. Wang, Y., Liu, Z., Zhou, L.: Key-styling: learning motion style for real-time synthesis of 3D animation. Computer Animation and Virtual Worlds 17, 229–237 (2006)
4. Shapiro, A., Cao, Y., Faloutsos, P.: Style Component. In: Proceeding of the 2006 conference on Graphics interface, pp. 33–39 (2006)
5. Kovar, L., Gleicher, M.: Automated extraction and parameterization of motions in large data sets. ACM Transactions on Graphics 23, 559–568 (2004)
6. Safonnova, A., Hodgins, J.K., Pollard, N.S.: Synthesizing physically realistic human motion in low-dimensional behavior-specific spaces. ACM Transaction on Graphics 23(3), 514–521 (2004)
7. Grochow, K., Martin, S.L., Hertzmann, A., Popovic, Z.: Style-based inverse kinematics. ACM Transaction on Graphics 23(3), 522–531 (2004)
8. Rose, C.F., Sloan, P.J., Cohen, M.F.: Artist-directed inverse-kinematics using radial basis function interpolation. Computer Graphics Forum 20(3), 239–250 (2001)
9. Carvalho, S.R., Boulic, R., Thalmann, D.: Motion pattern preserving IK operating in the motion principal coefficients space. In: International Conference in Central Europe on Computer Graphics, Visualization and Computer Vision, Plzen, pp. 97–104 (2007)
10. Tournier, M., Wu, X., Courty, N., Arnaud, E., Reveret., L.: Motion compression using principal geodesic analysis. Computer Graphics Forum 28, 355–364 (2009)
11. Raunhardt, D., Boulic, R.: Motion constraints. Visual Computer 25, 509–518 (2009)
12. Hyvarinen, A., Hoyer, P.: Emergence of phase- and shift-invariant features by decomposition of natural images into independent feature subspaces. Neural Computation, 1705–1720 (2000)
13. Liu, G., Pan, Z., Lin, Z.: Style subspaces for character animation. Computer Animation and Virtual Worlds 19(3-4), 199–209 (2008)
14. Wampler II, C.W.: Manipulator inverse kinematic solutions based on vector formulations and damped least squares methods. IEEE Transaction on Systems, Man and Cybernetics 16(1), 93–101 (1986)

Methodologies for the User Evaluation of the Motion of Virtual Humans

Sander E.M. Jansen[1,2] and Herwin van Welbergen[3]

[1] Department of Computer Science, Utrecht University, The Netherlands
[2] TNO Human Factors, The Netherlands
[3] Human Media Interaction, University of Twente Enschede, The Netherlands

Abstract. Virtual humans are employed in many interactive applications, including (serious) games. Their motion should be natural and allow interaction with its surroundings and other (virtual) humans in real time. Physical controllers offer physical realism and (physical) interaction with the environment. Because they typically act on a selected set of joints, it is hard to evaluate their naturalness in isolation. We propose to augment the motion steered by such a controller with motion capture, using a mixed paradigm animation that creates coherent full body motion. A user evaluation of this resulting motion assesses the naturalness of the controller. Methods from Signal Detection Theory provide us with evaluation metrics that can be compared among different test setups, observers and motions. We demonstrate our approach by evaluating the naturalness of a balance controller. We compare different test paradigms, assessing their efficiency and sensitivity.

Keywords: Evaluation of Virtual Agents, Naturalness of Animation.

1 Introduction

Virtual humans (VHs) are employed in many interactive applications, including (serious) games. The motion of these VHs should look realistic. We use the term *naturalness* for such observed realism [1]. Furthermore, VH animation techniques should be flexible, to allow interaction with its surroundings and other (virtual) humans in real time. Such flexibility is offered by procedural animation methods (for example [2,3]) and animation steered by physical controllers (for example [4]). We are interested in finding methods to evaluate the naturalness of motion generated by these techniques.

Both procedural models and physical controllers typically steer only a selected set of joints. Whole body movement is generated by a combination of different procedural models and/or physical controllers that run at the same time. Such whole body involvement is crucial for the naturalness of motion [1]. It is hard to determine exactly what motion model contributed to the (un)naturalness in motion generated by such a mix of controllers and/or procedural models. We propose the use of a mixed motion paradigm [5] to augment the motion generated by a single controller on a selected set of joints with recorded (and thus assumed natural) motion on the remaining joints, in a physically coherent manner.

Zs. Ruttkay et al. (Eds.): IVA 2009, LNAI 5773, pp. 125–131, 2009.

1.1   Motion Used to Demonstrate Our Approach

We demonstrate our approach by testing the naturalness of a balance controller (based on based on [4]) that acts on the lower body. This controller balances the body by applying torques to the ankles, knees and hips. We augment this motion with a motion captured recording of an actor clapping his hands at different tempos. These recordings are applied to the arms, neck and head. A mixed motion paradigm method [5] is used to couple the two motions: we calculate the torques generated by the arms and head from the motion capture specification, using inverse dynamics. These torques are then applied to the trunk, whose movement is physically simulated by the balancing controller. To asses the naturalness of the balance controller, we compare the following motor schemes:

- Motion 1: full body mocap of the original clapping motion
- Motion 2: upper body mocap + lower body balance model
- Motion 3: upper body mocap + no movement on lower body

Our evaluation is intended to answer questions like:

- Is Motion 1 rated as more natural than Motion 2 and Motion 3?
- Is Motion 2 rated as more natural and harder to discriminate from Motion 1 than Motion 3?

1.2   Selecting a Test Paradigm

Ideally, a test-paradigm would be efficient (needing only small number of participants to get significant results) and scalable, that is, provide metrics that can be compared with metrics obtained in previous tests. The measure d' from Signal Detection Theory (SDT) [6] is used in all our tests as a scalable measure of discriminability. We define the sensitivity of a test (given certain test conditions) as d'. An efficient test-paradigm has a d' with a low variance in each test condition and large differences between d'-s measured in different test conditions. We compare the d' and variability of d' for the following test-paradigms (see section 2 for a detailed description of procedures and analysis for each of these methods):

- 2 Alternative Forced Choice (2AFC): In each test item, participants viewed two short movie clips of animated characters in succession. Each time, one of the clips was driven by motion 1 and one by either motion 2 or motion 3. The task was to decide which of these showed natural human motion.
- Yes/No: Participants viewed one clip per test-item. The movement of the VH was controlled by either motion 1 or motion 2. They were asked to indicate if the movement was based on real human data or a computational model.
- Rating: Participants viewed one clip per test item. Movement was controlled by either motion 1, motion 2 or motion 3. They were asked to rate the naturalness of the movement on a scale of 1-10 (not at all - very much).

2AFC is commonly used to evaluate the quality of animation, using a direct comparison to a reference motion [7,8]. 2AFC discourages bias and does not suffer from contextual effects [6]. However, for some animations providing such a reference motion is impractical (extra motion capture recordings are needed, the mocap actor might no longer be available, it might be difficult to record motion with the exact conditions used in the model, there might be large stylistic differences between the reference and the modeled motion, etc). For the evaluation of such animations, Yes/No is an interesting testing alternative. Using a rating method [9] allows for a direct measurement of naturalness, rather than the indirect assessment (human/model) provided by the other methods.

Question 1. Do Yes/No and rating have a higher $var(d')$ and a lower variability between the d'-s measured in different test conditions than 2AFC?

We expect 2AFC to be more sensitive than Yes/No and Rating because each test provides a direct reference to compare to. Macmillan and Creelman [6] propose using a $\frac{1}{\sqrt{2}}$ correction factor for d' obtained by a 2AFC test so that its value can be compared with the value of a d' obtained by a Yes/No test. They note that different values of this correction factor are found empirically.

Question 2. Is there a relationship between the sensitivities of the different test-paradigms?

2   Methods

2.1   Participants

29 participants (25 male, all between 24 and 52 years of age) took part in this experiment. All were free from any known neurological disorders as verified by self-report. Experience with motion capture and creating animations varied from 'not at all' to 'very much', creating a diverse group of participants.

2.2   Stimuli

18 separate clips were used during the experiment. One for each combination of the variables *motion input* (3), *viewing orientation* (2, see Fig. 1) and *clapping frequency* (3). Each clip showed a scene of a virtual human clapping its hands with a speed of 50, 110, 180 claps/minute. Motion was controlled as described in section 1.1 The runtime of each clip was approximately 4 seconds. Stimulus presentation and data collection was performed with Medialab v2008. [1].

Embodiment. We project the motion captured human movement onto the same embodiment as the VH. The fingers and face do not move in our experiment. To make sure that the unnaturalness of these unmoved body-parts does not dominate the naturalness judgment, we have selected an embodiment for our

---

[1] http://www.empirisoft.com/medialab.aspx

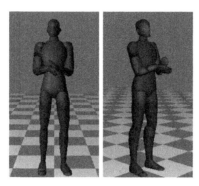

Fig. 1. Frontal and off-axis view used in the experiment

VH with simplified hands and minimal facial features (see Fig. 1). The physical model of our VH consists of 15 rigid bodies, connected by 14 joints. Each of the rigid bodies is represented by a mesh shaped as the corresponding body part in our motion captured actor. We determine the mass, CoM and inertia tensor of these bodies in a similar manner as in [5]. The physical body of the VH has roughly (within 5kg) the same total mass as our motion captured actor.

2.3   Design and Procedures

The experiment consisted of three sessions. The 2AFC and Yes-No sessions concern the discrimination between different motion inputs and the rating session required the users to rate the naturalness of a given animation. To counter learning effects, the order of the two discrimination sessions was randomized with the rating session always in between them. This was done because participants needed a certain amount of practice before they could come to a reliable rating. At the beginning of each of the three sessions, instructions were given and two test items were provided to familiarize participants with the procedure. At the end of each session, they were asked to describe what criteria they used to make their decision. A short description of each of the sessions is given in section 1.2.

2.4   Statistical Analyses

To analyze the rating data (naturalness score of 1-10), we performed a 3 (motion input) x 2 (viewing orientation) x 3 (clapping frequency) full factorial analysis of variance (ANOVA).

Signal Detection Theory is used to determine the sensitivity and variance of sensitivity for each of the *test paradigms*, (Yes/No , 2AFC and rating), *viewing orientations* (off-axis vs frontal) and *clapping frequencies* (50, 110 and 180 bpm). d' is a measure of perceptual difference between two observations that is not influenced by response bias (that is, a general tendency by subjects to favor the selection of one class over another) and that is comparable between different tests [6]. $d' = 0$ indicates that two observations cannot be discriminated, $d' = 4.65$

is considered an effective ceiling that indicates near perfect discrimination. d' is given by

$$d' = z(H) - z(F) \tag{1}$$

where H is the hit rate, F is the false alarm rate and z is the inverse of the normal distribution function. In the Yes/No paradigm, $H = P(\text{"human"}|human)$ and $F = P(\text{"human"}|model)$. In the 2AFC test $H = P(\text{"human left"}|humanleft)$ and $F = P(\text{"human left"}|humanright)$. Note that we do not employ the $\frac{1}{\sqrt{2}}$ correction factor for d' in 2AFC, since we are interested in determining whether the relation between d'-s found by 2AFC and Yes/No in similar test conditions is captured by this factor or any other linear relationship. The variance of d' is given by

$$var(d') = \frac{H(1-H)}{N_2(\phi(H))^2} + \frac{F(1-F)}{N_1(\phi(F))^2} \tag{2}$$

With N_2 the number of mocap trails, N_1 number of 'model' trails and $\phi(p)$ the height of the normal density function at $z(p)$.

For the rating test, we choose the area under the receiver operating characteristic (ROC) curve A_z as a measure for sensitivity (see [6], chapter 3). A_z and its variance are calculated using ROCKIT. [2]

3   Results

3.1   Comparing Motion Inputs

Motion input has a significant effect on naturalness ratings $F(2, 56) = 18.357, p < 0.001$. Tukey post-hoc analysis shows that motion input 1 was rated as more natural than motion input 2 ($p < 0.001$) and motion input 3 ($p < 0.001$). The average rating for motion input 2 although higher, was not significantly different from that of motion input 3 ($p = 0.12$).

Participants can discriminate between motion 1 and motion 2 as well as between motion 1 and motion 3 for all tests and conditions ($d' \neq 0$, $p < 0.05$). Subjects incorrectly identified motion 2 as human only in the yes/no test at 50bpm, off-axis. All other d' scores show that the subjects correctly identify motion 1 as human and motion 2 and motion 3 as nonhuman.

In the 2AFC test, subjects can discriminate between motion 1 and motion 3 significantly better than between motion 1 and motion 2 at all off-axis views and the 50bpm front view ($p < 0.001$). The rating test shows only significantly better discrimination of motion 1 and motion 3 versus motion 1 and motion 2 for the off-axis view at 50bpm ($p < 0.05$). These and other significant rating and discrimination results are illustrated in Fig. 2.

3.2   Comparing Evaluation Methods

No significant differences in $var(d')$ are found between the test paradigms. The variance between d'-s in the different test conditions is 0.95 for 2AFC, 0.25

---

[2] http://xray.bsd.uchicago.edu/krl/KRL_ROC/software_index6.htm

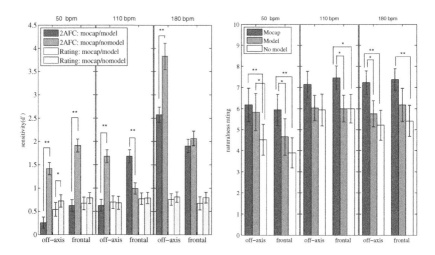

Fig. 2. Left: sensitivity as function of *viewing orientation* and *clapping frequency* for the 2AFC and rating tests. Right: mean naturalness ratings as a function of *motion input, viewing orientation* and *clapping frequency*. Vertical bars denote the 95% confidence intervals and. Significant differences are illustrated by * ($p < 0.05$) and ** ($p < 0.001$).

for Yes/No and 0.0058 for the rating paradigm. These values are significantly different ($p < 0.001$). We conclude that, for our test conditions, 2AFC is the most efficient test and that rating is not a good test for discrimination.

There is a strong correlation between the d' values obtained by the rating test and the d' values obtained by the Yes/No test (Pearson's $\rho = 0.906$, $p < 0.05$). Possibly the rating test as it was used in our experiment, was experienced by the subjects as a Yes/No test with an expanded grading scale. The correlation between 2AFC and Yes/No was strong ($\rho = 0.785$), but only marginally significant ($p = 0.064$). The correlation between 2AFC and rating was moderate ($\rho = 0.665$, $p < 0.05$). Significant observations made with the different test paradigms generally agreed, with the exception of the one specific case mentioned above.

4   Discussion

We have demonstrated the applicability of a mixed paradigm animation technique to evaluate physical controllers in isolation. Setting up such an evaluation is relatively easy, because the used mixed paradigm technique integrates with any existing physical simulation environment used to animate VHs [5].

Differences in variability between the d' for different test conditions show that 2AFC is the most efficient test, followed by Yes/No. Rating is not a good test for discrimination, but it does offer possibly valuable information on the naturalness of motion capture and model based motion separately, rather than just their discriminability. When significant observations were made by multiple test paradigms, their results agreed. While we have shown that the 2AFC test is more efficient than a Yes/No test, there might be valid reasons to opt for a Yes/No test (see 1.2). In fact, for all results we obtained using both tests (that is, those dealing with only motion 1 and motion 2) the Yes/No test provided the same (significant) result as the 2AFC test did.

For procedural motion, generating a mix of coherent motion captured and procedurally generated motion to evaluate a procedural controller in isolation is more challenging. Perhaps one of the motion combination methods discussed in [1] can be used there.

Chaminade et al. [7] show that the sensitivity measure d' obtained from a 2AFC test that compared motion captured locomotion with key-framed locomotion is independent of the embodiment of a VH. If this result holds for other movement types and movement models, d' could prove an interesting measure to compare naturalness of motion models generated by different research groups.

Acknowledgments. This research has been supported by the GATE project, funded by the Netherlands Organization for Scientific Research (NWO) and the Netherlands ICT Research and Innovation Authority (ICT Regie). We would like to thank Rob van der Lubbe for his help with SDT.

References

1. van Welbergen, H., van Basten, B.J.H., Egges, A., Ruttkay, Z., Overmars, M.H.: Real Time Animation of Virtual Humans: A Trade-off Between Naturalness and Control. In: Eurographics - State of the Art Reports, Eurographics Association, pp. 45–72 (2009)
2. Hartmann, B., Mancini, M., Pelachaud, C.: Formational parameters and adaptive prototype instantiation for mpeg-4 compliant gesture synthesis. In: Computer Animation, pp. 111–119. IEEE Computer Society, Los Alamitos (2002)
3. Kopp, S., Wachsmuth, I.: Synthesizing multimodal utterances for conversational agents: Research articles. Comput. Animat. Virtual Worlds 15(1), 39–52 (2004)
4. Wooten, W.L., Hodgins, J.K.: Simulating leaping, tumbling, landing, and balancing humans. In: International Conference on Robotics and Animation, pp. 656–662 (2000)
5. van Welbergen, H., Zwiers, J., Ruttkay, Z.: Real-time animation using a mix of dynamics and kinematics. Submitted to Journal of Graphics Tools (2009)
6. Macmillan, N.A., Creelman, D.C.: Detection Theory: A User's Guide, 2nd edn. Lawrence Erlbaum, Mahwah (2004)
7. Chaminade, T., Hodgins, J.K., Kawato, M.: Anthropomorphism influences perception of computer-animated characters' actions. Social Cognitive and Affective Neuroscience 2(3), 206–216 (2007)
8. Weissenfeld, A., Liu, K., Ostermann, J.: Video-Realistic Image-based Eye Animation System. In: Eurographics 2009 - Short Papers, pp. 41–44. Eurographics Association (2009)
9. van Basten, B., Egges, A.: Evaluating distance metrics for animation blending. In: Proceedings of the 4th International Conference on Foundations of Digital Games, pp. 199–206. ACM, New York (2009)

A Study into Preferred Explanations of Virtual Agent Behavior

Maaike Harbers[1,2], Karel van den Bosch[2], and John-Jules Ch. Meyer[1]

[1] Utrecht University, P.O. Box 80.089, 3508 TB Utrecht, The Netherlands
{maaike,jj}@cs.uu.nl
[2] TNO Human Factors, P.O. Box 23, 3769 ZG Soesterberg, The Netherlands
karel.vandenbosch@tno.nl

Abstract. Virtual training systems provide an effective means to train people for complex, dynamic tasks such as crisis management or firefighting. Intelligent agents are often used to play the characters with whom a trainee interacts. To increase the trainee's understanding of played scenarios, several accounts of agents that can explain the reasons for their actions have been proposed. This paper describes an empirical study of what instructors consider useful agent explanations for trainees. It was found that different explanations types were preferred for different actions, e.g. conditions enabling action execution, goals underlying an action, or goals that become achievable after action execution. When an action has important consequences for other agents, instructors suggest that the others' perspectives should be part of the explanation.

1 Introduction

This paper presents a study about explanations of intelligent virtual agents about their own behavior. Several accounts for such self-explaining agents for virtual training have been proposed [1,4,7,11]. In general, self-explaining agents act in virtual training systems used to train people for complex, dynamic tasks in which fast decision making is required, e.g. the persons in command in crisis management, military missions or fire-fighting. During a training session, a trainee interacts with the virtual agents, which play the role of e.g. team-member or opponent. After the training session is over, the agents can be queried or give explanations on their own initiative about their actions in the played session, aiming to give trainees better insight in the played training session.

Explanations exist in a wide variety of forms. Explanations of why one should wear seat belts, why trees grow, and why Anna was angry with John last week, each have different properties and are created according to different mechanisms. Even single phenomena or processes can be explained in different ways. For instance, the vase fell because of the gravity force, because Chris pushed it, or because Chris was distracted by his cat. As there are so many possible ways to explain phenomena, events and processes, explaining all facets is usually neither possible, nor desired [6]. Thus, in order to provide useful explanations one should

Zs. Ruttkay et al. (Eds.): IVA 2009, LNAI 5773, pp. 132–145, 2009.
© Springer-Verlag Berlin Heidelberg 2009

choose an explanation type and select the information that fits the domain and the people to whom the explanation is directed.

A way to categorize explanations is according to the *explanatory stance* to be adopted for framing the explanation [6]. Dennett distinguishes three explanatory stances: the mechanical, the design and the intentional stance [3]. The mechanical stance considers simple physical objects and their interactions, the design stance considers entities as having purposes and functions, and the intentional stance considers entities as having beliefs, desires, and other mental contents that govern their behavior. Humans usually understand and explain their own and others' behavior by adopting the intentional stance. Most accounts of self-explaining agents give explanations in terms of an agent's beliefs [7] or motivations [4,1] that were responsible for its actions. We believe that the intentional stance distinguishes explanations of agents from explanations provided by expert systems, in which no intentionality is involved [12].

In earlier work we have proposed an account of self-explaining agents which is able to provide explanations in terms of beliefs and goals [5]. Though the scope of these agents' possible explanations is restricted by adopting the intentional stance, they can still explain one action in several ways. There are usually several mental concepts that underly one action, but not all of them are equally relevant in an explanation. Especially when the agent models are complex, providing all beliefs and goals underlying an action does not result in useful explanations. Instead, explanations containing a selection of the explaining mental concepts are probably more effective.

The purpose of the study presented in this paper is twofold. First, it serves to examine whether the explanatory stance we used in our approach for self-explaining agents is considered useful by instructors. We aim to find empirical indications that explanations which are considered useful by instructors are compatible with the intentional stance. We consult instructors' on what they consider useful explanations for trainees, as instructors have knowledge about both the task domain and didactic aspects. Second, we want to use the results of this study to further develop our approach of self-explaining agents, so that within the scope of possible explanations, useful ones are selected. We will consider several properties of explanations: explanation length, abstraction level and explanation type. The experiments in this paper aim to shed light on instructors' preferences on these aspects.

2   Methods

The subjects participating in the experiments had to play a training session involving several virtual agents. After the scenario was completed, the subjects were provided by possible explanations for actions performed by the virtual agents, and asked to select the explanation which they considered most useful for a trainee. In this section we will discuss the virtual training system that was used, the generation of possible explanations, and more details on the experimental setup.

2.1   Training on-Board Fire Fighting

The subjects played a training session with the Carim system[1], a virtual training system developed for the Royal Netherlands Navy to train the tasks of an Officer of the Watch (for a more extensive overview of the system see [10]). The Officer of the Watch is the person who is in command when there is a fire aboard a navy frigate. From the Technical Center of the ship he collects information, makes an assessment of the situation, develops plans to solve the incident, instructs other people, monitors the situation, and adjusts his plans if necessary. The Officer of the Watch communicates with several other officers, of which the Chief of the Watch, the Leader Confinement Team, and the Leader Attack Team are the most important. In a typical incident scenario, the Officer of the Watch and the Chief of the Watch remain in the Technical Center, the Leader Attack Team is situated close to the location of the incident, and the Leader Confinement Team moves between both locations. One training session takes about half an hour to complete.

Fig. 1. A snapshot of the Carim system: communication with a virtual agent

The Carim system is a stand-alone, low-cost desktop simulation trainer, to be used by a single trainee who is playing the role of Officer of the Watch. The trainee can freely navigate through the Technical Center. All equipment that the Officer of the Watch normally uses is simulated and available to the trainee, e.g. a map of the ship, information panels and communication equipment. Communication from agent to trainee happens by playing pre-recorded speech expressions, and a trainee can communicate with an agent by selecting speech acts from a menu (figure 1). These menus are agent-specific and may change over the course of a training session.

_____

[1] The Carim system has been developed by TNO and VSTEP.

The course of a training session in the Carim system is guided by a scenario script. The script defines for each possible situation what should happen, which is either an event in the environment or an action of an agent. The trainee has certain freedom to act the way he wants to act, but if he deviates from the storyline in the scenario, the simulation redirects the trainee back to the intended scenario. For instance, if it is necessary that the trainee contacts the Leader Attack Team, the Chief of the Watch will repeat an advice to contact the Leader Attack Team till the trainee does so. Currently, a new version of the Carim system is being developed in which the behavior of agents is not scripted, but generated online by intelligent agents. Advantages of intelligent agents are that they are able to deal with unexpected trainee behavior, and thus yield more freedom for the trainee and more diverse courses of a training scenario. Moreover, intelligent agents can more easily be reused in different scenarios. However, the improved version of the Carim system was not available yet at the time the experiments in this paper were performed.

2.2   Explanation Generation by Simulation

In the ideal case, the behavior of the virtual characters in the training system would be generated autonomously and online by self-explaining agents. Then, the agents would create logs about their decisions and actions during the scenario, and based on these logs, give explanations for their behavior in the scenario afterwards. However, because no connection between intelligent agents and virtual environment had been established yet, we had to obtain explanations of agents in another way. We did so by running a separate simulation with only agents, and no visualization of the environment. These agents were not scripted, but instead, generated behavior in an intelligent way. During the simulation, the self-explaining agents built up a log about their decisions and actions, and based on these logs we could derive explanations. We run the simulation before the actual experiment took place, and in the experiment we presented the beforehand obtained explanations to the subjects.

We have modeled and implemented three of the agents in the Carim scenario: the Chief of the Watch, the Leader Confinement Team, and the Leader Attack Team. While modeling the agents, we ensured that they would generate the same behavior as the scripted virtual agents with whom the subjects would interact. The behavior of the scripted agents was almost completely known because the scenario script of the Carim system only allows for little deviation from the intended storyline. The difference between modeled agents and the scripted agents is that the modeled agents make reasoning steps in order to generate behavior and the scripted agents do not. These reasoning steps are stored in a log, and from this log explanations can be derived. Because the actions of the scripted and modeled agents are equal, the derived explanations are exactly the same as when there would be a connection between agents and virtual environment.

We used the approach for developing self-explaining agents that we recently proposed [5]. In this approach, the conceptual model of an agent is a task hierarchy containing all its possible tasks. A task hierarchy representation language is used to represent an agent's tasks, subtasks and the conditions for adopting and achieving tasks. It is specified how such a task hierarchy can be translated to an agent implemented in a BDI-based (Belief Desire Intention) agent programming language. The translation is based on similarities between task hierarchies and BDI models[9]. Tasks are implemented as goals, actions (tasks at the bottom of a hierarchy) are implemented as plans, and adoption conditions are implemented as beliefs.

Following this approach, we constructed task hierarchies of the Chief of the Watch, the Leader Confinement Team, and the Leader Attack Team in the Carim scenario, and implemented them in the agent programming language 2APL [2]. For the construction of the task hierarchies, we used task descriptions provided by the Navy and interviews with experts. Figure 2 shows a part of the task hierarchy of the Leader Attack Team agent. The task *Initiate fire attack*, for instance, has three subtasks: *Go to location*, *Develop a plan*, and *Instruct team*. Only for two tasks (*Initiate fire attack* and *Develop a plan*) the conditions under which they are adopted are shown, but all other tasks have adoption conditions as well. For instance, for achieving the task *Initiate fire attack* one can only adopt the task to *Develop a plan* when one is *At location*.

By developing agents according to this approach, the elements in the deliberation process generating behavior can also be used to explain that behavior, i.e. the goals and beliefs underlying an action also explain that action. In figure 2, for instance, the tasks and adoption conditions underlying and thus explaining the action *Contact the OW* are marked by a bold line. To enable agents to provide explanations, they need to have knowledge about their own internal structure, which is realized by adding a representation of the agent's own task hierarchy to its belief base. Moreover, when the agent is executed, a log of the agent's actions

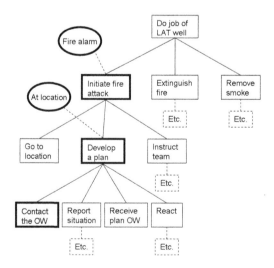

Fig. 2. Part of task hierarchy of the Leader Attack Team containing tasks (boxes) and adoption conditions (circles)

is created in its belief base. With knowledge about its task structure and past actions, an agent can explain its actions by providing the beliefs and goals that were involved in the generation of that action.

We equipped the three Carim agents with explanations capabilities and run them. Figure 3 shows a part of the Leader Attack Team agent's belief base after it was run. The left part of the code represents the agent's beliefs about its task hierarchy, and the right part shows the log that was created during the execution.

```
task(DoJobWell,                                      log(t(1), goToLocation).
   [(InitiateFireAttack, alarm),                     log(t(2), contactOW).
   (ExtinguishFire, attackInitiated),                log(t(3), reportFire).
   (RemoveSmoke, fireExtinguished and smoke)]).      log(t(4), reportVictims).
task(InitiateFireAttack,                             etc.
   [(GoToLocation, not atLocation),
   (DevelopPlan, atLocation),
   (InstructTeam, planDevleoped)]).
etc.
```

Fig. 3. Part of the belief base of the Leader Attack Team after execution

The left part of the code shows a representation of a part of the Leader Attack Team's task hierarchy. Each task in the hierarchy is represented by a belief containing information about the identity of the task, the identity of its subtasks, and the adoption conditions of the subtasks. For example, the task *DoJobWell* has three subtasks, *InitiateFireAttack*, *ExtinguishFire* and *RemoveSmoke*, with adoption conditions *alarm*, *attackInitiated*, and *fireExtinguished and smoke*, respectively. The right part of the code shows log beliefs containing information about the actions that were executed and the time of their execution. From these two types of information in the agent's belief base, several explanations for one action can be derived. For example, the Leader Attack Team went to the location of the incident because a) it had to do its job well, b) the alarm bell rang, c) it had to initiate the fire attack, or d) it was not at the location of the incident yet.

2.3   Experimental Setup

We conducted two experimentation sessions in which subjects had to play a scenario in the Carim system and indicate their preferences about explanations of the behavior of the agents in the scenario. The subjects, 15 in total, were all instructors of the Dutch Navy with knowledge about the task domain, and experience in teaching. Before they started, the subjects received instructions about the objective of the experiments and what they were expected to do. None of them had used the Carim system before. To get acquainted to the system, they received some time to practice with navigating their avatar, communicating with other agents, and marking an incident on a damage panel. The subjects were asked to fill in a questionnaire after playing the session.

The questionnaires consisted of two parts. In part I, the subjects were asked to explain 12 actions which had been performed by the virtual agents in the scenario, four actions of each of the three agents we modeled. For example, the subjects had to explain why the Leader Attack Team contacted the Officer of the Watch. They were instructed to provide explanations from the perspective of the agent that executed the action, and to keep in mind that the explanations should help the trainee to achieve a proper understanding of the situation. In part II, the same 12 actions were presented to the subjects, and this time they were asked to select the best out of four possible explanations. The explanations were derived from the agents' belief bases after the offline simulation with intelligent agents. We translated the programming code explanations to sentences in natural language by hand. For example, the subjects had to indicate their preferred explanation for the following question.

The Leader Attack Team contacted the Officer of the Watch because...
- *there was a fire alarm*
- *he wants to initiate the fire attack*
- *he arrived at the location of the incident*
- *he wants to develop an attack plan*

The four explanations are, respectively, an abstract belief, an abstract goal, a detailed belief and a detailed goal. Abstract explanations contain goals and beliefs higher in the agent's task hierarchy, and detailed explanations contain goals and beliefs higher and lower in the agent's task hierarchy. In part II, the subjects were again instructed to keep in mind that the explanations should increase trainees' understanding of the situation. The subjects had to give their own explanations before they saw the agents' explanations to ensure that their own explanations were not influenced by the explanations provided to them in the second part of the questionnaire.

The first session was conducted with 8 subjects, and mainly focused on the question whether explanations preferred by instructors are compatible with the intentional stance. Namely, the answers in part II of the questionnaire, in which subjects select one out of several intentional explanations, are only valuable if the instructors consider intentional explanations useful at all. The compatibility of the instructors' preferred explanations with the intentional stance was obtained by analyzing the instructors' own explanations in part I of the questionnaire. We expected that the instructors' preferred explanations would be compatible with the intentional stance.

The second experimentation session aimed to obtain more detailed information on the nature of preferred explanations, such as preferred explanation length, type and abstraction level. Concerning explanation length, we expected that short explanations would be preferred over long ones because not all information that explains an action is relevant. Concerning explanation type, we expected that explanations containing a belief with the precondition for an action, or a goal to be achieved by an action would be preferred over other types of explanations. Finally, concerning preferred abstraction level, we expected that explanations containing detailed, low-level information would be preferred over explanations with abstract, high-level information.

3 Results

All of the subjects were able to solve the incident presented to them in the training scenario. Though some of the subjects had some difficulties with navigating their avatar, they generally rated the training system positively. Section 3.1 discusses the results of experimentation session 1, and presents data obtained from part I of the questionnaire. Section 3.2 discusses the results of experimentation session 2, and presents data obtained from part II of the questionnaire. Note that some of the data obtained in session 1 from part II of the questionnaire are also presented in section 3.2.

3.1 Session 1

The first experimentation session was conducted with 8 subjects. From part I of the questionnaire we obtained 88 explanations of virtual agent actions, provided by the subjects themselves. Note that in 8 occasions, a subject was unable to provide an explanation, as 8 times 12 should deliver 96 explanations.

Subjects' own explanations: explanation length. The first categorization of explanations is according to their length. We defined explanation length by the number of elements, where an element is a goal, a belief, a fact, etc. Table 1 shows the frequencies of the number of elements in the subjects' explanations. The results show that most explanations contained only 1 element (70%). All others contained 2 elements (30%). No explanations with more than 2 elements were given.

Table 1. Frequencies of the number of elements in the provided explanations (n=8)

Length	# explanations
1 element	62
2 elements	26
>2 elements	0

Subjects' own explanations: explanation type. A second way to categorize the subjects' explanations is according to type. More specifically, explanation elements can be categorized according to type. Our aim was to examine whether the subjects' explanations are compatible with the intentional stance. We thus tried to map the provided explanation elements to intentional concepts such as beliefs, goals and intentions.

An examination of the provided explanations resulted into five types of explanation elements: the condition for executing an action, background information concerning an action, the goal to be achieved an the action, the goal that becomes achievable after executing an action, and others' goals that become achievable after executing an action. A *condition* for an action was for example 'I went to the location of the incident because I heard the alarm message'. An example of *background information* is 'the Officer of the Watch and the Leader Attack Team communicate by a headphone'. An explanation with a *goal to be achieved* is for instance 'I put water on the fire to extinguish it'. An explanation containing an *enabled goal* is e.g. 'I prepared fire hoses to extinguish the fire'. Finally, an example of an explanation in terms of an *other's goal* is 'if I make the location voltage free, my colleague can safely use water in the room'.

The first two types, condition and background information can be considered as beliefs, and the last three types, own goal, enabled goal and other's goal, are all goals. We do not claim that our classification is the only one possible. These results should rather be seen as an explorative examination of whether the provided explanations are compatible with the intentional stance. Table 2 shows the number of provided elements per explanation type. If an explanation contained two elements, e.g. a goal and background information, both elements were counted as a half. A remark about table 2 is that some of the explanations

Table 2. Number of explanations per explanation type (n=8)

Type	# elements
Belief (condition)	10
Background information	10
Goal	12.5
Enabled goal	34
Other's goal	21.5

classified as enabled goals could also be classified as goals. For instance, the explanation 'the Leader confinement team goes to the TC to report to the Officer of the Watch' can be classified in two ways. Namely, the explaining element 'to report to the Officer of the Watch' can be seen as a goal of which going to the TC is a subgoal, but also as an enabled goal that can be achieved after the Leader Confinement Team arrived in the TC. In the first interpretation the explanation would be classified as a goal, and in the second as an enabled goal. In case of such ambiguity, we have chosen for the second interpretation, and classified the explanation as an enabled goal.

In the first experimentation round, the second part of the questionnaire only contained explanations in terms of beliefs forming a condition and goals to be achieved by the action. However, the results in table 2 show that many of the explanations were in terms of enabled goals and others' goals. Therefore, we decided to add more possible explanations to the second part of the questionnaire. In figure 2 one can see that an explanation in terms of an enabled goal for the action 'The Leader Attack Team contacted the Officer of the Watch' is that 'The Leader Attack Team wants to report the situation to the Officer of the Watch'. Explanations in terms of others' goals cannot be derived from an agent's own belief base, but it is possible to look at task hierarchies of other agents and formulate explanations in terms of others' goals.

3.2   Session 2

The second experimentation session was conducted with 7 subjects. Part II of the questionnaire was adjusted by adding an explanation in terms of an enabled goal to the answers where possible, and adding an explanation in terms of an other's goal to the answers for all actions. As explanations in terms of others' goals were not derivable from the agents' own belief bases, preferences on this type of explanations were asked in a separate question.

Multiple choice: explanation type (3 choices) and abstraction level.
There were five actions for which an explanation in terms of an enabled goal could be derived from the agents' task hierarchies, and for these actions the subjects could select one of five possible explanations in part II of the questionnaire. Table 3 shows for these actions which explanation type was preferred, and whether at least 75% or 50% of the subjects agreed on that. Thus, the italic numbers in the table are action numbers and not frequencies. The general agreement among

Table 3. Preferred explanation types and abstraction levels for actions 1,2,5,7,8 (n=7)

Type	Abstraction	>75%	>50%
Belief	Detailed	*8*	-
	Abstract	-	-
Goal	Detailed	-	*1*
	Abstract	-	*7*
Enabled Goal	-	*2,5*	-

the subjects expressed in a multi-rater kappa coefficient [8] was 0.55. The results show that for some actions (action 2 and 5) a large majority of the subjects preferred an explanation in terms of an enabled goal. However, explanations in terms of enabled goals were not always preferred. Subjects even agreed for more than 75% that action 8 could best be explained in terms of a detailed condition belief.

Multiple choice: explanation type (2 choices) and abstraction level.
For the actions for which no explanation in terms of an enabled goal could be derived from the agents' belief bases, subjects could choose between four options. As these questions were equal to those in the first experimentation session, table 4 shows the results based on the answers of all 15 subjects. Out of seven actions,

Table 4. Preferred explanation types and abstraction levels for actions 3,4,6,9,10,11,12 (n=15)

Type	Abstraction	>75%	>50%
Belief	Detailed	10	3
	Abstract	-	-
Goal	Detailed	9	11,12
	Abstract	-	6

only for two actions (9 and 10) more than 75% of the subjects agreed on the preferred explanation type, which is reflected in a rather low kappa coefficient of 0.33. For action 4, no preference on which at least 50% of the sujects agreed was found.

Multiple choice: explanations involving other agents' perspectives. In the second experimentation session, the 12 multiple choice questions in part II were each followed up by a second question concerning explanations in terms of others' goals. After indicating their preference of four or five possible explanations, subjects were asked to compare their first answer to another (fifth or sixth) option. This extra option was an explanation in terms of an other's goal, for instance as follows.

The Leader Attack Team contacted the Officer of the Watch because...
  - < answer given in part a >
  - the Officer of the Watch knows he is there

The results of the follow up question are presented in table 5. A kappa of 0.43

Table 5. Amount of explanations and the actions per explanation type (n=7)

Type	>75%	>50%
First choice	1	7,8
Other's goal	4,5,9,10,11,12	2,3,6

for the overall agreement among the subjects was found. The results show that for 9 out of 12 actions, the subjects preferred explanations in terms of an other's goal over their first choice. For six of the actions (4,5,9,10,11,12) more than 75% of the subjects preferred an explanation in terms of an other's goal and only for one action (1) more than 75% of the subjects agreed on a preference for an explanation not based on an other's goal. As explanations in terms of others' goals were not based on the belief bases of the agents we modeled, the data in table 5 should not be considered as final results, but as an exploration of possibly preferred explanations.

4   Discussion

The first objective of the study was to examine whether preferred explanations are compatible with an intentional perspective. In part I of the questionnaire, the subjects were asked to provide explanations without any constraints concerning explanation types to be used. We were able to classify the elements in the subjects' own explanations in five explanation types, which were all either belief-based or goal-based (table 2). Though the explanations might be classifiable in other ways, possibly in non-intentional explanation types, it was possible to understand the explanations from an intentional perspective. We may thus conclude that the preferred explanations are compatible with the intentional stance, and that using a BDI-based approach is an appropriate method for developing self-explaining agents.

In section 2.3, we formulated three expectations about the nature of preferred explanations. Concerning explanation length, we expected that short explanations would be preferred over long ones. In part I of the questionnaire, the subjects were asked to provide their own explanations, whereby no restrictions on explanation length were given. Table 1 showed that their explanations in most cases only contained one element, and never more than two elements. These results thus confirm our expectations. Consequently, self-explaining agents should make a selection of elements which they provide in an explanation.

Concerning preferred explanation type, we expected that most of the instructors' explanations about an action would either involve a belief with the condition enabling execution of the action, or a goal for which the action is executed. Though part of the instructors' explanations in part I could be classified into one of these categories, the results in table 2 show that three other explanation types were also used, namely background information, enabled goals and others' goals. Results from part II of the questionnaire confirmed the results of part I. Namely, table 3 and 5 show that the instructors sometimes selected other explanation types than the ones we originally expected. We may conclude that our expectations were partly supported by the results. Within our approach of self-explaining agents it was already possible to provide explanations in terms of enabled goals, but the agents should be extended with the capability to provide explanations in terms of others' goals as well.

Our last expectation involved the abstraction level of preferred explanations. We expected that detailed explanations would be preferred over abstract ones. In this study, detailed and abstract explanations consisted of mental concepts low (just above action level) and high in an agent's task hierarchy, respectively. We cannot give a general conclusion concerning preferred abstraction level because the data only give information about the preferred abstraction level of two types of explanations, condition beliefs and own goals. For belief-based explanations, the results clearly show that detailed explanations are preferred over abstract ones (table 3 and 4). For goal-based explanations, the results in table 3 and 4 also show that detailed explanations are preferred over abstract ones, but not as convincingly as for belief-based explanations.

A possible explanation for the low score on abstract belief-based explanations is that condition beliefs are often directly related to events in the environment. Abstract beliefs take place earlier in time than detailed beliefs, for example, the fire alarm rings before the Leader Attack Team reaches the location of the incident, and it is plausible that more recent cues are preferred over older ones.

5   Conclusion and Future Work

In this paper we described a study of preferred explanations of virtual agents in a training context. Our goal with this study was twofold. First, it aimed to explore whether our BDI-based approach of self-explaining agents as described in section 2.2 is appropriate for the generation of explanations. The results of the experiments supported our expectation that preferred explanations of virtual agent behavior are compatible with an intentional perspective. Thus, explanations in terms of beliefs and goals are expected to enhance trainees' understanding of the training situations.

Second, the study was meant to obtain information on how our approach for developing self-explaining agents could be improved. An important finding was that for some actions, instructors preferred explanations in terms of enabled goals and others' goals. Explanations in terms of enabled goals can already be derived from the self-explaining agents' belief bases in the current approach. However, to generate explanations in terms of others' goals, the agents' models need to be extended with beliefs about other agents' goals. We are currently working on extending the self-explaining agents with a theory of mind, i.e. the agents are equipped with a 'theory' about the beliefs and goals of other agents. With this extension it should be possible to generate explanations that are based on other agents' goals.

Another outcome of the study was that different actions were explained in different ways. In future work we will examine different situations in which actions are executed in relation to their preferred explanation. For instance, only if an action has important consequences for other agents, an explanation in terms of others' goals may be preferred. Finding such relations will help to develop a mechanism that selects a useful explanation among possible explaining mental concepts.

After improving the approach of self-explaining agents, we plan to perform a new set of experiments. These experiments will not be meant to explore, as the study described in this paper, but rather to validate the approach. Consequently, the subjects of the experiments will be trainees instead of instructors. The results of such a study can give insight on whether the explanations really enhance trainees' understanding of the training situations.

Acknowledgments. This research has been supported by the GATE project, funded by the Netherlands Organization for Scientific Research (NWO) and the Netherlands ICT Research and Innovation Authority (ICT Regie).

References

1. Core, M., Traum, T., Lane, H., Swartout, W., Gratch, J., van Lent, M.: Teaching negotiation skills through practice and reflection with virtual humans. Simulation 82(11), 685–701 (2006)
2. Dastani, M.: 2APL: a practical agent programming language. Autonomous Agents and Multi-agent Systems 16(3), 214–248 (2008)
3. Dennett, D.: The Intentional Stance. MIT Press, Cambridge (1987)
4. Gomboc, D., Solomon, S., Core, M.G., Lane, H.C., van Lent, M.: Design recommendations to support automated explanation and tutoring. In: Proc. of the 14th Conf. on Behavior Representation in Modeling and Simulation, Universal City, CA (2005)
5. Harbers, M., Van den Bosch, K., Meyer, J.: A methodology for developing self-explaining agents for virtual training. In: Decker, Sichman, Sierra, Castelfranchi (eds.) Proc. of 8th Int. Conf. on Autonomous Agents and Multiagent Systems (AAMAS 2009), Budapest, Hungary, pp. 1129–1130 (2009)
6. Keil, F.: Explanation and understanding. Annual Reviews Psychology 57, 227–254 (2006)
7. Johnson, W.L.: Agents that learn to explain themselves. In: Proc. of the 12th Nat. Conf. on Artificial Intelligence, pp. 1257–1263 (1994)
8. Randolph, J.: Online kappa calculator (2008),
   http://justus.randolph.name/kappa (retrieved March 6, 2009)
9. Sardina, S., De Silva, L., Padgham, L.: Hierarchical planning in bdi agent programming languages: A formal approach. In: Proceedings of AAMAS 2006. ACM Press, New York (2006)
10. Van den Bosch, K., Harbers, M., Heuvelink, A., Van Doesburg, W.: Intelligent agents for training on-board fire fighting (to appear, 2009)
11. Van Lent, M., Fisher, W., Mancuso, M.: An explainable artificial intelligence system for small-unit tactical behavior. In: Proc. of IAAA 2004. AAAI Press, Menlo Park (2004)
12. Ye, R., Johnson, P.: The impact of explanation facilities on user acceptance of expert systems advice. Mis Quarterly 19(2), 157–172 (1995)

Evaluating Adaptive Feedback in an Educational Computer Game

Cristina Conati and Micheline Manske

Computer Science Department, University of British Columbia
2366 Main Mall, Vancouver, BC, V6T1Z4, Canada
conati@cs.ubc.ca

Abstract. In this paper, we present a study to evaluate the impact of adaptive feedback on the effectiveness of a pedagogical agent for an educational computer game. We compare a version of the game with no agent, and two versions with agents that differ only in the accuracy of the student model used to guide the agent's interventions. We found no difference in student learning across the three conditions, and we report an analysis to understand the reasons of these results.

Keywords: Educational games, student modeling, evaluation.

1 Introduction

Educational computer games (edu-games) are an increasingly popular paradigm embedding pedagogical activities in highly engaging, game-like interactions. While edu-games usually increase student engagement and motivation, there is still limited evidence on their pedagogical potential (see [1] for an overview). One possible reason for these results is that most edu-games are designed based on a one-size-fits-all approach, rather than being able to respond to the specific needs of individual students. We aim to overcome this limitation with intelligent pedagogical agents that can provide individualized support to student learning during game playing [2].

Providing this support is challenging because it requires a careful trade-off between fostering learning and maintaining engagement. Our long-term goal is to enable our agents to achieve this trade-off by relying on models of both student learning and affect [2]. In this paper, however, we analyse the performance of an agent that acts only on the basis of a model of student learning. In particular, we describe a study to evaluate the effect of improving model accuracy on the agent's pedagogical effectiveness.

Although there is widespread interest in educational computer-games, adaptive versions of these learning tools are still relatively new, and empirical evaluations of the learning benefits of having adaptive game components are rare (see next section).

The evaluation we discuss in this paper focuses on Prime Climb, an adaptive edu-game for number factorization. Our evaluation is novel because it is the first in adaptive edu-games research to combine an analytical evaluation of the accuracy of the game's student model with an empirical evaluation of the effectiveness of adaptive interventions based on this model. Although our study shows no advantage in having an accurate student

Zs. Ruttkay et al. (Eds.): IVA 2009, LNAI 5773, pp. 146–158, 2009.

model, our methodology allows us to provide insights into the reasons for this null-result, representing a step towards understanding how to devise effective adaptive edu-games. In the rest of this paper, we first discuss related work. Next, we describe Prime Climb and the versions of its agent and student model that we evaluated. We then present the study and its results, and discuss implications for future work.

2   Related Work

Because of the highly motivating nature of electronic games, there has been growing interest in investigating whether they could be utilized to assist learning, especially for those children who lost interest in math or other science courses [15,16]. Results on the effectiveness of these educational tools, however, are mixed. There is evidence that these games can increase student engagement and motivation (e.g., 17, 18), but the results on their pedagogical potential are limited (e.g., [1],[15],[19]), unless the interaction is led by teachers and integrated with other instructional activities [e.g., 16]. There is also initial evidence that, for some students, educational games can be less engaging and motivating than more traditional e-learning tools [14].

One of the main reasons for these limitations of educational games is that learning how to play the game does not necessarily imply learning the target instructional domain. Learning happens when students actively build the connections between game moves and underlying knowledge. However, building these connections on one own is a form of exploratory or discovery learning, and there is extensive evidence that not all students are proficient in these activities , because they lack relevant meta-cognitive skills such as self-explanation and self-monitoring) [10, 20]. These students tend to perform better in more structured pedagogical activities [10], thus they may benefit from having some form of tutorial guidance when playing educational games.

In light of these findings, researchers have started investigating *adaptive* educational games, that is games that can autonomously tailor the interaction to the specific needs of each individual player. Although adaptive techniques have been successfully applied to other types of computer-based instructional environments [12], research on adaptive educational games is still in its infancy, and there are very few formal evaluations that explicitly target the pedagogical impact of adding adaptive function-alities to educational games. Both [9] and [13] showed that it is possible to devise user models that can capture student learning in educational games. The work in [9] relates to the educational game targeted by this paper and described in the next sec-tion. The work in [13] describes a model of student learning for Zombie Division, an educational game designed to help elementary school students learn about division. None of these works, however, show that having an adaptive component built on their student models supports learning. KMQuest [3], an adaptive edu-game for business decision-making, was shown to significantly improve student learning, but was not compared with a non-adaptive version. The Tactical Language and Culture Training System (TLCTS) supports language learning by combining an ITS component (the Skill Builder) and two games [4]. TLCTS is being actively used by the US military, and there is substantial evidence of its pedagogical effectiveness. However, in TLCTS the adaptive behaviors reside primarily in the ITS component, and the only results on how the games contribute to system effectiveness relate to increasing student motivation [5]. The Elektra project [6] is a large research initiative aiming at defining a general methodology and tools to devise effective educational games. The proposed methodology includes having cognitive and motivational student models to allow a game to react adequately to the individual learner's cognitive and motivational needs. One of the games built as part of the project for teaching the physics of optics was evaluated and the study results showed positive trends in students perceived effectiveness of the game's adaptive interventions. The results, however, failed to provide results on actual learning gains [6]. McQuiggan et al. [7] evaluate the impact of rich narrative in a narrative-based adventure game for teaching microbiology, but there is no adaptive component in this system.

3   The Prime Climb Game, Its Agent and Student Model

In Prime Climb, students in 6th and 7th grade practice number factorization by pairing up to climb a series of mountains. Each mountain is divided into numbered sectors (see Figure 1), and players must try to move to numbers that do not share common factors with their partner's number, otherwise they fall. To help students, Prime Climb includes the Magnifying Glass, a tool that allows players to view the factorization for any number on a mountain in the PDA device displayed at the top-right corner on the game interface (see Figure 1). Each student also has a pedagogical agent (Figure 1) that provides individualized support, both on demand and unsolicited, when the student does not seem to be learning from the game. In the next subsections, we describe two versions of the agent, built through an iterative cycle of design and evaluation.

Fig. 1. The Prime Climb Interface

3.1 First Version of the Prime Climb Agent

To provide appropriate interventions, the agent must understand when incorrect moves are due to a lack of factorization knowledge vs. distraction errors, and when good moves reflect knowledge vs. lucky guesses or playing only based on game heuristics. Thus, Prime Climb includes a student model, based on Dynamic Bayesian networks, that assesses the student's factorization knowledge for each of the numbers involved in a Prime Climb session (*factorization skills* from now on) based on the student's game actions [8]. A first version of the agent gave hints at incremental levels of detail based on this model, as is commonly done in several ITS [21], with the goal of triggering student reasoning about number factorization as they play.

- The first (*focus*) level aims to channel the student's attention on the skill that requires help. For instance, the agent says *"Think about how to factorize the number you clicked on"* if the student model predicts that the student doesn't know how to factorize that number;

- the second (*tool*) level is a hint that encourages the student to use the magnifying glass to see relevant factorizations.

- The third (*bottom-out*) level gives either the factorization of a number or which factors are in common between two numbers [8].

Students can choose to progress through the various levels by asking for further help. Otherwise, the agent goes through the progression when it needs to intervene on the same skill more than once. Hints are provided regardless of the correctness of the student's move, if the student model assesses that the student needs help with the relevant number factorization skills.

Table 1. Sample revised hinting sequence triggered by a student not knowing the factorization of a number

Focus	Think carefully how to factorize the number you clicked on.
Definition 1	Factors are numbers that divide evenly into the number. Here's an example.
Definition 2	Factors are numbers that multiply to give the number. Look at this example.
Tool	You can use the magnifying glass to see the factors of the number you clicked on.
Bottom-out	You fell because x and y share z as a common factor. x can be factorized as $x_1*x_2*...*x_n$. y can be factorized as $y_1*y_n*...*y_m$.

An empirical study showed that this first version of the Prime Climb agent generated better student learning than the game with no agent [8]. A follow-up analysis of the student model used in this study showed limited accuracy (50.8%), due to various limitations of the model, discussed in [9]. The fact that an agent based on this model could still trigger learning indicates that even hints based on an almost random model are better than no hints at all. However, there was still room for improvement in the post-tests of the agent-condition (the post-test average was 77%), suggesting that a more accurate student model may yield even more substantial learning gains.

3.2   Second Version of the Prime Climb Agent

Following the results of the evaluation of the first version of the Prime Climb agent, we devised a new version of its student model that addressed the limitations uncovered by the study and that achieved an accuracy of 78% in assessing student factorization knowledge [9]. We also changed the agent's hinting strategy. We added a fourth hinting level (*definition*), to provide reteaching of the *factorization* and *common factor* concepts via definitions and examples. The original set of hints did not include an explanation of these concepts, thus students who still needed to understand them could only do so via some form of discovery learning during game playing. There is ample evidence, however, that for many students discovery or inquiry based learning is less effective than more structured instruction in the early stages of learning [10]. This effect may be more prominent with edu-games, when students are too busy playing to engage in non-spontaneous learning processes. Table 1 shows a sample revised hinting sequence.

Fig. 2. Sample example that the agent presents to accompany Definition 1 in table 1

As the table shows, we provide two different factorization definitions, because there is no common unifying definition for this concept. The agent alternates which definition to give first, and gives the second the next time it needs to provide an unsolicited hint on the same skill. Figure 2 shows a screenshot of an example that accompanies Definition 1 in Table 1. The examples at this level are general (i.e., do not relate to the number targeted by the current hint) and serve both to solidify the student's understanding of the definition and as a template for finding the factors of other numbers that the student sees on the mountain. *Definition* hints are given before the *tool* hint the first time the student goes through the hinting sequence, as shown in Table 1. Subsequently, they are given after the *tool* hint, because at this stage the student may just need a trigger to put together the definitions and examples seen earlier in order to find the answer by herself. All hints and examples were designed based on the experience of the second author, a former elementary school teacher (and award-winning university teaching assistant), and then extensively pilot-tested.

In the rest of the paper, we describe a study that we ran to test if and how the more accurate model we developed for Prime Climb impacts the effectiveness of the Prime Climb agent with this new hinting strategy.

4   Study Design

The study was run in two local elementary schools with sixth grade students, with the constraint that each study session had to be held during a class period (40 minutes) to avoid disrupting regular class schedule. The students were randomly assigned to one of three conditions: *No Agent*: game with no agent nor any other form of adaptive support (13 students); *Old-model*: game with the pedagogical agent and the original version of the student model (14 students). *New-model*: game with the pedagogical agent and the new, more accurate, version of the student model (17 students).

The morning of the study, all students wrote a pre-test in class, designed to assess the students' factorization knowledge of various numbers involved in the Prime Climb game. The rest of the study was conducted with pairs of students in a separate room, due to constraints on computer availability. The two students were excused from the class for that period and joined the experimenters in a room provided by the school for the experiment. Following the set-up that had been successfully adopted in [8], each session was designed to last at most 30 minutes so that there would be sufficient time for students to get to the study room and return to their class for the next period. Students were told that they would be playing a computer game, and received a demo of Prime Climb. They were told that the game contained a computer-based agent that was trying to understand their needs and help them play the game better. Next, students played with one of the three versions of Prime Climb for approximately 10 minutes. We had to limit playing time to 10' to allow for sufficient time for post-tests and post-questionnaires, because they could not be taken during regular class hours. It should be noted that, although these were relatively short sessions, sessions of the same length in the study on the older version of the Prime Climb agent [8] were sufficient to show learning effects. Each student played with an experimenter as her partner, to avoid confounding factors due to playing with partners with different knowledge and playing behaviors. Experimenters made sure that students obtained help only from the pedagogical agent. After game play, all students wrote a post-test equivalent to the pre-test, and students in the *old-model* and *new-model* conditions filled out a questionnaire on their impressions of the agent.

5   Results

5.1   Impact on Learning

We measure learning gains as the difference between post-test score and pre-test score. The study hypotheses are the following:

H1: *Students in the new-model condition will learn significantly more than students in the old-model condition.*

H2: *Students in conditions with the agent will learn more than students in the no-agent condition.*

Table 2 shows the results by condition. An ANOVA using learning as the dependent variable, condition as main factor, and pre-test scores as covariate (to control for student incoming knowledge) shows no significant differences between the three conditions.

Table 2. Pre-test, post-test and learning gain results by condition (maximum test score is 30)

	Average score (st. dev)		
	No-Agent	**Old-Model**	**New-model**
Pre-test	20.62 (2.83)	25.53 (1.81)	25.77 (1.72)
Post-test	19.39 (3.41)	25.40 (1.88)	25.35 (1.84)
Learning	-1.23 (1.33)	-0.13 (0.42)	-0.41 (0.64)

Thus, we have not been able to prove either of our two hypotheses. The fact that we did not manage to reproduce the results in [8], i.e., to show that having a pedagogical agent is better than not having one (H2 above), is especially surprising, given that, compared to the agent in [8], the new agent used in the study had a more accurate model and an improved set of hints, carefully designed by an experienced teacher. Students in the current study did have a higher level of knowledge than students in [8], scoring an average of 83% on the pre-test compared to 60% in [8], so it was indeed harder to see an effect of pedagogical interventions with this student population. But there were still several occasions in which agent interventions could have triggered learning (as we will discuss in the next sub-section). We investigate two possible reasons for the null effect of the improvements we made to both the agent and its model: (1) in this study, the new model was not more accurate than the old model; (2) elements of the new hinting strategy obstructed learning.

5.1 Comparison of Models' Accuracy

The accuracy of the old and new model reported in previous sections referred to model assessment of student factorization skills at the end of the interaction, compared with student post-test performance [9]. A measure that is more informative for understanding model impact on learning (or lack thereof) is accuracy during game playing, influenced by how quickly the model stabilizes its assessment of student knowledge. We can't determine this accuracy on all the target factorization skills, because we do not have a ground-truth assessment of how the related knowledge evolves during game playing. We can, however, restrict the analysis to skills for which the student's answer did not change from pre-test to post-test, i.e., the related knowledge was constant throughout the interaction. Since there was little learning in the study (see Table 2), this selection covers a substantial fraction of our data points.

Table 3. Confusion matrices (# of raw data points) for the accuracy of the old model (left) and new model (right)

	Old Model			New Model		
	Test assessment			Test assessment		
Model Assessment	Known	Unknown	Total	Known	Unknown	Total
Known	369	84	453	354	27	381
Unknown	19	4	23	54	76	130
Total	388	88	476	408	103	511

Table 4. Confusion matrices (percentages) for the accuracy of the old model (left) and new model (right)

	Old Model			New Model		
	Test assessment			Test assessment		
Model Assessment	Known	Un-known	Total	Known	Un-known	Total
Known	77.5%	17.6%	95.1%	69.3%	5.3%	74.6%
Unknown	4%	0.9%	4.9%	10.5%	14.9%	25.4%
Total	81.5%	18.5%	100%	79.8%	20.2%	100%

The logs files from the old-model and new-model conditions included, for each student action, the model's assessment of the student factorization knowledge after that action. We searched these log files for all episodes in which a student encountered a number with the same pre-test and post-test results (*known* vs. *unknown*), and compared these results with the model's assessment for that number at that point (also expressed in terms of *known* vs. *unknown*). Table 3 and Table 4 show the confusion matrices (with raw data and percentages, respectively) for the two models across students and all relevant episodes. We calculate from these matrices two standard measures of accuracy: recall (fraction of all *unknown* data points that the model classifies as such) and precision (fraction of all data points that the model classifies as *unknown* and that are actually unknown). Recall and precision are important from the pedagogical point of view, because they define, respectively, how good the model is at detecting situations in which the student's knowledge is low, and how good the model is at generating interventions that are justified.

The old model has very poor performance in both recall (4.5%), and precision (17.4%). With 73.7% recall and 58.5% precision, the new model clearly outperforms the old model. We conclude that we can reject lack of difference in model accuracy as a reason for the null result with respect to H1 (more learning in the new-model condition than in the old-model condition). We now explore the second reason, i.e., that elements of the agent's hinting behavior obstructed learning.

5.2   Effects of the Agent's Hinting Behavior

One factor that may disrupt learning is how often the agent intervenes, influenced by the student model. The last row of each confusion matrix in Table 4 shows that the breakdown of *known* and *unknown* data points is approximately 80%:20% for both conditions, indicating that the underlying student knowledge is the same in both groups (confirmed by a lack of significant differences in their pre-test scores). However, the last column in Table 4 shows that the old model judges factorization skills to be unknown 4.9% of the time, compared to 25.4% for the new model. Thus, the new model causes the agent to intervene much more often. In fact, there is a significant difference ($p < 0.001$, as per a two-tail t-test) between the average number of hints each student received in the old-model condition (mean 7.6, st. dev. 3.6) and in the new-model condition (mean 16.3, st. dev. 5.5). This difference is mostly due to the model's assessment, given that students in both agent conditions rarely asked for hints (The requested hints were only 3.4% of all given hints. [8] reports similar results with respect to student hints requests).

The fact that students in the old-model condition received very few justified hints explains why they did not learn from the interaction with Prime Climb. It should be noted that while the study in [8] used the same model as the old-model condition, in that study students likely learned because they had less factorization knowledge to start with, thus there were more occasions to generate learning, even for a model with limited recall/precision. As for the more frequent hints generated by the new model, although more of these are justified (58.4%) than the old model's hints (14.4%), students may not like to have their game playing interrupted by didactic interventions, especially when about 40% of these interruptions are not justified. This may have caused students to stop paying attention to the hints. To verify this conjecture, we looked at whether students in the new-model condition are taking the time to read the hints and accompanying examples.

Our log files do not contain the action of closing a hint, so we can't use the time between the appearance of a hint and its closure as an estimate for reading time. We use instead the difference between the average time taken to make a move after getting a hint (12.82 sec., st. dev. 4.22), and the average time taken to make a move when there is no hint (9.14 sec., st. dev. 3.02). We obtain 3.42 seconds (st. dev. 2.62) as an estimate of the average amount of time each student spent reading a hint. The average adult reader can read 3.4 words per second [11]. With hints that were 22.5 words on average, an adult would take 6.62 seconds on average to read the hints.

Thus, it is conceivable that students were not taking time to read the hints thoroughly and think about their meaning. This conclusion is supported by the fact that there are no significant correlations between the estimated time spent reading hints, or the number of hints received, and learning. As further evidence of lack of attention to hints, we compare the times between receiving a hint and performing an action for the *Focus* and *Definition* hints, the first time they are presented (see Table 5). The second row reports the number of hint words, not including the words in the accompanying examples.

Table 5. Average (and st.dev.) time (in seconds) between receiving a hint for the first time and acting

Hint Type	Focus	Definition 1	Definition 2
Words	19	26	27
Avg. time (st.dev.)	12.03 (4.53)	13.57 (4.41)	13.00 (3.75)

As expected, students spend more time between receiving a hint and performing an action with hints that involve examples (*Definition 1* and *Definition 2*) than with the *focus* hint. However, the additional time spent does not account for their higher number of words in *Definition* hints. For instance, *Definition 1* hint is 7 words longer than the focus hints, thus we would expect an average (adult) reader to spend approximately 2 seconds longer to read it, plus time to examine the example. Table 5 shows that students are not taking the time, and thus are probably not reading the hints thoroughly. If students are not finding the hints generated by the agent in the new-model condition useful, this should affect their perception of the agent. To see if this is the case, we look at the students' post-questionnaire answers.

5.3 Student's Perception of the Prime Climb Agent

The post-questionnaires on agent perception included six questions rated on a Likert scale from 1 (*strongly disagree*) to 5 (*strongly agree*). The average score (and standard deviation) for each question in the two agent conditions are shown in Table 6. We see that all the questions are in favor of the old-model condition, although the only difference that is statistically significantly is Q1: the agent in the old-model condition is rated as more helpful than the other agent ($p = 0.017$). This result is consistent with the picture that emerged from the previous sections: more students in the new-model condition received a hint, but they tended not read it, so the hint was not helpful to them. It is not surprising that more of these students rated the agent as "unhelpful", and that it received a quite high score for "intervening too often". Interestingly, the agent in the old-model condition also scored quite poorly on this item, despite the fact that it intervenes much less than the other agent. This may be due to a general student dislike of any interruption of their game playing.

Table 6. Average responses (and st. dev.) in the post-questionnaire

Question	Old-model	New-model
Q1: the agent is helpful	3.60 (0.22)	2.56 (0.34)
Q2: the agent understands my needs	3.00 (1.05)	2.67 (1.41)
Q3: the agent helps me play better	2.80 (0.92)	2.44 (1.13)
Q4: the agent helped me learn factorization	3.20 (0.92)	2.56 (1.13)
Q5: the agent intervenes too often	3.20 (1.48)	3.89 (1.05)
Q6: I liked the agent	3.60 (1.07)	3.11 (1.36)

6   Discussion, Conclusions and Future Work

We have presented a study to evaluate the impact of adaptive feedback on the effectiveness of a pedagogical agent for an educational computer game. We compared a version of the game with no agent, and two versions with agents that differ only in the accuracy of the student model used to guide their interventions. We found no difference on student learning across the three conditions, so we combined an analysis of model accuracy during game playing with an analysis of log data on student relevant behaviors to understand the reasons for these results. We eliminated lack of difference in model accuracy as a possible cause for the null results, because the student model that was known to be more accurate in assessing student knowledge at the end of the interaction (new model) was also more accurate in assessing student knowledge during game playing. This model generated significantly more justified hints than the other model (old model). However, over 40% of the hints it generated addressed skills that students already had. This is likely one of the reasons why students seem to not pay attention to the hints, and thus failed to learn from the game.

Ironically, the old, less accurate model with simpler hints used by the first version of the Prime Climb agent (described in section 3), did generate more learning than the game with no agent [8]. This result is likely due to the combination of two factors. The study participants had low factorization knowledge, and thus there were more occasions for the few justified system interventions to have an effect than in the study presented here, where students scored 83% in the pre-test, on average. Because the system did not interrupt game playing often and because the hinting sequence was shorter and simpler, students did not perceive it as intrusive, paid more attention to the hints and sometime they learned.

An obvious direction to improve the effectiveness of the adaptive hints' is to improve model precision, so that more of the agent's interventions are justified. However, students may resent being interrupted often during game play even when most interruptions are justified. Our results suggest a simple solution: some learning can be achieved with an inaccurate model, by favoring unobtrusiveness over intervening when it seems necessary. In Prime Climb, we could achieve this by lowering the probability threshold that dictates when a skill is considered known in the student model. A more interesting, although more challenging solution is to endow the model with the ability to reason about the expected effects of its interventions on both student learning and affect, to achieve a trade-off between maintaining engagement and promoting maximum learning. A decision-theoretic approach that combines a model of student learning with a model of student affect is one way around this issue [2]. We plan to explore both solutions, to determine their relative impact on game effectiveness. For the latter, we plan to combine the model of student learning described here with the model of affect we have been developing in parallel [21,22]. Another direction of investigation relates to the *form* of the agent's hints, i.e. how to devise pedagogical hints that can be perceived as less didactic and intrusive [e.g., 23, 24] and can thus be more acceptable for students during game playing.

References

[1] Van Eck, R.: Building Artificially Intelligent Learning Games. Games and Simulations in Online Learning: Research and Development Frameworks. In: Gibson, D., Aldrich, C., Prensky, M. (eds.) Information Science Pub., pp. 271–307 (2007)

[2] Conati, C., Klawe, M.: Socially Intelligent Agents in Educational Games. In: Dautenhahn, K., et al. (eds.) Socially Intelligent Agents - Creating Relationships with Computers and Robots. Kluwer Academic Publishers, Dordrecht (2002)

[3] Christoph, N., Sandberg, J., Wielinga, B.: Added value of task models and metacognitive skills on learning. In: AIED 2005 Workshop on Educational Games as Intelligent Learning Environments (2005)

[4] Johnson, W.L.: Serious use for a serious game on language learning. In: Proc. of the 13th Int. Conf. on Artificial Intelligence in Education, Los Angeles, USA (2007)

[5] Johnson, W.L., Beal, C.: Iterative Evaluation of a Large-scale, Intelligent Game for language Learning. In: AIED 2005: Proceedings of the 12th International conference on Artificial Intelligence in Education. The Netherlands, Amsterdam (2005)

[6] Peirce, N., Conlan, O., Wade, V.: Adaptive Educational Games: Providing Non-invasive Personalised Learning Experiences. In: Second IEEE International Conference on Digital Games and Intelligent Toys Based Education (DIGITEL 2008), Banff, Canada (2008)

[7] McQuiggan, S.W., Rowe, J.P., Lee, S.Y., Lester, J.C.: Story-based learning: The impact of narrative on learning experiences and outcomes. In: Woolf, B.P., Aïmeur, E., Nkambou, R., Lajoie, S. (eds.) ITS 2008. LNCS, vol. 5091, pp. 530–539. Springer, Heidelberg (2008)

[8] Conati, C., Xhao, X.: Building and Evaluating an Intelligent Pedagogical Agent to Improve the Effectiveness of an Educational Game. In: Proceedings of IUI 2004, International Conference on Intelligent User Interfaces, Island of Madeira, Portugal (2004)

[9] Manske, M., Conati, C.: Modelling Learning in Educational Games in AIED 2005. In: Proceedings of the 12th International Conference on AI in Education. The Netherlands, Amsterdam (2005)

[10] Kirschner, P., Sweller, J., Clark, R.: Why minimal guidance during instruction does not work: an analysis of the failure of constructivist, discovery, problem-based, experimental and inquiry-based teaching. Educational Pshychologist 41(2), 75–86 (2006)

[11] Just, M., Carpenter, P.: The Psychology of Reading and Language Comprehension, A. Bacon, Boston (1986)

[12] Wool, B.: Building intelligent interactive tutors. Morgan Kauffman, San Francisco (2008)

[13] Baker, R.S.J.d., Habgood, M.P.J., Ainsworth, S.E., Corbett, A.T.: Modeling the acquisition of fluent skill in educational action games. In: Conati, C., McCoy, K., Paliouras, G. (eds.) UM 2007. LNCS (LNAI), vol. 4511, pp. 17–26. Springer, Heidelberg (2007)

[14] Rodrigo, M.M.T., Baker, R.S.J., d'Mello, S., Gonzalez, M.C.T., Lagud, M.C.V., Lim, S.A.L., Macapanpan, A.F., Pascua, S.A.M.S., Santillano, J.Q., Sugay, J.O., Tep, S., Viehland, N.J.B.: Comparing Learners' Affect While Using an Intelligent Tutoring Systems and a Simulation Problem Solving Game. In: Proceedings of the 9th International Conference on Intelligent Tutoring Systems, pp. 40–49 (2008)

[15] Randel, J.M., Morris, B.A., Wetzel, C.D., Whitehill, B.V.: The effectiveness of games for educational purposes: A review of recent research. Simulation & Gaming 23(3), 261–276 (1992)

[16] Klawe, M.: When Does The Use Of Computer Games And Other Interactive Multimedia Software Help Students Learn Mathematics? In: NCTM Standards 2000 Technology Conference, Arlington, VA (1998)

[17] Alessi, S.M., Trollip, S.R.: Multimedia for Learning: Methods and Development, 3rd edn. Allyn & Bacon, Needham Heights (2001)

[18] Lee, J., Luchini, K., Michael, B., Norris, C., Solloway, E.: More than just fun and games: Assessing the value of educational video games in the classroom. In: Proceedings of ACM SIGCHI 2004, Vienna, Austria, pp. 1375–1378 (2004)

[19] Vogel, J.J., Greenwood-Ericksen, A., Cannon-Bowers, J., Bowers, C.: Using virtual reality with and without gaming attributes for academic achievement. Journal of Research on Technology in Education 39(1), 105–118 (2006)

[20] Conati, C., Fain Lehman, J.: Toward a Model of Student Education in Microworlds. In: 15th Annual Conference of the Cognitive Science Society. Erlbaum, Hillsdale (1993)

[21] Conati, C., Maclaren, H.: Empirically Building and Evaluating a Probabilistic Model of User Affect. In: User-Modeling and User-Adapted Interaction (2009) (in press)

[22] Conati, C., Maclaren, H.: Modeling User Affect from Causes and Effects. To appear in Proceedings of UMAP 2009, First and Seventeenth International Conference on User Modeling, Adaptation and Personalization. Springer, Heidelberg (2009)

[23] Arroyo, I., Ferguson, K., Johns, J., Dragon, T., et al.: Repairing Disengagement With Non-Invasive Interventions. In: AIED 2007, pp. 195–202 (2007)

[24] Baker, R.S.J.d., Corbett, A.T., et al.: Adapting to When Students Game an Intelligent Tutoring System. Intelligent Tutoring Systems 2006, 392–401 (2006)

Media Equation Revisited: Do Users Show Polite Reactions towards an Embodied Agent?

Laura Hoffmann[1], Nicole C. Krämer[1], Anh Lam-chi[1], and Stefan Kopp[2]

[1] University Duisburg-Essen, Forsthausweg 2, 47057 Duisburg, Germany
[2] University of Bielefeld, Sociable Agent Group, 33549 Bielefeld, Germany
laura.hoffmann@uni-due.de, nicole.kraemer@uni-due.de,
anh.lam-chi@uni-due.de, skopp@techfak.uni-bielefeld.de

Abstract. In human-computer interaction social behavior towards computers like flattery, reciprocity, and politeness have been observed [1]. In order to determine whether the results can be replicated when interacting with embodied conversational agents (ECA), we conducted an experimental study. 63 participants evaluated the ECA Max after a 10-minute conversation. The interview situation was manipulated in three conditions: Being questioned by Max himself, being questioned by paper-and-pencil questionnaire in the same room facing Max, and being questioned by means of a paper-and-pencil questionnaire in another room. Results show that participants were more polite to the ECA in terms of a better evaluation when they were questioned by Max himself compared to when they were questioned more indirectly by paper-and-pencil questionnaire in the same room. In contrast to previous studies [2] it was ruled out that some participants thought of the programmer when they were asked to evaluate the ECA. Additionally, user variables (e.g. gender, computer literacy) show an impact on the on the evaluation of the ECA.

Keywords: evaluation study, social effects, politeness, media equation.

1 Introduction

As by now is widely known the Computer as Social Actors research group (CASA-group) [3] demonstrated that social effects that occur in interpersonal interaction (e.g. praise and criticism, reciprocity, stereotypes, flattery or politeness) can also be observed in human-computer interaction. The phenomenon has been termed media equation: "media equals real life" [1]. Empirical studies in the CASA-paradigm demonstrated that people responded socially to computers by evaluating a computer better if it was praised by another computer than by itself [4], by helping a computer which has helped them before rather than a computer that has not helped them before [3], and by assuming that a computer with a female voice knows more about love and relationships than a computer with a male voice [3].

More recent technological developments like embodied conversational agents (ECAs) have the aim to make conversations more intuitive and natural for the users. In order to achieve this goal ECAs not only look human-like but also use human-like

Zs. Ruttkay et al. (Eds.): IVA 2009, LNAI 5773, pp. 159–165, 2009.
© Springer-Verlag Berlin Heidelberg 2009

communication means such as voice and nonverbal behavior. Thus, the question arises whether this increase in social cues leads to the same or even more pronounced social reactions on the part of the user. The study reported here focuses on one of the aspects analyzed by the CASA-group, politeness behavior towards technology. Reeves and Nass transferred a common politeness-rule from interpersonal interaction to HCI, namely: "When a computer asks a user about itself, the user will give more positive responses than when a different computer asks the same questions." [1, p. 21]. In their study, politeness behavior was measured by an evaluation-score user gave a tutor-computer when they were asked a) by the tutor-computer itself b) a different computer, or c) a paper-and-pencil questionnaire. The results showed that people made higher evaluations in a) than in b) and c). Hence they concluded that people behaved polite towards the tutor-computer in order not to offend it [5].

Although empirical testing of the CASA-paradigms in human-agent-interaction is still at its beginning, several studies already suggest that people react socially when confronted with embodied agents. Examples for studies and corresponding results are given in the next paragraph.

Social effects in human-agent interaction. Numerous studies yield social effects, demonstrating that humans' reactions towards virtual agents are remarkably similar to those towards human interlocutors [3, 6]. It has been shown that virtual humans elicit attention just as real humans do [8], person perception was shown to be like that of real humans [8], tasks are facilitated or inhibited by the "social" presence of a virtual agent [8], and socially desirable behavior is triggered [9]. Additionally, it was shown that users employ conversational politeness strategies such as small talk and etiquette towards embodied agents [10]. This result already suggests that embodied agents influence the politeness behavior of humans. However, this has not been tested in more detail or been extended to politeness evaluation instead of politeness behavior.

In general, it can be concluded that social responses exist when a human user is confronted with an embodied agent. Several explanations for these responses have been suggested: Most prominently, the "ethopoeia" approach [3] has been suggested. Nass, Moon, Morkes, Kim, and Fogg [11] propose that users automatically and unconsciously apply social rules to their interactions with computers - due to the fact that humans are inherently social and that computers display social cues. Additionally, Nass and Sundar [2] falsified the notion that human participants address the social behavior towards the programmer instead of the computer.

Research questions and hypotheses. If social cues are prerequisites for social effects, the amount of social cues an ECA summarizes (e.g. an anthropomorphic body, and the ability to interact with humans) should lead to distinct social effects. We hypothesize that participants will be more polite towards an ECA (in the sense of evaluating the interaction more positively) when asked directly by the ECA, than when asked indirectly by a paper-and-pencil questionnaire.

Based on the ethopoeia approach [3] we also expected that people who respond socially towards an ECA deny to do so and deny that they addressed the programmer when asked for evaluation of the ECA. Additionally, we asked how user variables (gender and computer literacy) influence the social effects towards an ECA.

2 Method

Stimulus material: ECA Max. In this study, the participants were confronted with the embodied conversational agent Max (see figure 1) who was developed by the Artificial Intelligence Group of Bielefeld University (Germany). Max is displayed in human-like size on a screen, and his synthetic voice is presented via loud speakers.

Fig. 1. Agent Max

In previous scenarios users had to communicate with Max by using a keyboard. In this study we used a so-called "Wizard of Oz" scenario (e.g., [12]), so that participants could orally address Max. The hidden human wizard acted as "speech recognizer" and made the participants' natural language utterances accessible for Max by concurrently typing in everything the participants said.

Independent variables: interview situation. In order to determine whether participants will give more polite, i.e. positive answers when asked by the agent directly, there were three versions of the interview situation: a) participants were asked by Max himself to evaluate him (N=20), b) participants were asked to evaluate Max on a paper-and-pencil questionnaire while they were still in the same room with him (N=22) and c) participants were asked to evaluate Max on a paper-and-pencil questionnaire in a separate room (N=21) [5]. Thus, we used a one-factorial experimental design with three conditions and chose a between-subjects-design to test our hypothesis.

Dependent variables: politeness. Politeness was operationalized by means of the evaluation participants attributed to Max. The evaluation was measured by 16 adjectives which the participants rated on a ten-point Likert-scale. We chose the same 12 adjectives Nass et al. [5] utilized in their politeness-study (e.g. "polite", "friendly" - translated into German to ensure that participants understand their meaning) and amended 4 items: "Self-confident", "dominant" and "active", derived from the semantic differential established by Osgood, Suci, and Tannenbaum [13]. and "anthropomorphic", to find out how natural participants experienced Max. Additionally, the participants' attitude towards the sociability of technology was assessed on a five-point Likert-scale with ad-hoc items such as "I treated Max like a human being." and "I thought of the programmer when I was asked for evaluation". The data was collected with the intention to determine whether the participants were aware of their attitudes respectively their behavior and to achieve further insights on the reasons for social behavior towards embodied agents.

Procedure. After a short briefing, all participants had to fill in a questionnaire assessing their experiences with computers and virtual entities. When they had finished, the experimenter led them into the laboratory where Max was displayed on a life-sized screen. Participants were instructed to start their conversation with "hello" and continue with small-talk or the animal game. In the animal game Max asked participants to think of an animal which he then tried to guess by asking closed questions (participants could only answer with "yes" or "no").

Participants were randomly assigned to one of the three experimental conditions: In condition a), Max asked questions about its own performance (e.g. "How competent did you think I was?") and the participants spoke their rating out loud (e.g said "eight"). The wizard in the other room heard the ratings of the participants via headphones and noted them on a copy of the questionnaire. Max showed idle behavior until the wizard initialized the next question. In condition b) the experimenter asked the participants to end the conversation and fill out the questionnaire with Max still visible on the screen displaying idle behavior. In condition c) the experimenter led the participants out of the laboratory before they were handed the second questionnaire.

Participants. 63 persons aged from 19 to 38 years (mean value= 23.60 years; sd = 4.22 years), recruited at the University of Bielefeld, participated in the study. The sample consisted of 32 female and 31 male persons. All of them received 5 Euros for participating, and signed informed consent forms.

3 Results

Dependent variable: Evaluation of Max. In sum, the evaluation of Max by the participants was rather positive. As a prerequisite for analyses of variance, the items of Max`s evaluation were reduced by factor analysis.

Four factors could be extracted which explained 67.62% of the total variance. We labeled each factor according to the meaning of the constituting items: Competence, Friendliness, Naturalness and Activity and Dominance (see table 1).

A one-factorial ANOVA with the interview situation as fixed factor and the extracted factors from the adjectives of Max`s evaluation as dependent variables showed no significant differences between the three conditions. But a post hoc test yielded a significant difference between condition a (participants are asked by Max directly) and b (participants fill in a questionnaire in Max`s presence). Therefore we compared only these two conditions by means of a t-test.

The t-test reflected that participants gave significantly better evaluations with regard to Max`s competence when they were asked by Max directly (condition a, mean value= 0.25; sd= 0.75) than when they were indirectly asked by paper-and-pencil questionnaire in the same room (condition b, mean value= -0.36; sd= 1.05, $t(40)$= 2.15; p= .038). There were no significant differences for the other factors.

Effects of programmer thought. The average agreement with the statement "I thought of the programmer when I was asked for the evaluation of Max" indicated that on average participants rather rejected the notion (mean value = 2.48; sd = 1.49). After the dichotomization of the parameter values by a median split, 37 participants with a "programmer-thought", and 26 "without a programmer-thought" resulted.

Table 1. Factor analysis for the evaluation of Max (main component analysis with varimax rotation)

	Factor			
Item	Competence	Friendliness	Naturalness	Activity and Dominance
Helpful	.80			
Useful	.76			
Competent	.73			
Knowledgeable	.73			
Analytical	.72			
Informative	.71			
Friendly		.88		
Enjoyable		.77		
Likable		.75		
Polite		.74		
Fun		.64		
Anthropomorphic			.82	
Warm		.58	.60	
Self-Confident			.59	
Dominant				.82
Active				.95
Total variance (%)	23.47	21.57	12.83	9.74
Cronbachs α	.87	.86	.65	.56

Table 2. Interaction between the independent variable interview situation and the moderating variable programmer-thought

	Mean values			Standard deviations		
	S_1	S_2	S_3	S_1	S_2	S_3
Factor: Competence						
With programmer-thought	0.46	-0.53	0.93	0.72	1.01	0.77
Without programmer-thought	0.11	-0.24	-0.45	0.76	1.10	0.92

S_1: interview situation: questioning by Max; S_2: interview situation: questioning by paper-and-pencil questionnaire in the same room; S_3: interview situation: questioning by paper-and-pencil questionnaire in another room

When using "programmer-thought" as an additional independent variable, besides several main effects, a significant ($F_{(2; 62)} = 4.51$; $p = .015$; $\eta^2 = .130$) interaction between the interview situation and the programmer-thought was observable for the factor competence (see table 2). If participants did not think of the programmer the evaluation of Max was best in the questioning by Max condition (a), worse in the questioning by paper-and-pencil questionnaire in the same room condition (b), and worst in the questioning by paper-and-pencil questionnaire in another room condition (c). Else if participants thought of a programmer instead of Max the factor competence received the highest evaluation-score in the questioning by paper-and-pencil questionnaire in another room condition. The evaluation in the "questioning by Max" condition was lower than the latter, but higher than in the questioning by paper-and-pencil questionnaire in the same room condition. For the other factors, no significant interactions emerged.

4 Discussion

The aim of the present study was to empirically verify whether social effects as described in the CASA-studies can be replicated within human-agent-interaction. Therefore we created three interview situations to determine if people respond in a polite way to the ECA Max. Politeness was measured by the ratings participants made for adjectives which described Max.

Main effects of the interview situation were indeed found between condition a) and b): The comparison showed that participants who were questioned by Max were more polite in the sense that they rated Max as more competent than participants who were questioned by paper-and-pencil questionnaire in the same room. Similarly as in the corresponding study in human-computer-interaction [5] we were thus able to demonstrate that participants tended to refrain from giving negative evaluations when they addressed Max explicitly and directly during the rating process. There was, however, no significant difference to the third condition in which participants were instructed to fill in the questionnaire in another room. Nevertheless, this condition did also not differ from the second condition (filling in the questionnaire while Max was present in the room) either and can thus not be assumed to be even more indirect.

In sum, we gained evidence for the notion that participants reacted in a way that would also have been socially appropriate in human-human interaction. It is still important to consider potential alternative explanations for the behavior: An explanation might be that only participants who were questioned by Max got an impression of his ability to interview someone else. Therefore it is possible that participants in condition a found him more competent as only they had the chance to observe this ability. This seems unlikely, though, as this ability is less sophisticated as the small-talk and animal guessing abilities that Max demonstrated earlier.

In order to gain insights on the causes for social behavior towards agents we also considered whether participants thought of the programmer when evaluating the agent. Unlike in the CASA-studies, here, several participants agreed that they thought of the programmer. We thus tested whether participants who agreed to having thought of the programmer differed from those who disagreed. And certainly, the results of the two-factorial analysis of variance show an interaction between the condition and the fact of whether the participants thought of the programmer: If the participants did not think of the programmer they rated condition a best, followed by b and c. This finding was consistent with the findings reported previously and supports the hypothesis that people were polite to an ECA who asks for its own evaluation. However, for those participants who reported to think of the programmer, the ratings were most positive in condition c when filling in the questionnaire alone. This is plausible as those participants were no longer confronted with Max and other aspects – such as the abilities of the programmer - might have become more salient.

In general, further aspects might limit the study and its comparability to the early CASA-studies: For instance, the variation of the interview situation can be criticized. A condition in which the participants were questioned by another ECA was missing.

Therefore a direct comparison like same computer versus different computer [5] was not possible. Further research should take this into account.

In conclusion we state that the manipulation of the interview situation indeed led to different evaluation of Max. This can be interpreted as a hint for social effects in human-agent interaction. With regard to the application of these results we would thus suggest to not use the agent itself to ask for evaluations. If an ECA should be evaluated objectively the evaluation should not be conducted by the ECA itself because interviewer-effects could occur which are known from interpersonal interaction. In this sense agents thus have to be treated as "social actors" who are capable of influencing other social actors - namely the human who reacts in a social way.

References

1. Reeves, B., Nass, C.: The Media Equation: How People Treat Computers, Television, and New Media Like Real People and Places. Cambridge University Press, New York (1996)
2. Nass, C., Sundar, S.: Are Programmers Psychologically Relevant to Human-Computer Interaction? Paper presented at the annual meeting of the International Communication Association, San Francisco, CA (1994)
3. Nass, C., Moon, Y.: Machines and Mindlessness: Social Responses to Computers. Journal of Social Issues 56(1), 81–103 (2000)
4. Nass, C., Steuer, J.: Voices, Boxes and Sources of Messages: Computers and Social Actors. Human Communication Research 19(4), 504–527 (1993)
5. Nass, C., Moon, Y., Carney, P.: Are People Polite to Computers? Responses to Computer-Based Interviewing Systems. Journal of Applied Social Psychology 29(5), 1093–1110 (1999)
6. Krämer, N.C.: Social effects of virtual assistants. A review of empirical results with regard to communication. In: Prendinger, H., Lester, J.C., Ishizuka, M. (eds.) IVA 2008. LNCS (LNAI), vol. 5208, pp. 507–508. Springer, Heidelberg (2008)
7. Bente, G., Krämer, N.C., Petersen, A., de Ruiter, J.P.: Computer Animated Movement and Person Perception. Methodological Advances in Nonverbal Behavior Research. Journal of Nonverbal Behavior 25(3), 151–166 (2001)
8. Rickenberg, R., Reeves, B.: The Effects of Animated Characters on Anxiety, Task Performance, and Evaluations of User Interfaces. In: Proceedings of the CHI 2000 Conference, pp. 49–56. ACM Press, New York (2000)
9. Krämer, N.C., Bente, G., Piesk, J.: The Ghost in the Machine. The Influence of Embodied Conversational Agents on User Expectations and User Behaviour in a TV/VCR Application. In: Bieber, G., Kirste, T. (eds.) IMC Workshop 2003, Assistance, Mobility, Applications, pp. 121–128. Frauenhofer IRB Verlag, Stuttgart (2003)
10. Kopp, S., Gesellensetter, L., Krämer, N.C., Wachsmuth, I.: A conversational agent as museum guide – design and evaluation of a real-world application. In: Panayiotopoulos, T., Gratch, J., Aylett, R.S., Ballin, D., Olivier, P., Rist, T. (eds.) IVA 2005. LNCS (LNAI), vol. 3661, pp. 329–343. Springer, Heidelberg (2005)
11. Nass, C., Moon, Y., Morkes, J., Kim, E.-Y., Fogg, B.J.: Computers Are Social Actors: A Review of Current Research. In: Friedman, B. (ed.) Moral and Ethical Issues in Human-Computer Interaction, pp. 137–162. CSLI Press, Stanford (1997)
12. Dahlbäck, N., Jönsson, A., Ahrenberg, L.: Wizard of Oz Studies – Why and How. In: Proceedings of the ACM International Workshop on Intelligent User Interfaces, pp. 193–200. ACM Press, New York (1993)
13. Osgood, C.E., Suci, G.J., Tannenbaum, P.H.: The Measurement of Meaning. University of Illinois Press, Urbana (1965)

The Lessons Learned in Developing Multi-user Attentive Quiz Agents

Hung-Hsuan Huang[1], Takuya Furukawa[1], Hiroki Ohashi[1],
Aleksandra Cerekovic[2], Yuji Yamaoka[3], Igor S. Pandzic[2],
Yukiko Nakano[4], and Toyoaki Nishida[1]

[1] Graduate School of Informatics, Kyoto University, Japan
[2] Faculty of Electrical Engineering and Computing, University of Zagreb, Croatia
[3] Department of Computer, Information and Communication Sciences,
Tokyo University of Agriculture and Technology
[4] Department of Computer and Information Science, Seikei University, Japan
`huang@ii.ist.i.kyoto-u.ac.jp`

Abstract. This paper presents two attempts in integrating attentive-ness into a virtual quiz agent in the situation when multiple game partic-ipants present. One of them features an utterance strategy to determine when and whom to talk to among the participants. The other one fea-tures a SVM (support vector machine) triggered transition state model of the agent's attitude toward the participants in expressing observable behaviors. Both of them are driven by timings determined on video and audio information of the participants' activity while they are trying to solve the quizzes. To evaluate these two prototype systems, we applied GNAT (Go/No-go Task) method in addition to questionnaires. From the joint results of the subject experiments, the direction in finding appro-priate action timings of the agent is proved to be able to improve user impressions.

1 Introduction

Making virtual agents to go public in exhibitions or museums is an emerging challenge in recent years. Handling the situation when there are multiple users is a requirement because visitors usually come in groups. Traum [1] provided a principal literature on general issues to realize multi-party human-agent inter-actions, In multi-user configurations, the conversation situation is more unpre-dictable and thus more difficult to be realized. Gamble [2] is a dice game where an agent interacts with two human players. Rehm and Andre [3] found the hu-man players' mixed behaviors interacting with the agent or the other player in the game. The human players showed similar reactions to the agent as what they do to the other player but also some behaviors what are considered as impolite or rude. The round based game rules fixed the system's scenario and resulted in basically three dyadic interactions. Max [4] is a guide agent installed in a computer museum. A keyboard is used for the interface of him and the museum visitors, but this limits him only be able to interact with the visitors one by

Zs. Ruttkay et al. (Eds.): IVA 2009, LNAI 5773, pp. 166–173, 2009.

one. It counts the number of the visitors standing in front of him by using skin color detection techniques what cannot distinguish two visitors if they stand closely.

In our case, we have exhibited a virtual quizmaster agent [5] in four events of the National Food Research Institute (NFRI) of Japan. From the observation on how the game participants interacting with the agent, we have the following findings. (1) Most of the game participants come in groups and answer the quizzes as a collaborative task. (2) The activity of this discussion is dynamic, i.e. sometimes participants discuss enthusiastically or sometimes they consider the answers separately. (3) There is usually one participant who leads the discussion and negotiate the final answer of certain quiz. In order to improve the interaction experience of the participants with the quiz agent and its life-likeness, we are motivated to integrate the agent with the attentiveness toward multiple participants by monitoring their activity. Here, two aspects of attentiveness that are complementary to each other can be considered: *As the effects on the agent's intentional behaviors toward the world external to it.* They include when the agent should utter and who is the addressee of the utterances. *As the effects on the agent's own attitude but expressed as observable behaviors.* They include the postures or other nonverbal behaviors expressed by the agent.

Nevertheless, we do not have very concrete ideas about how the agent should behave to make the participants perceive that the agent is attentive from its behaviors. In order to explore the effects of these two aspects more thoroughly without interfering each other, two variations of improved quiz agent (attentive quiz agent A and B) are then developed with corresponding hypothesized strategies and are evaluated, respectively.

2 Quiz Agent Who Utters Attentively to Multiple Participants (Agent A)

For attentive quiz agent A, we define its attentiveness as: the task of the agent is to proceed the quiz game smoothly. The agents utters for that purpose at the timings when the participants do not feel annoying and are likely to listen to. In order to improve the effectiveness of the agent's utterances which are expected to affect the participants, the addressee of each those utterances is the participant who is most likely to have influences on the other participants. The personality of the quiz agent is neutral, i.e. do not try to help the participants and do not try to confuse the participants, either. We hypothesize that the following heuristics are representative factors in deciding appropriate utterance behaviors for it.

Interaction Activity (AT): It indicates whether the users are active in their discussions. *High* and *low* are the two possible measured status. AT is high when all of the members of the participant group reacted to an utterance done by one of them with successive utterances and intensive face movements. AT is low otherwise.

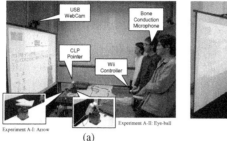

(a)   (b)

Fig. 1. The hardware configuration of (a) attentive quiz agent A (b) attentive quiz agent B

Conversation Leading Person (CLP): It is the participant who is most likely leading the group at certain time point. It is estimated by counting who spoke at most and initiated most AT status of the group.

The intensity of face movements is approximated from the face orientation information measured by a WebCam and Omron's OkaoVision [6] face detection library. Whether the participants are speaking or are in a conversation is detected only with acoustic information. A two-second silent period is used to detect speaking segments from the voice streams of the microphone attached on each participant. The information is combined from all participants to detect whether a conversation is existing if their successive utterances do not break longer than two seconds. The changing AT status is used to further partition the conversation segments, the participant who is the starting point of each AT period is counted to initiate AT status once. CLP is then estimated by tracking how many times each user spoke and how many times he or she initiated an AT status of the participant group. Each participant is ranked according to these two criteria. The participant who spoke most is assigned with three points while who spoke least is assigned with one point. The participant who initiated most AT is assigned three points and who initiated least AT is assigned one point. These two scores are then summed with the same weight, the user who has highest points is judged as the CLP at that time point. AT and CLP estimations are then used to drive the following utterance policy:

- The agent does not say anything when the users' discussion is very active (high AT status)
- The agent always talk to (point to by the pointer) the CLP user
- During the period after issuing the quiz and before the user's answer. If there was an high AT status detected from the users at the beginning, the agent indicates the availability of hint if the AT status becomes low. The agent will urges the users to answer the quiz if low AT status last for long time (50 sec)
- After the users' answer and the explanation of the correct answer by the agent is done. If the AT status is low, the agent will say additional comments to this quiz. If the AT status is high, the agent waits for a while before going

to next quiz. The agent will issues next quiz immediately if the AT status goes to low

As shown in Fig. 1(a), each user is equipped with a Nintendo Wii remote controller so that everyone can answer the quiz directly without the constraints of the distance to the touch panel that may have influences on the computation of CLP. Each one of them is also equipped with a bone conduction microphone to prevent the voice from the other users to be collected. Due to the limitation of the 2D agent, the users can not correctly perceive the gaze direction of the agent except the center one [7]. A physical pointer is introduced for the quiz agent as the pointer showing whom it is talking to.

3   Quiz Agent with Attentive Attitudes toward Multiple Participants (Agent B)

Machine learning methodology is adopted in this agent. SVM classifier is chosen because its stability to achieve high accuracy. To acquire the training data, a woz (wizard-of-oz) experiment with two three-people groups is conducted. Instead of the CG character, one of the authors played as the agent in another room and he is shown on the screen and interact with the participants in real-time. This author then categorized his attitude during the experiment into three situations.

Calm: the participants are paying attention to the quiz game (the screen) and the discussion is active. The agent should not disturb them and should keep watching them for a while.

Anxious: the participants are paying attention to the screen but the discussion of the answer is not active. The agent should stimulate the discussion by providing the hint and so on.

Impatient: a fairly long time past but the participants are still actively discussing so the game got stock and can not get progress. The agent should urge the participants to answer the quiz soon.

Both of Anxious and Impatient states are further divided into *weak* and *strong* and therefore formed a five-state attitude model of the quiz agent. The video corpus collected in the woz experiment is then labeled to the five states by the author. In addition to the state label, the following four criteria are used in the training of SVM [8]. (1) the averaged face orientation of the participants (2) the volume of the voice collected (3) the category of the quiz (4) time past since the agent issued the quiz. By using radial basis function kernel, the accuracy 73.2% is achieved in 10-fold cross verification. In contrary to agent A, a touch panel is used as the input device and only one environment microphone is used in this system (Fig. 1(b)). In order to let the participants feel the agent's attitude more easily, instead of the female character used in exhibited quiz agent prototype and attentive quiz agent A, an abstract character is designed for attentive quiz agent B. Exaggerated nonverbal behavior animations that express the five attitude states are then specially designed for this character.

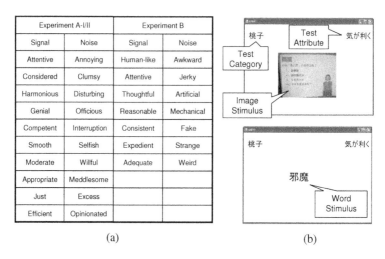

Experiment A-I/II		Experiment B	
Signal	Noise	Signal	Noise
Attentive	Annoying	Human-like	Awkward
Considered	Clumsy	Attentive	Jerky
Harmonious	Disturbing	Thoughtful	Artificial
Genial	Officious	Reasonable	Mechanical
Competent	Interruption	Consistent	Fake
Smooth	Selfish	Expedient	Strange
Moderate	Willful	Adequate	Weird
Appropriate	Meddlesome		
Just	Excess		
Efficient	Opinionated		

(a)   (b)

Fig. 2. (a) Word stimuli for the experiments (b) The screen-shot of the GNAT test program. Image and word stimuli change frequently in the test, and the participants need to judge whether the stimulus coincide to the being tested agent in that period. The error rates are then used to compute the participant's sensitivity.

4   Evaluation Experiments

In the ECA research field, the usual research goal is to achieve human likeness that is an internal feeling and can not be objectively measured by an instrument. ECA researchers usually used questionnaire evaluation up to now. However, questionnaire investigation is considered to be not reliable, not objective and not a scaled measurement. Therefore, in addition to the regular questionnaires, we adopted GNAT [9] to evaluate the subjects' implicit impressions toward agent A and agent B. GNAT is a method indexing an implicit attitude or belief by assessing the strength of association between a target category and two poles of an attribute dimension (Fig. 2).

Considering the functionalities of CNP pointer, to attract the participants' attention and to indicate the addressee of the agent's utterances. Three subject experiments are conducted for evaluating the effects, experiment A-I/II for attentive quiz agent A and experiment B for attentive quiz agent B.

Experiment A-I: Agent A who utters with timing policies is compared with an agent who utters at fixed timing. That is, the compared agent always indicates the availability of hints, urges the participants to answer the quiz and comments the answer at predefined timing without considering the participants' status. The CLP pointer points upward while the agent is in its stand-by status and randomly points to one of the participants while the agent is acting. The relationship between the pointer and the 2D character was not explicitly defined in the instructions to the participants, but the meaning of its movements were explained.

Experiment A-II: The same settings of experiment A except that the CLP pointer looks like a robot head with two eye balls.

Experiment B: Agent B whose internal state transits according to the participants' status with trained SVM classifier is compared to an agent whose internal state transits randomly. The behaviors corresponding to each state are the same on these two agents.

The experiment participants are recruited students in Kyoto University with only one prerequisite that they must enroll as three-people groups. Finally we got 72 participants in 24 groups (57 males, 15 females, 21.5 years old in average). Eight groups are assigned to each experiment randomly. Each group played quiz game with agent A or agent B for one session and their compared system for one session. Questionnaires are answered immediately after each session, and the GNAT test is taken after the two experiment sessions.

4.1   Experiment Results

In experiment A-I and A-II, the result of GNAT test were stable and similar. The difference between agent A and fixed-timing agent was not significant, but agent A is slightly more associated with *attentive* by the participants in both experiments. It also applies in the comparison based on number of persons, 11:8 in experiment A-I and 14:12 in experiment A-II.

In questionnaires, most of the questions did not have significant results. But the results in the questions, "there were silent periods in our conversation (p=.09, p=1.0, two-tailed sign test if not mentioned hereafter)" and "the progress is smooth (p=.12, p=.06)" tend to get relatively lower scores. This is supposed to be caused by the more conservative attitude of agent A because it may utter later or stop saying something depends on the visitors' status.

About the effects of the CLP pointer, the participants thought that the indication were not comprehensive in both systems in experiment A-I (both have low average 2.38, p=.75), but in experiment A-II, the indication of CLP pointer is more comprehensive (p=.08) but felt more uncomfortable (p=.29, p=.05). In both experiments, the participants paid more attentions on agent A's CLP pointer (p=.08, p=.08). The participants also discussed more in experiment A-II (p=1.0, p=.27) and think they discussed more because the behaviors of the agent (p=1.0, p=.50).

To sum up the results from GNAT test and questionnaires in experiment A-I and A-II, it suggests that the estimations of AT and CLP seemed to work fine so that agent A could cause positive impressions on its utterance timing and could drive the CLP pointer to do more meaningful movements that catches the participants' attention. On the contrary, the hypothesis of the utterance policies could be more deliberated because the results were not obvious, and the participants felt that the game was not smooth. Despite the robot head CLP pointer is considerably more effective working as a pointer, it does not contribute to make the participants feel that the agent is more attentive. The indication of a head shape with eyes also seem to be more offensive than an arrow pointer to make the participants feel uncomfortable. This shows that using a physical pointing device with the 2D agent is an effective way to specify the addressee of the agent's attention, but the utterance policy that always treats the person who is leading the conversation as the addressee is not effective. Whom to point and what to say at that time should be more carefully and detailedly designed.

The participants showed significantly higher sensitivity (t test: p <.01) toward agent B associating the attribute, *natural* than that with the random agent (on number of person based comparison, it was 11:3). Despite the considerably clear difference in the GNAT test, the questionnaire results between agent B and the random agent were not significant. From both of the results from objective GNAT measure and subjective questionnaires suggest a hypothesis that nonverbal behaviors play an essential role in the feeling of human-likeness but they are relatively implicit and do not leave so strong impressions as subjective memories.

Attentive agent A and B have the same quality of graphics, TTS and nonverbal animations as their compared systems, but the only difference is the *timings* to take actions are attentive to the participants' status. Still, in the evaluation experiments, the participants reflected more positive impressions on the attribute "attentive" and "nature", this shows an alternative way to improve the life-likeness of ECAs rather than realistic looking character and animations. Second, attentive agent B mainly distinguishes its compared system from the timing of non-verbal behaviors while agent A differs its compared system with the timings to utter. The considerably better performance of agent B in under-conscious GNAT test may imply that the non-verbal behaviors of ECA contribute to life-likeness than verbal behaviors.

5   Conclusions and Future Works

This paper presented our investigations on the issues involved in the communication with multiple users for ECAs in the context of quiz game. Two approaches are proposed for improving the attentiveness aspect of life-likeness of the quiz agent, a utterance policy and internal attitude adaptive to the users' status. The preliminary evaluation results using GNAT method was quite encouraging. The partial inconsistencies with the results from questionnaires are interesting and we will do more thorough analysis from video and log data collected in the subject experiments. The ideas proposed in this paper will then be improved and integrated to next version of our NFRI quiz agent which is deployable in practical exhibitions. The effects of the CLP pointer and how it should collaborate with the CG character are not clear. We would like to do deeper investigations on the CLP pointer.

References

1. Traum, D.R.: Issues in multiparty dialogues. In: Dignum, F.P.M. (ed.) ACL 2003. LNCS (LNAI), vol. 2922, pp. 201–211. Springer, Heidelberg (2004)
2. Rehm, M., Andre, E., Wissner, M.: Gamble v2.0 - social interactions with multiple users. In: The 4th international joint conference on Autonomous agents and multiagent systems (AAMAS 2005), pp. 145–146 (2005)

3. Rehm, M.: "she is just stupid"-analyzing user-agent interactions in emotional game situations. Interacting with Computers 20(3), 311–325 (2008)
4. Kopp, S., Gesellensetter, L., Krämer, N.C., Wachsmuth, I.: A conversational agent as museum guide – design and evaluation of a real-world application. In: Panayiotopoulos, T., Gratch, J., Aylett, R.S., Ballin, D., Olivier, P., Rist, T. (eds.) IVA 2005. LNCS (LNAI), vol. 3661, pp. 329–343. Springer, Heidelberg (2005)
5. Huang, H.-H., Inoue, T., Cerekovic, A., Pandzic, I.S., Nakano, Y., Nishida, T.: A quiz game console based on a generic embodied conversational agent framework. In: Pelachaud, C., Martin, J.-C., André, E., Chollet, G., Karpouzis, K., Pelé, D. (eds.) IVA 2007. LNCS (LNAI), vol. 4722, pp. 383–384. Springer, Heidelberg (2007)
6. Omron Corp.: OKAO Vision (2008)
7. Morikawa, O., Maesako, T.: Hypermirror: Toward pleasant-to-use video mediated communication system. In: Proceedings of the 1998 ACM conference on Computer supported cooperative work (CSCW1998), pp. 149–158. ACM Press, New York (1998)
8. Chang, C.C., Lin, C.J.: LIBSVM – a library for support vector machines (2008)
9. Nosek, B.A., Banaji, M.R.: The go/no-go association task. Social Cognition 19(6), 625–664 (2001)

On-Site Evaluation of the Interactive COHIBIT Museum Exhibit

Patrick Gebhard[1] and Susanne Karsten[2]

[1] DFKI, Saarbrücken and Berlin, Germany
patrick.gebhard@dfki.de
[2] TU Illmenau, Illmenau, Germany
susanne.karsten@tu-illmenau.de

Abstract. This paper presents the results of a field study of the CO-HIBIT museum exhibit. Its purpose is to convey knowledge about car-technology and virtual characters in an entertaining way. Two life-sized virtual characters interact with the visitors and support them in constructing car models with specific tangible car modules. The evaluation should reveal what makes the exhibit successful in terms of an overall user impression and how users rate the employed virtual characters. The focus of the evaluation is to measure the user experience that manifests in aspects like attraction, rejection and entertainment. Based on an analysis of relevant systems and evaluation models, an on-site evaluation for the COHIBIT exhibit has been designed. The results show that the positive user experience of the exhibit is mainly based on the non-task-specific aspects like virtual characters, joy of use and entertainment.

1 Introduction

Virtual characters (VCs) have been used in many applications in various fields for more than ten years [1]. Their human-like communication skills can be exploited for the creation of powerful and engaging interfaces. Besides, VCs can easily take different roles, e.g. a guide, a companion, a trainer or an entertainer. Their appearances and their communication skills enrich interactive systems, like kiosk systems [2], virtual training systems [3,4,5], physical interaction based games [6], and museum guides [7,8]. Creators of such applications have to ensure that all features and the communication interfaces fit harmonically together in order to provide users with a compelling experience. In general, a user's acceptance of an interactive application is tightly related to the experience a user makes with the system. *User Experience* (UX) is described by Norman with *"... all aspects of the user's interaction with the product: how it is perceived, learned, and used."* [9]. Overbeekes et al. state: *"Don't think ease of use, think enjoyment of the experience"* [10, p. 11]. Thus, UX represents the overall quality of using a system from a user's point of view. Its core theme are non-task-oriented aspects, which are mainly responsible for a positive experience, such as *Joy-of-Use*. Joy-of-Use describes a user's positive, subjective experience while interacting with an application [11, p. 3f]. In terms of HCI research it can be seen an extension

Zs. Ruttkay et al. (Eds.): IVA 2009, LNAI 5773, pp. 174–180, 2009.

to usability engineering by emotional aspects. Hence, UX considers not merely functional aspects (e.g. ergonomics) which were mainly in the focus of HCI-researchers and developers up to now, but rather non-task-oriented aspects. In general, it remains unclear which aspects lead to an overall positive UX and finally to the acceptance of a system, because there is no general evaluation framework. This paper presents an evaluation approach to measure the UX of the COHIBIT system under on-site conditions.

2   The COHIBIT Exhibit

Since the summer of 2006, the COHIBIT exhibit has been accessible for the general public in the Volkswagen technical museum in Wolfsburg, Germany. Visitors are confronted with two human-sized VCs that provide help during a car assembly task in the role of guides and construction partners (see Fig. 1).

Cameras are used to detect the presence of users. The detection of location and orientation of tangible car pieces is realized using RFID technology. Museum visitors entering the exhibit area are detected by cameras and welcomed by the two VCs. The VCs point out the possibility of assembling a car using the model car pieces in the shelf and offer their (verbal) assistance. Visitors can use the 10 tangible car-model pieces (instrumented with passive RFID tags) to construct a car-model on a table with 5 adjacent areas with RFID readers. For the

Fig. 1. The COHIBIT exhibit

speech output, we use the commercial hi-end text-to-speech (TTS) synthesis system rVoice (Rhetorical) by Nuance. The VCs are animated with a real-time animation engine by Charamel featuring 3D-based keyframe animation and motion blending. The nonverbal behavior of our agents consists of a total repertoire of 28 actions (including idle time behaviors) for each character.

3   Related Work and Research Questions

Evaluations of virtual character systems are crucial for the understanding of their acceptance [12]. There is an ongoing discussion about the effects of employing VCs in user interfaces [13]. There is some evidence that they can improve the human machine interaction substantially because of their simulated natural interactive behavior. In addition, VCs can act proactively, reducing initial misunderstandings about the systems functionality. All this implies that users are potentially more motivated and can be guided in an entertaining way by VCs. As a result, the UX of systems may be positively influenced by them [14,15]. On the other hand, VCs can influence the UX negatively by giving users the impression of losing control or by frightening them with unexpected behavior [16]. For the CO-HIBIT exhibit, we investigated which aspects of VCs contribute to the UX. We distinguish between *task-oriented aspects* and *non-task-oriented aspects*. The evaluation of task-oriented aspects (e.g. helping to solve a technical problem) has been addressed in several studies [17]. Findings show that VCs can influence the UX in a positive way. Other studies do not confirm these positive findings [16]. It was empirically confirmed, that non-task-oriented aspects of VCs can motivate and entertain users and, as a result, positively influence the overall UX [18,14]. In order to get a more fine-grained understanding which non-task-oriented aspects are relevant, we rely on existing evaluation concepts for VCs [13,19]. Moreover, we rely on the evaluation concepts of the 4 main categories in VC research: believ-ability, sociability, their application domain/role, and general operative system features/handling [20]. For the design of the presented field study, we carefully identified similar systems and evaluations with focus on interaction and edutain-ment. Those are the interactive information system Hans Christian Andersen [14], MAX - the museum guide [15], and Ritchie – The virtual anatomy assistant [21]. All systems are designed for public spaces in order to entertain and inform visitors interactively. The systems are evaluated in labs or under special conditions and were mostly based on quantitative analysis. There has been no qualitative eval-uation under real conditions. Regarding the results of the studies it can be said that all systems were rated positive. The employed virtual characters were seen as adequate for there respective tasks and they gave users the illusion of life.

4   Method

4.1   Participants

The initial 39 subjects are reduced by 2 subjects due to inconsistencies of their answers. 37 subjects (13 female) successfully participated in the evaluation. Their age ranges from 12 to 67. All subjects understood German, most of them were Germans (32), the others were from the Netherlands (2) and Austria (1), Poland (1), and Vietnam (1). The participants cover a broad range of professions.

4.2   Procedure

The study took place in the Autostadt technical museum in Wolfsburg, Germany, May 5-9, 2008. Each 30 minutes, a subject was acquired after s/he has used the exhibit. This helped in getting a representative visitor distribution. Subjects were informed with a defined instruction. They had the option to participate or to decline. All subjects were interviewed based on a semi-standardized ques-tionnaire. This procedure helped subjects in understanding the questions and reduced outtakes due to wrong answers. Each interview took about 10-20 min. In pretests, the understandability of the questions and 2 options for the final evaluation procedure were tested: 1. a standard questionnaire and 2. a guided interview based on a semi-standardized questionnaire. The second option was chosen for the final evaluation due to location and time issues.

4.3   Questionnaire

The construction of the questionnaire is based on known approaches for the systematic evaluation of VCs [13,20,19]. Furthermore, relevant criteria for the evaluation of the UX (e.g. Joy-of-Use) have been taken into account. Besides, factors that contribute to the acceptance of innovative technologies were considered (e.g. Ease of Use, Usefulness). The questionnaire consists of 39 (open and closed) question in the areas: (1) UX, (2) Virtual Characters, (3) Joy-of-Use and (4) Entertainment. For closed questions, mostly 5-ary rating scales were used. Subjects had to rate the likability of the VCs, their appearance, and behavior. The latter has to be judged with a 16 bipolar adjective rating scale. This semantic differential relies mainly on items of common self-rating scales that are based on the California-Psychological-Inventory. Furthermore, the subjects had to rate the VCs' communication channels (gestures, mimic, voice, and speech) and as how natural they are perceived. In addition, it is questioned how the VCs' information and feedback behavior influence the behavior of the user. Subjects also had to judge the interaction experience or respectively the overall impression of the VCs in 9 statements. These statements rely mainly on the aspects of the 7 suggested qualities of life-likeness [22]. In addition, the subjects had to rate the quality of using the system and the quality of the interaction experience with a semantic differential that consists of 7 bipolar opposed adjectives. It was developed by means of the AttrakDiff^{TM} questionnaire [23] and general usability criteria. Finally, Joy-of-Use, the degree of Entertainment and information, and the overall impression of the installation were questioned.

4.4   Results

For the data analysis appropriate methods and techniques were used. Most items of the questionnaire were unidirectional on a 5-ary scale ("very bad" to "very good"). All items the negative end of the scale was assigned to "1" and the positive end to "5". Since rating scales can be treated as interval scales [24], we used parametrical tests (t-Tests) for the statistical analysis. In addition, we used contingency coefficients (e.g. the correlation coefficient r) to measure correlations.

Virtual Characters and Interaction.   The subjects rate the VCs *positive* $(t(36) = 6.31; p < 0.0001)$. The subjects have a positive UX in respect of the VCs. This is supported by a high significant correlation and a high regression coefficient $(r = 0.53; t = 3,67; p < 0.001)$. There is a positive linear correlation of average strength between these factors. The VCs were judged *as being aware of visitors* $(t(36) = 5.50; p < 0.001)$ and their dialog behavior was rated *human-like* $(t(36) = 2.61; p < 0.01)$. They have a mean rating for the *integration of visitors into the conversation* $(t(36) = 1.06; p = .09)$ and for *individual treatment* $(t(36) = -1.11; p = .09)$. The overall *interaction experience* was judged *positive* $(t(36) = 4.08; p < 0.001)$. This is supported by the rating of the VCs being perceived as *supportive* $(t(36) = 4.48; p < 0.001)$, *motivating* $(t(36) = 4.77; p < 0.001)$, *informative* $(t(36) = 2.91; p < 0.005)$ in an entertaining way, and they show a *agreeable* $(t(36) = 6.15; p < 0.001)$ feedback behavior.

Their *answers are mostly appropriate* ($t(36) = 1.52; p < 0.06$) and *understandable* ($t(36) = 6.73; p < 0.001$).

User Experience, Entertainment and Joy-of-Use. The subjects have a positive UX in respect of the COHIBIT museum exhibit ($t(36) = 8.99; p < 0.0001$). Looking at the task-oriented aspects, it can be stated that the exhibit was rated *easy to use* ($t(36) = 16.19; p < 0.0001$), *entertaining* ($t(36) = 10.73; p < 0.0001$), *informative* ($t(36) = 3.96; p < 0.001$), *supportive during a car assembly task* ($t(36) = 4.48; p < 0.001$), and *reactive to actions (e.g. placement of a car piece)* ($t(36) = 3.39; p < 0.001$). However, the subjects give the system a mean rating for *being treated individually* ($t(36) = .772; p = .22$). There is a positive correlation between the entertainment experience and the positive UX of the exhibit ($r = 0.529; p < 0.001$). The experience was rated as *joyful* ($t(36) = 11.20; p < 0.0001$). Together with the mainly positive answers of the open questions that address some of Reeps' Joy-of-Use criteria [11, p. 76], it can be concluded that visitors have the Joy-of-Use experience that contributes to the positive User Experience. There is a moderately positive correlation between these variables ($r = 0.538; p < 0.001$). Thus, the UX of the exhibit is more positive if the Joy-of-Use is positive. For identify which factor contributes positively to the overall UX, the factors are correlated to each other. As a result, the correlations reveal that the non-task-oriented aspects (VCs, Joy-of-Use, and Entertainment) are related positively to the UX. The correlation shows that non-task-oriented aspects are more important for the positive UX than task-oriented ones. This can be inferred from the correlations between the non-task-oriented aspects and the UX. In each case, they were very significant ($rVC = 0.527; p < 0.001$; and $rJoyofUse = 0.538; p < 0.001$ and $rEntertainment = 0.529; p < 0.001$). In contrast, the correlations between task-oriented aspects ("VCs are supportive", "VCs are reactive") and UX are not significant ($rSupport = 0.240; p > 0.05$ and $rReaction = 0.409; p < 0.01$). The correlation between the information factor and the UX is not significant ($rInformation = 0.247; p > 0.05$) as well.

5   Discussion and Conclusion

The presented on-site evaluation addresses important questions about the overall UX of the COHIBIT exhibit in particular and about VCs, Joy-of-Use, and Entertainment in general. Overall, the exhibit and the VCs are rated positive. It can be concluded, that besides the task-oriented aspects the non-task-oriented aspects, which are related to VCs, Joy-of-Use, and Entertainment, are essential for the overall positive UX of the COHIBIT exhibit. The employed VCs are perceived as life-like dialog partners in the roles of assistants and entertainers. There is some evidence that the VCs have a positive impact on a visitor's impression of the exhibit. According to the results, the VCs have an average importance for users of the exhibit during the interaction. In addition, the VCs' behavior is neither perceived as natural nor as unnatural. The information and the help given by the VCs during the interaction satisfied the visitors in total. The results mostly confirm the existing results of the lab study of the exhibit [25]. In contrast to this results and the findings in the MAX evaluation [15], the lifelikeness of the COHIBIT VCs is average. In detail, they are not perceived as human-like characters, but they show some life-like traits in their interaction behavior. This could be explained by the fact that they have limited communication skills (they cannot understand spoken questions, requests, or comments). Most of our subjects would have liked to communicate via spoken language. Results of other studies on aspects of VCs and similar exhibits are confirmed. Especially, it was found that the general acceptance of VCs mainly depends on 3 factors: (1) the personality and their related aspects, (2) the domain, and the (3) task itself [18]. Our study provides a clue that the interaction design is an important factor of the overall User Experience. Overall, the evaluation procedure of a guided interview based on a semi-standardized questionnaire is suitable for on-site studies of interactive installations like COHIBIT because of the limitation of misunderstandings and failures. It has to be investigated, if the evaluation design can be used for evaluations of similar installations with VCs in order to identify factors that are related to a positive UX and to the acceptance in general.

Acknowledgments. The work reported here was supported by the Volkswagen Autostadt technical museum in Wolfsburg, Germany. The authors would like to thank Lübomira Spassova for supporting us with her expertise.

References

1. Cassell, J., Bickmore, T., Billinghurst, M., Campbell, L., Chang, K., Villhjálmsson, H., Yan, H.: An architecture for embodied conversational characters. In: Proceedings of the First Workshop on Embodied Conversational Characters (1998)
2. Babu, S., Schmugge, S.J., Barnes, T., Hodges, L.F.: "What would you like to talk about?" an evaluation of social conversations with a virtual receptionist. In: Gratch, J., Young, M., Aylett, R.S., Ballin, D., Olivier, P. (eds.) IVA 2006. LNCS (LNAI), vol. 4133, pp. 169–180. Springer, Heidelberg (2006)
3. Dorfmüller-Ulhaas, K., André, E.: The synthetic character ritchie: First steps towards a virtual companion for mixed reality. In: Proceedings of IEEE International Symposium on Mixed and Augmented Reality (ISMAR 2005), pp. 178–179 (2005)
4. Kenny, P., Parsons, T.D., Gratch, J., Rizzo, A.A.: Evaluation of justina: A virtual patient with PTSD. In: Prendinger, H., Lester, J.C., Ishizuka, M. (eds.) IVA 2008. LNCS (LNAI), vol. 5208, pp. 394–408. Springer, Heidelberg (2008)
5. Ruttkay, Z., van Welbergen, H.: Elbows higher! performing, observing and correcting exercises by a virtual trainer. In: Prendinger, H., Lester, J.C., Ishizuka, M. (eds.) IVA 2008. LNCS (LNAI), vol. 5208, pp. 409–416. Springer, Heidelberg (2008)
6. Gebhard, P., Schröder, M., Charfuelan, M., Endres, C., Kipp, M., Pammi, S., Rumpler, M., Türk, O.: IDEAS4Games: Building expressive virtual characters for computer games. In: Prendinger, H., Lester, J.C., Ishizuka, M. (eds.) IVA 2008. LNCS (LNAI), vol. 5208, pp. 426–440. Springer, Heidelberg (2008)
7. Kopp, S., Jung, B., Leßmann, N., Wachsmuth, I.: Max - a multimodal assistant in virtual reality construction. In: KI, vol. 4, pp. 17–23 (2003)

8. Ndiaye, A., Gebhard, P., Kipp, M., Klesen, M., Schneider, M., Wahlster, W.: Ambient intelligence in edutainment: Tangible interaction with life-like exhibit guides. In: Maybury, M., Stock, O., Wahlster, W. (eds.) INTETAIN 2005. LNCS (LNAI), vol. 3814, pp. 104–113. Springer, Heidelberg (2005)
9. Norman, D.: Invisible Computer: Why Good Products Can Fail, the Personal Computer Is So Complex and Information Appliances Are the Solution. MIT Press, Cambridge (1999)
10. Overbeeke, K., Djajadiningrat, T., Hummels, C., Wensveen, S., Frens, J.: Let's make things engaging. In: Funology: from usability to enjoyment, pp. 7–17. Kluwer Academic Publishers, Norwell (2005)
11. Reeps, I.E.: Joy-of-use - a new quality for interactive products. Master's thesis, Universität Konstanz (2004),
    http://kops.ub.uni-konstanz.de/volltexte/2004/1386/
12. Ruttkay, Z., Pelachaud, C.: From Brows to Trust: Evaluating Embodied Conversational Agents. Springer, Heidelberg (2004)
13. Catrambone, R., Stasko, J., Xiao, J.: Eca as user interface paradigm. In: From brows to trust: evaluating embodied conversational agents, pp. 239–267. Kluwer Academic Publishers, Norwell (2004)
14. Bernsen, N.O., Dybkjaer, L.: User evaluation of conversational agent h. c. anderson. In: Proceedings of INTERSPEECH, pp. 237–241 (2005)
15. Kopp, S., Gesellensetter, L., Krämer, N.C., Wachsmuth, I.: A conversational agent as museum guide – design and evaluation of a real-world application. In: Panayiotopoulos, T., Gratch, J., Aylett, R.S., Ballin, D., Olivier, P., Rist, T. (eds.) IVA 2005. LNCS (LNAI), vol. 3661, pp. 329–343. Springer, Heidelberg (2005)
16. Shneidermann, B., Maes, P.: Direct manipulation vs. interface agents. Interaction 4, 42–61 (1997)
17. Rickenberg, R., Reeves, B.: The effects of animated characters on anxiety, task performance, and evaluations of user interfaces. In: Letters of CHI., pp. 49–56 (2000)
18. Dehn, D.M., Van Mulken, S.: The impact of animated interface agents: A review of empirical research. International Journal of Human-Computer Studies 52, 1–22 (2000)
19. Ruttkay, Z., Dormann, C., Noot, H.: Embodied conversational agents on a common ground. In: From brows to trust: evaluating embodied conversational agents, pp. 27–66. Kluwer Academic Publishers, Dordrecht (2004)
20. Isbister, K., Doyle, P.: The blind man and the elephant revisited. In: From Brows to Trust: Evaluating Embodied Conversational Agents., pp. 3–26. Kluwer Academic Publishers, Dordrecht (2004)
21. Wiendl, V., Dorfmüller-Ulhaas, K., Schulz, N., André, E.: Integrating a virtual agent into the real world: The virtual anatomy assistant ritchie. In: Proceedings of the Seventh International Conference on Intelligen Virtual Agents. LNCS, pp. 211–224. Springer, Heidelberg (2007)
22. Hayes-Roth, B.: What makes characters seem life-like? In: Prendinger, H., Ishizuka, M. (eds.) Life-like Characters. Tools, Affective Functions and Applications, pp. 447–462. Springer, Berlin (2003)
23. AttrakDiff^{TM}. UI Design GmbH (2009), http://www.attrakdiff.de/en/home/
24. Westermann, R.: Empirical tests of scale type for individual ratings. Applied Psychological Measurement 9 (1985)
25. Kipp, M., Kipp, K.H., Ndiaye, A., Gebhard, P.: Evaluating the tangible interface and virtual characters in the interactive COHIBIT exhibit. In: Gratch, J., Young, M., Aylett, R.S., Ballin, D., Olivier, P. (eds.) IVA 2006. LNCS (LNAI), vol. 4133, pp. 434–444. Springer, Heidelberg (2006)

Evaluating an Algorithm for the Generation of Multimodal Referring Expressions in a Virtual World: A Pilot Study

Werner Breitfuss[1], Ielka van der Sluis[2], Saturnino Luz[2],
Helmut Prendinger[3], and Mitsuru Ishizuka[1]

[1] University of Tokyo, 7-3-1 Hongo, Bunkyo-ku,
Tokyo, 113-8656, Japan
`werner@mi.ci.i.u-tokyo.ac.jp`
[2] Trinity College Dublin
Dublin Ireland
`{ielka.vandersluis,luzs}@cs.tcd.ie`
[3] National Institute of Informatics,2-1-2 Hitotsubashi,Chiyoda-ku,
Tokyo, 101-8430, Japan
`helmut@nii.ac.jp`

Abstract. This paper presents a quest for the most suitable setting and method to assess the naturalness of the output of an existing algorithm for the generation of multimodal referring expressions. For the evaluation of this algorithm a setting in Second Life was built. This paper reports on a pilot study that aimed to assess (1) the suitability of the setting and (2) the design of our evaluation method. Results show that subjects are able to discriminate between different types of referring expressions the algorithm produces. Lessons learnt in designing questionnaires are also reported.

Keywords: Embodied Conversational Agents, Automatic Behavior Generation, Generation of Multimodal Referring Expressions, Virtual Worlds.

1 Introduction

Research in Human Computer Interaction (HCI) shows an increased interest in developing interfaces that closely mimic human communication. The development of "embodied conversational agents" (ECAs) with appropriate verbal and non-verbal behavior with regard to a concrete spatial domain clearly fits this interest (e.g. [10]; [6]; [1]). Currently, the ability of an ECA to interact with human users is very limited. Interactions rely mostly on pre-scripted dialogue, whereby the manual generation of natural and convincing agent behavior is a cumbersome task.

An issue addressed in many HCI systems is that of identifying a certain object in a visual context accessible to both user and system. This can be done by an ECA that points to the object combined with a linguistic referring expression. The work presented in this paper uses one of these algorithms, which is arguably the most flexible in the sense that it can generate referring expressions that uniquely identify objects, which may include pointing gestures that vary in their precision.

Zs. Ruttkay et al. (Eds.): IVA 2009, LNAI 5773, pp. 181–187, 2009.

Although many evaluations of ECAs have been performed, systematic studies on specific aspects of interaction are scarce (cf. [15] and [8]). This paper presents a carefully designed evaluation method to assess the quality of automatically generated multimodal referring expressions by ECAs in a virtual environment. The method is demonstrated through a pilot study conducted within a setting built in Second Life.

2   Generating Multimodal Referring Expressions

The generation of referring expressions (GRE) is a central task in Natural Language Generation (NLG), and various algorithms which automatically produce referring expressions have been developed ([19]; [20]; [9]; [11]). Most GRE algorithms assume that both speaker and addressee have access to the same information. This information can be represented by a knowledge base that contains the objects and their properties present in the domain of conversation. A typical algorithm takes as input a single object (**the target**) and a set of objects (**the distractors**) from which the target object needs to be distinguished (borrowing terminology from [7]). The task of a GRE algorithm is to determine which set of properties is needed to single out the target from the distractors.

The multimodal GRE algorithm that was taken as a starting point for the work presented in this paper, approaches GRE as a compositional task in which language and gestures are combined in a natural way and in which a pointing gesture does not always need to be precise. The algorithm co-relates speech and gesture dependent on the distance between the target referent and the pointing device. The decision to point is based on a notion of effort that is defined by a cost function. In practice, an ECA can identify an object located far away, by moving close to the object to distinguish it with a very precise pointing gesture and the use of only limited linguistic information. Alternatively, the algorithm could generate a less precise pointing gesture that also includes other objects in its scope. In this case more linguistic information has to be added to the referring expression to ensure that the object can be uniquely identified by the addressee. As an example, an ECA can say `the large blue desk in the back' and accompany this description with an imprecise pointing gesture directed to the location of the desk. For a detailed description of the algorithm we refer to [21], for other multimodal GRE algorithms see (c.f., [12]; [13]; [2]).

3   Evaluating the Output of a Multimodal GRE Algorithm

3.1   Virtual Reality, Scripted Dialogue and Referring Expressions

For the evaluation design we use the virtual world Second Life (SL) for the design of evaluation experiments. It enables us to choose a specific domain of conversation in which all objects and their properties are known. This allows for complete semantic and pragmatic transparency, which is important for a content determination task like the generation of referring expressions.

Fig. 1. The agents and the furniture shop

The stage built for the experiment is a virtual furniture shop (Figure 1, right), in which two agents (Figure 1, left), a buyer and a seller interact with each other. The furniture shop contains over 43 objects, 13 of which are actually referred to in the dialogues. The other items in the shop are used as distractor objects.

In recent years, an alternative paradigm for computational work on agents has emerged ([1], [23]), with which entire dialogues are produced by one generator. Initially, scripted dialogues made heavy use of canned text, but recently this approach has been integrated with Natural Language Generation techniques, resulting in the Fully Generated Scripted Dialogue (FGSD) ([18]; [14]). FGSD allows us to produce dialogues, without implementing a full natural language interpretation module.

For our evaluation we manually prepared a dialogue, consisting of 19 utterances with 5 references to furniture items (3 singletons and 2 sets), featuring a conversation between an agent purchasing furniture for her office, and a shop-owner guiding her through the store while describing different items. The dialogue was used as a template in which the referring expressions that indicated particular pieces of furniture were varied. The referring expressions that were used to fill the slots in the dialogue were automatically produced with the algorithm discussed above.

Three types of output were implemented in three dialogues, with referring expressions ranging over two extremes with respect to linguistic and pointing information. One extreme, the imprecise version, used a version of the algorithm that generates very detailed linguistic descriptions of objects in which all the attributes of the target object were included. The pointing gestures generated to accompany these descriptions are, however, vague and the ECA can direct them from a considerable distance from the target object. The other extreme, the precise version, used another version of the algorithm that generates limited linguistic information (e.g. "this one") combined with precise pointing gestures. Between these two extremes a `mixed version' was implemented, in which 2 targets in the dialogue were identified with precise pointing gestures (1 singleton and 1 set) and 3 targets were identified with imprecise pointing gestures (2 singletons and 1 set).

3.2 Script Generation and Method of Evaluation

To control and animate our agents we use an existing gesture generation system that automatically adds nonverbal behavior to a dialogue and produces a play-able script.

We extended this system to add pointing gestures based on the algorithm. This gesture generation system consists of three steps. First the system analyzes the input text based on semantic and morphological information. Then the data used to suggest gestures which should appear along with the spoken utterance, like beats, metaphoric gestures and iconic gestures. In a third step the system filters the gestures, adds the most appropriate ones and produces a playable MPML3DSL script (c.f. [17]). The system is described in detail in ([3]; [4]). This system was extended to generate three levels of pointing gestures, precise, very precise and imprecise, as suggested in [21]. This involved: (1) object identification by the ECA, (2) detection of the position of these objects in relation to the ECA to select the right direction for the pointing gesture, and (3) choice of pointing gesture to be displayed.

To evaluate our setting, subjects were first introduced to the environment and asked to complete a questionnaire designed to obtain general judgments on the setting. They were then instructed to view and judge three presentations. Finally subjects were asked to compare the three presentations. Three kinds of questionnaires were used, which we will refer to as A, B and C. A aimed at obtaining a baseline and contained ten questions about the agents, the setting and the conversation plus some general questions about the subject's background. Some questions were open and some used a Likert scale that ranged from one ("strongly agree") to seven ("strongly disagree"). B was used for evaluating the three presentations and consisted of four sections addressing the interaction between the agents, the agents themselves, their role-play and the conversation. In total there were twenty-one questions. For all questions, questionnaire B used the same Likert scale as A. C compares the three presentations. Possible answers were (`Dialogue 1', `Dialogue 2', `Dialogue 3', `Don't know', `Now Difference'). All questionnaires allowed subjects to enter free comments.

4 The Pilot Study, Results and Discussion

Ten people participated in the study, all native speakers of English (4 males and 6 females). Half of them were familiar with virtual worlds, but no one visited SL regularly. After entering the experiment room individually they received a written introduction to the experiment. First, subjects were asked to familiarize themselves with the environment by moving and looking around in the shop. When ready, subjects were told to sit down at a predefined location and watch the three life versions of the dialogue presented in a random order. For the evaluation, we used the method described in 3.2, showing them three different settings and letting them fill out questionnaires A, B and C. Each Sessions lasted around 45 minutes per person. Subjects were not paid and participated voluntarily.

In general, the data obtained with A showed that subjects were content with their view of the stage, found the presentation easy to follow and enjoyable. With respect to the characters, they rated the female voice as more pleasant, and clearer than the male voice. The outcomes of B showed that the ECAs were perceived as friendly, trustworthy and talkative, and that the conversations were easy to follow. It proved difficult for the subjects to judge the naturalness of the acting and conversation.

Table 1. Means for questions targeting movement and talkativeness of the seller (standard deviations in brackets)

Question	Precise	Imprecise	Mixed
The male agent moved a lot	2.2 (1.398)	6.5 (0.707)	3.1 (1.663)
The male agent was talkative	2.6 (1.173)	3.0 (1.490)	2.7 (0.674)
It was clear which item the male agent was talking about	2.6 (1.080)	3.8 (1.813)	3.1 (1.100)

Table 1 shows that in the precise presentation, (i.e. precise pointing gestures + "this one"), subjects found that the furniture seller moved around a lot and that the conversation was easy to follow. A similar result was found for the mixed presentations. In contrast, in the Imprecise presentation, (imprecise pointing + detailed linguistic descriptions), subjects judged that the agent did not move around a lot and that it was not so clear which item was under discussion.

Table 2 presents the highlights from questionnaire 3, which asked subjects to compare the three presentations. For this small set of subjects it seems that the precise and the mixed version were preferred. Surprisingly, eight out of ten subjects found that there was no difference in how much the furniture seller talked while the presentations, while the imprecise dialogue contained five referring expressions of the type `the large blue desk in the back of the shop' and the precise version used `this one' in all these cases. Note also that none of the subjects used the answer `I don't know', all were able to remember and judge accordingly.

Table 2. Results of a comparison between the three settings

Question	Precise	Imprecise	Mixed	No Diff
The Seller acted more naturally in	5	1	4	0
If I were a buyer I would prefer Seller	5	1	4	0
The Seller moved more in	8	0	2	0
The Seller talked more in	1	1	0	8
The conversation most easy to follow in	4	1	4	1
The conversation was most naturally in	3	1	4	2

The results of the study show that subjects were able to perceive differences between the three types of GRE outputs used in the presentations, each one using a different kind of referring expressions. The study also gave us a number of pointers to improve the setup of the study. It turned out that in the questionnaires some of the questions were not very useful. In particular, the questions where subjects had to judged the naturalness of the conversation and the characters seemed problematic and need to be rephrased. This is not surprising as the setting is highly artificial (cf. [16]). Probably other types of evaluation (cf. [6]; [12], [22]) will be necessary (e.g. performance, behavior, preference etc.) to evaluate multimodal GRE algorithms.

Another issue was that some subjects found it difficult to tell which of the three furniture sellers they preferred. This is interesting because it addresses both the physical distance from which they were asked to view the presentation as well as our use of scripted dialogue. In our setting subjects were watching a play from a stand of the type that is used in theatres and arenas. Apart from the fact that there was a physical distance between the subjects and what was happening on the stage, subjects had no actual interest in the furniture itself. As a result, it appeared that subjects had different preferences dependent on whether the goal was to comprehend the dialogue, or whether they were asked to imagine themselves in the shoes of the customer.

Some pilot results related to technical problems in SL. For instance, it was not possible to turn the characters in a particular direction other than towards each other. Also movement was still very imprecise, which makes it difficult to be sure that the agent walks precisely the predefined route in the shop. An issue that remains open is the TTS system, which sometimes rendered the prosody somewhat unnatural.

5 Conclusion and Future Directions

In this paper we presented our approach to evaluate an existing algorithm for the generation of multimodal referring expressions embedded in an automatic gesture generation system. We employed two ECAs acting as a seller and a buyer in a virtual furniture shop. The setting aimed to test three types of referring behavior by the seller in which the precision of the pointing gestures and the linguistic descriptions were varied. A pilot study was carried out to test the setting and the methods used. The results of this study gave us some useful feedback to improve the current setup.

With respect to the questionnaires, especially the questions that aimed at the naturalness of the agents' behaviour and the conversation need to be rephrased. Other changes in the experimental setup will be of a presentational nature. In future studies we will use video of our SL presentations instead of displaying the scripts live as done in the pilot study. In the video, the camera can follow the agents through the furniture store, possibly reducing the 'overhearer' effect that is inherent to FGSD. In addition, we plan to remove the non-deictic gestures from the utterances that contain point gestures. Initially, these non deictic gestures were included to increase the naturalness of the characters. However, the pilot has shown that these gestures can have a distracting effect on the viewer. In the near future a cross-cultural study is planned, that focuses on differences and similarities in the perception of multimodal referring expressions between subjects in Dublin and in Tokyo.

Acknowledgements

This research was part-funded by Science Foundation Ireland under the CNGL grant.

References

1. André, E., Rist, T., Van Mulken, S., Klesen, M., Baldes, S.: The Automated Design of Believable Dialogues for Animated Presentation Teams. In: Cassell, J., Prevost, S., Sullivan, J., Churchill, E. (eds.) Embodied Conversational Agents. The MIT Press, Cambridge (2000)
2. Andre, E., Rist, T.: Coping with temporal constraints in multimedia presentation. In: Proc. of the 13th Conference of the AAAI, pp. 142–147 (1996)
3. Breitfuss, W., Prendinger, H., Ishizuka, M.: Automatic generation of gaze and gestures for dialogues between embodied conversational agents. Int'l J of Semantic Computing 2(1), 71–90 (2008)

4. Breitfuss, W., Prendinger, H., Ishizuka, M.: Automatic generation of conversational behavior for multiple embodied virtual characters: The rules and models behind our system. In: Prendinger, H., Lester, J.C., Ishizuka, M. (eds.) IVA 2008. LNCS (LNAI), vol. 5208, pp. 472–473. Springer, Heidelberg (2008)
5. Byron, D., Koller, A., Striegnitz, K., Cassell, J., Dale, R., Moore, J., Oberlander, J.: Report on the First NLG Challenge on Generating Instructions in Virtual Environments (GIVE). In: Proc. of ENLG 2009 (2009)
6. Cassell, J., Stocky, T., Bickmore, T., Gao, Y., Nakano, Y., Ryokai, K., Tversky, D., Vaucelle, C., Vilhjalmsson, H.: MACK: Media lab Autonomous Conversational Kiosk. In: Proc. of the IMAGINA 2002 (2002)
7. Dale, R., Reiter, E.: Computational interpretations of the Gricean maxims in the generation of referring expressions. Cognitive Science 18, 233–263 (1995)
8. Dehn, D., Van Mulken, S.: The impact of animated interface agents: a review of empirical research. Int. J. Human-Computer Studies 52, 1–22 (2000)
9. Jordan, P., Walker, M.: Learning content selection rules for generating object descriptions in dialogue. Journal of Artificial Intelligence Research 24, 157–194 (2005)
10. Kopp, S., Jung, B., Lessmann, N., Wachsmuth, I.: Max - A Multimodal Assistant in Virtual Reality Construction. KI Künstliche Intelligenz 4(3), 11–17 (2003)
11. Krahmer, E., Van Erk, S., Verleg, A.: Graph-based generation of referring Expressions. Computational Linguistics 29(1), 53–72 (2003)
12. Kranstedt, A., Lücking, A., Pfeiffer, T., Rieser, H., Wachsmuth, I.: Deictic object reference in task-oriented dialogue. In: Rickheit, G., Wachsmuth, I. (eds.) Situated Communication, pp. 155–207 (2006)
13. Lester, J., Voerman, J., Towns, S., Callaway, C.: Deictic believability: Coordinating gesture, locomotion and speech in lifelike pedagogical agents. Applied Artificial Intelligence 13(4-5), 383–414 (1997)
14. Piwek, P.: Presenting Arguments as Fictive Dialogue. In: Grasso, F., Green, N., Kibble, R., Reed, C. (eds.) Proc.of 8th of the CMNA (2008)
15. Ruttkay, Z., Pelachaud, C.: From Brows to Trust: Evaluating Embodied Conversational Agents. Kluwer, Dordrecht (2004)
16. Slater, M.: How colorful was your day? Why questionnaires cannot assess presence in virtual environments. Presence-Teleoperators and Virtual Environments 13(4), 484–493 (2004)
17. Ullrich, S., Prendinger, H., Ishizuka, M.: MPML3D: Agent authoring language for virtual worlds. In: Proc. of the Int'l Conf on Advances in Computer Entertainment Technology (ACE 2008), pp. 134–137. ACM Press, New York (2008)
18. Van Deemter, K., Krenn, B., Piwek, P., Klesen, M., Schroeder, M., Baumann, S.: Full Generated Scripted Dialogue for Embodied Agents. AI Journal (2008)
19. Van Deemter, K., Krahmer, E.: Graphs and booleans. In: Bunt, H., Muskens, R. (eds.) Computing Meaning, vol. 3. Kluwer Academic Publishers, Dordrecht (2006)
20. Van Deemter, K.: Generating Referring Expressions that Involve Gradable Properties. Computational Linguistics 32(2), 195–222 (2006)
21. Van der Sluis, I., Krahmer, E.: Generating Multimodal Referring Expressions. Discourse Processes. In: Piwek, P., Kuhnlein, P. (eds.) Special Issue on Dialogue Modelling: Computational and Empirical Approaches vol. 44(3), pp. 145–174 (2007)
22. Van der Sluis, I., Krahmer, E.: The Influence of Target Size and Distance on the Production of Speech and Gesture in Multimodal Referring Expressions. In: Proc. of the ICSLP 2004 (2004)
23. Williams, S., Piwek, P., Power, R.: Generating monologue and dialogue to present personalised medical information to patients. In: Proc. of the 11th European Workshop on Natural Language Generation, pp. 167–170 (2007)

Expression of Emotions Using Wrinkles, Blushing, Sweating and Tears

Celso M. de Melo and Jonathan Gratch

Institute for Creative Technologies, University of Southern California,
13274 Fiji Way, Marina Del Rey, CA 90292, USA
demelo@usc.edu, gratch@ict.usc.edu

Abstract. Wrinkles, blushing, sweating and tears are physiological manifestations of emotions in humans. Therefore, the simulation of these phenomena is important for the goal of building believable virtual humans which interact naturally and effectively with humans. This paper describes a real-time model for the simulation of wrinkles, blushing, sweating and tears. A study is also conducted to assess the influence of the model on the perception of surprise, sadness, anger, shame, pride and fear. The study follows a repeated-measures design where subjects compare how well is each emotion expressed by virtual humans with or without these phenomena. The results reveal a significant positive effect on the perception of surprise, sadness, anger, shame and fear. The relevance of these results is discussed for the fields of virtual humans and expression of emotions.

Keywords: Expression of Emotions, Wrinkles, Blushing, Sweating, Tears.

1 Introduction

Communicating one's emotions serves an adaptive purpose [1, 2, 3, 4]. A person might express anger to signal another to cease some action which might be hindering his goals. A person might express shame to convey regret for breaking some accepted social rule. In fact, emotions play a significant role in social interaction where participants continuously monitor and respond to each other's emotions while pursing their own goals. As to the manner emotions are expressed, besides facial expression, vocalization and appropriate gestures, several other autonomically mediated signals accompany emotions such as changes in coloration that result in local blood flow (e.g., flushing, blushing, blanching and bulging of arteries), whereas others involve additional detectable changes such as piloerection, sweating (and accompanying odors), tearing and crying [5]. As we try to build embodied virtual agents, or virtual humans, which communicate emotions effectively and naturally with humans [6], we should also simulate these autonomically mediated signals.

This paper describes a model to express emotions in virtual humans using wrinkles, blushing, sweating and tears. Regarding wrinkles, two kinds can be distinguished [7]: (a) *permanent wrinkles*, which are caused by aging and habitual facial expressions as the skin looses elasticity; (b) *temporary wrinkles*, which are caused by deformations of the skin layers as a result of muscle contraction. In this work we are

Zs. Ruttkay et al. (Eds.): IVA 2009, LNAI 5773, pp. 188–200, 2009.

interested in the subset of the latter which is associated with emotional facial expressions. The argument here is that wrinkles can be an important, if not crucial, clue to the perception of the emotion the agent is trying to convey. In particular, the work focuses on simulation of wrinkles in the forehead caused by the expression of surprise, sadness and anger.

Blushing manifests physiologically as a spontaneous reddening of the face, ears, neck and upper chest as the small blood vessels in the blush region dilate, increasing blood volume in the area [7]. Blushing, aside from being associated with self-consciousness, can be accompanied by social anxiety, uneasiness, embarrassment, shame or happiness (e.g., when someone receives an undeserved praise) [8]. Several theories of blushing have been proposed: (a) the *interpersonal appraisal theory* argues that blushing arises from being self-aware and thinking about what others are thinking of us [9]; (b) the *communicative and remedial theory* argues that blushing is a save-face action which acknowledges and apologizes for breaking an accepted social rule [10]; the *social blushing theory* expands on the previous one (e.g., explaining cases where blushing occurs with positive emotions) and argues that blushing will occur when undesired social attention is given to someone [8]. In this work we are interested in the fact that blushing serves an important communicative function and is associated with certain characteristic emotions. In particular, the work focuses on simulation of blushing associated with two self-conscious emotions - shame (with negative valence) and pride (with positive valence).

Sweating is primarily a means of thermoregulation but can also be caused by emotional stress [7]. This latter form is referred to as *emotional sweating* and manifests physiologically in the palms of the hands, soles of the feet, axillae and head [11, 12]. This form of sweating may occur in situations where an individual is subjected to fearful situations or the scrutiny of others (e.g., talking in public or to a superior) and is particularly evident in shy and social phobic individuals [13]. This work focuses on the simulation of sweating in the forehead associated with fear.

Crying is usually associated with the experience of intense emotions in situations of personal suffering, separation, loss, failure, anger, guilt or joy [14]. Crying manifests physiologically through the shedding of tears and a characteristic noise (which might become concealed with age). Several explanations have been advanced for crying: (a) in one view, crying is seen as being cathartic and a release after an intense experience [15]; (b) in another view, attachment theory explains crying as an appeal for the protective presence of a parent [16]. For the infant, crying is used to call the attention of its care-takers in face of some urgent need (e.g. danger). Later in adulthood, crying continues to be a reaction to a loss and to carry an attachment message which seeks to trigger a response from its "care-takers" (e.g., spouse or friends). Thus, two factors motivate the simulation of tearing in our work: first, the important communicative function it serves; and second, its association with the expression of strong emotions. The focus of the work is in the simulation of tearing which occurs when experiencing intense sadness.

A study was also conducted to evaluate the influence of our model of wrinkles, blushing, sweating and tears on the perception of surprise, sadness, anger, shame, pride and fear. The study follows a repeated-measures design where subjects compare images of a virtual human expressing each of the aforementioned emotions with or without wrinkles, blushing, sweating and tears.

The rest of the paper is organized as follows: Section 2 describes related work; Section 3 describes the model for simulation of wrinkles, blushing, sweating and tears; Section 4 describes the experiment conducted to assess the influence of the model on the expression of sadness, anger, surprise, fear, shame and pride; finally, Section 5 discusses the results and future work.

2 Related Work

Three kinds of methods have been explored to simulate wrinkles: *texture mapping*, *physically-based* and *geometric* methods. Texture mapping methods rely on the *bump mapping* technique [17] to simulate wrinkles. Bump mapping simulates small details in an object's surface by locally changing the vertices' normals and, thus, affect the lighting calculation without deforming the object's geometry. Normal deformation can be defined using a texture, called a *normal map*, or calculated on-the-fly. Physically-based methods [18, 19] approximate the biomechanical properties of skin and, dynamic wrinkles emerge naturally as a consequence of skin deformation under the influence of muscle contraction. These methods tend to produce very realistic visual results and dynamic behavior for the wrinkles but, are very expensive computationally. Geometric methods avoid the computational cost of physical models by deforming the geometry, so as to simulate dynamic wrinkles, based on geometrical properties [20, 21]. This work uses bump mapping to render the wrinkles and normal map interpolation to simulate wrinkle dynamics.

There have been fewer systems developed for the simulation of blushing. Kalra et al. [22] define several textures with appropriate coloration of the face which are then interpolated appropriately according to the prevailing emotion. Jung et al. [23] also rely on predefined textures to simulate coloration of the face. The model presented here does not rely on textures and applies color to user-defined regions in the face.

Regarding tearing and sweating, several researchers [24, 25] have simulated the physical properties of water drops as well as its interactions with other water drops and solid surfaces. These systems, even though producing very realistic visual results, are far from being real-time. Jung et al. [23] propose a rare implementation of real-time tearing. Their system simulates refraction of light and strong highlights in tear drops. Tearing dynamics rely on 3D textures, which define a sequence of keyframe normal maps with a gloss map in the alpha channel, to animate the tears in real-time. This work also uses 3D textures to simulate dynamics but also explores another simpler technique. Furthermore, besides simulating strong highlights in the tears, highlights in the eyes are also simulated. Finally, sweating is easily implemented with the tears model by using appropriate normal and dynamic textures.

3 The Model

The model for wrinkles, blushing, sweating and tears has strict real-time requirements. First, following the paradigm of human face-to-face conversation, virtual humans need to integrate several verbal and nonverbal modalities [6]. Therefore, these new forms of expression need to integrate with the usual facial, bodily and vocal expression channels. Effectively, in this work the proposed model is integrated with an existent platform for virtual humans [26]. Second, virtual humans' behavior unfolds in time subject to various sub-second temporal constraints [6]. For instance, gestures which accompany speech must closely follow voice cadence. If these timing requirements are not met, the effectiveness of the communication breaks down. Therefore, the challenge is not to simply integrate the state-of-the-art in the techniques for simulation of each expression modality but to strike a balance between *visual realism* and *behavioral realism*. The idea of a believable character, which need not be visually realistic, but whose behavior provides the illusion of life and thus permits the audience's suspension of disbelief, applies here [27]. Therefore, this work steers away from physical models of wrinkles, blushing, sweating and tears which, even though creating visually realistic results, are very expensive computationally. Furthermore, our model makes extensive use of the *graphics processing unit* or *GPU*. The GPU implements a hardware-supported programmable graphics rendering pipeline where certain stages can be set to run user-defined programs, called *shaders*, written in a special language [28]. The advantage of using the GPU over pure software solutions is the considerable increase in speed we gain from hardware acceleration. This factor is likely to play a significant role in virtual human research as the models for expression modalities become more and more complex and new modalities are integrated.

3.1 Wrinkles

Wrinkles are simulated using bump mapping with normal maps. One normal map represents a typical temporary wrinkle pattern associated with a certain emotion. Wrinkle dynamics are then synchronized with the underlying pseudo-muscular model for facial expressions [26]. To implement this, three steps are taken. First, the vertex structure is augmented to contain binormal and tangent vectors which, together with the normals in the normal map, define a frame of reference on which lighting calculations, accounting for bump mapping, are performed [28]. Second normal maps for the wrinkle patterns are created. For each, the following procedure is realized, Fig.1: (a) a picture is taken with a person doing the respective wrinkle configuration; (b) the picture is cropped and converted to grayscale; (c) the picture is composited onto the virtual human texture; (d) the composited picture is edited to remove color information everywhere but in the wrinkle region, a Gaussian filter is applied to blur the image and the side borders are faded into the background color; (f) finally, the NVIDIA's normal map tool[1] is used to create the normal map. The third and final step is to create a shader program to run in the GPU which, given the data from the previous steps, actually applies the bump mapping technique while at the same time providing the following expression parameters: (a) one or more normal maps to apply; (b) the interpolation level between the images with and without bump mapping applied. The first parameter supports composition of wrinkle patterns, whereas the second implements wrinkle dynamics by synchronizing it with changes in the pseudo-muscular model of the face [26]. The results for the emotions of surprise, anger and sadness are shown in Fig.2-(a) to (c). Fig.2-(d) shows how this effect can also be applied to simulate bulging of arteries in anger.

---

[1] Available at: http://developer.nvidia.com/object/nv_texture_tools

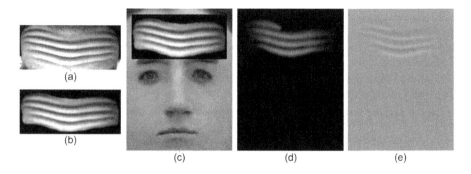

Fig. 1. Methodology to get normal maps for wrinkle patterns

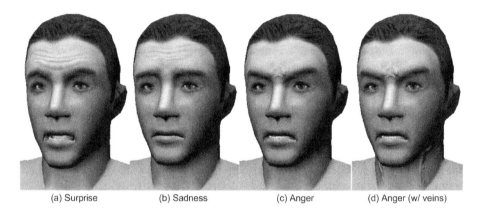

(a) Surprise   (b) Sadness   (c) Anger   (d) Anger (w/ veins)

Fig. 2. Expression of surprise, sadness and anger using wrinkles

3.2 Blushing

The basic idea for simulating blushing is having a way to selectively apply a color tint over certain vertices in the virtual human mesh (e.g. the vertices in the cheek). To accomplish this, four steps are taken. First, a floating-point value, called *mask*, is added to the virtual human vertex structure (which already has position, normal, skinning blend weights and texture coordinates). This value provides the foundation for defining custom subsets of the virtual human mesh, which we call *mesh masks*. A coding scheme, not described in the paper, is adopted which supports the association of up to 8 masks with each vertex. Thus, mesh masks can be overlapping. Second, a tool is developed to support the interactive creation of mesh masks. Once the mask is finished, the tool allows saving the mask in XML format. Having developed the tool, the third step is to use it to define masks for the areas of the face where blushing is to occur. Two masks are created: one for the cheeks; and one for the cheeks, forehead, nose and ears. The fourth and final step is to create a shader program to run in the GPU which tints the vertices in the specified mask. An important detail is that the tint is multiplied with the diffuse light component and, thus, the portion of the mask in the dark does not get painted. Several expression parameters are defined for this shader: (a) color of the tint (e.g., reddish for blushing); (b) mask to apply the tint; (c) fadeoff at the boundary, which defines how far the pixels in the (outside of the) mask boundary get affected by the color tint. Blushing of the cheeks and the full face, which can be associated with shame or pride, are shown in Fig.3-(b) and (c).

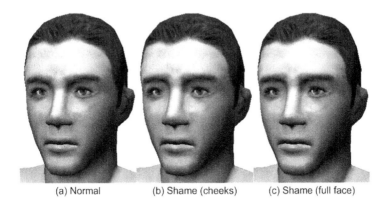

(a) Normal   (b) Shame (cheeks)   (c) Shame (full face)

Fig. 3. Expression of shame and pride using blushing

3.3 Tearing and Sweating

Simulation of tearing consists of modeling the properties of water and its dynamics. Regarding the former, the material properties of water were defined to have a very high specular component, a low diffuse component (e.g. RGB color of [10, 10, 10]) and a null ambient component. The water is, then, rendered using bump mapping with a normal map of a typical pattern of tears. The normal map's alpha channel is set to a nonzero value in the tearing (sweating) zone and to zero elsewhere. This channel is then used to composite the tears (or sweat) on top of the virtual human image. Moreover, the specular component of the eyes is increased to simulate accumulation of water in the eyes in the case of tearing. Regarding dynamics, two approaches are explored: (a) *volume textures*, which consist of a sequence of normal maps defining keyframes which are then interpolated to animate the tears (or sweat); (b) *definition of a dynamics texture*, which consists of a unique grayscale texture which defines how tears (or sweat) evolve in time being black the earliest and white the latest. This texture can then be used to interpolate a value which defines how much of the normal map is rendered at each instant. Each one of these mechanisms has its advantages and disadvantages. The first allows greater expressive control but at the cost of higher memory requirements and artistic effort. The second has lower memory requirements and requires less artistic effort but is less flexible than the former. Finally, both the properties of water and its dynamics are defined in a shader program to run in the GPU which defines parameters to set which animation mechanism to use and the current time in the animation. Results for the expression of sadness using tears are shown in Fig.4-(a) to (c). Fig.4-(d) shows simulation of sweating in fear.

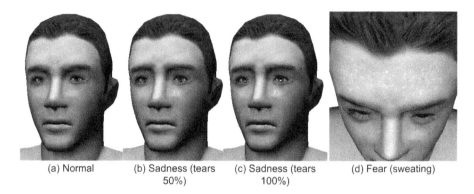

(a) Normal   (b) Sadness (tears   (c) Sadness (tears   (d) Fear (sweating)
                          50%)   100%)

Fig. 4. Expression of sadness using tears and fear using sweating

4 Evaluation

4.1 Design

A study was conducted to evaluate the influence of the wrinkles, blushing, sweating and tears model on the perception of surprise, sadness, anger, shame, pride and fear. The experiment followed a repeated-measures design with two conditions per emotion: the *control virtual human*, which uses only facial expression to convey the emotion; the *expressive virtual human*, which uses facial expression and wrinkles, blushing, sweating and tears to convey the emotion. Subjects are asked to classify, for each condition, whether the virtual human expresses the emotion on a scale from *1* (meaning 'doesn't express the emotion at all') to *10* (meaning 'perfectly expresses the emotion'). The order of presentation of the emotions is randomized. The order of presentation of the conditions, given an emotion, is also randomized.

The control and expressive conditions for each emotion are shown in Fig.5. The virtual human, in both conditions, assumes a typical muscular configuration of the face [29]. The virtual human in the expressive condition rely, additionally, on wrinkles, blushing, sweating and tears as follows: surprise, sadness and anger are given typical wrinkle patterns in the forehead; sadness is also associated with tears and shiny eyes; anger is also associated with bulging of arteries in the neck region and a light reddening of the face; pride and shame are associated with blushing of the cheeks; and, fear is associated with sweating of the forehead.

4.2 Procedure

The survey was implemented as an online survey. Forty-four participants were recruited with the following age distribution: *11-20* years, 6.8%; *21-30* years, 47.7%; *31-40* years, 31.8%; *41-50* years, 6.8%; and, *51-60* years, 6.8%. Gender distribution was as follows: *female*, 54.6%; *male*, 45.4%. Most had college education or above (90.9%) from diverse fields. Participants had diverse origins: *North America*, 38.6%; *Europe*, 36.4%; *Asia*, 13.6%; and, *Africa*, 11.4%.

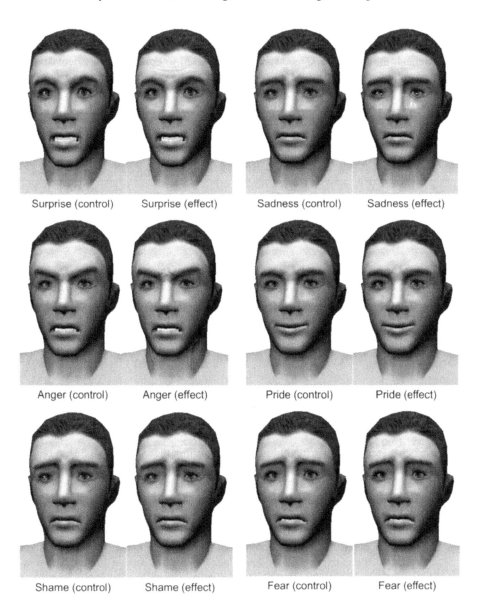

Fig. 5. Control and expressive conditions for surprise, sadness, anger, pride, shame and fear

4.3 Results

The Kolmogorov-Smirnov test was applied to assess the normality of the data in each condition in each emotion. The results show that the control conditions for surprise ($D(44)=0.12$, $p>.05$), sadness ($D(44)=0.13$, $p>.05$) and shame ($D(44)=0.10$, $p>.05$) are significantly non-normal. Therefore, the dependent t test was used to compare means between the expressive and control conditions in pride, anger and fear as shown in Table 1; and, the *Wilcoxon* signed-rank test was used to compare ranks between the expressive and control conditions in surprise, sadness and shame as shown in Table 2.

Table 1. Dependent t test statistics for difference in means between the expressive and control conditions for the following emotions: PRIDE; ANGER; and, FEAR ($df = 43$)

Variables	Mean	Std. Dev.	Std. Error Mean	95% CI		t	Sig. 2-sd
				Lower	Upper		
PRIDE	-0.182	1.369	0.206	-0.598	0.234	-0.881	0.383
ANGER*	1.886	1.186	0.179	1.526	2.247	10.555	0.000
FEAR*	0.523	1.338	0.202	0.116	0.930	2.592	0.013

* Significant difference, p < 0.05

Table 2. *Wilcoxon* signed-rank test statistics for difference in mean ranks between the expressive and control conditions for the following emotions: SURPRISE; SADNESS; and, SHAME ($N = 44$)

Variables	N			Mean Rank		Z	Sig. 2-sd
	Neg.	Pos.	Ties	Neg.	Pos.		
SURPRISE*	19	8	17	14.39	13.06	-2.069	0.039
SADNESS*	34	2	8	19.32	4.50	-5.152	0.000
SHAME*	29	6	9	19.02	12.69	-3.952	0.000

* Significant difference, p < 0.05

The results in Table 1 show that, on average:

- Subjects perceived the virtual human with blushing (M=5.73, SE=0.33) to be less expressive of pride than the control virtual human (M=5.91, SE=0.34). However, this result was not significant: $t(43)$=-0.881, p>.05, r=0.133[2];
- Subjects perceived the virtual human with wrinkles, veins and blushing (M=7.91, SE=0.28) to be significantly more expressive of anger than the control virtual human (M=6.02, SE=0.314, $t(43)$=10.555, p<.05, r=0.849);
- Subjects perceived the virtual human with sweating (M=6.89, SE=0.31) to be significantly more expressive of fear than the control virtual human (M=6.36, SE=0.32, $t(43)$= 2.592, p<.05, r=0.368).

The results in Table 2 show that, on average:

- Subjects perceived the virtual human with wrinkles (M=5.84, SE=0.31) to be significantly more expressive of surprise than the control virtual human (M=5.36, SE=0.32, Z=-2.069, p<.05, r=-0.312[3]);
- Subjects perceived the virtual human with wrinkles and tears (M=7.93, SE=0.27) to be significantly more expressive of sadness than the control virtual human (M=6.18, SE=0.27, Z=-5.152, p<.05, r=-0.777);

[2] Effect size for the dependent t test statistic is calculated as suggested by Rosenthal [30].
[3] Effect size for the *Wilcoxon* signed-rank test is calculated as suggested by Rosenthal [30].

- Subjects perceived the virtual human with blushing (M=6.55, SE=0.31) to be significantly more expressive of shame than the control virtual human (M=5.52, SE=0.31, Z=-3.952, p<.05, r=-0.596).

5 Discussion

This paper presents a real-time model for the expression of emotions in virtual humans using wrinkles, blushing, sweating and tears. Wrinkles are rendered using bump mapping with normal maps representing typical wrinkle patterns and its dynamics simulated using normal map interpolation synchronized with the underlying pseudo-muscular facial model. Simulation of blushing relies on application of color to selected subsets of the virtual human's mesh and interpolation of color at the pixel-level. Tears and sweating are rendered using bump mapping with a normal map for typical patterns and by simulating some of the properties of water. The dynamics of tearing and sweating are simulated using either volume textures or a special dynamics texture which maps time into grayscale values. The model is also integrated with a virtual humans platform which supports bodily, facial and vocal expression and, moreover, is implemented making extensive use of the GPU.

A study is also described to assess the influence of the model on the perception of surprise, sadness, anger, shame, pride and fear. The results show a large effect on the perception of anger, sadness and shame; a medium effect on the perception of fear and surprise; and, no effect on the perception of pride. This suggests that the model can improve the perception of anger, sadness, shame, fear and surprise. One explanation for this might be that the communicative functions wrinkles, blushing, sweating and tears serve in human-human interactions [5, 8, 12, 14] can also carry to human-virtual human interactions. The fact that no effect is achieved with blushing in pride could be explained for three reasons: (a) the physiological manifestation of pride is not successfully simulated by our model; (b) the facial expression of pride is not universal [29]; (c) further contextual cues are necessary for the association of blushing with pride (e.g., the knowledge that an individual's accomplishments could have been easily missed in virtue of the quality of the work of others) [8].

The results also suggest that wrinkles, blushing, sweating and tears can be used to convey *intensity* of emotion. Effectively, even in the control condition, where the virtual human relied only on proper configuration of the muscles in the face to convey emotion, subjects, on average, were already giving relatively high classifications (surprise: 5.36; sadness: 6.18; anger: 6.02; shame: 5.52; pride: 5.91; fear: 6.36). Still, the expressive conditions managed to increase the average classification for all emotions (surprise: 5.84; sadness: 7.93; anger: 7.91; shame: 6.55; fear: 6.87) but pride (5.73). Being able to control the intensity of the expressed emotion is, of course, useful in regulating human-virtual human interactions [6]. However, display of strong emotions should be used with care. For instance, it would be unreasonable to always use bulging of arteries to express anger or tearing to express sadness as these occur only in specific cases in human-human interactions [5, 16].

Future work consists of developing computational cognitive models for blushing, sweating and tears. Notice wrinkles occur naturally with the deformation of the underlying muscles and, therefore, can be considered to be a physical, rather than cognitive, phenomenon. Regarding the other phenomena, the cognitive models need to define clearly the respective eliciting conditions. In this work we assumed a simple association between emotions and blushing, sweating and tears. However, this association is not that simple and there are several factors influencing the magnitude and whether these physiological manifestations occur when experiencing the corresponding emotions [5, 8, 12, 14]. For instance, individual factors are known to influence the display of blushing [8], sweating [11] and tears [14].

Furthermore, a study needs to be conducted to evaluate the dynamics of emotion expression using the proposed model. The way emotion expression unfolds in time is known to influence its perception. For instance, it has been shown that subtle variations in facial dynamics can have an impact on how much people are willing to trust and cooperate with a person [31]. Subjects in our study compared only static images of the virtual human. What is required is a second study which asks subjects to compare videos of the virtual human in a control and expressive conditions.

The proposed model can also be used to display more autonomically mediated signals. The wrinkles model is used to display bulging of arteries in the neck but, this effect can also be used to simulate bulging of arteries in other regions of the body and, thus, possibly support the display of more emotions. The blushing model can be used to simulate blanching, pallor and flushing of the face which are known to be associated with the occurrence of emotions [32]. The sweat model can be used to simulate perspiration in other regions from the body, aside from the forehead. In fact, emotional sweating is believed to occur significantly in the palms of the hands, soles of the feet and axillae [11]. This might also explain why perspiration of the forehead only caused a medium effect on perception of fear in our study.

Finally, the proposed model can be used to influence the perception of more emotions. This work focuses on the display of surprise, sadness, anger, shame, pride and fear. These are emotions commonly associated with the phenomena being simulated [5, 8, 12, 14]. However, looking at the eliciting conditions suggested by Ortony, Clore and Collins' emotion appraisal theory [33], it seems likely that resentment, reproach, disappointment, disgust and remorse can benefit from display of wrinkles, blushing and sweating. Furthermore, the display of autonomically mediated signals has also been argued to play a major role on the display of moral emotions such as reproach, anger, shame, remorse, admiration, gratitude and sympathy [34, 35, 36].

Acknowledgments

This work was sponsored by the U.S. Army Research, Development, and Engineering Command and the National Science Foundation under grant # HS-0713603. The content does not necessarily reflect the position or the policy of the Government, and no official endorsement should be inferred.

References

1. Smith, J.: The behavior of communicating: An ethnological approach. Harvard University Press, Cambridge (1977)
2. Krebs, J., Dawkins, R.: Animal signals: Mind reading and manipulation. In: Krebs, J.R., Davies, N.B. (eds.) Behavioural ecology: An evolutionary approach, pp. 380–402. Sinauer Associates, Sunderland (1984)

3. Owings, D., Morton, E.: Animal vocal communication: A new approach. Cambridge University Press, Cambridge (1998)
4. Darwin, C.: The expression of emotions in man and animals. John Murray, England (1872)
5. Levenson, R.: Autonomic specificity and emotion. In: Davidson, R.J., Scherer, K.R., Goldsmith, H.H. (eds.) Handbook of Affective Sciences, pp. 212–224. Oxford University Press, New York (2003)
6. Gratch, J., Rickel, J., Andre, E., Badler, N., Cassell, J., Petajan, E.: Creating Interactive Virtual Humans: Some Assembly Required. IEEE Intelligent Systems 17(4), 54–63 (2002)
7. De Graaff, K.: Human Anatomy, 6th edn. McGraw Hill, New York (2002)
8. Leary, M., Britt, T., Cutlip, W., Templeton, J.: Social Blushing. Psychological Bulletin 112(3), 446–460 (1992)
9. Harris, P.: Shyness and embarrassment in psychological theory and ordinary language. In: Crozier, W.R. (ed.) Shyness and embarrassment: Perspectives from social psychology, pp. 59–86. Cambridge University Press, Cambridge (1990)
10. Castelfranchi, C., Poggi, I.: Blushing as a discourse: Was Darwin wrong? In: Crozier, W.R. (ed.) Shyness and embarrassment: Perspectives from social psychology, pp. 230–254. Cambridge University Press, Cambridge (1990)
11. Kuno, Y.: Human Perspiration. Charles C. Thomas, Springfield (1956)
12. McGregor, I.: The sweating reactions of the forehead. Journal of Physiology 116, 26–34 (1952)
13. Scheneier, F., et al.: Social Phobia. In: DSM-IV Sourcebook, vol. 2, pp. 507–548. American Psychiatric Association (1996)
14. Miceli, M., Castelfranchi, C.: Crying: Discussing its Basic Reasons and Uses. New Ideas in Psychology 21, 247–273 (2003)
15. Efran, J., Spangler, T.: Why Grown-Ups Cry: A Two-Factor Theory and Evidence from the Miracle Worker. Motivation and Emotion 3(1), 63–72 (1979)
16. Nelson, J.: The meaning of crying based on attachment theory. Clinical Social Work Journal 26(1), 9–22 (1998)
17. Blinn, J.: Simulation of wrinkled surface. In: Proc. SIGGRAPH 1978, pp. 286–292. ACM Press, New York (1978)
18. Terzopoulus, D., Waters, K.: Physically-based facial modeling, analysis and animation. Journal of Visualization and Computer Animation 1, 73–80 (1990)
19. Boissieux, L., Kiss, G., Magnenat-Thalmann, N., Kalra, P.: Simulation of skin aging and wrinkles with cosmetics insight. In: Proceedings Eurographics Workshop on Computer Animation and Simulation 2000, pp. 15–27 (2000)
20. Bando, Y., Kuratate, T., Nishita, T.: A simple method for modeling wrinkles on human skin. In: Pacific Graphics 2002 (2002)
21. Larboulette, C., Cani, M.-P.: Real-Time Dynamic Wrinkles. In: Proceedings of Computer Graphics International (CGI 2004), vol. 6(16), pp. 522–525 (2004)
22. Kalra, P., Magnenat-Thalmann, N.: Modeling of Vascular Expressions. In: Computer Animation 1994, pp. 50–58 (1994)
23. Jung, Y., Knopfle, C.: Dynamic aspects of real-time face-rendering. In: Proceedings of the ACM symposium on Virtual reality software and technology, pp. 193–196 (2006)
24. Wang, H., Mucha, P., Turk, G.: Water drops on surfaces. ACM Transactions on Graphics 24(3), 921–929 (2005)
25. Tong, R., Kaneda, K., Yamashita, H.: A volume-preserving approach for modeling and animating water flows generated by metaballs. The Visual Computer 18(8), 469–480 (2002)

26. de Melo, C., Paiva, A.: Multimodal Expression in Virtual Humans. In: Proc. of the Computer Animation and Social Agents 2006 (CASA 2006) Conference and Computer Animation and Virtual Worlds vol. 17(3-4), pp. 239–248 (2006)

27. Bates, J.: The role of emotion in believable agents. Communications of the ACM 37(7), 122–125 (1994)

28. Akenine-Moller, T., Haines, E., Hoffman, N.: Real-Time Rendering, 3rd edn. A. K. Peters, Ltd., Natick (2008)

29. Ekman, P.: Facial expressions. In: Dalgleish, T., Power, M. (eds.) Handbook of Cognition and Emotion. John Wiley & Sons, New York (2003)

30. Rosenthal, R.: Meta-analytic procedures for social research (revised). Sage, Newbury Park (1991)

31. Krumhuber, E., Manstead, A., Cosker, D., Marshall, D., Rosin, P., Kappas, A.: Facial Dynamics as Indicators of Trustworthiness and Cooperative Behavior. Emotion 7(4), 730–735 (2007)

32. Drummond, P.: Correlates of facial flushing and pallor in anger-provoking situations. Personality and Individual Differences 23(4), 575–582 (1998)

33. Ortony, A., Clore, G., Collins, A.: The Cognitive Structure of Emotions. Cambridge University Press, Cambridge (1988)

34. Haidt, J.: The Moral Emotions. In: Davidson, R.J., Scherer, K.R., Goldsmith, H.H. (eds.) Handbook of Affective Sciences, pp. 852–870. Oxford University Press, New York (2003)

35. Morris, M., Keltner, D.: How Emotions Work: The Social Functions of Emotional Expression in Negotiations. Research in Organizational Behaviour 22, 1–50 (2000)

36. Frank, R.: Introducing Moral Emotions into Models of Rational Choice. In: Manstead, A.S., Frijda, N., Fischer, A. (eds.) Feelings and Emotions: The Amsterdam Symposium, pp. 422–440. Cambridge University Press, New York (2004)

Impact of Expressive Wrinkles on Perception of a Virtual Character's Facial Expressions of Emotions

Matthieu Courgeon[1], Stéphanie Buisine[2], and Jean-Claude Martin[1]

[1] LIMSI-CNRS, B.P. 133, 91403 Orsay, France
{courgeon,martin}@limsi.fr
[2] Arts et Métiers ParisTech, LCPI, 151 bd Hôpital, 75013 Paris, France
stephanie.buisine@paris.ensam.fr

Abstract. Facial animation has reached a high level of photorealism. Skin is rendered with grain and translucency, wrinkles are accurate and dynamic. These recent visual improvements are not fully tested for their contribution to the perceived expressiveness of virtual characters. This paper presents a perceptual study assessing the impact of different rendering modes of expressive wrinkles on users' perception of facial expressions of basic and complex emotions. Our results suggest that realistic wrinkles increase agent's expressivity and user's preference, but not the recognition of emotion categories. This study was conducted using our real time facial animation platform that is designed for perceptive evaluations of affective interaction.

Keywords: Facial animation, Evaluation of virtual agents, Affective interaction, Advanced 3D modeling and animation technologies.

1 Introduction

Facial expressions are *"rapid signals produced by the movements of the facial muscles, resulting in temporary changes in facial appearance, shifts in location and shape of the facial features, and temporary wrinkles"* [12]. Since this early definition, facial expressions have been extensively studied. Expressive virtual characters based on Ekman's work are now widely used. However, most virtual agents do not display wrinkles. Indeed, most of them use the MPEG-4 animation system, which does not integrate wrinkles. Thus, few perceptive studies on expressive virtual faces have assessed the role of expressive wrinkles on the perception of emotions. Does their presence vs. absence play a role in emotion decoding? Does expressive wrinkles depth influence emotions perception? Does realism influence user's preference?

This paper presents a perceptive study on the influence of different levels of expressive wrinkles rendering on subjects' perception of emotion. We considered not only basic emotions, but we also explored more complex emotions. A video presenting this study is available on the web[1].

In section 2, we present some related works. We review theories of emotions and studies on the perception of wrinkles in psychology distinguishing permanent and

---

[1] URL : http://www.limsi.fr/Individu/courgeon/static/IVA09/

Zs. Ruttkay et al. (Eds.): IVA 2009, LNAI 5773, pp. 201–214, 2009.

expressive wrinkles. We also provide an overview of virtual character animation and expressive wrinkles generation. Section 3 presents MARC, our interactive facial animation system, extending the MPEG-4 model to display expressive wrinkles and enabling different wrinkle rendering modes. Section 4 presents our experiment, the results of which are discussed in section 5. Section 6 concludes this paper and presents future directions.

2   Related Work

An emotion can be seen as an episode of interrelated, synchronized changes in five components in response to an event of major significance to the organism [31]. These five components are: the cognitive processing, the subjective feeling, the action tendencies, the physiological changes, and the motor expression.

Ekman suggests different characteristics which distinguish basic emotions from one another and from other affective phenomena [10]. He lists distinctive clues for the facial expressions of Surprise, Fear, Disgust, Anger, Happiness, and Sadness [12]. Each of the basic emotions is not seen as a single affective state but rather as a family of related states. Several researchers (Tomkins, Izard, Plutchik and Ekman) consider different lists of fundamental emotions. For example Izard's list includes Contempt, Interest, and Guilt. Five emotions are nevertheless common to the lists proposed by these four researchers (Anger, Disgust, Joy, Fear and Surprise). Baron-Cohen proposes a more general and detailed list of 416 mental states including for example Fascination [13]. Although less literature is available about the facial expressions of these mental states (some of which are called complex emotions by Baron-Cohen), the MindReading database includes 6 audiovisual acted expressions for each of these mental states [13].

In this paper we wish to address the influence of wrinkles on emotional expression or perception. Following Ekman's distinction [9], we consider separately wrinkles as rapid signs vehicles of emotional expression (i.e. when they are temporarily produced by the activity of the facial muscles) and slow sign vehicles (i.e. permanent wrinkles emerging over the life span). Outside Ekman's descriptions of wrinkles in expressions of basic emotions [12], temporary wrinkles are sometimes mentioned anecdotally, e.g. crow's feet typically involved in Duchenne smile [11]. However, we failed to find in psychology literature any formal attempt to model the influence of these temporary wrinkles on emotional expression.

Besides, the role of permanent wrinkles is sometimes discussed in emotional aging research and we briefly review this literature. The dominant theory in this field states that emotional processes (experience and expression) should be submitted to the general decline associated to aging. Self-report surveys from elderly people tend to confirm a decrease in emotional experience, although this decline may arise in different ways for positive and negative affects [14, 25]. Physiological reactions to emotional experience also decline with age [18]. An alternate theory suggests that these phenomena may be due to a greater emotional control rather than a decline [3, 14, 21], but the consequences on emotional expression are the same. Indeed, several experimental data show that elderly people's facial expressions are harder to decode, be they voluntarily elicited [18, 22] or produced by mood-induction procedures [23].

However, opposite results were also reported, showing no difference in emotional expressiveness between older and younger adults [16, 21]. Results from Borod et al. [3] might provide a nice hypothesis to account for such discrepancy as well as for the forementioned theoretical assumptions. These authors instructed young, middle-aged and old women to produce negative, positive emotions, and neutral facial expressions. These posed expressions were subsequently evaluated by independent judges, and the results highlight two opposite phenomena: on the one hand, the expressions of older posers proved to be less accurate and decoded with less confidence than those of younger posers, which is consistent with either a decline of emotional expression over age, or a greater emotional control with more masking and blends. On the other hand, the neutral poses of older subjects were rated as more intense than those of younger people, which can be due to age-related morphological changes in the face, i.e. permanent wrinkles and folds [3]. Furthermore, these permanent wrinkles remaining visible on neutral expressions can convey personality information [22], e.g. anger dominance in a personality trait tends to leave a permanent imprint on the face.

Following this set of results, we can hypothesize that wrinkles should increase facial expressiveness, although in humans this effect is sometimes compensated by a decline or a greater control in emotional expression, possibly resulting in a global absence of difference between young and old peoples' level of expressiveness, or in confusing blends in older people. Therefore, in virtual characters systems, wrinkles are expected to enhance expressiveness, as far as no decline, control or interference process is simulated.

Since the early 70s, research in computer graphics tries to simulate the human face, perceived as a powerful communication tool for human-computer interaction. Parke animated a virtual human face with a short number of parameters [28], creating an animation by linear interpolation of key expressions and using a simple face representation. This method is still used in several systems by interpolating between key expressions or keypoints' position [30]. For example, the MPEG-4 model [27] is widely used for expressive virtual agents [26, 30]. However, interpolation based models have limitations, e.g. the non-compliance to face anatomical constrains. Several approaches were proposed to model multiple layers of the face (e.g. bones, muscles, and skin), e.g. Anatomic models such as Waters' muscles models [37] and Terzopoulos' model [32]. However, they require more computational time than parametric models. Most of these models are not real-time.

In the early 90s, the increasing performance of computers and the emergence of programmable GPUs (Graphic Processing Unit) gave a new impetus to facial animation. Viaud generated procedural expressive wrinkles [34]. Wu simulated skin elasticity properties [39]. Anatomical models also benefited of these new hardware performances, and real-time anatomically accurate models have appeared.

Facial animation addresses another issue: credibility. Synchronized animations all over the face and linear interpolation of facial expressions are perceived as unnatural motions [29]. Pasquariello *et al.* [30] divide the face into 8 areas, and involve a local area animation at different speed rates.

On a real human face, expressions create expressive wrinkles, with varying intensity and depth, depending on age and morphology. However, simple models like

MPEG-4 do not offer a systematic way to simulate wrinkles. Several techniques have been proposed to simulate such effects, and they are not specific to facial animation, e.g. cloth simulation [15]. Wrinkle generation can be divided in two approaches. Firstly, predefined wrinkles, manually edited or captured, and triggered during animation [15, 20]. This technique requires one or several wrinkle patterns for each model. Larbourlette et al. [17] used a compression detection algorithm applied to mesh triangles to trigger predefined wrinkles. The wrinkles progressively appear as the mesh is compressed.

The second main approach is the generative method, e. g. physical computation of muscles and skin elasticity. It does not need predefined wrinkle patterns. This approach is generally much more complex, and requires more computational time. However, the resulting wrinkles are generated automatically, without manual edition [4, 38]. Some physical models are specifically developed for wrinkles generation [38]. In contrast, some models generate wrinkles as a side effect of their anatomically based facial animation system. Several generative models have been proposed, based on length preservation, energy functions [36], or mass-spring systems [40].

As generative models require more computation time, some use the GPU to generate wrinkles [19]. The method is similar to Larboulette's work [17], but the wrinkle pattern is dynamically generated in the GPU. However, this approach uses a large part of GPU capacities that recent facial animation systems need for realistic skin rendering. Combining procedural and generative models, Decaudin et al. [7] propose an hybrid approach for clothes simulation, defining manually folding lines, and generating wrinkles automatically.

Several methods exist to create facial animation and expressive wrinkles. Evaluations of these methods are often limited to technical criteria, such as frame rate, computational complexity, or the fuzzy concept of "realism". However, in a context in which virtual faces are used to convey an affective content, perceptive evaluations are required. As argued by Deng [8], human perception is one the most effective measuring tool for expressivity of a virtual agent. Some perceptive studies provide recommendations for conception and design of virtual agents. For example, studies on the "uncanny valley" [35], assess the interaction between visual and behavioral realism of an agent. The "persona effect"[33] reports how the presence of an agent modifies user's perception of a task and can improve his performance and/or preference. But no such study was conducted on expressive wrinkles. Some studies on complex emotions show that they can modify user's perception. For example, as argued by Becker-Asano [2], agents expressing both basic and complex emotions are perceived to be older than agents expressing only basic emotions.

To summarize, few expressive virtual agents are displaying sophisticated wrinkles. Most of them use the MPEG-4 system, which does not include wrinkles generation. Thus, no detailed studies have been conducted to assess the impact of different features of wrinkles, e.g. depth, visual and dynamic realism. However, the technology to generate such expressive wrinkles does exist. In this paper, we present a perceptual study led with our facial animation platform, extending the MPEG-4 to display dynamic expressive wrinkles. Our study assesses the impact of the presence vs. absence of expressive wrinkles, and the impact of wrinkles realism of the recognition of emotions.

3   MARC: A Facial Animation Platform for Expressive Wrinkles

MARC (Multimodal Affective and Reactive Character)[5] is designed for real-time affective interaction. It relies on GPU programming to render detailed face models and realistic skin lighting. This technique enables a more realistic rendering than most of the existing interactive virtual agents. Our animation system extends the MPEG-4 model [27] and uses additional techniques to render expressive wrinkles. As in the MPEG-4 animation system, key expressions are predefined as a set of keypoints displacements, and our system achieves real-time animation by blending several key expressions. Thus, we can create complex facial expressions from predefined ones. We developed a dedicated offline 3D edition software, enabling direct 3D edition of keypoints position, displacement, and influence on the facial mesh. This software enables manual edition of wrinkles directly on the face. All outputs are compatible with our real-time rendering engine. During online animation, live blends of key expressions are performed. In addition, several automatic features are computed from the dynamic facial expression, e.g. expressive wrinkles activation and eyelids position. Visual realism is achieved using recent graphic computing techniques for skin rendering [6]. We compute real-time simulation of skin translucency (BSSRDF) and cast shadows.

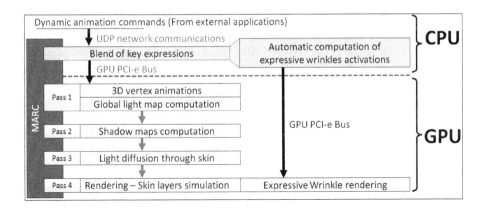

Fig. 1. Rendering and animation pipeline of our animation system

Fig. 1 shows the multi-pass rendering and animation pipeline. Pass #1 performs "per vertex" animation and computes a light map. This map is used in pass #2 to generate shadow maps. Pass #3 simulates light diffusion through the skin to generate final illumination maps. Finally, pass #4 uses all resulting information to render a realistic face and generate wrinkles.

Dynamic facial expression is achieved by blending key expressions. Expressive wrinkles are then triggered from facial deformation. Triggering is based on an adaptation of clothes wrinkling [17] to MPEG-4 facial animation. Instead of computing global mesh compression to deduce wrinkles visibility, we compute the compression of the keypoints' structure to deduce wrinkles visibility. These compression rules are designed to match the different expressive wrinkles described in Ekman's descriptions of facial expressions [12].

Fig. 2 shows the different compression rules. Joy triggers crow's feet wrinkles (C, and F axes) and naso-labial folds (A and B axes). Anger triggers vertical lines between the brows (H axis).

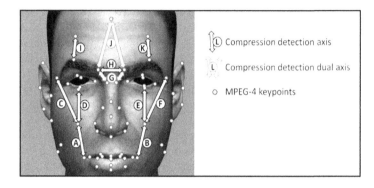

Fig. 2. Compression detection axis for wrinkles triggering

From the compression rules, we obtain wrinkles visibility percentages that we use in the GPU (Pass #4) to draw wrinkles with variable intensity. Our platform enables different modes of rendering. The "No-Wrinkles" mode does not render wrinkles (e.g. only the movements of eyebrows, lips etc. are displayed; the texture remains the same). The "Realistic-Wrinkles" mode renders smooth bumpy wrinkles. The "Symbolic-Wrinkles" mode renders black lines instead of realistic wrinkling effect, generating non realistic but visible wrinkles. Finally, the "Wrinkles-Only" mode is displaying realistic wrinkles without any actual movement on the face (e.g. the face shape remains unchanged, but its texture seems to fold). Fig. 3 shows the Anger expression with all wrinkle modes.

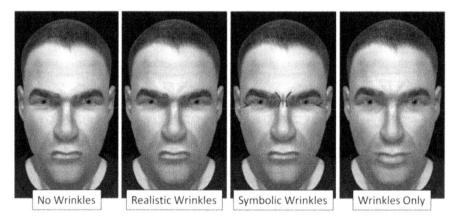

Fig. 3. Anger expression using the 4 wrinkle modes

4 Experiment

Our study aims at assessing the impact of the presence vs. absence of expressive wrinkles, and the impact of expressive wrinkles realism. Facial expressions of basic emotions have been specified in detail including expressive wrinkles [12]. Nevertheless, it has been shown that a larger set of affective states than 6 basic emotions exists [1, 24] . Thus, our goal in this experiment is to study wrinkles effects on a larger set of affect, including some complex emotions (cf. below).

Our first hypothesis is that basic emotions will be better recognized than complex affective states as they were proved to be universally recognized. We also hypothesize that different wrinkles rendering models will show differences in recognition rates. Finally, as we will use different intensities, we suppose that expressions with higher intensities will be better recognized. We defined the full intensity of an expression as the facial movements' threshold over which we perceived the expression as too exaggerated. The low intensity expression is defined as a proportional reduction of full-intensity facial movements. Finally, we hypothesize that differences between wrinkle rendering modes will be less significant with lower emotion intensities.

4.1 Experimental Setup

Participants. 32 subjects (10 females, 22 males), aged from 16 to 40 (25 years old on average, SD=4.6) participated in the experiment.

Material. The expression of 8 emotions were designed: 4 basic emotions (Joy, Anger, Fear, and Surprise) and 4 complex emotions (Interest, Contempt, Guilt, and Fascination). To limit the number of stimuli, only emotions with positive Arousal [24] were selected. We selected a basic emotion and a complex emotion on each quarter of the Pleasure/Dominance [24] space. A facial expression of each basic emotions was defined using Ekman's description [12]. Facial expressions of selected complex emotions (Interest, Contempt, Guilt, and Fascination) were inspired by the MindReading database [1] where each mental state is acted by six actors (we extracted facial expressions features, e.g. brows movements, appearing in at least half of the videos). Emotion categories were selected within the intersection of Russell and Mehrabian [24] set of affective states and Baron-Cohen mental states [1]. This selection method was used in order to have for each emotion its location in the PAD space, and a video corpus of its facial expression.

Each selected emotion was expressed using the 4 wrinkles models (No wrinkle, Realistic wrinkles, Symbolic wrinkles, Wrinkles only) with 2 different intensities. Each animation started with a neutral face, then expressed progressively the current emotion, sustained it for 4 seconds, and got back to a neutral face. Animations were rendered in real-time using 2 nVidia 8800GT graphic cards (SLI), and displayed on a 24" screen with a 1920x1200 pixels resolution. A video describing these stimuli was submitted to IVA 2009 along with the current paper.

Procedure. Subjects were invited to provide some personal information (age, gender, occupation, etc.). The experiment was divided in 2 phases. The first phase consisted in watching successively 64 short animations displaying a facial expression. For each animation, subjects had to select a single label in a set of 16 emotional descriptors. Fig. 4 shows the 16 descriptors we selected as possible answers. 8 were the displayed emotions. 4 adjectives were selected by neutralizing the Pleasure axis or the Dominance axis, and 4 adjectives selected with a negative Arousal.

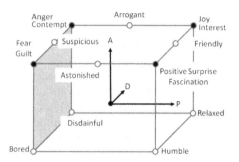

Fig. 4. Selected emotions (*black dots*) and descriptors (*white dots*) in the PAD space

4 animations served as a training session, with no time limit. From the 5th animation, subjects had only 30 seconds to choose a label. We set up this timeout procedure in order to ensure a relative spontaneity of answers and to limit the total duration of the experiment. The presentation order of the 64 stimuli was randomized across the subjects' sample. Participants were allowed to take a short break between 2 animations by clicking on a pause button.

In the second phase, for each emotion, participants were shown static images of the emotional expression at the maximum intensity and using the 4 graphical rendering modes side by side in a randomized order (emotion and rendering). Participants had to rank these renderings modes according to their expressivity level for each emotion. They also had to choose their favorite rendering for each emotion. The whole experiment lasted about 30 to 40 minutes by subject.

Data collected. The recognition of emotion was collected as a binary variable (right answer=1, wrong answer=0). The ranking of expressivity (1st rank representing the stimulus perceived as most expressive) was converted into expressivity scores (1st rank became a 3-point score of expressivity) and the preferences were collected as a binary variable (favorite rendering=1, other=0).

4.2 Results

Recognition performance, Expressivity scores and Preference scores were analyzed by means of ANOVAs with Gender as between-subject variable, Emotional category, Graphical rendering and Intensity as within-subject variables. Fisher's LSD was used for post-hoc pair-wise comparisons. All the analyses were performed with SPSS.

Recognition performance. Among the 64 stimuli × 32 users (i.e. 2048 items), there were 56 timeouts, which corresponds to 2.7% of data. They were analyzed as wrong recognition answers. The average answer time over the whole sample of items was 15.6 seconds (SD=1.99). The global recognition score was 26.6%, the chance level being at 6.25% (drawing lots out of 16 emotional labels). The main effect of Emotional category proved to be significant (F(7/630)=16.24, p<0.001, see Fig. 5 left panel): the recognition score was higher than the chance level, except for Guilt and Fascination (9.3% and 9.8%) whose scores were not significantly different from the chance level.

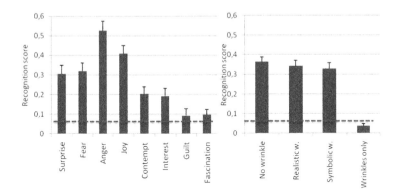

Fig. 5. Global recognition scores for each Emotional category (left panel) and each Graphical rendering (right panel). The dotted horizontal line represents the chance level (0.0625).

Moreover, basic emotions were better recognized (39%) than complex emotions (14.6%, p<0.05). Anger was best recognized (52.7%) among basic emotion (marginally from Joy, p=0.059, and significantly from all other emotions, p<0.002).

The main effect of Graphical rendering was also significant (F(3/630)=59.39, p<0.001, see Fig. 5 right panel): the No-wrinkle, Realistic-wrinkle and Symbolic-wrinkle renderings all enabled equivalent recognition scores, significantly higher than the chance level (34.5%, p<0.001). Conversely the recognition score with Wrinkles-only rendering (3.7%) was not different from the chance level.

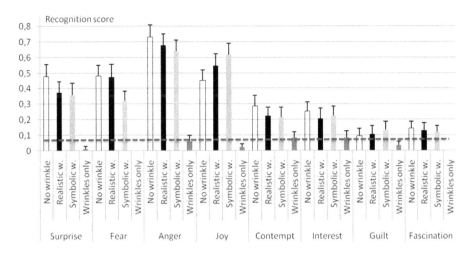

Fig. 6. Recognition scores for each Emotional category × Graphical rendering combination. The dotted horizontal line represents the chance level (0.625).

We also observed an Emotional category × Graphical rendering interaction (F(21/630)=5.27, p<0.001 see Fig. 6), showing that the previous pattern (No-wrinkle, Realistic-wrinkle, and Symbolic-wrinkle renderings equivalent and better than Wrinkles-only rendering) was not true for all emotional categories. For Interest and Guilt there was no effect of graphical rendering. Besides, for Joy the Symbolic rendering gave rise to marginally better performance than the No-Wrinkle rendering (p=0.078). Finally, for the recognition of Fear, the Symbolic rendering was associated to a marginally lower performance than No wrinkle (p=0.065) and Realistic wrinkles (p=0.073).

The stimuli intensity also had a significant influence on the recognition score (F(1/630)=12.01, p=0.002): items displayed with high intensity were better recognized (30%) than items displayed at medium intensity (23.7%). However, an Emotional category × Intensity interaction (F(7/630)=2.95, p=0.006) showed that this pattern was true only for Fear (p<0.001) and Anger (p=0.014). For all other emotions, the Intensity of stimuli had no influence on the recognition performance.

Finally, subject's Gender had no influence on the recognition performance.

Expressivity. Regarding the subjective evaluation of Expressivity, the Graphical rendering proved to have a significant main effect (F(3/630)=97.39, p<0.001, see Fig. 7 left panel). The Realistic-wrinkle rendering was rated as significantly more expressive (2.4/3) than the 3 other renderings (p<0.001). The scores of No-wrinkle and Symbolic-wrinkle renderings (1.6 and 1.7) were not significantly different while the Wrinkles-only rendering was significantly the least expressive (0.2, p<0.001).

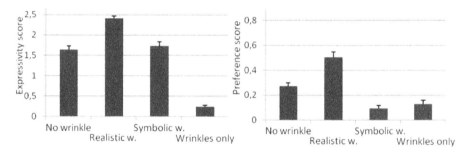

Fig. 7. Expressivity scores (left) and Preference scores (right) for each Graphical rendering

An Emotional category × Graphical rendering interaction (F(21/630)=5.96, p<0.001) showed several patterns according to the Emotional category:

- For Surprise, Guilt and Fascination: the main effect is verified (Realistic wrinkles most expressive; No-wrinkle and Symbolic equivalent; Wrinkles-only least expressive).
- For Fear and Anger: Realistic wrinkles most expressive; Symbolic rendering more expressive than No-wrinkle rendering; Wrinkles-only rendering least expressive.
- For Joy and Contempt: Wrinkles-only is still the least expressive rendering, but no significant difference between the 3 other renderings.
- For Interest: Realistic wrinkles most expressive; then No-wrinkle; Symbolic and Wrinkles-only equivalent and least expressive.

Subject's Gender had no significant influence on Expressivity ratings.

Preferences. The Graphical rendering had a significant main effect on the Preference scores ($F(3/630)=25.80$, $p<0.001$, see Fig. 7 right panel). The realistic wrinkles (with a preference score of 0.51/1) were preferred to the 3 other renderings ($p<0.001$). Then the No-wrinkle rendering (0.27) was preferred to Symbolic wrinkles (0.09) and to Wrinkles-only (0.13, $p<0.001$). Symbolic and Wrinkles-only had equivalent preference scores.

An Emotional category × Graphical rendering interaction ($F(21/630)=2.58$, $p<0.001$) showed 4 preferences patterns according to the Emotional category:

- For Surprise, Fear and Anger: the Realistic rendering is preferred ($p<0.037$) while the 3 other renderings are not different.
- For Joy, Guilt and Fascination: the No-wrinkle rendering is not significantly different from the Realistic rendering.
- For Interest: The difference between the Wrinkles-Only mode and the Realistic mode is not significant.
- For Contempt: The effect of the graphical rendering is not significant, which means that no rendering was consistently preferred.

5   Discussion

Our results provide hints about the validity of our experimental stimuli. The fact that the recognition scores were higher than the chance level tends to validate the design of our animations, except for Guilt and Fascination which were not better recognized than the chance level. Therefore, we will no longer discuss the results about these 2 emotional expressions. When the recognition data about Guilt and Fascination are excluded, the recognition score on the remaining expressions amounts to 32.6%. Such performance level may still seem low, but we would like to underline that only strictly exact answers were taken into account in our analyses and that slight vs. major recognition errors were not distinguished within wrong answers. For example, confusion between Contempt and Arrogance was considered as a wrong answer although people may overlook the difference between the expressions of these emotions. We adopted this conservative rule in order to prevent our data from a ceiling effect and maximize the likelihood of observing differences between our graphical renderings.

The global effect of intensity on recognition scores also tends to validate our stimuli, as high intensities lead to better recognition rates. However, this improvement is only significant for Fear and Anger expressions. Indeed, the recognition of the other emotional expressions is not significantly better with intense stimuli. We hypothesize that our way of manipulating intensity is responsible for this result. High intensity of an emotion may not be expressed only by a wider expression, but using different facial expressions for a single emotion and other modalities, such as head and gaze movements, and skin coloration. Further studies should be conducted to validate this hypothesis.

The main goal of this experiment was to compare several graphical renderings related to wrinkle display. In this respect, the major, original and unexpected result of this study is the effect of renderings on the recognition of emotions. The presence of wrinkles did not improve the recognition performance: neither realistic nor symbolic wrinkles seemed to provide more information than the no-wrinkle rendering. Hence the key factor for facial expression recognition appears to be face movements rather than wrinkles, since the absence of movements (wrinkles-only condition) made the recognition performance dramatically fall to the chance level. However, the realistic-wrinkle rendering proved to be rated as the most expressive and the favorite one of our subjects. Such result is sufficient to ground the usefulness of including realistic wrinkles into virtual characters design. Regarding expressivity, one may wonder why our participants rated realistic rendering as more expressive although it did not provide effective recognition improvement. We hypothesize that these ratings of expressivity were influenced by users' preferences, which may have led them to pick up this rendering first in the ranking exercise of the experiment.

The 3 interaction effects between emotional categories and graphical renderings (on recognition, expressivity and preference scores) provide us with finer information as to whether some renderings fit more or less to particular emotional expressions. However, when synthesizing the results from the 3 variables, some patterns appear inconsistent or confusing; therefore they cannot be used directly as generic design recommendations. For example, for Joy the symbolic wrinkles tended to improve recognition but had lower preference scores than the realistic and no-wrinkle renderings. For Fear, the symbolic wrinkles were rated as more expressive than the no-wrinkle rendering but tended to disrupt the recognition. For Interest, the wrinkles-only rendering obtained a preference score equivalent to that of realistic wrinkles but was rated as least expressive.

Basic emotions were better recognized than complex ones. This can be explained by the lack of detailed descriptions of facial expressions of complex emotions in the literature. We also hypothesize that definition of these emotions are more subjective. Thus, selecting an adjective for these emotions is a fuzzier task.

6 Conclusion and Future Directions

We presented an experiment using our platform for interactive facial animation. Our goal was to evaluate the impact of expressive wrinkles on user's perception of emotion expressed by a virtual character. The major result of this experiment is that wrinkles simulation did not improve categorical recognition of emotions. However, wrinkles influence user's preferences and improve perceived expressivity of a virtual character. We were unable to provide systematic design recommendations for the conception of virtual face, mainly because of the recognition differences between emotions. However, we cannot conclude that wrinkles have no effects on categorical recognition. For this experiment, we only used two kinds of wrinkle simulation, only one "realistic", and none of them were generated by a physical system. Thus, other types of wrinkle simulation may have an effect on categorical recognition. Similar experiments on anatomically accurate wrinkles simulation have to be conducted.

Moreover, our study was limited in several ways. A single emotion was displayed at a time, whereas wrinkles might also have a role to play in the perception of blends of emotions. We only used a male virtual face. We did not consider static wrinkles due to aging. Finally, an emotion was always expressed with one single expression.

To summarize, our study suggests that expressive wrinkles should be realistically rendered on a virtual face, as it improves user's preference and agent's expressivity. Virtual agents are now used in a wide range of applications. It is thus important to take into account such results in the design of expressive virtual agents.

References

1. Baron-Cohen, S.: Mind Reading: The Interactive Guide to Emotions. Jessica Kingsley Publishers (2007)
2. Becker-Asano, C., Wachsmuth, I.: Affect Simulation with Primary and Secondary Emotions. In: Proceedings of the 8th international conference on Intelligent Virtual Agents. Springer, Tokyo (2008)
3. Borod, J., Yecker, S., Brickman, A., Moreno, C., Sliwinski, M., Foldi, N., Alpert, M., Welkowitz, J.: Changes in posed facial expression of emotion across the adult life span. Experimental Aging Research 30, 305–331 (2004)
4. Bridson, R., Marino, S., Fedkiw, R.: Simulation of clothing with folds and wrinkles. In: ACM SIGGRAPH 2005. ACM, Los Angeles (2005)
5. Courgeon, M., Martin, J.-C., Jacquemin, C.: User's Gestural Exploration Of Diffirent Virtual Agents' Expressive Profiles. In: 7th Int. Conf. on Autonomous Agents and Multiagent Systems (AAMAS 2008), Estoril - Portugal (2008)
6. D'Eon, E., Luebke, D.: Advanced techniques for realistic real-time skin rendering. In: nguyen (ed.) GPU Gems, vol. 3, pp. 293–348. Addison Wesley, Reading (2007)
7. Decaudin, P., Thomaszewski, B., Cani, M.-P.: Virtual garments based on geometric features of fabric buckling. In: INRIA (2005)
8. Deng, Z., Ma, X.: Perceptually Guided Expressive Facial Animation. In: SCA 2008: Proc. of SIGGRAPH/EG SCA, pp. 67–76 (2008)
9. Ekman, P.: Facial signs: Facts, fantasies, and possibilities. In: Sebok, T. (ed.) Sight, sound and sense, pp. 124–156. Indiana University Press, Bloomington (1978)
10. Ekman, P.: Basic emotions. In: Dalgleish, T., Power, M.J. (eds.) Handbook of Cognition & Emotion, pp. 301–320. John Wiley, New York (1999)
11. Ekman, P., Davidson, R.J., Friesen, W.V.: The Duchenne Smile: Emotional Expression and Brain Physiology II. Journal of Persotutlity and Social Psychology 50(2), 342–353 (1990)
12. Ekman, P., Friesen, W.V.: Unmasking the face. A guide to recognizing emotions from facial clues. P-H, Englewood Cliffs (1975)
13. Golan, O., Baron-Cohen, S., Hill, J.: The Cambridge Mindreading (CAM) Face-Voice Battery: Testing Complex Emotion Recognition in Adults with and without Asperger Syndrome. Journal of Autism and Developmental Disorders 36(2) (2006)
14. Gross, J.J., Carstensen, L.L., Pasupathi, M., Tsai, J., Götestam-Skorpen, C., Hsu, A.Y.C.: Emotion and aging: Experience, expression and control. Psychology and Aging 12, 590–599 (1997)
15. Hadap, S., Bangerter, E., Volino, P., Magnenat-Thalmann, N.: Animating wrinkles on clothes. In: Proceedings of the conference on Visualization 1999: celebrating ten years. IEEE Computer Society Press, San Francisco (1999)
16. Kunz, M., Mylius, V., Schepelmann, K., Lautenbacher, S.: Impact of age on the facial expression of pain. Journal of Psychosomatic Research 64, 311–318 (2008)
17. Larboulette, C., Cani, M.-P.: Real-Time Dynamic Wrinkles. Computer Graphics International (2004)

18. Levenson, R.W., Carstensen, L.L., Friesen, W.V., Ekman, P.: Emotion, physiology, and expression in old age. Psychology and Aging 6, 28–35 (1991)
19. Loviscach, J.: Wrinkling coarse meshes on the GPU. CGF 25, 467–476 (2006)
20. Maddock, S., Edge, J., Sanchez, M.: Movement realism in computer facial animation. In: 19th British HCI Group Annual Conference, Workshop on Human-animated Characters Interaction (2005)
21. Magai, C., Consedine, N.S., Krivoshekova, Y.S., Kudadjie-Gyamfi, E., McPherson, R.: Emotion experience and expression across the adult life span: Insights from a multimodal assessment study. Psychology and Aging 21, 303–317 (2006)
22. Malatesta, C.Z., Fiore, M.J., Messina, J.J.: Affect, personality, and facial expressive characteristics of older people. Psychology and Aging 2, 64–69 (1987)
23. Malatesta, C.Z., Izard, C.E., Culver, C., Nicolich, M.: Emotion communication skills in young, middle-aged, and older women. Psychology and Aging 2, 193–203 (1987)
24. Mehrabian, A., Russell, J.A.: Evidence for a three-factor theory of emotions. Journal of Research on Personality, 273–294 (1977)
25. Mroczek, D.K.: Age and emotion in adulthood. Current Directions in Psychological Science 10, 87–90 (2001)
26. Niewiadomski, R., Ochs, M., Pelachaud, C.: Expressions of empathy in eCAs. In: Prendinger, H., Lester, J.C., Ishizuka, M. (eds.) IVA 2008. LNCS (LNAI), vol. 5208, pp. 37–44. Springer, Heidelberg (2008)
27. Pandzic, I., Forchheimer, R.: MPEG-4 Facial Animation: The Standard, Implementation and Applications. John Wiley & amp; Sons, Inc, Chichester (2003)
28. Parke, F.I.: A parametric model for human faces. Univ. of Utah (1974)
29. Parke, F.I.: Parameterized Models for Facial Animation. IEEE Comput. Graph. Appl. 2(9), 61–68 (1982)
30. Pasquariello, S., Pelachaud, C.: Greta: A Simple Facial Animation Engine. In: 6th Online world conf. on soft computing in industrial applications (2001)
31. Scherer, K.R.: Emotion. In: Stroebe, M.H.W. (ed.) Introduction to Social Psychology: A European perspective, pp. 151–191, Blackwell, Oxford (2000)
32. Terzopoulos, D., Waters, K.: Analysis and Synthesis of Facial Image Sequences Using Physical and Anatomical Models. IEEE Trans. Pattern Anal. Mach. Intell. 15(6), 569–579 (1993)
33. Van Mulken, S., André, E., Müller, J.: Persona Effect: How Substantial Is It? In: Proceedings of HCI on People and Computers XIII. Springer, Heidelberg (1998)
34. Viaud, M.-L., Yahia, H.: Facial animation with wrinkles (1992)
35. Walters, M.L., Syrdal, D.S., Dautenhahn, K., te Boekhorst, R., Koay, K.L.: Avoiding the Uncanny Valley. Robot Appearance, Personality and Consistency of Behavior in an Attention-Seeking Home Scenario for a Robot Companion. Journal of Autonomous Robots 24(2), 159–178 (2008)
36. Wang, Y., Wang, C.C.L., Yuen, M.M.F.: Fast energy-based surface wrinkle modeling. Computers & Graphics 30(1), 111–125 (2006)
37. Waters, K.: A muscle model for animation three-dimensional facial expression. In: Proceedings of the 14th annual conference on Computer graphics and interactive techniques. ACM, New York (1987)
38. Wu, Y., Magnenat Thalmann, N., Thalmann, D.: A dynamic wrinkle model in facial animation and skin ageing. Journal of Visualization and Computer Animation 6(4), 195–205 (1995)
39. Wu, Y., Thalmann, N.M., Kalra, P.: Simulation of static and dynamic wrinkles of skin. In: Proceedings of Computer Animation 1996, pp. 90–97 (1996)
40. Zhang, Y., Prakash, E., Sung, E.: Real-time physically-based facial expression animation using mass-spring system. Computer Graphics International 2001 (2001)

Real-Time Crying Simulation

Wijnand van Tol and Arjan Egges

Games and Virtual Worlds group
Utrecht University, the Netherlands
wijnandvantol@gmail.com, egges@cs.uu.nl

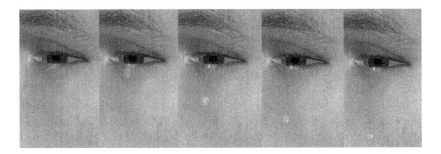

Fig. 1. A few frames from a tear rolling over the character's face. Both the fluid and trail are clearly visible. Also note the reduction in tear volume over time.

Abstract. Displaying facial motions such as crying or laughing is difficult to achieve in real-time simulations and games. Not only because of the complicated simulation of the physical characteristics such as muscle motions or fluid simulations, but also because one needs to know how to control these motions on a higher level. In this paper, we propose a method that uses the MPEG-4 Facial Animation standard to control a realistic crying face in real-time. The tear simulation is based on the Smoothed Particle Hydrodynamics technique, which we optimized for real-time tear generation and control. Through simple parameters, a wide range of expressions and tears can be generated on the fly. Additionally, our method works independently of the graphics and physics engines that are used.

1   Introduction

Virtual characters in games and simulations are becoming more realistic, not only through more detailed geometry but also because of better animations. Due to motion capturing and automatic blending methods, both facial and body motions can be displayed convincingly. One of the main goals of using virtual characters in 3D environments is to make an affective connection with the user.

Zs. Ruttkay et al. (Eds.): IVA 2009, LNAI 5773, pp. 215–228, 2009.

An important aspect of establishing this connection between the virtual character and the user is by using emotions. Virtual characters are already capable of displaying a variety of emotions, either by employing different body motion styles[1] or facial expressions[2]. However, the range of emotions for virtual characters is still quite limited. For instance, more extreme expressions such as laughing out loud, screaming in anger, or crying are rarely seen in games. The absence of these extreme expressions results in a less emotionally involving experience, as opposed to movies, where such expressions are used regularly to entice the viewer.

Displaying extreme expressions is a complicated task. It requires precise muscle modeling and skin deformation, and in the case of crying: real-time fluid simulation that realistically interacts with the face. Because of the technical challenges, few games try to incorporate extreme expressions, and if they do, it is mostly done by using manually defined motions. In this paper, we propose a system for automatically generating and displaying crying motions in real-time. We achieve this by using a real-time fluid simulation method, which we optimized for crying synthesis. We will also show that with a simple extension of the MPEG-4 facial animation standard[2], the real-time crying engine can be controlled by an animator, without having any knowledge of the physical processes that govern the crying simulation.

This paper is organized as follows. In the next section, we will discuss related research. Section 3 describes our real-time crying simulation method. In Section 4, we discuss how to control the crying engine as a part of an MPEG-4 facial animation engine. Then, some results of our approach are shown in Section 5. Finally, we present our conclusions and recommendations for future work.

2 Related Work

In order to accurately reproduce crying motions for virtual characters, we first need to determine what the phenomena of crying are and when crying occurs. There have been several studies that investigate why people cry, and these have been summarized by Vingerhoets et al. [3]. In particular, we would like to mention Borgquist [4] who did a study among students, which pointed out three mood states in which crying occurs: anger, grief or sadness, and joy. He also pointed out accompanying physical states such as fatigue, stress and pain. Young [5] studied crying on college students, but made no clear distinction between moods and situations. He classified the reasons for crying as follows: disappointment, lowered self esteem, unhappy mood, organic state, special events and laughter to the point of tears. William and Morris [6] proposed a list of possible crying inducing events or moods, containing situations such as deaths of intimates, broken love relations or sad movies. Nelson [7] states that adult crying is mostly associated with grief, but makes a distinction between angry and sad crying. Also, much research has been done on crying behavior in infants[8], which is usually related to a need for attention, however in this paper we will focus on crying in adults. Tears are a very important aspect of crying. This is explained by Vingerhoets in [9]. People will more easily identify the emotions associated with crying if the subject is indeed crying. Another phenomenon of crying is sobbing. Sobbing is the convulsive inhaling and exhaling of air with spasms of the respiratory muscle groups. This is, for example, explained by Patel [10]. Other phenomena include an increased heart rate and flow of blood to the head, as researched by Ax [11].

Expressions and emotions are clearly very important for visualizing crying. If one wants to simulate crying convincingly, a facial animation system that can reproduce expressions effectively is paramount. Facial animation is a research domain that started around the 1970s with the pioneering work done by Parke [12]. Several facial animation techniques have also been developed that try to abstract from the geometrical model. Apart from basic key-frame animation, models have been developed based on muscle physics [13] as well as a pseudo-muscle approach [14]. Not only the model used to deform the face is of importance. Also a system of parameterization is required so that animations can be played on different faces. Several parameterizations have been proposed, notably the Facial Action Coding System (FACS) [15], which was originally a way of describing expressions, and the MPEG-4 standard [16]. The MPEG-4 standard generally uses geometrical deformation of the face vertices according to a set of Facial Animation Parameters (FAPs). Because of the existing work already done on MPEG-4 facial animation [2,17,18] and the generic way of controlling facial motions, we have adopted the MPEG-4 standard in this work.

A major drawback of any existing facial animation engine is that they only allow for geometrical deformation of a face mesh. For displaying a crying motion, a more elaborate animation model is required, involving a physical simulation of fluids. Fluid simulation can be done in different ways, the most common approaches are grid-based (Eulerian) and particle-based methods. Grid-based simulations, such as [19], use a grid of points connected by springs. For each point at each time step, the next position is calculated using Euler integration. Grid based simulations for liquids usually involve Navier-Stokes equations to calculate the momentum of the fluid, and need additional formulas to conserve the mass and energy of the system. These computations can be quite complex. Additionally, the grid-based approach is not suitable for simulating drops of water, since multiple meshes are required. A more popular method for simulating such types of fluids is based on particles.

The Smoothed Particle Hydrodynamics (SPH) approach [20] is a particle-based method that uses particles with a fixed mass. Each particle represents a volume, which is calculated by dividing the mass by the density of the particle. SPH is a very general method which can be used for any application where field quantities have to be calculated. Müller [21] proposed a method where he applies SPH to fluid simulation. He uses SPH to solve a simplified version of the Navier-Stokes Equations, which describe the dynamics of fluids. By calculating the density of the fluid at discrete particle locations, the pressure and viscosity of the fluid, as defined by the Navier-Stokes Equations, can be evaluated anywhere in space. An additional advantage of the SPH method is that the simulation can be partially implemented on the GPU [22]. While the physical behavior is simulated by the particle system, the visualization step is generally done by applying a point-splatting technique [23] or a marching cubes algorithm [24]. SPH is a suitable approach for simulating smaller bodies of water such as drops or tears. However, a challenge lies in integrating this method into a facial animation engine, in a way that allows an animator to control the fluid behavior as a part of the facial animation. Also, existing visualization techniques do not take interaction with the skin into account. Finally, real-time performance is a requirement for such an integrated system.

In the next section, we will propose a novel SPH approach, optimized for the simulation of crying motions. Our tear simulation technique takes the skin into account by defining an additional skin adhesion force, as well as a realistic tear trail synthesizer. Furthermore, we show that the crying engine can be controlled through simple parameters, similar to controlling facial animations using the MPEG-4 standard.

3   Real-Time Crying Simulation

In this section, we will present our SPH-based real-time crying engine. First we will discuss the generic SPH approach and our added extensions for the physical simulation of tears and their interaction with the skin. Next, we will discuss the visualization of the fluid using marching cubes and a simple method for simulating the trail of a teardrop.

3.1   Smoothed Particle Hydrodynamics

We will first briefly explain the SPH-based method proposed by Müller et al.[21]. The SPH method consists of a few basic steps to be executed for each frame. First, the densities of the particles need to be calculated based on their current position. Then, the pressure and viscosity forces of the Navier-Stokes equations have to be calculated for each particle. In [21], also an additional surface tension force is suggested for better fluid stability. Finally the external forces, such as gravity and collision have to be applied to the particles. Then, a scalar field based on the location of the particles is defined to estimate the surface and the normal of the simulated fluid. Following [21], we will call this scalar field the *color field* in the remainder of this paper. The color field can be visualized using a mesh generation algorithm, such as marching cubes [24] or point-splatting [23].

The Navier-Stokes equations calculate the velocities of the fluid anywhere in the area of the fluid. Since these are continuous functions for calculating velocity fields, they need to be discretised. Smoothed Particle Hydrodynamics uses discrete particle locations at which field quantities are defined. The value of the field can then be calculated anywhere in space using smoothing kernels, which distribute the quantities in the neighborhood of a particle. A smoothing kernel is a function which returns a value for a position anywhere in space based on the distance of that position to the center of the smoothing kernel. A scalar quantity A at location $\mathbf{r}$ is defined by a weighted sum of all the particles as shown in the following formula:

$$A\left(\mathbf{r}\right) = \sum_j m_j \frac{A_j}{\rho_j} W\left(\mathbf{r} - \mathbf{r}_j, h\right).$$

(1)

where j iterates over all particles, m_j and ρ_j are the mass and density of particle j and $\mathbf{r}_j$ its location. The scalar quantity A_j is the discrete field quantity at location $\mathbf{r}_j$. The function $W\left(\mathbf{r} - \mathbf{r}_j, h\right)$ is called the smoothing kernel with a maximum influence radius of h. The smoothing kernel gives us a value based on r, the distance between $\mathbf{r}$ and $\mathbf{r}_j$. This means that the smoothing kernel are centered at the particle j. Any r larger than h will produce a value of 0, meaning that particle j has no influence on location $\mathbf{r}$ if the distance between them is more than h. The gradient of a smoothing kernel, $\nabla W\left(\mathbf{r}, h\right)$, gives us a vector in the direction of the center of the kernel. This gradient can be seen as the change in influence of this particle, and the direction of this change. This is needed in some equations where derivatives of a field quantity are needed. To find the density at any location $\mathbf{r}$ in a scalar field, the following function is used:

$$\rho\left(\mathbf{r}\right) = \sum_j m_j W\left(\mathbf{r} - \mathbf{r}_j, h\right).$$

(2)

We use the location of a particle for $\mathbf{r}$ to get the density of a particle. So before calculating the forces, we first need to calculate the density of all the particles.

According to [21], particles have three forces acting on them: the pressure, the viscosity and finally the external forces. The main external forces used in our simulation are gravity and friction. The pressure force on a particle is the derivative of the pressure at the location of the particle. By applying Equation 1 and using p for the scalar quantity, the pressure force on particle i is calculated as follows:

$$\mathbf{f}_i^{\text{pressure}} = -\sum_j m_j \frac{p_i + p_j}{2\rho_j} \nabla W\left(\mathbf{r}_i - \mathbf{r}_j, h\right).$$

(3)

The pressure values at the particle locations, p_i and p_j, are calculated by multiplying the density ρ of the particle with a gas constant k. Note that we use the derivative of the smoothing kernel, since this results in the direction of the change of pressure. Also, [21] made some modifications to this formula to achieve a more stable simulation. For the viscosity force equations, we also need to know the velocity of the other particles. The viscosity causes particles to adjust their velocity to match each other, and is present in the Navier-Stokes equations with the term $\mu \nabla^2 \mathbf{v}$, where μ is the viscosity constant for the fluid. Using SPH, the viscosity force can be found using the following equation:

$$\mathbf{f}_i^{\text{viscosity}} = \mu \sum_j m_j \frac{\mathbf{v}_j - \mathbf{v}_i}{\rho_j} \nabla^2 W\left(\mathbf{r}_i - \mathbf{r}_j, h\right).$$

(4)

where $\nabla^2 W\left(\mathbf{r}_i - \mathbf{r}_j, h\right)$ is the derivative of the gradient, or: the Laplacian of the kernel. The velocities of the particles i and j are given by $\mathbf{v}_i$ and $\mathbf{v}_j$.

Müller also defines another force called the surface tension. This force is not in the original Navier-Stokes equations. It is used to balance the forces on the surface of the fluid, so that a cohesive fluid is guaranteed. Normally in a fluid, all the molecules are pulled toward each other but because the forces come from every direction they balance each other. The molecules on the surface, on the other hand, are only pulled by the particles 'below' them, causing them to be pulled inwards. This is the surface tension of a fluid. In order to calculate the surface tension force, a representation of the surface represented by the particles is needed. This surface is estimated by defining the color field, which is 1 at particle locations and 0 at every other location. By applying Equation 1 and substituting A_j by 1, a smoothed color field can be computed at any location with the following equation:

$$c_s\left(\mathbf{r}\right) = \sum_j m_j \frac{1}{\rho_j} W\left(\mathbf{r} - \mathbf{r}_j, h\right). \tag{5}$$

The gradient of the color field can be computed at any location ($\mathbf{r}$) in the color field, but the gradient will only be significant near the surface of the fluid. Inside the fluid, because there are a lot of particles, the color field will be 1 or almost 1 everywhere, so the gradient will be small. Near the surface, the color field will go from 1 to 0 over the course of h, the smoothing kernel size. So the color field gradient $\mathbf{n}$ of the smoothed color field, shown in Equation 6, will point inward in the direction of the normal of the surface. The surface normals can be determined by evaluating $\mathbf{n}$ near the surface, normalising $\mathbf{n}$ and inverting it. The smoothed color field can later also be used for identifying and visualising the surface of the fluid.

$$\mathbf{n} = \nabla c_s. \tag{6}$$

The surface tension depends on the curvature of the surface κ and a tension coefficient σ, which depends on the two materials (in this case air and water) that form the substance. The curvature of the surface κ is the divergence of the surface normal, also the Laplacian of the smoothed color field, and is given by the following equation:

$$\kappa = \nabla \frac{-\mathbf{n}}{|\mathbf{n}|} = \frac{-\nabla^2 c_s}{|\mathbf{n}|} \tag{7}$$

And this leads to the formula for the surface tension field as follows:

$$\mathbf{f}_i^{\text{surface}} = \sigma \kappa \mathbf{n} = -\sigma \nabla^2 c_s \frac{\mathbf{n}}{|\mathbf{n}|} \tag{8}$$

To calculate the surface tension on particle i, we need to evaluate the surface normal and the Laplacian of c_s at location $\mathbf{r}_i$, which is the location of particle i. Note that this force should only be applied on particles near the surface, since the normals at other locations are meaningless.

Once the hydrodynamic forces for the particles are computed, we can apply the external forces. In the original SPH approach [21], only gravity and a collision force are defined. The method does not take friction into account. After contact with a surface, a particle is simply sent in a direction mirroring its incoming direction on the surface. The reflected particle is kept in place by the particles above it, resulting in a stable simulation. However, in the case of tears, we are dealing with a limited number of particles, which leads to an unstable fluid simulation. To solve this we chose to apply friction to the particles as an additional external force in our simulation. A benefit of this is that the friction can be handled by the physics engine.

Another external force that is missing is adhesion. In real life, the small molecular forces between the water and a surface cause the water to stick to the surface. The lack of skin adhesion causes the particles to lose contact with the surface as soon as the surface starts facing downward. We approximate this behavior by adding a force to the particles that are in contact with the skin surface. The direction of this force is in the opposite direction of the normal of the skin surface (thereby attracting the particles into the skin). The formula for this force is as follows:

$$\mathbf{f}_i^{\text{adhesion}} = -\alpha \frac{\mathbf{n}_s}{\rho_i}. \tag{9}$$

where $\mathbf{n}_s$ is the normal of the skin surface and α is a coefficient which determines how adhesive the surface is. Because the density ρ of a particle is taken into account, the attraction to the surface depends on the volume a particle represents. A lower density means a particle represents a larger volume, which means that a larger area of fluid contacts the skin, causing a stronger adhesion to the skin for the particle.

3.2   Mesh Generation

In the previous section we discussed how the physical behavior of tears are simulated using the SPH method, extended with a skin adhesion force. The second step is to visualize the fluid by generating a mesh. Two established methods exist to render the surface generated by the particle system. One is point splatting [23] and the other is the marching cubes algorithm [24]. The point splatting technique is more efficient than the marching cubes approach, but it requires an extension of the renderer. Our goal is to make our implementation so that it would be independent of the render engine. This means we are using the marching cubes algorithm to visualize the isosurface of the fluid. The marching cubes algorithm can be used to visualize an isosurface of a scalar field, such as the color field generated by SPH. The algorithm traverses the scalar field through a grid. At each point on this grid, the algorithm samples 8 neighboring locations, forming an imaginary cube, then moves to the next 'cube' on the grid. Each of the points on a cube has a value in the scalar field. The isosurface is determined by an iso-value. If the value of a point is higher than the iso-value it is inside the surface, otherwise it is outside the surface. So a cube can be fully inside the surface, if all the points have a higher value than the iso-value, fully outside it, or partially inside it. Through rotations and reflections there are only 15 unique polygon configurations for a cube [24], formed by the points determined by the iso-values. The next step is calculating the correct normals for each polygon. Since the mesh is created for the isosurface of the smoothed color field c_s, we can use the gradient of the smoothed color field at the location of the vertices as the normal. Finding the normal is done using Equation 6 and explained in the previous subsection.

By traversing the grid and creating the right polygons and normal for each cube a mesh is generated that resembles the isosurface. Because marching cubes is not as efficient as point splatting, the number of particles in the simulation needs to be limited to ensure real-time operation. In order to maximize this number, we propose an optimization to the marching cubes technique.

Using marching cubes in a traditional grid means that we will probably have a lot of empty cells because of the space that the tear can pass through is quite large in comparison to the tear. This is computationally very expensive because even the empty cells have to be checked during the marching cubes algorithm. In order to avoid this extra cost, we store the particles in an octree. By giving the octree a maximum depth, and keeping track of the nodes that contain particles at the maximum depth, we use only those nodes for the marching cubes algorithm. However, using an octree for the marching cubes algorithm introduces a problem. Some cells that do not contain particles need to be checked as well during the marching cubes algorithm, because the particles have an influence on the smoothed colorfield based on their smoothing kernel (see Figure 2). To solve

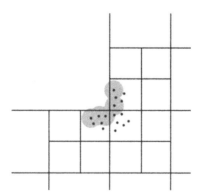

Fig. 2. Not only the cubes with particles in them need to be checked for the marching cubes algorithm. The blue circles around the particle show their area of influence and show that cubes without particles are within their influence.

this problem we slightly change the octree data structure. We add a particle to a node if it is within distance h of a node, where h is the size of the smoothing kernel of a particle. This is shown in Figure 3. This way, when we check the particles of a certain node, we only need check them against the other particles

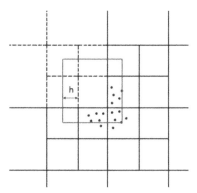

Fig. 3. Our addition to the oct-tree data structure. Nodes now contain particles that are within h of their boundaries.

that belong to the node. An additional advantage is that this representation also speeds up the calculation of the forces on the particles. To avoid checking the same particle several times (since a particle can belong to several nodes now), we keep track of which particles of a node are actually inside the node.

3.3   Fluid Trail Synthesis

In real life, a water drop leaves a trail as it slides down a surface. This is partly because of the adhesive force. Water molecules stick to the surface, decreasing the volume of the drop. A simulation with that level of detail requires a very large number of particles, so creating a trail by using particles is nearly impossible. Therefore, we created a method that simulates the trail and the decreasing volume of a tear. The method identifies all the different drops of the tear and then it stores their boundaries. These boundaries are then used to create a mesh which represents the trail.

Every step, we first identify the different tear drops and which particles are part of which drop. To identify a drop, we take a random node from a list of nodes with particles in them. We add the particles in this node to the collection of particles that create this drop and flag this node as checked. Then we look at its neighboring cells and do the same if they contain particles. We repeat this until we do not find any new neighboring cells with particles in them, meaning we have found a complete drop. From the collection of particles that are part of this drop, We store the right- and leftmost particle. Then, we select a new random node from the nodes we have not checked yet and repeat the algorithm to find a new drop. We repeat this until we have run out of nodes.

For each drop, we now have the leftmost en rightmost position. We will call those the boundaries of the teardrop. We will use those points to create a mesh which represents the trail of the drop. First, we create a point in the middle of the boundary and we elevate this point slightly in the direction of the normal of

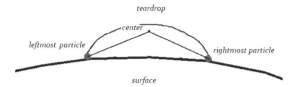

Fig. 4. A schematic top view of a teardrop. The particles which are marked red are the left- and right most particles of the drop. These are the basis for the left- and rightmost points of the trail. As seen, the middle point is slightly elevated, to make the trail appear to have a volume and lying on top of the skin.

the skin. The middle point can not be raised more than h, the smoothing kernel size. This would cause the trail to become thicker than the teardrop itself. The positioning of these points is best explained in Figure 4.

Every frame, we create these three points. With those three points and the points from the previous frame, we create four triangles, which simulate a small part of the trail. If we do this every frame, a complete trail of the teardrop will be created.

Calculating a new part of the trail every frame will be a waste of triangles and computation time. So first, at every frame, we compute the new boundaries of the tear. We store the boundaries of this tear only if the distance d between the current and previously stored center is larger than d_{min}, a variable we set beforehand. This variable resembles the minimum distance a teardrop has to travel before creating a new part of the trail. Only then do we create a new set of triangles for the trail, using the previous and the new boundaries of the drop.

A result of a drop leaving a wet trail is that it reduces in size because of the water molecules that stick to the surface. Because we do not simulate the trail with particles, we have no accurate way of diminishing the size of the drop. Because of this we alter the mass of the particles in the drop, based on how far the drop has traveled over the surface. Decreasing the mass has two important effects. First, the mass has an effect on the density and pressure of the particle. This causes a particle to represent a smaller volume of liquid, making the teardrop smaller. Second, a lower mass causes friction to have a greater effect on the particle. So the further a tear travels the slower it will most likely go, depending on obstacles and gravity.

4   Controlling Crying Motions

In the previous section we explained how a tear is simulated using an extended version of SPH in combination with a marching cubes algorithm. Equally important is how we control the generation of these tears. First we will present how we control the amount of tears that are generated. Then we will identify some physical parameters which control the shape and behavior of the tear.

4.1 MPEG-4 Facial Animation

The MPEG-4 Facial Animation Standard is a simple and effective way of describing facial expressions, by defining a set of FAPs that control different logical areas of the face. Through these FAPs, an animator can quickly generate facial expressions without having to think about the geometrical deformations of the face mesh. The goal of our approach is to be able to have a similar way of controlling tears, but we do not want the animator to have to think of the physical behavior of tears. To show that this is possible, we have added two additional FAP parameters, one for each eye. The value of each FAP represents the number of particles that are present at that frame in the animation. This way, the animator has complete control over the lifespan and the number of particles that are generated by the crying engine, for both left and right eyes. In addition, the source of both tear generating FAPs can be set, so that the animator can choose from where on the face tears are generated. Since the focus of this paper is not on the facial animation itself, we used a geometrical deformation method as discussed in [2].

4.2 Physical Parameters

A lot of different physical parameters are involved in simulating a fluid. In this section, we try to give an overview of these parameters and how they affect the simulation. First, one has to provide the four main parameters for the four forces used in our implementation of SPH. These are the pressure, the viscosity, the surface tension and the adhesion. The pressure determines how wide the particles of the tear will spread. Using a high pressure will result in large tears with low density particles. The viscosity will determine how strongly the particles drag each other along and stay together as one drop. The surface tension will also keep the particles together, but is less sensitive to obstacles and friction than the viscosity force. A high skin adhesion force means that the tear will follow the surface of the face better and will be more affected by friction. The friction parameter itself is the most direct way of controlling how fast a tear moves across the skin. Next to these forces, one also has to choose the size of the smoothing kernel of a particle. A lower value for this will result in a more incoherent particle system because particles have less influence on each other. This value also influences the color field, so a smaller value means that the mesh will follow the actual shape of the particles more closely.

Next to the previously discussed physical parameters, the mesh generation system also introduces some parameters. The node size determines how small the octree nodes containing the particles will be. A smaller node size results in more nodes but this can speed up the force calculations if the kernel size is small. Second, the marching cube size needs to be set to a value smaller than or equal to the octree node size. A smaller marching cube size results in a finer mesh. Finally, we also set an iso-value in the marching cubes algorithm.

A higher iso-value results in a smaller mesh, following the particles more closely. The tear trails are generated automatically and they do not introduce additional parameters. In the next section, we will propose a few sample settings of these parameters that result in realistic tear simulation.

5 Results

We ran our simulation on a Pentium 4 Duo CPU 2.66 Ghz with 4 Gb RAM. We generated tears consisting of 100 particles and achieved an average frame rate of 12.7 fps. For these tests we used a pressure of $0.4e-2$, a viscosity of 0.9, a tension of 0.2 and an adhesion of 20. The friction of the skin was set at 3.8. The size of the marching cubes value was half that of the node size. The iso-value was set to 0.02. We set the kernel size to 0.5. The values of these parameters are mostly found by trial and error, since in our application, the real physical properties of water did not produce satisfying results. This may be because we have a small number of particles or because the weight of the particles is different from the weight of amount of water they represent. For each eye, a particle source is defined. The position of the sources is set at the middle of each eye. Finally, we added a blending texture to simulate the moist skin around the eyes. We created a texture to represent wet or irritated skin, and used alpha blending to mix it with the existing texture of the face. The alpha value of this texture depends on the number of particles that is generated. The results of this can be seen in Figure 5 and Figure 1. Additional examples, rendered in real-time, can be seen in the accompanying demonstration video[1].

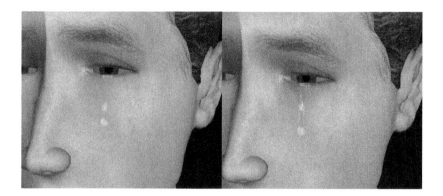

Fig. 5. An example of real-time trail synthesis. In the left image, only the fluid simulation is shown. In the right image, the automatically generated tear trail is shown. In addition, we used a subtle texture blend to represent wetness and irritation of the skin.

---

[1] http://people.cs.uu.nl/egges/files/Crying.wmv

6   Conclusions

We have presented a real-time crying simulation framework, by using an extended SPH approach, optimized for crying fluid simulation. Our framework integrates with an existing facial animation system, and it is independent of the renderer and physics engine that is used. The shape of the fluid and the material used create a convincing simulation of tears. By adding a skin adhesion force, the motion of the tear neatly follows the skin without falling off. Also, the addition of a wet trail is a great improvement to the realism of the tear. Because of the easy integration with existing facial animation frameworks, animators will be able to control crying motions using only a few parameters in addition to the FAP values as defined in the MPEG-4 standard.

Although we have set the first steps in the direction of creating a more expressive face, a lot of work still needs to be done. In this paper we have mainly focused on generating fluids to simulate tears, but our current method for simulation tear-skin interaction is limited. If someone cries, this effect is still visible after a while. In order to correctly simulate this, more elaborate skin modeling is required. Second, extreme expressions such as laughing and crying are difficult to simulate convincingly without properly modeling muscle motions. In the future, we are going to look at what muscle motions are important in crying and laughing animations in order to improve our simulation, while retaining the real-time constraint. Finally, another important consideration is the control of the facial expression and tears. As we have discussed, several motivations and emotions are related with crying. An interesting research objective would be to investigate how such motivations and emotion can be incorporated in embodied conversational agents, so that tears and crying motions may be controlled automatically.

Acknowledgements

This research has been supported by the GATE project, funded by the Netherlands Organization for Scientific Research (NWO) and the Netherlands ICT Research and Innovation Authority (ICT Regie).

References

1. Egges, A., Magnenat-Thalmann, N.: Emotional communicative body animation for multiple characters. In: First International Workshop on Crowd Simulation (V-Crowds), pp. 31–40 (2005)
2. Garchery, S., Magnenat-Thalmann, N.: Designing mpeg-4 facial animation tables for web applications. In: Multimedia Modeling 2001, May 2001, pp. 39–59 (2001)
3. Vingerhoets, A.J.J.M., Cornelius, R.R., van Heck, G.L., Becht, M.C.: Adult crying: a model and review of the literature. In: Review of General Psychology, vol. 4(4), pp. 354–377. Educational Publishing Foundation (2000)
4. Borgquist, A.: Crying. American Journal of Psychology 17, 149–205 (1906)

5. Young, P.T.: Laughing and weeping, cheerfulness and depression: A study of moods among college students. Journal of Social Psychology 8, 311–334 (1937)
6. Williams, D.G., Morris, G.H.: Crying, weeping or tearfulness in british and israeli adults. British Journal of Psychology 87, 479–505 (1996)
7. Nelson, J.K.: The meaning of crying based on attachment theory. Clinical Social Work Journal 26(1), 9–22 (1998)
8. Barr, R.G.: Crying behaviour and its importance for psychosocial development in children (2006)
9. Vingerhoets, A.J.J.M.: Adult Crying, A Biopsychosocial Approach. Psychology Press (2001)
10. Patel, V.: Crying behavior and psychiatric disorder in adults: A review. Comprehensive Psychiatry 34(3), 206–211 (1993)
11. Ax, A.F.: The physiological differentiation between fear and anger in humans. Psychosomatic Medicine 14(5), 433–442 (1952)
12. Parke, F.I.: Computer generated animation of faces. In: Proceedings ACM Annual Conference, pp. 451–457. ACM Press, New York (1972)
13. Platt, S.M., Badler, N.: Animating facial expression. Computer Graphics 15(3), 245–252 (1981)
14. Noh, J.Y., Fidaleo, D., Neumann, U.: Animated deformations with radial basis functions. In: Proceedings of the ACM Symposium on Virtual Reality Software and Technology, pp. 166–174. ACM Press, New York (2000)
15. Description of facial action coding system,
    http://face-and-emotion.com/dataface/facs/description.jsp
    (accessed November 2007)
16. Mpeg-4 standard homepage,
    http://www.chiariglione.org/mpeg/standards/mpeg-4/mpeg-4.htm
    (accessed January 2009)
17. Kshirsagar, S., Garchery, S., Magnenat-Thalmann, N.: Feature point based mesh deformation applied to mpeg-4 facial animation. In: Proceedings Deform'2000; Workshop on Virtual Humans by IFIP Working Group 5.10 (Computer Graphics and Virtual Worlds), pp. 23–34. Kluwer Academic Publishers, Dordrecht (2000)
18. Lavagetto, F., Pockaj, R.: The facial animation engine: towards a high-level interface for the design of mpeg-4 compliant animated faces. IEEE Transactions on Circuits and Systems for Video Technology, 277–289 (March 1999)
19. Chen, J.X., da Vitoria Lobo, N., Hughes, C.E., Moshell, J.M.: Real-time fluid simulation in a dynamic virtual environment. IEEE Computer Graphics and Applications 17(3), 52–61 (1997)
20. Monaghan, J.J.: Smoothed particle hydrodynamics. Annual review of astronomy and astrophysics 30, 543–574 (1992)
21. Müller, M., Charypar, D., Gross, M.: Particle-based fluid simulation for interactive applications. In: SCA 2003: Proceedings of the 2003 ACM SIGGRAPH/Eurographics symposium on Computer animation, Aire-la-Ville, Switzerland, pp. 154–159. Eurographics Association (2003)
22. Harada, T., Koshizuka, S., Kawaguchi, Y.: Smoothed particle hydrodynamics on gpus. Computer Graphics International (2007)
23. Zwicker, M., Pfister, H.P., van Baar, J., Gross, M.: Surface splatting. In: SIGGRAPH 2001, pp. 371–378 (2001)
24. Lorensen, W.E., Cline, H.E.: Marching cubes: A high resolution 3rd surface construction algorithm. In: SIGGRAPH 1987: Proceedings of the 14th annual conference on Computer graphics and interactive techniques, pp. 163–169. ACM, New York (1987)

Breaking the Ice in Human-Agent Communication: Eye-Gaze Based Initiation of Contact with an Embodied Conversational Agent

Nikolaus Bee, Elisabeth André, and Susanne Tober

Institute of Computer Science, Augsburg University,
86135 Augsburg, Germany
{bee,andre}@informatik.uni-augsburg.de

Abstract. In human-human conversation, the first impression decides whether two people feel attracted by each other and whether contact between them will be continued or not. Starting from psychological work on flirting, we implemented an eye-gaze based model of interaction to investigate whether flirting tactics help improve first encounters between a human and an agent. Unlike earlier work, we concentrate on a very early phase of human-agent conversation (the initiation of contact) and investigate which non-verbal signals an agent should convey in order to create a favourable atmosphere for subsequent interactions and increase the user's willingness to engage in an interaction with the agent. To validate our approach, we created a scenario with a realistic 3D agent called Alfred that seeks contact with a human user. Depending on whether the user signals interest in the agent by means of his or her gaze, the agent will finally engage in a conversation or not.

1 Introduction

In human-human conversation, the first impression decides whether two people feel attracted by each other and whether contact between them will be continued or not. A large industry has developed around the production of training material that intends to give advice to people that wish to present themselves in a positive light to new people (for example, see [Cohen, 1992], for a guidebook on flirting). A recommendation that can be found in almost any guidebook that prepares people for such first encounters, whether be it in a date or a job interview, is to show a genuine interest in the conversational partner using eye gaze and smiles. In this way, instant rapport is built up which creates a good starting point for subsequent interactions (see [Argyle and Cook, 1976] and [Kleinke, 1986]).

Recently, there has been a significant amount of work on embodied conversational agents that make use of non-verbal behaviors to establish rapport with a human user. There is empirical evidence that rapport-building tactics also work for human-agent communication, see, for example, [Gratch et al., 2006]. Most work focuses on the use of non-verbal signals during a dialogue taking it for

Zs. Ruttkay et al. (Eds.): IVA 2009, LNAI 5773, pp. 229–242, 2009.

granted that the human has an interest in communicating with the agent. Unlike earlier work, our paper concentrates on a very early phase of human-agent communication (the initiation of contact) and investigate which non-verbal signals an agent should convey in order to create a favourable atmosphere for subsequent interactions and increase the user's willingness to engage in an interaction with the agent. In particular, we are interested in the question of whether it is possible to give a human user the feeling that an agent has a genuine interest in him or her. We consider work on flirt tactics as a useful resource to implement agents that have these capabilities.

To validate our approach, we created a scenario with a realistic 3D agent called Alfred that seeks contact with a human user. Depending on whether the user signals interest in the agent by means of his or her gaze, the agent will finally engage in a conversation or not. Alfred is able to convey emotional and attentive states via facial displays, head movements and gaze shifts. In addition, we employ a contact-free eye tracker that provides us continuously with information on the user's eye gaze. In order to use means to analyze and generate social signals effectively, the agent has to sense the user's eye gaze and to align it in parallel with its own behaviors. The challenge of our work is to tightly synchronize the agent's non-verbal behaviors with the user's non-verbal feedback.

2   Related Work

So far, embodied conversational agents have rarely been used as flirt partners. An exception includes the work by [Pan and Slater, 2007] who present a virtual party-like environment in which a female character called Christine approaches a male user and involves him into a conversation. The character shows her interest into the male user by smiles and head nods. She leans her upper body forward towards the user, looks at him and maintains eye contact with him. After some time, the character moves closer and formulates personal questions and statements. Using physiological measurements, [Pan and Slater, 2007] found out that the participants' level of arousal was correlated to compliments and intimate questions of the character. In addition, some of them indicated in a questionnaire that they had the feeling to have flirted with a real woman.

Unlike Pan and Slater, we do not make use of a full-body character, we just show the upper body of the agent in order to make sure that the users are able to perceive the subtle signals in the agent's face. Furthermore, Pan and Slater's agent is not fully responsive since it is not able to recognize the user's eye gaze. Finally, the courtship behaviors of our agent are much more subtle concentrating on eye gaze behaviors and light smiles. We are less interested in the simulation of flirting per se, but rather aim at investigating to what extent courtship behaviors may contribute to the creation of instant rapport.

[Gratch et al., 2006] developed a so-called rapport agent which acts as a silent listener. The agent tries to create rapport by providing rapid non-verbal feedback, expressed by head nods, posture shifts and eye gaze behaviors, through a shallow real-time analysis of the human's voice, head motion and body posture. An empirical study revealed that the agent increased speaker fluency and engagement.

The robotic penguin developed by [Sidner et al., 2004] is able to track the face of the conversational partner and adjusts its gaze towards him or her. Even though the set of communicative gestures was strongly limited, an empirical study revealed that users indeed seem to be sensitive to a robots conversational gestures and establish mutual gaze with it.

While most research focuses on how to create rapport in short-term interactions, [Cassell and Bickmore, 2003] investigate how to establish and maintain a relationship between a user and an agent over a series of conversations. They performed a series of experiment with a virtual character acting as a real-estate agent which revealed that the character's use of social language had an important impact on the creation of rapport.

Most studies analyzing the user's non-verbal feedback behavior make use of head trackers. They are able to roughly assess in which direction the user is looking, but do not have more detailed information on the user's eye gaze direction. One of the earliest work of using eye trackers for agent-based human interaction comes from [Starker and Bolt, 1990]. They adapt "The Little Prince" to the users current interest in a virtual scene that shows one planet from the story by Antoine de Saint-Exupéry. Dependent on the duration and focus of the user's gaze further details of the scene are described via a text-to-speech system. Another exception includes the work by [Eichner et al., 2007] who made use of an eye tracker. In an experiment, they showed that agents that adapted the content of their presentation to a user's eye gaze were perceived as more natural and responsive than agents that did not have that capability.

The studies above show that embodied conversational agents are to a certain extent able to establish rapport with human conversational partners through appropriate verbal and non-verbal behaviors. Unlike the approaches described above, we focus on the first seconds of an encounter and investigate how to create a friendly and natural atmosphere for human-agent communication by appropriate courtship behaviors of the agent. We make use of an eye tracker to monitor the user's gaze behaviors. A particular challenge of our work is to align and synchronize the user's gaze behaviors with the agent's courtship behaviors.

3   Eye Gaze Model for Human-Agent Interaction

As a basis for our research, we rely on the approach by [Givens, 1978] who distinguishes between five phases of flirting:

- The *attention phase* describes the phase in which men and women arise each other's attention. It is characterized by ambivalent non-verbal behavior, such as a brief period of mutual gaze broken by downward eye aversion, reflecting the uncertainty of the first seconds.
- In the *recognition phase*, one interactant recognizes the interest of the other. He or she may then disencourage the other interactant, for example, by a

downward gaze, or signal readiness to continue the interaction, for example, by a friendly smile.

- After mutual interest has been established, the man or woman may be initiated the *interaction phase* and engage in a conversation.
- In the *sexual-arousal* and *resolution phases*, the relationship between man and woman intensifies. These two phases are not further described here because of their missing relevance to human-agent communication.

Our system will cover the attention, recognition and the initiation of the interaction phase. In addition to the work by Givens, our eye gaze based interaction system incorporates findings from [Tramitz, 1992] and [Bossi, 1995]. In particular, we rely on their work to determine the timing of gazes. [Tramitz, 1992] analyzed the flirt behavior in a study with 160 school students. She found that the initiation of a first encounter decides on the continuation of the flirt interaction. [Bossi, 1995] used the same study but analyzed couples with different levels of interest on each other. Flirting couples seemed to use more time, up to three times, to gaze at each other. Further, the first gaze and following single gazes lasted longer.

Attention Phase. The implementation of the attention phase (see Fig. 1 left) is motivated by typical behavior sequences described in [Givens, 1978]. The attention phase starts at the point when the human and the virtual agent take notice of each other. The virtual agent shows a slightly friendly facial expression and the gaze is averted from the user. First, the agent's eyes only wander around

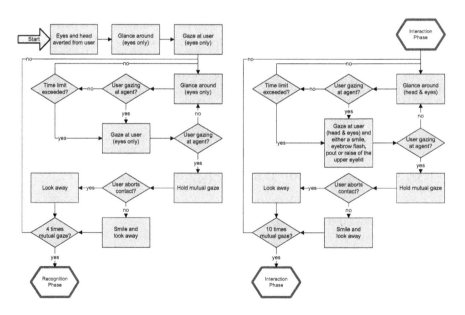

Fig. 1. Attention phase (left) and recognition phase (right)

the room for a while until they meet the user's eyes. After that, the virtual agent will engage in an interplay of mutual and averted gaze.

While the virtual agent gazes randomly around the room, the system checks whether the user gazes at the agent. If this is the case, the agent establishes gaze contact with the user. The system is now in the hold-mutual-gaze-state and the agent tries to hold eye contact until a specified time interval elapses. It then breaks off eye contact by a downward gaze accompanied by a smile. To avoid that unconscious very brief sweep gaze behaviors of the user are by mistake categorized as mutual gaze, eye contact with the user will be taken into account only after a certain duration. In case the user breaks off eye contact before the maximal time interval elapses, the agent will look away as well, however, without showing a smile since the user would not recognize the facial expression anymore. If the user does not respond to eye contact established by the agent, the agent will avert its gaze again. After each successful or failed eye contact, the system will return to the state of looking around trying to establish eye contact again or to respond to the user's eye gaze.

This loop is repeated until one of the following terminating conditions is fulfilled. In the positive case, a certain number of mutual gazes could be established and the system transits to the next phase. In the negative case, the agent has attempted to established gaze contact with user in vain and breaks off the complete interaction due to missing interest of the human flirt partner. After each successful gaze contact, the emotional state of the agent improves and its facial display becomes more joyful. After each failed attempt to establish gaze contact, the emotional state of the agent becomes worse and it looks more sad.

Recognition Phase. Similar to the attention, the recognition phase (see Fig. 1 right) is based on the interplay between mutual and averted gaze behavior, save that the durations of the mutual gazes increase. Further, the virtual agent smiles more often and uses more distinct flirt signals (i.e. eyebrow flash, pout or raise of the upper eyelid). Since the agent's self confidence has increased after the successful attention phase, it tries to establish eye contact more often and eye movements are supported by head movements to show a more obvious interest in the human interactant. Just as the attention phase, the recognition phase can still fail. Namely, in case the agent unsuccessfully tried to establish mutual gaze for several times. Or, if a particular number of mutual gazes has been set up, the recognition phase was successful and completed. This will lead to the next phase, which is the interaction phase.

Interaction Phase. After successfully completing the two previous phases, verbal communication will be initiated in the interaction phase. The virtual agent verbally addresses the user using small talk strategies adopted from [Tramitz, 1992].

4   System

The system for eye gaze based interaction between the virtual agent and human consists of an eye tracker, an virtual character and the program logic for the interaction. We use a contact-free eye tracker (SMI iView X RED) which allows the user to move relatively free.

4.1   Eye Tracker

The SMI iView X RED eye tracker operates with sampling rate of 50 Hz, the latency for a gaze point is less than 35 ms and the tracking accuracy is less than 0.5°. The distance between the eye tracker and the user should be about 60 - 80 cm [SMI, 2008]. The advantages of an unobtrusive, contact-less eye tracker include that users do not have to wear a sometimes bulky apparatus and thus are not steadily reminded that their gaze is tracked. Further, the SMI iView X RED eye tracker allows head movements horizontally and vertically up to 20 cm in each direction.

4.2   Virtual Agent

We used a fully controllable virtual head which was developed by Augsburg University and which is freely available [Augsburg University, 2008]. The head is based on Ekman and Friesen's Facial Action Coding System (FACS). FACS was developed to classify human facial expressions [Ekman and Friesen, 1975]. It divides the face into action units (AU) to describe the different expressions a face can display (e.g. inner brow raiser, nose wrinkler, or cheek puffer). Although FACS was originally designed to analyze natural facial expressions, it turned out to be usable as a standard for production purposes, too. That is why FACS based coding systems are used with the generation of facial expressions displayed by virtual characters, like Kong in Peter Jackson's King Kong. But the usage of FACS is not only limited to virtual characters in movies. The gaming industry with Half-Life 2 by Valve also utilizes the FACS system to produce the facial expressions of their characters.

Alfred (see Fig. 2), a butler-like character, uses the FACS to synthesize an unlimited set of different facial expressions. The action units were designed using morph targets and thus gives the designer the full power in defining the facial expression outlook. The system includes a tool to control the single action units [Bee et al., 2009]. The tool allows to store the result in a XML file for later usage in our agent system.

Alfred's mesh has a resolution of about 21.000 triangles. For displaying more detailed wrinkles in the face, normal maps baked from a high-resolution mesh are used. The morph targets for the action units are modeled using the actor's templates from the [Facial Expression Repertoire, 2008] (FER).

4.3   System for Interaction

To be able to detect where the user is looking at, we connected the eye tracker with the virtual 3D-world. Ray casting allows us to map the screen coordinates obtained from the eye tracker to the objects in the virtual world. In this vein, we are able to detect whether the user looks at the virtual agent, the left eye or

Fig. 2. The virtual character Alfred with a skyline in the background

the right eye or something else in the virtual scene. This was necessary for the eye gaze based interaction on a level of mutual gaze and to see, if the user is looking at Alfred or not.

The flirt behavior can be varied by parameters. A confidence value defines the agent's level of self assurance and influences the probability that the agent initiates gaze interaction. The maximal and minimal duration of mutual gaze can be set as well. Furthermore, we may indicate the maximal duration the virtual agent gazes around. For the attention and recognition phases, the maximum number of trials to initiate mutual gaze before it fails can be defined. Finally, we may specify how long the virtual agent waits until the user responds with mutual gaze. These parameters are stored in a XML file and can be easily adjusted.

The virtual agent is able to direct his gaze using his eyes only or his head and his eyes in combination.

Flirt signals are displayed whenever mutual gaze occurs. In the attention phase, flirt signals are rarely sent whereas in the recognition phase, flirt signals are an integral part of the interaction. Whenever mutual gaze occurs, the virtual agent sends with a probability of $1/3$ one of the following flirt signals: an eyebrow flash, a pout, a raise of the upper eyelid or a smile.

The agent's mood changes dependent on the number of successful mutual gazes. The more mutual gazes occur, the friendlier Alfred's facial expression becomes. Vice versa, the agent's happiness declines if there is no reaction from the user to an attempt to establish mutual gaze.

5   Evaluation

We conducted an empirical study to demonstrate the benefits of eye gaze based interaction in combination with flirting tactics. Our main focus was to figure out if the users realize the virtual agent's interest. Further, we would like to investigate the impact of an eye gaze based interaction system on user engagement. Finally, we were interesting in finding out whether an eye gaze based interaction system works with a life-size setting. Thus, the study focuses on the following points:

1. The flirting agent is able to show the user that it has an interest in him through its gaze and facial expression behavior, and the user will perceive this behavior as flirting.
2. The integration of flirting tactics has a positive impact on the perception of the agent and the interaction with him and thus contributes to the user's engagement.
3. By tracking the user's eye gaze and responding to it in real-time, the effects can be increased.

5.1   Setting

The optimal dimensions for such a video projector based eye tracking setting are limited. The user is placed in front of a table on which the eye tracker was placed. The eye tracker with an incline of 23° is placed 80 cm above ground and 140 cm away from the projection surface. The user is seated 60 - 80 cm in front of the eye tracker. In total the user is about 2 m away from the virtual agent, which is within the *social space* according to [Hall, 1963]. The projection surface sizes 120 × 90 cm, which displays the virtual agent in life-size (see Fig. 3).

To avoid that the user automatically stares at the virtual agent (which would happen if it was placed in the center of the visual display), we placed it on the left side. To offer an enriched scene where the user has the choice to look away from the virtual agent, we added a city skyline (see Fig. 2).

Interaction Modes. Apart from the fully interactive version where the agent recognizes and responds to the user's eye gaze behavior in real-time, two further gaze behavior variants were created to demonstrate the benefits of the gaze behavior model described in Section 3: a non-interactive version which implements an *ideal* flirt behavior derived from the literature and a non-interactive version which implements an *anti-flirt* behavior.

In the non-interactive ideal version the virtual agent behaves like in the interactive version except for that it does not respond to the user's eye gaze behavior, but assumes a perfect eye gaze behavior from the user and thus follows a fixed sequence. The gaze directions while glancing around the scene are still randomly selected, but the virtual agent gazes at the user always with the same duration, no matter whether the user returns the gaze or not.

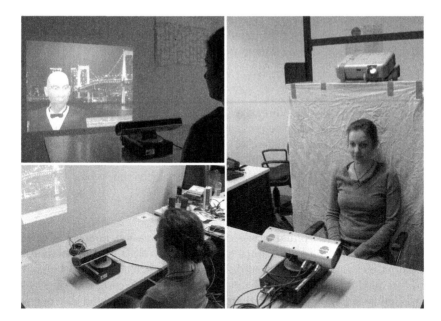

Fig. 3. Set-up for the eye gaze based interaction application from different perspectives

In the non-interactive anti-flirt version, by contrast, the virtual agent behaves contrarily to the typical flirt behaviors previously described. The duration of the mutual gaze is increased from 3 seconds to 7 seconds, which is commonly considered as staring. Furthermore, the facial expression remains neutral, which can be interpreted as a bored attitude towards the user. Finally the virtual agent looks away upwards after gazing at the user instead of downwards.

We had to disable the break after an unsuccessful attention phase in the interactive version as the interaction duration would have been significantly shorter and thus not comparable to the two non-interactive versions.

5.2   Study

For the study, we recruited 16 subjects, solely women due to the male virtual counterpart, and presented them with all three interaction modes. The order of the three interaction modes (i.e. *interactive, non-interactive ideal* and *non-interactive anti-flirt*) was randomized for each subject to avoid any bias due to ordering effects. The procedure was as follows: First, the subjects were asked to fill in the first part of the questionnaire about demographic data. After placing the subjects in front of the eye tracker, a calibration, which took less than 2 minutes, was carried out. The subjects were told that they would be presented with a flirting agent and should try to engage in a flirt with the agent themselves using their eye gaze. They were informed that they would have to run the interaction sequence three times, but they did not know that there were different modes of interaction. After accomplishing one interaction sequence, the subjects had to fill in a post-sequence questionnaire about the interaction with the virtual agent. The study took about 20 minutes including the calibration for the eye tracker and answering the questionnaire.

5.3 Questionnaire

The post-sequence questionnaire used 13 attitude statements with a 5-point Likert scale to evaluate how the participants perceived the interaction with the system. The questions were related to the user's engagement of the interaction (five questions: E1 – E5), the exclusion of external influences (three questions: I1 – I3) and the quality of the gaze behavior model (five questions: Q1 – Q5).

5.4 Results

The analyses of the questionnaires were based on the one-way analysis of variance (ANOVA) across the different groups and the Tukey-HSD for the posthoc two-sided pairwise comparisons. Two subjects had to be excluded from the analysis due to technical difficulties with the eye tracker. In their case, the eye tracking data stream was discontinuous and thus the interactive version did not work properly.

Engagement of the Interaction. The one-way ANOVA for the questions regarding the engagement revealed significant differences among the means for question E1 ($F(2, 39) = 3.02, p < 0.05, \eta^2 = 4.02$), E2 ($F(2, 39) = 6.07, p < 0.01, \eta^2 = 6.5$), E3 ($F(2, 39) = 5.98, p < 0.01, \eta^2 = 6.38$) and E5 ($F(2, 39) = 3.35, p < 0.05, \eta^2 = 2.31$). E4 did not reveal significant differences. The Tukey-HSD posthoc test for pairwise comparisons revealed a significant difference for E1 between the *interactive* and *anti-flirt* mode ($p < 0.05$), for E2 between the *interactive* and *anti-flirt* mode ($p < 0.01$) and for E3 between the *ideal* and *anti-flirt* mode ($p < 0.05$) and the *interactive* and *anti-flirt* mode ($p < 0.01$).

Questions E1 – E5 (see Fig. 4) were related to the users' engagement in the eye gaze interaction with the virtual agent. All these questions resulted into a higher mean for the interactive mode, where the agent's gaze behavior was aligned to the user's eye gaze. In the interactive mode, the subjects rated Alfred's eye gaze behavior and mimics more realistic (E1) and enjoyed the interactions with Alfred more (E2). Furthermore, they uttered a higher interest in continuing the interaction with Alfred (E3) and in actually engaging in a conversation with him (E4). They also thought that their own interaction behavior was more natural in the interactive mode than in the two non-interactive modes.

Exclusion of External Influences. The one-way ANOVA for the questions (I1 – I3) regarding the exclusion of external influences revealed no significant differences (see Fig. 4). Unaffected by the mode of interaction, the subjects felt hardly watched by the equipment (I1). Furthermore, they gave similar subjective ratings for their flirting capabilities independent from the mode of interaction

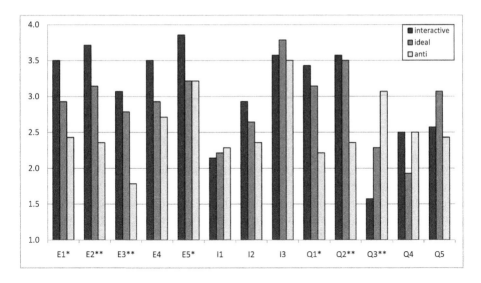

Fig. 4. Results of the questionnaire for the interactive, non-interactive ideal and non-interactive anti-flirt mode ($^*p < 0.05$, $^{**}p < 0.01$)

(I2) which we take as further evidence that they did not feel more disturbed in the interactive version. Finally, in all three modes of interaction, the subjects had the feeling that Alfred was looking into their eyes when he was looking at them (I3). Consequently, we can exclude artefacts due to different user sizes and the resulting different positions relative to the agent.

Quality of the Gaze Behavior Model. The one-way ANOVA tests reveal significant differences for all questions regarding the quality of the gaze behavior model, for question Q1 ($F(2, 39) = 4.27$, $p < 0.05$, $\eta^2 = 5.64$), Q2 ($F(2, 39) = 5.27$, $p < 0.01$, $\eta^2 = 6.5$) and Q3 ($F(2, 39) = 6.00$, $p < 0.01$, $\eta^2 = 7.88$). The Tukey-HSD posthoc test for pairwise comparisons reveals significant difference for Q1 between the *interactive* and *anti-flirt* mode ($p < 0.05$), for Q2 between the *ideal* and *anti-flirt* mode ($p < 0.05$) and the *interactive* and *anti-flirt* mode ($p < 0.05$) and for Q3 between the *interactive* and *anti-flirt* mode ($p < 0.01$).

Questions Q1 and Q2 referred to the ability of the virtual agent to convey interest through its gaze behavior and mimics. The subjects had the impression that Alfred was more interested in them (Q1) and flirting more with them (Q2) in the interactive version than in the other two versions. Nevertheless, they did not have the feeling that Alfred's gaze behaviors were obtrusive (Q3).

Q4 and Q5 did not reveal any significant differences. The subjects felt that the agent gazed at them directly (Q4) and was interactive (Q5) with a medium score in all three conditions. Surprisingly, the user did not perceive the interactive agent as more interactive even though this agent was more positively rated (E1 – E5).

5.5   Analyzing the User's Eye Gaze Behavior During the Interaction

In the following, we perform a more careful analysis of the interactive mode. Here, the overall interaction took between 59.1 and 107.8 seconds, 82.6 seconds on average. The first part of the interaction was completed on average after 24.5 seconds (17.1 seconds minimum and 32.0 seconds maximum) which corresponds to the observation by [Tramitz, 1992] that the first 30 seconds of an interaction lay the foundations for further interactions.

As it turned out, the user was more pro-active than the agent in establishing and breaking off eye contact. In 76.9% of the cases, the gaze contacts were initiated by the human user. In 85.7% of the cases, the human user decided to break off eye contact.

Four subjects did not execute downward gazes after breaking off eye contact which are typical of flirting situations. Also the remaining candidates showed this behavior only one to three times.

Not every attempt to establish gaze contact also led to mutual gaze. Each subject experienced at least once (at a maximum five times) the situation that the agent did not respond to his or her attempt to establish mutual gaze. As a reason we indicate that the user was averting his gaze immediately after meeting the agent's eyes. That is in some cases, Alfred's response came too late. On the other hand, in 12 out of 14 interactions, it happened only once that the agent tried in vain to establish eye contact.

5.6   Discussion

Overall, the experiment led to promising results. In the interactive and the ideal mode, the agent was able to show the users that he had an interest in them and the users also had the feeling that he was flirting with them (Hypothesis I). Furthermore, we found that the effect was increased when moving from the ideal to the interactive mode (Hypothesis II). Although significant differences were only detected between the interactive and the anti-flirt version, the means of the interactive version were always rated higher than the ideal version and the means of the ideal version were always rated higher than the anti-flirt version. In addition, the experiment revealed that the interactive version contributed to the user's enjoyment, increased their interest to continue the interaction or even to engage in a conversation with Alfred even though the differences were only significant for the interactive and the anti-flirt version (Hypothesis III). The users did not have the feeling that the agent was significantly more responsive in the interactive than in the non-interactive versions. The result is in conflict with a result we obtained for an earlier experiment with an eye-gaze controlled agent. In the earlier experiment, the interactive agent was perceived as more responsive than the non-interactive agent. The subjects felt, however, also more disturbed by the perceptive agent [Eichner et al., 2007]. Obviously, the users enjoyed the interactive version more and found it more engaging without perceiving it, however, as more interactive. The higher level of engagement was also reflected by the users' behavior. We were seeking more often for eye contact with the agent than in the non-interactive versions. Furthermore, the subjects found the inter-active agent more realistic and indicated that it was more natural to interact with it.

6   Conclusion

In this paper, we presented an eye-gaze based interaction model for embodied conversational agents which incorporates studies of flirting in human-human in-teraction. The approach was tested using a 3D character that enables realistic gaze behaviors in combination with expressive mimics. We successfully inte-grated an eye tracker in a life-size application with a quite huge interaction screen display. The contact-free eye tracker has proven appropriate and reliable for a life-size interactive setting with a large interaction screen display. It was not perceived as intrusive or disturbing and thus the users could interact in a relatively natural manner. As we did not give the subjects special instructions how they should behave in front of the eye tracker, they moved freely without taking care of the eye tracker. The usage of such eye tracker is promising, as only 2 of 16 subjects had to be removed from the recordings as the eye tracker did not work trouble-free with them.

To enable smooth interactions, a high amount of alignment and coordination was required. In particular, the agent had to sense and respond to the user's gaze behavior in real-time. Despite of the technical challenges involved in this task, the interactive version was perceived as more natural than the non-interactive versions. The user's also had the impression that the agent had an interest in them without perceiving it as obtrusive. Both subjective user ratings as well as objective user observations revealed that the users were more eager to continue interaction with the agent.

Usually, attractiveness is considered as a prerequisite for successful flirting. Our subjects rated Alfred as sympathetic, but also little attractive. Nevertheless, the incorporation of flirting tactics has proven beneficicial. Thus, this can be taken as evidence that the flirting tactics as implemened in this work are of benefit to a much broader range of situations with agents than just dating, e.g. initiate human-agent interaction or regulating turn-taking in dialogues.

Acknowledgements

This work has been funded in part by the European Commission under grant agreement IRIS (FP7-ICT-231824).

References

Argyle and Cook, 1976. Argyle, Cook: Gaze & Mutual Gaze. Cambridge University Press, Cambridge (1976)
Augsburg University, 2008. Augsburg University, Horde3D GameEngine (2008), http://mm-werkstatt.informatik.uni-augsburg.de/projects/GameEngine/

Bee et al., 2009. Bee, N., Falk, B., André, E.: Simplified facial animation control utilizing novel input devices: A comparative study. In: International Conference on Intelligent User Interfaces (IUI 2009), pp. 197–206 (2009)

Bossi, 1995. Bossi, J.: Augen-Blicke. Zur Psychologie des Flirts, Huber, Bern (1995)

Cassell and Bickmore, 2003. Cassell, J., Bickmore, T.W.: Negotiated collusion: Modeling social languageand its relationship effects in intelligent agents. User Model. User-Adapt. Interact. 13(1-2), 89–132 (2003)

Cohen, 1992. Cohen, D.: Body Language in Relationships. Sheldon Press (1992)

Eichner et al., 2007. Eichner, T., Prendinger, H., André, E., Ishizuka, M.: Attentive presentation agents. In: Pelachaud, C., Martin, J.-C., André, E., Chollet, G., Karpouzis, K., Pelé, D. (eds.) IVA 2007. LNCS (LNAI), vol. 4722, pp. 283–295. Springer, Heidelberg (2007)

Ekman and Friesen, 1975. Ekman, P., Friesen, W.: Unmasking the Face. Prentice Hall, Englewood Cliffs (1975)

Facial Expression Repertoire, 2008. Facial Expression Repertoire, Filmakademie Baden-Württemberg (2008), http://research.animationsinstitut.de/

Givens, 1978. Givens, D.B.: The nonverbal basis of attraction: flirtation, courtship, and seduction. Psychiatry 41(4), 346–359 (1978)

Gratch et al., 2006. Gratch, J., Okhmatovskaia, A., Lamothe, F., Marsella, S., Morales, M., van der Werf, R., Morency, L.P.: Virtual rapport. In: Gratch, J., Young, M., Aylett, R.S., Ballin, D., Olivier, P. (eds.) IVA 2006. LNCS (LNAI), vol. 4133, pp. 14–27. Springer, Heidelberg (2006)

Hall, 1963. Hall, E.T.: A system for notation of proxemic behavior. American Anthropologist 65, 1003–1026 (1963)

Kleinke, 1986. Kleinke, C.L.: Gaze and eye contact: A research review. Psychological Bulletin 100(1), 78–100 (1986)

Pan and Slater, 2007. Pan, X., Slater, M.: A preliminary study of shy males interacting with a virtual female. In: PRESENCE 2007: The 10th Annual International Workshop on Presence (2007)

Sidner et al., 2004. Sidner, C.L., Kidd, C.D., Lee, C., Lesh, N.: Where to look: a study of human-robot engagement. In: IUI 2004: Proceedings of the 9th international conference on Intelligent user interfaces, pp. 78–84. ACM Press, New York (2004)

SMI, 2008. SMI. SMI iView X RED (2008),
http://www.smivision.com/en/eye-gaze-tracking-systems/products/
iview-x-%red.html

Starker and Bolt, 1990. Starker, I., Bolt, R.A.: A gaze-responsive self-disclosing display. In: CHI 1990: Proceedings of the SIGCHI conference on Human factors in computing systems, pp. 3–10. ACM, New York (1990)

Tramitz, 1992. Tramitz, C.: Auf den ersten Blick. ADMOS Media GmbH (1992)

An Approach for Creating and Blending Synthetic Facial Expressions of Emotion

Meeri Mäkäräinen and Tapio Takala

Helsinki University of Technology
P.O. Box 5400, FIN-02015 HUT, Finland
{meeri.makarainen,tapio.takala}@tkk.fi

Abstract. We introduce a physically-based facial animation system for natural-looking emotional expressions. Our system enables creation of simple facial expressions using Facial Action Coding System (FACS) and complex facial expressions by blending existing expressions. We propose a method for blending facial actions, based on a parameterization that combines elements of FACS and MPEG-4 standard. We explore the complex expression space by examining the blends of basic emotions produced with our model.

1 Introduction

Expression of emotions is an important feature of lifelike virtual agents, and usually this requires appropriate facial displays. In current research, the focus is largely on facial expressions beyond the six basic expressions, which are joy, sadness, fear, anger, surprise and disgust. One approach for broadening this range is complex facial expressions that occur when two emotions are felt simultaneously. It has been shown that complex facial expressions in embodied conversational agents can improve human-machine interaction by increasing the perceived empathy of the agent [1]. We introduce a model for creating and blending facial expressions, and explore the range of complex expressions produced by the model. Figure 1 shows an example of facial expressions produced with our model.

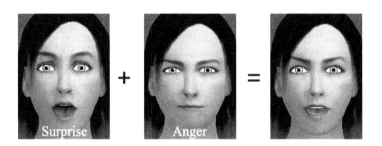

Fig. 1. Two basic expressions blended

Zs. Ruttkay et al. (Eds.): IVA 2009, LNAI 5773, pp. 243–249, 2009.
© Springer-Verlag Berlin Heidelberg 2009

Several approaches have been applied to blending basic expressions into complex expressions. Sometimes basic expressions are located in certain positions in a two-dimensional emotion space, and intermediate expressions are interpolated [2], [3]. For example, Raouzaiou et al. [2] define the position of a facial expression in a two-dimensional space by using psychological parameters of the corresponding emotion. However, while several emotions can occur simultaneously, the face can only have one display at a time. This approach cannot solve the problem of how to display two opposite emotions, such as joy and sadness, simultaneously.

Another approach to blending emotions is to display one emotion on one part of the face and another emotion on another part [4], [5]. In many cases this works, but problems arise when one region conveys essential signs of several emotions. For instance, in a believable blend of joy and surprise the mouth should be open and smiling and the same time. Another problem is that sometimes the entire face is needed to convey a single expression. An example is the Duchenne smile, the expression of genuine enjoyment [6]. The eye region is essential to distinguish the Duchenne smile from a social or a faked smile, but the mouth region is often needed to recognize the expression as a smile in the first place.

In some systems, blends are created by calculating a weighted average of individual expressions [7], [8]. This enables blends of any expressions, also those that are psychologically opposite. However, when the averaging is done on the level of facial features, the results are not necessarily anatomically correct expressions. Another drawback is that in many cases the intensity of the original expressions is reduced. For instance, a frown in the combination of anger and disgust may be less intense than in the pure expression of anger, thus perhaps misleadingly implying a less angry emotion. The reduction of intensity is avoided in systems that use additive methods to combine facial expressions [9].

We introduce a system that uses a modified additive method for blending facial expressions. We apply physically-based facial animation and we use a parameterization that combines elements of Facial Action Coding System (FACS) and MPEG-4 standard. Finally, we explain how several expressions are combined using our model. This should be thought of as an exploration of the complex expression space more than a conclusive solution for blending expressions. The paper is based on the author's M.Sc. thesis [10].

2 Physically-Based Facial Model

We built a three-dimensional, animated model of a human head. To achieve realistic facial behavior, we applied physically-based facial animation. We modeled facial muscles and deformable skin tissue based on human anatomy.

The musculature is based on Zhang et al.'s model [11]. However, we use only linear and sphincter muscles, and not sheet muscles. Anatomically the Frontalis muscle is a sheet muscle, but since the inner and outer parts can be contracted separately, we modeled it as two linear muscles. We also developed the sphincter muscle model further. In our model, the sphincter muscle force can be different in the horizontal and the vertical directions, and the muscle force can be greater for the upper lip or lid or the lower lid or lip.

The facial skin tissue was implemented using the mass-spring-damper model. We used two layers of cubical hexahedral elements that were cross-strutted to build a structurally stable lattice. Muscles are attached to the lower nodes in the top layer in one end and to bone surface in the other end. We used Zhang et al.'s semi-implicit integration [11] for solving the equations in the mass-spring-damper system. The skin surface is smoothened before rendering.

3   Parameterization of Facial Actions

Our parameterization for facial action combines Facial Action Coding System (FACS) [12] and MPEG-4 standard [13]. In FACS, Action Units (AUs) represent smallest elements of observable facial movement, and most of them correspond to an activation of a particular muscle. In MPEG-4 Facial Animation Parameters (FAPs) define precise movements for each point on the face from an animator's viewpoint. MPEG-4 is sometimes seen just as a formalization of FACS, but what makes it a fundamentally different approach is that, unlike FACS, it lacks the direct correspondence between animation parameters and facial muscles.

We use FACS as the main principle for coding facial displays. Because of the direct link to facial muscles, we attain a naturalistic range of anatomically correct facial expressions. Think, for instance, the expression when one tries to restrict one's smile. Certain muscles pull mouth corners upwards and other muscles downwards, but the resultant is not a neutral expression with a relaxed mouth. MPEG-4 coding would lose the nuances of this expression, since opposite movements cancel each other out. However, we use MPEG-4 coding for details that are not covered by the physically-based model. For MPEG-4-parameterised facial actions, we also define a mapping between AUs and FAPs, to enable specifying an entire facial expression in FACS.

3.1   FACS-Based Actions

Each FACS-based action was implemented by either a linear or a sphincter muscle in the physically-based model. The configuration of linear muscles and sphincter muscles is shown in Fig. 2.

The musculature of the facial model was designed so that each muscle corresponds to one AU. This is mainly congruent with anatomical modeling of muscles, but where conflicts exist, we favored the AU-based approach. These instances include modeling one muscle as several AUs, modeling several muscles as one AU, and modeling a muscle as a different type of muscle. These choices were done because actions of muscles are here more important than anatomical details.

3.2   MPEG-4-Based Actions

We created separate models for eyelids, lips and jaw, and we used MPEG-4 for coding their positions. The eyelid model is controlled by FAPs 19, 20, 21 and 22. The upper lid and the lower lid move along the eyeball surface.

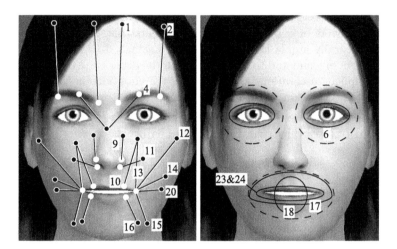

Fig. 2. Left: The configuration of linear muscles. The white dots mark muscle insertion to skin and the black dots mark muscle origin attached to bone. Right: The configuration of sphincter muscles. The numbers in both diagrams refer to action units.

The mouth opening is fundamentally a hole in the spring lattice. However, the equilibrium position of the mass-spring-damper system would leave the mouth open, and therefore we added springs connecting the upper lip to the lower lip. The stiffness of the springs is adjusted according to the FAPs 4 and 5. Finally, jaw movement is described by FAP 3. This parameter defines the rotation of the jawbone, and the deformable skin tissue takes care of the rest.

4   Combining Facial Actions

In our system, facial actions are combined on two different levels. Firstly, actions of different AUs are combined to form a single facial display. Secondly, two or more facial displays can be blended to form a composite display.

To combine a facial display from AUs, all actions are performed independently and the skin tissue finds the equilibrium position under all the forces acting on it. Some muscles may draw the skin in opposite directions, but usually they do not cancel each other out completely, and the effect of both forces can be seen on the skin. This is what actually happens when one, for example, tries to restrict one's smile.

Analogously to a facial expression being a sum of action units, we now also think a composite facial expression as a sum of the constituent expressions. This way any expression can be blended with any other expression, all parts of the face are available for each expression, and the expressions are not diluted. For FACS-based facial actions, the parameters of the blend are calculated by summing the original parameters. Since the summation is performed on muscle tension values and not facial movements directly, this method does not easily produce unnatural facial displays. For MPEG-4-based facial actions the summing method can not be used, because FAPs describe the position of a certain part of a face and not muscle tension. In these cases, we use the average position. For eye and mouth openings, all average positions are anatomically correct.

5   Facial Expressions of Emotion

Our system enables creation of facial expressions in two ways: defining new expressions as combinations of AUs and blending existing expressions. First we show the expressions of the six basic emotions. For each basic emotion, we chose one prototypical AU combination defined in FACS [14]: joy 6+12 modified with AU7, sadness 1+4+15, fear 1+2+4+5+20+26, anger 4+5+7+23, surprise 1+2+5+27 and disgust 10+17. These expressions are shown in Fig. 3.

To explore the facial expression space, we have formed complex expressions by blending pairs of basic expressions. In our model, any two basic expressions can be blended. This is reasonable, because all pairs of basic emotions can also mix in reality – one can be simultaneously sad and joyful, or surprised and

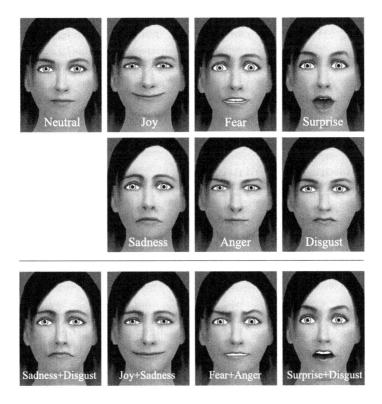

Fig. 3. Top two rows: Expressions of the six basic emotions and a neutral face. Bottow row: Example blends of two basic expressions.

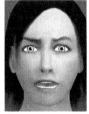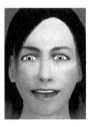

Fig. 4. Examples of blends of three basic expressions. From left to right: joy + sadness + fear, surprise + sadness + anger, joy + surprise + anger.

angry, for example. The bottom row in Fig. 3 shows example blends of two basic expressions. We also tried blending three emotions into one facial display, and got results such as shown in Fig. 4. Even these facial displays seem quite meaningful.

So, we have produced meaningful-looking facial expressions by blending two or three basic expressions. But what exactly is the nature of these expressions? A complex expression is a simultaneous expression of two different emotions, but does this mean that both of the two emotions should be clearly distinguishable from the facial expression, or can it happen that a complex facial expression represents a new emotion apart from both constituent emotions? For instance, in the blend of sadness and disgust one may see a bored face. Is it just a coincidence that summing the AUs that produce the expressions of sadness and disgust produces a facial display quite similar to a bored expression, or could it be possible that the feeling of boredom would somehow include elements of the emotions of sadness and disgust?

6   Conclusions and Future Work

We have presented a method for generating synthetic facial expressions also beyond the six basic expressions. We used physically-based facial animation with a parameterization combining elements of FACS and MPEG-4. Our system provides a possibility to define facial expression using AUs and enables blending two or more existing facial expressions. These new expressions broaden the scope of synthetic facial expressions from the basic expressions to the more complex ones in a natural way.

Subsequent research will focus on finding the meaning of different blends of basic expressions. This will be done by examining how people perceive the composite displays and what emotions they see in them. This research will help in finding the answer to the question about the nature of the produced blends. Maybe it will also shed some light on the questions about the nature of complex facial expressions in general and how they should be created.

Acknowledgments

We thank Mikko Sams and Michael Frydrych for guidance in building the facial model, and Kari-Jouko Räihä and Maira Carvalho for commenting the paper. This research has been supported by the Academy of Finland (projects Interactive Emotional Embodied Experience and Enactive Media) and the Graduate School in User Centered Information Technology.

References

1. Niewiadomski, R., Ochs, M., Pelachaud, C.: Expressions of empathy in ECAs. In: IVA, 37–44 (2008)
2. Raouzaiou, A., Tsapatsoulis, N., Kollias, S.: Parameterized facial expression synthesis based on MPEG-4. EURASIP Journal on Applied Signal Processing 2002(10), 1021–1038 (2002)
3. Arya, A., DiPaola, S., Parush, A.: Perceptually valid facial expressions for character-based applications. International Journal of Computer Games Technology (2009)
4. Paradiso, A.: An algebra for combining MPEG-4 compliant facial animations. In: Proc. Int. Workshop Lifelike Animated Agents: Tools, Affective Functions, and Applications (2002)
5. Martin, J.-C., Niewiadomski, R., Devillers, L., Buisine, S., Pelachaud, C.: Multimodal complex emotions: Gesture expressivity and blended facial expressions. International Journal of Humanoid Robotics 3(3), 269–291 (2006)
6. Ekman, P., Davidson, R.J., Friesen, W.V.: The Duchenne smile: Emotional expression and brain physiology II. Journal of Personality and Social Psychology 58(2), 342–353 (1990)
7. Ostermann, J.: Animation of synthetic faces in MPEG-4. In: CA 1998: Proceedings of the Computer Animation, DC, USA, p. 49. IEEE Computer Society, Los Alamitos (1998)
8. Deng, Z., Neumann, U., Lewis, J.P., Kim, T.-Y., Bulut, M., Narayanan, S.: Expressive facial animation synthesis by learning speech coarticulation and expression spaces. IEEE Transactions on Visualization and Computer Graphics 12(6), 1523–1534 (2006)
9. Pelachaud, C., Badler, N.I., Steedman, M.: Generating facial expressions for speech. Cognitive Science 20(1), 1–46 (1996)
10. Mäkäräinen, M.: Expressions of emotion on an animated face model. Master's thesis, Helsinki University of Technology, Finland (2006)
11. Zhang, Y., Prakash, E.C., Sung, E.: Face alive. Journal of Visual Languages and Computing 15(2), 125–160 (2004)
12. Ekman, P., Friesen, W.V., Hager, J.C.: Facial Action Coding System: The Manual. A Human Face, 666 Malibu Drive, Salt Lake City UT 84107, USA (2002)
13. ISO/IEC 14496-2:1999: Coding of audio-visual objects, Part 2: Visual
14. Ekman, P., Friesen, W.V., Hager, J.C.: Facial Action Coding System: Investigator's Guide. A Human Face, 666 Malibu Drive, Salt Lake City UT 84107, USA (2002)

Animating Idle Gaze in Public Places

Angelo Cafaro[1], Raffaele Gaito[1], and Hannes Högni Vilhjálmsson[2]

[1] Università degli Studi di Salerno, Italy
angelcaf@inwind.it, raffaele@cosmopoli.it
[2] Center for Analisys and Design of Intelligent Agents, School of Computer Science,
Reykjavik University, Iceland
hannes@ru.is

Abstract. In realistic looking game environments it is important that virtual characters behave naturally. Our goal is to produce naturally looking gaze behavior for animated agents and avatars that are simply idling. We studied people standing and waiting, as well as people walking down a shopping street. From our observations we built a demo with the CADIA Populus multi-agent social simulation platform.

Keywords: Social animation, gaze, idling, avatars, game environments.

1   Introduction

It is well established that gaze is an important aspect of human behavior that exhibits regular patterns during social activity [1,2,3]. Different social situations call for different gaze patterns, and within the same situation, different personal, inter relational and environmental factors also play a role [4]. A pervasive personal factor is cognitive activity [1], which at least will always produce a base-line gaze behavior in the background. In this paper we explore and simulate this base-line behavior in two different social situations: (1) Waiting for a Bus; and (2) Walking down a shopping street. In both situations our subjects are "idling alone" to minimize external factors, but they are still part of the dynamic social environment of a public place.

2   Related Work

Animated characters in games should foster a sense of co-presence: the sense of actually being with another person rather than simply being a graphical object on a computer screen [5]. Static screen shots may look convincing, but during actual game play the behavior has to keep up with the visual realism. The complete lack of gaze behavior in online avatars was addressed by [6] in BodyChat by fully automating it based on existing theory like [2] and [3]. BodyChat focused on social interaction, but did not model idling behavior. We build on the same theory, but add our own empirical results to fill in the idling gaps. Similar to BodyChat, [5] highlighted the importance of secondary behavior, generated

Zs. Ruttkay et al. (Eds.): IVA 2009, LNAI 5773, pp. 250–256, 2009.

autonomously for an avatar. They show a technique to add automated gaze to user-defined task execution, but base the generation on informal observations, while we rely on detailed video analysis. [7] focuses on generating gaze during the execution of certain tasks. While our work relates to their "Spontaneous Looking" situation, we extend it further with new well defined social situations and new observations. [8] presented a statistical eye movement model, which is based on both empirical studies of saccades and acquired eye movement data. Unlike our work, they analyzed people having face-to-face conversations. In recent work [1] remarked that gaze plays a large number of cognitive, communicative and affective roles in face-to-face human interaction, which is led us to think more about the cognitive base-line before engaging in interaction.

3   Video Studies

We performed two studies that we will refer to as study 1 and study 2. In the following descriptions we will refer to the study subjects as Ss.

Study 1. We picked Hlemmur, the main bus terminal in Reykjavik, as our setting for waiting behavior. Ss were filmed for a duration between 1 and 2 minutes with the camera placed 30 m away from the bus station as depicted in figure 1 (left).

Study 2. We picked Laugavegur, the main shopping street downtown Reykjavik, as our setting for walking behavior. Ss were filmed along a 30 m walking-path with the camera placed 30 m away from the end of the walking-path as depicted in figure 1 (right).

In both studies we first chose a S and, then, we recorded him/her for the whole study duration with two cameras, one focused on the S's eyes and another focused on the S's surroundings using a larger field of view. We analyzed all collected video frame-by-frame, annotating the following for each subject: Eye direction (combinations of up/center/down and left/center/right relative to head), head

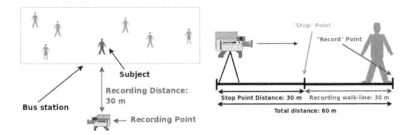

Fig. 1. The setup of the two studies. In study 1 (left), the camera recorded subjects outside a bus terminal on the other side of the street. In study 2 (right), the camera recorded a subject walking towards the camera on the sidewalk.

orientation (combinations of up/center/down and left/center/right relative to torso), torso facing (left, forward or right relative to line to camera), eyelids state (open or closed)[1] and target of attention. For these we also annotated duration. Moreover, for the eyes, head and torso we annotated the time interval in which movement happens and the speed of that movement (slow, neutral or fast). For study 1 we also annotated the following: Potential gaze targets for the Ss (categorized as objects or persons), proxemics area in witch the potential target appears [9] and instances when a potential target in a given area produced actual gaze movement. In study 1 we annotated 9 subjects for a total duration of 14'30", during which 142 gaze shifts were observed. In study 2 we annotated 16 subjects for a total duration of 5'40", during which 216 gaze shifts were observed (excluding a few at the camera).

The results include both general observations and empirical data extracted from the annotations. The observations for Study 1, include:

1. Ss that produce short glances were observed to keep their glances short throughout the study;
2. Conversely, Ss producing longer glances or gazes were observed to keep them long throughout the study;
3. The shorter glance Ss were observed to pick many different targets around them;
4. The longer glance Ss were picking targets from a narrower set;

The empirical data describes: The gaze attraction of potential targets that were either objects or persons, in relation to the proximity of the target. This is based on how much of the total time an object or a person spent at a given proximity was spent being looked at by the subject. In addition the duration of each gaze was recorded. This is shown in Table 1.

For Study 2, the main discovered patterns are:

1. Ss frequently look to the ground while walking down the street;
2. Related to that, Ss first choice is to look down to the ground when exercising gaze-aversion;
3. Ss usually close their eyelids just before moving their head (or changing gaze direction);
4. Ss almost never look up, up-left or up-right.

The empirical data describes: How often a target of a given type gets looked at compared to other target types. Information about timing including the average, minimum and maximum gaze length. This is shown in Table 2.

We are at an early stage of a more in-depth statistical analysis of the massive amount of data we have gathered, but the patterns we have already discovered along with the first set of numerical data has been the basis for new autonomous idle gaze behavior generation algorithms for the two social situations we studied.

---

[1] We annotated this only for study 2 due to the high frequency of gaze movement.

Table 1. Observations about the relationship between gaze targets and proxemics from Study 1 where the subject is waiting alone for a bus. It is noticeable that objects at a close range receive complete attention while persons at a similarly close range are avoided. All durations are in seconds.

	Objects			Persons		
Proxemics Area	Time on Target	%	Avg. Dur.	Time on Target	%	Avg. Dur.
Intimate	84.11 out of 84.11	100%	6	0 out of 6.43	0%	-
Personal	10.26 out of 10.26	100%	5.13	7.3 out of 61.16	12%	2.43
Social	14.36 out of 22.56	64%	4.80	45.17 out of 96.68	47%	22.60
Public	1.33 out of 1.33	100%	1.33	6.90 out of 29.46	23%	2.30
Extra	5.90 out of 8.66	68%	5.90	9.00 out of 35.56	25%	3.00

Table 2. Observations about where people look when walking down a shopping street from Study 2. The first two target types refer to other people on the sidewalk, of which there were equal number of males and females. Cars refer to those coming up the street and passing the subjects. All durations are in seconds.

	Targets		Durations		
Target Type	%	Time on Target	Avg.	Min.	Max.
Same Gender	3%	7.75	0.64	0.24	1.24
Opposite Gender	5%	12.92	0.72	0.29	1.15
Shops	13%	33.58	0.74	0.14	1.34
Cars	9%	23.25	0.93	0.1	1.8
Ground	25%	64.58	1.5	0.5	2.5
Camera	7%	18.08	-	-	-
Other Side	16%	41.33	-	-	-
Unknown	22%	56.83	-	-	-
Total	100%	258.32			

4 Autonomous Generation of Idle Gaze Behavior

We implemented the idle gaze generation with a new tool for constructing social behaviors for avatars and agents in game environments: CADIA Populus [10]. The process was simply a matter of plugging in new steering behaviors along with conditions to activate them during the particular situations that we were modeling. The new behaviors fit nicely into the steering behavior framework of CADIA Populus, adding a new set of motivations for turning the head and eyes when appropriate.

Both of our steering behaviors follow the same working principle, they differ only in their update frequency[2]. The *idle gaze waiting* required a lower update frequency than the *idle gaze walking*. This makes intuitive sense. The goal of the entire autonomous gaze generation process is to continuously obtain a target and a gaze duration for that target. The target can be an entity of the environment (other avatars or objects), a point in space or a direction relative to the avatar

---

[2] CADIA Populus updates each steering behavior with a given frequency.

itself. In order to achieve this goal the process starts analyzing the entities around the avatar, using the perception system provided by CADIA Populus, and creates a list of potential targets for the decision step. At this stage several factors are combined to obtain the final target and its duration: First the social situation dependent steering behavior, that incorporates the observation data, is applied and then additional features from the avatar's profile and preferences are incorporated. We limited the profile to a simple personality variable (extrovert or introvert) and gender, while a preferences held a possible bias towards any kind of entity. The underlying perception system already provided in CADIA Populus allows access to two kinds of information: the social high-level environment and the low-level avatar visual perception. Information related to the social environment is retrieved through a social perception interface; examples of social perception include how many individuals are within a certain proximity range (using the proxemics notation intimate, personal, social and public zones). Notice that the perception of social and public space has a blind cone behind the avatar, of respectively 90 and 150 degrees [10]. The avatar visual perception is divided into central view and peripheral view. Our basic attention model is realized using the intersection between the social and visual perception information, obtaining the three areas as we can see in Fig. 2. In order to produce a list of potential targets the system collects them from these areas by priority, starting from Area 1 and ending when the mentioned targets are found. Finally, only entities in remaining areas that are moving toward the avatar are added, as they represent high potential for upcoming interaction. A detailed attention model implementation is beyond the purpose of this paper, in fact ours is primarily a way to obtain a reasonable list of targets to work with.

The decision phase is a core process and is based on four values from our data: *Choice Probability, Look Probability, Minimum* and *Maximum Duration.* To use these differently for each situation. For study 1, in each proxemics area we identify two general target types: Objects or Persons. Then, fixing a target type in one specific area we assigned the four above-mentioned values. For study 2, since the setting was the same for all recordings, all the potential targets were classified into five main categories. Three of them including targets able to move (Cars, Same Gender People or Opposite Gender People), the remaining two

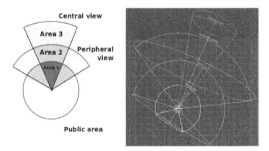

Fig. 2. The area subdivision in our basic attention model for the potential target selection (left). The social and visual perception systems in CADIA Populus (right).

included fixed targets (Shops and Other[3]). Finally, for each target category we assigned the four above-mentioned values. Next we pick *a single* target of possible interest by using the *Choice Probability* to select among potential targets. An example of this probability is given in Table 2. Then, for this single target, we may or may not decide to actually look at it. This decision is left to what we call a *Look Probability* for a particular type of target. An example of a probability of this sort is given in Table 1. Finally, if a gaze is produced, the duration of the gaze for that target is a random value between *Minimum Duration* and *Maximum Duration* as seen in the data.

In some cases the decision process could not select a target for two possible reasons: there aren't potential targets surrounding the avatar or the decision process chose not to produce gaze towards the most likely target (due to *Look Probability*). In these cases we generated a gaze behavior with a relative direction based on the discovered common patterns mentioned earlier. To make the gaze behavior even more dynamic, the avatars are always attentive to changes in surrounding potential targets. This means that even during a gaze shift to a chosen target. These changes are being monitored in the background. Another important detail is that repeated targets are avoided using a simple memory structure.

5   Conclusions and Future Work

This paper has introduced one approach to design and animate avatar gaze behavior for game environments based both on existing literature and on data gathered through carefully planned observation. As we can see in Fig. 3, we have constructed a virtual model of the places where we gathered our data in order to test our steering behaviors. We have not performed user studies yet to independently evaluate the believability of the resulting gaze behavior, but it is clear from the accompanying video[4] that compared to no gaze or purely random gaze, our results look promising. Some limitations should be considered. First of all, the data was gathered in a single location, which may or may not generalize to other locations or cultures. Secondly, the videos were gathered in a natural setting so it was impossible to obtain detailed data on many of the personal state factors that we know can influence gaze, for example how the subjects were feeling. Thirdly, only certain types of potential targets were present so even if we tried to keep target types general some new scenes may require more data. Finally, CADIA Populus currently lacks vertical head movement, which constrains looking down to eye movement only.

This is work in progress, so future work is extensive. For example we would like to incorporate the speed of head and torso movement. Including the closing of the eyes could improve believability. We have already analyzed the data for that and just have to implement it. Regarding the video studies, the next steps include a more thorough statistical data analysis and hypothesis testing for contributing

---

[3] We grouped in this category all the other objects present on the scene, i.e. pickets, lamps, etc...

[4] Available at http://cadia.ru.is/projects/cadiapopulus/cafaro2009.avi

Fig. 3. Screenshot of our gaze behaviour inside CADIA Populus

to the body of theoretical work on gaze behavior. Finally, we would like to construct new studies with different configurations to cover more factors and social situations.

Acknowledgements

Big thanks to the CADIA team and Claudio Pedica in particular. This work was made possible with the support of the Humanoid Agents in Social Game Environments Grant of Excellence from The Icelandic Research Fund and the ERASMUS European student exchange programme.

References

1. Lee, J., Marsella, S.C., Traum, D.R., Gratch, J., Lance, B.: The rickel gaze model: A window on the mind of a virtual human. In: Pelachaud, C., Martin, J.-C., André, E., Chollet, G., Karpouzis, K., Pelé, D. (eds.) IVA 2007. LNCS (LNAI), vol. 4722, pp. 296–303. Springer, Heidelberg (2007)
2. Kendon, A.: Conducting Interaction: Patterns of Behavior in Focused Encounters (Studies in Interactional Sociolinguistics). Cambridge University Press, Cambridge (1990)
3. Argyle, M., Cook, M.: 5. In: Gaze & Mutual Gaze, pp. 98–124. Cambridge University Press, Cambridge (1976)
4. Argyle, M., Furnham, A., Graham, J.A.: Social Situations. Cambridge University Press, Cambridge (1981)
5. Gillies, M.F.P., Dodgson, N.A.: Behaviourally rich actions for user controlled characters. Journal of Computers and Graphics 28(6), 945–954 (2004)
6. Vilhjllmsson, H.H., Cassell, J.: Bodychat: Autonomous communicative behaviors in avatars. In: Proceedings of the 2nd International Conference on Autonomous Agents (Agents 1998), pp. 269–276. ACM Press, New York (1998)
7. Chopra-Khullar, S., Badler, N.I.: Where to look? automating attending behaviors of virtual human characters. In: Proceedings of the third annual conference on Autonomous Agents (Agents 1999), pp. 16–23. ACM, New York (1999)
8. Lee, S.P., Badler, J.B., Badler, N.I.: Eyes alive. In: Proceedings of of ACM SIGGRAPH 2002, vol. 21, pp. 637–644. ACM, New York (2002)
9. Hall, E.T.: The Hidden Dimension, 1st edn. Doubleday, Garden City (1966)
10. Pedica, C., Vilhjálmsson, H.H.: Social perception and steering for online avatars. In: Prendinger, H., Lester, J.C., Ishizuka, M. (eds.) IVA 2008. LNCS (LNAI), vol. 5208, pp. 104–116. Springer, Heidelberg (2008)

Virtual Agents and 3D Virtual Worlds for Preserving and Simulating Cultures

Anton Bogdanovych[1], Juan Antonio Rodriguez[2], Simeon Simoff[1],
and Alex Cohen[3]

[1] School of Computing and Mathematics,
University of Western Sydney, NSW, Australia
{a.bogdanovych,s.simoff}@uws.edu.au
[2] IIIA, Artificial Intelligence Research Institute
CSIC, Spanish National Research Council Campus UAB, Bellaterra, Spain
jar@iiia.csic.es
[3] Federation of American Scientists, 1725 DeSales Street, Washington, DC, USA
acohen@fas.org

Abstract. Many researchers associate a culture with some form of knowledge; other scholars stress the importance of the environment inhabited by the knowledge carriers; while archaeologists learn about cultures through the objects produced in the environment as a result of utilizing this knowledge. In our work we propose a model of virtual culture that preserves the environment, objects and knowledge associated with a certain culture in a 3D Virtual World. We highlight the significance of virtual agents in our model as, on the one hand, being the knowledge carriers and, on the other hand, being an important element establishing the connection between the environment, objects and knowledge. For testing the resulting model we have developed a research prototype simulating the culture of the ancient City of Uruk 3000 B. C. (one of the first human-built cities on Earth) within a Virtual World of Second Life.

1 Introduction

There is a disturbing lack of agreement amongst researchers as to what constitutes a culture. Most existing definitions of culture come from anthropologists, but even amongst them there is no solidarity. Stone axes and pottery bowls are culture to some, but no material object can be culture to others [1]. Some researchers claim that the environment itself constitutes an important part of the culture and strictly defines how the culture evolves [2], other researchers consider cultures being the knowledge transmitted by non-genetic means [3] and neither objects nor the environment are related to the culture in their view.

We do not take any side in this debate, but consider culture being tightly connected with both the environment and the material products created as the result of utilizing the cultural knowledge. This consideration is made based on

Zs. Ruttkay et al. (Eds.): IVA 2009, LNAI 5773, pp. 257–271, 2009.

the following observations. First of all, the majority of the existing methods of culture preservation and methods used for learning about extinct cultures are structured around discovering, preserving and learning from the objects produced by this culture. The environment also provides important clues that help to fill the gaps in the existing knowledge. Moreover, in some cultures, i.e. the culture of indigenous Australians, the environment is so tightly integrated with all human actions, beliefs and traditions that ruling it out as being irrelevant to the culture makes it impossible to understand most of the cultural knowledge.

The *aim* of our work is to discover the elements that are associated with learning and preserving cultures and to produce an integrated framework enabling culture preservation and learning that incorporates all those elements.

While studying the existing techniques for cultural preservation we have identified printed materials as the most popular way of preserving cultural knowledge and museums as the way of preserving a culture in terms of objects. The most popular techniques that link a culture to a particular environment are movies and 3D virtual environments. Through further analysis of these techniques we have selected 3D virtual environments (and their subclass 3D Virtual Worlds) as the most affordable, dynamic and interactive option for integrating the environment, objects and knowledge associated with a culture.

Using 3D virtual environments to reconstruct lost sites of high historical significance has become very popular during the last decade [4]. Initially, 3D heritage applications were only focused on reconstructing destroyed architecture (e.g. Roman Colosseum). While such an approach creates a unique possibility for general audiences to examine the architectural details of the heritage site it still does not help an observer to understand how this site has been enacted in the past. Therefore, at a later stage, some researchers started to populate these virtual sites with so-called virtual crowds [5]. Such crowds normally consist of a large number of avatars dressed as local citizens of the reconstructed site. The state of the art in combining crowd simulation and 3D heritage can be observed on the example outlined in [6] where a virtual City of Pompeii is populated with a large number of avatars that walk around the city avoiding collisions.

Introducing virtual humans into cultural heritage applications, in our view, is an important step towards integrating all the three key dimensions of a culture: knowledge, environment and objects. However, current approaches focused on crowd simulations are not normally concerned with having virtual agents as immersed knowledge carriers, but rather use them as moving decorations.

In this paper we analyze the mechanisms that are required for capturing and preserving cultural knowledge through virtual agents. To do so we suggest focusing on individual agents rather than crowds. In order to avoid the debate about the role of environment and objects in a culture we introduce the notion of *virtual culture*, which is a combination of cultural knowledge, environment and objects preserved in a 3D Virtual World. Further we investigate the phenomenon of virtual cultures. The key *contributions* of our work are as follows:

- Specifying the role of virtual agents as an important element in the preservation of virtual cultures.
- Producing a formal model of virtual culture enabling successful culture preservation, facilitating the learning of a particular culture by the visitors and providing the foundations for the computational enactment of a culture.
- Testing the developed model through a case study.

The remainder of the paper is structured as follows. In Section 2 we identify the key elements that constitute a culture by using existing definitions and mathematical models. As the result of it, Section 3 proposes a formal model of virtual culture. In Section 4 the resulting model is applied to the development of a prototype aiming at preserving the culture of the ancient city of Uruk, 3000 B.C. Finally, Section 5 presents concluding remarks and directions of future work.

2 Background

When trying to replicate a culture inside a computer simulated environment it is important to have a formal model of the culture. The majority of research efforts focused on creating such artificial cultures originates in the field of artificial life [7]. To our knowledge, none of the existing works provide a comprehensive formal model of the culture that can be utilized for preserving a culture along its multiple dimensions. Therefore, in this section we will analyze the existing models and the available informal definitions of culture in order to understand which existing models to rely upon and how they should be extended.

2.1 Definitions

Most of the existing conceptualizations consider culture being some sort of knowledge. One of the first and most popular definitions of culture that is still accepted by the majority of modern researchers was produced by Edward Burnett Tylor. He defines culture as "that complex whole which includes knowledge, belief, art, morals, law, custom, and any other capabilities and habits acquired by man as a member of society" [8].

The telling point of the definition proposed by [8] is that, although labelled a whole, culture is actually treated as a list of elements, which motivates us to look through other available definitions and identify those elements that can be included into the resulting formal model.

Through the analysis of the definitions linking culture to knowledge we identified the following elements that constitute such knowledge: Beliefs [8], Morals [8], Law [8], Customs [8], Habits [9], Techniques [9], Ideas [9], Values [9], Behavior Patterns [9], Standards of Behavior [2], and Rules of Behavior [2].

Culture is also believed to have a functional dimension, as suggested by [1]. It is not only considered as knowledge, but also as an evolving mechanism of utilizing this knowledge to better adapt to the environment and control it.

While not making a direct connection to physical objects in his definition, in his works Tylor also connects culture to human possessions. Specifically, he enumerates beliefs, customs, objects – "hatchet, adze, chisel," and so on – and techniques – "wood-chopping, fishing, fire-making," and so on [8]. The view that the concept of the culture is associated with certain objects created by its carriers is also shared by [9]. Herskovits in [2] takes an extreme materialistic view and considers culture being "the man-made part of the environment".

In [8] many of the attributes constituting a culture correspond to humans. In contrast to the majority of existing approaches to cultural heritage we are focused on including humans into both preservation and simulation of the culture and make them exhibit these attributes. So, in our model we will relate the knowledge aspect of a culture to humans and make humans the carriers of this knowledge. Additionally, the aforementioned definitions mention rules of behavior, techniques, standards and patterns of behavior and customs. While those elements are distributed amongst the culture carriers they have some kind of a unifying nature and can be preserved independently from their carriers. Therefore, we introduce the notion of institutions, which should be understood as the concept uniting all the aforementioned terms. While strongly associated with knowledge, the institutions are rather a global type of knowledge with individual agents having little impact on changing this knowledge. We find the notion of institutions being a central concept for culture preservation.

Generalizing the above considerations we can say that a culture is associated with institutions accepted by the virtual society, objects produced by culture carriers, culture carriers themselves together with their knowledge and behaviors.

2.2   Existing Models

Culture has been studied by social and computer scientists in the realm of the emergence of social consensus (e.g. [10,11]), of which culture is a particular case. Here we examine these works as a basis for a general model of culture.

In [10] Axelrod observes that individuals can be characterised by their cultural features, such as language, religion, technology, style of dress, and so forth. Hence, the cultural traits of such features characterise each individual. Therefore, given a population of agents Ag, Axelrod characterises each agent $ag_i \in Ag$ by a vector of cultural features $\langle \sigma_i^1, \ldots, \sigma_i^m \rangle$, each one taking on a value to define an agent's cultural traits. Some of these traits change over time with the dissemination of culture, whereas other traits remain unchanged because an agent might be closed-minded or simply a given trait is not under its control (e.g. ethnicity). Similarly, in [11] Carley considers that culture is a distribution of facts among people, namely who knows what facts (e.g. a belief in God). Therefore, both Axelrod and Carley propose basic models to characterise *cultural knowledge*.

Despite the many definitions in the literature about culture, everyone agrees that people learn from each other. Hence, the dissemination of culture among people is based on the notion of social influence. In [10,11], Axelrod and Carley incorporate a well-known regularity in the social world: "homophily" [12], or the tendency to interact with similar people. Thus, similarity among people's cultural features drives interactions. As a result of an interaction, two agents start sharing cultural features or knowledge that were different prior to their interaction.[1] Therefore, existing models of dissemination of culture agree on the need for a *local dissemination function* that each agent uses for changing her cultural knowledge or features based on her social influences (interactions).

Recent studies (mostly in the area of complex systems) on the emergence of social conventions agree on the importance of the structure (topology) of social relationships (e.g. the network of interactions among agents accounts for the local geography in Axelrod's model). Indeed, the work in [13] empirically shows that the network of interactions is important to reach consensus on either a single, global culture or on multiple cultures.[2] Hence, a model of culture must also take into account a model of social relationships.

At this point we can compile the fundamental components identified in the literature to computationally model a culture. Thus, a culture can be characterised in terms of models of: (i) cultural knowdledge or features; (ii) dissemination of culture; and (iii) social relationships. And yet, we believe that there is something missing. In section 2.1 we have highlighted the role of institutions. Hence here we advocate that institutions shape social relationships with varying degrees of social influence. This is particularly true in ancient societies where institutions like the family, the law, religions, or tribes play a fundamental role in the dissemination of culture. For instance, consider the influence of the head of a tribe or the father in a family.

3   Formal Model of Virtual Culture

Based on the analysis of the definitions and existing formal models of culture presented in Section 2 we have produced a formalization of virtual culture. Our aim was to develop a model allowing for preserving a culture along as many of its attributes as possible. This aim is very different to the aims behind the models presented in Section 2.2, where the key motivation was to investigate a very particular aspect of cultures (dissemination) and the simplicity of the model was rather a positive than a negative factor. In our work we rely on those existing models, but extend them with additional elements identified in Section 2.1.

In our formalization a virtual culture develops in a virtual environment, mimicking the actual physical environment where a culture is *situated*, and populated by virtual agents whose interactions occur in the framwork of and are constrained by institutions (e.g. families, law, religion). The institutions are associated with a certain space within the virtual environment (e.g. temples, markets). Moreover, we consider that virtual agents employ virtual objects in their interactions, namely virtual replicas of artifacts that mimic the actual physical objects (e.g. spears, pottery) being used by the members of a culture. Therefore, we can regard virtual places along with artifacts as the objects produced by a culture. Wrapping all the above elements, we can characterise a virtual culture as a tuple:

---

[1] Notice that considering homophily as part of a model of dissemination of culture assumes that social influences and interactions can only be positive.

[2] Moreover, San Miguel et al. [13] also investigate cultural drift, namely the effects of spontaneous changes of cultural traits.

$$VirtualCulture = \langle E, P, O, Ag, I, l \rangle \tag{1}$$

where E is the virtual environment; P stands for the set of virtual places occupied by a virtual culture; O stands for the objects produced by a virtual culture (buildings and artifacts); Ag stands for a set of virtual agents; I stands for a set of institutions constraining the interactions of virtual gents; and $l : I \to P$ is a function mapping each institution to a location, namely to some virtual place.

Institutions are used to regulate the interactions amongst the participating individuals by enforcing strict rules, norms and conventions on their behavior [14]. Researchers working in the field of Distributed Artificial Intelligence have been working on formalizing the concept of "institution" for over a decade. One of the most successful institutional formalisms from this area is the concept of "Electronic Institutions" [15].

In our work we rely on the concept of Electronic Institution as a basis for producing the formal definition of a culture. Here an institution is treated as a composition of: roles and their properties and relationships, norms of behavior in respect to these roles, a common language (ontology) used by virtual agents for communications with each other (e.g. this ontology must allow virtual agents to refer to places and artifacts), acceptable interaction protocols representing the activites in an institution along with their relationships, and a role flow policy establishing how virtual agents can change their roles. As mentioned in Section 2.2 we take the stance that social relationships in the realm of an institution establish social influences of varying degrees that must be considered for culture dissemination. So, an institution in our model can be characterised as:

$$I = \langle R, ssd, sub, N, Ont, PS, \mathcal{I} \rangle \tag{2}$$

where R is a set of roles; $ssd \subseteq R \times R$ and $sub \subseteq R \times R$ stand for relationships among roles (incompatibility of roles and subsumption of roles respectively); N is a set of norms of behaviour; Ont is a common language (ontology); PS stands for a graph defining the relationships among interaction protocols and role flow of the agents; and $\mathcal{I} \subseteq R \times R$ stands for a set of directed arcs between roles, where $w : \mathcal{I} \to \mathcal{R}^+$ labels each arc with a degree of social influence.

From the agent perspective, we take the stance that virtual agents are culturally characterised by their appearance (e.g. dress, facial features, etc.) and their cultural knowledge, namely their beliefs. We also assume that virtual agents are endowed with patterns of behaviour[3], namely plans of actions, which allow them to act in different institutions. Based on its beliefs, a virtual agent selects a pattern of behaviour to perform in each institution. Moreover, the definition of culture presented in [3] suggests that culture is not transmitted by genetic means amongst agents and that culture can be transmitted from one agent to another via *social learning* mechanisms. Hence, a virtual agent requires a social learning function modelling the dissemination of culture, namely the way a virtual agent's knowledge changes after interacting with some other agent in the

---

[3] Eventually these patterns are obtained either by cultural transmission or by learning.

framework of an institution depending on the role each agent plays (since a role determines the degree of social influence). Following the above considerations, we can characterise the components of a virtual agent as a tuple:

$$Ag = \langle Ap, K, B, \pi, \delta \rangle \qquad (3)$$

where Ap is the appearance of a virtual agent; K is the agent's knowledge; B is a set of patterns of behaviour the agent can perform; $\pi : K \times I \rightarrow B$ is a behaviour selection function that allows a virtual agent to choose a behaviour, a plan of actions; and $\delta : K \times R \times I \times Ag \times R \rightarrow K$ is a social learning function.

4   Case Study: The City of Uruk, 3000 B.C.

The case study aims at recreating the ancient city of Uruk from the period around 3000 B.C. in the Virtual World of Second Life letting the history students experience how it looked like and how its citizens behaved in the past (more about the Uruk Project as well as the prototype video can be found in [16]). The Virtual World of Second Life provides a unique collaborative environment for history experts, archaeologists, anthropologists, designers and programmers to meet, share their knowledge and work together on making the city and the behavior of its virtual population historically authentic.

Uruk was an ancient city located in present day Iraq. Many historians and archaeologists believe that Uruk was one of the first human built cities on Earth. Uruk played a major role in the invention of writing, emergence of urban life and development of many scientific disciplines including mathematics and astronomy.

4.1   Approach

Our approach to preserving and simulating the Uruk culture is shown in Figure 1.

The 3D Virtual World is used for both preserving the culture and for teaching the resulting culture to the visitors. It is accessible by two types of participants: Visitors and Experts. Visitors are participating in the environment to learn about the given culture through exploration of the Virtual World and through embodied interactions with its virtual inhabitants. Experts are a key element in culture preservation. Through embodied interactions with other experts in the Virtual World they share their knowledge and refine the appearance of the heritage environment, validate the correctness of the reconstructed buildings and artifacts, as well as help to refine the behavior of virtual agents. As the result of the joint work of historians, archaeologists, designers and programmers the resulting heritage site is recreated in the virtual world and populated with virtual agents that look and behave similar to the actual people that used to live in the given area. With the help of the Virtual Institutions technology [17] the agents are able to engage into complex interactions with other agents and humans, while following the social norms of the reconstructed ancient culture.

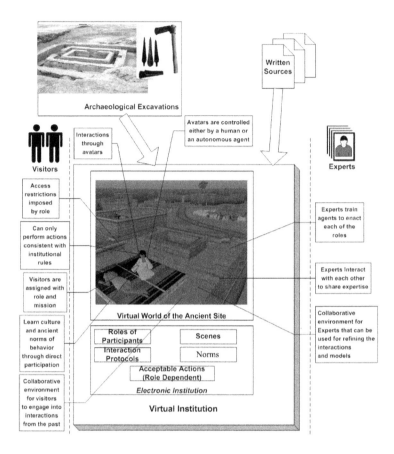

Fig. 1. Our Approach to Preserving and Simulating Cultures

4.2   The Prototype

The prototype aims at showing how to enhance the educational process of history students by immersing them into daily life of the ancient city of Uruk, so that they gain a quick understanding of the advance of technological and cultural development of ancient Sumerians. The prototype was built following the formal model outlined in Section 3. It does not currently feature culture dissemination and agent actions are limited to non-verbal behaviors.

4.3   Uruk Environment

Based on the available data we have recreated the environment of the city of Uruk in the Virtual World of Second Life. The environment features a flat desert-like area with very little vegetation. It contains animals: donkeys, sheep, eagles and fish. These animals are known to be living in the city of Uruk in 3000 B.C.

4.4   Uruk Objects

Based on the results of archaeological excavations and the available written sources we have recreated the buildings and artifacts that were available in Uruk. Both modeling of the city and programming of the virtual humans populating it were conducted under the supervision of subject matter experts. The object designers used input from our subject matter experts, who provided them with sketches, measurements and positions of the objects. Many of the artifacts were replicated from the artifacts available in museums.

4.5   Uruk Agents

Our model presented in Section 3 identifies some functionalities a virtual agent must implement to successfully operate within a virtual culture. In particular, each virtual agent must incoroporate a machinery to "decide" how to behave within institutions (through patterns of behaviour) and how to handle the social influences. To make this possible the agent must have access to the institutional formalization. Such access is provided by the virtual institutions technology [17].

For the purpose of this study we have selected fishermen daily life of ancient Uruk in order to illustrate our model of virtual culture. We created four agents that represent members of two fishermen families (see Figure 3 and figure 4). Each family consists of a husband and a wife. Every agent has a unique historically authentic appearance and is dressed appropriately for the period around 3000 B.C.

The agents literally "live" in the virtual world of Second Life. Their day is approximately 15 minutes long and starts with waking up on the roof of the house (where they slept to avoid high temperatures). The wives would wake up first to collect some water from the well and prepare breakfast for their husbands. The husbands normally start their day by having a morning chat while waiting for the breakfast to be prepared (eating and cooking are not currently implemented).

After breakfast the fishermen would collect their fishing gear and walk towards the city gates – Figure 2 a). Outside the gates on the river bank they would find their boat which they will both board and start fishing. One of the agents would be standing in the boat with a spear trying to catch the fish and the other agent would be rowing. Figure 2 b) illustrates the fishing process.

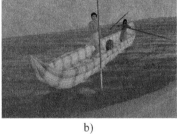

a)   b)

Fig. 2. The City of Uruk Prototype

Fig. 3. Fisherman Family 1: Fisherman1 Andel and Wife1 Andel

Fig. 4. Fisherman Family 2: Wife2 Jigsaw and Fisherman2 Jigsaw

After fishing, the men exit the boat, collect the fishing basket and spear and bring them back to their homes. This daily cycle is then continuously repeated with slight variations in agent behavior.

Each of the agents enacts one of the four social roles. Agent Fisherman1 plays the "SpearOwner" role. He is the young male fisherman. He possesses the fishing spear and is capable of catching the fish with it. He and his brother also jointly own a fishing boat. His daily routine consists of waking up on the roof, having a morning chat with fisherman 2, fishing, bringing the fishing gear back home and climbing back on the roof to sleep.

Wife1 Andel enacts the "WaterSupplier" role. She is the young wife of Fisherman1, who is responsible for collecting water from the well. Her daily routine consists of waking up on the roof, collecting the water from the well, doing house work and climbing back on the roof to sleep there. As any other typical fisherman wife in Uruk she does not have any recreation time and is constantly working.

Agent Fisherman2 is the older brother of Fisherman1 playing the social role "BoatOwner". He lives with his wife in the separate house next to his brother. Both families are very close and spend most of their day together. Fisherman2 possesses a fishing basket and paddles for rowing the fishing boat. His daily routine consists of waking up on the roof, having a morning chat with Fisherman1, fishing, bringing the fishing gear back home and climbing on the roof to sleep.

Wife2 Jigsaw, the wife of Fisherman2, plays the "FireKeeper" role. She is older than Wife1 and, therefore, is the key decision maker for controlling the integrity of both households. She makes fishing baskets and trades them for other household items. Starting the fire and preparing food are her direct responsibilities. Her daily routine consists of waking up on the roof, starting a fire for cooking, routine house work and climbing back on the roof to sleep there.

In the current prototype we employ an incomplete model of an agent as compared with the model described in Section 3. Each agent has an appearance, a number of behavior patterns and a behaviour selection function, but has a very limited knowledge about the culture and no social learning function to realise the dissemination of culture. These features are left for the future work.

4.6   Uruk Institution

The extended description of the process and the methodology used for formalizing the Uruk institution are presented in [18]. For the purpose of this presentation we only focus on the key components present in the resulting Uruk institution.

Figure 5 outlines the Performative Structure, Roles of participants and gives an example of a Norm and an interaction protocol (Scene). The Performative Structure is a graph defining the role flow of participants among various activities. The nodes of this graph feature the identified scenes and the arcs define the permission of participants playing the given role to access certain scenes. Arcs labelled with "new" define which participants are initializing the scene, so that no other participants can enter it before the initialization occurs.

The institution can be accessed by the agents playing the following four roles: SpearOwner, BoatOwner, WaterSupplier and FireKeeper. Here SpearOwner and BoatOwner are two subroles of the role Fisherman and WaterSupplier and Fire-Keeper are the subroles of role wife. The Performative Structure also includes the following roles (Fire, Boat, House1, House2, Well). These roles correspond to dynamic objects that change the state of the environment by performing some actions in it. The interaction of the agents with such objects must be formalized appropriately in the specification of the institution to ensure correct behavior.

The "root" and "exit" scenes are not associated with any patterns of behavior and simply define the state of entrance and exit of participants into the institution. Apart from them each of the scenes in the Performative Structure is associated with a Finite State Machine defining the interaction protocol for the participants that are accepted into the scene. To change the scene state a participant has to perform an action accepted by the institutional infrastructure.

The scene protocol here defines in which sequence agents must perform the actions, at which point they can join and leave the scene and what they should do to change the scene state. In Virtual Institutions we consider every action that changes the state of the institution being a speech act (text message). Every action (i.e. grabbing an object or clicking on it) a participant performs in a Virtual World is captured by the institutional infrastructure.

As an example, Figure 5 outlines the institutional formalization of the Fishing Scene (associated with the area around the boat). Once a scene is initialized its initial state becomes "W0". While the scene is in this state Fisherman2 and Boat can join the scene and both Fisherman1 and Fisherman2 can leave the scene

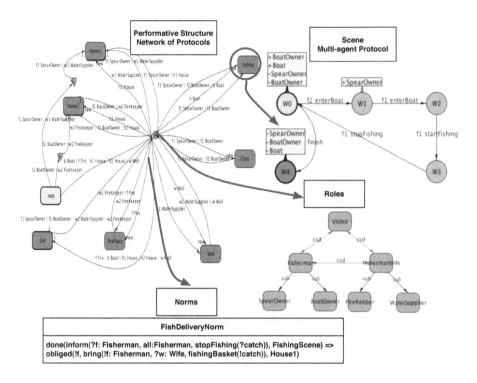

Fig. 5. Some Components of the Uruk Institution

(the "Boat" is part of the scene when this is activated). Fisherman1 can only enter the scene after Fisherman2 successfully enters the boat. This occurs when the avatar of Fisherman2 boards the boat by performing the action "f2:enterboat" (labelling the transition from "W0" to "W1"), making the scene evolve from state "W0" to state "W1" (BoatOwner on board). After Fisherman1 enters the boat, by performing the "f1:enterBoat" action, the institutional infrastructure makes the scene evolve to state "W2" (SpearOnwer on board) and notifies all participants about the state change. Then Fisherman1 may request to start the fishing, by performing action "f1:startFishing", which would bring the scene into "W3" (Fishing). The result of this is the change of the boat state from "standing" to "afloat", Fisherman2 will start rowing and the boat object will move. In state "W3" the only action that can be performed is informing all the participants by Fisherman1 that fishing is finished. When the fishing is finished Fisherman2 must return the boat to the initial position, park it there, drop the paddles, take the fishing basket and exit the boat. Fisherman1 will also have to exit the boat. No participants can leave the scene in this state and must wait until the scene evolves to "W0". While the scene is in "W0" again, the Boat object will change its state to "docks", this being captured as a "finish" action by the institutional infrastructure that makes the scene evolve to its final state "W4".

This deactivates the scene and makes it impossible for the participants to join it and act on it (no participant will be able to sit inside the boat).

Similar to the Fishing scene the interaction protocols have to be specified for other scenes present in the Performative Structure. We would like to point out that the scene protocol does not define how the actual fishing should take place, but simply provides the key states within the scene so that the agents can have a formal understanding of the performed actions.

4.7 Validation

Our approach to modeling cultures is based on the 3D Virtual Worlds technology. The importance of this technology for transmitting knowledge was highlighted by the outcomes of the research summit on the role of computer games in the future of education [19]. The outcomes suggest that 3D Virtual Worlds is an important technology for teaching higher-order thinking skills such as strategic thinking, interpretative analysis, problem solving, plan formulation and execution, and adaptation to rapid change. Based on the opinions of over 100 experts in education the summit concludes that virtual experience is beneficial for learning as it helps the students to maintain a high level of motivation and goal orientation (even after failure); enables personalized learning and, under certain conditions, is associated with unlimited patience. The key identified benefits of using Virtual Worlds for learning are: personalization, active learning, experiential learning, learner-centered learning and immediate feedback [19].

In order to test the validity of our particular approach to modeling the selected culture in a Virtual World we conducted additional validation from two different perspectives. The first perspective is *Expert Validation*. To verify our simulation of the culture of the city of Uruk, 3000 B.C. we have collaborated with 2 subject matter experts. The experts helped us in revising the scenarios and 3D models of the objects. Once the prototype was completed, the experts confirmed that the created prototype indeed reflects the way of life of ancient Sumerians from the city of Uruk and confirmed its historical authenticity.

The second perspective of validation is *Learners Feedback*. In order to conduct this validation, we have selected 10 people (students and staff members) from two Australian universities. The key selection criteria for our *sample* was that those people are supposed to have very little [next to nothing] previous knowledge about ancient Mesopotamia and the city of Uruk. To ensure this, before conducting the study all participants were asked about their previous knowledge in this respect. We aimed at analyzing the impact of our simulation on people from different genders and different age groups. To ensure this, another level of candidate screening was associated with their age and gender. As the result we have selected 10 people (5 males and 5 females) with their age evenly distributed between 23 to 63 years old. All the participants claimed to have no previous knowledge about ancient Mesopotamia and the city of Uruk.

During the *study* each test subject was asked to sit in front of the computer screen and was given a very brief introduction. The introduction mentioned that what is shown on the screen is the 3D reconstruction of the city of Uruk in 3000

B.C. After this the participant was given instructions on how to navigate in the Virtual World and was asked to follow each of the 4 virtual agents present in our prototype. The interviewee was giving commands as to which direction to go and which avatar to follow. Once the participant successfully observed the key activities in the life cycle of the selected agent he/she was asked to follow another avatar. For the purpose of this study we kept the duration of this experience under 20 minutes for each participant.

At the end of this experiment the Virtual World browser was closed and the participant was interviewed about the Virtual World experience. The aim of these interviews was to verify whether the users of our simulation are able to learn about the culture of ancient Mesopotamia along all the dimensions we have identified. Each *interview* consisted of 18 questions. The first 16 questions aimed to test what was learned by the participant about the Uruk culture along each of the 4 dimensions covered by our model. For example, some of the questions focused on the environment, asking the test subject to describe the climate, vegetation and weather. Other questions targeted the institutional structure, i.e. social relationship between the observed virtual agents as well as information about their social roles and interaction protocols. Another two groups of questions focused on agent behavior and on objects in Uruk city. Finally, the last two questions aimed at evaluating the overall experience, asking the test subjects to briefly summarize what they have learned about the culture, identify any of their concerns and list the key highlights of the virtual experience.

The *results* of the study confirm that participants were able to acquire new knowledge about the Uruk culture along every dimension we have identified. None of the participants gave 100% correct answers, but all of them provided at least 70% of correct information. The incorrect responses were not biased along any of the dimensions and seemed to be highly individual. Some of the wrong answers had clear correlation with the lack of skills in controlling the interface.

5   Conclusion and Future Work

We have presented a formal model of a virtual culture that is suitable for preserving a variety of cultural attributes and for simulating a giving culture to the public. Our model is based on the Virtual Institutions technology [17] with Virtual Agents being the carriers of the cultural knowledge, while the 3D Virtual World provides a necessary environment for visualizing a culture. The resulting model was used for creating the research prototype of the city of Uruk 3000 B.C. The prototype aims at simulating the culture of two fishermen families in ancient Mesopotamia. The validation of the developed prototype ensures the feasibility of the selected approach and suggests that it is possible to preserve the cultural knowledge along all the dimensions we have identified trough our research.

Future work includes extending the scenarios with more agents, improving the agent architecture, introducing more variety in agent behavior and further formalization of the Uruk institution. In the future we will support the dissemination of culture, namely how culture spreads and evolves. We will also work on gathering more scientific evidence in favor of our approach to modeling cultures by comparing it with traditional approaches. In particular, we will investigate whether the users of our simulation are able to learn more about a particular culture than those accessing the same information through printed materials.

References

1. White, L.: The Concept of Culture. American Anthropological Association (1959)
2. Herskovits, M., Jean, M.: Cultural anthropology, Knopf New York (1955)
3. Dictionary.Com: Definition of Culture. Published Online (accessed February 15, 2009), `http://dictionary.reference.com/browse/culture`
4. Addison, A.C.: Emerging trends in virtual heritage. IEEE MultiMedia 7(2), 22–25 (2000)
5. Gutierrez, D., Frischer, B., Cerezo, E., Gomez, A., Seron, F.: AI and virtual crowds: Populating the Colosseum. Journal of Cultural Heritage 8(2), 176–185 (2007)
6. Mam, J., Haegler, S., Yersin, B., Mller, P.: Populating Ancient Pompeii with Crowds of Virtual Romans. In: 8th International Symposium on Virtual Reality, Archeology and Cultural Heritage - VAST (2007)
7. Upal, M.A.: From Artificial Intelligence to Artificial Culture. In: Papers from the AAAI- 2006 Workshop, pp. 1–5. AAAI Press, Menlo Park (2006)
8. Tylor, E.B.: Primitive Culture. J.P. Putnams Sons, New York (1871)
9. Kroeber, A., Kluckhohn, C.: Culture: A critical review of concepts and definitions. Random House, New York (1952)
10. Axelrod, R.: The dissemination of culture: A model with local convergence and global polarization. Journal of Conflict Resolution 41(2), 203–226 (1997)
11. Carley, K.M.: A theory of group stability. American Sociological Review 56, S331–S354 (1991)
12. Cohen, J.M.: Sources of peer homogeneity. Sociology of Education 50(4), 227–241 (1977)
13. Miguel, M.S., Eguiluz, V.M., Toral, R., Klemm, K.: Binary and multivariate stochastic models of consensus formation. Computing in Science and Engineering 7, 67–73 (2005)
14. Schotter, A.: The Economic Theory of Social Institutions. Cambridge University Press, Cambridge (1981)
15. Esteva, M.: Electronic Institutions: From Specification to Development. PhD thesis, Institut d'Investigació en Intelligència Artificial (IIIA), Spain (2003)
16. Uruk Project, `http://www-staff.it.uts.edu.au/~anton/Research/Uruk_Project`
17. Bogdanovych, A.: Virtual Institutions. PhD thesis, UTS, Australia (2007)
18. Bogdanovych, A., Rodriguez, J., Simoff, S., Cohen, A., Sierra, C.: Developing Virtual Heritage Applications as Normative Multiagent Systems. In: Proceedings of the AOSE 2009 Workshop. Springer, Heidelberg (2009)
19. Summit on Educational Games: Harnessing the Power of Video Games for Learning. Public report, Federation of American Scientists (October 2006)

One for All or One for One? The Influence of Cultural Dimensions in Virtual Agents' Behaviour

Samuel Mascarenhas, João Dias, Rui Prada, and Ana Paiva

INESC-ID, Av. Prof. Cavaco Silva,
2780-990 Porto Salvo TagusPark, Portugal
{samuel.mascarenhas,joao.dias,rui.prada}@gaips.inesc-id.pt,
ana.paiva@inesc-id.pt

Abstract. With the increase in the development of autonomous agents, there is a bigger demand on their capability of interacting with other agents and users in ways that are natural and inspired by how humans interact. However, cultural aspects have been largely neglected so far, even though they are a crucial aspect of human societies. Our goal is to create an architecture able to model cultural groups of agents with perceivable distinct behaviour. In particular, this paper focus on how to use two cultural dimensions proposed by Hofstede in order to influence the agent's goal selection and appraisal processes. Using our cultural architecture, we created two cultural groups of agents and asked users to visualise them performing a short emergent story. We then asked them to describe the two groups visualised. Results confirmed that users did perceived differences in the groups, and those differences were congruent with the cultural parametrisation used.

1 Introduction

Nowadays, we are witnessing an increasing research on creating richer Intelligent Virtual Environments (IVEs). In the current development of these applications, many research challenges arise from the desire of leading users to experience the same kinds of social dynamics they would experience in the real world.

Consequently, there has been a large increase on studies related to agent architectures that take into account human social interactions, such as human dialogue and emotional responses. In particular, current architectures have acquired the capacity to create characters with distinguishable "personalities". This is usually done by associating the characters with different emotional profiles and personal goals.

However, culture which is a fundamental aspect of human societies, has been largely neglected so far in current agent systems. Research in culture specific agents has mainly focused on communication aspects [17] [7]. As a consequence, the social richness of the IVEs is diminished, since the behaviour of the characters ends up being distinguishable by their individual differences. While not

Zs. Ruttkay et al. (Eds.): IVA 2009, LNAI 5773, pp. 272–286, 2009.

having culture embedded in the minds of the characters can be sufficient for representing simple real-world situations, we believe it is important for dealing with more complex scenarios and essential if we wish to build IVEs to represent multicultural worlds.

With this problem in mind, the aim of this research is to create an agent architecture that recreates general cultural aspects of human behaviour, not only related to different gestures or communication styles, but also to other important elements such as: rituals, goals and emotions. This architecture can then facilitate the creation of different cultural groups of agents with perceivable differences in their patters of behaviour, similar to the patterns found in real human cultures.

As described in [12], some previous work was done towards this goal by defining and implementing the notion of cultural rituals into an emotional agent architecture. Differently, in this paper we explore the use of an explicit model of *Cultural Dimensions* to influence the agent's behaviour. These dimensions were proposed by Hofstede in [6] and according to him, they indicate certain behavioural tendencies that are present in every human culture. In order to assess the model's capability to express different cultural behaviour, we performed a small evaluation with two sets of agents representing cultures with opposing dimensions. The results show that user's correctly classify the agent's behaviour as collectivist or individualist.

The structure of this paper is described as follows. In the next section we present some background on culture and describe in detail Hofstede's dimensional model. In section 3 we discuss related work in the area of culture specific agents in order to situate our approach. In section 4 we present the conceptual approach we used to model Hofstede's dimensions. Its implementation into an agent architecture is described in section 5. We then present a case study used to perform an evaluation where users watched two cultural groups with a different dimensional parametrisation. Finally, after analysing and discussing the results obtained, we draw some conclusions and present some future work.

2   Background

Culture is a vast concept, not easy definable. In 1952, a list containing 164 possible definitions of culture was compiled by Alfred Kroeber and Clyde Kluckhonn [8]. Still, no consensus has yet been reached in the present day.

The notion of culture here adopted is the one proposed by Geert Hofstede. The foundation for his theory is a large empirical study conducted in more than 70 countries. According to him, culture is "the collective programming of the mind that distinguishes the members of one group or category of people from another" [6]. These "mental programs" refer to patterns of thinking, feeling, and potential acting that are shared and learnt by members of the same culture. The patterns can manifest themselves at an implicit level, under the form of values, or at a more clearly observable level, under the form of rituals, heroes and symbols. These four types of manifestations can be described as follows:

Values - represent cultural preconceptions about what is desirable/undesirable;

Rituals - are essential social activities that are carried out in a predetermined fashion;

Heroes - are persons, alive, dead or even imaginary, that serve as role models.

Symbols - words, gestures, pictures, or objects that members of a given culture have assigned a special particular meaning.

Asides from the cultural manifestations presented above, Hofstede proposes five dimensions on which cultures vary [6]. Different from the previous manifestations, which can be very specific to a certain culture or subculture (e.g. the Japanese tea ceremony), Hofstede argues that these dimensions are universal. They are directly based on the culture's values and indicate general behavioural tendencies shared by the members of the culture. These tendencies should be not considered deterministic, since other factors such as the individual's personality, also play an important role on human behaviour. Hofstede's five dimensions can be described as follows:

1. **Power Distance Index (PDI) -** the degree to which less powerful members of the group expect and accept that power is distributed unequally. In small PDI cultures (e.g. Austria), people tend to regard others as equals despite their formal status. In high PDI cultures (e.g. Malaysia) powerful people have more privileges and like to wear symbols that reflect their status.

2. **Individualism (IDV) -** versus its opposite, collectivism, indicates the extent to which individuals see themselves integrated into groups. In collectivistic cultures (e.g Guatemala), everyone looks out for one another in exchange for unquestioning loyalty. On the other hand, in individualistic cultures (e.g. USA) people stress the importance of personal achievements and individual rights. Everyone is expected to be only responsible for themselves and their immediate family.

3. **Masculinity (MAS) -** versus its opposite, femininity, refers to the distribution of roles between genders. In very feminine cultures (e.g. Sweden), relationships and quality of life are very important. Both sexes should have equal rights and responsibilities. Very masculine cultures (e.g. Japan), favours assertiveness, ambition, efficiency, competition and materialism. Also, differences between gender roles are accentuated.

4. **Uncertainty Avoidance Index (UAI) -** this dimension indicates to what extent people prefer structured over unstructured situations. In low UAI cultures (e.g. Singapore), people have as few rules as possible and unfamiliar risks and ambiguous situations cause no discomfort. In an opposite manner, in high UAI Cultures (e.g. Portugal), people tend to have strict laws and rules and also various safety measures to avoid situations that are novel, unknown, or different from usual.

5. **Long-Term Orientation (LTO) -** indicates to what extent the future has more importance than the past or present. Short-Term oriented cultures (e.g Nigeria), value the respect for tradition, quick results, fulfilling social

obligations and reciprocation of gifts. On the other hand, in long-term oriented cultures (e.g. China), people give more importance to the future than the past and present.

The main advantage of this model is the fact that it gives a clear and detailed notion of universal differences between cultures. As such, we believe the model serves the purpose of our work by indicating how we should characterise general cultural aspects of behaviour.

3   Related Work

A substantial part of the research done on culture in virtual agents involves the adaptation of the agents to the user's culture. This research is strongly motivated by the study conducted by Lee and Nass in [9], which showed that users tend to prefer to interact with a virtual agent that has a similar cultural background. In this line of investigation, CUBE-G is an interesting project that uses Hofstede's dimensions. They are used for exclusively modelling nonverbal communication aspects of the different national cultures. During a conversation with virtual agents, the cultural background of a user is inferred by sensing his nonverbal behaviour using a Nintendo's Wii remote controller. Then the nonverbal behaviour of the virtual agents is dynamically adapted according to the culture inferred. In [10], the manual adaption of a virtual agent to achieve believability in several cultural audiences was also studied.

To a lesser degree, virtual agents have also been adapted to specific cultures that are intentionally different from the user's culture. For example, in the Tactical Language Training System [7], users interact with autonomous characters from a foreign culture in order to train the culture's spoken language and gestures. The goal is to teach communicative skills in languages that are less commonly taught in USA, such as Arabic, Chinese or Russian. Learning such languages with traditional courses can be very time-consuming, due to their unfamiliar writing systems and cultural norms. However this system only addresses communicative aspects of a culture, namely spoken language and gestures.

As for agent architectures that include social and cultural factors in virtual agents' internal knowledge and reasoning, research is quite new. In the Tactical Language Training System the architecture that drives the behaviour of the characters in called Thespian [19]. It embeds cultural norms in the character's conduct by using social relationships such as trust and by allowing the definition of cultural obligations between agents. Thespian was built on top of PsychSim [16], a architecture for social behaviour. PsychSim implements a social theory called Theory of Mind, which is defined in [14] as the human ability of attributing mental states such as intentions, beliefs, and values, not only to oneself but to others as well. A similar feature was required in our cultural agents in order to model collectivistic cultures where people care a lot about the consequences their actions have on others.

More recently, the Culturally Affected Behaviour (CAB) model [20] allows the encoding of specific ethnographic data on cultural norms, biases and stereotypes, which is used to influence the behaviour of virtual agents. In addition to the Theory of Mind, the model is also inspired by the Schema Theory proposed by D'Andrade [2]. This theory postulates that a culture can be represented as a shared organisation of schemas. The main difference with our work is that CAB's cultural norms are tied to very particular tasks or actions such as giving alcohol or showing pictures of one's wife to a stranger. Our dimensional model addresses more general predispositions and behavioural tendencies.

4   Cultural Dimensions in Agents

Hofstede's model has five different cultural dimensions which normally range from 0 to 100. Our intention was to use similar values to change the agent's behaviour in a way that is congruent with Hofstede's findings. As described in section 3, the work done in CUBE-G already maps these dimensions to expressive nonverbal behaviour. We wish to pursue a different approach. As such, we decided to use similar dimensions to influence two other important aspects that are strongly influenced by culture in humans [2,13]: (1) goal utility and (2) emotional appraisal. The first one is used for the agent to make more rational decisions about what he should do at any given moment. The latter serves to simulate human emotional responses to events.

For simplification purposes, we decided to encompass only two of the five dimensions (the ones that seemed to be more easily recognisable in a short-term interaction and easier to start from): (1) Individualism vs Collectivism and (2) Power Distance. As such, the other dimensions are left as future work.

4.1   Goal Utility - Individualism Dimension

So, how can culture affect goal utility? Hofstede states that, in an individualistic culture, "people are expected to be only responsible for themselves and their immediate family." [6] Also, close friendships are very important. On the other hand, in a collectivistic culture "everyone looks out for one another in exchange for unquestioning loyalty". As such, it seems clear that our cultural characters should evaluate a goal's utility under two different perspectives: (1) the impact the goal has to themselves and (2) the impact the goal has to others (which requires the ability to form mental models of others, like the agents from PsychSim). Individualistic characters are much more concerned with the first perspective as the second one is only important if the character has a strong interpersonal attraction (symbolising a close bond) with any of the other characters. Oppositely, collectivistic characters are equally concerned with both perspectives and treat everyone alike (regardless of social bonds). Based on these facts the following equation (1) was proposed for calculating a goal's utility based on the individualism score (IDV), the impact the goal has on the character's self (SI), the impact the goal has on others (OI), and a positive relationship factor (PREL), which considers interpersonal attractions between the targets of the goal and the character:

$$Utility(g) = SI(g) + OI(g)(\frac{100 - IDV}{100} + \frac{IDV}{100} \times PREL(g)) \qquad (1)$$

Note that $PREL(g)$ is normalised to a scale of 0 (no positive relationships) to 1 (maximum positive relationships) and the exact equations for $SI(g)$ and $OI(g)$ are domain-dependent. To explain the rationale behind this particular equation, we will use the following situation: character A is considering the goal of giving an apple to character B versus the goal of giving the apple to character C. A has plenty of apples so loosing just one has a small negative impact, such as $SI(g)$ = -1. However, B is hungry and poor, so receiving an apple would have a considerable positive impact like $OI(g)$ = 5. On the other hand, C is also hungry but wealthy, so the impact for him of receiving the apple is a little lower, for example $OI(g)$ = 4. Moreover, A has a negative interpersonal attraction towards B, thus $PREL(g)$ = 0. On the other hand, A has a positive interpersonal attraction towards C, which makes $PREL(g)$ return a positive multiplier depending on the intensity of the relation (in this particular scenario, we'll assume that it returns 0.5).

Using the previous situation, let's examine three different cultural scenarios: (1) an extreme collectivistic culture; (2) an extreme individualistic culture and (3) a neutral culture. In the first scenario IDV is equal to zero, so both goal impact functions are weighted equally which means that a character considers his own well-being to have the same importance as the well-being of others, regardless of the existent relationships. As such, regarding the example depicted, the utility of giving B the apple is higher ($Utility(g)$ = 4) than giving it to C ($Utility(g)$ = 3).

In the second scenario IDV is equal to 100, so the others well-being depends only on the existence of a positive relationship. Since in the previous situation A disliked B, then PREL(g) = 0. Thus, A now will never create an intention to give B the apple, since the goal has a utility of -1. But for C, since A has a positive relation with him it makes PREL(g) return a positive multiplier (e.g. 0.5). Thus, the utility of giving C the apple will now be equal to 2.

In the third scenario with a neutral culture (IDV = 50), i.e. a culture that is neither inclined to individualism or collectivism, the utility for giving B the apple is equal to 1.5. It is not negative but is lesser than the utility of giving it to C, which is equal to 2. This means that generally characters of a neutral culture care for all other agents but will give preference to their friends.

4.2   Goal Utility - Power Distance Dimension

According to Hofstede [6], in low-power distance cultures people tend to regard others as equals despite their formal status. Oppositely, in high power distance cultures powerful people are expected to be privileged. As such, we want characters that belong to a high power culture to favour goals that positively affect others who have a higher status. To achieve this result, we propose to augment equation 1 with a component related to the power distance score (PDI), and a power distance factor (DIST) that considers the differences of power between the targets of the goal and the character:

$$Utility(g) = SI(g) + OI(g)(\frac{100 - IDV}{100} + \frac{IDV}{100} \times PREL(g) + \frac{PDI}{100} \times DIST(g)) \tag{2}$$

Similar to the positive relationship factor (PREL), DIST is also normalised to a scale of 0 (power equal or lower than self) to 1 (power is higher than self). Consider that in the previous "giving apple" situation, character A has a power of 5, character B a power of 3, and C a power of 10. Since B has lower power than A, DIST(g) is equal to zero towards him. However, C has a power that is two times higher than the power of A, thus DIST(g) will return a value greater than zero (e.g. DIST(g) = 0.5). In the extreme collectivistic scenario (IDV = 0), we previously concluded that A would prefer to give the apple to B (Utility(g) = 4) than to give it to C (Utility(g) = 3). Now, considering also the power distance dimension, the situation can change when PDI becomes greater than zero. If we consider the extreme case (PDI = 100). The goal of giving the apple to C has now an utility of 5 and so A prefers to give him the apple instead of giving it to B (which remains with an utility of 4).

4.3   Emotional Appraisal

The idea that emotions are elicited by subjective evaluations (appraisals) of events or situations is the basis of several appraisal theories [18]. But how does culture affects emotions? According to Mesquita and Frijda [13], "cross-cultural differences as well as similarities have been identified in each phase of the emotional process." Regarding cultural differences that we can relate to the appraisal process and to Hofstede's dimensions, there are distinctions related to the Individualism dimension, proposed by Markus and Kitayama in [11]. They argue that in individualistic cultures the individual "appears as focused on his or her independence and self-actualization", while in a collectivistic culture the individual is "focused predominantly on his or her relationship with in-group members or with the in-group as a whole." Consequently, individualists appraise events in "terms of their individual achievements and properties" while collectivists appraise events in "terms of group the person belongs to or as affecting the interpersonal relationships." Concerning the Power Distance, so far we could not find any distinctions that we could correlate directly to Power Distance. However, based on the notions previously presented, we propose equation (3) for calculating one of OCC's [15] appraisal variables - the praiseworthiness of an event. As stated in the OCC theory of emotions [15], events with a positive praiseworthiness will potentially cause the character to feel pride or admiration, and a negative praiseworthiness result will potentially cause the character to feel shame or reproach.

$$Praiseworthiness(e) = \begin{cases} 0, & \text{if } AI(e) > OI(e) \geq 0 \\ (OI(e) - AI(e)) \times \frac{100 - IDV}{100}, & \text{if otherwise} \end{cases} \tag{3}$$

The equation proposes is based on the impact the event has on the character who caused it (AI), the sum of impacts the event has on the other characters (OI), and the individualism score (IDV). In general terms, the first branch of the equation refers to events that did not harm others $(OI(e) \geq 0)$ but had a more beneficial effect for the character who caused them (AI(e) >OI(e)). As such, no matter how collectivistic a culture is, a character will not be ashamed if, for example, he has just eaten an apple (an event that had a positive effect on himself but a neutral effect on others). As for the second branch, it provides the following results: (1) the more collectivistic a culture is (i.e. the lower the IDV), the more an event that is undesirable for others (OI(e) <0) but is beneficial for the responsible character (AI(e) >0) will be blameworthy (e.g. stealing something); and also (2) the more collectivistic a culture is, the more an event that is good for others (OI(e) >0) but is bad for the responsible character (AI(e) <0) will be highly praiseworthy (e.g. giving food). In other words, collectivistic characters will find highly admirable a spirit of self-sacrifice for the well-being of the group and will find highly reproachable selfish acts.

To give an example, consider the following situation: agent B has asked directly agent A for an apple and A denies it. This has a positive impact on A considering he keeps the food for future use (e.g. AI(e) = 1). However, it has a negative impact on B who is very hungry (e.g. OI(e) = -3). Let's consider that agent A and agent B are from a culture that has an IDV of 27 (a value representing a collectivist culture). Applying the equation, agent's A decision will have a praiseworthiness value of -3 approximately. This means that A will potential feel ashamed, while B would feel reproach for A. Instead, if A decides to give B the apple, it will have a negative impact on A (e.g. AI(e) = -2) but a positive effect on B (e.g. OI(e) = 3). The praiseworthiness value of this decision will be 3.6. As such, A will likely feel pride, while B will feel admiration for A. Finally, if we re-examine both decisions, now considering the characters belong to a culture with an IDV of 91 (the value of the USA culture), we'll confirm that both decisions have a very low praiseworthiness. Namely, the decision of giving B the apple will be equal to 0.4, while keeping it -0.3.

5   Integration into an Agent Architecture

For the implementation of our cultural model, we have extended an emotional agent architecture [4]. Asides from the added cultural elements, agents have also individual behaviour, determined by their emotions, needs, quick reactions to events, and goals. The concept of emotions is based on the OCC cognitive theory of emotions [15], which defines emotions as valenced (good or bad) reactions to events. The subjective evaluation of events that causes such reactions is called the appraisal process. Motivational needs (grounded on a psychological model of human action regulation called PSI [5]) are used to select between alternative goals. The extended architecture is shown in Figure 1.

In this paper we will provide a brief description of the overall behaviour, without detailing previous existing components. For more information about them

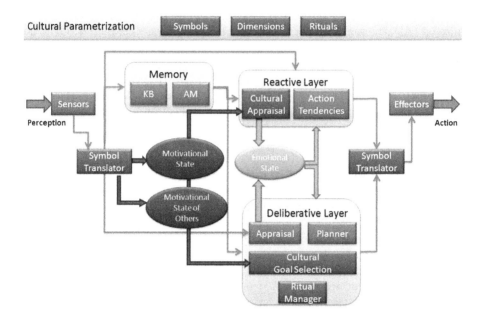

Fig. 1. Cultural Agent Architecture

please see [3]. When an event is perceived it passes through a Symbol translator that translates the meaning of the event according to a culture's symbols (for instance a waving hand may considered greeting in one culture and insulting in another one). The event is then used to update the agent's Knowledge Base (KB) and Autobiographic Memory. At the same time is used to update the agent's motivational state. For instance, if the agent finished an eating action, its need for energy will go down. The agent needs to model the same process for others, and so it builds and updates a motivational state of others according to events perceived. This information is used later in the cultural goal selection and cultural appraisal processes.

After updating the motivational states, the event is finally appraised. There are two main appraisal processes, the deliberative one that handles emotions related to the achievement of goals (e.g. satisfaction, disappointment), and the reactive one that consists in associating predefined appraisal values to the event (and then generating the corresponding emotions). The Cultural Appraisal was integrated in the reactive appraisal component. The Praiseworthiness appraisal variable is now automatically determined using equation (3) where AI(e) is equal to the effect the event had on the motivational state of the agent responsible for causing the event while OI(e) is equal to the effect the event had on the motivational state of the other agents affected by the event. This effects are manually defined for each possible action. The resulting emotional state is then used to trigger Action Tendencies (reactive actions).

In the deliberative layer, the event perceived will also activate predefined goals, and the agent will have to select between competing alternative goals. Here we introduced the Cultural Goal Selection process that calculates the expected cultural utility for each active goal using equation 2, where SI(g) was associated to the expected impact the goal will have on the agent's motivational state and OI(g) to the expected impact the goal will have on the goal's target (determined using the representation of that agent's motivational state). The goal with highest expected cultural utility will be selected as the agent's current intention, and the planning component will develop and execute a plan to achieve the goal.

6 Case Study

The implemented cultural architecture was used for the development of ORIENT [1], an agent-based educational role-playing game that aims to promote intercultural empathy for young teenagers. Even tough it is a promising project, the game currently has only a single culture. Hence, we could not use it to measure the power of our architecture in creating various distinct cultures. Instead, for evaluating the architecture we created two different cultural groups of five autonomous characters to enact a common real-life situation in a 3D virtual world, namely, a dinner party (see Figure 2). The only difference between the two groups is that one of them was defined as extremely individualistic (IDV = 100) and the other extremely collectivistic (IDV = 0).

Fig. 2. Characters at the dinner table

For simplicity reasons, the overall plot is very short: the characters arrive at the party location; greet each other; socialise for a while; and then sit together at a dinner table and start to eat. Despite the fact that the characters all look alike, they have some individual differences. For example, one character feels sick and another has some medicine with him. Also, the character that has the medicine has just built a new house and needs someone to help him paint it. These individual differences were made for originating situations to explore the parametrisation of the culture's dimensional scores. For instance, in the collectivistic culture the agent will give the medicine to the sick character.

7   Evaluation

Using the case study presented, we performed an evaluation to determine the differences the users could recognise in the behaviours of the two groups of characters created. Again, the groups are only different in their associated value for the Individualism dimension. Thus, we wanted to check if users did in fact could recognise one group as more individualistic and the other as more collectivistic.

7.1   Methodology

Two videos were created with the system working and generating the situations. The actions of the characters allowed for the emergence of the stories enacting a dinner party situation. Both videos were then used in an online questionnaire which starts by asking participants to watch one video and then answer two groups of questions about the characters depicted in it. Afterwards, the participants were asked to watch the other video and again answer the same groups of questions. Since repeated measures were used, participants were randomly assigned to a visualization order.

In the first question group participants had to decide if a given statement was appropriate to the conduct of the characters or not (in a scale from -3 to 3). These statements (see Table 1) were based on the questions used by Hofstede in his cultural questionnaire and represent cultural values associated either to Individualism/Collectivism. The idea was to see if users would associate the Individualistic/Collectivistic agents to the corresponding statements.

In the second question group, participants had to choose a number between two opposite adjectives in a scale from -3 to 3, according to what they thought to fit best with the characters. The adjectives chosen were: Individualist / Collectivist; Approachable / Distant; Equal / Biased; Independent / Sharing; Polite / Impolite; Pleasant / Unpleasant; Unfriendly / Friendly; Relaxed / Tense; Compassionate / Indifferent; Serious / Cheerful; and Warm / Cold.

Finally, the questionnaire consists in two additional questions that tries to access if any differences between the videos presented were perceived, and if so, if participants understood those differences as being caused by the culture of the characters, or by their personalities, or by neither one of these factors.

7.2   Results

We had a total of 42 participants (36 Portuguese, 5 German, and 1 British), aged between 18 and 34 years old of which 76% were male. Concerning the group of questions about the value statements we applied the Wilcoxon test to see if there was significant differences in the user's classification. For every statement

Table 1. Results for the statements related to individualism/collectivism

Value Statement (Culture Associated)	Culture	Avg.	StD.	Differences between cultures
They are concerned with everyone's well-being (Collectivism)	Col.	1,62	1,56	|ΔAvg| = 1
	Ind.	0,62	2,16	p = 0,003 r = 0,33
Personal achievements are very important (Individualism)	Col.	0,74	1,43	|ΔAvg| = 0,43
	Ind.	1,17	1,15	p = 0,006 r = 0,30
Direct confrontations should be avoided (Collectivism)	Col.	0,50	1,64	|ΔAvg| = 0,5
	Ind.	0,00	1,81	p = 0,033 r = 0,23
They like to trust and cooperate with other people (Collectivism)	Col.	2,05	1,08	|ΔAvg| = 1,43
	Ind.	0,62	2,22	p = 0,00 r = 0,38
It is important for them to be independent (Individualism)	Col.	0,07	1,31	|ΔAvg| = 0,48
	Ind.	0,55	1,42	p = 0,015 r = 0,27

related to Individualism or Collectivism (see Table 1) the results were statistically significant (p <0,05). Users found the individualistic/collectivistic values to be more appropriate for the individualistic/collectivistic culture respectively. The highest effect (r=0,38) was for "They like to trust and cooperate with other people" statement. This suggests that users can recognise appropriate differences related to cultural values in groups of characters, by simply changing their parametrisation of our dimensions component accordingly.

For the adjective's classification we used the Wilcoxon test once more. Except for the *Equal/Biased* and *Warm/Cool* every other pair of adjectives yielded significant results. As such, we can affirm that there was a significant effect of the Individualism dimension score in the user's classification of most adjectives. Amongst them are the adjectives *Individualistic/Collectivistic* (which had the largest difference in averages) and *Independent/Sharing*. Therefore, user's interpretation of the characters' behaviour matched the parametrisation used for the dimensions component. Interestingly, the majority of users formed a more positive opinion of the characters in the collectivistic video by rating them more Friendly, Polite, and Pleasant. We believe the fact most users are from Portugal (a strongly collectivistic culture) might have caused this effect. In the last two questions to assess directly if users perceived the videos as being different, only 1 did not found any differences. This corresponds to only 3% of the participants. From the resulting 41 participants (which answered they had perceived differences), 63% associated the differences to personality, 30% to culture and only 7% answered neither. We performed a a Chi-square test to determine if the result was not obtained by chance. The Chi-square value obtained was 5,158 and was significant (p=0,023).

The results indicate that the different parametrisation, used for the Individualism dimension, was strong enough to cause users to perceive significant differences in the cultural groups. Yet, most of the users did not attributed those differences to culture. This is congruent with Hofstede's argument that the behavioural tendencies associated to his dimensions are harder to interpret as cultural by the average person.

8   Concluding Remarks

In this paper we have argued the importance of considering culture in order to enhance the social dynamics of virtual agents. The research in culture-specific agents is quite novel and the work existent has mainly focused on communication aspects. Differently, we have proposed a model that tries to recreate more general cultural behavioural aspects, inspired by an well-established anthropological theory on human cultural variation. This theory, proposed by Hofstede in [6], encompasses five different dimensions that exist in every human culture.

Two of these dimensions (Individualism vs Collectivism and Power Distance) were integrated into an agent architecture for autonomous synthetic characters. They are used to influence the emotions of the characters and the utility of their goals. The main idea for achieving this was to make characters more or less concerned with the needs and social statuses of others, according to the dimensional parametrisation established.

The cultural architecture was then used to create two different cultures, one extremely individualistic and the other extremely collectivistic. An evaluation was performed to determine the effect the dimensions implemented had on the user's characterisation of the created cultures. The results show that the different dimensional parametrisation used was strong enough to cause users to perceive significant differences in the two cultures. Users classified the cultures as individualistic or collectivistic in congruence with the parametrisation used. This is a very encouraging result as it shows that our model is able to create cultures with perceivable differences, just by changing a simple dimensional parameter. As future work, we would like to perform additional evaluations of the model. For instance, to perform the same experiment but with users from an highly individualistic culture. Also, we want to explore additional ways to use the dimensions implemented and consider the inclusion of the other dimensions as well.

Acknowledgements

This work was partially supported by a scholarship (SFRH BD/19481/2004) granted by the Fundação para a Ciência e a Tecnologia (FCT) and by European Community (EC) and is currently funded by the eCIRCUS project IST-4-027656-STP with university partners Heriot-Watt, Hertfordshire, Sunderland, Warwick, Bamberg, Augsburg, Wuerzburg plus INESC-ID and Interagens. The authors are solely responsible for the content of this publication. It does not represent the opinion of the EC or the FCT, which are not responsible for any use that might be made of data appearing therein.

References

1. Aylett, R., Paiva, A., Vannini, N., Enz, S., Andre, E., Hall, L.: But that was in another country: agents and intercultural empathy. In: Proceedings of AAMAS 2009, Budapest, Hungary, May 2009, IFAMAAS/ACM DL (2009)
2. D'Andrade, R.: Schemas and motivation. In: D'Andrade, R., Strauss, C. (eds.) Human motives and Cultural models, pp. 23–44. Cambridge University Press, Cambridge (1992)
3. Dias, J.: Fearnot!: Creating emotional autonomous synthetic characters for empathic interactions. Master's thesis, Universidade Técnica de Lisboa, Instituto Superior Técnico, Lisboa (2005)
4. Dias, J., Paiva, A.C.R.: Feeling and reasoning: A computational model for emotional characters. In: Bento, C., Cardoso, A., Dias, G. (eds.) EPIA 2005. LNCS (LNAI), vol. 3808, pp. 127–140. Springer, Heidelberg (2005)
5. Dorner, D.: The mathematics of emotions. In: Prooceedings of the Fifth International Conference on Cognitive Modeling, Bamberg, Germany, pp. 75–79 (2003)
6. Hofstede, G.: Culture Consequences: Comparing Values, Behaviors, Intitutions, and Organizations Across Nations. Sage Publications, Thousand Oaks (2001)
7. Johnson, W.L., Beal, C.R., Fowles-Winkler, A., Lauper, U., Marsella, S.C., Narayanan, S., Papachristou, D., Vilhjálmsson, H.H.: Tactical language training system: An interim report. In: Lester, J.C., Vicari, R.M., Paraguaçu, F. (eds.) ITS 2004. LNCS, vol. 3220, pp. 336–345. Springer, Heidelberg (2004)
8. Kroeber, A., Kluckhohn, C.: Culture: A Critical Review of Concepts and Definitions. Peabody Museum, Cambridge (1952)
9. Lee, E., Nass, C.: Does the ethnicity of a computer agent matter? an experimental comparison of human-computer interaction and computer-mediated communication. In: Emobied Conversational Agents (1998)
10. Maldonado, H., Hayes-Roth, B.: Toward cross-cultural believability in character design. In: Payr, S., Trappl, R. (eds.) Agent Culture: Human-Agent Interaction in a Multicultural World, pp. 143–175. Lawrence Erlbaum Associates, London (2004)
11. Markus, H., Kitayama, S.: Culture and the self: Implications for cognition, emotion, and motivation. Psychological Review 98, 224–253 (1991)
12. Mascarenhas, S., Dias, J., Afonso, N., Enz, S., Paiva, A.: Using rituals to express cultural differences in synthetic characters. In: Proceedings of AAMAS 2009, Budapest, Hungary, May 2009, IFAMAAS/ACM DL (2009)
13. Mesquita, B., Frijda, N.: Cultural variation in emotions: A review. Psychological Bulletin 112, 179–204 (1992)
14. Nichols, S., Stich, S.: Mindreading. An Integrated Account of Pretence, Self-Awareness, and Understanding of Other Minds. Oxford University Press, Oxford (2003)
15. Ortony, A., Clore, G., Collins, A.: The Cognitive Structure of Emotions. Cambridge University Press, Cambridge (1988)
16. Pynadath, D.V., Marsella, S.: Psychsim: Modeling theory of mind with decision-theoretic agents. In: IJCAI, pp. 1181–1186 (2005)

17. Rehm, M., Bee, N., Endrass, B., Wissner, M., André, E.: Too close for comfort?: Adapting to the user's cultural background. In: HCM 2007: Proceedings of the international workshop on Human-centered multimedia, pp. 85–94. ACM, New York (2007)
18. Roseman, I., Smith, C.: Appraisal Processes in Emotion: Theory, Methods, Research. Oxford University Press, Oxford (2001)
19. Si, M., Marsella, S.C., Pynadath, D.V.: Thespian: Modeling socially normative behavior in a decision-theoretic framework. In: Gratch, J., Young, M., Aylett, R.S., Ballin, D., Olivier, P. (eds.) IVA 2006. LNCS (LNAI), vol. 4133, pp. 369–382. Springer, Heidelberg (2006)
20. Solomon, S., van Lent, M., Core, M., Carpenter, P., Rosenberg, M.: A language for modeling cultural norms, biases and stereotypes for human behavior models. In: BRIMS (2008)

Combining Facial and Postural Expressions of Emotions in a Virtual Character

Céline Clavel[1], Justine Plessier[2], Jean-Claude Martin[1], Laurent Ach[2], and Benoit Morel[2]

[1] LIMSI CNRS, BP 133
91403 Orsay cedex, France
[2] Cantoche, 68, rue d'Hauteville
75010 Paris, France
{celine.clavel,martin}@limsi.fr,
{jplessier,lach,bmorel}@cantoche.com

Abstract. Psychology suggests highly synchronized expressions of emotion across different modalities. Few experiments jointly studied the relative contribution of facial expression and body posture to the overall perception of emotion. Computational models for expressive virtual characters have to consider how such combinations will be perceived by users. This paper reports on two studies exploring how subjects perceived a virtual agent. The first study evaluates the contribution of the facial and postural expressions to the overall perception of basic emotion categories, as well as the valence and activation dimensions. The second study explores the impact of incongruent expressions on the perception of superposed emotions which are known to be frequent in everyday life. Our results suggest that the congruence of facial and bodily expression facilitates the recognition of emotion categories. Yet, judgments were mainly based on the emotion expressed in the face but were nevertheless affected by postures for the perception of the activation dimension.

Keywords: evaluation of virtual agents, affective interaction, conversational and non-verbal behavior, multimodal interaction with intelligent virtual agent.

1 Introduction

An emotion can be seen as "an episode of interrelated, synchronized changes in five components in response to an event of major significance to the organism" [33]. These five components are: the cognitive processing, the subjective feeling, the action tendencies, the physiological changes, and the motor expression. Thus the synchronization of expressions of emotion across different modalities is expected to be of major importance to our understanding of emotion perception. Yet, few studies explored jointly the contribution of the different nonverbal modalities such as posture and face to the overall perception of emotions [24] and did not use virtual characters as potential stimuli. Furthermore, several emotion theorists postulated the existence of emotion blends [8, 12, 13, 28, 31]. Klaus Scherer described three experiments in which the superposition of several emotions was observed.

Zs. Ruttkay et al. (Eds.): IVA 2009, LNAI 5773, pp. 287–300, 2009.
© Springer-Verlag Berlin Heidelberg 2009

Virtual characters are now able to express basic emotions in individual modalities such as facial expressions and more recently bodily expressions. Computational models for generating nonverbal behaviors for expressive characters need to integrate the distribution of the expression of emotion across modalities based on how such combinations are perceived by users. Some models and related experimental studies considered the perception of superposition of emotions but mostly in facial expressions [26].

Our research aims to study how the face and the body posture jointly contribute to a multimodal congruent perception of a single emotion in terms of categories and dimensions. We also aim at studying the impact of incongruent facial and postural expressions on the perception of superposed emotions which are known to frequently occur in everyday life.

Section 2 summarizes related work in Psychology and Affective Computing. Section 3 describes the virtual character animation technology that we used for conducting experimental studies about the perception of combined facial and postural expressions. Sections 4 and 5 detail the two experiments that we conducted about the perception of congruent and incongruent expressions. After discussing the results, we provide possible directions for continuing to study nonverbal expression of superposed emotions, and assess their usefulness for computational models of nonverbal behaviors. A video presenting this research has been submitted along with the paper[1].

2 Related Work

2.1 Emotions

Ekman proposed a set of characteristics that distinguish basic emotions from other affective phenomena (distinctive universal signals, distinctive physiology, automatic appraisal, distinctive universals in antecedent events, distinctive appearance developmentally, presence in other primates, quick onset, brief duration, unbidden occurrence, distinctive thoughts, distinctive subjective experience). Different sets of basic emotions have been proposed such as Joy, Surprise, Fear, Anger, Sadness, Disgust and Contempt [10]. Izard [21] also considers Interest, Shame and Guilt.

Independent and bipolar dimensions have also been proposed for representing emotional states. Russell proposed a 2D circumplex model of affects using a pleasure-displeasure dimension and an arousal-sleep dimension [29]. Other additional dimensions are also proposed such as dominance-submissiveness [30] or unpredictability [14].

In everyday life, several emotions often occur at the same time resulting in the expressions of blends of emotions [12, 32].

2.2 Facial and Bodily Expressions of Emotions

Ekman suggested that a given emotion can be expressed by a family of facial expressions. The number of expressions depends on the emotion [9, 10]. Joy and Contempt have a small set of expressions; Surprise and Disgust might have around 10 expressions; Fear, Sadness and Anger might have around 20 expressions. The recognition

---

[1] http://www.limsi.fr/Individu/martin/permanent/2009-iva/IVA09-Cantoche-comp.avi

rate was also observed to depend on the emotion. Gosselin and Kirouac [15] evaluated the recognition of 30 pictures of facial expressions collected by Ekman and Friesen. They observed that Joy, Anger, Surprise and Sadness were well recognized, whereas Fear and Disgust were less recognized.

A few studies considered how the body expresses emotion. Some researchers observed that body actions might provide information regarding the intensity of the felt emotion [7, 11]. Harrigan suggests that the body's positions and actions provide a backdrop for helping to interpret the meaning of more subtle facial and vocal affect [18]. Wallbott [36] nevertheless observed discriminative features of emotion categories in both posture and movement quality of acted behaviors collected in lab.

Digital corpora have been collected to get detailed information on the expression of emotion in the different modalities. The Geneva Multimodal Emotion Portrayal database is an audiovisual corpus containing more than 7,000 videos recordings of portraits of 18 emotions acted by 10 professional actors [3].

Postural expressions of emotions were collected by Berthouze et al. [4, 6, 25, 37] using a VICON motion-capture system. 12 subjects acted Anger, Joy and Sadness. Their movements were recorded at 34 points of the body. The VICON system did not record the position of the fingers, thus creating confusions between some emotions. Kleinsmith and Bianchi-Berthouze [22] tried to identify the postural features that enable us to recognize the emotional dimensions such as valence and arousal. 111 affective postures were presented to 5 observers who had to judge the postures according to emotional dimensions. The authors observed that some postural features inform the level of dimensions (e.g. the opening of the body is used to assess the activation).

Whereas the importance of synchronization of changes in the various components of emotion is acknowledged [33], few studies considered how the face and the body do combine to express emotions.

Gunes and Piccardi [16] observed that emotions were better recognized when subjects were able to rely on facial expressions and gestures rather than when limited to either facial expressions or gestures.

Scherer and Ellgring [35] compared the expression of emotion across acoustic, face and body modalities. Different emotions, including members of the same emotion family were selected: Hot Anger, Cold Anger, Panic Fear, Anxiety, Despair, Sadness, Elation, Happiness, Interest, Boredom, Shame, Pride, Disgust, and Contempt. Facial actions were coded using FACS [9]. The coding of body expression combined both functional and anatomical approaches. According to Scherer and Ellgring [34], the multimodal response pattern is driven by the presence or absence of behavioral urges produced by appraisal rather than triggered by emotion-specific affect programs. Indeed, the respective multimodal pattern occurs frequently for several emotions, including positive emotions.

Hietanen and Leppänen [20] studied the perception of combinations of static facial expressions and dynamic manual actions of the hands. The emotions (Happiness, Anger and "Neutrality") expressed by the face and hands were the same (congruent expressions) or different (incongruent expressions). They observed that the judgments were mainly based on the facial expressions, but were also affected by the manual expressions. An effect of hand movement quality was observed for facial expressions of Happiness. When the happy face was combined with either happy or neutral hand movements, the happy response was the same. But the proportion of happy responses dropped when the happy face was combined with angry hand movements as compared to happy responses when the happy face was combined with either neutral or happy hand movements. Thus, the perception of facial expressions of emotions can be affected by the expressive qualities of hand movements.

Meeren et al. [24] studied subjects' perception of emotion displayed in static pictures combining facial expressions and body postures. The two modalities conveyed the same or different emotions (Fear, Anger). They observed that when the emotions conveyed by the two modalities differ, the recognition of the emotion conveyed by the facial expression is influenced by the emotion conveyed by the posture. Congruent emotional body language improves recognition of facial expression, and incongruent emotional postural expression biases facial judgment toward the emotion conveyed by the body.

2.3 Nonverbal Expression of Emotion in Virtual Characters

Virtual agents have been designed to display facial expressions of emotions including blends of several emotions using a decomposition of the face in several areas [1, 26]. Models of gesture expressivity have also been proposed focusing on movement quality represented by parameters such as overall activation, spatial extent, temporal extent, fluidity, power and repetition [27]. Postural expressivity was considered to enable virtual characters to display interpersonal attitudes [2, 27].

Few studies considered the combinations of facial expressions and bodily expression of emotion in virtual agents. Using a multimodal corpus exploratory approach, Buisine et al. [5] defined a method for replaying annotated gestures and facial expressions. The authors describe an experimental study exploring how subjects perceive different replays but do not compare how facial and postural expressions are perceived individually vs. jointly.

To summarize, expressions of emotions via the face and the posture have been studied individually in Psychology but rarely jointly. Current computational models for generating multimodal expressions of emotion in intelligent virtual agents are also limited with this respect.

3 A Virtual Agent Technology for Studying Facial and Postural Expressions of Emotions

The Living Actor™ technology was developed by Cantoche and launched in January 2002 for the Major Accounts market which includes e-marketing and e-learning. Our client's objectives depend on the mission of the Living Actor™ avatar (assistant, guide, tutor …) and all clients understand that emotional full body avatars are a unique personalized solution to communicate with the young generation as they are similar to the avatars they are used to interact with in video games. Today, more than 200 large companies in Europe and in the USA use Living Actor™ and the market is growing. According to Gartner (April 2007), by the end of 2011, 80 percent of active Internet users (and Fortune 500 enterprises) will have a "second life", but not necessarily *in* the virtual world called *Second Life*.

Living Actor™ is an innovative real time process for emotion-rich avatars driven solely by the user's voice that allows end users and companies to generate advanced personalized video calls, video content on mobile and chat-based services, or interactive content on web applications.

The system is based on speech-to-animation engine, which provides automatic animation of avatars by a human voice: Avatars' mouth, expressions, and gestures move in sync with the speech. After analyzing the audio signal (recorded or streamed) and detecting sound volume, pace of the speech, prosody, and others parameters, the engine associates and synchronizes it with the virtual character's animation data and the best behaviors and actions are automatically generated to realize the speech visualization by full-body avatars.

A multi-export engine enables the display of avatars in different formats (3D, Flash, AVI, 3GP, FLV). The avatars are compatible with various types of interfaces and devices depending on the technological specifications—ranging from PCs, and mobile phones to set-top boxes for interactive television, or large screen displays for mass audiences.

This industrial animation technology can benefit from experimental studies to evaluate how users will perceive the expressions of emotions displayed by the characters.

4 First Study: Facial and Postural Expressions of Congruent Emotion

This first study aimed at providing answers to the following question: how do different nonverbal modalities (face only, posture only, face and posture) compare in terms of how human subjects perceive the emotion expressed by a virtual character? As the study of combinations of facial and postural expressions of emotion is still exploratory, we decided to test a subset of basic emotions for which there is at least a minimum data in the literature to which we would be able to compare our results: Sadness, Fear, Anger, Surprise and Joy. For the same reason, we focused on a single expression for each emotion.

4.1 Methodology

We designed facial expressions of these emotions based on a selection of some of the distinctive clues described by Ekman [12]. We also designed postural expressions of emotions. We inspired from a database of acted postures [23]. This set of nonverbal expressions was implemented using the virtual character technology presented above. Some of the resulting set of stimuli used for the two experiments described in this paper is illustrated in a video submitted along with the current paper.

For this first study, we designed 15 canned animations of 3 seconds each (from a neutral pose to the expression of emotion and back to neutral pose). 5 animations were face-only expressions of the emotions that we selected (the rest of the body is hidden), 5 animations displayed the postural expression of the same emotions (the head is hidden), and 5 animations displayed combined facial and bodily expressions of emotions (Fig. 1). We decided to hide the irrelevant part of the body rather than involving a "neutral" expression to avoid any influence of this neutral expression on the expressive part.

59 students from an engineering school participated in this first study. They were divided randomly into two groups. Each group viewed only half of the animations.

Fig. 1. Expressions of anger in the face only (left), posture only (middle), and combination of face and posture (right)

A first animation of the character displaying a deictic gesture was used as a training animation so that subjects had seen the character once before evaluating its emotional expressions. After viewing an animation, subjects had to answer a questionnaire. They had to report how much they perceived each of the emotions in the animation using 5 points Likert scales. Subjects were able to select several emotion labels for each animation. They also had to rate the activation and the valence of the emotion.

4.2   Results

Emotion categories perceived in each animation. We computed repeated measures ANOVA in order to estimate the degree of recognition of the intended emotion in each modality (Table 1).

Anger was the most perceived emotion in our animations of Anger for the three modalities. *Sadness* was the most perceived emotion in our animations of Sadness for the three modalities. *Joy* was the most perceived emotion in the Face animation and Face+Posture designed for Joy. Nevertheless the Posture animation designed for Joy was equivalently perceived as Joy or Surprise. The Face animation designed for *Surprise* was equivalently perceived as Fear, Surprise, or Sadness. Surprise was the most perceived emotion in the Posture animation designed for Surprise. The Face+Posture animation designed for Surprise was equivalently perceived as Fear or Surprise. The Face animation designed for *Fear* was equivalently perceived as Sadness or Neutral. The Posture and Face+Posture animations designed for Fear were equivalently perceived as Surprise or Fear.

In summary, the animations designed for Anger, Sadness and Joy were well recognized. Animations designed for Surprise and Fear were both perceived as blends of Surprise and Fear.

These results are similar to Hall & Matsumoto where people perceived blends of emotions in static pictures intended to express a single emotion [17].

These results are also in line with those observed by Gosselin and Kirouac [15]. They observed that Ekman's pictures of facial expressions of Joy, Anger, Sadness and Surprise were better recognized than facial expressions of Fear and Disgust. Yet, in

Table 1. Average perception of emotion in the various modalities (min = 0, max = 4). Averages that are significantly different from others are displayed in bold.

Animations	Modalities	Joy	Anger	Fear	Surprise	Sad	Neutral	ANOVA $p<,001$
	Face	0,05	**3,21**	0,16	0,63	0,42	0,05	$F(5, 90)=61,79$
ANGER	Posture	0,05	**3,47**	0,28	0,5	0,28	0	$F(4, 68)=100,82$
	Face+Posture	0,05	**3,63**	0,21	0,05	0,31	0,05	$F(5, 90)=176,44$
	Face	**2,31**	0,05	0,1	0,22	0,1	0,79	$F(5, 85)=31,43$
JOY	Posture	**2,47**	0,84	0,26	**2,26**	0,16	0	$F(4, 72)=14,90$
	Face+Posture	**3,74**	0,05	0	1,58	0	0,5	$F(3, 54)=124,44$
	Face	0,16	0,1	0,68	0,26	**3,16**	0,26	$F(5, 90)=51,32$
SAD	Posture	0,05	0,28	0,22	0,44	**1,95**	0,89	$F(5, 85)=7,90$
	Face+Posture	0	0,05	0,58	0,37	**3,47**	0,37	$F(4, 72)=67,86$
	Face	0,12	0,28	**1,53**	**1,7**	1,69	0,39	$F(5, 150)=18,95$
SURPRISE	Posture	1,23	0,32	1,46	**2,89**	0,09	0,06	$F(4, 132)=32,28$
	Face+Posture	0,34	0,26	**2,38**	**3,02**	0,32	0,17	$F(5, 165)=76,01$
	Face	0,21	0,12	0,39	0,15	1,12	**1,8**	$F(5, 150)=19,50$
FEAR	Posture	0,64	0,17	**2,77**	**2,63**	0,67	0,08	$F(5, 170)=48,17$
	Face+Posture	0,26	0,41	**2,54**	**2,79**	0,6	0	$F(4, 132)=59,59$

our study, we observed that Surprise was confused with Fear for the three conditions. This means that the way we specified this animation has to be improved.

Emotional dimension perceived in each animation. With respect to the perception of dimensions of emotions, our results show that subjects perceived the intended valence for each condition, but not the intended activation. When rating face only animations of each emotion, we did not observe any significant difference between animations intended to display active versus passive emotions. Yet, subjects perceived correctly the activation dimension from our posture only animations (Table 2).

Table 2. Average perception of activation and valence for each emotion and for each modality (min = 0, max = 4)

Animations	Modalities	Active	Passive	Positive	Negative
	Face	1,42	1,37	0,31	**3,42**
ANGER	Posture	**3,16**	0,21	0,42	**3,31**
	Face+Posture	**3,21**	0,47	0,16	**3,63**
	Face	0,78	**2,26**	**2,94**	0,37
JOY	Posture	**3,21**	0,1	**2,36**	1,16
	Face+Posture	**3,37**	0,21	**3,63**	0,05
	Face	1,47	1,31	0,53	**2,89**
SAD	Posture	1,05	**1,84**	0,47	**2,37**
	Face+Posture	1,22	**2,05**	0,33	**3,1**
	Face	1,42	**2,11**	0,65	**2,64**
SURPRISE	Posture	**3**	0,32	1,85	1,21
	Face+Posture	**2,71**	0,62	0,82	**2,14**
	Face	0,77	**2,25**	0,71	**1,64**
FEAR	Posture	**2,78**	0,38	1	**2,15**
	Face+Posture	**2,82**	0,97	0,76	**2,26**

This effect of correct perception of activation via the posture and incorrect perception of activation via the face might be explained by the way we designed our animations. Yet, the fact that the effect was found for all our facial animations and not for any postural animation might also suggest that facial expressions might not be as appropriate as postural expressions for perceiving the activation of emotions.

Comparing the recognition of each emotion in the three modalities. Finally, we proceeded to a one-way ANOVA to compare the different modalities. Our goal was to study if the perceived emotion depends on the modality (e.g. does the level of perceived Anger depends on the modality? Do subjects perceive more Anger when this emotion is displayed both in the face and in the posture than when it is displayed in a single modality? Do face only and posture only are equivalent?).

The perception of *Anger* did not differ between the three conditions. The perception of *Joy* was higher in the Face+Posture condition than in the Face condition and in the Posture condition. The perception of *Sadness* was higher in the Face and in the Face+Posture conditions than in the Posture condition. The perceptions of *Surprise* and *Fear* were higher in the Posture and Face+Posture modalities than in the Face modality.

4.3 Discussion

This first study enabled us to validate some of our animations. The expressions of Joy, Anger and Sadness are well recognized by the subjects in the three modalities (Face only, Posture only and Face+Posture). The expressions of Surprise and Fear are more ambiguous and are less well recognized.

The results also show that the contribution of the different modalities depends on the emotion. For Anger, subjects recognize its expression regardless of the modality. For the other emotions, the mode of presentation influences recognition. However, it is still difficult to say if this is due to our animations or to a differentiated perceptive processing. Nevertheless, the results concerning the perception of the level of activation suggest that the perceptive processing is different for the two modalities.

5   Second Study: Facial and Postural Expressions of Incongruent Emotions

This second study aimed at providing answers to the following questions: how are perceived animations that blend two different emotions expressed in the face and in the posture? What is the influence of one modality over the other modality?

5.1 Methodology

We kept the emotions which were well recognized in the first study (Anger, Sadness and Joy) so as to avoid an effect of a bad recognition of a single emotion on the overall perception of a blend. Furthermore, these three emotions cover positive and negative valence, as well as low and high arousal.

We designed 6 canned animations of incongruent emotions (left column of Table 4). We also kept the 3 congruent animations combining the same emotion in both the Face and the Posture (Anger, Sadness and Joy) in order to compare them with the incongruent animations in the same experiment settings (Fig. 2 illustrates congruent and incongruent expressions). Each animation lasted 3 seconds (from a neutral pose to the expression of emotion and back to neutral pose).

Another group of 21 subjects (12 females, 9 males, average age 20 years) participated in the experiment. All of them were first or second year students at the University.

Fig. 2. Frame of congruent expressions of sadness in the face and in the posture (left) and incongruent facial expression of Joy and postural expression of Sadness (right)

As in the first study, a first animation of the character displaying a deictic gesture was used as a training animation so that subjects had seen the character once before evaluating its emotional expressions. After viewing an animation, the subjects had to answer a questionnaire. They had to report how much they perceived each of the emotions in the animation using 5 points Likert scales. Subjects were able to select several emotion labels for each animation. They also had to rate the level of activation and the valence of the emotion.

5.2 Results

Collected data was analyzed by repeated measures ANOVA and using t-test.

Emotion categories perceived in each animation. As observed in the first study, the intended emotion is well recognized in each congruent animation (Table 3).

Table 3. Average perception of emotion in congruent animations

	Joy	Anger	Fear	Surprise	Sadness	ANOVA $p<,001$
Face+Posture of Anger	0,00	**3,52**	0,05	0,19	0,10	$F(4, 76)=283,20$
Face+Posture of Joy	**3,67**	0,00	0,00	1,24	0,00	$F(1, 20)=85,00$
Face+Posture of Sadness	0,10	0,14	0,19	0,33	**2,19**	$F(5, 100)=34,75$

Regarding the 6 incongruent combinations, in all but one of the animations subjects reported perceiving only the emotion expressed via the face. The only exception is the animation combining the facial expression of Sadness with the postural expression of Anger. This animation was perceived as a blended expression of Sadness and Anger (Table 4).

Table 4. Average perception of emotion in incongruent animations

Face	Posture	Joy	Anger	Fear	Surprise	Sadness	Neutral	ANOVA $p<,001$
Joy	Sad	**2,05**	0,10	0,05	0,76	0,10	0,29	$F(5, 100)=17,35$
Joy	Anger	**2,43**	0,10	0,00	0,67	0,00	0,19	$F(3, 60)=41,62$
Anger	Joy	0,00	**3,00**	0,19	0,48	0,14	0,00	$F(3, 60)=126,76$
Anger	Sad	0,00	**2,81**	0,10	0,29	0,24	0,19	$F(4, 80)=54,85$
Sad	Anger	0,14	**1,52**	0,62	0,33	**1,29**	0,14	$F(5, 100)=9,21$
Sad	Joy	0,29	0,48	0,71	1,00	**1,95**	0,33	$F(5, 100)=8,10$

Table 5. Average perception of emotional dimension in incongruent animations

Face	Posture	Active	Passive	Positive	Negative
Joy	Sad	1,57	1,33	**2,62**	0,62
Joy	Anger	**2,52**	0,52	**2,95**	0,33
Anger	Joy	**2,95**	0,29	0,33	**2,95**
Anger	Sad	**2,05**	1,24	0,24	**3,14**
Sad	Anger	**2,38**	0,65	0,71	**2,52**
Sad	Joy	**2,67**	0,48	0,67	**2,52**

Perception of congruent and incongruent animations. Each congruent animation was compared to the four incongruent animations. For example, the animation of Anger was compared to 1) the animation combining the facial expression of Sadness with the postural expression of Anger, 2) the animation combining the facial expression of the Joy with the postural expression of Anger, 3) the animation combining the facial expression of Anger with the postural expression of Sadness, 4) and the animation combining the facial expression of Anger with the postural expression of Joy. The results show that the *Valence* and the *Activation* are better perceived when the congruent animations are displayed (Table 5). The only exception is the animation combining the facial expression of Anger with the postural expression of Joy. The perception of *Activation* for this animation is the same as for the congruent animations of Joy and of Anger. This result is not surprising since Anger and Joy are two emotions which have a high level of activation.

Comparison of incongruent animations displaying the same postural expression. Subjects perceive the emotions displayed in the facial expression. For example, the perception of *Sadness* was higher in the animation combining the facial expression of Sadness with the postural expression of Anger than in the animation combining the facial expression of Joy with the postural expression of Anger. Concerning the valence (Table 5), when the postural expression is negative, the perception of *Negative Valence* is higher in the animation combining the same negative valence for the facial and postural expression than in the animation combining different valence. Thus, the subjects perceive the emotion and the valence conveyed by the facial expressions.

Comparison of incongruent animations displaying the same facial expression. Subjects consider less the posture in order to elaborate their emotional judgment. Indeed, they do not report more the emotion displayed by the postural expression. For example, the perception of *Anger* is not higher in the animation combining the facial expression of Sadness with the postural expression of Anger than the animation combining the facial expression of Sadness with the postural expression of Joy. However, the perception of *Activation* is higher in the animation combining the same level of activation for the facial and postural expression than in the animations combining different levels of activation (Table 5).

Comparing incongruent animations. The results suggest that the categorical recognition is more influenced by the facial expression modality than by the postural modality. Furthermore, subjects preferentially used the postural modality to establish a judgment about the level of activation. For example, the perceptions of *Activation*, of *Negative Valence* and of *Sadness* were higher in the animation combining the facial expression of Sadness with the postural expression of Joy than in the animation combining the facial expression of Joy with the postural expression of Sadness. The perception of *Joy* was higher in the animation combining the facial expression of Joy with the postural expression of Sadness than in the animation combining the facial expression of Sadness with the postural expression of Joy. Thus, Joy and Sadness seem to be better identified when they are conveyed by facial expressions.

In summary, facial expressions are crucial to develop a perceptual judgment. The emotions are better recognized when they are conveyed by facial expressions than by the postural expressions.

6 Conclusions

Interest in body movement and gestures as components of emotional expression is relatively recent. Wallbott [36] observed some features of posture and movement quality that enabled him to discriminate between some emotion categories. On the contrary, Ekman and Friesen [11] suggested that bodily movements inform about the intensity of emotion, but not about emotion categories.

In this paper we described two experimental studies exploring how human subjects perceive combinations of facial and postural expressions of emotions. The first study aimed at assessing the relative contributions of the face and the posture in the perception of a single emotion. We observed that emotional congruence at the level of the body and the face facilitates the recognition of emotion categories and dimensions compared to face only or posture only presentations. Nevertheless, face only and posture only also enabled us to recognize emotion categories. The second study considered the influence of incongruent expressions. Judgments were mainly based on the facial expressions, but were nevertheless affected by postural expressions. In such incongruent case, posture revealed to be useful for assessing the perceived activation of the emotion.

Our results support the two theoretical positions mentioned above. Indeed, our first study shows that when postures are presented alone, subjects are able to perceive the emotion category. When postures are presented with an incongruent emotional combination, subjects rely on the posture to make judgments about the emotional activation. However in our studies, the dynamics of each emotional expression were not specified. Each expression had the same global duration, the same duration for attack, sustain and decay. These expressive properties of movement quality will be investigated jointly with postures since they also play a major role in the perception of emotion.

Coordination and synchronization of nonverbal modalities is an important issue for virtual characters to express emotions. Computational models of expressive characters need to consider how such combinations are perceived. Current studies seldom consider combinations of posture and face, and when they do, they consider static pictures [24] or stimuli what are not virtually integrated as a single body [19]. The originality of our work also lies in our integrated and animated stimuli. This methodology has the advantage of confronting the subjects to stimuli similar to virtual agent encountered on the web. It also helps us to understand how we perceive combinations of non-verbal expressions of emotion.

Acknowledgments

The research was partly supported by the project "ANR-07-TLOG-Affective Avatars". The authors thank the students who participated in the study.

References

1. Albrecht, I., Schröder, M., Haber, J., Seidel, H.-P.: Mixed feelings: Expression of non-basic emotions in a muscle-based talking head. Special issue of Journal of Virtual Reality on Language, Speech & Gesture 8(4) (2005)
2. Ballin, D., Gillies, M., Crabtree, B.: A Framework For Interpersonal Attitude And Non-Verbal Communication In Improvisational Visual Media Production. In: The First European Conference on Visual Media Production IEE, London (2004)
3. Bänziger, T., Scherer, K.: Using Actor Portrayals to Systematically Study Multimodal Emotion Expression: The GEMEP Corpus. In: Paiva, A., Prada, R., Picard, R.W. (eds.) ACII 2007. LNCS, vol. 4738, pp. 476–487. Springer, Heidelberg (2007)
4. Bianchi-Berthouze, N., Kleinsmith, A.: A categorical approach to affective gesture recognition. Connection Science 15(4), 259–269 (2003)
5. Buisine, S., Abrilian, S., Niewiadomski, R., Martin, J.C., Devillers, L., Pelachaud, C.: Perception of blended emotions: From video corpus to expressive agent. In: Gratch, J., Young, M., Aylett, R.S., Ballin, D., Olivier, P. (eds.) IVA 2006. LNCS (LNAI), vol. 4133, pp. 93–106. Springer, Heidelberg (2006)
6. De Silva, R., Bianchi-Berthouze, N.: Modelling human affective postures: an information theoretic characterization of posture features. Computer Animation and Virtual Worlds 15(3-4), 269–276 (2004)
7. Dittman, A.T.: The role of body movement in communication. In: Nonverbal behavior and communication. Lawrence Erlbaum, Mahwah (1987)
8. Ekman, P.: An argument for basic emotions. Cognition and Emotion 6, 169–200 (1992)
9. Ekman, P., Friesen, W.: Manual for the facial action coding system. Consulting Psychology Press, Palo Alto (1978)
10. Ekman, P., Friesen, W.: A new pan-cultural facial expression of emotion. Motivation and Emotion 10, 159–168 (1986)
11. Ekman, P., Friesen, W.V.: Nonverbal behavior and psychopathology. In: Friedman, R.J., Datz, M.M. (eds.) The psychology of depression: contemporary theory and research, pp. 203–232. Winston & Sons, Washington (1974)

12. Ekman, P., Friesen, W.V.: Unmasking the face. A guide to recognizing emotions from facial clues. Prentice-Hall Inc., Englewood Cliffs (1975)
13. Ekman, P., Friesen., W.: Unmasking the face: a guide to recognizing emotions from facial clues. Prentice-Hall, Englewood Cliffs (1975)
14. Fontaine, J.R., Scherer, K.R., Roesch, E.B., Ellsworth, P.: The world of emotion is not two-dimensional. Psychological Science 18(2), 1050–1057 (2007)
15. Gosselin, P., Kirouac, G.: Le décodage de prototypes emotionels faciaux. Canadian journal of experimental psychology 49(3), 313-329 (1995)
16. Gunes, H., Piccardi, M.: Bi-modal emotion recognition from expressive face and body gestures. Journal of Network & Computer Applications 30(4), 1334–1345 (2007)
17. Hall, J.A., Matsumoto, D.: Gender differences in judgments of multiple emotions from facial expressions. Emotion 4(2), 201–206 (2004)
18. Harrigan, J.A.: Proxemics, kinesics, and gaze. In: Harrigan, J.A., Rosenthal, R., Scherer, K. (eds.) The new handbook of methods in nonverbal behavior research. Series in Affective Science, pp. 137–198. Oxford University Press, Oxford (2005)
19. Hietanen, J.K., Leppänen, J.M.: Judgment of other people's facial expressions of emotions is influenced by their concurrent affective hand movements. Scandinavian Journal of Psychology 49, 221–230 (2008)
20. Hietanen, J.K., Leppänen, J.M.: Judgment of other people's facial expressions of emotions is influenced by their concurrent affective hand movements. Scandinavian Journal of Psychology 49, 221–230 (2008)
21. Izard, C.: Human Emotions. Plenum, New York (1977)
22. Kleinsmith, A., Bianchi-Berthouze, N.: Recognizing affective dimensions from body posture. In: Paiva, A.C.R., Prada, R., Picard, R.W. (eds.) ACII 2007. LNCS, vol. 4738, pp. 48–58. Springer, Heidelberg (2007)
23. Kleinsmith, A., De Silva, R., Bianchi-Berthouze, N.: Cross-Cultural Differences in Recognizing Affect from Body Posture. Interacting with Computers 18(6), 1371–1389 (2006)
24. Meeren, H.K.M., van Heijnsbergen, C., de Gelder, B.: Rapid perceptual integration of facial expression and emotional body language. Proceedings of the National Academy of Sciences of the USA, 16518–16523 (2005)
25. Mota, S., Picard, R.W.: Automated posture analysis for detecting learner's interest level. In: Workshop on Computer Vision and Pattern Recognition for Human-Computer Interaction (2003)
26. Niewiadomski, R.: A model of complex facial expressions in interpersonal relations for animated agents. PhD Thesis, University of Perugia (2007)
27. Pelachaud, C.: Multimodal expressive embodied conversational agents. In: Proceedings of the 13th annual ACM international conference on Multimedia. ACM, Hilton (2005)
28. Plutchik, R.: A general psychoevolutionary theory of emotion. In: Plutchik, R. (ed.) Emotion: Theory, research, and experience, Theories of emotion, Academic, New York. vol. 1, pp. 3–33 (1980)
29. Russell, J.A.: A circumplex model of affect. Journal of Personality and Social Psychology 39(6), 1161–1178 (1980)
30. Russell, J.A., Mehrabian, A.: Evidence for a three-factor theory of emotions. Journal of Research in Personality 11, 273–294 (1977)
31. Scherer, K.R.: The nonverbal dimension: A fad, a field, or a behavioral modality? The social dimension: European developments in social psychology, 160–183 (1984)
32. Scherer, K.R.: Analyzing Emotion Blends. In: Fischer, A. (ed.) Proceedings of the Xth Conference of the International Society for Research on Emotions, pp. 142–148 (1998)

33. Scherer, K.R.: Emotion. In: Stroebe, M.H.W. (ed.) Introduction to Social Psychology: A European perspective, pp. 151–191. Blackwell, Oxford (2000)
34. Scherer, K.R., Ellgring, H.: Are facial expressions of emotion produced by categorical affect programs or dynamically driven by appraisal? Emotion 7(1), 113–130 (2007)
35. Scherer, K.R., Ellgring, H.: Multimodal Expression of Emotion: Affect Programs or Componential Appraisal Patterns? Emotion 7(1) (2007)
36. Wallbott, H.G.: Bodily expression of emotion. European Journal of Social Psychology 28, 879–896 (1998)
37. Woo, W., Park, J., Iwadate, Y.: Emotion Analysis from Dance Performance Using Time-Delay Neural Networks. In: JCIS-CVPRIP 2000, pp. 374–377 (2000)

Expression of Moral Emotions in Cooperating Agents[*]

Celso M. de Melo[1], Liang Zheng[2], and Jonathan Gratch[1]

[1] Institute for Creative Technologies, University of Southern California,
13274 Fiji Way, Marina Del Rey, CA 90292, USA
demelo@usc.edu, gratch@ict.usc.edu
[2] Information Sciences Institute, University of Southern California,
4676 Admiralty Way, Suite 1001, CA 90292
liang.zheng@usc.edu

Abstract. Moral emotions have been argued to play a central role in the emergence of cooperation in human-human interactions. This work describes an experiment which tests whether this insight carries to virtual human-human interactions. In particular, the paper describes a repeated-measures experiment where subjects play the iterated prisoner's dilemma with two versions of the virtual human: (a) neutral, which is the control condition; (b) moral, which is identical to the control condition except that the virtual human expresses gratitude, distress, remorse, reproach and anger through the face according to the action history of the game. Our results indicate that subjects cooperate more with the virtual human in the moral condition and that they perceive it to be more human-like. We discuss the relevance these results have for building agents which are successful in cooperating with humans.

Keywords: Moral Emotions, Virtual Humans, Expression of Emotions, Cooperation, Prisoner's Dilemma.

1 Introduction

The expression of moral emotions has been argued to influence the emergence of cooperation in human-human interactions [1]. Moral emotions are associated with the interests or welfare of either society as a whole or people other than the self [2]. They show disapproval of another's actions (reproach and anger), regret for one's own actions (shame and remorse) and praise for someone else's action (admiration and gratitude). To understand the effect of moral emotions on emergence of cooperation, consider first the decision model of self-interested agents. In this model agents cooperate only if that improves their own condition, without regard to the other agents' welfare. Now, even though attractive in its simplicity, researchers were quick to notice that people more often than not consider the welfare of others and cooperate [3]. But, cooperation isn't blind and will tend to emerge in situations where participants

---

[*] This work was sponsored by the U.S. Army Research, Development, and Engineering Command. The content does not necessarily reflect the position or the policy of the Government, and no official endorsement should be inferred.

Zs. Ruttkay et al. (Eds.): IVA 2009, LNAI 5773, pp. 301–307, 2009.

are willing to cooperate as opposed to trying to take advantage of each other. There-fore, being able to identify when someone is willing to cooperate is key to the emergence of mutual cooperation. Moral emotions take on an important role in this identification process as their display constitutes a cue that someone might be consid-erate of the welfare of others and is willing to cooperate [1,4].

This paper explores whether the expression of moral emotions can also have an ef-fect on the interaction between people and embodied agents. Embodied agents, or virtual humans, are a special kind of agents which have bodies and are capable of ex-pressing themselves through gesture, face and voice [5]. There has already been much work in trying to promote cooperation, through trust- and reputation-building models, in computational multi-agent systems [6]. However, agents in these systems are opti-mized to cooperate with other agents. With embodiment, agents can now promote cooperation-building mechanisms which rely on nonverbal behavior, as in human-human interactions [7]. However, whether these mechanisms carry to human-virtual human interactions is not clear. Evidence exists that people interact with machines in similar ways as with people [8]. Further evidence has also been provided that embod-ied agents can induce social-emotional effects similar to those in human-human inter-actions [9]. This work seeks evidence that the expression of moral emotions in virtual humans influences people's willingness to cooperate with it.

The paper describes an experiment where humans are asked to play the iterated prisoner's dilemma game with two virtual humans that follow the same action policy but differ only in that one expresses moral emotions and one does not. Expression of moral emotions consists of expressing gratitude, distress, remorse, reproach and anger through the face according to how the game is unfolding. We expect this manipula-tion to produce an effect on the subjects' willingness to cooperate. The goals of the experiment are to get insight into: (a) whether the expression of moral emotions has an effect on the emergence of cooperation between virtual humans and humans; (b) the magnitude of such effect, if it does exist; and, (c) the importance of embodiment for the emergence of cooperation between agents and humans.

2   Method

Design. The experiment follows a within-subjects design where each participant plays the iterated prisoner's dilemma with two different virtual humans. The virtual humans differ in their expression of moral emotions: a *neutral virtual human*, (the control condition) expresses no emotions; a *moral virtual human* expresses moral emotions. After playing two rounds of the prisoner's dilemma to familiarize them-selves with the game, participants play twenty-five rounds of prisoner's dilemma with each agent. The order of the agents is randomized across participants (i.e., one half of the subjects play the neutral virtual human first whereas the other half play the moral virtual human first).

The Game. The iterated prisoner's dilemma game was chosen because it is regularly used in game theory to understand cooperative behavior between two agents [10]. The (non-iterated) prisoner's dilemma game was described in the experiment as follows: "You and your partner are arrested by the police. The police have insufficient evidence for a conviction, and, having separated you both into different cells, visit each in turn to offer the same deal. If one testifies for the prosecution against the other and the other remains silent, the betrayer goes free and the silent accomplice receives the full 3-year sentence. If both remain silent, both prisoners are sentenced to only 3 months in jail for a minor charge. If each betrays the other, each receives a 1-year sentence". The two actions in this game were presented to the subject as 'Remain SILENT' or 'TESTIFY against other'. However, in the rest of the paper, we shall refer to the first as 'cooperate' and the second as 'defect'. According to the self-interested model of agents, the only rational action strategy is to defect as this maximizes the expected utility. In the iterated version of the prisoner's dilemma, the game is played several times. Importantly, in our experiment the game is played a finite number of times (25) and subjects are aware of this. Furthermore, subjects are told that they will be playing each round with the same partner (i.e., virtual human) and that each will have the opportunity of learning what the other did in the previous round. Again, the self-interested model states that the optimal strategy for the finite iterated prisoner's dilemma is to defect in every round. Finally, subjects were instructed to play the game as if they were actually experiencing the dilemma and to follow the best strategy they saw fit. In particular, subjects were not told about the strategies predicted by the self-interested model.

The Action Policy. Virtual humans in both conditions play a variant of tit-for-tat. Tit-for-tat is a strategy where a player begins by cooperating and then proceeds to repeat the action the other player did in the previous round. Tit-for-tat is argued to strike the right balance of punishment and reward with respect to the opponent's previous actions [11]. So, the action policy used in our experiment is as follows: (a) in rounds 1 to 5, the virtual human plays randomly; (b) in rounds 6 to 25, the agent plays tit-for-tat. Importantly, the random sequence of actions in the first five rounds is the same in both conditions and is chosen at the beginning of each trial with a new subject. The rationale for having some randomness in the first rounds was to make it harder for the subjects to guess the virtual humans' strategy.

Expression of Emotions. The moral virtual human expresses emotions after each round of the game. The emotion which is expressed reflects not only the outcome of the last round but also the outcome of (recent) rounds in the past. The way we map the outcome history of the game into emotions follows the eliciting conditions for moral emotions as described by Haidt [2]. The mapping we propose is not meant to be the correct one but only one which is intuitive and reasonable. The mapping is described by the following ordered rules:

a. If in the present round both players cooperate, gratitude is expressed;
b. If in the present round the subject defects and the virtual human cooperates:
   1. If in the previous two rounds both cooperated, anger is expressed;
   2. If in the previous round both cooperated, reproach is expressed;
   3. If in the previous round the subject defected and the virtual human cooperated, reproach is expressed;
   4. Otherwise, distress (or sadness) is expressed;
c. If in the present round the subject cooperates and the virtual human defects, remorse is expressed;
d. If in the present round both players defect:

1. If in the previous round the subject cooperated and the virtual human defected, don't express any emotion;
2. Otherwise, express distress.

Virtual Humans. The virtual human platform we use supports expression of emotions through gesture, face and voice [12]. The focus on this work, however, is on
expression of moral emotions through the face. Facial expression relies on a pseudo-
muscular model of the face and on simulation of wrinkles and blushing. The facial
expressions for the moral virtual human condition are shown in Fig.1. These expressions are elicited after the subject chooses its action and the outcome of the round is
shown. The neutral condition uses the neutral face. Aside from facial expression,
Perlin noise to the neck and torso and blinking was added to both conditions to keep
the virtual human from looking stiff while the subject is choosing its actions. Finally,
a different shirt (i.e., texture) is chosen to help distinguish the two virtual humans the
subject plays with. Shirts vary according to letter (A or B) and color (blue or yellow).
The letter 'A' is always assigned to the first player and the letter 'B' to the second.
The shirt colors are assigned randomly to each player. Neutral images of the respective virtual humans, with the respective shirts, are also shown in the debriefing questions to help subjects remember the players.

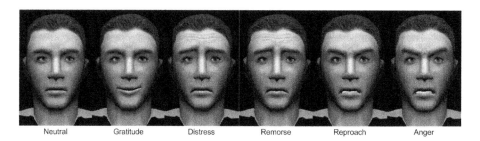

Neutral	Gratitude	Distress	Remorse	Reproach	Anger

Fig. 1. The facial expressions used for the moral virtual human condition. Usual facial configurations are used for gratitude, distress, remorse, reproach and anger. Typical wrinkle patterns
are used for distress, remorse, reproach and anger. Blushing of the cheeks is used for remorse
and (light) redness of the face is used in anger.

Survey Software. The survey was implemented in software and structured into four
phases: (1) *profile*, where data about the subject is collected (e.g. age, sex and educa-
tion-level) while assuring anonymity; (2) *tutorial*, where the subject plays a two-
round game of the iterated prisoner's dilemma to get comfortable with the game and
interface; (3) *game*, where the subject plays the 25-round iterated prisoner's dilemma
twice, once for each condition; finally, (4) *debriefing*, where the subject answers the
debriefing questions. Fig.2 shows a snapshot of the software.

The Dependent Variables. While the subject is playing the games, the following
dependent variable is measured: NCOOP – The number of times the subject cooperates.
After game playing, a set of questions is asked to the subjects in the debriefing section
of the survey. The questions refer to the players as 'Player A', which is the first the

subject plays with and is in either the neutral or moral condition, and 'Player B', which is the second the subject plays with and is in the other condition. From these questions, the following dependent variables are measured: HL – Classification of how human-like was the virtual human (1 – 'totally unlike a human' to 6 – 'extremely like a human'); WELF – Classification of how much was the virtual human considerate of the subject's welfare (1 – 'never' to 6 – 'always'). Subjects were also asked to choose which player they preferred to play with - the neutral, moral or no preference.

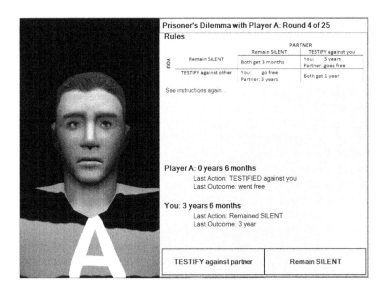

Fig. 2. A snapshot of the survey software in the game phase

The Hypotheses. The hypotheses we set forth for this experiment are: H1 – The subject will cooperate more with the moral virtual human than with the neutral; H2 – Subjects will perceive the moral virtual human as being more human-like than the neutral; H3 – Subjects will perceive the moral virtual human to be more considerate of the subjects' welfare than the neutral.

Participants. Twenty-eight (28) subjects were recruited at the University of Southern California and related institutions. Subjects' were, on average, 25.2 years of age; 42.9% were males; and, all had at least college-level education but, in diverse areas.

3 Results

The dependent t test was used to compare means for the dependent variables in the moral and neutral conditions. Table 1 shows descriptive statistics and the results of the t test. The results show that hypotheses H1 and H2 are accepted, whereas H3 is not. Subjects also self-reported that they preferred to play against the moral virtual human: fifteen subjects (53.57%) preferred the moral agent; nine subjects (32.14%) preferred the neutral agent; and four subjects (14.29%) had no preference.

Table 1. Descriptive statistics and dependent t test for the following dependent variables ($df = 27$): NCOOP, HL and WELF

Vars	Moral		Neutral		Diff.	Diff.	t	Sig.	r
	Mean	SD	Mean	SD	Means	SE		2-sd	
NCOOP[*]	16.571	6.563	12.893	7.320	3.679	1.402	2.624	0.014	0.451
HL[*]	4.36	1.224	3.32	1.188	1.036	0.358	2.892	0.007	0.486
WELF	3.96	1.453	3.25	1.602	0.714	0.496	1.441	0.161	0.267

* Significant difference, p < 0.05

4   Discussion

The results suggest that people cooperate more with virtual humans if these express moral emotions. This is in line with Frank's view that participants in social dilemmas look for contextual cues in their trading partners that they are likely to cooperate [1]. One such cue is the expression of moral emotions. As to why this cue works in our case, we look at Keltner & Kring social-functional characterization of emotions [13]. Accordingly, the display of emotions serves three functions: *informative*, signaling information about feelings and intentions to the interaction partner; *evocative*, eliciting complementary or similar empathic emotions in others; *incentive*, to reinforce, by reward or punishment, another's individual social behavior within ongoing interactions. So, under this view, the expression of moral emotions in the virtual human is likely to be promoting cooperation because: it is informative of its willingness to engage in cooperative behavior; and, it is providing incentive for mutual cooperation through appropriate facial feedback. Regarding the evocative role of emotions, our results do not clarify whether subjects perceive the virtual human to actually be experiencing the moral emotions it expresses and whether any complimentary or empathic emotion is actually being experienced by the subjects.

The results also show that the moral virtual human is perceived as being more human-like than the neutral virtual human. This could have led to a sense of closer psychological distance between subject and moral virtual human. Psychological distance, in turn, is argued to influence the establishment of bonds of sympathy between interacting partners which, in turn, positively influences the potential for cooperation [14]. The argument here is that because subjects perceive the virtual human to be more human-like they are more likely to be sympathetic towards it and, thus, more likely to attempt cooperation. This might have also been the reason why subjects tended to prefer playing the game with the moral virtual human.

The results do not show a statistically significant difference in the perception of consideration for the subject's welfare between the neutral and moral virtual humans. Nevertheless, subjects did cooperate more with the moral virtual human. This suggests that the expression of moral emotions could be having an unconscious influence on subjects' decision-making and so, even though subjects were cooperating more with the moral virtual human, they were not conscious of it. This would be in line with Damasio's account of the influence of emotions in human decision-making at an unconscious level [15] and with Reeves & Nass [8] perspective that humans unconsciously treat interactions with the media (in our case, virtual humans) in the same way as with humans. The result, however, did not generalize to all subjects, as many referred explicitly to emotions (or some aspect of it) as the reason they preferred the moral virtual human to the neutral one.

In general, the results emphasize the importance of embodiment in virtual agents to the emergence of cooperation with humans. Effectively, in our study, even though the action policies were the same in both conditions, subjects cooperated more with the moral virtual human. Furthermore, this work has only begun to explore the many ways in which embodiment can play a role in the emergence of cooperation. Two promising lines of future work are the building of sympathetic bonds and rapport [16] which rely heavily on embodiment and that, in human-human interactions, contribute to the emergence of cooperation.

References

1. Frank, R.: Introducing Moral Emotions into Models of Rational Choice. In: Manstead, A.S., Frijda, N., Fischer, A. (eds.) Feelings and Emotions: The Amsterdam Symposium, pp. 422–440. Cambridge University Press, Cambridge (2004)
2. Haidt, J.: The Moral Emotions. In: Davidson, R.J., Scherer, K.R., Goldsmith, H.H. (eds.) Handbook of Affective Sciences, pp. 852–870. Oxford University Press, Oxford (2003)
3. Lowenstein, G., Lerner, J.: The Role of Affect in Decision Making. In: Davidson, R.J., Scherer, K.R., Goldsmith, H.H. (eds.) Handbook of Affective Sciences, pp. 619–642. Oxford University Press, Oxford (2003)
4. Frank, R.: Cooperation through emotional commitment. In: Hesse, R. (ed.) Evolution and the capacity for commitment, pp. 57–76. Russell Sage, New York (2001)
5. Gratch, J., Rickel, J., Andre, E., Cassell, J., Petajan, E., Badler, N.: Creating Interactive Virtual Humans: Some Assembly Required. IEEE Intellig. Systems 17(4), 54–63 (2002)
6. Sabater, J., Sierra, C.: Review on computational trust and reputation models. Artificial Intelligence Review 24, 33–60 (2005)
7. Morris, M., Keltner, D.: How Emotions Work: The Social Functions of Emotional Expression in Negotiations. Research in Organizational Behaviour 22, 1–50 (2000)
8. Reeves, B., Nass, C.: The Media Equation: How People Treat Computers, Television, and New Media Like Real People and Places. University of Chicago Press (1996)
9. Kramer, N.: Social Effects of Virtual Assistants. A Review of Empirical Results with Regard to Communication. Intelligent Virtual Agents 2008, 507–508 (2008)
10. Poundstone, W.: Prisoner's Dilemma. Anchor Books (1992)
11. Axelrod, R.: The Evolution of Cooperation. Basic Books (1984)
12. de Melo, C., Paiva, A.: Multimodal Expression in Virtual Humans. Computer Animation and Virtual Worlds 17(3-4), 239–248 (2006)
13. Keltner, D., Kring, A.: Emotion, Social Function, and Psychopathology. Review of General Psychology 2(3), 320–342 (1998)
14. Sally, D.: A general theory of sympathy, mind-reading, and social interaction, with an application to the prisoner's dilemma. Social Science Information 39(4), 567–623 (2000)
15. Damasio, A.: Descarte's Error: Emotion, Reason, and the Human Brain. G.P. Putnan's Sons (1994)
16. Capella, J.: On defining conversational coordination and rapport. Psychological Inquiry 1(4), 303–305 (1990)

Evaluating Emotive Character Animations Created with Procedural Animation

Yueh-Hung Lin[1], Chia-Yang Liu[2], Hung-Wei Lee[3], Shwu-Lih Huang[2],
and Tsai-Yen Li[1]

[1] Department of Computer Science, National Chengchi University, Taiwan
{g9339,li}@cs.nccu.edu.tw
[2] Department of Psychology, Research Center for Mind, Brain, and Learning,
National Chengchi University, Taiwan
{95752003,slh}@nccu.edu.tw
[3] Department of Applied Psychology, Hsuan Chuang University, Taiwan
spoon@hcu.edu.tw

Abstract. How to create effective body animations for virtual agents with emotions remains the state of the art for human animators and a great challenge for computer scientists. In this paper, we propose to use a model of hierarchal parameters to represent body animations: *emotional*, *style*, *motion,* and *procedural* parameters. Based on this model, we have created motions for a virtual character with generic animation procedures and mapped these procedural parameters into style parameters as proposed in the literature. The expressiveness of the generated animations was verified through experiments in our previous work. In this paper, we further report the results of two experiments attempting to verify how the style parameters are mapped into various emotions. The results reveal that the participants can successfully distinguish emotions based on the manipulation of style parameters for neutral motions such as walking. When these style parameters were used for emotive motions, including pounding, shivering, flourishing and crestfallen, the generated animations were even more effective for intended contexts.

1 Introduction

Modeling and expressing emotions for virtual agents remains a key issue for believability because of the subtleness involved. Most previous research focused on facial expression since it was the most common way to communicate emotions. Nevertheless, body movements are also crucial for the expression of emotion especially in the virtual world where avatars are usually seen in a distance and their facial expressions become too vague to discern.

Not until recent years, the principles used in analyzing human body motions were extended to computer animations for the composition of expressive motions for virtual characters/agents [5]. Nevertheless, the expressiveness of a character animation remains a subjective matter. In recent years, some research in psychology has started to analyze the relationship between motion and emotion (e.g. [6]) but the body

Zs. Ruttkay et al. (Eds.): IVA 2009, LNAI 5773, pp. 308–315, 2009.
© Springer-Verlag Berlin Heidelberg 2009

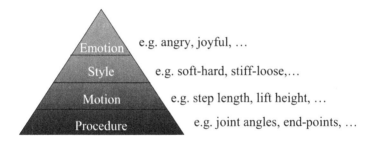

Fig. 1. Hierarchy of parameters for expressing emotive motions

motions used in these experiments were usually performed by professional actors. Therefore, it remains an open question how to generate expressive animations by the computer in a systematic manner in order to deliver emotions to the viewers.

In this work, we aim to design a systematic way to generate human body animations and study the linkage between motion and emotion. We propose to stratify the variables related to expressive motions into four layers: *emotion, style, motion,* and *procedure* layers with their own respective sets of parameters, as shown in Fig. 1. In the emotion layer, emotions can be modeled with either the basic emotions approach or the dimensional approach [4]. The style layer serves as an intermediate layer for describing the expressiveness of an animation while the parameters specific to a motion are defined in the motion layer. And in the procedure layer, generic animation procedures are used to generate parameterized motions.

In our previous work [6], we have shown that, in terms of style parameters, the expressiveness of an animation can be successfully generated through our animation procedures for walking. In this paper, we investigate how to generate emotive animations by designing appropriate animation procedures for virtual characters and verifying the effectiveness of these generated animations. We conducted two psychological experiments to study the mapping between emotion parameters and style parameters.

2 Related Work

Human body motion always contains subtle emotional ingredients. Wallbott [10] attempted to find the relationship between emotions and body motions by asking motion analyzers to code the characteristics of emotional body movements performed by professional actors. Montepare et al. [6] studied how people of various ages perceive emotions from motions differently. Camurri et al. [2] attempted to find the motion characteristics of expressing emotions in dances. The results of these studies all revealed that human body motions were indeed affected by the emotional states possessed by the human actor.

Most of the studies on the relationship between motion and emotion used professional actors to perform emotional motions for observations. However, in the modeling of virtual agents, it is required to generate these emotive motions by the computer. On the other hand, in the literature of computer animation, there has been much research on analyzing and synthesizing emotional human motions. For example,

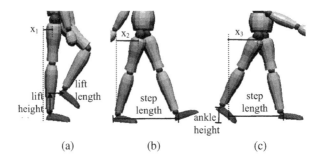

Fig. 2. Definition of the motion parameters for the walking motion

Unuma, et al. [9] used Fourier transform to analyze captured motion clips and synthesized new motions containing various styles. Pelachuad [8] based on a 6-dimesion model to modify gestures of a virtual agent and evaluated its emotional expressiveness. However, for all these approaches, the quality of the final animation relies highly on the quality of the source motions.

Another common approach to the generation of computer animation is by designing parameterized procedures. For example, Bruderlin and Calvert [1] designed a procedure embedded with empirical knowledge to generate the animation of human running. Chi et al. [3] proposed the EMOTE model that made use of the Effort and Shape concepts in Laban Motion Analysis [5] to implement emotional upper-body gestures and full-body postures.

3   Design of Animation Procedures

In this section, we will describe the generic animation procedures that we have implemented to realize parameterized motions for the lower body. We will use the walking motion as an example to illustrate the animation procedures.

The kinematics model that we have used is an LOA1 (Level of Articulation 1) model in the H-Anim standard [11]. We define each branch of the limbs as a 5-bar linkage (including the base) on a plane with four joints. We need to specify at least two constraints in order to uniquely determine this type of mechanism. One common simplification is that we usually make the toes compliant to the ground or parallel to the foot (if it is in the air). Therefore, we need to specify one more constraint to determine the final configuration. According to the type of constraints that we would like to specify in order to determine a key frame, we can classify the procedures for determining the configuration of a leg branch into four different types, each of which is used as a fundamental procedural for composition of a motion.

We use the walking motion as an example to illustrate the generation of a motion with fundamental procedures. We divide the walking motion into three phases separated by three keyframes. In the first keyframe, the two ankles are aligned; the second keyframe is defined when the front leg touches the ground; and the third keyframe is defined when the rear leg leaves the ground. Several motion parameters at various phases are defined to specify the motion, as shown in Fig. 2. These parameters include how the swinging leg is lifted at keyframe 1 (lift_length, lift_height), how two legs are separated (step_length) at keyframes 2 and 3, how the ankle of the rear leg is lifted (ankle_height) at keyframe 2, and how the sacroiliac moves over time (x_1, x_2, and x_3). These motion parameters are used to compute the parameters for the lower-level animation procedures. In addition, the interpolation of in-between frames between two keyframes is performed on the procedural parameters such as joint angles or points in the 3D space.

4   Mapping Motion Parameters into Style Parameters

We have adapted the style attributes defined in [6] as our *style* parameters which originally include *smooth-jerky, stiff-loose, slow-fast, soft-hard, expanded-contracted*, and no action-a lot. Since we use only one type of motion at a time, the last attribute (i.e. no action-a lot) is not considered. There could be many ways to map motion parameters into style parameters. Our current implementation is described as follows.

- **Jerky-Smooth:** This parameter is related to the dimension of "fluidity" in [8]. By discretizing the timing curve with different temporal resolution, we can produce different degrees of smoothness/jerkiness.
- **Stiff-Loose:** This parameter is used to specify the stiffness of a motion. We assume that cyclic motions (e.g. walking) are due to a virtual spring embedded in each joint. Therefore, the stiffness can be modeled as the stiffness constant of a spring with a force proportional to its displacement. A stiff joint tends to change acceleration more rapidly than a loose joint.
- **Slow-Fast:** This parameter bears the usual meaning of modifying the tempo or speed of a motion and is related to the dimension of "temporal extent" in [8]. The relative timing between the phases remains fixed.
- **Soft-Hard:** This parameter is related to the dimension of "power" in [8] and is defined on the amount of joint torque (and its angular acceleration) to be applied to each joint. A softer motion results from a smaller torque.
- **Expanded-Contracted:** The parameter is realized by changing the expansiveness of keyframes and is related to the dimension of "spatial extent" in [8].

In our previous work [6], we conducted an experiment to test the effectiveness of the mapping between *motion* parameters and *style* parameters. Participants compared the *target* stimulus (manipulated) with the *standard* stimulus (neutral) and rated the target according to all of the five style parameters listed above. We found that most style parameters are successful except for the soft-hard parameter. As for the ineffectiveness of the soft-hard parameter, we considered a possible explanation that while the zero-order spatial-temporal relationship (i.e. the positions of an object or its displacement) remains fixed, it is difficult to discern second-order changes (i.e. the acceleration of object motion) with human perception. Nevertheless, we have shown that most style parameters have been implemented with satisfactory results on expressiveness.

5   Mapping from Style Parameters to Emotion Parameters

As mentioned above, it is our ultimate goal to have the mapping all the way from *procedure, motion, style* to *emotion* parameters. For the last step, we need to verify

Table 1. Biserial correlations between style and emotion parameters

style \ emotion	jerky-smooth	stiff-loose	slow-fast	soft-hard	expanded-contracted
Angry	-0.24	-0.19	0.27	0.17	0.77**
Fear	0.07	0.61**	-0.56**	-0.01	-0.50**
Joy	-0.11	-0.49**	0.73**	0.06	0.39*
Sadness	0.14	0.43**	-0.73**	-0.04	-0.47**

$* p < .05$ ，$** p < .01$

the effectiveness of these *style* parameters on expressing various kinds of *emotions*. We follow the basic emotions approach to accept primary emotional responses as *anger, joy, fear, sadness*, disgust and surprise [4]. But we have excluded the last two in this study because the expressions for them depend mostly on facial expressions.

In addition, we regard *walking* as an *emotionally neutral motion*. It means that walking does not relate closely to any kind of emotion.. But we do confront scenarios repeatedly that someone pounds heavily in his rage or that another one flourishes wildly when he is very happy. In other words, there are some kinds of human motions used to express certain emotions. In the present study, we regard *pounding, shivering, flourishing* and a *crestfallen* posture as *emotional motions* which always come with anger, fear, joy and sadness, respectively. We are not only interested in the expressiveness of style parameters for the emotionally neutral motion of walking but also the adding or canceling effect of these parameters for the emotional motions listed above. To achieve the goal, we designed two experiments.

5.1 Experiment 1: Emotional Expressiveness for Walking

First, we verify the emotional expressiveness of style parameters for the emotionally neutral motion of *walking*. Participants are asked to see two animation movie clips (*standard* and *target* stimuli) shown side by side. The standard stimulus is fixed on all of the five style parameters which are set to the middle range of their intensities. The target stimulus can be one of the 32 (i.e. 2^5) combinations with either high or low in intensity of the five style parameters. Participants need to compare the two stimuli and rate the target from -100 to 100 points to indicate if the virtual character is angry, fearful, joyful or sad (with the standard stimulus as the reference of 0 point).

Thirty-two participants are recruited and the whole procedure is divided into five blocks. The first one is the practice block which is followed by four formal blocks of anger, fear, joy and sadness. The sequence of formal blocks and the presentation of 32 movie clips in each block are set randomly for every participant. Ratings are recorded and then analyzed with biserial correlation.

As shown in Table 1, we have found many significant correlations between *style* parameters and *emotion* parameters. In terms of different kinds of emotions, we can see that anger correlates with only the extend of body expanding while other three basic emotions correlate to stiffness, speed and expanding significantly with different patterns. For example, when the character is fear, its body movement is stiffer, slower and more contracted. On the contrary, when the character is joyful, its movements are more relaxed (loose), faster and more expanded. However, when the character is sad, it will become stiff, contracted and even slower in motion than its fearful reaction.

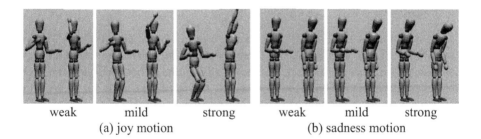

weak	mild	strong	weak	mild	strong
	(a) joy motion			(b) sadness motion	

Fig. 3. Examples of emotive motions with different strengths for joy and sadness

Table 2. Ratings of emotive motions by compatibilities of style parameters

emotion strength	mean	stdev	emotion strength	Mean	stdev
angry (incompatible)	35.3	11.5	joy (incompatible)	25.7	12.1
(compatible)	78.9	10.8	(compatible)	85.4	10.4
fear (incompatible)	37.4	15.4	sadness(incompatible)	42.4	10.2
(compatible)	86.8	13.8	(compatible)	68.1	10.3

5.2   Experiment 2: Emotional Expressiveness for Other Motions

Next, we continue to evaluate the adding or canceling effects of style parameters for some emotional motions. We use *pounding* as the typical motion for anger, *shivering* for fear, *flourishing* for joy and a *crestfallen* posture for sadness (Fig. 3). In the movie clips of this experiment, the virtual character starts to talk with some one invisible for a few seconds and then ends up with a particular emotional motion. Participants have to rate the degree of the character's anger, fear, joy and sadness under the conditions of pounding, shivering, flourishing and crestfallen, respectively.

As for the manipulation of style parameters, we design two versions of animations, either *compatible* or *incompatible*, for each emotional dimension. For example, according to the results on Table 1, more expanded motion is compatible with anger while more contracted motion is incompatible with it. For the same reason, motions high in stiffness and low in speed and expanding are compatible with fear while motions with the opposite pattern of style parameters are incompatible. The same rule can be used on the condition of sadness, too. However, for the sake of joy, the motion needs to be low in stiffness and high in both speed and expanding to be compatible.

Thirty-four participants are recruited to compare the target stimulus with the 50-point standard stimulus and rate the character's emotions from 0 to 100 points. The results are summarized on Table 2. For all of the 4 emotional dimensions, compatible conditions always lead to higher ratings of target emotions. We have also verified the effects with t-tests between compatible/incompatible conditions and all of the tests are significant with the standard of $p<0.01$. It means that the style parameters can actually have their adding effects on emotional motions.

5.3 Discussions

Based on the results of these two experiments, we can see that three but not all of the five *style* parameters are significantly related to the *emotion* parameters with different patterns. And whether the motions are emotionally neutral or not, the style parameters work as well. The inefficiency of jerky-smooth and soft-hard can be due to the same reasons that we have discussed in Section 4 previously. But it can also be possible that these two style parameters do not matter at all. We need more studies to find out the answer. But up to now, we do have satisfactory results of the mapping from procedure, motion, style to emotion parameters. That is to say, we have verified the emotional expressiveness of the lower-level parameters in our hierarchical model.

6 Conclusions

The objective of our research is to study how to generate emotional animations for virtual agents with a systematic procedural approach. The expressiveness of these animations is determined by the appropriate design of parameters at various abstraction levels. In this paper, we have proposed and implemented such a design and conducted two psychological experiments on human walking and other motions to verify the expressiveness of these parameters. Based on the two experimental studies and previous works, we conclude that three out of five style parameters are implemented with satisfactory expressiveness. We believe that the current work can lead to various applications such as an emotive virtual character on the interactive television. We also believe that this work is one step toward the establishment of affective computers [8] which can recognize, express and even have emotions. We will continue to pursue these two lines of developments, both applicative and theoretical, in the future.

Acknowledgement

This work was supported by the National Science Council of Taiwan under contract NSC 97-2627-E-004-001.

References

1. Bruderlin, A., Calvert., T.W.: Knowledge-Driven, Interactive Animation of Human Running. Graphics Interface 1996, 213–221 (1996)
2. Camurri, A., Lagerlof, I., Volpe, G.: Recognizing Emotion from Dance Movement: Comparison of Spectator Recognition and Automated Techniques. Intl. Journal of Human-Computer Studies 59(1), 213–225 (2003)
3. Chi, D., Costa, M., Zhao, L., Badler, N.: The EMOTE Model for Effort and Shape. In: Proc. of SIGGRAPH (2000)
4. Ekman, P.: Argument for basic emotions. Cognition and Emotion 6, 169–200 (1992)

5. Laban, R.: The Mastery of Movement, 2nd edn. MacDonald & Evans LTD, London (1960)
6. Lin, Y.-H., Liu, C.-Y., Lee, H.-W., Huang, S.-L., Li, T.-Y.: Verification of Expressiveness of Procedural Parameters for Generating Emotional Motions. In: Prendinger, H., Lester, J.C., Ishizuka, M. (eds.) IVA 2008. LNCS (LNAI), vol. 5208, pp. 514–515. Springer, Heidelberg (2008)
7. Montepare, J., Koff, E., Zaitchik, D., Albert, M.: The Use of Body Movements and Gestures as Cues to Emotions in Younger and Older Adults. Journal of Nonverbal Behavior, 133–152 (1999)
8. Pelachaud, C.: Studies on Gesture Expressivity for a Virtual Agent. Speech Communication 51, 630–639 (2009)
9. Unuma, M., Anjyo, K., Takeuchi, R.: Fourier Principles for Emotion-based Human Figure Animation. In: Proc. of SIGGRAPH (1995)
10. Wallbott, H.G.: Bodily Expression of Emotion. European Journal of Social Psychology 28(6), 879–896 (1998)
11. H-Anim, http://www.h-anim.org/

Modeling Emotional Expressions as Sequences of Behaviors

Radosław Niewiadomski[1], Sylwia Hyniewska[1], and Catherine Pelachaud[2]

[1] Telecom ParisTech, Paris, France
{niewiado,hyniewska}@telecom-paristech.fr
[2] CNRS-LTCI, Paris, France
pelachau@telecom-paristech.fr

Abstract. In this paper we present a system which allows a virtual character to display multimodal sequential expressions i.e. expressions that are composed of different signals partially ordered in time and belonging to different nonverbal communicative channels. It is composed of a language for the description of such expressions from real data and of an algorithm that uses this description to automatically generate emotional displays. We explain in detail the process of creating multimodal sequential expressions, from the annotation to the synthesis of the behavior.

Keywords: virtual characters, emotional expressions, multimodality.

1 Introduction

In this paper a novel approach to the generation of emotional displays of a virtual character is presented. The aim is to develop a model of multimodal emotional behaviors that is based on data from literature and on the annotation of a video-corpus. For this purpose a language was developed to describe the appearance in time of single signals as well as the relations between them.

Recent studies (e.g. [1,2,3]) show that several emotions are expressed by a set of different nonverbal behaviors which include different modalities: facial expressions, head and gaze movements, gestures, torso movements and posture. We call *multimodal sequential expressions of emotions* emotional displays that go beyond the description of facial expressions of emotions in their apex. They might be composed of nonverbal behaviors (called in this paper *signals*) displayed over different modalities or/and as a sequence of behaviors.

Several models of emotional expressions have been proposed to enrich virtual characters' behavior. A tool to modify manually the course of the animation of any single facial parameter was proposed in [4]. In Paleari and Lisetti [5] and Malatesta et al. [6] the emotional expressions are manually created from sequences predicted in Scherer's appraisal theory [7]. Both papers focus on the temporal relations between different facial actions predicted by the theory. In Xueni Pan et al. [8] a motion graph is used to generate emotional displays from

Zs. Ruttkay et al. (Eds.): IVA 2009, LNAI 5773, pp. 316–322, 2009.

sequences of signals like facial expressions and head movements. The arcs of the graph correspond to the observed sequences of signals while nods are possible transitions between them. New animations can be generated by reordering the observed displays. Finally Lance and Marcella [9] model head and body movements in emotional displays focusing on the correlation between them.

In next sections we present a system that allows the generation of multimodal sequential expressions.

2   Multimodal Sequential Expressions Language

In this section we present the representation scheme that encompasses the dynamics of emotional behaviors. The scheme is based in observational studies. We use a symbolic high level notation which gives us flexibility in the generation of possible behaviors. Our XML-based language defines multimodal sequential expressions in two steps: *behavior set* and *constraint set*. Single signals like a *Duchenne smile*, *shake* or *bow* are described in the repositories of the character's nonverbal behaviors. Each of them may belong to one or more *behavior sets*. Each emotional state has its own behavior set, which contains signals that might by used by the character to display that emotion. A number of regularities occur in expressions that concern the signal duration and the order of displaying (see e.g. [1,2]). Consequently for each signal in a behavior set one may define the following five characteristics: *probability_start* and *probability_end* - probability of occurrence at the beginning (resp. towards the end) of an expression (a value in the interval [0..1]), *min_duration* and *max_duration* - minimum (resp. maximum) duration of the signal (in seconds), *repetitivity* - number of repetitions during an expression.

According to the observational studies (e.g. [2]) the signals occurrence in an emotional display is not accidental. The relations that occur between the signals of one behavior set are more precisely described in the *constraint sets*. This set introduces a set of constraints on the occurrence and duration (i.e. on the values for $start_{s_i}$ and $stop_{s_i}$) of the signal s_i in relation to others signals. We introduced two types of constraints:

- *temporal constraints* define relations on the start time and end time of a signal using arithmetical relations: $<$, $>$ and $=$;
- *appearance constraints* describe more general relations between signals like inclusion or exclusion e.g. "signals s_i and s_j cannot co-occur" or "signal s_j cannot occur without signal s_i".

The constraints of both types are composed using the logical operators: *and, or, not*. The constraints take one or two arguments.

Three types of *temporal constraints* are used *morethan, lessthan*, and *equal*. These arithmetical relations may involve one or two signals: for example the observation: "signal s_i cannot start at the beginning of animation" will be expressed as following $start_{s_i} > 0$, while "signal s_i starts immediately after the signal s_j finishes" will be $start_{s_i} = stop_{s_j}$.

In addition, five types of *appearance constraints* were introduced:

- $exists(s_i)$ - is true if the s_i appears in the animation;
- $includes(s_i, s_j)$ - is true if s_i starts before the signal s_j and ends after the s_j ends;
- $excludes(s_i, s_j)$ - is true if s_i and s_j do not co-occur at the same time t_k i.e.: if $start_{s_i} < t_k < stop_{s_i}$ then $stop_{s_j} < t_k$ or $start_{s_j} > t_k$ and if $start_{s_j} < t_k < stop_{s_j}$ then $stop_{s_i} < t_k$ or $start_{s_i} > t_k$;
- $precedes(s_i, s_j)$ - is true if s_i ends before s_j starts;
- $rightincludes(s_i, s_j)$ is true if s_i starts before the signal s_j ends, but s_j ends before s_i ends.

During the computation of the animation constraints are instantiated with signals appearance times (i.e. $start_{s_i}$ and $stop_{s_i}$). By the convention the constraints that cannot be instantiated (i.e. one of the arguments does not appear in the animation) are ignored. An animation is consistent if there is no constraint that is not satisfied.

3   From Annotation to Behavior Representation

In this section we present how the definition of behavior and constraint sets are created from the manual annotation. One coder annotated the modalities of the face, head, gaze and body movements. The facial changes have been annotated with FACS [10], while the head, gaze and body movements were described verbally. For practical reasons a *signal* is defined as a configuration of body actions that can occur at the same time in a particular modality. Thus one signal per modality is displayed at a time. Usually different body actions of one modality were defined as independent signals, e.g. *a hand touching the face* and *a hand hiding the mouth* gestures are two signals. The same body actions can be part of several signals, if they can occur in different configurations and with different co-occurrences, e.g. a smile is a signal, a smile with an open mouth is another one even if they have some AUs in common.

Figure 1 presents the FACS annotation of a segment of a panic fear expression. The following signals were individuated in this sample:

- *signal 1*: eyebrows very raised and drawn together, eyes extremely open, mouth extremely open,
- *signal 2*: inner eyebrows slightly raised, slightly drawn together, mouth slightly open with lowered mouth corners,
- *signal 3*: upper lid raised widening the eye, mouth open,
- *signal 4*: eyebrows drawn together, upper lid raised to widen the eye, lower lid raised,
- *signal 5*: outer eyebrows raised, eyebrows drawn together, mouth open with lowered corners.

In three of the four panic fear videos, extreme facial displays of fear with the very widely open eyes and mouth (signal 1) were followed by milder facial expressions of fear like an open mouth with falling lip corners and the inner or outer part of the eyebrows raised (signal 2). As a consequence, a rule was written to state besides others that *signal 2* occurs *immediately* after *signal 1* (see Figure 1). This information might be described in the constraint set as a *temporal* constraint: the start time of *signal 2* is equal to the end time of *signal 1* (i.e. $stop_{signal1} = start_{signal2}$).

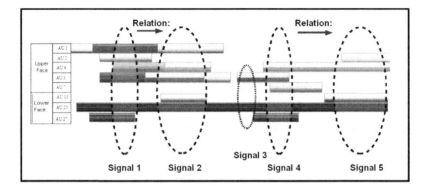

Fig. 1. Annotation of facial expressions of panic fear

Then analyzing expressions of panic fear across different modalities the following signals were individuated: hands to the face (*signal 6*), shoulders up (*signal 7*), hand suspended in the air (*signal 8*), hand that hides the mouth than comes to rest on the chest (*signal 9*), both hands on the chest (*signal 10*), hand hides the mouth (*signal 11*), head (*signal 12*) and gaze turns to the side (*signal 13*). By looking at the panic fear videos one could argue that *signal 6* (i.e. a gesture with hands to the face) is a signal that cannot occur in panic fear if *signal 1* (i.e. facial expressions of eyebrows very raised and drawn together, eyes and mouth extremely opened) has not started before. It also stops before the end of *signal 1*. This information might be described in the constraint set by *appearance constraints* of the type *includes* and *exists*. When *signal 6* cannot appear without *signal 1* we obtain the constraint: *exists(signal 1) and includes(signal1,signal6)*.

4   Generation of Multimodal Sequential Expressions

In our model, the behavior and constraint sets are used to generate multimodal sequential expressions of emotions. The input to the system is one emotional label e (e.g. *panic fear* or *embarrassment*) from a predefined set of emotional labels and its expected duration, t. Our system generates sequences of multimodal expressions, i.e. the animation A of a given duration t composed of a sequence of signals $s_{i(j)}$ on different modalities. It does so by choosing a coherent subset of signals from the behavior set BS_e as well as their timing $start_{s_i}$, $stop_{s_i}$.

4.1   Algorithm

Let A be the animation to be displayed by a virtual character. A can be seen as a set of triples $A = \{(s_i, start_{s_i}, stop_{s_i})\}, start_{s_i}, stop_{s_i} \in [0..t], start_{s_i} < stop_{s_i}$ where s_i is the name of the signal, $start_{s_i}$ is the start time of the signal s_i and $stop_{s_i}$ is its stop time. At the beginning A is empty. In the first step the algorithm chooses the behavior set $BS_e = \{s_k\}$, the constraint set $CS_e = \{c_m\}$ corresponding to the emotional state e, and the number n of uniform intervals, time stamps, for which the t is divided. Next, at each time step, t_j, (j=0..n-1, t_n=t), the system randomly chooses a signal-candidate s_c between the signals of the behavior set BS_e considering their probabilities of occurrence. For this purpose it manages a table of probabilities that contains, for each signal s_k, its current probability value $p_{k(tj)}$. Obviously, at the first time stamp, $t_0 = 0$, the values of this table are equal to the values of the variable *probability_start*, while at the last time stamp t_{n-1} the probabilities are equal to the *probability_end*. At each time stamp, t_j, the probabilities $p_{k(tj)}$ of each signal $s_k \in BS_e$ are updated. The candidate for a signal to be displayed s_c in a time stamp t_j is chosen using the values $p_{k(tj)}$. Next, the start time $start_c$ is chosen from the interval $[t_j, t_{j+1})$ and the consistence of CS_e with the partial animation $A(t_{j-1}) \cup (s_c, start_{s_c}, \emptyset)$ is checked. If all the constraints are satisfied the stop time $stop_c$ is randomly chosen between two values:

$$stop_{c1} = min_{s_c} + R * \frac{M}{2}, \qquad stop_{c2} = max_{s_c} - R * \frac{M}{2}, \qquad M = max_{s_c} - min_{s_c}$$

while R is a value from the interval $[0..1]$, max_{s_c} is the maximum duration of s_c while min_{s_c} is the minimum duration of s_c. Otherwise, i.e. if there is a constraint that is not satisfied, another signal from BS_e is chosen as candidate. The consistency of the triple $(s_c, start_{s_c}, stop_{s_c})$ with the partial animation $A(t_{j-1})$ is checked again. If all the constraints are satisfied the signal s_c starting at $start_{s_c}$ and ending at $stop_{s_c}$ is added to A. The table of probabilities is updated and the algorithm chooses another signal, moves to the next time stamp, or finishes generating the animation.

In our approach we do not scale the timing of an observed sequence of behaviors to t. Rather the system chooses between the available signals of a behavior set in order to generate animations. The choice of our approach is motivated by research results showing that the duration of signals is related to their meaning. For example, spontaneous facial expressions of felt emotional states are usually not longer than four seconds, while the facial display of surprise is much shorter [11]. Similarly, gestures have also a minimum duration. Moreover the same gesture performed with different expressivity parameters (e.g. velocity) might convey different meanings.

The algorithm intentionally does not use any backtracking mechanism as it is implemented in near real-time applications that generate the animation rapidly. Thus in each computational step it adds a new signal that starts not earlier than the previous one. It allows the animation generation pipeline to be more efficient.

The algorithm is able to generate a number of animations that is consistent with the constraints. In this way we avoid the repetitiveness of the character's behavior and we obtain a variety of animations, each of which is consistent with the annotator's observation but go beyond a set of annotated cases.

4.2   Example

We used the Greta agent [12] to generate animations using our model. In Figure 2 an animation generated by our algorithm from the description of panic fear (see section 3). The following signals are displayed: 2a) *signal 1* - eyes and mouth extremely open, 2b) *signal 1* with *signal 6* - hand to the eyes, 2c) *signal 1* and *signal 10* i.e. hands on chest, 2d) *signal 2* accompanied by *signal 12* and *signal 13* - eyebrows slightly raised and drawn together, mouth open with lowered lip corners, head and gaze turns to the side.

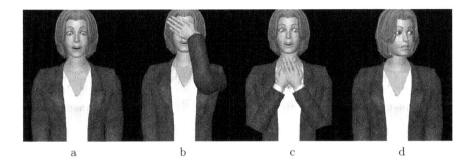

| a | b | c | d |

Fig. 2. An example of a multimodal expression, based on the annotation of panic fear

5   Conclusions

In this paper a multimodal sequential expressions model for a virtual character was introduced. These expressions go beyond facial displays defined in their apex. For this purpose a language was proposed that allows formalizing the observational data and an algorithm that generates multimodal sequential expressions coherent with their descriptions. We have conducted a perceptual study [13] of eight expressions (anger, anxiety, cheerfulness, embarrassment, panic fear, pride, relief, tension) generated by our algorithm. The results show that multimodal sequential expressions enable the recognition of affective states, such as relief, that are not prototypical expressions of basic emotions. In the case of all emotions the recognition rate surpassed chance level [13].

Acknowledgement

Part of this research is supported by the EU FP6 Integrated Project CALLAS IP-CALLAS IST-034800.

References

1. Haidt, J., Keltner, D.: Culture and facial expression: Open-ended methods find more expressions and a gradient of recognition. Cognition and Emotion 13(3), 225–266 (1999)
2. Keltner, D.: Signs of appeasement: Evidence for the distinct displays of embarrassment, amusement, and shame. Journal of Personality and Social Psychology 68, 441–454 (1995)
3. Wallbott, H.: Bodily expression of emotion. European Journal of Social Psychology 28, 879–896 (1998)
4. Ruttkay, Z.: Constraint-based facial animation. International Journal of Constraints 6, 85–113 (2001)
5. Paleari, M., Lisetti, C.: Psychologically grounded avatars expressions. In: First Workshop on Emotion and Computing at KI 2006, 29th Annual Conference on Artificial Intelligence, Bremen, Germany (2006)
6. Malatesta, L., Raouzaiou, A., Karpouzis, K., Kollias, S.D.: Towards modeling embodied conversational agent character profiles using appraisal theory predictions in expression synthesis. Appl. Intell. 30(1), 58–64 (2009)
7. Scherer, K.R.: Appraisal considered as a process of multilevel sequential checking. In: Scherer, K., Schorr, A., Johnstone, T. (eds.) Appraisal Processes in Emotion: Theory, Methods, Research, pp. 92–119. Oxford University Press, Oxford (2001)
8. Pan, X., Gillies, M., Sezgin, T.M., Loscos, C.: Expressing complex mental states through facial expressions. In: Second International Conference on Affective Computing and Intelligent Interaction (ACII), pp. 745–746. Springer, Heidelberg (2007)
9. Lance, B., Marsella, S.: Emotionally expressive head and body movements during gaze shifts. In: Proceedings of the 7th International Conference on Intelligent Virtual Agents (IVA), pp. 72–85. Springer, Heidelberg (2007)
10. Ekman, P., Friesen, W.: Facial Action Coding System. Consulting Psychologists Press (1978)
11. Ekman, P., Friesen, W.: Unmasking the Face. A guide to recognizing emotions from facial clues. Prentice-Hall, Inc., Englewood Cliffs (1975)
12. Bevacqua, E., Mancini, M., Niewiadomski, R., Pelachaud, C.: An expressive ECA showing complex emotions. In: Proceedings of the AISB Annual Convention, Newcastle, UK, pp. 208–216 (2007)
13. Niewiadomski, R., Hyniewska, S., Pelachaud, C.: Evaluation of multimodal sequential expressions of emotions in ECA. In: Proceedings of the International Conference on Affective Computing and Intelligent Interaction (ACII), Amsterdam, Holland. Springer, Heidelberg (2009)

I Feel What You Feel: Empathy and Placebo Mechanisms for Autonomous Virtual Humans

Julien Saunier, Hazaël Jones, and Domitile Lourdeaux

Laboratoire Heudiasyc
UMR CNRS 6599
Université de Technologie de Compiègne
{jsaunier,joneshaz,dlourdea}@hds.utc.fr

Abstract. Computational modeling of emotion, physiology and personality is a major challenge in order to design believable virtual humans. These factors have an impact on both the individual behavior and the collective one. This requires to take into account the empathy phenomenon. Furthermore, in a crisis simulation context where the virtual humans can be contaminated by radiological or chemical substances, empathy may lead to placebo or nocebo effects.

Stemming from works in the multiagent systems domain, our virtual human decision process is designed as an autonomous agent. It has been shown that the environment can encapsulate the responsibility of spreading part of the agent state. The agent has two parts, its mind and its body. The mind contains the decision process and is autonomous. The body is influenced by the mind, but controlled by the environment which manages the empathy process. Combined with biased reasoning, favorable personality traits and situational factors, empathy can lead some agents to believe they are contaminated although they are not. We describe these mechanisms and show the results of several experiments.

1 Introduction

The context of this research is a project of crisis simulation for the improvement of multi-institutional response to terrorist attacks. The goal is to propose a training tool for both security and rescue teams (command and action roles). Civilians are virtual autonomous humans / agents represented in a virtual environment. In order to improve crisis simulation, designers have to take into account personality, emotion and physiology in decision making [15]. However, these mechanisms are described through many conflicting and/or shallow-defined models [16]. Another pitfall is that scripted scenarios limit the re-playability of the training exercise, but non-scripted simulation is hard to achieve and resource hungry. Multiagent systems (MAS) are a way to simulate virtual humans via cognitive agents. There are two main approaches to obtain an intelligent behavior : imitate the cognitive process [5], or manipulate a set of observed behaviors [10]. Our research follows an hybrid path that simulates interdependencies in behavior choice, in order both to explain the cognitive factors that lead to simulated situations and to keep the agents complexity coherent with the simulation needs. This architecture uses ergonomics task models, in the same way as [4].

In this article, we focus on the social mechanisms of the system. Collective behavior is not an aggregate of individual behaviors [9], in particular because of empathy

Zs. Ruttkay et al. (Eds.): IVA 2009, LNAI 5773, pp. 323–329, 2009.

[13] and, combined with biased reasoning, placebo/nocebo effects. Empathy is "the intellectual identification with or vicarious experiencing of the feelings, thoughts, or attitudes of another" (Dictionary). Basically, it means that the agents influence each other through some kind of affective interaction. In the crisis context where virtual humans can be contaminated by radiological or chemical substances, empathy may lead to nocebo effects [1]: someone believing he is contaminated and possibly even showing physical symptoms although he is safe. In section 2, we show the motivations of our work. Section 3 is a brief overview of our architecture named PEP $\rightarrow$ BDI. Section 4 describes the inter-agent empathy mechanism and how it can lead to nocebo. We show the results of several experiments in section 5, and draw conclusions and perspectives in section 6.

2   Social Phenomena

Studies from the psychology field, such as [2], highlight the individual and social dimensions of crisis. At the individual level, disasters engender high levels of stress, which can either be adapted stress or overwhelming stress. Adapted stress mobilizes the mental and physiological capacities, while overwhelming stress exhausts the energetic reserves through one of four modalities: stuporous inhibition, uncontrolled agitation, individual panic flight, and automatic behavior. Symmetrically, collective behaviors can be adjusted or maladjusted. Maladjusted behaviors such as panic and violence may arise when the rescue teams are weakly organized and when the victims believe they are poorly informed or treated. Mutual awareness [3] and empathy are necessary for collective behavior to appear [9]. Empathy is the low-level mechanism which enables the agents to perceive each other physical and emotional state. At a higher level, mutual awareness involves a symbolic representation of the activities of the others.

Stemming from works in the multiagent systems domain, our virtual human decision process is designed as an autonomous agent. The environment has been recently put forward as a first-order abstraction [17] which can encapsulate the responsibility of spreading a part of the agent state. Following this principle, the agent has two parts: its mind and its body [14]. The mind contains the decision process and is the autonomous part of the agent. The body is influenced by the mind, but controlled by the environment. One may try to fly, it does not mean one can. Practically, the agent state is public and its modification is regulated by the environment. Hence, the functionalities are clearly separate and the agent architecture is centered on the decision process. In terms of computation costs, encapsulating services in the environment does not increase the global load, but may create a bottleneck.

3   System Overview

Figure 1[1] shows our global architecture. The virtual environment is an external module called EVE which manages the 3D representation of the scene. The MAS platform manages the agents life cycle and communications and each virtual human is driven by an agent. The virtual environment and the MAS platform are synchronized in order to ensure consistency during the simulation. Our architecture (PEP $\rightarrow$ BDI) is an

---

[1] Screenshot: EVE©, EMI Informatique.

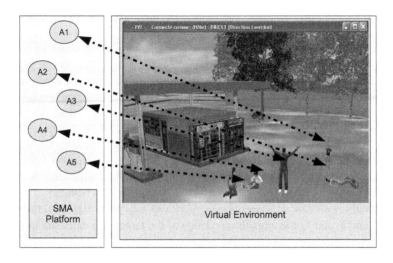

Fig. 1. Global Architecture

extension of eBDI framework [7]. It considers emotion, personality and physiology in the agent decision process. The agent gets new information (perception, message and body) from the environment. This information generates immediate emotions, and the agent changes its beliefs in function of its emotions. The selection of desires and intentions is similar to the classical BDI scheme except for the emotion, physiology and personality influence. Once intentions are selected, the agent updates its emotions again. If its emotions change, it updates again its beliefs, physiology, desires and intentions. Finally, it plans its actions and executes its new plan.

Basically, emotions are based on OCC [12]. Emotions are grouped by pair like, for example, pride and shame. In this article, the focus is put on empathy in a terrorist attack simulation. Relevant factors are fear, anger and stress (physiological parameter). Personality is formed by parameters that indicate personality traits. In a crisis situation, agents evolve on a short time period (a few hours) where only some prominent behavior elements are expressed. As a consequence, we chose to simplify the personality model and to use only personality traits relevant for the simulation. The personality of an agent does not evolve during the simulation.

4   State Spreading and Its Influence on the Agents

4.1   Empathy

As stated in the introduction, empathy enables the agents to be impacted by the other agents state. Proximity, either spatial or psychological, is a requirement for empathy to take place. The functional separation of mind and body means that the agent knows its physical / emotional state, but can only influence it. In fact, its emotions will be updated through two mechanisms: internal and external dynamics. Emotions and physiology evolve in function of time towards an equilibrium (internal dynamics), and in function of events and stimuli (external dynamics).

Internal dynamics are managed by the agent itself. Emotions and stress are calculated as $emotion = emotion \times emotion\_tendency$.

External dynamics are managed by the perception function of the environment, in order to give the right information to the right agent(s). Concerning the empathy mechanisms specifically, the environment updates regularly the agents state. The empathy manager module of the environment gets the current state of the agent and updates accordingly its global state of the world. The state of the world contains the body properties of each agent. Then, the empathy manager calculates the effects of empathy on the agents' neighbours in function of their previous state and their tendency to empathy. Finally, the environment spreads these into the concerned agents bodies.

The formula is $stress = \frac{1}{dist(origin,target)} stress * t_e$, with $dist(a, b)$ the distance between a and b, and t_e the empathy tendency of the target. We calculate in the same way the two emotions, namely fear and anger.

4.2 Placebo

In our crisis scenario, part of the civilians inhale and/or touch chemical and radiological substances. These civilians quickly develop symptoms, which range from itching to suffocation. A major problematic for the rescuers is to isolate the contaminated victims. However, a part of the population will mimic reactions to the toxics without real exposure [11,8]. Four categories of factors are involved in the nocebo effect: personality, physiology, emotion and beliefs.

Personality- Studies show that in clinical experiments 30 to 40 % of the patients are placebo-responsive, but that there is no obvious personality trait which may lead to placebo or nocebo responsiveness [6]. Two main personality factors were identified: optimism -one who believes in a positive outcome tends to be less responsive to nocebo than one who does not- and empathy tendency -one who is prone to assimilate the others feelings can also share perceptible symptoms-.

Physiology- Although optimism and empathy tendency play a role in placebo responsiveness, of greater importance are immediate situational and interpersonal factors. The first of these factors is stress. Nervous tension is a consequence of general adaptation. It is influenced [15] by temporal pressure, tiredness, positive or negative events and actions success / failure. Generally, it follows the same curve as emotions.

Beliefs- New information can be obtained by perception (sight, hearing, smelling, ...), by communication (messages) or by sensing the semi-controlled body (injury, tiredness, ...). Primary emotions are a direct reaction to a percept. For example, if an agent perceives several agents suffocating, it will feel fear. In our representation, emotions and personality have an impact on the way the new beliefs are interpreted. This leads the agent to either modify the input, for example a coward agent is more inclined to believe the situations to be dangerous, or build biased beliefs. In the simulation, because of the crisis situation, it is important for agents to have a risk representation. This includes the agents' beliefs about the other agents contamination, and about their own contamination. The other agents contamination is assessed through their visible symptoms. Furthermore, emotions influence the agents survival prediction belief. The agent starts showing symptoms when it has persuaded itself of its own contamination.

Calculation- All these factors increase or decrease the probability for the agent to be placebo-responsive, but there is no predictive rule. The calculation is realized when an event likely to cause placebo/nocebo happens. These events are (i) information or rumour about the presence of a contaminating substance, (ii) a new belief evaluating an agent to be contaminated, and (ii) the survival prediction belief crossing the lower threshold. Stress and emotions are evaluated in $[0, 100]$, emotion tendencies belong to $[1 - t, 1 + t]$. The calculation is $threshold(contam(itself)) =$

$$\left(\sum \frac{1}{dist(itself, agent)} contam(agent) + stress * pessimism \right) \times t_e \times p$$

with p the probability to be subjected to nocebo.

When an event triggers this calculation, a random number is generated and compared with the threshold. If $threshold(contam(itself))$ is crossed, the agent believes it is contaminated and starts to mimic the symptoms of nearby seemingly contaminated agents. Doing so, it triggers the same calculation for its neighbours while increasing the probability their result is positive.

5 Experiments

We have run experiments using the MadKit[2] platform. MadKit is a general-purpose multiagent system platform written in Java. In these simulations, the agents are pseudo-randomly located in a two-dimensional space. The darker the point is, the higher the agent stress it represents is.

Figure 2 shows the simulation evolution over one minute. It starts just after a stressful event occurred (such as an explosion). Consequently, the agents have various levels of stress, depending on their perception, their personality and how they assessed the situation. After one minute, the agents' stress is stabilized.

The middle screenshot shows that clusters of agents with the same stress level are forming, because the agents are sensible to the state of their neighbours. The right screenshot shows what happens if no empathy mechanism is implemented: only the stress tendency of the agent is taken into account, and no collective phenomenon can take place.

We have run experiments in which no stressful event occurs. Although the agents have a tendency to get stressed, social regulation limits the impact of this tendency in normal situations. These experiments show that our empathy mechanism is sound both in normal situations and after events modifying physiological and emotional factors.

Figure 3 shows the simulation evolution when nocebo effects are added. The points are shadowed when the agents show symptoms of contamination.

---

[2] http://www.madkit.org

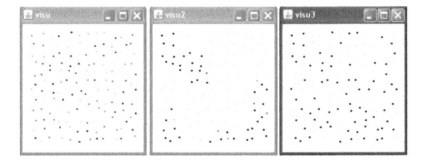

Fig. 2. Left: initial state. Middle: final state with empathy. Right: final state and without empathy.

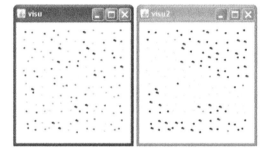

Fig. 3. Left: initial state. Right: final state.

Only the agents showing symptoms at the beginning of the simulation are really contaminated ($\frac{1}{10}$ of the agents). In these experiments, the agents do not move. Hence, events triggering the calculation are only (i) after the initialization, once the agents perceive their surroundings (and therefore the contaminated agents in their area), and (ii) the agents showing nocebo-induced symptoms. The results of our experiments are consistent with the principles discussed in section 4.2. Nearly one half of the agents exhibiting symptoms are not contaminated. Immediate proximity is a major factor, combined with stress and pessimism. Finally, we note the high correlation between symptoms spreading and clusters of agents whose stress is important.

6 Conclusion and Perspectives

Simulation of human behavior, in particular in a crisis situation, needs to consider physiology, personality and emotion in order to be plausible. Furthermore, collective behavior simulation requires the instantiation of social phenomena such as empathy and nocebo effects. An originality of this work is to delegate to the environment the task of spreading the states of the agents. Combined with the agents decision process, this mechanism enables the representation of complex social behavior.

We have run experiments to validate our model, which have shown the soundness of our environment-driven empathy mechanism and of the nocebo simulation. Further works include a thorough validation of simulated behaviors. This work of calibration will require users and expert feedbacks to improve the simulation.

References

1. Benson, H.: The nocebo effect: History and physiology. Preventive Medicine 26(5), 612–615 (1997)
2. Crocq, L.: Special teams for medical/psychological intervention in disaster victims. World Psychiatry 1(3), 154 (2002)
3. Dugdale, J., Pavard, J., Soubie, B.: A pragmatic development of a computer simulation of an emergency call center. In: Designing Cooperative Systems: The Use of Theories and Models, pp. 241–256. IOS Press, Amsterdam (2000)
4. Edward, L., Lourdeaux, D., Lenne, D., Barthes, J., Burkhardt, J.: Modelling autonomous virtual agent behaviours in a virtual environment for risk. IJVR: International Journal of Virtual Reality 7(3), 13–22 (2008)
5. Gratch, J., Marsella, S.: A domain-independent framework for modeling emotion. Cognitive Systems Research 5(4), 269–306 (2004)
6. Harrington, A.: The placebo effect: an interdisciplinary exploration. Harvard University Press (1997)
7. Jiang, H., Vidal, J.M., Huhns, M.N.: Ebdi: an architecture for emotional agents. In: AAMAS 2007: Proceedings of the 6th international joint conference on Autonomous agents and multiagent systems, pp. 1–3. ACM, New York (2007)
8. Lacy, T., Benedek, D.: Terrorism and Weapons of Mass Destruction: Managing the Behavioral Reaction in Primary Care. Southern Medical Journal 96(4), 394 (2003)
9. Le Bon, G.: The Crowd: A Study of the Popular Mind (1895)
10. Maes, P.: The agent network architecture (ana). SIGART Bull. 2(4), 115–120 (1991)
11. Noy, S.: Minimizing casualties in biological and chemical threats (war and terrorism): the importance of information to the public in a prevention program. Prehospital and Disaster Medicine 19(1), 29–36 (2004)
12. Ortony, A., Clore, G.L., Collins, A.: The Cognitive Structure of Emotions. Cambridge University Press, Cambridge (1988)
13. Paiva, A., Dias, J., Sobral, D., Aylett, R., Sobreperez, P., Woods, S., Zoll, C., Hall, L.: Caring for agents and agents that care: Building empathic relations with synthetic agents. In: AAMAS 2004: Proceedings of the Third International Joint Conference on Autonomous Agents and Multiagent Systems, Washington, DC, USA, pp. 194–201. IEEE Computer Society, Los Alamitos (2004)
14. Platon, E., Sabouret, N., Honiden, S.: Tag interactions in multiagent systems: Environment support. In: Weyns, D., Van Dyke Parunak, H., Michel, F. (eds.) E4MAS 2006. LNCS, vol. 4389, pp. 106–123. Springer, Heidelberg (2007)
15. Silverman, B.G., Johns, M., Cornwell, J., O'Brien, K.: Human behavior models for agents in simulators and games: Part i: Enabling science with pmfserv. Presence 15(2), 139–162 (2006)
16. Sloman, A.: Beyond shallow models of emotion. In: Cognitive Processing: International Quarterly of Cognitive Science, pp. 177–198 (2001)
17. Weyns, D., Omicini, A., Odell, J.: Environment as a first-class abstraction in multi-agent systems. Autonomous Agents and Multi-Agent Systems 14(1), 5–30 (2007); Special Issue on Environments for Multi-agent Systems

Predicting User Psychological Characteristics from Interactions with Empathetic Virtual Agents

Jennifer Robison[1], Jonathan Rowe[1], Scott McQuiggan[2], and James Lester[1]

[1] Department of Computer Science, North Carolina State University, Raleigh, North Carolina
[2] SAS Institute, Cary, North Carolina

Abstract. Enabling virtual agents to quickly and accurately infer users' psychological characteristics such as their personality could support a broad range of applications in education, training, and entertainment. With a focus on narrative-centered learning environments, this paper presents an inductive framework for inferring users' psychological characteristics from observations of their interactions with virtual agents. Trained on traces of users' interactions with virtual agents in the environment, psychological user models are induced from the interactions to accurately infer different aspects of a user's personality. Further, analyses of timing data suggest that these induced models are also able to converge on correct predictions after a relatively small number of interactions with virtual agents.

Keywords: User modeling and adaptive agents, Evaluation of virtual agents, Agents in narrative, Affective interaction.

1 Introduction

A central feature of social intelligence is the ability to infer psychological characteristics of an interlocutor from a relatively limited number of observations. Quickly sizing up another participant in social settings is both common and useful in human-human interactions. Providing virtual agents with the ability to infer users' psychological characteristics could contribute to increased agent believability. This, in turn, could contribute to greater immersion in narrative games [1, 2] and increased effectiveness of game-based learning environments [3, 4] and agent-based training systems [5]. Alternatively, the same information could be obtained by requiring users to fill out lengthy questionnaires or to be extensively questioned by virtual agents. This approach, though frequently used, is invasive and for some applications may be undesirable or infeasible. Enabling a virtual agent to quickly and accurately infer users' psychological characteristics such as their personality could support a broad range of applications in education, training, and entertainment.

This paper presents an inductive framework for inferring users' psychological characteristics from observations of their interactions with virtual agents in a narrative-centered learning environment. Psychological user models are trained on traces of users' interactions with virtual agents in the environment. As users perform tasks,

Zs. Ruttkay et al. (Eds.): IVA 2009, LNAI 5773, pp. 330–336, 2009.

they engage in pre-scripted branching dialogue-like interactions with multiple virtual agents. Three families of attributes are monitored and logged: situational attributes (users' locations, tasks, actions), affective attributes (user-reported emotion states), and conversational attributes (frequency and duration of user-agent interactions). Psychological user models are then induced from the interactions to infer various aspects of user personality (based on Big Five models of personality [6]). Further, analyses of timing data suggest that these induced models are able to rapidly converge on correct predictions after a relatively small number of interactions with virtual agents.

2 Related Work

Recent work on intelligent virtual agents has investigated a range of models for the expression of virtual characters' social behaviors. Gratch *et al.* found that virtual agents exhibiting contingent non-verbal feedback could effectively engender feelings of rapport while listening to human speakers [7]. Other work has sought to construct computational models of socially normative conversational behavior [8, 9]. The characterization of different social relationships that can exist between humans and virtual agents has also received considerable attention. In their seminal work, Reeves and Nass asserted that humans treat computers as social actors, and the same social rules that govern human-human interactions also apply to human-machine interactions [11]. This has led to several lines of investigation examining the social-cognitive impacts of different factors on short-term and long-term human-agent interactions [12, 13].

The ability to automatically attribute traits to others, to assign stereotypes and to perform related inferences almost instantaneously, is a powerful and pervasive social phenomenon [11]. This ability to quickly "size up" another individual provides humans valuable knowledge about how to proceed during an interaction. Some recent work on social inference in virtual agents has focused on developing and evaluating a computational framework of social causality [14], but to our knowledge, little work to date has focused on automatically inferring users' psychological characteristics, such as personality.

3 Experimental Method

In this study, personality profiles of human subjects and traces of subjects' interactions with virtual agents are used to learn predictive models of user personality. These interactions took place within CRYSTAL ISLAND, a narrative-centered learning environment targeting eighth-grade (12-13 year old) students studying microbiology. Within this environment, students are attempting to solve a science mystery by gathering information from objects and interactions with virtual characters. For more information on the CRYSTAL ISLAND environment, please see [4, 15]

3.1 User Study

To investigate the inductive framework for inferring users' psychological characteristics from interactions with empathetic virtual agents, a human participant study was conducted with 35 college students ranging in age from 21 to 60 (M = 24.4, SD = 6.41) including 9 females and 26 males. Human-agent interaction histories acquired from monitoring and logging these subjects' interactions with virtual agents in the CRYSTAL ISLAND learning environment offer a rich substrate for developing empirically grounded models of cognition, affect, and social behavior. Previously they have been used to study empathy in virtual agents [15] and affect in students [3], and here they provide training data for inducing predictive models of user psychological characteristics.

Though many psychological characteristics may be of interest, this study focused on learning models of user's personality. Individuals' *personalities* are dispositions over a long duration, in contrast to emotions or moods which are more limited in their duration [16]. The Big 5 Personality Questionnaire [6] was used to assess subjects' personality. It employs five principal categories: *openness, conscientiousness, extraversion, agreeableness* and *neuroticism*. Subjects indicated their agreement with 45 statements across each of these five dimensions using a 5 point Likert scale [6]. Each of these measures may impact the receptiveness of a student towards various agent behaviors [17, 18].

In the study, participants were given an overview of the experiment agenda, and then completed several pre-experiment instruments, including the Big 5 Personality Questionnaire. Following completion of these materials, participants were given 45 minutes to solve the mystery. During this time, users interacted with each of six virtual agents who inhabit CRYSTAL ISLAND, each playing a distinct role in the environment. For consistency, each time a subject decided to interact with a virtual agent, a set schema was used to provide an empathetic interaction. Students were first greeted with an introduction of "Hi Alex, how are you feeling?" to which students were able to respond by selecting one of 10 emotional states (*anger, anxiety, boredom, confusion, delight, excitement, fear, flow, frustration and sadness*). The characters then responded with a short, one or two sentence empathetic response, followed by content related to the narrative environment. At the end of the interaction, characters would conclude by asking students "How are you feeling now?" to which students could respond using the same set of emotions.

3.2 Inductive Framework

As subjects interacted with the virtual agents in the learning environment, all of their interactions were monitored and logged. In addition to "snap-shot" attributes that offer a view onto the interaction at a particular moment, the value of "higher-order" attributes that summarize interactions up to that moment were also periodically computed, e.g., the number of interactions that a subject has had with all of the agents up to that point in time. Three categories of attributes were used to induce predictive models for user psychological characteristic modeling: situational attributes, affective attributes, and conversational attributes. *Situational attributes* are extracted directly from behavior trace data, and include users' locations within the environment, their tasks, and the actions they take to perform those tasks. *Affective attributes* feature higher-order attributes derived from users' self-report responses to agents' inquiries about how they feel, as well as the relative frequency of each emotion reported up to the current moment. *Conversational attributes* record the frequency and duration with which users communicate with the environment's virtual agents.

From these three categories of attributes, four separate datasets were created. Dataset 1 (*Situational-Only*) consisted solely of situational attributes taken directly from the user logs. Dataset 2 (*Situational/Affective*) and Dataset 3 (*Situational/Conversational*) supplemented the situational attributes with either affective or conversational attributes, respectively. Dataset 4 (*All*) included all three types of attributes.

4 Results

For each trait (e.g., *extraversion*) which makes up a personality profile, each subject was classified as being either "High" or "Low" on that trait by splitting on the median value for that trait across all subjects. Since this median is likely specific to the population studied, further investigation will be required to create comprehensive models applicable to a variety of populations. Using the behavior traces of the subjects interacting with the virtual agents as training data, predictive models were learned for each individual trait and then aggregated to form models of personality. Using the WEKA machine learning toolkit [19], three types of models were learned for each of the 5 traits using each of the four datasets above: Naïve Bayes, Decision Tree, and Support Vector Machines. All models were learned using a tenfold cross-validation scheme for producing training and testing datasets. In this scheme, data is decomposed into ten equal partitions, nine of which are used for training and one of which is used for testing. The equal parts are repeatedly swapped between training and testing sets until each partition has been used for both training and testing. Tenfold cross-validation is widely used for obtaining an acceptable estimate of error [19].

The accuracy of aggregated models for each dataset and model type are presented in Table 1. All of the models outperformed baseline measures with statistical significance. The baseline for each trait is computed by choosing the most frequent class label and applying it to all test data. The baselines for each specific trait are then aggregated to provide the average baseline measure (54.4%) for overall personality (high agreeableness, conscientiousness, extraversion and openness – low neuroticism). For instance, the worst performing model that was learned, which was the naïve Bayes model of *concientiousness*, used only situation attributes but was still significantly higher than the baseline (56.02%, $p<0.05$). The model with the highest accuracy was the decision tree model of *agreeableness*, which was learned from situation, agent and affect-based attributes (96.9%). Overall, decision tree models outperformed support vector machines ($M_1=84.9\%$, $SD_1=15.7\%$, $M_2=73.6\%$, $SD_2=11.2\%$, $p<0.0001$), which in turn outperformed naïve Bayes models ($M=67.0\%$, $SD=8.7\%$, $p<0.0001$).

Models also varied significantly based on the attributes used to train them. The inclusion of affect attributes (the *Situational/Affective* Dataset) increased the accuracy of user psychological characteristics predictions over the situational attributes alone (the *Situational-Only* Dataset) ($M_1=81.7\%$, $SD_1=10.1\%$, $M_2=58.1\%$, $SD_2=1.1\%$, $p<0.0001$). The inclusion of conversational attributes (the *Situational/Conversational* Dataset) also increased the accuracy of user psychological characteristics predictions over the situational attributes alone (the *Situational-Only* Dataset) ($M_1=75.0\%$, $SD_1=14.3\%$, $M_2=58.1\%$, $SD_2=1.1\%$, $p<0.0001$). Overall, affect information provided a larger increase in performance than conversational information ($p=0.14$). However, the

Table 1. Accuracies by model type and dataset (clockwise from top-left: Datasets 1, 2, 4, 3)

	Without Affective Attributes		With Affective Attributes	
Without Conversational Attributes	NB	57.8%	NB	72.5%
	DT	58.6%	DT	93.4%
	SVM	58.1%	SVM	79.4%
With Conversational Attributes	NB	60.0%	NB	73.6%
	DT	91.3%	DT	96.4%
	SVM	73.8%	SVM	84.0%

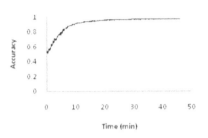

Fig. 1. Speed of convergence on accurate personality traits

largest performance increase came from the inclusion of these two sets of attributes together, which provided a slight increase in performance over affective data alone (M_2=84.3%, SD_2=10.7%, M_2=81.7%, SD_2=10.1%, p<0.50).

Because the overarching objective of this work is not only to infer a user's psychological characteristics after observing her for an extended period of time, but also to predict these characteristics at runtime so that agents can utilize the information to guide their social behaviors with the user, it is important to understand how quickly each individual's traits can be accurately predicted. Models that quickly and accurately converge on the correct prediction are highly desirable. To assess convergence properties, the models with the highest accuracy (decision tree models trained with situational, affective, and conversational attributes) were used to create incremental estimations of users' personality traits.

To simulate runtime estimation, we applied the model to the existing logs of the users' interactions at moments when new information was obtained. These estimates provided a best guess, given current knowledge, of each of the user's traits. Over time the history of these guesses is accumulated to provide confidence estimates for the classification of each trait. The chart presented in Figure 1 shows the convergence of estimates on the accurate classification as a function of time. These results indicate that models reach a 75% confidence in the correct classifications of user traits in approximately 4 minutes of interaction time. Given 10 minutes, predictive accuracy climbs to 90%, and with 19 minutes, 95% accuracy is achieved. With character interactions taking place, on average, approximately every 4 minutes, we can see that user personality traits can be learned in very few interactions with characters.

The results indicate that interactions with empathetic virtual agents can be used to accurately infer users' overall personality as well as each of their individual traits. For all of these traits, the inclusion of both affective and conversational attributes yielded the most accurate models. This suggests that the more information agents have about the user's situation, emotions and conversational interactions, the more likely they will be to effectively adapt their behavior to suit individual users. While both affective and conversational attributes were useful for informing models, the largest gain in insight was gleaned from the affective information, suggesting that in the case of limited computational resources, this mode of data collection would prove to be the most useful. In addition to being able to learn models of personal traits, the convergence analysis of these models reveals that they can be applied and used with an individual user and within a relatively short amount of time.

5   Conclusions and Future Work

Humans have the ability to quickly assess the personality and dispositional traits of those around them through social interaction. In virtual agents, these capabilities can be provided by empirically grounded models that are induced from observations of human-agent interactions. Induced models show promise for enabling agents to accurately infer user psychological characteristics such as personality, as well as the individual traits that make up an individual's personality profile. Initial results indicate that models trained on a pool of representative users can relatively quickly converge on accurate predictions during an evolving interaction with a particular user.

The results suggest important directions for future work. For example, it will also be interesting to explore the impact of enriching the interactions between agents and users by adding less constrained, multimodal communication functionalities. It will be important to explore how incorporating the predictive models into virtual agents can be leveraged to improve agent believability and effectiveness.

Acknowledgements

The authors would like to thank the other members of The IntelliMedia Group at North Carolina State University for useful discussions and support. We are grateful to Omer Sturlovich and Pavel Turzo for use of their 3D model libraries, and Valve Software for access to the Source^{TM} engine and SDK. This research was supported by the National Science Foundation under Grants REC-0632450, IIS-0757535, DRL-0822200 and IIS-0812291. This material is based upon work supported under a National Science Foundation Graduate Research Fellowship. Any opinions, findings, and conclusions or recommendations expressed in this material are those of the authors and do not necessarily reflect the views of the National Science Foundation.

References

1. Mateas, M., Stern, A.: Structuring Content in the Façade Interactive Drama Architecture. In: First Conference on Artificial Intelligence and Interactive Digital Entertainment, pp. 93–98. AAAI Press, Menlo Park (2005)
2. Mott, B., Lester, J.: U-Director: A Decision-Theoretic Narrative Planning Architecture for Storytelling Environments. In: 5th International Conference on Autonomous Agents and Multiagent Systems, pp. 977–984 (2006)
3. McQuiggan, S., Robison, J., Lester, J.: Affective Transitions in Narrative-Centered Learning Environments. In: 9th International Conference on Intelligent Tutoring Systems, pp. 490–499 (2008)
4. McQuiggan, S., Rowe, S., Lester, J.: The Effects of Empathetic Virtual Characters on Presence in Narrative-Centered Learning Environments. In: 26th Annual SIGCHI Conference on Human Factors in Computing Systems, pp. 1511–1520. ACM Press, New York (2008)
5. Johnson, W.L.: Serious Use of a Serious Game for Language Learning. In: 13th International Conference on Artificial Intelligence in Education, pp. 67–74. IOS Press, Amsterdam (2007)

6. McCrae, R., Costa, P.: Personality in Adulthood: A Five-Factor Theory Perspective, 2nd edn. Guilford Press, New York (2003)
7. Gratch, J., Wang, N., Gerten, J., Fast, E., Duffy, R.: Creating rapport with virtual agents. In: Pelachaud, C., Martin, J.-C., André, E., Chollet, G., Karpouzis, K., Pelé, D. (eds.) IVA 2007. LNCS (LNAI), vol. 4722, pp. 125–138. Springer, Heidelberg (2007)
8. Si, M., Marsella, S.C., Pynadath, D.V.: Thespian: Modeling socially normative behavior in a decision-theoretic framework. In: Gratch, J., Young, M., Aylett, R.S., Ballin, D., Olivier, P. (eds.) IVA 2006. LNCS (LNAI), vol. 4133, pp. 369–382. Springer, Heidelberg (2006)
9. Pedica, C., Vilhjálmsson, H.H.: Social perception and steering for online avatars. In: Prendinger, H., Lester, J.C., Ishizuka, M. (eds.) IVA 2008. LNCS (LNAI), vol. 5208, pp. 104–116. Springer, Heidelberg (2008)
10. Reeves, B., Nass, C.: The Media Equation: How People Treat Computers, Television, and New Media Like Real People and Places. Cambridge University Press, New York (1996)
11. Uleman, J.S.: A Framework for Thinking Intentionally About Unintended Thoughts. In: Uleman, J.S., Bargh, J.A. (eds.) Unintended Thought, pp. 425–449. Guilford Press, New York (1989)
12. Bickmore, T., Picard, R.: Establishing and Maintaining Long-Term Human-Computer Relationships. ACM Transactions on Computer-Human Interaction 59(1), 21–30 (2005)
13. Kim, Y., Baylor, A.: A Social-Cognitive Framework for Pedagogical Agents as Learning Companions. Educational Technology Research & Development 54(6), 569–590 (2006)
14. Mao, W., Gratch, J.: Modeling Social Inference in Virtual Agents. Journal of Artificial Intelligence and Society 24(1), 5–11 (2009)
15. McQuiggan, S., Robison, J., Phillips, R., Lester, J.: Modeling Parallel and Reactive Empathy in Virtual Agents: An Inductive Approach. In: 7th International Joint Conference on Autonomous Agents and Multi-Agent Systems, pp. 167–174 (2008)
16. Rusting, C.: Personality, Mood, and Cognitive Processing of Emotional Information: Three Conceptual Frameworks. Psychological Bulleti 124(2), 165–196 (1998)
17. Isbister, K., Nass, C.: Consistency of personality in interactive characters: verbal cues, non-verbal cues, and user characteristics. International Journal of Human Computer Interaction Studies 53, 251–267 (2000)
18. Kang, S., Gratch, J., Wang, N., Watts, J.: Agreeable People Like Agreeable Virtual Humans. In: Prendinger, H., Lester, J.C., Ishizuka, M. (eds.) IVA 2008. LNCS (LNAI), vol. 5208, pp. 253–261. Springer, Heidelberg (2008)
19. Witten, I., Frank, E.: DataMining: Practical Machine Learning Tools and Techniques, 2nd edn. Morgan Kaufmann, San Francisco (2005)

When Human Coders (and Machines) Disagree on the Meaning of Facial Affect in Spontaneous Videos

Mohammed E. Hoque, Rana el Kaliouby, and Rosalind W. Picard

Media Laboratory, Massachusetts Intitute of Technology
20 Ames Street, Cambridge, MA 02142
{mehoque,kaliouby,picard}@media.mit.edu

Abstract. This paper describes the challenges of getting ground truth affective labels for spontaneous video, and presents implications for systems such as virtual agents that have automated facial analysis capabilities. We first present a dataset from an intelligent tutoring application and describe the most prevalent approach to labeling such data. We then present an alternative labeling approach, which closely models how the majority of automated facial analysis systems are designed. We show that while participants, peers and trained judges report high inter-rater agreement on expressions of delight, confusion, flow, frustration, boredom, surprise, and neutral when shown the entire 30 minutes of video for each participant, inter-rater agreement drops below chance when human coders are asked to watch and label short 8 second clips for the same set of labels. We also perform discriminative analysis for facial action units for each affective state represented in the clips. The results emphasize that human coders heavily rely on factors such as familiarity of the person and context of the interaction to correctly infer a person's affective state; without this information, the reliability of humans as well as machines attributing affective labels to spontaneous facial-head movements drops significantly.

Keywords: facial expression analysis, affective computing, action units, spontaneous video.

1 Introduction

One important application area for intelligent virtual agents is intelligent tutoring systems (ITS). These systems are much more effective in maximizing learning goals when the virtual agent is equipped with the ability to understand the learner's facial affect. Building an automated system that recognizes spontaneous facial expressions remains a challenging endeavor: human facial muscle activations can occur in over twenty thousand combinations and there is no codebook to describe the mapping from facial expressions to affective state. Despite the immense diversity in human facial expressions, impressive results have been reported in the literature in recognizing small sets of prototypic facial expressions. However, when examined carefully, the reported results are dependent on the dataset, environment, and simplicity of affective state categorizations. For example, a study may be based on a dataset of professional

Zs. Ruttkay et al. (Eds.): IVA 2009, LNAI 5773, pp. 337–343, 2009.
© Springer-Verlag Berlin Heidelberg 2009

actors/random participants feigning particular affective states in a laboratory environment. While pattern recognition algorithms can be made to perform really well on such data, those algorithms do not generalize as well to spontaneous natural emotions. A more accurate validation of automated facial analysis systems uses emotional clips from movies/TV shows that have obvious emotional tags, optimized camera views and lighting conditions. These clips are carefully selected, clipped and validated by human judges and do not contain the variability of difficult and imperfect natural data. Another approach employs carefully selected movie clips which are believed to elicit natural spontaneous emotions from humans. A small group of participants are asked to view those clips while agreeing to be video taped. One limitation of such dataset is that it does not provide a task dependent environment where context becomes an inevitable part of elicited affective states. After building a framework to analyze and recognize affective states, most researchers also use a relatively limited set of individuals and a small set of possible labels to validate their framework. When individuals are given more labeling choices (e.g. both "proud" and "happy" for a smiling face) then agreement in labeling tends to go down.

For automated classification of facial expression data, given the lack of a robust theory that maps expressions to labels; one needs to have some portion of the data labeled by human judges. The judges are often instructed to equate a specific set of facial Action Units (AUs) with a particular affective state [3]. For example, the nose wrinkler (AU 9) is often considered a distinguishing feature of disgust. A brow lowerer (AU 4) is a common feature of confusion. Combination of lip AUs such as jaw drop (AU 26), low intensity lip corner puller (AU 12), lips funneler (AU 22), and lips part (AU 25) are often regarded as signatures of happiness. This direct mapping between AUs and affective states may work well in synthetic data, resulting in high agreement among the human judges, but it may not converge well in real life data. For example, in Figure 1 [1], the same face with identical facial expression is used in two different contexts, resulting in completely different meanings. While humans are more likely to tag Figure 1 (a) as angry and Figure 1 (b) as disgust, an automated algorithm would not be influenced by the context and would not differentiate between the two images. This is an example of how our perception of something can be biased by context and prior experience, even when the input pattern is constant.

   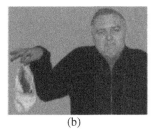

(a)   (b)

Fig. 1. The prototypic facial expression of disgust is placed in two different contexts, where the majority of the participants label (a) as anger, and (b) as disgust (Figure used by permission, copied from Aviezer et al. [1])

The remaining part of the paper is divided into the following sections – Section 2 presents details regarding experimental setup, data collection and labeling. Section 3 provides the results of how the inter-rater reliability among coders drops when context information is removed. It also shows details of correlation between a set of AUs and affective states, based on manual labeling. Section 4 summarizes the lesson learned through this study which may prove to be useful towards customizing an automated AU detection framework to work with natural data.

2   Data Collection Methods

In this paper, we have used data collected from an experiment where humans interact with a computer agent – Autotutor [2]. Autotutor is designed to simulate a human tutor while having the ability to interact with the learner using natural language. Autotutor engages students in learning by asking them questions on a given topic and then providing them useful clues to get to the correct or complete answer.

2.1   Materials, Data Size and Procedure

The participants consisted of 28 undergraduate at the University of Memphis who participated for extra course credit. In this paper, 10 sessions consisting of 10 participants were randomly selected. Each session was about 30 minutes long.

2.2   Tagging of Affective States

The affective states that were considered in this experiment were boredom, confusion, flow, delight, frustration, surprise and neutral (surprise and flow were not included in the manual discriminative AU analysis, described in Section 4.1, due to the infrequency of occurrences). These categories were ones that were frequently experienced in a previous experiment with Autotutor. Boredom was defined as lack of interest, whereas confusion was defined as lack of understanding. Flow symbolized a state that was a mix of drive, alertness, interest, concentration, and being self-determined that results from pleasurable engagement in an activity that is challenging but not too challenging. Delight indicated a high degree of satisfaction from accomplishment or comprehension. Frustration was described as a state of disappointment or annoyance with the Autotutor interaction. Surprise was labeled as an amazement being triggered from something unexpected. Neutral was equivalent to having no apparent affect or feeling.

There were four levels of tagging that took place in order to collect ground-truth data. In the first phase, learners (Coder 1) watched their own video of interacting with Autotutor, and then, were asked to label the affective states that they had experienced during the interaction; this was termed *self-judgment.* The second phase of the tagging included each participant returning to the lab after a week and then tagging a video of another participant interacting with Autotutor; this was termed as *peer judgment* or Coder 2. In the third level of tagging, two trained judges (Coders 3 and 4) with experience of facial expression tagging were asked to tag all the videos for a particular set of affective states. Both judges were undergraduate research assistants with extensive training on tutorial dialogue characteristics and FACS coding. Inter-rater reliability was measured using Kohen's kappa between self vs. peer (Coder 1 vs. Coder 2), self vs. judge1 (Coder 1 vs. Coder 3), self vs. judge2 (Coder 1 vs. Coder 4), peer vs. judge1 (Coder 2 vs. Coder 3), peer vs. judge2 (Coder 2 vs. Coder 4), judge1 vs. judge2 (Coder 3 vs. Coder 4). Among all these pairs, judge1 and judge2 had the highest agreement (kappa =0.71). We took the subset of videos where these two judges perfectly agreed and used these videos with the judges labels as the ground-truth data.

Next, we extracted 8-second clips around those points that the trained judges had identified. Then, those clips for all participants were presented in random order to three independent coders. The coders were expected to watch the 8 seconds of clips and assign one of the affective states label to each clip. The main rationale behind producing small segments of videos around each point that the trained judges labeled, was to produce a set of training and test examples that one would use to train a classifier to recognize affective states. However, the trained judges had the opportunity to view the entire video to tag affective states versus a machine counterpart that is typically trained on smaller video segments in random order. Therefore, we felt that it is more appropriate to analyze the agreement among humans on smaller segments of videos to get an idea of how difficult it may be for humans to label affective states without context.

3   Results

Coders 5, 6, and 7 were given the ground truth video clips where the expert judges agreed 100% of the time. Therefore, it was expected that coders 5, 6 and 7 would agree with the ground truth labels more often than "chance" to the least. Chance was calculated as 1-B.

Using Bayes Error, $B= \sum_{i} P_i (1 - P_i)$, where

P_i = i-th class prior probability based on the frequency of seven different labels in the training set. Based on the frequency of labels in the given dataset, chance was 51%. If the distribution of the labels in the training data set was uniform, then chance would have been $1/7 = 14.28\%$ for the 7 classes.

Table 1 demonstrates the kappa and percentage agreement between ground truth labels and Coder 5, 6 and 7. Both kappa and percentage agreement between ground truth values and independent coders were lower than chance which was 51%. Results indicated high agreement (above 80%) on delight, while disagreeing significantly on other categories. The lowest percent agreement was for frustration and confusion while the highest was for delight and surprise.

4.1   Analysis of Discriminative Power of AUs

Most automated facial expression analysis systems assume a one-to-one mapping between facial expressions and affect. However, it has been shown that when affective states beyond the six basic emotions [4] are considered, or when non-prototypic expressions of an affective state are included, the discriminative power of action units

Table 1. Kappa and percentage agreement among the ground truth labels and Coders 5, 6, 7. Ground truth corresponds to the labels agreed upon by Coders 3 and 4.

Combinations	Kappa	% agreement
Ground truth vs. Coder 5	0.25	0.38
Ground truth vs. Coder 6	0.38	0.50
Ground truth vs. Coder 7	0.28	0.39
Coder 5 vs. Coder 6	0.35	0.45
Coder 5 vs. Coder 7	0.31	0.41
Coder 6 vs. Coder 7	0.46	0.54

drops. In other words, the relationship between a single AU or facial expression and an affective state is not direct, and the same AU can appear in more than one affective expression. In this study, we trained judges manually coded a randomly chosen 20% of the original data for AUs. The main goal was to distinguish a smaller subset of AUs which may be unique to a particular affective state.

After the manual recognition of AUs, an analysis was done to predict how good of a discriminator a particular AU is, given a mental state. We define a heuristic variable, $H = P(Y_j \mid X_i) - P(Y_j \mid \sim X_i)$, where Y = AUs, and X = mental states. The magnitude of H quantifies the discriminative power of a display for a mental state; the sign depicts whether an action unit increases or decreases the probability of a mental state. To explain how the heuristic works, consider the following hypothetical cases of the discriminative ability of a lip corner pull in identifying delight:

Assume that a lip corner pull (AU 12) is always present in delight $P(Y_{j=12} \mid X_i=delight) = 1$, but never appears in any of the other mental states $P(Y_{j=12} \mid X_i \neq delight) = 0$. The heuristic is at its maximum value of one, and its sign is positive. The presence of a lip corner pull is a perfect discriminator of delight. Similarly, suppose that a lip corner pull (AU 12) never shows up in agreeing, $P(Y_{j=12} \mid X_i=agreeing) = 0$, but always shows up in all other mental states $P(Y_{j=12} \mid X_i \neq agreeing) = 1$. The magnitude of H would still be one, but its sign would be negative. In other words, the lip corner pull would be a perfect discriminator of agreeing, even if it never occurred in that state. (Again, this example is not actually true). Finally, if a lip corner pull is always observed in delight, and is also always observed in all other mental states, then $P(Y_{j=12} \mid X_i=delight) = P(Y_{j=12} \mid X_i \neq delight) = 1$. In this case, H has a value of 0, and the lip corner pull is an irrelevant feature in the classification of delight.

The result of computing H for each mental state is shown in Table 2. Table 2 helps identify a particular set of AUs which are either significant discriminators or non-discriminators of an affective state. Table 2 provides such a list, where outer brow-raiser (AU 2), mouth stretch (AU 27), eyes closed (AU 43), head turn left (AU 51) etc were positive discriminators of boredom. Lip corner pull (AU 12), lid lightener (AU 7), brow lowerer (AU 4), Jaw drop (AU 26), inner brow raiser (AU 1) were negative discriminators of boredom. Lip corner pull (AU 12) turned out to be the best discriminator for both delight and frustration and least for boredom, confusion and neutral. The highest discriminatory value of all the AU's went to AU 12 for delight (note that coders were able to identify delight more often than other categories). It was also evident that several AUs were positively correlated with more than one affective state.

Table 2. Discriminatory and non-discriminatory AUs per mental state. The AUs are listed in order of their contribution (most significant to least).

Mental states	Discriminatory Aus	Negatively discriminatory Aus
Boredom	2, 27, 43, 51	12, 7, 4, 26, 1
Confusion	4, 7, 17, 52	12, 53
Delight	12, 25, 26, 7	43
Frustration	43, 12, 7	57, 25, 54,
Neutral	None	7, 12, 4, 25, 43

4 Discussions and Future Work

In this paper, we provide a methodical approach to facial expression analysis when dealing with challenging natural data obtained from interaction with an automated agent in a learning context. Over 300 minutes of video data were collected from experiments where a human interacted with an animated agent, where the human played the role of learner and the agent played the role of tutor. The data were manually coded for seven different mental states of boredom, confusion, flow, delight, frustration, neutral and surprise by two human judges with inter-rater reliability being 0.7. These ground truth videos were then segmented into 8-second clips and given to 3 independent coders for tagging. The percent agreement among the independent coders was less than chance. This finding is very important because in pattern recognition, classifiers are typically trained on similarly short video clips and in most cases, the classifiers do not perform well with natural data.

Developing a system that reliably recognizes over 31 different AUs is a difficult problem. In this study, we have manually coded a random 20% of our data to detect the most discriminative and least discriminative AUs for the relevant affective states. Due to the experimental set up of our study, participants had to sit very close to the camera. Therefore, even a slightest movement/tilt of the head as part of natural movement would trigger most of the Action Descriptors (AD) related to head movement (AD 51 to AD 58 and AD 71 to AD 76). Therefore, it is probably not useful trying to incorporate those AUs in our analysis. Based on observation and manual coding of the data, AUs related to lip movement (AU 12, AU 15, AU 18, AU 25), eye/lid/brow movement (AU 1, AU 2, AU 7) were more relevant. From this experience, given the task, camera position, and context, it may be possible to group a bunch of AUs based on relevance and importance.

In the past, there has been a trend to associate a set of AUs with particular affective states regardless of the task and context. However, even faces made of AU's that correspond to basic emotions can take on a label of a different basic emotion if the context is modified [1]. In this paper, we argue that a blind association between a set of AUs and a particular affective state could potentially confuse the automated classifier.

Instead of looking for one-to-one or many-to-one association between AUs and affective states, it is important to investigate the interplay among AUs in sequence for a given affective state. Even though a video clip may contain AU signatures not unique to one affective state, the sequence in which the AUs appear and interact with each other may reveal unique patterns.

In the 8-second video clips, it was often the case that participants moved away from the viewable range of the camera, looked to the side with a tilted face, and occluded their face with their hands. While it is not possible to fully address these concerns with the current state of computer vision algorithms, it may be possible to add meaning to these phenomena, given a context.

Our immediate future work involves incorporating all these lessons learned towards modifying our existing AU detection framework for the given dataset. While it is desirable to develop a one-size-fits-all affect recognition system by inferring meaning from the detected AUs, it is very likely that we may have to perform a fair bit of customization of the framework and manual work depending on the dataset. Future work will also involve conducting similar exploratory studies of different real-world datasets to statistically model the way affect is communicated through natural data. It is also a possibility to incorporate and fuse other features such as shoulder movement, hand gestures, task-related behaviors, and prosodic aspects of speech towards affect recognition for animated agents.

Acknowledgement

This research was partially supported by NSF (IIS 0325428). Any opinions, findings, and conclusions or recommendations expressed in this material are those of the authors and do not necessarily reflect the views of the funding institution. The authors would like to acknowledge their colleagues at the University of Memphis for sharing the Autotutor data.

References

1. Aviezer, H., Hassin, R., Ryan, J., Grady, G., Susskind, J., Anderson, A., Moscovitch, M., Bentin, S.: Angry, Disgusted or Afraid? Studies on the Malleability of Emotion Perception. Psychological Science 19, 724–732 (2008)
2. Graesser, A.C., McDaniel, B., Chipman, P., Witherspoon, A., D'Mello, S., Gholson, B.: Detection of Emotions During Learning with AutoTutor. In: Proceedings of the 28th Annual Meeting of the Cognitive Science Society, Vancouver, Canada, pp. 285–290 (2006)
3. Ekman, P., Friesen, W.: Facial Action Coding System: A Technique for the Measurement of Facial Movement. Consulting Psychologists Press, Palo Alto (1978)
4. Ekman, P., Friesen, W.V., Ellsworth, P.: Emotion in the Human Face: Guidelines for Research and an Integration of Findings. Pergamon Press, New York (1972)

Spontaneous Avatar Behavior for Human Territoriality

Claudio Pedica[1,2] and Hannes Högni Vilhjálmsson[1]

[1] Center for Analysis and Design of Intelligent Agents, School of Computer Science,
Reykjavik University, Iceland
[2] School of Computer Science, Camerino University, Italy

Abstract. The challenge of making a virtual world believable includes a requirement for AI entities which autonomously react to a dynamic environment. After
the breakthroughs in believability introduced by modern lightning and physics
techniques, the focus is shifting to better AI behavior sophistication. Avatars and
agents in a realistic virtual environment must exhibit a certain degree of presence
and awareness of the surroundings, reacting consistently to unexpected contingencies and social situations. Unconscious reactions serve as evidence of life,
and can also signal social availability and spatial awareness to others. These behaviors get lost when avatar motion requires explicit user control. This paper
presents a new approach for generating believable social behavior in avatars. The
focus is on human territorial behaviors during social interactions, such as during conversations and gatherings. Driven by theories on human territoriality, we
define a reactive framework which allows avatars group dynamics during social
interaction. This approach gives us enough flexibility to model the territorial dynamics of social interactions as a set of social norms which constrain the avatar's
reactivity by running a set of behaviors which blend together. The resulting social
group behavior appears relatively robust, but perhaps more importantly, it starts
to bring a new sense of relevance and continuity to virtual bodies that often get
separated from the simulated social situation.

1 Introduction

Most of Multiplayer Massively Online Games (MMO) available nowadays portray their
players as animated characters or avatars, under the user control. One of the open challenges for the state of the art in interactive character animation is to measure up to the
standard of visual quality that the game industry reached with their environments. There
are numerous examples of 3D rendered characters in films and digital media that look
quite realistic when you see a screenshot or a still frame, but once they start moving,
they look totally non-lifelike giving to the viewer a slight sense of discomfort. This feeling is explained in robotics as the "uncanny valley", a terminology first introduced by
Masahiro Mori in 1970 [1]. Applying the "uncanny valley" hypothesis to an animated
character, the conclusion is that the more a virtual creature looks realistic the more we
will expect a realistic behavior when it is moving. For those companies which plan to
create close to photorealistic characters, it must be ensured that their behavior matches
the quality of the visual rendering. This is particularly true when they need to simulate
human communicative behavior in face-to-face interactions, such as conversations.

Zs. Ruttkay et al. (Eds.): IVA 2009, LNAI 5773, pp. 344–357, 2009.

In most commercial avatar-based systems, the expression of communicative intent and social behavior relies on explicit user input [2]. For example, in both Second Life[1] and World of Warcraft[2] users can make their avatars emote by entering special emote commands into the chat window. This approach is fine for deliberate acts, but as was argued in [3], requiring the users to think about how to coordinate their virtual body every time they communicate or enter a conversation places on them the burden of too much micro-management. When people walk through a room full of other people, they are not used to thinking explicitly about their leg movements, body orientation, gaze direction, posture or gesture, because these are things that typically happen spontaneously without much conscious effort [4]. Some of these behaviors are continuous and would require very frequent input from the user to maintain, which may be difficult, especially when the user is engaged in other input activities such as typing a chat message. In the same way that avatars automatically animate walk cycles so that users won't have to worry about where to place their virtual feet, avatars should also provide the basic behavioral foundation for socialization.

Interestingly, even though users of online social environments like Second Life appear sensitive to proximity by choosing certain initial distances from each other, they rarely move when approached or interacted with, but rely instead on the chat channel for engagement [5]. Since locomotion, positioning and social orientation is not being naturally integrated into the interaction when relying on explicit control, it is worth exploring its automation. For the particular case of a conversation, some have suggested that once an avatar engages another in such a face-to-face interaction, a fixed circular formation should be assumed [6]. Even though the idea matches with our common sense and daily experience, it is in fact a simplification. A conversation is indeed a formation but a more dynamic one. The circle we often see is merely an emergent property of a complex space negotiation process, and therefore the reliance on a fixed structure could prevent the avatars from arranging themselves in more organic and natural ways, with the net result of breaking the illusion of believability.

2   Related Works

2.1   Automating Avatar Control

As we summarized in [7] automating the generation of communicative behaviors in avatars was first proposed in BodyChat [3] and then further explored in the Spark system, that incorporates the BEAT engine [8] to automate a range of discourse related co-verbal cues in addition to cues for multi-party interaction management. With a special interest for postural shifts, the Demeanor system [9] generates avatar posture based on affinity between conversation partners. A study [2] showed how automating avatars' communicative behaviors provides some level of support to their users.

In this current work we focus on the yet "unconquered land" of simulating small scale group dynamics, while keeping in mind that other layers of behavior control introduced in previous work will need to be added for fully supporting the social interaction process.

---

[1] http://secondlife.com/
[2] http://www.worldofwarcraft.com/

2.2 Simulating Group Dynamics

Simulating group dynamics concerns with modelling and imitating the kinetic evolution over time of a group of individuals. This is different from another plausible definition of group dynamics which concerns how the social relationships evolves amongst the members of a group, like for example when two persons become friends. In the domain of our definition we can talk about large scale group dynamics and small scale group dynamics, and the difference between them is just in the order of magnitude of the number of individuals we consider. For our purposes we are more interested in the second kind of dynamics even though the scientific community has been much more prolific in dealing with large groups. Of course, simulating large scale groups is different from simulating small scale groups but the approaches used for modelling the former can be adapted for the latter. Numerous works have been published in the area of large scale group dynamics. Most of them simulate natural systems like crowds of people or formations of animals such as flocks of birds or schools of fish. These sort of global collective phenomena have been modeled with different approaches but the most interesting and successful of them define the group dynamics as an emergent behavior. In this direction, there are two main approaches to the problem:

– The particle-based system approach, where particles are animated in real time by application of forces.
– The agent-based systems approach, in which each agents are managed in real time by rules of behavior.

The main difference between them is how much sophistication we want for the behavior of each single individual. The first approach focuses more on the collective group behavior as a whole whereas the second focuses of the richness of behavior of each single individual.

Most of the Crowd Simulators use a particle-based approach because it is well suited for modeling global collective phenomena (such as group displacement and collective events) where the number of individuals is huge and they are all quasi-similar objects. Usually each individual is not doing more than just moving toward a destination, therefore its motion is easily modeled as a particle. One of the classical work on particle-based systems is the one of Helbing and Molnár [10] which clearly describes the concept of a social force model for simulating dynamics of walking pedestrians. Social forces are defined as a psychological tension toward acting in a certain way. Quoting the authors, a social force is a "[...] quantity that describes the concrete motivation to act". An interesting extension to the basic social force model has been introduced by Couzin et al. [11]. They define three concentric proximity zones around a particle where each zone exerts a different prioritized force on the particle's constant velocity. In the work of Pelechano et al. [12] the social force model is taken a step further with the introduction of line formation and psychological factors which induce a pushing behavior in panicking situations.

A social force model is not the only way of modelling crowds of people. Heigas et al. [13] use a model of fluid dynamics that incorporates two elementary repulsive forces to simulate jamming and flowing found in real life situations. Besides the specificity of the solution, as argued in [14] fluid dynamics not always can correctly model individual interactions which can be better described with a gaskinetic model. Another different approach is the one of Treuille et al. [15] which presents a model for crowd dynamics continuously driven by a potential field. The integration of global navigation planning and local collision avoidance into one framework produces very good video results. Furthermore, their model seems to integrate well with several agent-based models promoting interesting future integrations. Yet another approach consists of recording a crowd and then directly replicating the phenomenon using the recorded data. This is for example the approach taken by Lee et al. [16]. In this work the authors have been recording a crowd of people from a top down view and then used computer vision to extract motion trajectories out of it. Afterwards the data are fed into an agent model which can learn how to replicate the crowd motion driving each individual. Interestingly, the work also addresses some small group management but individuals are not aware of their social context and do not react to unexpected contingencies unless the centralized agent model has been trained specifically for that.

Thalmann et al. [17] use complex finite automata to determine the behavior of actors. The purpose of the model is still to simulate human crowds but this time the introduction of structured behavior of groups and individuals is remarkable. A hierarchical model describes the behavior of each part, but still the set of norms of social interactions such as conversations are not taken into account. Very comprehensive is also the work of Shao and Terzopoulos [18], which presents fully autonomous agents interacting in a virtually reconstructed Pennsylvania Station. The integration of motor, perceptual, behavioral, and cognitive components within a single model is particularly notable. Apart from the outstanding video realized with this technology, it is also very interesting to see how they use perceptual information to drive low-level reactive behaviors in a social environment. What is missing is how to constrain an agent's reactivity outside the special situation of walking down the hall of a train station. Rehm et al. [19] use a more fine-grained approach for conversations, recognizing the value of social proxemics and formation theories. They use them to inform their models of dynamic distance and orientation between pairs of humanoid agents based on their interpersonal relationship. While interpersonal relationships are necessary to fully simulate small scale group dynamics, they are not sufficient as is evident from Kendon's work [4].

In a pure agent-based approach the action generation loop produces a discrete sequence of behavior, that turns to be a downside. Human behavior is not discrete but rather continuous. One of the main advantage of the particle-based approach is in the continuity of the simulated behavior, which looks quite believable once animated. A sequential generation of behaviors is a discretization of the continuous process of perceiving and acting which take place at the lower levels of the artificial intelligence. Abstract high level behaviors can be decomposed in lower level, more fine grained, behaviors until they eventually merge into a continuum of behavioral control. For this reason we believe that the best approach for simulating social interaction territorial dynamics is to use a combination of the agent-based and particle-based approaches, where a set of reactive behaviors generates motivational forces which eventually are merged together in a continuous input control for the agent's motion generation layer. From this perspective, the work of Reynolds on the so called Steering Behaviors has been very helpful.

2.3   Reynolds Steering Behaviors

In 1999 Craig Reynolds [20] presented a simple and elegant solution, to allow simulated characters to navigate around their world in a life-like manner. These behaviors continuously generate steering forces to drive the underlying model of locomotion. So to speak they are slightly higher level than motor controllers and lower level than the actions selected by a planner for example. The advantage of using steering forces is that they can be easily combined before being applied to the agent's body. The composable nature of the steering behaviors allows building complex commands like 'go from here to there following a given path, while avoiding obstacles along the way without getting too close to the walls and maintaining a minimal distance from your neighbors'. When multiple commands are called at the same time, they generate steering forces which have to be blended. One of the simplest blending schema consists of linearly combining the steering vectors but, unfortunately, suffers of a common problem called cancellation. Basically, it could happen that the combination results in a null steering force. Amor et al. [21] recognize how sometimes a combination of behaviors result in a suboptimal steering force with the net result of having the agent behaving not in such an intelligent way, for example trying to avoid an incoming obstacle and ending up bumping into a wall. Instead of steering the agent toward a desired velocity, they invert the process by assigning a cost to a set of sampled directions. Afterwards they perform a heuristic to select the cheapest direction to follow. So far it is not clear how many sampled directions are necessary to create good behaviors while keeping the computational costs low. Some behaviors may require a large span of directions but with a very low sample resolution, while others require exactly the converse.

2.4   Small Scale Group Dynamics

The pioneering work of Jan et al. [22], for the first time exploits some of the techniques used in the field of Crowd Simulators to replicate small scale group dynamics with a special interest in conversations. In their work, the authors recognize the importance of managing the correct positioning and orientation of agents in conversation to avoid breaking the fragile illusion that makes a social virtual environment believable. They report an evaluation made in one of their previous works [23] where agents could group together and move from a group to another one but always maintaining a fixed position, and quoting the authors "[...], this significantly decreased believability when conversation groups did not coincide with positioning of the agents". To solve this problem, they took the social force field model idea from the Crowd Simulators literature and applied it to dynamically rearranging a group of agents engaged in a situated conversation inside a virtual training environment. While the approach looks promising, the main problem is that motivational forces applied to agent orientation are not taken into consideration. Reorienting is also part of the behavior expressed by people during social interactions. Moreover as we know from Scheflen [24] the orientation of some bodily regions normally express temporary membership to a group or a subgroup, or more generally our claim of territory. Such claims should be maintained as long as a member attends to that social interaction. Therefore it is important to extend the social force field model in such a way that reorientations can be also motivated. Furthermore, we should remember that a conversation is a unit at interactional level and has a territorial domain [4] and therefore we can think of it as an abstract social context but also as situated region of space. The conversation's spatial domain delimits a region which casts a behavioral influence not only on the participants but also on external individuals who stop close or just pass by [4].

Since this behavioral influence is common to other forms of territory [24] as well, we could use the name *social place* to refer to the spatial domain of a social interaction and the name *social situation* to refer to its abstract social context. Thus, a complete model of small scale group dynamics should also take into account the behavioral influence that any social situation casts in the environment, concretely bounded by its social place.

3   Conversations and Human Territories

A conversation is an example of human territorial organization. The space around it is structured in a certain fashion and specific behaviors take place demonstrating that, not only the same idea about the social context is shared amongst the participants, but also the same idea about the territorial domain of such context. These kinds of behaviors have been classified by Scheflen [24] as territorial behaviors. They don't have to be considered in isolation but rather as a particular way of looking at the behavioral relationship amongst the participants in a social interaction and as such, they are influenced by affiliation, involvement and social status. An automation of human communicative intent must take into account such a special class of behaviors in order to properly simulate individuals engaged in a social interaction, especially when we account not only for conversations but also for a variety of different social situations each of which could have is own territorial form. Territorial behaviors are intrinsically unconscious and reactive, therefore they as well are ill suited for explicit user control and must be automated.

Like some of the more interesting previous works, our primary inspiration has been Kendon's research on face-to-face interaction [4]. Individuals in a conversation tend to arrange in a way that gives all of them equal, direct and exclusive access to a common space. This positional and orientational arrangement is called an F-formation and the set of the behavioral relationships among the participants defines a behavioral system called the F-formation system (Fig. 1). From the definition of the F-formation comes an explanation of the usual circular arrangement of people in conversation with more than two participants: it is simply the best way to give everybody equal access to a common focused space. Since participants in a focused social interaction share a common space with equal access rights to it, a series of compensatory movements has to be simulated before one can hope to completely model social group dynamics.

Kendon explains a connection between the F-formation system and Goffman's concept of a frame [25]. A frame is a set of rules and social norms that all the participants in an interaction silently accept. The frame comes from the experience of the individual and states what behaviors are meaningful and what conduct is expected in that particular face-to-face interaction. The process of frame-attunement is tightly linked to the F-formation system. By actively maintaining a formation, participants inform each other that they share the same frame for the situation. This further reinforces the definition of an F-formation as a system and moreover describes the system as a unit of behavior at the interactional level of organization, not at the individual level (Fig. 1).

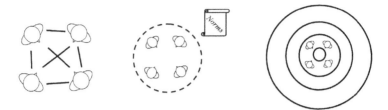

Fig. 1. A schematic representation of the three main concepts of a conversation as an instance of F-formation. The first picture shows how the participants are involved in a behavioral relationship which sustains a stable formation. The second picture shows a conversation as a unit at interactional level which states a set of norms silently accepted by its participants. The third picture shows how these set of norms organize a conversational human territory.

Scheflen [24] further proposes a general paradigm of human territorial organization (Fig. 2). He proposes a central space called *nucleus*, which comprises a common orientational space and a space of the participants, surrounded by a *region* which is commonly used as a buffer area for potential newcomers or as a passageway for passersby. Such general structure of space is applicable to all levels of territorial organization and frames the whole area in six concentric zones. The first three are called o, p and q spaces and they belong to the nucleus of the territory, while the remaining zones are called r, s and t spaces and they belong to the region or court. For small territories such as conversations or gatherings in a living room, the s and t spaces are irrelevant and the r and q spaces can be merged. Therefore, for simple and small formations the whole region around the nucleus can be unstructured. Notice that the concentric spaces define zones of progressive growing status, starting from the outermost and moving toward the innermost. In fact the region is meant for passersby, spectators and associated people while the nucleus is for the participants that get direct access to the o-space and have a claim on the territory.

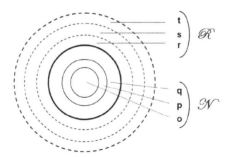

Fig. 2. The paradigm of territorial organization proposed by Scheflen and applicable to all levels of territorial organization. The o, p and q spaces belong to the nucleus N whereas the r, s and t spaces belong to the region R.

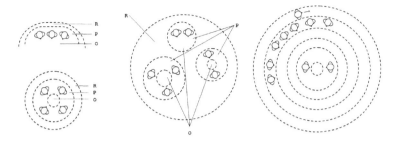

Fig. 3. From left to right, element, F-formation, gathering and hub. These are the main territorial fields of Scheflen's classification. Each of them can be seen as increment of the previous one for required space and complexity. In addition, more complex territory can contain simpler ones. The O and P in the picture stand for o and p spaces whereas the R stands for an unstructured region.

The classification of the territorial organization of small groups goes from the *element* to the *hub* in order of size and complexity, where the latter can get quite big in some situations (Fig. 3). An *element* is an array of people sufficiently close to each other and commonly oriented. Usually people arrange in adjacent locations but sometimes they also crowd in a single location. Participants in an element show a certain degree of affiliation because they are engaged in a common activity or involved in a special relationship. Examples of elements include a couple in a normal conversation, a queue of people waiting in line or a row of persons walking down a street. The next kind of simple and small territorial organization is the face formation, or *F-formation*, which has been extensively covered above and elsewhere. Here we want to point out that the region of an F-formation comprises the q and the r space in the paradigm of territorial organization (Fig. 2). The q-space is meant for salutations when joining and leaving the conversation or just as a buffer area for people who may want to join. The r-space could be used as a passageway by the participants themselves or for less close salutations. What in Kendon's work is called the c-space of a conversation is in fact an s-space in the Scheflen's territorial paradigm meant mainly for spectators and outsiders, conversely to the innermost q and r spaces where, whoever stops by, gets the higher status of being associated with the conversation. When elements and F-formations combine we have a more complex territorial organization called the gathering.

A *gathering* generalizes social situations like a group of people chilling out in a living room or at a party. Participants in a gathering do not share the same orientational spaces but rather there are many o-spaces sustained by several small groups. Indeed, a gathering is a collection of elements and F-formations which share a common region (Fig. 3). Another way of looking at it is considering the gathering as an increment of the F-formation. As such, we can have gatherings that naturally evolve from an F-formation which splits into more subgroups due, for example, to a higher number of participants. Notice that a gathering can also be just a collection of individuals clustered together a in closed space but not affiliated in any way. An example would be a waiting room where people do not interact. Usually a gathering consists of less than a dozen of people and takes the space of a room. Thus, in a bar situation we could find multiple gatherings, one for each room or floor, or multiple gatherings in the same room when several social contexts take place. The largest territorial field in terms of size and complexity is called *hub*. The hub is an increment of the gathering where the inner and outer zones are differentiated by role and status of the individuals. Unlike a gathering, the hub has a nucleus of people which perform for the spectators in the region. Thus, people in the region orient toward the nucleus while the performers can orient everywhere. The nuclear formation can be a single individual, an element, an F-formation or a gathering. Examples of hubs are a crowded theater or a cluster of persons watching at a street performer. The region of the hub, which is called surround, is usually structured in two levels of spectators plus an extra zone which is used as a passageway by passersby or people who simply want to join and attend the performance (Fig. 3).

4   Reaction Generation Paradigm

In our approach, the group dynamics of a simulated social interaction emerges from the avatars' territorial behavior. We have chosen to simulate such class of behavior as an avatar's reactive response to the environment and social context. The term reactive response should be clearly distinguished from other agent-based solutions where the agent goes through a higher level cognition process which involves some reasoning about its internal state and the state of the environment, to come up with a plan or a strategy to reach a given goal. There are fewer reasoning steps involved in our avatar's reactivity, which by definition should provide a quick response to changes in the environment, and therefore we can think of it as the simulation of a low level mental process much closer to perception than higher levels of reasoning. Thus in our reaction generation paradigm, low level perceptual information is analyzed by a set of reactive behaviors which motivate an immediate motion to accommodate contingent changes in the perceived surroundings (Fig. 4).

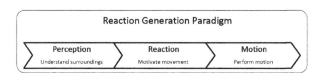

Fig. 4. Outline of our Reaction Generation Paradigm. The agent understands its surroundings through its senses. Successively, perceptual stimuli are used for generating motivations to move. Finally, motivations are transformed into physical forces which steer the agents motion.

The reaction paradigm is in effect a loop of continuous control of the avatar's motion. The surrounding environment stimulates the avatar's perceptual apparatus producing information which is later used by the reactive behaviors to generate motivations to move. Movement changes the state of the environment and therefore the set of perceptual information the avatar will perceive in the next round of the control loop.

At first, the avatar perceives its surroundings through a sense of vision and proximity both of which can be tailored to a specific individual (Fig. 5). The sense of proximity is a simple way of simulating the human awareness over the four distances of the Proxemics Theory [26]. A sensor structured in four concentric areas continuously informs the avatar about who or what is in the range of its intimate, personal, social or public zone. The public and the social zones cover a larger area of space which is also more distant from the avatar than the intimate and personal zones. Therefore we have two blinded cones for the public and social zones which extend from the avatar's back. For the sense of vision we have a peripheral and central visual area, where the former is larger and shorter whilst the latter is the converse. At the moment vision is at its early stage of design and we are planning to extend it with a more accurate model where one can specify a specialized perceptual ability for each area. For example, the peripheral vision should perceive movement better whereas central vision should be better at shapes and detail. These two senses continuously gather information about the avatar's surroundings, producing perceptual data which can be analyzed and used for generating reactions.

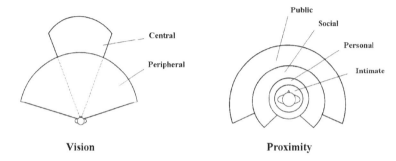

Fig. 5. Two diagrams showing the spatial structure of the sense of vision and proximity. Notice that proportions have not been respected to make the drawing more readable.

A set of reactive behaviors computes motivations for performing movement. For example, a *keep-personal-distance* behavior lets an avatar react by generating a motivation for moving away when other individuals come too close. Motivations are vectorial quantities that represent a psychological stimulation in performing a linear or rotational motion. The reactive framework permits applying motivations virtually to every part or joint of the avatar's body or to a higher level motor controllers such as a gaze controller. However, in our current implementation we limit our control to motivating the linear motion of the whole body and the rotational motion of eyes, head and rest of the body (torso and legs). When all the motivations have been generated, they are grouped per type and then blended into a composition which results in a net final motivation of each type. The combination of motivations allows multiple behaviors to stimulate the body at the same time. Several composition algorithms can be chosen for this step. In fact, motivations for linear motion usually need to be composed in a different way than motivation for rotational motion. After computing the set of final motivations, each of them is sent to the actuation module which performs a movement that respects the constraints imposed by the physical motion model.

5   Social Situation and Territorial Awareness

Now we are going to explain how, in our system, an avatar can show a certain degree of context awareness when engaged in a social interaction. To seem aware of the social context, a person has to show its acceptance of the norms that regulate the social interaction as we saw in [4] and [24]. Such norms state territorial rights and responsibilities of participants and outsiders and the acceptance of them makes the interaction possible. Thus, the attunement to such norms declares an intent of interaction and therefore the awareness of the social situation and its territorial organization. The spatial boundaries of a social situation, that we call social place, determine when the context should start influencing an avatar's behavior. In our system, such behavioral influence is realized by the activation of a set of reactive behaviors, each of which realizes a norm underlying the social situation that the avatar is participating in (Fig. 6). The activation of this set of behaviors produces the reactive dynamics expected from a group of people that has accepted the same social context.

In order to provide an example of how the behavioral influence works, we are going to succinctly describe how an avatar joins a conversation. As soon as an individual gets close enough to an ongoing conversation, it steps inside the conversation's territory. If it keeps moving closer to the nucleus, the individual receives an *associated* status. An associated person will be allowed to join a conversation if certain requirements are met. Since we assume that the conversation takes place amongst friends, the requirements are very loose. In fact it is sufficient to have the body oriented toward the o-space

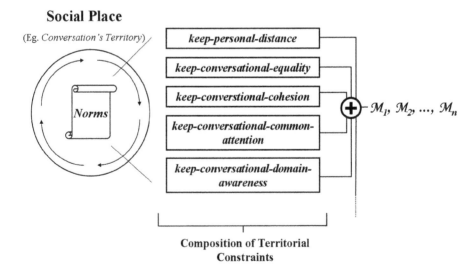

Fig. 6. A diagram to explain how social situation awareness is realized. Inside the border of the social place, the territorial organization states a set of norms that constraints the avatar's reactivity. Thus, the set of norms maps into a set of reactive behaviors that implements a composition of territorial constraints. The composition blends with other behaviors leading to a behavioral influence marked on the resulting final motivations $M_1, M_2, ..., M_n$.

and stop in front of it claiming access rights on the common space. Once an avatar is allowed to join, it is considered inside the conversation social situation, and therefore it is necessary to activate the proper set of territorial constraints in order to adapt the agent's behavior to the ongoing social situation and smoothly blend in. Conversely, an avatar can leave a conversation simply by going away from the nucleus. Moving out of the territory will stop the behavioral influence, releasing the avatar from its territorial constrains. This example is not meant to explain how an avatar should generally join or leave a conversation, but how the avatar's behavior is immediately and smoothly influenced by the simple fact that it enters or leaves a social place.

6   Conclusions and Future Work

The approach described here has been implemented in the CADIA Populus social simulation platform for virtual environments [7]. An important contribution is in the field of graphical avatars for games. With the advent of even more powerful 3D engines, faster and more robust physics engines and affordable dedicated hardware, games are rapidly growing as complex, fully dynamic and photorealistic worlds. Such rich and complex environments are now much more effective in providing the feeling of presence, immersion or intense atmosphere, than only few years ago. This generates higher expectation for behavioral AI, which has to perform at the same level of believability as the graphics and physics in order to not break the illusion. Today we have many commercial AI middleware software packages that address the need for better game AI with elegant and effective solutions, but all of them deal primarily with combat or explorative behaviors which are not suitable for social environments.

While evaluation of the effectiveness of our approach for multi-player games has not been performed yet, the visual results[3] and informal interaction tests support our direction. Having agents and avatars powered by this technology will ensure that they will immediately show a certain degree of social presence when placed in a virtual situation. Moreover, this technology will demonstrate the validity of some of the theories of Kendon on face-to-face interaction and Scheflen on human territories. These theories cannot be formally proven because of the intrinsic nature of dealing with human behavior. However, an application of their principles demonstrates their consistency as behavioral models and proposes possible extensions to clarify some of their ambiguities.

A current system limitation that we are working on is that motion generation is currently restricted to a simple point mass model plus head and eyes rotations that, while good in its simplicity, is really far from producing believable animations. Since the framework is totally independent from the implementation we are using to realize the avatar's motion, it sounds natural to plug an animation engine into it. Thus a Motion Generation module will provide an interface to control the avatar's embodiment while translating motivations into requests for the animation system. For example, a strong motivation to moving to the left would be translated into a walking cycle toward the a destination point while a weaker motivation would result just in a posture shift. Plugging

---

[3] See companion video at: http://cadia.ru.is/projects/cadiapopulus/pedica2009.avi

an animation engine into our framework will allow the generation of far more convincing movement. At that point, we will have the possibility of realistically evaluate our technology to its practical contribution to believability.

Acknowledgments. We are grateful to Dr. Adam Kendon for discussions and sending the unobtainable Scheflen's book. Also big thanks to the CADIA and CCP team. This work is supported by the Humanoid Agents in Social Game Environments Grant of Excellence from The Icelandic Research Fund.

References

1. Mori, M.: The uncanny valley. Energy 7(4) (1970)
2. Cassell, J., Vilhjalmsson, H.: Fully embodied conversational avatars: Making communicative behaviors autonomous. Autonomous Agents and Multi-Agent Systems 2(1), 45–64 (1999)
3. Vilhjalmsson, H., Cassell, J.: Bodychat: Autonomous communicative behaviors in avatars. In: Autonomous Agents, pp. 477–486. ACM Press, New York (1998)
4. Kendon, A.: Conducting Interaction: Patterns of behavior in focused encounters. Cambridge University Press, Cambridge (1990); Main Area (multimodal commnication)
5. Friedman, D., Steed, A., Slater, M.: Spatial social behavior in second life. In: Pelachaud, C., Martin, J.-C., André, E., Chollet, G., Karpouzis, K., Pelé, D. (eds.) IVA 2007. LNCS (LNAI), vol. 4722, pp. 252–263. Springer, Heidelberg (2007)
6. Salem, B., Earle, N.: Designing a non-verbal language for expressive avatars. In: Collaborative Virtual Environments, pp. 93–101. ACM, New York (2000)
7. Pedica, C., Vilhjálmsson, H.H.: Social perception and steering for online avatars. In: Prendinger, H., Lester, J.C., Ishizuka, M. (eds.) IVA 2008. LNCS (LNAI), vol. 5208, pp. 104–116. Springer, Heidelberg (2008)
8. Cassell, J., Vilhjalmsson, H., Bickmore, T.: Beat: the behavior expression animation toolkit. In: SIGGRAPH 2001, August 12-17, pp. 477–486. ACM Press, New York (2001)
9. Gillies, M., Ballin, D.: Integrating autonomous behavior and user control for believable agents. In: Autonomous Agents and Multi-Agent Systems, July 19-23, pp. 336–343. ACM Press, New York (2004)
10. Helbing, D., Molnár, P.: Social force model for pedestrian dynamics. Physical Review E 51(5), 4282 (1995)
11. Couzin, I., Krause, J., James, R., Ruzton, G., Franks, N.: Collective memory and spatial sorting in animal groups. Journal of Theoretical Biology, 1–11 (2002)
12. Pelechano, N., Allbeck, J.M., Badler, N.I.: Controlling individual agents in high-density crowd simulation, pp. 99–108 (2007)
13. Heigeas, L., Luciani, A., Thollot, J., Castagne, N.: A physically-based particle model of emergent crowd behaviors. In: Proc. of GraphiCon, September 5-10 (2003)
14. Helbing, D., Molnar, P., Schweitzer, F.: Computer simulations of pedestrian dynamics and trail formation (1994)
15. Treuille, A., Cooper, S., Popovic, Z.: Continuum crowds. In: SIGGRAPH 2006 Papers, pp. 1160–1168. ACM, New York (2006)
16. Lee, K.H., Choi, M.G., Hong, Q., Lee, J.: Group behavior from video: a data-driven approach to crowd simulation, pp. 109–118 (2007)
17. Musse, S.R., Thalmann, D.: Hierarchical model for real time simulation of virtual human crowds. IEEE Transactions on Visualization and Computer Graphics 7(2), 152–164 (2001)
18. Shao, W., Terzopoulos, D.: Autonomous pedestrians. Graph. Models 69(5-6), 246–274 (2007)

19. Rehm, M., André, E., Nischt, M.: Let's come together — social navigation behaviors of virtual and real humans. In: Maybury, M., Stock, O., Wahlster, W. (eds.) INTETAIN 2005. LNCS, vol. 3814, pp. 124–133. Springer, Heidelberg (2005)
20. Reynolds, C.W.: Steering behaviors for autonomous characters. In: Proc. of the Game Developers Conference, pp. 763–782. Miller Freeman Game Group, San Francisco (1999)
21. Amor, H.B., Obst, O., Murray, J.: Fast, neat and under control: Inverse steering behaviors for physical autonomous agents
22. Jan, D., Traum, D.: Dynamic movement and positioning of embodied agents in multiparty conversation. In: Proc. of the ACL Workshop on Embodied Language Processing, June 2007, pp. 59–66 (2007)
23. Jan, D., Traum, D.R.: Dialog simulation for background characters, pp. 65–74 (2005)
24. Scheflen, A.E.: Human Territories: how we behave in space and time. Prentice-Hall, New York (1976)
25. Goffman, E.: Frame Analyses: An Essay on the Organization of Experience. Harvard University Press, Cambridge (1974)
26. Hall, E.T.: The Hidden Dimension. Doubleday, New York (1966)
27. Vilhjalmsson, H.: Animating conversation in online games. In: Rauterberg, M. (ed.) ICEC 2004. LNCS, vol. 3166, pp. 139–150. Springer, Heidelberg (2004)

Tree Paths: A New Model for Steering Behaviors

Rafael Araújo Rodrigues[1], Alessandro de Lima Bicho[3], Marcelo Paravisi[1],
Cláudio Rosito Jung[2], Léo Pini Magalhães[3], and Soraia Raupp Musse[1]

[1] Graduate Programme in Computer Science - PUCRS
Av. Ipiranga, 6681 - Building 32 - Porto Alegre/RS - Brazil
{rafael.rodrigues,marcelo.paravisi,soraia.musse}@pucrs.br
[2] Graduate Programme in Applied Computing - UNISINOS
Av. Unisinos, 950 - São Leopoldo/RS - Brazil
crjung@unisinos.br
[3] School of Electrical and Computer Engineering - UNICAMP
Av. Albert Einstein, 400 - Campinas/SP - Brazil
{bicho,leopini}@dca.fee.unicamp.br

Abstract. This paper describes a model for generating steering behaviors of groups of characters based on the biologically-motivated space colonization algorithm. This algorithm has been used in the past for generating leaf venation patterns and tree structures, simulating the competition for space between growing veins or branches. Adapted to character animation, this model is responsible for the motion control of characters providing robust and realistic group behaviors by adjusting just a few parameters. The main contributions are related with the robustness, flexibility and simplicity to control groups of characters.

1 Introduction

Behavioral animation has been proposed by Reynolds [1] in 1987, with the main goal to provide easy manners to control groups of individuals. Since that, many models have been proposed in order to provide different ways to steer behaviors of groups, as discussed in Section 2. However, in spite of all existing methods, the current state-of-the-art lacks of flexibility. In this context, we expect to provide different types of behaviors with simple changes in the proposed model: robustness, in order to provide realistic behaviors in low and medium density of people, and simplicity to control (only a small number of parameters are required). In addition, the steering behaviors should serve to control groups of any type of entities (fishes, birds and virtual humans) in virtual spaces.

The application of steering behaviors is very broad, including games, films, simulation tools, among others. Indeed, this technology can be applied in any situation in which mobile entities can be simulated. However, the scope of this paper is focused on groups of individuals and not crowds. The main point is that groups of individuals can only be recognized if density of people is not high, since group structures are not visible in highly dense crowds.

The main advantages of proposed model are robustness, simplicity and flexibility to control groups of individuals in virtual spaces, by populating the environment with markers points. Our model is inspired in a biological algorithm based on competition

Zs. Ruttkay et al. (Eds.): IVA 2009, LNAI 5773, pp. 358–371, 2009.

for space in a coherent growth of veins and branches [2]. We adapted this idea in order to generate motion behavior of groups, which also compete for space in order to move realistically, as described in Section 3. Another important contribution is the connection between two distinct areas such as steering behaviors and the algorithms for generating leaf venation patterns and tree structures.

The remainder of this paper is organized as follows: in next section we discuss some works found in literature, while in Section 3 we describe our model to steer behaviors of groups. Section 4 discusses some obtained results, and draws final considerations.

2 Related Work

Virtual groups have been studied since the early days of behavioral animation. Two seminal papers are related to models based on agents, which have some level of autonomy and individuality. Reynolds [1] simulated flocks of bird-like entities called *boids*, obtaining realistic animation by using only simple local rules. Tu and Terzopoulos [3] created groups of artificial fishes endowed with synthetic vision and perception of the environment, which control their behavior.

Researches are being conducted to the use of path planning algorithms associated to generation of realistic movements of the found path. Lavalle [4] introduced the concept of a Rapidly-exploring Random Tree (RRT) as a randomized data structure for path planning problems. An RRT is iteratively expanded by applying control inputs that drive the system slightly toward randomly-selected points. Choi et al. [5] proposed a model based on a probabilistic path planning and hierarchical displacement mapping to generate a sequence of realistic movements of a human-like biped figure to move from a given start position to a goal with a set of prescribed motion clips. Metoyer and Hodgins [6] proposed a method for generating reactive path following based on the user's examples of the desired behavior. Dapper et al. [7] proposed a path planning model based on a numerical solution for boundary value problems (BVP) and field potential formalism to produce steering behaviors for virtual humans. Rodríguez et al. [8] proposed a heuristic approach to planning in an environment with moving obstacles using dynamic global roadmap and kinodynamic local planning.

More specifically concerning groups motion, Kamphuis and Overmars [9] introduced a two-phase approach, where a path for a single agent (a backbone path) is generated by any motion planner. Next, a corridor is defined around the backbone path and all agents will stay in this corridor. Rodríguez et al. [10] proposed a model using a roadmap providing an abstract representation of global environment information to achieve different complex group behaviors that cannot be modeled with local information alone. Lien and collaborators [11] proposed ways using roadmaps to simulate a type of flocking behavior called shepherding behavior in which outside agents guide or control members of a flock. Data-driven models are quite recent in comparison with other methods, and aim to record motion in a pre-production stage or to use information from real life to calibrate the simulation algorithms. One example is proposed by Musse et al. [12] describing a model for controlling groups motion based on automatic tracking algorithms.

This paper proposes a new model for steering behaviors, where group behaviors can be easily calibrated, while keeping diversity of generated results. Considerations about the methods cited in this section and the proposed model are presented in Section 4.

3   The Proposed Model

This section describes our model to provide steering behaviors for groups of entities. First we discuss some aspects of our model[1], and then we focus on specific behaviors attained for groups control. Next, we present the original model of space colonization algorithm and performed adaptations for describing groups motion.

3.1   The Space Colonization Algorithm

The basic model for agents navigation is based on the space colonization algorithm, which has been previously used to develop leaf venation patterns [14] and tree structures [15]. The venation model simulates three processes within an iterative loop: leaf blade growth, the placement of markers in the free space, and the addition of new veins. The markers correspond to sources of the plant hormone auxin, which, according to a biological hypothesis, emerge in the growing leaf regions not penetrated by veins. A set of markers S interacts with the vein pattern, which consists of a set of points V called *vein nodes*. This pattern is extended iteratively toward the markers in the free space. The markers that are approached by the advancing veins are gradually removed, since the space around them is no longer free. As the leaf grows, markers in the free space are added in the space between existing veins and markers. This process continues until the growth stops, and there are no markers left. The interplay between markers in the free space and vein nodes is at the heart of the space colonization algorithm. During each iteration, a vein node is influenced by all the markers closer to it than any other vein node. Thus, veins compete for markers, and thus space, as they grow.

In the present paper, the venation model has been adapted to animate groups. Indeed, the key idea is to represent the space in a explicit way, using a set of markers (dots in the space). The markers define the "walkable space" through a discrete set of points, which are used to compute the paths of agents. These markers should be randomly distributed (according to a uniform probability density function) over the portions of the space that can be effectively occupied by the virtual agents, meaning that obstacles and other regions where agents should not move must not be filled with markers. Fig. 1(a) illustrates an environment populated with markers. The markers allow the organization and facilitates the steering of group behaviors, as discussed in next sections.

The amount of existing markers, as well as their position, have great impact in the generated trajectories. For instance, a higher density of markers uniformly distributed yields a wider range of movements, since there are more possibilities of trajectory for the entities. On the other hand, a lower density of markers tends to generate smaller number of trajectories, but presenting a smaller computational cost. Furthermore, the possibility of restricting use of markers have also impact in generated trajectories for agents and groups. Let is consider that markers are never restricted to only one path.

---

[1] Details are described in PhD thesis authored by Alessandro Bicho [13].

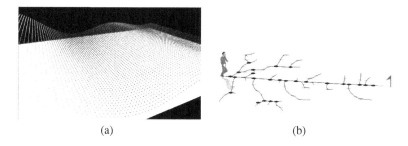

Fig. 1. (a) Markers (dots) are discrete representation of walkable space; (b) Agent wants to go reach its goal, illustrated with a red flag. Darker dots describe key positions, lighter dots are related with each simulated step that generates path nodes, and between two path nodes there is the path segment.

In this case, different paths share markers, and it can cross in some region. On the other hand, if markers are temporarily restricted to only one path, more diversity in trajectories can emerge. This characteristic is very important in our model, since we can provide different behaviors by changing few aspects in the algorithm. The following sections describe further details of this model.

3.2   The Algorithm for Characters Motion

Our model based on space colonization algorithm can be used to provide path planning (from initial position to a fixed or mobile goal), as well as to direct motion of virtual agents without specific goals. The main difference between these two cases is that motion planning generates one or more coherent paths (called *tree paths* in this work) to reach a specific position, while the direct motion takes into account desired directions. So, in the last possibility, local minima are allowed, since a global path is never planned. The main application of direct motion is in situations where a specific goal is not possible, like group behavior for alignment, for instance.

Let I denote an agent in the group, having a position $p(t)$ at each iteration t. Depending on the behavior to be applied, agents can have specific goals or not. If agents have an objective, its position at each time[2] t is denoted by $g(t)$. Also, there is a *personal space* for each agent, modeled as a spherical region (with radius R), that represents a "perception field" that limits the range of markers which can be used by each agent.

Let G denote the tree path for an agent, computed by using the venation model proposed by Runions et al. [14] and adapted to group animation. The main difference between [14] and our approach is that, in [14], veins grow everywhere to occupy free space, while the proposed method guides the creation of branches toward the position of goal $g(t)$ of the agent.

A tree path is a set of locations (key positions) organized in a directional graph. Each step created in the path corresponds to a *path node*, while a path segment joins two path nodes. In our model, paths from the current position of a given agent to its

---

[2] For sakes of clarity, the time index t will be removed from this point on, and used only when necessary.

goal are described through a tree, as illustrated in Fig. 1(b). In this figure, the goal is illustrated through a red flag, darker dots describe key positions where bifurcations occur, and lighter dots are related with each simulated step that generates path nodes. Between two path nodes there is a path segment, and all segments have the same length. Drawing all segments we can see the tree path generated from one agent to a specific goal.

Computing Tree Paths for Agents: The tree path G is computed through a two-stage algorithm within an iterative loop: i) markers processing, and ii) the addition of new path nodes. The markers in [14] correspond to sources of the plant hormone auxin, which emerge in the growing leaf regions not penetrated by veins, according to a biological hypothesis. For path planning, markers describe the "walkable space", in order to define the direction of a path node. During each iteration, a path node is influenced by all the markers closer to it than any other path node.

For a path node n, located at the position $\boldsymbol{n}$, the set of markers (located at positions $\boldsymbol{m}_i$) that are closer to n than any other node is denoted by

$$S(n) = \{\boldsymbol{m}_1, \boldsymbol{m}_2, ..., \boldsymbol{m}_N\}, \tag{1}$$

where N is the number of markers associated with node n. If $S(n)$ is not empty, a new path node n' will be created and attached to n by an edge representing a path segment. Each path node has an action region[3], that limits the markers that can be evaluated (if they are not closer to any other path node) in order to compute the new direction of growth of the tree path. Fig. 1(b) shows an example of tree path computed from an agent to its goal. To provide a diversity of branch orientations generated for G, increasing the space occupation, the markers closer to each segment are allocated to it, and they can not be used by other path segments from same agent I. On the other hand, the tree path G^* associated to another agent can use the same markers of the tree path G. Consequently, tree paths from different agents can intercept each other. However, this fact could bring a collision situation, which is not desirable. In order to deal with collision-free behaviors, we used the method for minimum distance enforcement among agents, proposed by Treuille et al. [16], and detailed in "Computing the Motion of Agents", in this section.

Mathematically, the algorithm for building the tree path is described as follows. Given a tree node n and a non-empty $S(n)$, a decision must be made whether a child node n' related to n will be created or not. This decision is made in such a way that nodes closer to the goal are more likely to have children, achieving a wider variety of paths in the vicinity of the goal. In fact, that the node n_g that is the closest to the goal will certainly have a child, guaranteeing that the goal will be reached by at least one trajectory. The probability $P(n)$ of any other node n having a child is given by:

$$P(n) = \frac{\|\boldsymbol{n}_g - \boldsymbol{g}\|}{\|\boldsymbol{n} - \boldsymbol{g}\|}, \tag{2}$$

where $\| \cdot \|$ is the L^2 norm of a vector. To decide whether a child will be created for n, a random variable ξ with uniform distribution in the interval $[0, 1]$ is generated, and the

---

[3] Its size can be calibrated, but normally we use the same radius R defined for the agent personal space.

the child is created if $\xi \leq P(n)$. Clearly, such probability rule prioritizes the creation of child nodes closer to the goal, since $P(n)$ decreases with its distance from the goal g. If a given node n is granted a child n', it will be created at a position n' through:

$$n' = n + \alpha \frac{d(n)}{\|d(n)\|}, \qquad (3)$$

where $d(n)/\|d(n)\|$ is a unit vector representing the growth direction of the branch at node n, and α is a constant step that controls the length of the path segments. Vector $d(n)$ is obtained based on the markers in $S(n)$ and their coherence to the goal g:

$$d(n) = \sum_{k=1}^{N} w_k (m_k - n), \qquad (4)$$

where

$$w_k = \frac{f(g - n, m_k - n)}{\sum_{l=1}^{N} f(g - n, m_l - n)} \qquad (5)$$

are the weights of the markers computed based on a non-negative function f. This function should prioritize both markers that lead to the goal, those that are closer to the current node n. Our choice for f satisfying these conditions is

$$f(x, y) = \begin{cases} \dfrac{1 + \cos\theta}{1 + \|y\|} = \dfrac{1}{1 + \|y\|}\left(1 + \dfrac{<x, y>}{\|x\|\|y\|}\right), & \text{if } \|x\|\|y\| > 0 \\ 0, & \text{otherwise} \end{cases}, \qquad (6)$$

where θ is the angle between x and y, and $< \cdot , \cdot >$ denotes the inner product. It can be observed that f decreases as the angle between $(g - n)$ and $(m_k - n)$ increases (so that markers that are aligned with the goal carry a larger weight), and also as $\|m_k - n\|$ increases (so that markers closer to the node carry a larger weight as well). If the number of markers is large, $d(n)$ will point approximately toward the goal (in fact, it can be shown that $d(n)$ points directly toward the goal if the number of markers grow to infinity). However, if the amount of markers is small, $d(n)$ may deviate from the goal, generating a variety of paths. The procedure described so far creates a sequence of nodes connected by path segments, but no bifurcations in the tree. To create bifurcations, one father node n must be connected to at least to two different children nodes n'_1 and n'_2. When the first child node n'_1 is created, it retrieves the markers around it according to a "restriction distance" (so that the number of markers available to n is reduced). Then, $S(n)$ is re-computed with this reduced set of markers, and Equations (2)-(3) are re-applied to obtain a second child node n'_2. This node also retrieves the markers around it, and the process for creating child nodes for n is repeated until there are no markers available to n. It should be noticed that, at each iteration, a new random variable ξ is created and compared to the probability $P(n)$ given in Equation (2) to decide if node n will have a child or not. Hence, some nodes may have more children than others (usually, the number of children increases near the goal). In fact, some nodes may have just one child, and do not present any bifurcation at all. Nodes that present at least two children are called "key positions", and there is a unique path between adjacent key positions (see darker dots in Fig. 1(b)).

Fig. 2 shows the generation of branches in the proposed model. The green branch (from green to black path nodes) is created first, and then some markers are restricted (due to restriction distance). The blue path node is then computed with the remaining markers associated to the father node n (black one), and the new node also restrict the markers around it. The same thing happens with the branch from black to red path nodes. Other branches could be still generated from the same father node (since there are remaining markers), but they were not created in this example because of the probability function $P(n)$. One difference from Runions' model to ours is the treatment of restricted markers. In Runions' model, markers around a newly created node are really removed and placed afterwards in data structure. On the other hand, our markers are only not available in the data structure for the agent to which the tree path is being computed, i.e. they are not deleted from data structure and can be used for other tree paths.

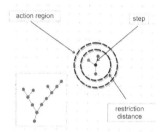

Fig. 2. New branches are generated and they restrict markers within the restriction distance

While a tree path is being computed, the agent is able to walk along the generated paths. Although other path planning algorithms can also be used (such as A^* search algorithm), the proposed model presents some advantages. First, for group behaviors (follow, escape and collaborative actions such as surround behavior), one important aspect is the diversity of paths (it is desirable that a group walks to a specific goal by occupying the space with different possible paths). Another interesting aspect is that we are able to recompute our trajectories from the needed position, e.g. when the target of the agent (in follow behavior) crosses the tree path, we can recompute the path from the intersection point. The next section describes how the agents move along the tree, after the path has been computed.

Computing the Motion of Agents: Tree paths provide local goals for agents. However, an important challenge in groups motion should be treated in this model: collision avoidance. As mentioned before, tree paths G and G^* related to different agents can share markers, consequently agents walking in tree paths can collide, passing by closer (or the same) path nodes. To address this problem, we used the method for minimum distance enforcement among agents, proposed by Treuille et al. [16]. Their method proposes iterations over all pairs of agents within a *threshold distance*, symmetrically pushing them apart, so that the minimum distance is enforced, as describes in Equation (7).

$$d_{\text{enf}}(\boldsymbol{p_i}) = \sum_{\{j \mid d_{i,j} < t_{\min}\}} \frac{\boldsymbol{p_i} - \boldsymbol{p_j}}{2}, \tag{7}$$

where $t_{\min}$ is minimum threshold distance allowed and $d_{i,j}$ is the distance between agents i and j. Consequently, modifying the position of one character impacts all other characters. We implemented a translation for pairs of agents which are closer than the minimum distance. Indeed, this strategy does not present any compromise in the computational time for small number of agents (main focus of this work). Anyway, more details about computational time are discussed later.

There are two manners to provide agents motion. The first one is used when agents have specific goal location; the second, when there are not goals. In the latter case agents are affected by the markers, which can have different weights. Indeed, markers are used as discretized information of the available space, but also they can affect differently the motion of agents, depending on associated weights. Given an agent I at the position $\boldsymbol{p}(t)$ and goal $\boldsymbol{g}(t)$, at each time iteration t and given its computed tree paths G, the next agent position is computed by:

$$\boldsymbol{p}(t+1) = \boldsymbol{p}(t) + \beta \frac{\boldsymbol{d}(\boldsymbol{p}(t))}{\|\boldsymbol{d}(\boldsymbol{p}(t))\|} + \boldsymbol{d}_{\text{enf}}(\boldsymbol{p}(t)), \tag{8}$$

where β is a constant that controls the length of the agent step, $\boldsymbol{d}(\boldsymbol{p}(t))$ is an orientation vector from the agent's current position $\boldsymbol{p}(t)$ to the next path node coming from tree path, indicating its local goal (and attaining the global goal $\boldsymbol{g}(t)$). Also, we compute $\boldsymbol{d}_{\text{enf}}(\boldsymbol{p}(t))$, a result vector for minimum distance enforcement among agents, proposed by Treuille et al. [16] to avoid collisions.

In the goal-based motion of the agent, which includes the tree path computing, three events should be iteratively managed:

1. Agent's decision: when an agent reaches a key position, it should take a decision to which tree branch it should follow. This decision is considered taking into account how close to the goal the tree branch brings the agent.
2. Branch death: There are two reasons to remove the branches in a tree: *i)* When a branch was not chosen by the agent (last item), the branch and its children are removed, and *ii)* When the goal changes position, the branches into a distance from the goal are removed and then recomputed to taking into account the new goal position (defined by *recomputing distance*).
3. Branch reaches agent's goal: tree path stops growing, but the agent keeps walking along the paths until it reaches the goal.

In addition to goal-based motion, there is another manner to compute the motion agents that is useful when goals are not explicit, e.g. in formation and alignment behaviors. In this case, there is no goal vector, but an agent motion direction $\boldsymbol{md}$ which is computed based on a variation of the weights of the markers within the agent's personal space.

Given an agent I at the position $p(t)$ at each iteration t, and given the set of M markers $S(p(t)) = \{m_1, m_2, ..., m_M\}$ within the personal space of the agent I (all markers are considered), we first find the set $S'(p(t))$ of M orientation vectors from agent I to all the markers in $S(p(t))$, in order to compute the agent direct motion md:

$$S'(p(t)) = \{v_1, v_2, ..., v_M\}, \quad \text{where } v_k = m_k - p(t). \tag{9}$$

The motion direction md of the agent is computed similarly to Equation (4), where w_k is a weight associated with orientation vector v_k, calculated according to the desired behavior (see Sections 3.4 and 3.5 for details):

$$md = \sum_{k=1}^{M} w_k v_k, \tag{10}$$

Therefore, the next agent position is given by:

$$p(t+1) = p(t) + \beta \frac{md}{\|md\|} + d_{\mathrm{enf}}(p(t)), \tag{11}$$

where β and $d_{\mathrm{enf}}(p(t))$ are the same parameters used in Equation (8). Next, we present some examples of behaviors that can be obtained using the two strategies for the motion of agents described in this Section: based on goals and based on directions.

3.3   Behaviors: Pursue, Escape and Surround the Goal

The best way to describe the pursuit action takes into account a path between only two individuals (one follower and one target agent). Moreover, as target location can change dynamically, and the path between follower and target should be re-computed iteratively (as described in last section). Fig. 3(a) illustrates such behavior.

In this case, once the target agent crosses the tree path of a follower agent, the tree path is recomputed from the intersection point. In the case of a group of agents following the same target, it is desirable to provide emergent behavior of surround. In this

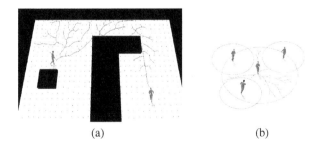

(a)   (b)

Fig. 3. (a) Pursue behavior: one agent tries to reach another one. The illustrated tree path shows the way for follower agent achieve the target; (b) Escape behavior: one agent tries to escape from a circular region, in which three follower agents are included.

Fig. 4. Surround behavior: two agents try to reach another one. It is possible to observe the diversity of generated tree paths causing the surround behavior.

case, a simple change in the rule to allocate markers can be used to obtain interesting results: the emergent behavior is defined by all markers used in a tree path being allocated to such path and not being shared by other path. Consequently, other agents should fight for space, by trying to find other possibilities to move. Fig. 4 illustrates this behavior.

Finally, another small change in the path planning algorithm can provide escape behavior. In path planning, the path node is accepted in tree path when it brings the agent closer to its goal. In a escape behavior, all agents should try to get away from a pre-defined position c. To cope with this condition, a path n node should be accepted (according to the probabilistic function in Equation (2)) when it gets agents far from the c. In fact, that can be accomplished by replacing Equation (2) with $P(n) = \frac{\|n-c\|}{\|n_c-c\|}$, where n_c is the node located the farthest away from c. Fig. 3(b) illustrates such behavior. In this figure, the escape region is automatically computed based on three follower agents, and consequently the tree path algorithm tries to bring agent outside such region.

3.4   Behavior: Groups Formation

This behavior aims to provide the formation of specific shapes, which is relevant in several entertainment applications. For instance, games and movies, as well as theatrical performances, can use such characteristics to provide group motion. There are at least two different ways to model such behavior. The predefined one considers the generation of specific goals into a shape, and the posterior distribution of the individuals into the group. The drawback of this approach is the low flexibility if a shape changes dynamically, or if more agents want to participate in the performance, since it requires the recomputation of specific goals for each agent. The second approach describes an emergent behavior of agents in order to occupy the space corresponding to the desired shape. We adopted the last approach in our model by using markers in the space.

Initially, a shape region should be defined (as illustrated in Fig. 5, where the shapes are the letters V and H). It can be done by using our markers spray. At the beginning, the environment has markers to allow the agents motion. Then, the user can spray markers to define the shape formation. Consequently, markers are painted over the environment, increasing the density of markers in formation shape. Yet, the markers into the target shape have increased weight to a defined constant (we experimentally set this value to 10). The consequence is that markers into the target shape will have more importance in Equation (10) than markers outside.

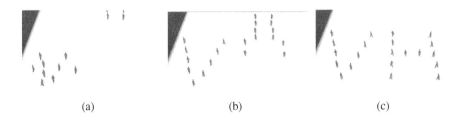

(a)   (b)   (c)

Fig. 5. Agents form explicit shapes of letters V and H

The algorithm is described in two steps. The first one takes into account the tree path algorithm described previously. In this case, an automatic goal into the target shape is attributed for each agent in the simulation, providing motion stimulus for each individual. The automatic goal takes into account the bounding box of the target shape, and it is selected as a random position within it. When the agent gets close to the shape region (it is identified through markers analysis, i.e. if one agent has a target marker into its personal space), the orientation vector computed in tree paths algorithm is not any more taken into account. In other words, Equation (8) is used initially to guide the motion of agents, and then it is replaced by a modified version of Equation (11), using the following weights w_k to obtain the motion direction $\boldsymbol{md}$:

$$w_k = \begin{cases} 10, & \text{if } \boldsymbol{m}_k \text{ is within the target shape} \\ 1, & \text{otherwise} \end{cases} \tag{12}$$

When other agents arrive in formation shape, they fight for space, but they tend to keep inside the formation shape, since the weight of the markers is greater than outside target shape markers. Moreover, if all agents should present same specific orientation in target shape, their distribution is easily regulated after the agent entries in the shape region. The final distribution of agents for the VH shape is given in Fig. 5(c).

3.5   Behavior: Groups Alignment

This behavior, as the one described in last subsection, is useful to provide group performances in entertainment applications. Alignment of people is an interesting feature that can be used in several applications. In our model, we are able to having people moving based on specific goals (using tree path algorithm - Section 3.2) as well as without goals, by changing the weights of markers into agent personal space, and then generating the motion of agents, as in last section.

For our group formation, we are able to create alignment regions with predefined weight masks for markers. One possible mask used to provide horizontal and vertical alignment is illustrated in Fig. 6, on the left. In this case, the markers into the formation mask have their weights increased according to $w_k = \text{dist}_{(I,k)}$, where $\text{dist}_{(I,k)}$ is the Euclidean distance from the current position of agent I to the marker $\boldsymbol{m}_k$. These weights are used to obtain the motion direction $\boldsymbol{md}$ used in Equation (11). If a given marker is within the personal space of more than one agent, these agents compete for the marker. In fact, the same marker may present different weights when viewed by different agents,

Fig. 6. On the left: weight masks are used in order to define alignement behavior. On the right: an example of generated behavior.

depending on their goals and relative position w.r.t. the marker. To minimize the chance of more than one agent reaching the same marker at the same time, the weight of the marker is increased for the agent that is the closest to it. More specifically, this weight is recomputed as the sum of the weights of that specific marker as viewed by all agents having the marker within their personal spaces, so that the closest agents tends to reach the marker faster than the others.

4   Final Considerations

This paper presented a new algorithm to provide motion of groups of agents. It is based on biologically-inspired technique used in the past for generating leaf venation patterns and tree structures, simulating the competition for space between growing veins or branches. In this paper, we presented some behaviors to simulate groups of agents, such as group path planning (we called tree paths), pursue behavior, surround behavior, escape behavior, groups formation and groups alignment. The key innovation is the simple way in which the paths are created, by "observing" and "occupying" free space, which is represented using a set of marker points, which leads to a simple yet computationally effective implementation of the competition for space. Global tree path is modeled by biasing the influence of the captured marker points according to their agreement with each agent's direction to its goal, which can be assigned to individual agents or groups. In addition, agents motion can be goal-based or, influenced by variation of weights attributed to markers, originating alignement and formation behaviors.

In terms of computational performance, such analysis is very dependent of generated tree paths, which also take into account the simulated environment (obstacles, number of agents, distance to the goal). In Fig. 7 we show the time[4] consumed for 1, 5 and 10 agents, including the number of iterations performed in the simulation. It is important to note that maximum number of iterations observed in our simulations is 49, meaning that at most 49 iterations are required by the agents to reach their goals in the simulated environment. Since our model is focused on low density scenarios, we have tested a

---

[4] Average of 20 simulated experiments; these results were obtained using monothread implementation without characters' rendering on Intel® Core™ 2 Duo 2.2GHz, 3GB DDR2 at 667MHz and NVIDIA® GeForce® 8400M GS 128MB.

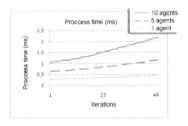

Fig. 7. Computational time (ms) for processing 1, 5 and 10 agents, considering the evolution of tree paths

maximum of 50 agents to better visualize the groups behavior, achieving real-time performance. However, according to the worst possibility (49 iterations to reach the goal) in Fig. 7, it is theoretically possible compute tree paths for thousands of agents.

Comparing with other models, while a RRT explores uniformly the "walkable space", defining positions randomly in this space that will guide the expansion of the search tree, in the proposed model the space is previously discretized using a uniform distribution. Once known the space, the proposed model considers weighted positions so that the growth of branches is directed to the goal. This difference allows optimizing the construction of the tree and the search for the path in this structure. Compared to roadmaps, the proposed model allows the generation of a connected tree using a small amount of edges. In a roadmap, the performance of the connected graph is impaired because to the number of edges necessary to explore the entire space. The proposed model also requires single nearest-neighbor queries, while roadmaps require more-expensive k-nearest neighbor queries. As future work, we intend to provide other group behaviors, focused on individualities, such as agents skills. Also, we are interested on integrating our model with crowds techniques, providing an adaptative framework in which methods can be applied depending on people density.

Acknowledgments

This work was developed in collaboration with HP Brazil R&D and Brazilian research agencies CNPq, FINEP and CAPES.

References

1. Reynolds, C.W.: Flocks, herds and schools: a distributed behavioral model. In: Proceedings of SIGGRAPH 1987, NY, USA, pp. 25–34 (1987)
2. Sachs, T.: Polarity and the induction of organized vascular tissues. Annals of Botany 33(2), 263–275 (1969)
3. Tu, X., Terzopoulos, D.: Artificial fishes: physics, locomotion, perception, behavior. In: Proceedings of SIGGRAPH 1994, NY, USA, pp. 43–50 (1994)
4. LaValle, S.: Rapidly-exploring random trees: A new tool for path planning. Technical Report TR98-11, Dep. of Computer Science, Iowa State University (1998)

5. Choi, M.G., Lee, J., Shin, S.Y.: Planning biped locomotion using motion capture data and probabilistic roadmaps. ACM Trans. Graph. 22(2), 182–203 (2003)
6. Metoyer, R.A., Hodgins, J.K.: Reactive pedestrian path following from examples. The Visual Computer 20(10), 635–649 (2004)
7. Dapper, F., Prestes, E., Nedel, L.P.: Generating steering behaviors for virtual humanoids using bvp control. In: Proc. of Computer Graphics International, RJ, Brazil, pp. 105–114 (2007)
8. Rodríguez, S., Lien, J.M., Amato, N.M.: A framework for planning motion in environments with moving obstacles. In: IEEE/RSJ Inter. Conf. on Intelligent Robots and Systems, November 2007, pp. 3309–3314 (2007)
9. Kamphuis, A., Overmars, M.H.: Finding paths for coherent groups using clearance. In: Proceedings of the ACM SIGGRAPH/Eurographics Symposium on Computer Animation, pp. 19–28. Eurographics Association, Switzerland (2004)
10. Rodríguez, S., Salazar, R., McMahon, T., Amato, N.M.: Roadmap-based group behaviors: Generation and evaluation. Technical Report TR07-004, Dep. of Computer Science, Texas A&M University (2007)
11. Lien, J.M., Rodríguez, S., Malric, J.P., Amato, N.M.: Shepherding behaviors with multiple shepherds. In: Proceedings of the IEEE Inter. Conf. on Robotics and Automation, pp. 3402–3407 (2005)
12. Musse, S.R., Jung, C.R., Jacques Jr., J.C.S.: Using computer vision to simulate the motion of virtual agents. Computer Animation and Virtual Worlds 18(2), 83–93 (2007)
13. de Lima Bicho, A.: From Plants to Crowd Dynamics: A bio-inspired model (in portuguese, to be published). PhD thesis, State University of Campinas, Campinas, Brazil (July 2009)
14. Runions, A., Fuhrer, M., Lane, B., Federl, P., Rolland-Lagan, A.-G., Prusinkiewicz, P.: Modeling and visualization of leaf venation patterns. ACM Trans. Graph. 24(3), 702–711 (2005)
15. Runions, A., Lane, B., Prusinkiewicz, P.: Modeling trees with a space colonization algorithm. In: Proc. of the Euro. Workshop on Natural Phenomena, Prague, Czech Republic, September 2007, pp. 63–70 (2007)
16. Treuille, A., Cooper, S., Popović, Z.: Continuum crowds. ACM Trans. Graph 25(3), 1160–1168 (2006)

A Virtual Tour Guide for Virtual Worlds

Dusan Jan, Antonio Roque, Anton Leuski, Jacki Morie, and David Traum

Institute for Creative Technologies, Marina del Rey, CA

Abstract. In this paper we present an implementation of a embodied conversational agent that serves as a virtual tour guide in Second Life. We show how we combined the abilities of a conversational agent with navigation in the world and present some preliminary evaluation results.

1 Introduction

Embodied Conversational Agents (ECAs) allow both verbal and non-verbal interactions [1]. Some ECAs are set within virtual worlds, but few are designed to be able to move around in the virtual world. They are usually placed in a fixed position where the user can interact with them. In this paper we present some of the challenges and our initial solutions for designing conversational agents that can move around in the virtual world and interact with human-controlled avatars and other computer agents.

We have implemented a conversational and navigational agent in Second Life, a virtual world developed by Linden Lab where users can explore, meet other users, socialize and participate in various activities. Our agent, Staff Duty Officer Moleno (SDO), is a junior officer who watches over two islands in Second Life where visitors can find information about the US Army and participate in activities such as a quiz, a helicopter ride, and a parachute jump. As a real staff duty officer would, he patrols the area to make sure everything is ok. Since this is primarily a tourist destination site, he is also equipped to interact with visitors and give them information about the island as well as giving a guided tour as he goes through his rounds. The avatar of SDO Moleno can be controlled either by our agent, or by a human operator.

The SDO's knowledge domain contains information about the two islands. He also is aware of knowledge sources for information such as facts about the army — if visitors ask about this, he tells them to investigate those sources. If someone asks a question that is out of his domain of expertise he promises to try to find the answer, and relays the question to a remote human monitor. In contrast with similar guide or question-answering agents [2,3,4] the SDO has to navigate the world, handle multiparty situations and has to play a more active role in interactions with visitors. Porting ECAs to Second Life is not new [5,6,7], but none of these included an ability to guide people through a virtual space.

In the following section, we give an overview of the agent architecture. In Sect. 3, we describe the agent's algorithms for navigating around the island. In Sect. 4 we describe the user modelling component and how different types of

Zs. Ruttkay et al. (Eds.): IVA 2009, LNAI 5773, pp. 372–378, 2009.
© Springer-Verlag Berlin Heidelberg 2009

visitors are dealt with in terms of when and how to contact them. In Sect. 5, we describe how conversations are managed. In Sect. 6, we show some examples of conversations visitors have had with SDO Moleno. Finally, in Sect. 7, we present our preliminary evaluation and further evaluation plans.

2   Agent Architecture

The agent is deployed as three separate executables: the main agent application, a text classifier, and a remote control application for human supervisor.

The main agent application is implemented in C# using LibOpenMetaverse (formerly libsecondlife), a .NET based client library used for accessing 3d virtual worlds. This library implements the Second Life client-server protocol and allows for a computer agent to connect to the Second Life virtual world in the same way a human user would connect to it using the Second Life client. The agent application also runs a web server that the remote control applications connect to using TCP protocol. It is used to inform the supervisor about the status of the SDO (whether controlled by computer agent, human operator or offline) and the list of questions that the agent needs help with. In order for the application to determine whether human operator is currently controlling the SDO avatar it connects to Second Life using a separate account while the agent is not running to query the online status of the SDO avatar. This way it can give an accurate status to the supervisor and it knows not to try to automatically connect with the agent when a human is controlling the avatar.

The agent interacts with visitors using text only over chat and instant messages. The understanding of visitor input works purely at the textual level, using cross-language information retrieval techniques to learn the best output for any input from a training set of linked questions and answers. This classification is performed by NPCEditor [8], to which the agent submits the visitor text and replies using the NPCEditor response, postprocessed using contextual information.

3   Navigation

SDO Moleno restricts his movements to two islands which include various buildings and objects of interest. He can move or teleport using kiosks designed to lead to points of interest.[1] Compared to other navigation systems such as [9] we have decided on a relatively simple implementation. Since the domain is fixed we have represented the navigation map as a graph representing the walkways and teleports that the SDO has access to.

SDO Moleno keeps track of which navigation node he is currently closest to. To find a path to a specific location we use the A* algorithm (using the QuickGraph library) from the current location to the navigation node closest to the target. For the final leg to the target the agent just moves directly to target location under the assumption that the navigation map is designed in a way that

---

[1] Flying is also possible, but SDO Moleno avoids flying to make guiding visitors easier.

the obstacles are accounted for in the graph. If the target is too far away from the navigation map it is treated as inaccessible.

We use two modes for costs of navigation links based on whether the SDO is traveling alone or guiding visitors. In the latter case there is an additional cost associated with teleporting to account for time spent on instructing visitors how to use the teleports and potential problems visitors might have in using them.

One of the features of the SDO is to be able to give a tour of the islands to visitors. This is a partly scripted tour where the SDO gives a brief description at various points of interest, but visitors may also ask questions along the way. The order of the tour is generated dynamically based on where the visitor is at the start using a simple solution of the traveling salesman problem.

4 Visitor Management

One of the main features of the SDO is to proactively assist visitors. Unlike question-answering agents such as [4,10] where the agent just responds to questions, the SDO actively seeks out the visitors that might need help.

The SDO keeps a user model for everyone he meets. This model persists between sessions. He classifies visitors in several categories that are used in deciding how to interact with them. Each visitor is either marked as a new user, advanced user, computer agent or human supervisor. The SDO also tracks information about visitors to help with decisions, such as last time the visitor was greeted and the time of last interaction with the visitor as well as realtime parameters such as online status, away from keyboard (AFK) status, whether they are typing a message and their location.

The SDO can be in one of several states which determine his behavior. He can be idle, following a path, approaching a visitor, engaged in conversation, guiding visitors or waiting for a visitor. When the SDO is idle he will perform routine rounds, checking if everything on the islands is in order. When he detects a visitor that he is not aware of he will approach their location to investigate.[2] For identified avatars the SDO will evaluate how important it is to approach them. In general he will only check on new users not marked as AFK to see if they need help, but not more than once every 5 minutes.

When approaching a visitor the SDO will first move to an appropriate distance from the visitor before engaging. The chat has a limit on how far one can see it. In addition the SDO tries to follow proxemics norms as they translate from the real world into virtual worlds [11,5]. Once he reaches the desired distance. SDO Moleno uses aspects of his information state, including the user model to decide how to address a visitor. If this is the first time he is interacting with a visitor he will introduce himself, give a calling card that enables them to send instant messages to him and offer assistance. For returning visitors he will greet them if he hasn't seen them for some time (more than 3 hours) or just ask if everything is ok. A similar greeting behavior is performed when visitors start an interaction as opposed to the SDO seeking them out.

---

[2] Beyond a certain distance, one can only see an avatar's location, not their identity.

When guiding visitors around the island he makes sure everyone in the group stays with him. If someone falls too far behind he first waits a bit and if they don't come, sends them an instant message, prompting to offer them a teleport if they got lost. During a guided tour, if anyone in the group starts to type the SDO will stop and wait to see what they have to say and enter conversation mode. During conversation if no one takes a turn for a while he will try to resume the guided tour if one is pending.

5   Conversation Management

Visitors can interact with the SDO either in chat or over instant messages (IM). Chat and IM differ in two regards: chat is public but local – everyone who is nearby can see and participate in the chat, but it can only be seen by those who are nearby. IM has no distance limitation, but is private. The SDO can only be in one chat conversation (potentially multiparty) while he can participate in any number of private, dyadic IM conversations going on at the same time. While we have tried to make the SDO human-like in behavior when using chat (e.g., using a typing animation and simulating the time needed to type the messages) we have opted for instantaneous responses in the case of instant messages.

Because of the differences in the media, the SDO responds differently to some content. In some cases visitors will ask the SDO for directions to some location, such as the gift shop. In this case, a good response is not just to answer with directions, but to actually guide the visitor there. This will only work, however, if the visitor is present in the local environment. Moreover, the SDO can only guide to one location at a time, which requires a serialization of interaction that is not required for informational question answering. Because these constraints line up well with the constraints for chat, these kinds of navigational responses are limited to chat conversations. IM conversations will have different responses to direction or action-seeking kinds of initiatives. This difference in chat and IM conversational behavior has been implemented by using several classifiers in NPCEditor[4]: a general one handles generic answers that apply in both situations and each one for chat and IM that inherit from the general one and extend it with answers that only apply in that situation.

When designing question answering agents one usually provides a number of off topic responses to cover the questions that are not understood by the agent [10]. For the SDO we took a different approach since the design goal was to allow a remote supervisor to answer questions that the agent does not have in his domain. Whenever the visitor text is not understood by the classifier we first pass the text to a spell checker. For this purpose we are using NetSpell library. NetSpell's suggestions for a misspelled word are generated using phonetic matching and ranked by a typographical score. In addition we are using a custom domain specific list of words that we use to modify the rank of results based on prior probability of those words appearing in our scenario. This helps us avoid misunderstandings in presence of typos by the visitor. When spellchecking also does not provide an answer by the classifier, the SDO first gives a prompt asking the visitor to rephrase the question. If he fails to understand two questions in a row he adds the questions to his remote assistance list and tells the visitor he is unable to answer the question, but will try to find out and get back to the visitor. A remote control application allows a human supervisor who can be outside the virtual world but in contact by IM or text message, to monitor the questions that the agent needs help with. The supervisor can either decide to drop the request or provide an answer for it. When the answer is given this is transmitted back to the agent. If he is still in conversation with the visitor he gives them the answer directly (indicating that this is in response to a previous question) or otherwise sends them an IM.

In multiparty conversations we take slightly different approach since we have observed that in many cases the out of domain questions come as a result of two visitors talking to each other about other things. We handle this by delaying the prompt for rephrasing and submission to supervisor. Instead of taking action immediately when he does not understand something SDO Moleno waits until no one is typing for a certain amount of time and only then takes the turn.

The answers that the classifier provides can be templates that include variables representing contextual information and other commands that the agent can interpret. These templates include variables for the current time or name of the addressee, which can be filled in at run-time according to the current context. This can also be used for positive/negative affirmations that need a response based on past context or to provide an answer that depends on contextual knowledge of the agent such as answering a question about who from the group they are waiting for. The annotations are also used for anaphora resolution. For example when a visitor asks "Where is the conference center?" and SDO Moleno replies with "The Army Conference Center is in the SE of Interaction Island." the answer is annotated with a landmark reference that links to a particular location in the world. This way when a visitor asks "Can you show me how to get there?" SDO Moleno knows how to respond appropriately. In addition the answers are also marked with commands used to generate nonverbal behavior such as gestures and sound as well as instruct the agent to perform specific actions such as guide visitors to a particular location, give them a tour, and offer a teleport.

6   Examples of Interaction

Figure 1 shows an example interaction with a visitor. In this example the interaction was started by the visitor greeting. The SDO identified the visitor as a returning user and returned a greeting appropriate for the current time of day, followed by an offer for assistance. The visitor asks some questions about the events and asks where he could find the helicopter. When the visitor asks the SDO to guide him to the location, SDO Moleno changes into guiding mode, instructs the visitor to follow him and instructs the visitor how to teleport there. Contrast this dialogue with the following example interaction with a new visitor:

SDO: Good afternoon, I'm Lt Moleno, the Army Island Staff Duty Officer.
SDO: Here is a calling card if you ever need to call me.

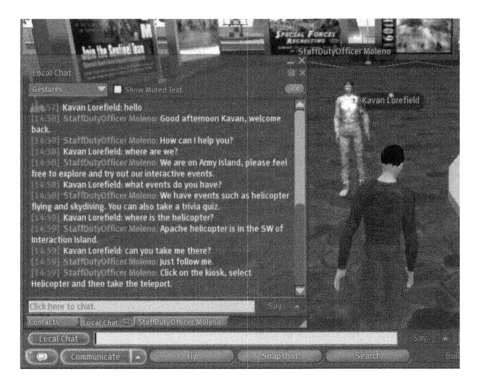

Fig. 1. Example interaction with a returning visitor

SDO: How can I help you?
Visitor: i am just looking around
SDO: Have a nice stay, please feel free to explore and try out our interactive events.

The following sample interaction shows an example of how the SDO handles an out of domain question that needs supervisor input:

Visitor: when will the island open for public?
SDO: Could you rephrase that?
Visitor: can you tell me when others will be able to come here?
SDO: I dont know, but I will find out and get back to you.
...
SDO: I found the answer to what you were asking me before.
SDO: We will be opening the islands for an education fair on April 29.
Visitor: thank you

7   Preliminary Evaluation and Plans

During the design of the agent we have performed an informal evaluation of the conversational capabilities of SDO Moleno in order to determine where we need to make more improvements. We had several users interact with the agent with a domain of about 300 questions and 70 answers. We have used two coders to annotate the questions into categories indicating what kind of response the agent should have given (in domain, no response needed, off topic, relay to supervisor).

The sample included 155 questions with agreement of 68% and a kappa score of 0.37 for the two coders. The average agreement between actual agent responses and the coders was 47% with kappa score 0.22. One main distinction we noticed was that the SDO relayed a lot more questions to the supervisor than expected. We have used this data to enhance the domain coverage and change the threshold parameters of the classifier. Once the islands open we plan a more extensive evaluation of the SDO performance and visitor satisfaction.

Acknowledgments. This work was sponsored by the U.S. Army Research, Development, and Engineering Command (RDECOM), and the content does not necessarily reflect the position or the policy of the Government, and no official endorsement should be inferred.

References

1. Cassell, J., Sullivan, J., Prevost, S., Churchill, E. (eds.): Embodied Conversational Agents. MIT Press, Cambridge (2000)
2. Gustafson, J., Lindberg, N., Lundeberg, M.: The august spoken dialogue system. In: Proceedings of Eurospeech 1999 (1999)
3. Kopp, S., Gesellensetter, L., Krämer, N.C., Wachsmuth, I.: A conversational agent as museum guide - design and evaluation of a real-world application. In: Panayiotopoulos, T., Gratch, J., Aylett, R.S., Ballin, D., Olivier, P., Rist, T. (eds.) IVA 2005. LNCS (LNAI), vol. 3661, pp. 329–343. Springer, Heidelberg (2005)
4. Leuski, A., Patel, R., Traum, D., Kennedy, B.: Building effective question answering characters. In: Proceedings of SIGdial Workshop, pp. 18–27 (2006)
5. Friedman, D., Steed, A., Slater, M.: Spatial social behavior in second life. In: Pelachaud, C., Martin, J.-C., André, E., Chollet, G., Karpouzis, K., Pelé, D. (eds.) IVA 2007. LNCS (LNAI), vol. 4722, pp. 252–263. Springer, Heidelberg (2007)
6. Endraß, B., Prendinger, H., André, E., Ishizuka, M.: Creating and scripting second life bots using MPML3D. In: Prendinger, H., Lester, J.C., Ishizuka, M. (eds.) IVA 2008. LNCS (LNAI), vol. 5208, pp. 492–493. Springer, Heidelberg (2008)
7. Weitnauer, E., Thomas, N.M., Rabe, F., Kopp, S.: Intelligent agents living in social virtual environments – bringing max into second life. In: Prendinger, H., Lester, J.C., Ishizuka, M. (eds.) IVA 2008. LNCS (LNAI), vol. 5208, pp. 552–553. Springer, Heidelberg (2008)
8. Leuski, A., Traum, D.: A statistical approach for text processing in virtual humans. In: 26th Army Science Conference, Orlando, Florida (2008)
9. Gayle, R., Manocha, D.: Navigating virtual agents in online virtual worlds. In: Proceedings of the Web3D 2008, pp. 53–56. ACM, New York (2008)
10. Artstein, R., Cannon, J., Gandhe, S., Gerten, J., Henderer, J., Leuski, A., Traum, D.: Coherence of Off-Topic Responses for a Virtual Character. In: 26th Army Science Conference, Orlando, Florida (2008)
11. Jan, D., Traum, D.: Dynamic movement and positioning of embodied agents in multiparty conversations. In: proceedings of AAMAS 2007, pp. 59–66 (2007)

Design and Implementation of a Virtual Salesclerk

Christopher Mumme, Niels Pinkwart, and Frank Loll

Clausthal University of Technology
Clausthal-Zellerfeld, Germany

Abstract. This paper describes the design and implementation of a virtual agent that is capable of providing customers in a 3D online shop with advice. Based on a product knowledge base, a conversation model and a model of the shop, the agent communicates with the customer through text based dialogues and leads the customer through the virtual world using gestures.

Keywords: Virtual Agents, 3D Environments, Online Shopping.

1 Introduction

Virtual Environments (VEs) are used in a variety of research fields including collaboration systems, marketing [1], medicine [2], computer graphics and psychology [3]. In contrast to traditional 2D representations used in websites or chats, VEs make possible a much higher level of social interaction due to several factors, including the identification of the user with the avatar embodiment, the possibility of expressing emotions and gestures, and the overall representation of the virtual world which may resemble reality much better than is possible in 2D [3]. These factors can also open up new possibilities for eBusiness applications: using 3D representations, products can be presented more realistically and can be arranged next to each other as is done in real shops, making use spatial contexts [1]. For instance, in 2006 the company Adidas made use of this way of presentation by displaying their new sports collection in a virtual shop on Second Life. Also numerous other companies like IBM, ABC.com, Toyota and Deutsche Telekom try to reach additional target groups through this new medium. In addition to saving costs for physical warehouses, virtual shops can offer the customer personalized representations of assortments of goods [4]. For instance, it is possible to show a coach suite in different variants to a customer within the customers' virtual imitated living-room, or to present a shelf of "his preferred products" to a customer within a virtual store. Such a personalization of products is not feasible in real-world shops.

Yet, a large range of products makes it hard for customers to decide. Therefore, many customers like to ask qualified salesclerks for help. This may lead to an increased shop turnover because it simplifies the decisions for the customers. Traditional 2D online shops like Amazon.com work with recommender systems to achieve similar effects. While these can be seen as anonymous agents without a visual representation, there are other approaches which apply the concept of agent in form of chatbots, i.e. graphical representations of agents one can communicate with. Examples for such

Zs. Ruttkay et al. (Eds.): IVA 2009, LNAI 5773, pp. 379–385, 2009.

agents on websites include the Coca Cola Company which replaced their FAQ by an agent, PayPal which guides their users through the payment process with an agent, or Bol.com which gives information about products via agents. Prominent advantages of using virtual salesclerk agents on websites are, among others, a simplification of navigation (users can ask the agent instead of browsing the website to find the searched information) as well as extended marketing potentials (the agent can actively seek contact with the customer to point his attention to specific products) [5, 6].

While using chatbots as sales agents works fine in 2D environments, a straightforward approach for developing virtual salesclerks for VEs by simply integrate existing chatbots into a virtual online shop is problematic. Typically, chatbots do not support actions like movements and non-verbal communication which are essential interaction techniques in VEs. To fully exploit the potential of 3D environments, more advanced agent models are required. A number of successful agents in differently targeted VEs have been developed. For instance, Kenny et al. [7] have described the use of virtual patients in the training of medical students. Other examples in the field of medicine are a virtual fitness trainer [8] and a virtual therapist [2]. Furthermore, 3D agents have been employed to escort visitors in real museums [9]. For the specific application area of online shops however, there are no research results yet – and sales agents in virtual shops are generally very rare also in environments like Second Life that are used by a number of companies.

Fig. 1. Product specification, shopping basket and product demonstration

We developed a virtual video store based on a modified OpenSim server and a Second Life client as a testing framework for a virtual salesclerk agent. To process interaction data (e.g. movement, communication), we made use of the framework described in [10] which also allows for sending feedback directly into the VE. The virtual video shop contains more than 2500 movies and about 500 seasons of series. The shop is designed close to video shops in the real world in order to ensure that the customers behave as they would in real life [11]. The only notable difference is the size of the DVD covers, which is larger than in reality. The reason for this design choice was that in the real world, humans can recognize DVDs covers from some distance. To enable this also in the virtual store with the limited screen resolution, we increased the cover size. To see information about a movie, a customer can open an extra window in the client by clicking on a virtual DVD (Figure 1, right). After that the user puts the movie into his shopping basket which also opens in an extra window (Figure 1, left). The basket is also used to purchase movies.

2 Agent Design

In this section, we discuss the requirements for a virtual salesclerk agent and describe the design of our agent in terms of embodiment, movement, language processing and provision of shopping advice.

2.1 Embodiment and Movement

Embodiment deals with the representation of artificial figures such as avatars and robots, including their appearance and their behaviour. Key research results to consider are that humans transfer social behaviours of real-life situations into virtual environments [11]. The degree of this transfer depends on the level of immersion, which is determined by the design of the virtual world [12]. Often, the question whether users accept a virtual environment is hard to predict and requires empirical studies. As a rule of thumb, a close-to-reality representation (such as offered by a Second Life based environment) is likely to reach a high acceptance [12, 13]. Another factor connected to embodiment is that humans using a virtual world would expect virtual agents to make use of the communication options that this framework offers. This includes moving around and exploiting the available space (in our case, for showing products) and making use of gestures. Figure 1 illustrates how our sales agent points to a DVD, recommending it. The availability of gestures and the sufficiently realistic visual representation were reasons to use OpenSim/SecondLife as a technical base for our implementations.

Concerning movements, our agent is able to go to and point at a DVD in the shop for recommending it. To calculate the shortest paths while avoiding obstacles, we use the Potentialfield/Wavefront algorithm [14]. In addition, in order to provide customers with advice, the agent also needs to select the customers he wants to counsel. It does so as follows (see Figure 2): First of all, the agent addresses customers that are in a logical waiting queue to which customers are added to when they want to get served while the agent already counsels another customer. In this case, the agent asks these clients to wait and then comes back to them. If the queue is empty, the agent updates a list of all users that are in the store. He then looks for the nearest costumer, provided that he hasn't served him within the last three minutes. That way, it is ensured that the agent does not address the same customer consecutively several times. If the agent finds a customer, he offers his assistance. If there are no clients in the shop, the agent moves to a sales counter.

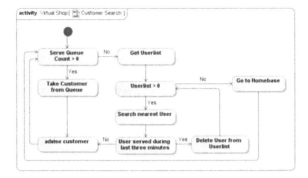

Fig. 2. Model for choosing customers

2.2 Language Processing and Provision of Shopping Advice

Evaluating user inputs is the most challenging task of a chatbot engine. Generally, there are two types of talks between a salesclerk and a customer: either the customer looks for a specific product or the customer has general ideas about the type of product he is looking for, but is, however, still undecided. While the former case requires only a comparison with the underlying knowledge base to retrieve the required information, the latter is more difficult, since the agent has to talk actively with the user to collect further information about his needs [6].

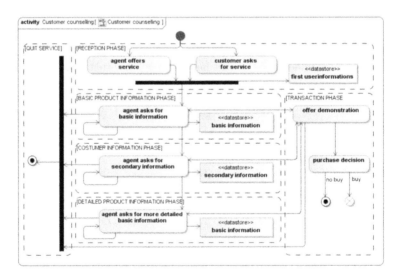

Fig. 3. Model of customer counselling

Thus, we developed a sales dialogue model (see Figure 3) consisting of five phases: (1) *Reception*: The welcome phase, initiated either by the customer or the agent. (2) *Basic Product Information*: The agent collects information about the product the customer is looking for and compares it to his database. If there are hits in the database, the agent offers the customer to lead him into an area of the shop or directly to the product, pointing on it before turning back to the customer. (3) *Customer Information:* After having asked specific questions about the product, the agent tries to collect personal data like age or sex about the customer. By comparing this information to statistical data, the agent can infer potentially good recommendations. For instance, kids will not be recommended horror movies, gender-specific typical genre preferences (for instance, men prefer action movies, while women prefer love films) will be considered, and more recent films will be recommended to younger people. (4) *Detailed Product Information:* In this phase, the agent repeatedly asks product specific questions in order to gain further insights into the preferences of the customer. (5) *Transaction:* Finally, the transaction phase introduces the end of the conversation. The agent invites the customer to look around, assuming that they are now at a place in the shop where the desired film is located and thus – due to the shop layout – also other potentially interesting films are. These phases are exemplified in the example interaction sequence in Table 1.

Table 1. Example dialogue between agent and user (including movements and gestures)

1 : [**Reception phase**]	17: Customer: 20 years old.
2: Agent: Hello, can I help you?	18: [**Detailed product information phase**]
3: Customer: Yes.	19: Agent: Can you tell me another genre
4: [**Basic product information phase**]	which you prefer?
5: Agent: What kind of genre do you prefer?	20: Customer: Yes
6: Customer: I´m looking for some action	21: Agent: So please tell me.
movies.	22: Customer: **Thriler**
7: Agent: Can I show you the action section?	23: Agent: Can I offer you the movie "War of
8: Customer: Yes, gladly.	the Worlds"?
9: Agent: Ok, please follow me.	24: Customer: Yes
10: … *Agent walks, customer follows*	25: Agent: Ok, please follow me.
11: Agent: Here we are, please take a look	26: … *Agent walks, customer follows.*
around.	27: [**Transaction phase**]
12: … *Agent waits near customer. After 30s:*	28: Agent: Here we are *(pointing at a DVD),*
13: Agent: Can I still help you?	please take a look around.
14: Customer: Yes.	29: Agent: Can I still help you?
15: [**Customer information phase**]	30: Customer: No, I think I´ll take this one,
16: Agent: Can you tell me how old the person	thank you!
is for whom you want to buy the movie?	31: Agent: You are welcome.

In each phase of the dialogue, it is possible for the customer to leave the service also without communicating this directly to the agent. Identifying this case when both the agent and the customer move around the shop is not trivial. In our implementation, we make use of timeouts (see Table 2). If a customer does not answer an agent's question within a certain time interval, the agent assumes that the customer does not wish a further consultation. An alternative approach would have been to check if the customer moves away from the agent and thus to use the growing distance between them as indicator whether the counseling should be continued. However, it is imaginable that a customer walks away, wishing the agent to follow. In this case it would be wrong to finish the service.

As a matter of fact, spelling mistakes occur in chats. Thus, the agent's chat engine must be able to deal with it. Therefore, we used the algorithm of Damerau-Levenshtein which delivers a string metric between two words. Depending on word length and distance, the algorithm can determine whether a spelling mistake is present (as in Table 1, line 22). Pilot tests with different parameters have shown that distance values of

Table 2. Timeouts for quitting counselling

Timeout	Handling
Agent follows customer for more than 30 seconds without customer talking to him	Finish counselling
Agent waits for an answer for more than 30 seconds	Repeat question
Agent waits for an answer for more than 60 seconds	Finish counselling
Agent arrives at a product while counselling and waits for more than 30 seconds for the arrival of the customer	Finish counselling

0 for word lengths of 0-4 characters, a distance of 1 for 5-8 character words, and a distance of 2 for longer words worked best.

In the different phases of the conversation, the agent has to give product recommendations to the customer on the basis of the collected information. Generally, recommendation algorithms can be classified into two groups: personalized techniques give advice based on a user profile of the customer (e.g., about his shopping behaviour), while non-personalized techniques give the same advice to any customer (e.g., based on sales volume) [15]. Our agent integrates personalized techniques (cf. "Customer Information phase") with a form of non-personalized recommendations that Schafer et al. [16] called attribute-based recommendations. In our implementation we compare the user input and the user information with the data that is available in the product specifications. The film with the best match is then recommended. For the matching algorithm, in order to consider the temporal structure of sales dialogues where statements made by clients recently are of higher priority than those made half an hour ago, the information collected by the agent during the counseling is evaluated using weights. New information receives a very high weight, while older data loses its weight increasingly (see Figure 4).

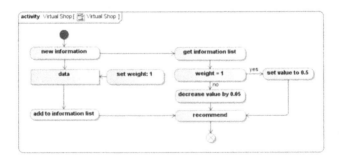

Fig. 4. Weighing information over time

3   Conclusion and Outlook

Shops in virtual worlds have a large potential for eBusiness applications. They enable a detailed representation and arrangement of products and a rich interaction in the environment. In this paper, we discussed some differences between classical 2D online shops and modern 3D virtual environments and the design challenges this imposes for implementing sales agents in virtual worlds.

The virtual salesclerk agent for a virtual movie store, presented in this paper, is able to provide customers with advice based on a product and a shop model, information about the user and a process model for the counseling activity. Interacting with the customer, the agent combines text based dialogues with movements and gestures in the virtual world. To evaluate the success of our approach, we conducted a study with 36 participants. While details about this study are not in the focus of this paper, the results showed that the participants generally followed the advice given by the agent and that they liked the interaction with our agent. Many users stated that they can imagine shopping in a virtual shop, receiving advice by a virtual shopping agent. Based on these positive results, we plan to further refine and evaluate the virtual shop and the agent in future studies.

References

1. Herder, J., Jaensch, K., Horst, B., Novotny, T.: Testmärkte in einer Virtuellen Umgebung. In: Workshop Augmented & Virtual Reality in der Produktentstehung, pp. 97–110 (2004)
2. Pontier, M., Siddiqui, G.F.: A virtual therapist that responds empathically to your answers. In: Prendinger, H., Lester, J.C., Ishizuka, M. (eds.) IVA 2008. LNCS, vol. 5208, pp. 409–416. Springer, Heidelberg (2008)
3. Benford, S., Bowers, J., Fahlen, L.E., Greenhalgh, C.: Managing Mutual Awareness in Collaborative Virtual Environments. In: Proceedings of VRST 1994. ACM Press, New York (1994)
4. Rogoll, T., Piller, F.: Product configuration from the customer's perspective: A comparison of configuration systems in the apparel industry. In: International Conference on Economic, Technical and Organisational aspects of Product Configuration Systems, Denmark (2004)
5. Mahbubur Rahman, S., Bignall, R.J.: Internet commerce and software agents. IGI Publishing (2001)
6. Braun, A.: Chatbots in der Kundenkommunikation. Springer, Heidelberg (2003)
7. Kenny, P., Parsons, T.D., Gratch, J., Rizzo, A.A.: Evaluation of justina: A virtual patient with PTSD. In: Prendinger, H., Lester, J.C., Ishizuka, M. (eds.) IVA 2008. LNCS (LNAI), vol. 5208, pp. 394–408. Springer, Heidelberg (2008)
8. Ruttkay, Z., van Welbergen, H.: Elbows higher! performing, observing and correcting exercises by a virtual trainer. In: Prendinger, H., Lester, J.C., Ishizuka, M. (eds.) IVA 2008. LNCS (LNAI), vol. 5208, pp. 409–416. Springer, Heidelberg (2008)
9. Satoh, I.: Context-aware agents to guide visitors in museums. In: Prendinger, H., Lester, J.C., Ishizuka, M. (eds.) IVA 2008. LNCS, vol. 5208, pp. 409–416. Springer, Heidelberg (2008)
10. Mumme, C., Olivier, H., Pinkwart, N.: A Framework for Interaction Analysis and Feedback in Collaborative Virtual Worlds. In: Proceedings of the 14th International Conference on Concurrent Enterprising, pp. 143–150 (2008)
11. Friedman, D., Steed, A., Slater, M.: Spatial social behavior in second life. In: Pelachaud, C., Martin, J.-C., André, E., Chollet, G., Karpouzis, K., Pelé, D. (eds.) IVA 2007. LNCS (LNAI), vol. 4722, pp. 252–263. Springer, Heidelberg (2007)
12. Schneider, E.: Mapping out the Uncanny Valley: a multidisciplinary approach. In: Proceedings of SIGGRAPH 2008, New York, USA (2008)
13. Benford, S., Bowers, J., Fahlén, L.E., Greenhalgh, C., Snowdon, D.: User embodiment in collaborative virtual environments. In: Proc. of SIGCHI 1995, Denver, USA, pp. 242–249 (1995)
14. Barraquand, J., Langlois, B., Latombe, J.-C.: Numerical potential field techniques for robot path planning. IEEE Trans. on Systems, Man and Cybernetics 22(2), 224–241
15. Runte, M.: Personalisierung im Internet - Individualisierte Angebote mit Collaborative Filtering. Dissertation, Christian-Albrechts-Universität zu Kiel (2000)
16. Schafer, J.B., Konstan, J., Riedl, J.: Recommender Systems in E-Commerce. In: Proceedings of ACM-EC 1999, Denver, USA (1999)

Duality of Actor and Character Goals in Virtual Drama

Maria Arinbjarnar and Daniel Kudenko

Department of Computer Science
The University of York
Heslington, YO10 5DD, York, UK
maria@cs.york.ac.uk, kudenko@cs.york.ac.uk

Abstract. Actor agents in a virtual reality and interactive drama must deliver a believable performance. This is challenging and many issues need to be resolved. One prominent problem is that the goals of a character in an emergent interactive drama may conflict with demands for coherency in the drama's progress. We propose an approach to resolve this that uses Object Oriented Bayesian networks and intelligent agents with dual roles: an actor role focused on the dramatic goals of the story, and a character role focused on believable actions in line with the character's personality and goals.

1 Introduction

The larger environments and grander stories in the newest games titles lead to an increasing need for intelligent characters with which the player can interact. These autonomous agents need to be able to respond to player actions fluently. This requires highly scalable techniques for partially observable environments in fast expanding game worlds. Probabilistic methods based on emergence rather than planning and pre-scripting, are more suitable because of their scalability and computational efficiency.

The agents need to respond in a coherent way to the user and the unfolding story. The experience should be similar to that of an audience member stepping onto the stage and taking a full part in a theatre play, with the other actors improvising rather than following a pre-authored script [8]. This *interactive drama* needs to conform to a specific intended drama genre, (for example; mystery, comedy, romance), and follow an expected dramatic arc to enhance the user experience. One specific problem occurs when the goals of a character directly contradict the needs of the drama. For example in an interrogation situation with a character's goals being to conceal motive, means and opportunity to preserve believability, (not to appear guilty). If the character is skilfully played by the autonomous agent then she can manage to avoid revealing clues which are necessary for the resolution of the mystery. This would be disastrous in a game as it would lead to unsolvable mysteries and quests, which would frustrate the user.

Zs. Ruttkay et al. (Eds.): IVA 2009, LNAI 5773, pp. 386–392, 2009.

In this article we address this coherency problem by incorporating both *actor goals* and *character goals* with each individual agents. Actor goals are needed by the agent to ensure a coherent drama. Character goals are needed by the agent to ensure a believable performance. We draw on lessons from improvisational theatre. Bayesian networks (BNs) are used as the agents' decision mechanism. The proposed methods are scalable and satisfy the need for real-time applicability. Our example case is an interrogation scene which is reminiscent of that in a mystery play.

The reason for choosing BNs is that they provide a means of calculating utility based on probabilities in a highly efficient manner. In addition they can easily be extended to allow for an efficient way of calculating Nash Equilibria [9]. BNs are flexible and very scalable when using Object Oriented Bayesian networks (OOBs) [10].

2   Improv

In improv, actors commonly use simple rules [15] and games that focus their efforts on joint goals [16]. For example, one rule is to never block or refuse other actors, another rule is to try to support your co-actors performance. Spolin's games [16] aim at concentrating actors' efforts on a specific goal to lead to a united effort towards achieving it. For example, the actors may act out a job interview several times, and each time they play their roles they may try to play a character that has a different level of confidence. For example, first they may play a very confident interviewer and with an interviewee who lacks confidence, following which they may switch so that the interviewer lacks confidence but the interviewee is very confident. We extend these improv techniques by having the agents assist each other within each scene so that they are free to play out their roles and fulfil their character goals. Because agents can pass messages between themselves (where actors cannot), the agents can contradict each other without this being a blocking action, because both agents will be in agreement that this will advance the drama.

3   Bayesian Networks

For efficiency reasons we use Bayesian networks to implement the reasoning of the interactive drama agents. The networks are manually authored for the example domain, which is a common practice when creating Bayesian networks for specific tasks [14]. The Bayesian networks build on previous work [2,3]

The network is divided into small objects, such that every node along with its parents is an object. This facilitates the option of calculating only the value of the relevant nodes each time. Additionally objects are grouped into larger objects which can be chosen by the author, for instance "suspect object" or "weapon object". This provides context for the reasoning algorithms, as they can use these larger objects to limit the search space.

3.1   The Approach and Algorithm

Our approach consists of defining autonomous agents that have dual roles, namely actor and character roles. A fully realized drama needs to fulfil both requirements of the overall drama consistency, progressing along the dramatic arc, and to fulfil expectations of engaging believable character portrayals. The goals of the drama have a dual nature, and this needs to be taken into account by the autonomous agents. This means that the agents have the same dual goals - consisting of actor goals preserving drama consistency, and character goals preserving character believability. Both types of goals constitute the overall drama goals.

The core idea behind our approach is for the agents' request aid from other agents when there is a conflict between their actor and character goals. We present the algorithm in pseudo-code in figure 1, and then explain it in the context of our case study which is an interrogation scene.

```
1  A1: Stimuli(sender_action,sender) {
2      If (sender_action.IsSpeech() and
3          sender_action.IsAddressedTo == actor_agent) {
4          speech_actions = GetSpeechActions(sender_action,actor)
5          action = PickAnAction(speech_action)
6          ExecuteAction(action)
7      }
8  }
9
10 A1, A2: ExecuteAction(action) {
11     SLIntereface.Act(action)
12     for ( each in actors ) { each.Stimuli(action,this.actor) }
13     if (ContradictionOfGoals(action) {
14         assistant_actor = PickActor()
15         assistant_actor.RequestResponce(action,this.actor)
16     }
17 }
18
19 A2: RequestResponce(sender_action,sender) {
20     speech_actions = GetSpeechActions(sender_action,sender)
21     action = PickAnAction(speech_actions)
22     action.IsAddressedTo = sender
23     ExecuteAction(action)
24 }
```

Fig. 1. The pseudo-code for agent conflict resolution

In our case study the user asks the suspect, played by agent (A1): "Do you have a motive?". A1 has two goals relevant to this example: an actor goal of maximising the motive's value for state true and a character goal of minimising

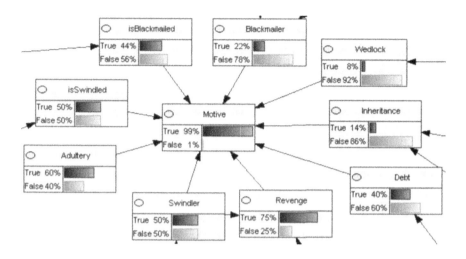

Fig. 2. The Motive variable and its parents

the motive's value for state true (see figure 2). These goals are explicitly declared before the drama begins. We now explain our algorithm in detail, in the context of this case study:

– First A1 maps the sentence to the corresponding motive variable in the OOBs. This is passed to the Stimuli() function (see line 1 in figure 1). It is mapped to ($motive_0$) because that is the representation of the motive variable being true for the agents in their knowledgebases, i.e. the respective agent having a motive for the crime.

– A1 then queries the knowledgebase with ($motive_0$), retrieving a set of speech actions from the parents of the variable queried, (see figure 2). For example the variable $revenge_1$ in 2 could be phrased by the suspect as: "I had nothing to revenge for".

– A1 compares each speech action to the current goals when querying the knowledgebase. The character goals have a higher priority than actor goals to ensure believability of the character. In our example the character goal of concealing motive will have priority, meaning that A1 will choose speech actions that conceal A1's motive. The Bayesian net is causal and facilitates precisely this type of reasoning. The query will return all speech actions that will decrease the value of ($motive_0$), as shown in figure 2. In this figure some classical motives are shown. If any of the variables are true then the motive variable becomes true. When the algorithm is given "motive" as a seed to search from, it will retrieve all of the parents. For each of the parents it tests which state of the parent (when instantiated) will satisfy the current character goal.

– A1 then randomly picks one of the resulting speech actions.

– When A1 executes an action that has goals which conflict with A1's actor goals then A1 will send a request to another agent (A2) for assistance (see line

10-15 in figure 1). The algorithm, (see line 13 in figure 1) compares actor goals with character goals where the variable names match. If the states do not match then there is a conflict, for example $(motive_0)$!= $(motive_1)$.

– A1 randomly picks an agent who is on the scene to assist. A1 uses the Pick-Actor() function (see line 14 in figure 1) to pick one actor agent to request a response. The PickActor() function returns a random agent. Unless there is already an active helper. This function keeps track of the chosen actors to ensure that the same one is not continuously returned.

– When A2 receives the request for a response, A2 does almost the same as A1 did, except that A2 queries her knowledgebase in reference to A1 rather than herself. The agents have a theory of mind which means that they maintain a knowledgebase containing their expectation of the knowledgebase of other agents, and the user.

– A2 has the same actor and character goals as A1. This means that A2 has an actor goal of revealing the motive of all other agents, but only to conceal his own motive. She will thus return speech actions revealing the possible motives for A1, pick one at random, address it to A1, and execute it.

– When actor agents execute an action they send it to all other actor agents. A2 marks this specific speech act as addressed to A1 so that A1 can recognise it and possibly respond to it if she finds something relevant to say.

– A1 recognises the response because it is marked as addressed to A1 by A2.

– A dialogue has started between A1 and A2. This will continue until either: the topic is exhausted; or A1 stops contradicting A1's actor goals.

4   Results

We used the virtual reality environment Second Life(SL) [11] to run our tests. In SL the user can create avatars and interact in a very free way with the environment. We use a C# library, libsecondlife [12] that allows us to implement our own agents. These agents log into SL as avatars and can act like any other avatar (such as those controlled by men).

We implemented an example of the interrogation scene. In which the user can interrogate a suspect and see the other actors start to aid the actor being interrogated in revealing motive. This is shown in the accompanying video clip (which can be seen online at http://www.youtube.com/watch?v=pfxz5RbmnFE)

To facilitate the input/understanding of speech we use a simple place holder system which recognizes certain keywords in user input and matches it to variables and states in the agent's knowledge base. The user speaks to the characters in Second Life using the local chat provided by Second Life, and the agents respond in the same manner. The responses are formulated by scripting a sentence for each state of the variables. An example in which the user "Valla Haggwood" asks Lydia whether the victim was blackmailing her is shown here:

– Valla Haggwood: Was Snorri blackmailing you Lydia?
– Lydia Philipp: Snorri was not blackmailing me.

– Kenneth Dawid: Snorri was blackmailing Lydia, Snorri knew all about Lydia's secrets, Lydia has deep dark secrets.
– Lydia Philipp: I'm sure Snorri knew nothing, I have no secrets.

The agents' response are buffered by 5 seconds so that the user can follow the interaction, and to ensure that the gestures seen in the video clip are in sync with the text.

5   Related Work

The main contribution of this paper is the proposal and realisation of the actor-character duality. This means that an agent has dual roles, i.e. it is simultaneously an actor and a character, and for each role the agent has specific goals which can conflict. Our proposed algorithm is specifically designed to address the conflicts between the character and actor goals. Additionally we give support for the claim that Bayesian networks are highly suitable for the domain of interactive drama. The main techniques previously applied are Planning, primarily STRIPS which is PSPACE-complete [5], and search, primarily A-star [4].

Within the fields of interactive drama and emergent story generation there has been previous research into the use of improvisation to facilitate coherency of autonomous agent actions in emergent architecture for instance Louchart and Aylett [13] and Swartjes and Vromen [17]. In our research improv is mainly used to structure the agents' actions by using the rules discussed in section 2, which ensure that agent should support and not block each other.

Bayesian reasoning has been used in research in many other fields. Allen-Williams [1] recently showed that Bayesian reasoning and learning is specifically suitable for agents in partially observable environments which need to make fast and optimised decisions, such as those which would be needed among rescue workers on disaster sites.

Although much previous research has been focussed on multi-agent systems and coordination as can for instance be seen in [18], none of this work has considered the duality of character and actors which we propose.

6   Summary and Conclusion

In this paper we address the need for scalable reasoning techniques for intelligent agents in an emergent interactive drama. We propose that Object Oriented Bayesian networks are a suitable choice to approach this challenge.

We discussed the need for coherent behaviour when character goals conflict and even contradict the needs of the drama. Our proposed algorithm uses intelligent agents with dual roles (actor and character), each with its own distinct set of goals. In our approach, the agents cooperate to resolve the conflict between the needs of the drama and the need to play believable characters.

The algorithm provided is real time applicable, as shown by the example in the video clip. In fact, the system response needs to be delayed to sync it with gestures displayed and to give the user time to understand/follow the action.

Acknowledgement

We would like to thank the anonymous reviewers for their constructive feedback.

References

1. Allen-Williams, M.: Bayesian learning for multi-agent coordination. PhD thesis, University of Southampton (2009)
2. Arinbjarnar, M.: Rational dialog in interactive games. In: Proceedings of AAAI Fall Symposium on Intelligent Narrative Technologies, Westin Arlington Gateway, Arlington, Virginia (2007)
3. Arinbjarnar, M.: Dynamic plot generation engine. In: Proceedings of the Workshop on Integrating Technologies for Interactive Stories, Playa del Carmen, Mexico (2008)
4. Arinbjarnar, M., Barber, H., Kudenko, D.: A critical review of interactive drama systems. In: AISB 2009 Symposium. AI & Games, Edinburgh (2009)
5. Bylander, T.: The computational complexity of propositional STRIPS planning. Artificial Intelligence 69(1-2), 165–204 (1994)
6. Fudenberg, D., Tirole, J.: Game Theory. The MIT Press, Cambridge (1991)
7. Harsanyi, J.C.: Games with Incomplete Information. The American Economic Review 85(3), 291–303 (1995)
8. Kelso, M.T., Weyhrauch, P., Bates, J.: Dramatic presence. PRESENCE: The Journal of Teleoperators and Virtual Environments 2(1) (1992)
9. Koller, D., Milch, B.: Multi-Agent Influence Diagrams for Representing and Solving Games. Games and Economic Behavior 45(1), 181–221 (2003), Full version of paper in IJCAI 2003
10. Koller, D., Pfeffer, A.: Object-oriented bayesian networks. In: Proceedings of the Thirteenth Conference on Uncertainty in Artificial Intelligence, San Francisco, pp. 302–313 (1997)
11. Linden Lab.: Second life (June 2009), http://secondlife.com/
12. Libsecondlife (June 2009), http://www.libsecondlife.org/wiki/Main_Page
13. Louchart, S., Aylett, R.: Building synthetic actors for interactive dramas. In: Proceedings of the AAAI Fall Symposium on Intelligent Narrative Technologies, pp. 63–71 (2007)
14. Jensen, F.V.: Bayesian Networks and Decision Graphs. Springer, Heidelberg (2001)
15. Johnstone, K.: Impro: Improvisation and the Theatre. Theatre Arts Books, New York (1979)
16. Spolin, V.: Improvisation for the Theater, 3rd edn. Northwestern University Press (1999)
17. Swartjes, I., Vromen, J.: Emergent story generation: Lessons from improvisational theater. In: Proceedings of the AAAI Fall Symposium on Intelligent Narrative Technologies, Arlington, Virginia (November 2007)
18. Wooldridge, M., Jennings, M.R.: Intelligent agents: theory and practice. The Knowledge Engineering Review 10(2), 115–152 (1995)

EMBR – A Realtime Animation Engine for Interactive Embodied Agents

Alexis Heloir and Michael Kipp

DFKI, Embodied Agents Research Group
Campus D3 2, 66123 Saarbrücken, Germany
`firstname.surname@dfki.de`

Abstract. Embodied agents are a powerful paradigm for current and future multimodal interfaces, yet require high effort and expertise for their creation, assembly and animation control. Therefore, open animation engines and high-level control languages are required to make embodied agents accessible to researchers and developers. In this paper, we present EMBR, a new realtime character animation engine that offers a high degree of animation control via the EMBRScript language. We argue that a new layer of control, the *animation layer*, is necessary to keep the higher-level control layers (behavioral/functional) consistent and slim, while allowing a unified and abstract access to the animation engine, e.g. for the procedural animation of nonverbal behavior. We describe the EMBRScript animation layer, the architecture of the EMBR engine, its integration into larger project contexts, and conclude with a concrete application.

1 Introduction

Turning virtual humans into believable, and thus acceptable, communication partners requires highly natural verbal and nonverbal behavior. This problem can be seen from two sides: creating intelligent behavior (planning context-dependent messages) and producing corresponding surface realizations (speech, gesture, facial expression etc.). The former is usually considered an AI problem, the latter can be considered a computer graphics problem (for nonverbal output). While previous embodied agents systems created their own solutions for transitioning from behavior planning to graphical realization (cf. [1,2,3]), recent research has identified three fundamental layers of processing which facilitates the creation of generic software components [4,5]: intent planner, behavior planner and surface realizer. This general architecture allows the implementation of various embodied agents *realizers* that can be used by the research community through a unified interface.

In this paper, we present a new realizer called EMBR[1] (Embodied Agents Behavior Realizer) and its control language EMBRScript. An embodied agents realizer has particularly demanding requirements: it must run at interactive speed,

---

[1] See also http://embots.dfki.de/projects.html

Zs. Ruttkay et al. (Eds.): IVA 2009, LNAI 5773, pp. 393–404, 2009.

animations must be believable while complying with high-level goals and be synchronized with multiple modalities (speech, gesture, gaze, facial movements) as well as external events (triggered by the surrounding virtual environment or by the interaction partners), it must be robust and reactive enough to cope with unexpected user input with human-like responses. The system should provide the researchers with a consistent behavior specification language offering the best compromise between universality and simplicity. Finally, all the components of such a system should be open and freely available, from the assets creation tools to the rendering engine. In the terminology of the SAIBA framework [4,5], users work on the level of intent planning and behavior planning and then dispatch high-level behavior descriptions in the behavior markup language (BML) to the realizer which transforms it into an animation. Because the behavior description is abstract, many characteristics of the output animation are left for the realizer to decide. There is little way to tune or modify the animations planned by existing realizers [6]. To increase animation control while keeping high-level behavior descriptions simple, we propose an intermediate layer between: the *animation layer*. The animation layer gives access to animation parameters that are close to the actual motion generation mechanisms like spatio-temporal constraints. It thus gives direct access to functionality of the realizer while abstracting away from implementation details.

On the one hand, the animation layer provides users with a language capable of describing fine-grained output animations without requiring a deep understanding of computer animation techniques. On the other hand, the concepts of this layer can be used as building blocks to formally describe behaviors on the next higher level (BML).

To sum up, the main contributions of this paper are:

- Introducing a new, free behavior realizer for embodied agents
- Presenting a modular architecture for realtime character animation that combines skeletal animation, morph targets, and shaders
- Introducing a new layer of specification called the *animation layer*, implemented by the EMBRScript language, that is based on specifying partial key poses in absolute time

In the following, we will first review related work, then describe the animation layer and EMBRScript. We then explain EMBR's modular architecture and conclude with a concrete application and future work.

2   Related Work

In the terminology of the SAIBA framework, the nonverbal behavior generation problem can be decomposed into behavior planning and realization. The problem of behavior planning may be informed by the use of communicative function [7], linguistic analysis [8], archetype depiction [9], or be learned from real data [10,3]. The problem of realization involves producing the final animation which can be done either from a gesture representation language [2,1] or from a set of active motion segments in the realizer at runtime [6].

Kopp et al. [2] created an embodied agent realizer that provides the user with a fine grained constraint-based gesture description language (MURML) that lets him precisely specify communicative gestures involving skeletal animation and morph target animation. This system allows a user to define synchronization points between channels, but automatically handles the timing of the rest of the animations using motion functions extracted from the neurophysiological literature. Their control language can be regarded to be on the same level of abstraction as BML, being, however, much more complex with deeply nested XML structures. We argue that a number of low-level concepts should be moved to what we call the animation layer.

The *SmartBody* open-source framework [6] relates to our work as a freely available system that lets a user build its own behavior realizer by specializing generic animation segments called *motion controllers* organized in a hierarchical manner. Motion controllers have two functions: they generate the animation blocks and manage motion generation (*controllers*) as well as blending policy, scheduling and time warping (*meta-controllers*). As *SmartBody* uses BML [4] as an input language, it must tackle both the behavior selection and the animation selection problem. Although extending the controllers to tailor animation generation is feasible, there is currently no easy way to modify the behavior selection as "each BML request is mapped to skeleton-driving motion controllers" [6]. Moreover, even if Smartbody lets users import their own art assets, the only supported assets creation tool is Maya (commercial) and used rendering engine is Unreal (also commercial). The *BML Realizer*[2] (BMLR) is an open source project that uses the SmartBody system as an engine and Panda3D as a realizer. It therefore remedies the drawbacks of commercial tools from the Smartbody system.

3   Animation Layer: EMBRScript

It has been proposed that an abstact behavior specification language like BML should be used to communicate with the realizer. Such a language usually incorporates concepts like relative timing (e.g. let motions A and B start at the same time) and lexicalized behaviors (e.g. perform head nod), sometimes allowing parameters (e.g. point to object X). While we acknowledge the importance of this layer of abstraction we argue that another layer is needed that allows finer control of animations without requiring a programmer's expertise. We call this layer the *animation layer*. It can be regarded as a thin wrapper around the animation engine with the following most important characteristics:

- specify *key poses* in time
- use absolute time
- use absolute space
- avoid deeply nested specification structures

---

[2] http://cadia.ru.is/projects/bmlr

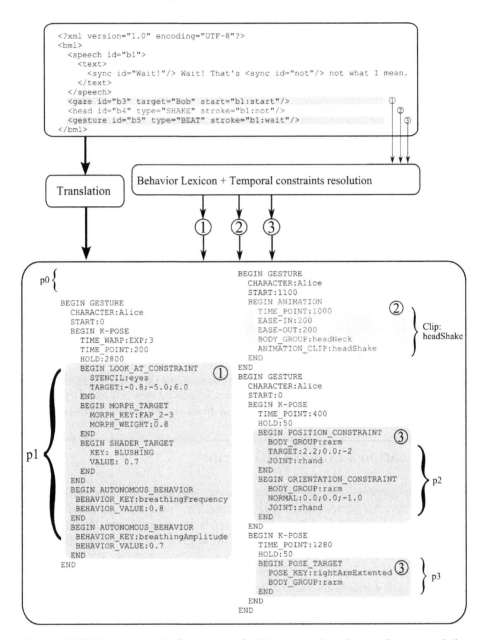

Fig. 1. EMBRScript sample (bottom box): The script describes realizations of the behavior specified in the original BML script (top box)

We incorporate the functionality of this layer in a language called *EMBRScript* (see Fig. 1 for a sample script). EMBRScript's main principle is that every animation is described as a succession of *key poses*. A key pose describes the state of the character at a specific point in time (TIME_POINT), which can be held still for a period of time (HOLD). For animation, EMBR performs interpolation between neighboring poses. The user can select interpolation method and apply temporal modifiers. A pose can be specified using one of four principal methods: skeleton configuration (e.g. reaching for a point in space, bending forward), morph targets (e.g. smiling and blinking with one eye), shaders (e.g. blushing or paling) or autonomous behaviors (e.g. breathing). Sections 3.1 to 3.3 describe each of these methods in detail. Since the animation layer is located between behavior planning (BML) and realizer (animation engine), one can implement a BML player by translating BML to EMBRScript, as depicted in Fig. 1[3].

3.1   Skeleton Configuration

Animating virtual humans using an underlying rigid skeleton is the most widely used method in computer animation. In EMBRScript, a skeleton configuration can be described in two different ways: (1) using forward kinematics (FK): all angles of all joints are specified, usually pre-fabricated with the help of a 3D animation tool, (2) using inverse kinematics (IK): a set of constraints (e.g. location of wrist joint, orientation of shoulder joint) are passed to an IK solver to determine the pose. In Fig. 1, the pose description labeled p2 in EMBRScript defines a key pose using two kinematic constraints on the right arm: a position constraint and a partial orientation, both defined in Cartesian coordinates. In EMBR, kinematic constraints modify parts of the skeleton called BODY_GROUPS which are defined in terms of skeleton joints. Pose description p3 referes to a stored pose in the engine's pose repository. The animation description *Clip:headShake* refers to a pre-fabricated animation clip (which is treated as a sequence of poses) also residing in the engine's repository.

3.2   Morph Targets and Shaders

The face is a highly important communication channel for embodied agents: Emotions can be displayed through frowning, smiling and other facial expressions, and changes in skin tone (blushing, paling) can indicate nervousness, excitement or fear. In EMBR, facial expressions are realized through morph target animation, blushing and paling are achieved through fragment-shader based animation. In EMBRScript, the MORPH_TARGET label can be used to define a morph target pose and multiple morph targets can be combined using weights. Like with skeletal animation, the in-between poses are computed by interpolation. In Fig. 1, pose p1 in the EMBRScript sample defines a weight for a morph target key pose which corresponds to the basic facial expression of anger in MPEG-4. For skin tone, one defines a SHADER_TARGET together with an intensity, like the blushing pose in p1.

3.3   Autonomous Behaviors

Autonomous behaviors are very basic human behaviors that are beyond conscious control. Such autonomous behavior include breathing, eye blinking, the

---

[3] BML examples are deliberately chosen to be similar to the ones used in [6].

vestibulo-ocular reflex, eye saccades and smooth pursuit, balance control and weight shifting. Although we don't want to completely describe such behavior in EMBRScript, we still want to specify relevant parameters like breathing frequency or blinking probability. However, we don't want the EMBRScript language to be restricted to a set of predefined autonomous behavior parameters but rather let the users define and implement their own autonomous behaviors and associated control parameters. The pose description labeled *p1* in the EMBRScript sample depicted in Fig. 1 shows how a user can modify autonomous behavior parameters like breathing frequency and amplitude.

3.4   Temporal Variation and Interpolation Strategies

Human motion is rarely linear in time. Therefore, procedural animations derived from interpolation between poses must be enhanced with respect to temporal dynamics. Therefore, EMBR supports time warp profiles that can be applied on any animation element and correspond to the curves depicted in Figure 2. Time warp profiles conveying *ease in*, *ease out* and *ease it and ease out* can be specified in the EMBR language with a combination of two parameters: function family and slope steepness. The first gesture described in the EMBRScript sample of Fig. 1 illustrates a possible usage of the `TIME_WARP` element.

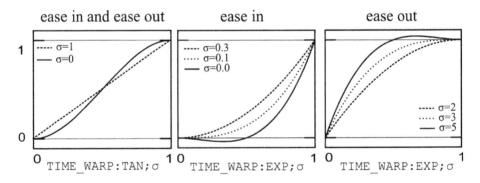

Fig. 2. Time warp profiles can be used to model *ease in*, *ease out* and *ease in and ease out*. EMBRScript offers two spline-based function families, **TAN** and **EXP**, where parameter σ roughly models steepness at $(0,0)$. A profile may (intentionally) result in overshoot (also used by [1]).

3.5   Immediate, High-Priority Execution

An agent may have to respond to an interruptive event (like dodging an incoming shoe). In order to specify behaviors which require immediate, high-priority execution, EMBRScript provides a special `TIME_POINT` label: `asap`. A behavior instance whose time stamp is `asap` is performed as soon as possible, overriding existing elements.

4   EMBR Architecture

The EMBR engine reads an EMBRScript document and produces animations in realtime. In practice, this means that EMBR must produce a skeleton pose for every time frame that passes. This process is managed by a three-component pipeline consisting of the motion factory, the scheduler and the pose blender (Fig. 3). This processing is independent of the concrete rendering engine (cf. Sec. 5 to see how rendering is managed).

To give an overview, EMBR first parses the EMBRScript document which results in a sequence of commands and constraints. The *motion factory* gathers and rearranges constraints according to their timestamp and type in order to create a set of time-stamped *motion segments*. Motions segments are sent to the *scheduler* which sorts out at regular intervals a set of motion segments whose timestamp matches the current time. Relevant poses are sent to the *pose blender*. The pose blender merges all input poses resolving possible conflicts and outputs a final pose.

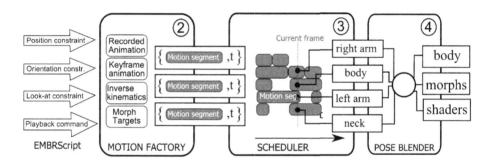

Fig. 3. The EMBR architecture

4.1   Motion Factory

The motion factory produces the building blocks of the animation called *motion segments* from the key poses specified in EMBRScript. A *motion segment* represents an animation for part of the skeleton[4] over a period of time . For instance, a motion segment may describe a waving motion of the right arm or the blushing of the face. Each motion segment contains an instance of a specialized *actuator* which drives the animation. The actuator's type depends on the motion generation method and the relevant pose component (recorded animation playback, skeleton interpolation, morph target weight and shader input interpolation). Motion segments are controlled in terms of absolute time and the timing can be warped (see Sec. 3.4) to model e.g. ease-in and ease-out.

---

[4] More precisely: for part of the pose which includes morph targets and shaders.

4.2   Scheduler and Pose Blender

The *scheduler* manages incoming motion segments, makes sure that active segments affect the computation of the final pose and removes obsolete segments. For each time frame the scheduler collects all active segments and assigns a weight according to the following algorithm:

- if segment is terminating (fade out), assign descreasing weight from 1 to 0
- else if segment contains a kinematic constraint, it is tagged with `priority`
- else segment is assigned weight 1

The pose components from the motion segments are merged in the *pose blender* according to their weights using linear interpolation (we plan to allow more blending policies in the future). For kinematic constraints it is often critical that the resulting pose is not changed (e.g. *orientation* and *hand shape* of a pointing gesture), therefore the pose is tagged `priority` and overrides all others.

5   Integrating EMBR Into Larger Projects

An open character animation engine is only useful if it can easily be integrated into a larger project context and if it is possible to extend it, specifically by adding new characters. For EMBR, one of our goals was to provide a framework whose components are freely available. Therefore, we rely on the free 3D modelling tool *Blender*[5] for assets creation and on the free *Panda3D* engine[6] for 3D rendering. This section describes the complete pipeline from assets creation to runtime system. To sum up our goals:

- components for assets creation and rendering are freely available
- modifying existing characters is straightforward
- creating a new agent from scratch is possible
- use of alternative assets creation tools or renderers is possible

The EMBR framework is depicted in Fig. 4: It can be characterized by an assets creation phase (top half of figure), a runtime phase (bottom half), and data modules connecting the two (boxes in the middle).

5.1   Assets Creation

When creating a new character, two mandatory steps are involved: creating 3D assets in a 3D modelling tool (Blender) and specifying the *EMBR character configuration*. Optionally, shader programs can be designed. In the 3D modelling tool, one first creates static resources: the character's mesh, skeleton, mesh-skeleton rigging, and textures. For facial animation, one usually creates a set of morph targets. Finally, one creates a repertoire of skeletal animations.

---

[5] http://www.blender.org
[6] http://panda3d.org

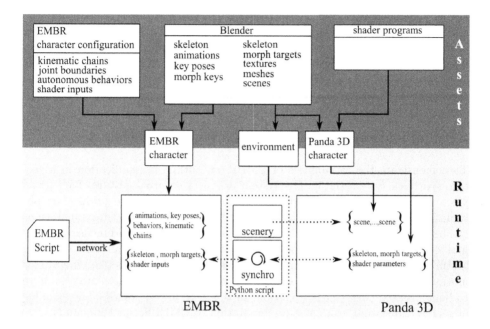

Fig. 4. The EMBR framework: Assets creation and runtime system

Since in the modelling stage the user is free to choose joint names and skeleton topology, the EMBR character configuration file must be created to inform EMBR about the character's kinematic chains (e.g. left/right arm) and joint limits. Autonomous behaviors (Sec. 3.3) can also be defined here. Finally, the user may create a set of programmable shaders, e.g. for changing skin tone at runtime (blushing/paling) or for improved rendering. Shader programming is highly dependant on the rendering engine. For instance, only the Cg[7] programming language is currently supported by Panda3D. Developers can expose parameters from the shader program and control them through EMBRScript. Shader input parameters must be declared in the EMBR character configuration file. Once the character is ready, export scripts package the data from Blender for later usage by the EMBR engine and the Panda3D renderer.

5.2 Runtime

At runtime, EMBR is initialized with the EMBR character data (Fig. 4). First, it dynamically populates the *animation factory* with *motion segment* producers corresponding to the character's attributes and capabilities (see Section 4). Second, it configures the EMBRScript parser according to the character's attributes and capabilities. EMBR uses the Panda3D rendering engine for interactive display of the character. Panda3D provides a Python scripting interface which we

---

[7] http://developer.nvidia.com/page/cg_main.html

use for synchronizing EMBR with Panda3D and for contolling the runtime system. During the lifespan of a character inside an EMBR session, two instances of the characters exist: one stored in EMBR representing the poses that result from processing EMBRScript, another one stored in Panda3D representing the display-optimized version of the character. Our Python synchronizer ensures that the Panda3D character is always in the same the state as the EMBR character.

6   Application in Procedural Gesture Synthesis

To demonstrate the capabilities of EMBR we outline its application in a gesture synthesis system [11,3]. The system produces coverbal gestures for a given piece of text using statistical profiles of human speakers. The profiles are obtained from a corpus of annotated TV material [12]. The gesture annotations can be considered a low-dimensional representation of the high-dimensional original motion, if the latter is seen as a frame-wise specification of all joint angles. In gesture synthesis the low-dimensional representation facilitates planning of new motions. However, at the final stage such low-dimensional representations have to be translated back to a full motion. In this section, we describe one example of such a translation: from gesture annotation to EMBRScript commands.

The annotation of gesture is performed by the hierarchical three-layered decomposition of movement [13,14] where a gestural excursion is transcribed in terms of phases, phrases and units. Our coding scheme adds positional information at beginning and end of strokes and independent holds. The transcription can be seen as a sequence of expressive phases[8] $s = < p_0, \ldots, p_{n-1} >$ where each phase is an n-tuple $p = (h, t_s, t_e, p_s, p_e)$ specifying handedness (LH, RH, 2H), start/end time, start/end pose. This description can be used to recreate the original motion which is useful for synthesizing new gestures or for validating how faithfully the coding scheme describes the form of the gesture.

For the translation to EMBRScript we separate the pose vector s into two *channels* for LH and RH, obtaining two pose vectors s_{LH} and s_{RH}. Each vector is then packaged into a single GESTURE tag (cf. Fig. 1). For each pose start/end information, a respective key pose is defined using positional constraints. Note that even two-handed (2H) gestures are decomposed into the described LH and RH channels. This is necessary to model the various possibilities that arise when 2H gestures are mixed with single handed gestures in one g-unit. For instance, consider a sequence of $< 2H, RH, 2H >$ gestures. There are now three possibilities for what the left hand does between the two 2H gestures: retracting to rest pose, held in mid-air or slowly transition to the beginning of the third gesture. Packaging each gesture in a single gesture tag makes modeling these options awkward. Using two channels for RH, LH allows to insert arbitrary intermediate poses for a single hand. While this solution makes the resulting EMBRScript harder to read it seems to be a fair trade-off between expressivity and readability.

---

[8] An expressive phase is either a stroke or an independent hold; every gesture phrase must by definition contain one and only one expressive phase [15].

Using this straightforward method we can quickly "recreate" gestures that resemble the gesture of a human speaker using a few video annotations. We implemented a plugin to the ANVIL annotation tool [16] that translates the annotation to EMBRScript and sends it to EMBR for immediate comparison between original video and EMBR animation. Therefore, this translation can be used to refine both coding schemes and the translation procedure. A coding scheme thus validated is then an ideal candidate for gesture representation in procedural animation systems.

7 Conclusion

We presented a new realtime character animation engine called EMBR (Embodied Agents Behavior Realizer), describing architecture, the EMBRScript control language and how to integrate EMBR into larger projects. EMBR allows fine control over skeletal animations, morph target animations, shader effects like blushing and paling and autonomous behaviors like breathing. The EMBRScript control language can be seen as a thin wrapper around the animation engine that we call the *animation layer*, an new layer between the *behavior layer*, represented by BML, and the realizer. While the behavior layer has behavior classes (a pointing gesture, a head nod) for specifying form, and allows for time constraints to specify time, the animation layer uses channels, spatial constraints and absolute time to control the resulting animation. The latter is therefore much closer to the animation engine while abstracting away from implementation details. We showed how to use EMBR in conjunction with gesture coding to visually validate the coding scheme. Thus encoded gestures can then be used to populate procedural gesture synthesis systems.

For the future we plan to make EMBR freely available to the research community. We also intend to work on extending the BML layer, e.g. providing descriptors of gesture form. We will use EMBRScript to prototype these extensions. Finally, for overall integration purposes we want to develop formal descriptions of embodied agents characteristics and capabilities, taking into account existing standards like h-anim.

Acknowledgements

This research has been carried out within the framework of the Excellence Cluster Multimodal Computing and Interaction (MMCI), sponsored by the German Research Foundation (DFG).

References

1. Hartmann, B., Mancini, M., Pelachaud, C.: Implementing expressive gesture synthesis for embodied conversational agents. In: Proc. of GW-2005 (2005)
2. Kopp, S., Wachsmuth, I.: Synthesizing multimodal utterances for conversational agents. Computer Animation and Virtual Worlds 15, 39–52 (2004)

3. Neff, M., Kipp, M., Albrecht, I., Seidel, H.P.: Gesture modeling and animation based on a probabilistic recreation of speaker style. ACM Trans. on Graphics 27(1), 1–24 (2008)

4. Kopp, S., Krenn, B., Marsella, S.C., Marshall, A.N., Pelachaud, C., Pirker, H., Thórisson, K.R., Vilhjálmsson, H.H.: Towards a common framework for multimodal generation: The behavior markup language. In: Gratch, J., Young, M., Aylett, R.S., Ballin, D., Olivier, P. (eds.) IVA 2006. LNCS (LNAI), vol. 4133, pp. 205–217. Springer, Heidelberg (2006)

5. Vilhjalmsson, H., Cantelmo, N., Cassell, J., Chafai, N.E., Kipp, M., Kopp, S., Mancini, M., Marsella, S., Marshall, A.N., Pelachaud, C., Ruttkay, Z., Thórisson, K.R., van Welbergen, H., van der Werf, R.J.: The behavior markup language: Recent developments and challenges. In: Pelachaud, C., Martin, J.-C., André, E., Chollet, G., Karpouzis, K., Pelé, D. (eds.) IVA 2007. LNCS (LNAI), vol. 4722, pp. 99–111. Springer, Heidelberg (2007)

6. Thiebaux, M., Marsella, S., Marshall, A.N., Kallmann, M.: Smartbody: Behavior realization for embodied conversational agents. In: Proc. of AAMAS-2008, pp. 151–158 (2008)

7. De Carolis, B., Pelachaud, C., Poggi, I., Steedman, M.: APML, a mark-up language for believable behavior generation. In: Life-like Characters. Tools, Affective Functions and Applications (2004)

8. Cassell, J., Vilhjalmsson, H., Bickmore, T.: BEAT: The Behavior Expression Animation Toolkit. In: Fiume, E. (ed.) Proc. of SIGGRAPH 2001, pp. 477–486 (2001)

9. Ruttkay, Z., Noot, H.: Variations in gesturing and speech by GESTYLE. Int. Journal of Human-Computer Studies 62, 211–229 (2005)

10. Stone, M., DeCarlo, D., Oh, I., Rodriguez, C., Stere, A., Less, A., Bregler, C.: Speaking with hands: Creating animated conversational characters from recordings of human performance. In: Proc. ACM/EUROGRAPHICS-2004 (2004)

11. Kipp, M., Neff, M., Albrecht, I.: An annotation scheme for conversational gestures: How to economically capture timing and form. Journal on Language Resources and Evaluation 41(3-4), 325–339 (2007)

12. Kipp, M., Neff, M., Kipp, K.H., Albrecht, I.: Toward natural gesture synthesis: Evaluating gesture units in a data-driven approach. In: Pelachaud, C., Martin, J.-C., André, E., Chollet, G., Karpouzis, K., Pelé, D. (eds.) IVA 2007. LNCS (LNAI), vol. 4722, pp. 15–28. Springer, Heidelberg (2007)

13. Kendon, A.: Gesture – Visible Action as Utterance. Cambridge University Press, Cambridge (2004)

14. McNeill, D.: Hand and Mind: What Gestures Reveal about Thought. University of Chicago Press, Chicago (1992)

15. Kita, S., van Gijn, I., van der Hulst, H.: Movement phases in signs and co-speech gestures, and their transcription by human coders. In: Wachsmuth, I., Fröhlich, M. (eds.) GW 1997. LNCS (LNAI), vol. 1371, pp. 23–35. Springer, Heidelberg (1998)

16. Kipp, M.: Anvil – a generic annotation tool for multimodal dialogue. In: Proc. of Eurospeech, pp. 1367–1370 (2001)

Augmenting Gesture Animation with Motion Capture Data to Provide Full-Body Engagement

Pengcheng Luo[1], Michael Kipp[2], and Michael Neff[1]

[1] UC Davis, USA
{pcluo,neff}@ucdavis.edu
[2] DFKI, Germany
michael.kipp@dfki.de

Abstract. Effective speakers engage their whole body when they gesture. It is difficult, however, to create such full body motion in animated agents while still supporting a large and flexible gesture set. This paper presents a hybrid system that combines motion capture data with a procedural animation system for arm gestures. Procedural approaches are well suited to supporting a large and easily modified set of gestures, but are less adept at producing subtle, full body movement. Our system aligns small motion capture samples of lower body movement, and procedurally generated spine rotation, with gesture strokes to create convincing full-body movement. A combined prediction model based on a Markov model and association rules is used to select these clips. Given basic information on the stroke, the system is fully automatic. A user study compares three cases: the model turned off, and two variants of our algorithm. Both versions of the model were shown to be preferable to no model and guidance is given on which variant is preferable.

Keywords: Embodied Conversational Agents, Posture Synthesis, Motion Capture.

1 Introduction

When creating virtual agents, the designer is caught between two main animation options, each with their inherent trade-offs. Procedural motion generation offers excellent control, allowing the agent to flexibly respond to a range of situations and generate a very large set of gestures. This flexibility, however, comes at the cost of extra work and/or realism as it is difficult to generate highly realistic motion using procedural methods. On the other hand, motion capture-based approaches provide an easier method to obtain realistic motion that engages the entire body, but control is generally limited.

In this paper, we present a hybrid system that uses procedural generation for arm gestures and motion capture data to add realistic body movement[1]. Our

---

[1] Animation samples can be found on
http://www.cs.ucdavis.edu/~neff/pengcheng/

Zs. Ruttkay et al. (Eds.): IVA 2009, LNAI 5773, pp. 405–417, 2009.
© Springer-Verlag Berlin Heidelberg 2009

procedural methods for arm gesture are based on previously published techniques [1,2]. The contribution of this work is a system for engaging the rest of
the body, using motion capture data to control the lower body, augmented with
procedural generation of body rotations. The approach leverages off the strengths
of the two animation techniques: using procedural generation for arm gestures,
where maximal control is necessary, while using motion capture to generate full
body engagement and increase the realism of the final motion.

Inspired by Lamb's theory of body-gesture merger [3], discussed below, our
algorithm aligns the character's body movement with the stroke phase of gestures
to engage the total body in creating a gesture. The rules for this alignment are
based on a statistical model built from a sample speaker. It uses both a Markov
model and association rules to predict a desired weight shift and body orientation
for each stroke. The system then searches for a short piece of motion capture
data to satisfy these goals and uses it to control the lower body movement during
the stroke. Rotation of the spine is also added procedurally. We evaluate our
model in a user study that compares three cases: our body-engagement model
turned off and two variants of our model, one that uses motion capture to in-fill
body motion between strokes and one that uses interpolation and hold phases
for this in-fill. The study showed with high significance that both models were
preferable to no model. It also showed that the motion capture gap filling model
was preferable to the gap filling based on interpolation. Sample frames from
animation produced by our system are shown in Figure 1.

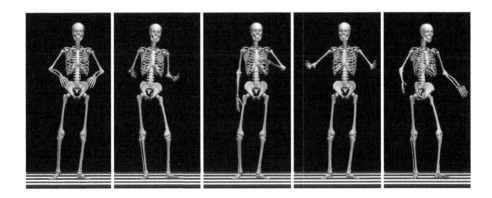

Fig. 1. Sample frames showing our algorithm used to add postural movement to a
gesture sequence

This paper makes two main contributions. First, it presents an effective algorithm for automatically augmenting animations of arm gestures with appropriate
postural movement. The resulting system allows a very wide range of gestures to
be generated with a higher degree of naturalness than was previously possible.
The algorithm is validated with a user study. The second contribution is a study
that indicates a strong preference for the continuous use of motion capture data

rather than a mix of motion capture data with interpolation and short holds. This suggests that continuous movement may be an important factor in the generating positive perceptions of virtual agents.

2 Background

2.1 Gesture and Posture Study

In his pioneering work, Lamb [3] argued that there were two broad classes of movers, those that made arm gestures largely independently of postural changes and those that effectively merged posture changes with gesture. He argued that this *posture-gesture merger* in the latter group led to much more effective movement. This idea provided the key motivation for aligning posture changes with gesture strokes in our model.

Cassell et al. [4] conducted an analysis of posture shifts in monologue and dialogues. They predicted posture shift as a function of discourse state in monologues and discourse state and conversation state in dialogues. We instead focus on more ongoing motion aligned with gesture strokes.

Gesture has been previously described in terms of phases, phrases and units [5,6,7,8], where a single gesture consists of a series of consecutive phases:

$$\text{GESTURE} \rightarrow [\ \textbf{preparation}\ ]\ [\ \textbf{hold}\ ]\ \text{STROKE}\ [\ \textbf{hold}\ ] \tag{1}$$

We use this same structure in our work and in particular, use the stroke placement to align our posture movement. Previous work has used this structure in recreating gesture animation [2,1].

For statistical modeling, Lee and Marsella [9] used a Hidden Markov model to generate head movements for virtual agents. In a very different domain, Khalil et al. [10] performed statistical modeling that combined association rules and a Markov model to predict web users' behavior and their next movement.

2.2 Animation Methods

There are a diverse set of papers on using motion capture in animation. A few of the most relevant works include Arikan et al.s'[11] synthesis of motions by controlling the qualitative annotations of motion clips. Pullen and Bregler [12] developed a conceptually similar approach for creating motions by considering the motion capture data as a texture to be applied to more simple key framed animation, but did not apply their work to gesturing characters, made no use of gesture structure and used a very different formulation based on a frequency decomposition. Arikan et al. [13] and Kovar et al. [14] proposed similar methods using motion graphs to connect motion clips together. Wang and Bodenheimer [15] studied the best parameters to use when doing linear blends to connect motion clips together.

Stone et al. [16] present a system for using motion capture to animate a conversational agent. They use motion capture to control the entire body, whereas our approach combines motion capture with a more flexible, procedural approach for gesture generation.

The procedural animation system for gestures follows the work of Neff et al. [1] which combines a statistical method for predicting gesture selection and placement with a procedural animation system to create an animated character that could gesture in synchrony with speech. In related work, the SmartBody engine [17] offers another way to combine different animation modalities.

3   Acquiring and Analyzing Input Motion

The algorithm augments procedural arm gestures with lower body motion and rotation. The rules for doing this are determined by analyzing sample data of a subject whose body engagement is considered desirable. This input data is used both in determining these rules and as the source motion data that is used in the reconstruction.

For our input data, we had a subject recite several versions of Shakespeare's famous Marc Antony speech "Friends, Romans, Countrymen..." while being both filmed and motion captured with an optical motion capture system [18]. This provided data of a long monologue, which we analyzed both in terms of speech and motion data. We manually annotated the data using the software package ANVIL [19]. This annotation included gesture *phrase*, gesture *phase*, the number of stroke repetitions and the hand used in each phrase (right hand, left hand or both hands). A trained coder can annotate 1 minute of video in ca. 25 mins.

The motion analysis began by reconstructing an animation skeleton from the motion capture data to obtain joint angle data. This data was then processed to extract a number of key parameters that were hypothesized to be important in lower body movement: center of mass (COM) and foot locations, swivel angles of the legs, pelvic rotation, and knee angles. A correlation analysis was performed across this data. It revealed that, taken together, the COM position and rotation of the pelvis around the vertical axis ($pelvis_Y$) were well correlated with the other data, having a correlation coefficient higher than 0.6. Some parameters correlated well with COM and others with pelvic rotation. Figure 2 shows an example of how the leg swivel data is correlated with the pelvis rotation. Based on this analysis, we determined that these two parameters effectively characterized the major lower body motion. We therefore focused on accurately reconstructing them in order to add lower body motion to new clips.

4   Statistical Model for Posture Prediction

For the domain of talking characters, lower body movement can be divided into two categories: movement co-occurring with gesture and movement not co-occuring with gesture, also known as idle movement. We segment the lower body motion based on this definition and use the posture information at the end of each gesture phrase for analysis and modeling.

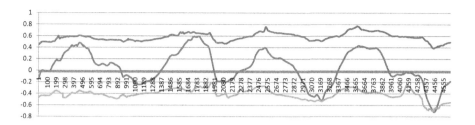

Fig. 2. In a plot of leg swivel data and pelvis data for a motion clip, a clear correlation can be seen between the data. Top: $Pelvis_Y$; middle: $LeftFootSwivel$; bottom: $RightFootSwivel$.

4.1 Markov Model

Posture configurations can be roughly defined into three categories for each of our posture parameters. For the center of mass, it contains the categories: weight shifted to the left foot, weight shifted to the right foot, and balance in the center of the two feet. The pelvis rotation around the vertical axis has three directions: facing left, facing right and facing front. Intuitively, having a variety of posture positions at the end of phrases makes motions more realistic. Imagine if a character consistently returns back to the exact same position at the end of a gesture, the motion will not be realistic. While using only three categories per parameter, our system will support a range of end poses within each category to avoid repetitive motion.

A Markov model is commonly used in modeling time series sequences. For example, Kipp et al. [2,1] used Markov models for modeling handedness and gesture sequences. Inspired by their work, we use a Markov approach for modeling the continuous posture sequence information. Let X be the end posture at each phrase, and n stands for the index of the phrase in the whole sequence. For a Markov chain:

$$P(X_{n+1}|X_n, X_{n-1}, \cdots) = P(X_{n+1}|X_n) \tag{2}$$

Or in words, the future state depends only on the present state and the past can be ignored. While this model captures some of the modeled individual's tendency to make weight shifts or rotations, it is not complete. For instance, it does not take into consideration the choice of synchronizing particular postures with given gestures. We turn our attention to that next.

4.2 Association Rules

We postulated that a person's posture changes (rotation and weight shifts) would be related to the form of the gesture they were performing. Different gestures would potentially lead to different posture changes. For example, a person may tend to shift his weight right when using his right hand. Modeling these properties has two benefits. It provides a better choice of posture change for a given gesture. It also adds more variation into the transition probability from one posture to the next. This will provide greater variation over a sequence.

Association rules are one of the most important concepts in data mining and commonly used in finding association patterns in a series of data sequences. Given a set of transactions, association rules will find useful hidden rules, given some threshold, to help predict values in the future. Generally speaking, there are two important metrics: one is the support and the other is the confidence. Suppose there are two itemsets X and Y where an itemset is just a set of observed attributes (e.g. a left body rotation with a left-handed cup gesture and no weight shift). The support count of X is the fraction of transactions in the database that contain X. Confidence measures how often items in Y appear in transactions that contain X and can be interpreted as an estimate of $P(Y|X)$.

We use association rules to model the relationship between gesture types and posture positions at the end of gestures. Each gesture phrase is a transaction in our model which contains the information of handedness (H), gesture lexeme (L) (e.g. a "cup" gesture or "frame" gesture) and an end of phrase posture description including the center of mass position (C) and the direction of body rotation (B).

To calculate the confidence of the center of mass position, we have the following formulas.

$Support(H) = count(H)/totalcount$
$Support(L) = count(L)/totalcount$
$Support(C) = count(C)/totalcount$
$Confidence(C|H) = count(C \cap H)/count(H)$
$Confidence(C|L) = count(C \cap L)/count(L)$
$Confidence(C|H, L) = count(C \cap H \cap L)/count(H \cap L)$

Where totalcount is the number of transactions appearing in the database.

Since there are many gesture lexemes and three handedness type, we will find a variety of association rules, but not all of them will have enough data support to be meaningful. Thus we first used a threshold filter on the itemsets to remove those that have too small a support number and are not considered meaningful. We then set up another threshold to filter the association rules whose confidence is small. The same strategy is used for prediction rules for body rotation. In the end, we are left with a list of useful association rules for each category of COM position and body rotation direction with satisfactory support and confidence values.

4.3 Combining Prediction Rules

The final prediction of the body movement is made by combining the output of the Markov model and the association rules. The input to the system is the initial center of mass position (IC), the gesture lexeme (L) and Handedness (H). We will get the probability of transition from IC to three categories of center of mass using the probability PM calculated from Markov model. In addition, we take the highest confidence value from our association rules and denote that as PC, which also describe the probability of transition from IC to the three categories of center of mass at the end of the phrase. The final probability distribution is defined as:

$$P = \alpha PM + \beta PC \tag{3}$$

where β was experimentally set to between 0.6 and 0.7 and $\alpha = 1 - \beta$. The same approach is used in predicting final body rotation direction. Since center of mass has three possibilities, and body rotation has three possibility, thus in total there are 9 possibilities in describing the final posture. We have a probability distribution that gives the odds of each of these occurring and we randomly sample from this distribution to choose the actual posture change. By changing our random seed, we can produce different motion sequences from a given distribution.

5 Animation Methods

5.1 Motion Capture

Motion capture has recently become a widely used alternative to keyframe or procedural techniques in the animation community. Compared with these traditional methods, motion capture will provide more detailed motions which were difficult to model previously. However few papers have addressed how to use this method to model lower body motion. Egges et al. [20] built up a general framework to insert idle movement into general animation. We use similar approaches in modeling idle movement but do so in a different reconstruction framework and within a larger system that focuses on aligning body motion with gesture.

5.2 Selection and Reconstruction of Co-occurring Motion Clips

The reconstruction method works in two stages. First, it finds appropriate motion capture clips to align with each stroke, as described below. Second, it fill in the gaps between these clips, as described in the following subsection.

The motion capture data used to generate posture movement is first preprocessed. The motions are divided into segments that co-occur with each gesture phrase in the sample and assigned to 9 groups based on their center of mass and pelvis rotation information. The motion samples used in the reconstruction are chosen one-by-one from this set according to the motion prediction rules to align lower body movement with co-occurring gestures. The motions are reconstructed as follows:

First, lower body motion clips are aligned with the end of stroke. Before working with our data, a butterworth filter is applied to the motion to smooth out small jerks. For our sample data, if there is an extreme value (minimum or maximum) within the phrase we then calculated the time difference between extreme values, where the velocity equals 0, and the end of the stroke. We found that the extreme for the pelvis rotation is usually between 0 and 10 percent of the average phrase duration before the end of the stroke. The end of the horizontal COM shift is usually between 0 and 20 percent of the average phrase time after the end of the stroke. This means that the pelvis usually stops a little before the end of stroke and the center of mass usually stops a little bit after the end of stroke which supports our assumption that the posture change usually stops around the end of stroke if it is going to pause within the phrase. While interesting, these conclusions are drawn on limited data for one speaker, so general conclusions about human movement should not be drawn.

Since there are many candidate motions for each clip selection, we select motions whose starting point has the smallest velocity difference from the average velocity over the idle duration as illustrated in Figure 3. The difference is calculated by

$$Diff = V_S - V_A \qquad (4)$$

where $Diff$ is the difference, V_S is the velocity at the starting point of the phrase for the next clip and V_A is the average velocity of the idle movement. The velocities are the summed difference velocities of the COM and pelvis rotation. Ensuring a small velocity difference helps ensure realistic motion.

Fig. 3. Clips are chosen to minimize the velocity difference in order to help produce smooth motion

In some cases, two consecutive selected motions will have a large gap between their end points that must be spanned in a short time. This can lead to unrealistically rapid movement. Instead, we find a path from the end of the previous motion to a point further ahead in time on the next motion that is closer to the previous motion's end state. This case is shown in Figure 4. The adjustment produces smoother overall motion.

Fig. 4. For rapid transitions, the next clip, shown in blue is truncated to allow a more direct transition from the previous clip

Sometimes, the postures predicted for the end of consecutive phrases will fall in the same category. In order to create more continuous motion in these cases, the algorithm finds longer, continuous motion clips from the mocap data to fit this sequence of motions.

Fig. 5. Once motion clips, the thick blue curves, are aligned with the gestures, the remaining gaps must be filled using either interpolatuion or additional clips, as represented by the thin red curve

5.3   Idle Motion Reconstruction

At this point, the system has a partial specification of lower body movement, with short clips aligned with each gesture stroke and gaps in between. The task now is to fill these gaps, the so-called *idle movement*, as shown in Figure 5. We designed two strategies for this. The first is to fill the gaps by selecting appropriate mocap clips and blending them into the overall motion stream. The second is to use a combination interpolation and short holds where the interpolation would be too slow. The effectiveness of the two strategies is compared in the user study presented in Section 6. The strategies are described below.

Motion Capture Gap Filling. When filling gaps with motion capture clips, we search the mocap database to find the correct duration of motion to fit the idle gap. Motion clips are selected based on their distance from the motions that have already been specified at the two ends of the gap. A sliding window is used to define how many frames are compared. Let the length of the window be L, and the motion clips already aligned with the gestures are represented by $M_1, M_2, \cdots M_m$, the source original motion clips are represented by $M'_1, M'_2, \cdots M'_n$. The distance

$$D(k, j, f, L) = \sum_{i=0}^{L} \alpha(M_{k-i} - M'_{j-i}) + \beta(M_{k+i+1} - M'_{j+f+i+1}) \tag{5}$$

where f is the number of frames in the gap, i is the index over the frames being compared, k is the start frame in the selected motion and j is the start frame in the source motion. α and β are adjusted to give greater weight to frames close to the gap and less weight further away. The sliding window ranges from 10 to 30 frames. This comparison combines the velocity comparison and distance comparison, which makes the selected motion the most similar to the motion on either end.

When motion clips are selected, we have to register the selected motion to the gaps, aligning them with the motion at either end. This is done by adding a linear offset to the fill clip which generates a good result. This can be represented formally as $F(x) = G(x) + O(x)$, where $O(x)$ is the linear offset, $G(x)$ is the selected motion clips, $F(x)$ is the final fitted motion for a frame index x. $G(x)$ and $O(x)$ have the same starting and ending index. Since $G(x)$ and $O(x)$ are both continuous functions, thus the final motion $F(x)$ is also continuous. However, sometimes the added offset will make the motion unrealistic by producing overly large movements. The sequence $F(x)$ can be multiplied by a scale factor to reduce the final motion to a more realistic range.

Interpolation and Hold Gap Filling. Another strategy explored is using interpolation to fill the gaps. The motivation for this strategy is to use the most complex movement for the stroke and relatively simple motion in between, the hope being that this would add greater emphasis to the stroke motion, where the communicative meaning is concentrated. The interpolation fill is combined with inserting short hold phases. These serve two purposes. First, they reflect the periods of stillness observed in our data. Second, they provide a way of ensuring the velocity of the movement is not unrealistically slow. If the gap requires a long duration interpolation with a relatively small change in posture, this would cause unrealistically slow movement. A hold phase is used to occupy some of the gap time, so the actual transition proceeds at a reasonable velocity.

This fill scheme is implemented as follows. To avoid a sudden stop in the motion, we extend the end point of the phrase clip into the gap by an amount $t = s_1 * GapDuration$ where s_1 is a scale factor set to 0.25. The new end position is calculated by multiplying the scaled velocity at the end of the clip ($V = 0.08*v$) by this time where v is the velocity at the end of last phrase. This allows the motion to fade out. A hold is then started at $HoldStart = p + V * t$ where p is the position at the end of last Phrase and the hold duration is $t' = s_2 * GapDuration$ where s_2 is a scale factor set to 0.25. The interpolation between the motion clips and hold is done using an ease-in, ease-out curve to connect the ends of the hold to the previous and next phrases.

5.4   Procedural Animation

Procedural animation is used to add body rotation to the motion. This is done by specifying an axial rotation along the spine. The desired body rotation direction is determined based on the same prediction used for the pelvis rotation. To determine the starting time for the rotation, we calculate the time difference between the phrase start time and the start time of body rotation for all samples in our source data. This offset can be modeled using a Gaussian distribution that has average AVE and standard deviation SD. During reconstruction, we sample from this distribution to determine the time difference between the starting point of phrase and the start of the rotation. The end time and the end value for body rotation is set up using default values which is similar to the approach in [1].

5.5   Motion Reconstruction

The approach described here is general enough to be adapted to various animation systems. Our specific animation system reconstructs the motion as follows, given as input a script that specifies the desired gestures and associated timings. First, the system solves for the arm posture associated with the start and end of each stroke. Interpolation functions are used to move between poses. Additional data such as hand-shape is also specified at this time, following the algorithm described by [1]. A similar approach is used for the procedural body rotation. Start and end poses for the effected spine degrees of freedom are specified and interpolation functions are associated with them to affect the transition. The algorithms described above generate a continuous sequence of motion capture data for controlling the lower body. Instead of representing this as joint angle data, our system stores this as a set of parameters that can be used to reconstruct the pose at each time step. Parameters include the COM position, foot positions, knee angles and pelvis angles. At each time step, a dedicated lower body solver uses this data to pose the lower body as the upper body is controlled by interpolating between the keyed values. Footskate is corrected by specifying periods during which each foot cannot move and then simply keeping the foot data constant during these times.

6   Evaluation

The algorithm provides visually pleasing motion that greatly adds to the overall liveliness of the animation. The accompanying video provides examples of the algorithm, including the motion capture fill and interpolation fill variants.

We conducted a user study to test the effects of our system. First, we wanted to make sure that adding body movements is an improvement at all. Second, we wanted to empirically find out which of the two variants of our model produces more natural motion. For our study we recruited 21 subjects (14 male, 7 female) from the US (11) and Germany (10), aged 23–46.

Material. We used a single clip from previous work of length 33 sec. to test different conditions [2]. Our conditions were: (N) no body motion, (F) body motion generated with the motion capture fill-in variant of our system, and (I) body motion with the interpolation variant. To gather sufficient power for the study we produced 4 different variations of each of conditions F and I using different random seeds in our probabilistic algorithm. We then cut the clips into 3 parts each. This resulted in 3 clips for N and 4x3=12 clips for F and I each. We intentionally left the audio track (speech) in the material because we considered the multimodal synchronization between speech, gesture and pose to be an important aspect for judging the naturalness of the motion.

Method. Each subject participated in two studies (A and B). In study A we presented *single clips* in random order. We used 12 clips for F, I and N each[2] So the user was exposed to 3x12 = 36 clips in total, clips could not be replayed. The user rated the "naturalness" of the motion on a 5-point scale where every option was numbered (-2 to +2) and the extremes labeled with *not at all* and *very much*. In study B, we presented all 12 clips of conditions F and I *side by side*, in random left-right order. The user was asked to decide which variant s/he found more "natural" in terms of movement. Below the two videos, which could be replayed multiple times, we displayed a fully labeled 5-point scale: -2 (left one), -1 (rather left one), 0 (both equal), +1 (rather right one), +2 (right one).

---

[2] To obtain 12 clips for condition N, we had to repeat each of the 3 clips 4 times.

Results. In study A, the subjects rated the three conditions on average: -0.63 (sd=.68) for no motion (N), +1.1 (sd=.38) for motion capture fill (M), and +0.65 (sd=.41)for interpolated fill (I). We found that conditions F and I were rated more natural than N (no motion) with high significance. For this, we used t-tests for N vs. F ($t(40)$=-10.19; $p < .001$) and N vs. I ($t(40)$=-7.36; $p < .001$). Moreover, condition F was clearly rated more natural than I ($t(40)$=3.75; $p < .001$). The latter was confirmed by study B where we mapped ratings such that F corresponded to -2 and I to +2. The mean of -0.73 indicated that users preferred F which was validated to be a significant deviation from zero in a one-sample t-test ($t(20)$=-5.78; $p < .001$).

Discussion. The highly significant preference of our proposed models to no motion (N) first ensures that our methods improve an animation instead of adding irritation. This finding underlines the importance of adding lower body motion at all in order to make an agent believable. The highly significant preference of I over F demonstrates how systematic studies can guide the algorithm design process and suggests the use of motion capture fill is a preferable option.

7   Conclusion

This paper presents an effective algorithm for adding full body postural movement to animation sequences of arm gestures. The system uses motion capture data and procedural animation to add lower body movement and spine rotation respectively. A combination of a Markov model and association rules are used to predict appropriate postural movement for specified gestures. The resulting motion has a much more lively, realistic feel while still maintaining the flexibility of a procedural gesture system capable of creating 38 different types of gestures in hundreds of variations.

A user study confirms the effectiveness of the algorithm. Two variants of the algorithm, using gap filling based on motion capture and gap filling based on interpolation, were both considered significantly preferable to not having a postural model. Interestingly, the motion capture gap filling was also considered significantly preferable to the interpolation based method. This suggests that continuous movement may be an important factor in subjects' judgement of animated motion.

Acknowledgments. We would like to thank Alexis Heloir and Tyler Martin for motion capture support. Financial support for part of this work was provided by the Department of Computer Science, UC Davis. Part of this research was conducted in the framework of the Excellence Cluster Multimodal Computing and Interaction (MMCI), sponsored by the German Research Foundation (DFG).

References

1. Neff, M., Kipp, M., Albrecht, I., Seidel, H.P.: Gesture modeling and animation based on a probabilistic re-creation of speaker style. ACM Transactions on Graphics 27(1), 5:1–5:24 (2008)

2. Kipp, M., Neff, M., Kipp, K.H., Albrecht, I.: Towards natural gesture synthesis: Evaluating gesture units in a data-driven approach to gesture synthesis. In: Pelachaud, C., Martin, J.-C., André, E., Chollet, G., Karpouzis, K., Pelé, D. (eds.) IVA 2007. LNCS (LNAI), vol. 4722, pp. 15–28. Springer, Heidelberg (2007)
3. Lamb, W.: Posture and gesture: an introduction to the study of physical behavior. Duckworth, London (1965)
4. Cassell, J., Nakano, Y., Bickmore, T., Sidner, C., Rich, C.: Annotating and generating posture from discourse structure in embodied conversational agents. In: Workshop on Representing, Annotating, and Evaluating Non-Verbal and Verbal Communicative Acts to Achieve Contextual Embodied Agents, Autonomous Agents 2001 Conference (2001)
5. McNeill, D.: Hand and Mind: What Gestures Reveal about Thought. University of Chicago Press, Chicago (1992)
6. Kita, S., van Gijn, I., van der Hulst, H.: Movement phases in signs and co-speech gestures, and their transcription by human coders. In: Wachsmuth, I., Fröhlich, M. (eds.) GW 1997. LNCS, vol. 1371, pp. 23–35. Springer, Heidelberg (1998)
7. Kendon, A.: Gesture – Visible Action as Utterance. Cambridge University Press, Cambridge (2004)
8. McNeill, D.: Gesture and Thought. University of Chicago Press, Chicago (2005)
9. Lee, J., Marsella, S.: Learning a Model of Speaker Head Nods using Gesture Corpora. In: 7th International Conference on Autonomous Agents and Multi-Agent Systems, Budapest, Hungary (2009)
10. Faten Khalil, J.L., Wang, H.: A framework of combining markov model with association rules for predicting web page accesses. In: Proc. Fifth Australasian Data Mining Conference, AusDM 2006, pp. 177–184 (2006)
11. Arikan, O., Forsyth, D.A., O'Brien, J.F.: Motion synthesis from annotations. ACM Transactions on Graphics 22(3), 402–408 (2003)
12. Pullen, K., Bregler, C.: Motion capture assisted animation: Texturing and synthesis. ACM Transactions on Graphics 21(3), 501–508 (2002)
13. Arikan, O., Forsyth, D.A.: Interactive motion generation from examples. ACM Transactions on Graphics 21(3), 483–490 (2002)
14. Kovar, L., Gleicher, M., Pighin, F.: Motion graphs. ACM Transactions on Graphics 21(3), 473–482 (2002)
15. Wang, J., Bodenheimer, B.: Synthesis and evaluation of linear motion transitions. ACM Transactions on Graphics 27(1), 1:1–1:15 (2008)
16. Stone, M., DeCarlo, D., Oh, I., Rodriguez, C., Stere, A., Lees, A., Bregler, C.: Speaking with hands: creating animated conversational characters from recordings of human performance. ACM Transactions on Graphics 23(3), 506–513 (2004)
17. Thiebaux, M., Marshall, A., Marsella, S., Kallman, M.: Smartbody: Behavior realization for embodied conversational agents. In: Proc. of 7th Int. Conf. on Autonomous Agents and Multiagent Systems, AAMAS 2008 (2008)
18. Vicon, Inc. (2008), http://www.vicon.com
19. Kipp, M.: Anvil: The video annotation research tool (2008), http://www.anvil-software.de/
20. Egges, A., Molet, T., Magnenat-Thalmann, N.: Personalised real-time idle motion synthesis. In: 12th Pacific Conference on Computer Graphics and Applications, October 2004, pp. 121–130 (2004)

ION Framework – A Simulation Environment for Worlds with Virtual Agents

Marco Vala, Guilherme Raimundo, Pedro Sequeira, Pedro Cuba, Rui Prada, Carlos Martinho, and Ana Paiva

INESC-ID and IST - Technical University of Lisbon
marco.vala@inesc-id.pt

Abstract. Agents cannot be decoupled from their environment. An agent perceives and acts in a world and the model of the world influences how the agent makes decisions. Most systems with virtual embodied agents simulate the environment within a specific realization engine such as the graphics engine. As a consequence, these agents are bound to a particular kind of environment which compromises their reusability across different applications. We propose the ION Framework, a framework for simulating virtual environments which separates the simulation environment from the realization engine. In doing so, it facilitates the integration and reuse of the several components of the system. The ION Framework was used to create several 3D virtual worlds populated with autonomous embodied agents that were tested with hundreds of users.

Keywords: Virtual Environment Simulation, Agent-Based Modelling, Embodied Agents, Guidelines.

1 Introduction

A virtual agent is by definition an entity that senses, reasons and acts within an environment. Usually, these agents have some components related to their behaviour, referred as the *agent mind*, and components related to their embodiment in a particular environment, referred as the *agent body*.

The environment is often simulated by the *realization engine*[1] that keeps a part of the simulation model while it provides a graphical representation to the elements in the simulation, including the agents. The *realization engine* plays the role of virtual space inhabited by the agents.

However, these *realization engines* do not provide the appropriate abstraction level required by the agents. For this reason, the minds are generally dependent on the environment and on a particular form of embodiment which, in turn, leads to components which are difficult to reuse across applications.

We argue that we need a set of guidelines to make components less interdependent thus fostering reusability across different applications. Our approach

---

[1] By realization engine we refer to a set of components that usually includes the graphics engine and the physics engine.

Zs. Ruttkay et al. (Eds.): IVA 2009, LNAI 5773, pp. 418–424, 2009.

separates the simulation environment from the *realization engine*. We named this simulation environment ION Framework[2].

The remainder of the paper is organised as follows. First we look at related work. Then, we describe the ION Framework and depict the guidelines of our approach using a concrete example. Then we present some other case studies to further demonstrate our results. Finally we draw some conclusions and outline future work.

2   Related Work

Several tools exist to aid in the development of autonomous embodied agents. Some of these tools support the development of the mind like Soar [11], JAM [7] or JESS [5]. Researchers frequently adopt game engines like Unreal Tournament [4], Source [16] or Ogre [14] for the embodiment.

Recent efforts from the virtual agents community lead to the SAIBA initiative [13] which specifies a framework for creating Embodied Conversational Agents (ECA). This framework lead to the definition of the FML (Function Markup Language) and BML (Behaviour Markup Language), which are an effort to provide a common language between the several components that form an ECA. There are currently systems[3] that use these markup languages like SmartBody [15] or ACE (ARticulated Communicator Engine) [10].

However, for most of these tools, the simulation environment depends on the application being developed. The components are integrated in a common environment but become dependent on each other. A good example is the use of game engines. The components around, like the agent's mind, usually become too dependent on how the game engine handles the embodiment and the environment, which reduces reusability across other applications.

On the other hand, we can borrow some ideas from tools to create agent-based simulations. Some provide conceptual frameworks and templates for the design and implementation of agent-based models, like Swarm [12] or JADE [8]. Other provide a complete simulation environment which is suitable for rapid development of prototype models, like NetLogo [17] or Breve [9].

3   ION Framework

Broadly speaking, a simulation using the ION Framework consists of a set of *Elements* whose state changes in a discrete manner over time when the simulation is updated.

Furthermore, to regulate the interactions between the several elements, the framework enforces a set guidelines which are applied to all the intervenients[4]

---

[2] The ION Framework is open-source under GNU LGPL license.

[3] For a complete list of tools and components within the SAIBA initiative go to http://wiki.mindmakers.org/projects:bml:main (updated in April 2009).

[4] By intervenient we mean any entity that intervenes in the simulation (either internal or external to the simulation).

in the simulation. These guidelines are: 1) coherent access to information, 2) mediation of conflicts, 3) active and passive gathering of information, and 4) dynamic configuration changes.

In order to introduce the framework and the guidelines behind it, we will present examples of FearNot! [1] which is an application aimed at reducing the bullying phenomena in schools. Several virtual characters interact with each other in a 3D environment throughout several episodes (Figure 1). Each episode portraits a situation involving a conflict between a victim and a bully. The user behaves like a friend of the victim and gives advices about the way the victim should solve its problems.

Fig. 1. FearNot!

3.1   Coherent Access to Information

Picture an example of two agents from FearNot!, John (the victim) and Luke (the bully), that decide to move depending on the position of each other. At each update cycle John looks at Luke and if he is too near John backs away. On the other hand, Luke tries not to be very far from John. So he looks at John and if he is farther than a given distance he moves closer.

Consider that John is the first to decide. John looks at Luke and since he has not moved yet they are still at a comfortable distance. Given this, John decides not to move. Next, Luke looks at John and he decides to move closer. Only Luke moves.

Now consider that Luke is the first to decide. As previously, he decides to move closer. But, when John looks at Luke, Luke is now too close because he moved closer. Thus, John decides to move away. The final outcome is that both agents have moved.

Notice that although the initial simulation state was the same for the two cases the outcome was different. The outcome depends on whom decided first and we believe this is undesirable in some situations.

The ION Framework provides *coherent access to information* and guarantees that all the intervenients get the same information if they do the same query to the simulation at a given instant. The agents always get the information as it was at the end of the last update cycle regardless of subsequent changes that will be carried out in the next update.

Therefore, all modifications to the simulation state in the ION Framework are not immediately carried out. We can schedule *Requests* on *Elements* which are handled at a later time during a specific phase of the update cycle denominated *Process Requests Phase*.

In the previous example, John and Luke were modelled with the ION Framework. Thus the outcome is always the first situation (only Luke moves) regardless of which agent decides first. This is due to the fact that even if one agent decides to move it will in practice only schedule a *Request* to do so. Therefore, both agents look at the same state of the simulation even if one of them has decided to change it before the other.

3.2   Mediation of Conflicts

In the ION Framework, changes to the simulation state are performed synchronously. As we have seen it ensures coherent access to information. But it also implies that intervenients are seen as acting simultaneously at each update cycle. Therefore, conflicts may arise between actions that try to modify the same portion of the simulation state at the same time.

An example from FearNot! happens when Luke and Paul (the bully assistant) decide to push John at the same time. We can have several outcomes: 1) John is pushed by Luke, 2) John is pushed by Paul, 3) John is pushed by both of them with their combined strength, etc.

The ION Framework ensures the *mediation of conflicts*. The previous setting corresponds to scheduling two push *Requests* on the *Element* that represents John in the simulation. When the *Process Requests Phase* takes place, a conflict arises and a decision has to be made on how the two push *Requests* are executed. The outcome will depend on the *Request Handler* that John has at that moment for executing push *Requests*.

Requests Handlers determine how *Requests* in general are executed. Every state change in the framework is performed by a *Request Handler*. This mechanism systematizes the mediation of conflicts by transmitting possible conflicting *Requests* to the same *Request Handler* which then acts as mediator.

3.3   Active and Passive Information Gathering

In the examples discussed so far the agents pro-actively gather information. John, Luke and Paul check each other's position when they need.

However, there are several circumstances in which it is preferable to be notified of a change in the simulation state. For example, in FearNot! there is an agent that manages the stories being created: the Story Facilitator. In order to decide when to advance to the next act, the Story Facilitator needs to be aware of certain events, such as whenever Luke goes away after bullying John. Instead of constantly polling for such information, it can be notified when that event happens.

The ION Framework offers both *active and passive gathering of information* which is the possibility of getting information by querying the simulation in a proactive way, or by subscribing a particular bit of information which will be delivered later. We use the observer pattern [6] to provide an event-driven paradigm. Hence, every time a change occurs in a particular *Element*, a corresponding *Event* is raised.

Similarly to what happens with *Requests*, *Events* are not processed immediately. Likewise, their handling is performed by *Event Handlers* at a specific phase of the update cycle denominated *Process Events Phase*. At that time all intervenients registered to get a particular *Event* are notified if that *Event* happened. Figure 2 depicts the simulation update cycle with both its phases.

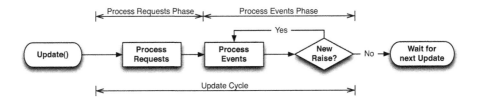

Fig. 2. Update Cycle

It should now be evident that there is a fundamental difference between *Requests* and *Events*. While *Requests* are the desired changes to the simulation state, *Events* are the information of which changes effectively took place.

3.4   Dynamic Configuration Changes

The ION Framework allows *dynamic configuration changes* and it is possible to completely change the simulation behaviour in runtime. We can add or remove *Elements* to the simulation, but also change how these *Elements* inherently behave by modifying their *Request Handlers*.

4   Case Studies

The ION Framework was used to model the virtual worlds in FearNot! [1] and Orient [2] which were tested with hundreds of users. It is also being used in the ongoing EU-funded project LIREC.

One of the most interesting aspects in FearNot! (introduced in the section 3) comes from the fact that characters are *Elements* of the ION Framework. These *Elements* provide an abstraction layer through *Requests* and *Events* which act as an interface between the mind components created in FAtiMA [3] and the embodiment provided by Ogre 3D [14]. Thus, each component can be replaced without having to change the rest of the environment.

A good example of how different applications can reuse components using the ION Framework is Orient. Orient is an application to enhance intercultural sensitivity towards people from other cultures. It has a very similar architecture and it used most of the components developed for FearNot!. A particular example was the interaction with users. In FearNot! the user was modelled as any other *Element* of the simulation and it had a single form of interaction (text input). Even though in Orient the user interacts with different devices (Wii, DanceMat, Mobile Phones) it had no impact on the other components of the simulation that still receive the same *Events* from the user *Element* regardless of the input device.

In LIREC we are exploring different forms of embodiment through the notion of competences. Competences represent specific abilities that the agent has (e.g. speech or facial expression). We are modeling these competences as ION *Elements* with a set of *Requests* and *Events* which are independent from a particular implementation. This way it is possible to change their implementation and the mind will still be able to use them as before. This possibility is particularly interesting in migration scenarios where the mind roams across different platforms which have different implementations for the same competence.

5   Conclusions

This paper introduced the ION Framework, a framework for simulating virtual environments. It uses a set of guidelines to regulate the interactions between the several elements, namely: 1) coherent access to information, 2) mediation of conflicts, 3) active and passive gathering of information, and 4) dynamic configuration changes.

Several examples depict how the ION Framework was used to address common problems in applications with multiple autonomous embodied agents.

In the future, the generic concepts we offer can be extended with patterns of use, providing an higher-level pool of components which may suit more particular applications or domains. We believe that it can establish a common ground that helps the community to share their research efforts.

Acknowledgments

This work was partially supported by European Community (EC) and is currently funded by the LIREC project FP7-215554. Guilherme Raimundo and Pedro Sequeira were supported by the Portuguese Foundation for Science and Technology (FCT), grant references SFRH/BD/25725/2005 and SFRH/BD/38681/2007.

The authors are solely responsible for the content of this publication. It does not represent the opinion of the EC and FCT, and the EC and FCT are not responsible for any use that might be made of data appearing therein.

References

1. Aylett, R., Louchart, S., Dias, J., Paiva, A., Vala, M., Woods, S., Hall, L.E.: Unscripted narrative for affectively driven characters. IEEE Computer Graphics and Applications 26(3), 42–52 (2006)
2. Aylett, R., Paiva, A., Vannini, N., Enz, S., Andre, E.: But that was in another country: agents and intercultural empathy. In: AAMAS (2009)
3. Dias, J., Paiva, A.: Feeling and reasoning: A computational model for emotional characters. In: EPIA, pp. 127–140 (2005)
4. Epic-Games. Unreal tournament website, `http://www.unrealtournament.com/` (last seen April 2009) (2008)
5. Friedman-Hill, E.: Jess in Action. Java Rule-based Systems. Manning Publications (2003)
6. Gamma, E., Helm, R., Johnson, R., Vlissides, J.: Design patterns: elements of reusable object-oriented software. Addison-Wesley Longman Publishing Co., Inc., Boston (1995)
7. Huber, M.J., Leto, J.: Jam: A bdi-theoretic mobile agent architecture. In: Proceedings of the Third International Conference on Autonomous Agents, Seattle, Washington, USA. ACM Press, New York (1999)
8. JADE. Java agent development framework (2009), `http://jade.tilab.com/` (last seen April 2009)
9. Klein, J.: Breve: a 3d environment for the simulation of decentralized systems and artificial life. In: ICAL 2003: Proceedings of the eighth international conference on Artificial life, Cambridge, MA, USA, pp. 329–334. MIT Press, Cambridge (2003)
10. Kopp, S.: Articulated communicator engine (ace) (2000), `http://www.techfak.uni-bielefeld.de/skopp/max.html` (last seen April 2009)
11. Laird, J.E., Newell, A., Rosenbloom, P.S.: Soar: An architecture for general intelligence. Artificial Intelligence 1(33), 1–64 (1987)
12. Minar, N., Burkhart, R., Langton, C., Askenazi.: The swarm simulation system, a toolkit for building multi-agent simulations. working paper 96-06-042 (1996)
13. SAIBA-Initiative. Situation agent intention behavior animation (2009), `http://wiki.mindmakers.org/projects:saiba:main` (last seen April 2009)
14. Steve, S.: Object-oriented graphics rendering engine (ogre) (2009), `http://www.ogre3d.org/` (last seen April 2009)
15. Thiébaux, M., Marsella, S., Marshall, A.N., Kallmann, M.: Smartbody: behavior realization for embodied conversational agents. In: AAMAS, pp. 151–158 (2008)
16. Valve. Source game engine (2004), `http://source.valvesoftware.com/` (last seen April 2009)
17. Wilensky, U.: Netlogo (1999)

DTask and LiteBody: Open Source, Standards-Based Tools for Building Web-Deployed Embodied Conversational Agents

Timothy Bickmore, Daniel Schulman, and George Shaw

Northeastern University College of Computer & Information Science,
360 Huntington Ave, WVH202, Boston, MA 02115, USA
{bickmore,schulman,shaw}@ccs.neu.edu

Abstract. Two tools for developing embodied conversational agents and deploying them over the world-wide web to standard web browsers are presented. DTask is a hierarchical task decomposition-based dialogue planner, based on the CEA-2018 task description language standard. LiteBody is an extensible, web-based BML renderer that runs in most contemporary web browsers with no additional software and provides a conversational virtual agent with a range of conversational nonverbal behavior adequate for many user-agent interaction applications. Together, these tools provide a complete platform for deploying web-based conversational agents, and are actively being used on two health counseling applications.

Keywords: Dialogue planning, embodied conversational agent, relational agent, open source, behavior markup language.

1   Introduction

There is a growing interest in building common, standards-based software frameworks to support Embodied Conversational Agent (ECA) development, such as the SAIBA/ BML/FML standardization efforts [8]. The motivation for this work is to reduce duplication of effort in developing new systems, and to enable modules from different developers to be assembled into working systems. The approach taken in much of this work is to identify a core set of common functionality, but then to define a framework in which all possible ECA functions and future extensions can be accommodated.

In contrast, for many applications, developers only need a tiny subset of this functionality. An example is an application in which there is only one ECA and it only talks directly to the user while displaying a well-defined range of nonverbal conversational behavior. Examples of such systems include pedagogical agents [6], health counseling agents [2, 3], and direction-giving agents [4]. For such applications, many existing tools represent significantly more overhead and developer learning time than should be necessary. Further, such applications are constrained enough in their functionality that they have the potential to be deployed over the web using standard browsers without additional software, greatly increasing the possibility of wide dissemination of ECAs built this way.

Zs. Ruttkay et al. (Eds.): IVA 2009, LNAI 5773, pp. 425–431, 2009.

Our approach has been to develop a minimal ECA framework for this class of applications, while still adhering to available standards as much as possible. The current result of our effort is two tools—a dialogue engine and an ECA renderer—which, together, provide a complete framework in which user interface ECAs with rich dialogue content can be built and immediately deployed over the web. In addition, because they are based on several standards, these tools should facilitate sharing of dialogue, character animation, and user interface content among researchers and application developers.

2   The DTask Dialogue Engine

DTask is a dialogue planner designed to model and execute system-directed dialogue, with multiple-choice user input. Dialogue is specified declaratively, as a hierarchical task decomposition. The DTask application functions as a network server and relies on a user interface client to provide an interface, such as an ECA, to the user. In our current work, LiteBody (described in Section 3) provides this client functionality, and includes a BML-driven ECA.

2.1   CEA-2018

Following Shared Plans theory [7, 9], we treat dialogue as a collaboration in which participants coordinate their action towards achieving a shared goal. The intentional structure of dialogue is modeled as a hierarchical task decomposition: sets of recipes (goal decompositions) and subtasks which may be used to achieve the overall goal of the collaboration. Dialogue context is modeled as a runtime focus stack, representing the subgoals currently adopted. DTask's hierarchical task model is an implementation of the ANSI/CEA-2018 standard [10], which is itself inspired by the COLLAGEN dialogue engine [11]. CEA-2018 specifies an XML-based representation for a set of tasks, and a set of recipes which can be used to achieve those tasks. A recipe describes one way of decomposing a goal into a partially-ordered set of subgoals and/or primitive actions. ECMAScript [1] is used to specify task preconditions and postconditions, recipe applicability conditions, constraints on task parameters, and grounding of atomic tasks.

DTask extends CEA-2018 with a mechanism for declarative specification of dialogue. A turn of dialogue is specified as an adjacency pair template (APT): an agent utterance and a list of possible user responses, which comprise a primitive action in the task description. An APT achieves a particular task in the task model; there may be an arbitrary number of APTs, as well as recipes, which can achieve a task.

The surface form of agent and user utterances may include both natural language, and variables to be filled in at the time the utterance is produced. Generally, nonverbal behavior of the ECA is not specified in the dialogue model, with the intent that it be added automatically at runtime by a system such as BEAT [5]. However, explicit annotations can be added in BML, or in any other format understood by the user interface client.

2.2 DTask Example

Fig. 1 shows an example of a fragment of a DTask dialogue model. This example implements a task ("RitualIntro") which is a short ritualized greeting to the user. There is one recipe provided which can achieve this task ("DoRitualIntro"), consisting of two subtasks ("HowAreYou" and "RespondToIntro").

Tasks can have locally-scoped input and output parameters. The "HowAreYou" task has one output slot, which defines the semantics of the user's utterance which will be represented. In this case, the semantics is simply a boolean value representing whether the user asked a reciprocal question of the agent.

The "RespondToIntro" task has one input parameter, and constraints on the recipe are used to bind the output of the earlier task to this input. The example shows one dialogue turn which can be used to achieve this task in the case where the user requested a reciprocal response. There may be any number of other dialogue turns specified with different applicability conditions.

```
<task id="RitualIntro"/>
<subtasks id="DoRitualIntro" goal="RitualIntro">
   <step name="ask" task="HowAreYou"/>
   <step name="respond" task="RespondToIntro"/>
   <binding slot="$respond.reciprocal" value="$ask.reciprocal"/>
</subtasks>
<task id="HowAreYou">
   <output name="reciprocal" type="boolean"/>
   <d:turn>
      <d:agent>Hi {USER.name}. How are you?</d:agent>
      <d:user>
         <d:say>I'm good.  How are you?</d:say>
         <d:result slot="reciprocal" value="true"/>
      </d:user>
      <d:user>
         <d:say>Good.</d:say>
         <d:result slot="reciprocal" value="false"/>
      </d:user>
   </d:turn>
</task>
<task id="RespondToIntro">
   <input name="reciprocal" type="boolean"/>
   <d:turn>
      <applicable>$this.reciprocal</applicable>
      <d:agent>Great. Thanks for asking!</d:agent>
   ...
```

Fig. 1. Example DTask Task Descriptions and Recipes

3 The LiteBody User Interface ECA

Many ECA applications could ideally be fielded on users' home computers where users could interact with the agents at their convenience. However, hardware requirements for 3D graphics and unwillingness to install custom software, especially for occasional use, represent barriers to wide dissemination of many of these ECA applications. LiteBody is a web-enabled, ECA-based user interface which renders an ECA given BML commands from a dialogue engine. This is accomplished, in part, by synthesizing speech on a server and dynamically streaming it to the user's browser as needed. The application also presents the user with a range of input widgets (under control of the dialogue engine) to elicit user contributions to the conversation, and returns input information to the dialogue engine for interpretation.

The ECA provides a range of common conversational nonverbal behavior, including: visemes and eyebrow raises synchronized to speech, head nods, facial displays of emotion, posture shifts, gazing at and away from the user, and idle behavior (blinking, etc.). While the character can appear only in (continuously variable) mid-range to close-up shots facing the user, it can hold up and point at 2D objects (e.g., images, documents, web pages) in front of it. The background behind the character can be any dynamically loadable image (actually any Flash file, including animations). The interface also supports an extensible set of user input widgets, but currently provides multiple choice input buttons (Fig. 2) and a free text input box.

Fig. 2. Example LiteBody Character with Multiple Choice User Input Buttons

3.1 LiteBody Architecture

The LiteBody architecture consists of a Dialogue Server, a Text-To-Speech (TTS) Server, and a web-based Flash Client (Fig. 3).

The Dialogue Server represents the LiteBody interface point for a dialogue engine or other application controlling the ECA. In response to a single BML command, the Dialogue Server causes the TTS Server to produce a web-accessible mp3-format audio file of the ECA's speech, along with an XML document that contains speech-synchronized timing information for animation and other actions to be performed by the ECA in the Flash Client. The XML document also contains the URL for the audio file that the Flash Client will use to stream the speech mp3 from. Once the audio file has finished production, the XML document is transferred to the Flash Client for execution.

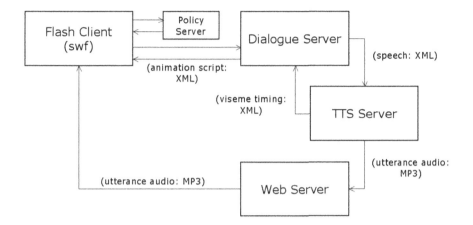

Fig. 3. LiteBody Architecture

The TTS Server uses any speech synthesizer that is compatible with the Microsoft Speech API (v5.1) to generate mp3 audio files for download to the FlashClient (via any standard web server) along with phoneme and word boundary timing information.

The Flash Client is built entirely in Adobe Flash using the ActionScript programming language and the standard Flash rendering engine for onscreen display. Flash provides a lightweight, near ubiquitous platform on which to deliver dynamic multimedia content via the web.

After being downloaded into the user's browser and initializing, the Flash Client makes a persistent socket connection with the Dialogue Server. Once a socket connection is made, the Dialogue Server may begin sending XML actions to the client for execution. Upon receipt of an action, the client inserts a new ActionObject into its animation queue. An ActionObject, contains any number of "untimed" commands such as loading documents or audio files, as well as any number of "timed" commands that must be synchronized with the speech audio. These timed actions each carry a timestamp in milliseconds relative to the beginning of performance of the action.

When the Flash Client begins a new action by taking the next ActionObject in the queue and sending it to the AnimationEngine, it first performs any untimed commands, such as the loading of a speech audio file. Flash has sophisticated streaming capabilities, which we leverage in order to begin realizing an utterance before the audio file has finished loading to minimize latencies between speaking turns. Once the audio file begins playing, a timer starts and the performance of timed actions begins, synchronized with the playback.

When the AnimationEngine determines that a particular action is due to be performed, it sends a message to the Rendering Engine telling it to make the appropriate changes to the onscreen ECA representation (for animation actions) or to perform other necessary commands (such as loading an external file or document). Animation actions are realized by either moving Flash's playhead to a new frame in the active movie clip, or by swapping the active movie clip for a new one.

Upon completion of all of an ActionObject's actions, a message is sent to the Controller. The Controller relays a message to the Dialogue Server that an action has been completed, and then checks the queue to see if another action is waiting. If not, the Controller either waits for another action to arrive from the server, or generates an idle action such as an eye-blink or a posture shift for the ECA.

User input actions are handled in a similar fashion to other actions, except that there is no timing information associated with a user input, and realization of the input interface is handled via a UserInputEngine class.

Fig. 4 shows an example BML command that LiteBody can execute. In this command, the ECA is being instructed to speak with the audio file URL specified in the "speech" command, and the visemes and their timing relative to the start of speech specified in the "lips" commands. BML extensions ("rag" namespace) are used to load a new background behind the character, modify the camera shot by zooming in to the ECA over the first 300ms of speech, and changing the ECA's facial expression to "happy" between 500ms and 800ms relative to the start of speech.

```
<BML>
<speech id="s1" start="0" type="xxx/mp3"
ref="http://localhost:8080/speech/file0000000001.wav.mp3" text="" />
<rag:background url="data/checkers.swf" />
<rag:zoom time="0" duration="300" timestamp="0" value="0.2" />
<rag:expression time="500" duration="300" timestamp="500" value="happy"/>
<lips viseme="1" time="870" />
<lips viseme="1" time="940" />
<lips viseme="9" time="1140" />
…
</BML>
```

Fig. 4. Example LiteBody BML Command

The Flash Client is designed to be extensible in several ways. Arbitrary user input widgets may be added to elicit information or conversational input from the user in a wide variety of ways. An input widget can be any Flash movie, with the only requirement being that it presents a button to submit its input, and returns the user input as a string to the server.

New animation sequences can also be added to the Flash Client with minimal effort. After adding the animation artwork, a new named keyframe is added that carries the name of the new animation, and the name and duration of the animation is added to a configuration file.

5   Conclusions and Future Plans

Our goals in developing DTask and LiteBody were to make the development of a certain class of conversational virtual humans significantly easier, allow for extensibility and modularity through adherence to public standards, and provide the ability for wide dissemination of developed systems over the web. These tools are currently being used in two health education and health behavior change projects funded by the

US National Institutes of Health. We have a commitment to our funding agency to release these tools as open source for the benefit of the virtual human and health informatics research communities, and welcome collaborations on the further development and application of these tools.

Acknowledgments. Thanks to Candace Sidner, Dolphy Fernandes, Rukmal Fernando, Langxuan Yin and the other members of the Relational Agents Group for their help with this work. This project was supported by NIH National Library of Medicine Grant R21LM008995.

References

1. Ecma International, http://www.ecma-international.org
2. Bickmore, T., Pfeifer, L., Paasche-Orlow, M.: Health Document Explanation by Virtual Agents. Intelligent Virtual Agents, Paris, 183–196 (2007)
3. Bickmore, T., Picard, R.: Establishing and Maintaining Long-Term Human-Computer Relationships. ACM Transactions on Computer Human Interaction 12(2), 293–327
4. Cassell, J., Stocky, T., Bickmore, T., Gao, Y., Nakano, Y., Ryokai, K., Tversky, D., Vaucelle, C., Vilhjálmsson, H.: MACK: Media lab Autonomous Conversational Kiosk. In: Imagina 2002, Monte Carlo (2002)
5. Cassell, J., Vilhjálmsson, H., Bickmore, T.: BEAT: The Behavior Expression Animation Toolkit. In: SIGGRAPH 2001, Los Angeles, CA, pp. 477–486 (2001)
6. Graesser, A., et al.: AutoTutor: A simulation of a human tutor. Cognitive Systems Research, 1
7. Grosz, B., Sidner, C.: Attention, Intentions, and the Structure of Discourse. Computational Linguistics 12(3), 175–204
8. Kopp, S., Krenn, B., Marsella, S., Marshall, A.N., Pelachaud, C., Pirker, H., Thórisson, K., Vilhjálmsson, H.: Towards a Common Framework for Multimodal Generation: The Behavior Markup Language. In: Intelligent Virtual Agents, Marina Del Rey, CA (2006)
9. Lochbaum, K.: A Collaborative Planning Model of Intentional Structure. Computational Linguistics 24(4), 525–572
10. Rich, C.: Building Task-Based User Interfaces With ANSI/CEA-2018. IEEE Computer (to appear)
11. Rich, C., Sidner, C.L.: COLLAGEN: A collaboration manager for software interface agents. User Modeling and User-Adapted Interaction 8(3-4), 315–350

A Combined Semantic and Motion Capture Database for Real-Time Sign Language Synthesis

Charly Awad[1], Nicolas Courty[1], Kyle Duarte[1], Thibaut Le Naour[1], and Sylvie Gibet[1,2]

[1] Université de Bretagne Sud, Laboratoire VALORIA, Bâtiment Yves Coppens, F-56017 Vannes, France
[2] IRISA, Campus de Beaulieu, F-35042 Rennes, France

Abstract. Over the past decade, motion capture data has become a popular research tool, and motion databases have grown exponentially. Indexing, querying, and retrieving data has thus become more difficult, and has necessitated innovative approaches to using these databases. Our aim is to make this approach feasible for virtual agents signing in French Sign Language (LSF), taking into account the semantic information implicitly contained in language data. We thus structure a database in two autonomous units, taking advantage of differing indexing methods within each. This allows us to effectively retrieve captured motions to produce LSF animations. We describe our methods for querying motion in the semantic database, computing transitory segments between concatenated signs, and producing realistic animations of a virtual LSF signer.

1 Introduction

Designing virtual humans that communicate in signed languages has been a serious challenge to the virtual agent animation community. Unlike gestures that accompany spoken language utterances, the signs of a signed language are themselves linguistic utterances; thus, signs require a more exacting understanding of their phonological structure in order to preserve communicative intent.

Our work sits squarely in the domain of computational linguistics as we consider the dynamics of French Sign Language (LSF) with the goal of designing a language-synthesis database. The structure we propose below considers the needs of the signal processing community by storing and segmenting motion-captured data for subsequent retrieval and processing, and also addresses the linguistic need to structure signs as pairs of semantic and phonological information. By keeping signal and annotation data separate, we are able to quickly search semantic data for a desired sign, retrieve its related motion chunk from the signal data, and send the query results to an animation engine, which creates transitions to complete a novel sign utterance.

Zs. Ruttkay et al. (Eds.): IVA 2009, LNAI 5773, pp. 432–438, 2009.

2   Related Work

Previous work on virtual intelligent agents focuses largely on modeling communicative gestures and sign language signs with high level specification languages, and on data-driven animation of virtual characters.

Several gesture taxonomies have already been proposed in [1] and [2], some of which identify specific phases that appear in gestures and signs [3]. Recent studies dedicated to expressive gesture rely on segmenting and annotating gestures for later re-synthesis [4]. In addition, a recent XML unified framework called BML [5] has been defined to contain several abstraction levels; BML interprets a planned multimodal behavior into a realized behavior, and may integrate different planning and control systems.

Regarding gesture generation, researchers have largely attempted to translate a gestural description into a sequence of commands that can be interpreted by an animation engine. Most of these works concern pure synthesis methods, for instance by computing specified postural goals in 3-dimensional space using inverse kinematics techniques, such as in [6,7,8]. Another approach uses annotated videos of human behaviors to synchronize speech and gestures, and a statistical model to extract specific gestural profiles; from textual input, a gestural script is formed and interpreted by a motion simulation engine [9].

Alternatively, data-driven animation methods can be substituted for these pure synthesis methods, as we will show. Much of the previous work on data-driven animation emphasizes the adapted re-use of captured motion chunks for creating new sequences of motion. Very few approaches deal with both motion-captured data and its implicit semantic content, and nearly nothing concerns communicative gestures. In [10], Arikan et al. use a semi-automatic annotation algorithm consisting of a manual annotation process paired with a Support Vector Machine to build animations of previously-captured movements.

As this work is the closest in nature to what we will discuss here, there are clearly new avenues to discover regarding the paired use of captured motion and semantic annotations for motion synthesis.

3   Sign Language Modeling

Phonetic studies of languages consider the formation of linguistic signals on both a simultaneous and sequential basis. At any moment in the signal, a series of features align to create a posture, and a string of postures combine temporally to create the signal.

Liddell and Johnson [11,12] describe Timing postures in signed languages as having Hand Configuration, Placement, and Orientation specifications, and propose complex notational schema to elaborate each of these domains for the purposes of detailed phonological study. Our goals do not require such phonetic specificity, but we must still consider the simultaneous and sequential nature of signs to create credible animations of novel sign streams. Here, we approach the sequential structure of signs and sign streams with semantic and phonological annotation files; on the contrary, simultaneous features of signs are encoded in the motion-capture data and manipulated by the animation engine.

In annotating our data, we adopt Kita et al's [3] model for dividing signs into general sections, represented as

$$Unit = \{Phrase\} \tag{1}$$

$$Phrase = [Preparation]Stroke[Retraction] \tag{2}$$

where { } requires at least one repetition, and [ ] is optional. In linguistic terms, Strokes are linguistic units (or signs) that provide semantic content to the discourse; Preparations and Retractions, which together form transitions, are non-linguistic segments that do not offer grammaticalized semantic information.

Despite lacking semantic value, transitions in signed languages are phonologically active, differing greatly from the easily hidden silent transitions of spoken language discourse. As signed language transitions are just as visible as the signs they connect, they must be fluid movements that allow the sign stream to continue intelligibly.

The difficulty of our assignment, then, is that only a very small part of the transition between two captured signs, if any of it, can be used in novel sequence animation, since each sign will be taken out of its recorded context, and its context-dependent transitions will therefore be rendered useless. We thus rely on the animation engine to consider the multimodal structure of transitions, creating transitions between two concatenated signs on a joint-by-joint basis.

4   Database Architecture

Figure 1 gives an overview of our methodology. In order to accelerate motion retrieval, data is indexed in two ways: first, by its annotated semantic content, and second, as raw data for synthesis purposes. Once motion is selected and retrieved, it is sent to the animation engine.

4.1   Data Indexation

After the data is annotated semantically, annotation files can be stored in a database in one of two ways: to optimize document load time, files can be stored sequentially without modifications, or to optimize query time, each file can be stored as an individual node. Given the small size of our semantic database, we have chosen the first method.

Due to the separate processing methods we use on each type of file, motion capture files are stored in a separate database from that for the annotation files. In preparation for processing, motion capture files are loaded from binary data and interpreted only once. The sequence of frames is divided into packets of p frames, such that one annotated motion of n frames will produce $\left[\frac{n}{p}\right]$ entries in the database.

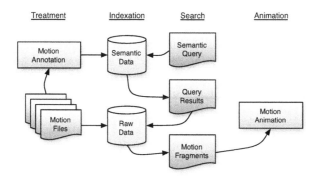

Fig. 1. Overview of the database architecture

Fragmenting motions in the database is advantageous for our purposes because only the small portion of the motion that we query will have to be reconstructed in the memory. The trade off, however, is that motion fragments increase the number of entries in the database, which could negatively affect search time.

4.2   Motion Search and Retrieval

Retrieving motion from the database begins by querying the semantic database with single- or multiple-condition queries called *PhaseQuery*. The result is a sequence of segments, with each segment represented by its containing file name and its beginning and ending time stamps. The corresponding motion fragments are then retrieved from the raw data database using these file name and time stamp results.

4.3   Motion Animation

For each pair of selected signs, a concatenation algorithm finds the Retraction phase R_i of the first sign S_i and the Preparation phase P_j of the second sign S_j. The algorithm then extracts the first m_i frames of the phase R_i and the last m_j frames of the phase P_j, so that the transition segment can be interpolated between the p last frames of the first sign and the p first frames of the second sign. The different parameters of the algorithm are chosen according to the desired transition length, as discussed in Sec. 5.2, below.

5   Experiments and Results

5.1   Data Acquisition and Annotation

The data for the present study consists of 82 seconds of LSF signs performed by a deaf signer, recorded by video camera as well as motion capture systems. The data includes two monologues describing weather forecasts and city names, which

were annotated using the ELAN XML annotation tool [13] following the
Kita et al. schema described above. A parent tier was elaborated with a semantic gloss for each sign in the discourse; its child tier described the Kita et al.
portions of the movement using the letters P for Preparation, S for Stroke, or R
for Retraction. With ELAN's signal-processing tool, we synchronized the video
of the signer (upon which we made our annotations) with the motion-capture
BVH data file.

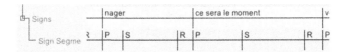

Fig. 2. A screenshot of the ELAN annotation tool. The "Signs" parent tier contains
annotations of the semantic glosses of each sign; the "Sign Segments" child tier is
elaborated with the segment schema proposed by Kita et al.

5.2 Animation Scenarios

Two animation scenarios were developed for the purposes of this study. Scenario
1 replaced signs of timing in the weather forecast sequence with the city name
signs VANNES, MARSEILLE, RENNES, and LE MANS, so that the forecast for
"this morning" became the forecast for Vannes, and so on. These replacements
were chosen to be especially challenging, as they require the right and left hands
to perform very different during the transitions into and out of the inserted city
name signs, as compared to their original motions.

Scenario 2 switched two weather predictions within the original production,
so that the prediction for "today" became the prediction for "Friday" and vice
versa. Again, this manipulation required that the two hands perform different
movements as compared with the original monologue, such as going from rest to
action.

As part of our attempt to make novel transitions between recalled signs appear
fluid and natural, we performed a statistical analysis of the captured transitions
for consideration in animating novel transitions. We analyzed the duration, displacement, and average velocity of the signer's hands over transitions, as shown
in Table 1. The data shows that the time duration of the transitions is more
stable than the displacement or average velocity of the transitions for both the
weather forecast and city names sequences.

Since the weather forecast sequence was more like natural sign sequences than
a simple list of city names, we have assumed that the lengths of transitions in the
course of natural conversations would follow the structure of transitions found
in our weather forecast data, having a mean length of approximately 735 frames
distributed naturally around a standard deviation of 224 frames. In animating
new transitions, we kept their time duration constant using these statistical
guidelines.

Table 1. A statistical analysis of transitions' displacements, durations, and velocities

Sequence	Δx	Δt	$V(t)$
Weather (N=23)	$\overline{\Delta x}=121.9(\sigma=72.7)$	$\overline{\Delta t}=735(\sigma=224)$	$\overline{V}=.168(\sigma=.098)$
Cities (N=14)	$\overline{\Delta x}=223.7(\sigma=131.8)$	$\overline{\Delta t}=1064(\sigma=289)$	$\overline{V}=.236(\sigma=.190)$

5.3   Motion Retrieval and Animation

We tested our architecture on the two scenarios described in Sec. 5.2 and computed the time needed to animate these scenarios, detailed in Table 2. Across our tests, the concatenation process took up a much larger portion of the total animation time than did semantic query and motion retrieval. It should be noted that the concatenation process requires aligning the simultaneous features of two motion chunks in placement and orientation, then concatenating these chunks with a generated transition, to arrive at a new bigger chunk. Thus, the concatenation time depends directly on the number of chunks to be concatenated, as well as each chunk's size in frames. As our motion-capture data had a frame rate of 100 frames per second (FPS), and as video is typically stored at 30 FPS, it should be possible to reduce the amount of frames in the data by two thirds to lower processing time while maintaining motion fluidity.

Table 2. Query and animation times for two synthesis scenarios

	Semantic Query (ms)	Motion Retrieval (ms)	Concaten- ation Time (ms)	Total Time (ms)	Number of Frames	Number of Concaten- ations
Scenario 1	557	1786	13856	20492	7050	8
Scenario 2	144	1418	5337	8733	6094	3

The experiments were run on a MacBook Pro with a 2.4 GHz Intel Core 2 Duo processor and 4 GB of memory, running Mac OSX 10.5.6. Two different database APIs, Oracle Berkeley DB and Tokyo Cabinet[1] yielded approximately similar results. We used a hash map as an index structure in all of our tests.

6   Conclusion

We have proposed a database architecture that utilizes different access methods for two databases, described database queries, and our motion animation process. Importantly, we have shown that the efficiency of sign language synthesis can be increased if data is pre-processed. In future work, we intend to generalize this approach to larger databases of French Sign Language signs containing both semantic and raw data. We would also like to investigate other indexing techniques, and to implement different motion retrieval techniques. In so doing, we

---

[1] http://tokyocabinet.sourceforge.net

hope to produce more complex real-time animations within different discourse contexts, and to evaluate these animations for their quantitative and qualitative merits.

References

1. Kendon, A.: Human gesture. In: Tools, Language and Cognition, pp. 43–62. Cambridge University Press, Cambridge (1993)
2. McNeill, D.: Hand and Mind: What Gestures Reveal about Thought. The University of Chicago Press, Chicago (1992)
3. Kita, S., van Gijn, I., van der Hulst, H.: Movement phases in signs and co-speech gestures, and their transcription by human coders. In: Wachsmuth, I., Fröhlich, M. (eds.) GW 1997. LNCS (LNAI), vol. 1371, pp. 23–36. Springer, Heidelberg (1998)
4. Kipp, M., Neff, M., Kipp, K.H., Albrecht, I.: Towards natural gesture synthesis: Evaluating gesture units in a data-driven approach to gesture synthesis. In: Pelachaud, C., Martin, J.-C., André, E., Chollet, G., Karpouzis, K., Pelé, D. (eds.) IVA 2007. LNCS (LNAI), vol. 4722, pp. 15–28. Springer, Heidelberg (2007)
5. Vilhjálmsson, H.H., Cantelmo, N., Cassell, J., E. Chafai, N., Kipp, M., Kopp, S., Mancini, M., Marsella, S.C., Marshall, A.N., Pelachaud, C., Ruttkay, Z., Thórisson, K.R., van Welbergen, H., van der Werf, R.J.: The behavior markup language: Recent developments and challenges. In: Pelachaud, C., Martin, J.-C., André, E., Chollet, G., Karpouzis, K., Pelé, D. (eds.) IVA 2007. LNCS (LNAI), vol. 4722, pp. 99–111. Springer, Heidelberg (2007)
6. Gibet, S., Lebourque, T., Marteau, P.F.: High-level specification and animation of communicative gestures. Journal of Visual Languages & Computing 12(6), 657–687 (2001)
7. Tolani, D., Goswami, A., Badler, N.I.: Real-time inverse kinematics techniques for anthropomorphic limbs. Graphical Models 62(5), 353–388 (2000)
8. Kopp, S., Wachsmuth, I.: Synthesizing multimodal utterances for conversational agents. Computer Animation and Virtual Worlds 15(1), 39–52 (2004)
9. Neff, M., Kipp, M., Albrecht, I., Seidel, H.P.: Gesture modeling and animation based on a probabilistic re-creation of speaker style. ACM Transactions on Graphics 27(1), 233–251 (2008)
10. Arikan, O., Forsyth, D.A., O'Brien, J.F.: Motion synthesis from annotations. ACM Transactions on Graphics 22(3), 402–408 (2003)
11. Liddell, S.K., Johnson, R.E.: American sign language: The phonological base. Sign Language Studies 64, 195–277 (1989)
12. Johnson, R.E., Liddell, S.K.: Sign language phonetics: Archiecture and description. Forthcoming (a)
13. Elan linguistic annotator, http://www.lat-mpi.eu/tools/elan/

Mediating Performance through Virtual Agents

Gabriella Giannachi[1], Marco Gillies[2], Nick Kaye[1], and David Swapp[3]

[1] Centre for Intermedia, Department of Drama,
University of Exeter, New North Rd, EX 4 4LA, UK
g.giannachi@exeter.ac.uk and n.kaye@exeter.ac.uk
[2] Department of Computing, Goldsmiths, University of London,
New Cross, London SE14 6NW, UK
m.gillies@gold.ac.uk
[3] Department of Computer Science, University College London,
Malet Place, London WC1E 6BT, UK
d.swapp@cs.ucl.ac.uk

Abstract. This paper presents the process of creation of virtual agents used in a virtual reality performance. The performance aimed to investigate how drama and performance could inform the creation of virtual agents and also how virtual reality could raise questions for drama and performance. The virtual agents were based on the performance of 2 actors. This paper describes the process of preparing the actors, capturing their performances and transferring them to the virtual agents. A second set of agents was created using non-professional 'naïve performers' rather than actors.

1 Introduction

This paper presents work that investigates both how research from drama can inform the creation of virtual agents and how virtual agents can create interesting findings for drama. A virtual reality scenario was created which featured two virtual agents that were based on actors' performances and explored the use of acting and non-professional, naïve performance for the creation of an appearance of interaction in an immersive VR theatre. We investigated what aspects of the live performance could be transferred to a virtual agent; what technology was needed to recreate the performance, and what effect the nature of the performance had on the final scenario. By comparison an equivalent scenario was created with untrained, naïve performers. This process builds on work using virtual agents for dramatic performance, starting with the work of Bates [1] to more recent work such as the work or Aylett et al.[2] or Mateas and Stern [3]. It also builds on recent performance work using virtual and mixed reality[4].

2 Context and Design of the Scenario

The scenario was designed with the intention of performing in a type of VR theatre commonly referred to as a CAVE [5]. In contrast with other mediated

Zs. Ruttkay et al. (Eds.): IVA 2009, LNAI 5773, pp. 439–445, 2009.

Fig. 1. Images from the scenario

experiences, the CAVE allows the spectator to inhabit the performance via a more complete immersion of the senses than other media – the environment and the virtual agents are seen stereoscopically in a very wide field of view, and the positions of the spectator's eyes are tracked so that the displayed environment is always perspective correct. This immersion of the visual senses provides good conditions for the elicitation of a sense of 'presence' in the person experiencing the performance (henceforth called the participant) – that is, in some sense they will act in and respond to the simulated environment as if it is real. This notion of presence in VR is subject to various interpretations (e.g. [6,7,8]). An extension of this notion of virtual presence is the idea of social presence [9,10], in which the participant's encounters with virtual agents elicit similar social behaviour to that observed in the real world. For such presence to become manifest, the simulated environment should exhibit some degree of believability to the participant.

A key question for designers of VR simulations, and a specific motivation in the design of our scenario, is how to engender believability. To this end, we wanted to investigate the role of interactivity in enhancing believability (and thus the elicitation of presence) by observing how participants behaved when afforded the opportunity to interact with or become involved in the performance.

The scenario involves an exchange between 2 virtual agents, both of which at some stage attempt to interact with the participant. The context of the perfor-mance is an experimental study, similar in many ways to the type of experimental investigation that commonly takes place in a CAVE. The scenario was thus de-signed as a fictitious psychological experiment conducted by the 2 virtual agents, with assistance from a real agent (the experimenter), who undertakes the tech-nical aspects of preparing the participant for the experiment. Images from the scenario are shown in figure 1.

A further design goal was that any interaction among the virtual agents, the participant and the real agent should be as naturalistic as possible, within the confines of a limited range of possible responses (both physical and verbal) on the part of the virtual agents. For example, the start of the "experiment" is delayed several times due to the virtual agents claiming to be "not ready yet", and then picking fault with the technical setup performed by the real agent. Such activities are designed to allow the participant to establish a sense of an existing relationship among the 3 agents (2 virtual, 1 real) in the performance. In particular, the virtual agents' criticism of the experimenter at an early stage is intended to cause the participant to be more willing to engage with the virtual agents (the subtext being that the experimenter is incompetent and should be ignored). The "experiment" then proceeds, albeit with further delays and interruptions, until a final scene in which the virtual agents appear out of character and they ask the participant direct questions about their experience.

Another important aspect of the scenario is a deliberate attempt to blur the boundary between the preamble and the immersive experience as much as possible, thus challenging the participant's explicit awareness of "being in an experiment". To this end, the participant's first encounter with the virtual agents takes place before they enter the laboratory – they can hear the virtual agents talking to the experimenter while they are still outside the lab.

3   Preparing the Performance

Script . As the final context of the scenario is a virtual reality experiment, it was decided to use a fictional experiment as the basis of the script. This was intended to blur conventional distinctions between virtual and real. The script consists of dialogue and interaction between two virtual agents and an experimenter who is played by the real experimenter. The script also involves interaction with the participant. At times the virtual agents directly address the participant and there are moments when a response from the participant is expected. The participant therefore becomes directly involved in the relationship between the agents. This reveals tensions and mistrust between them, and between the virtual agents and the experimenter, whose competency the agents question and consider.

Rehearal with actors. The actors were prepared using conventional methods for 'naturalistic' theatre performance, based broadly on the work of Stanislavski[11]. This enabled the actors to consistently express and reproduce specific emotional qualities and attitudes through their mode of speech, action and interaction with both the other actors and the hypothetical participant. This preparation included the development of an emotional context and backstory in which their behaviour was accounted for and through which each action to be performed in the scenario may be justified. This process involved, firstly, the detailing of fictional contexts that the script itself does not explicitly reveal, but which the actors use to define and understand the motivation behind the moment-to-moment performance the script demands. For example, during rehearsal it was determined that the male character was anxious about his performance and possibility he was considered incompetent by the female character. This was not explicit in the script but was used inform the emotional context of the actors performance. Through this process and to give expression to this detail, a 'Physical Score' was developed consisting of the movements and actions the actors would perform. These actions were always closely related to both the script and the backstory that had been developed. This process involved numerous iterations over a three-week period. At the end of this the actors were able to produce a consistent performance of plausible behaviour which could convey the sense of a unified and understandable 'character'. The rehearsal also removed any extraneous, unintended or irrelevant activity, which might detract from this aim.

While the rehearsal process resulted in the actors having a clear conception of the motivation behind each of the actions they performed, it would be incorrect to suppose that the actors have a complete grasp of the 'character' and that their conception of that character is conveyed to the participant in the CAVE experiment. In a conventional theatre performance, contemporary theatre and performance theory would suppose that 'character' is constructed by members of the audience from their perception of the actor's performance. This constructed 'character' is a function of the spectator's reading of the performance rather than the actors' intention. This becomes doubly important when a performance is mediated, for example through virtual agents. Some elements may be lost (for example, facial expression could not be captured) and others may be inadvertently added (for example noise or errors in the motion data). These elements are unlikely to be interpreted as simple errors, rather they will probably be interpreted as non-verbal cues that contribute to the participant's understanding of the virtual agent's behaviour and so the participant's conception of their 'character'. One aim of this research is to investigate this effect of mediation.

Naïve performers. In order to further investigate the relationship between an actor's preparation of a performance, its mediation and the participants interpretation, a second set of motion data was captured. This was from two naïve actors with no professional training or experience. These actors were not prepared in the way described above. Instead they were directed to exactly reproduce the actions and timings of the original actors. They were given precise instructions by the director of the actors' performance, without having seen the original performance themselves. As a result, the motion capture of the naïve actors provided a precise reproduction of the original actors' performance realized without the supporting structures and techniques intended to ensure fidelity between script, rehearsal and emotional affect. As a consequence, the structure and detail of the scenario and experimental design were fulfilled, but by performers who produced unself-conscious and undirected behaviours – including moments of distraction, inappropriate positions, stances, gazes, as well as tones and intonations – that had no specific design or purpose with regard to dramatic character. The experiment aims to investigate the participant's interpretation of these actions, in comparison with the more consistent performance by the actors.

4   Capturing and Animating the Performance

The two performances of the virtual agents were captured through the respective performances of the two actors and the two naïve performers. To capture the physical performance, a Vicon (www.vicon.com) motion capture setup using 32 markers per actor recorded and reconstructed their movements in 3D. This affords the capture of the performers' movements at a coarse level of detail, but not finer-grained movements such as lip movements, facial expression or hand gestures. Each motion capture session was also video and audio recorded. The recorded video was used as an aid in the motion capture data cleaning, to resolve ambiguities in marker placement. The audio recording was not of sufficient quality to be used in the virtual scenario, but was used as a reference for the studio recording of each audio clip, and for the accurate synchronisation of each clip with the corresponding animation.

In this way, each performer's actions were stripped of many significant details and distilled down to large-scale physical motions, which nevertheless still conveyed much of the original performance. This filtering-out of detail was in some ways akin to the removal, during the actors' rehearsals, of extraneous detail from the performance, with the principle difference being that the loss of detail through motion capture was indifferent to any desired qualities in the resultant performance. Indeed it subsequently became necessary to recreate much of the lost detail. Separately recorded audio samples were carefully synchronised with the resultant animations; the animations themselves, when stitched together to create the complete performance, were precisely positioned, with great care taken to match the performers' postures.

The motion capture took place within a small working volume with approximately 2.5m x 2.2m floor area. This was slightly smaller than the 3m x 3m virtual room in which the scenario takes place, thus it was necessary to spatially offset the recording of some captures. These offset captures could subsequently be repositioned, for example to allow the virtual agents to move within the entire virtual room, and to exit and enter through a doorway. The scenario was broken down into a number of shorter scenes which could be recorded separately and subsequently blended together. Some care had to be taken to ensure that the performers' positioning and posture at the start of each scene was similar to that at the end of the previous scene. The result is a number of different motion capture clips that needed to be combined together to make the final scenario. These captures were arranged into sequences which were played at run time with automatic smooth transitions between them. The script was largely linear so an animation engine structured around sequentially playing clips of motion data worked well. However, it was also important to support interaction of the virtual agents with the participant. An animation engine was therefore developed that supported both sequential, linear actions and more interactive, non-linear ones. This was done with two methods, Cue points and Interruptions.

Cue points. Throughout the scenario, several cue points were identified as locations on the timeline that we might want to instantaneously jump forward to. Typically this would be the case where the participant has answered a question and we want to move forward in the scenario without an unnatural pause. The initial captures contained a reasonably long (about 15 seconds) response phases in which the actor waited for a response from the participant. The response phases were designed to be long enough that the participant could respond comfortably during that time and that the agent would appear to be listening to the response. However, if the actual response is shorter than the captured response phase the animation should skip forward to the next action to avoid unnatural pauses. During each response phase the actors maintained relatively stable postures to allow naturalistic blending with the subsequent cue point. The animation engine was therefore able to interrupt the response phase anywhere and smoothly blend into the beginning of the next action.

Interruptions and stock responses. Although the transformation of the original performance into the virtual agents' performance filters away some of the salient detail, it also enables the performance to be reconstructed in novel ways that allow pseudo-spontaneous interaction between the participant and the virtual agents. For example, several points were identified as likely occasions that the participant might direct a question to the virtual agents. To allow the virtual agents to respond in some meaningful way, responses to such predictable questions, as well as several stock responses, were performed and processed in the same way as the core performance. All of the responses were captured so that they had similar start and end postures. The responses are animated in a similar way to the cue points, with smooth transitions from the main sequence to the response. However, these main sequences were less constrained than the response phases used for the cue points. For this reason good transition points were found by searching for points that were minimally different from the start and end of the interruptions. The interruptions were then animated by waiting for the next good transition point, smoothly transitioning to the response and then returning to the same point in the original motion.

5   Conclusion and Further Work

This paper has describe the development of a virtual reality dramatic scenario involving a participants interaction with virtual agents. One of our major interests was to investigate the effect of mediating a performance through virtual agents. In particular what effect this has on the participants' understanding of the virtual agents' behaviours and so conception of their 'character'. Actors were carefully prepared to ensure consistent motivation and behaviour, but the resulting performance was necessarily altered by being transferred to virtual agents. The effects of this alteration will be investigated with an experimental study. In this study the performance by the prepared actors will be compared to the performance by the naïve actors. This will help to understand the affect of aspects such as mediation, preparation, consistency and unself-conscious behaviour on the participant's perception of intention, meaning and so character.

Acknowledgements

Research for this paper was conducted in the context of Performing Presence: from the live to the simulated, a four-year collaboration between the University of Exeter, University College London and Stanford University funded by the Arts and Humanities Research Council (AHRC) UK. Performing Presence is available at: http://presence.stanford.edu.

References

1. Bates, J.: Virtual reality, art and entertainment. Presence 1(1), 133–138 (1992)
2. Aylett, R., Louchart, S., Dias, J., Paiva, A., Vala, M., Woods, S., Hall, L.E.: Unscripted narrative for affectively driven characters. IEEE Computer Graphics and Applications 26(3), 42–52 (2006)
3. Mateas, M., Stern, A.: The interactive drama façade. In: Young, R.M., Laird, J.E. (eds.) Proceedings of the First Artificial Intelligence and Interactive Digital Entertainment Conference, Marina del Rey, California, USA, pp. 153–154. AAAI Press, Menlo Park (2005)
4. Kaye, N.: Multi-Media: video – installation – performance. Routledge, London (2007)
5. Cruz-Neira, C., Sandin, D.J., DeFanti, T.A.: Surround-screen projection-based virtual reality: the design and implementation of the cave. In: Proceedings of the 20st Annual Conference on Computer Graphics and Interactive Techniques, SIGGRAPH 1993, pp. 135–142. ACM, New York (1993)
6. Lombard, M., Ditton, T.: At the heart of it all: The concept of presence. J. Computer-Mediated Communication 3(2) (1997)
7. Zahorik, P., Jenison, R.L.: Presence as being-in-the-world. Presence 7(1), 78–89 (1998)
8. Sanchez-Vives, M., Slater, M.: From presence to consciousness through virtual reality. Nature Reviews Neuroscience 6(4), 332–339 (2005)
9. Biocca, F.: The cyborg's dilemma: Progressive embodiment in virtual environments. J. Computer-Mediated Communication 3(2) (1997)
10. Garau, M., Slater, M., Pertaub, D.P., Razzaque, S.: The responses of people to virtual humans in an immersive virtual environment. Presence 14(1), 104–116 (2005)
11. Stanislavski, K., Benedetti, J.: An Actor's Work: A Student's Diary. Routledge (1938)

Teaching Computers to Conduct
Spoken Interviews:
Breaking the Realtime Barrier with Learning

Gudny Ragna Jonsdottir and Kristinn R. Thórisson

Center for Analysis & Design of Intelligent Agents and School of Computer Science
Reykjavik University
Kringlunni 1, IS-103 Reykjavik, Iceland
{gudny04,thorisson}@ru.is

Abstract. Several challenges remain in the effort to build software capable of conducting realtime dialogue with people. Part of the problem has been a lack of realtime flexibility, especially with regards to turntaking. We have built a system that can adapt its turntaking behavior in natural dialogue, learning to minimize unwanted interruptions and "awkward silences". The system learns this dynamically during the interaction in less than 30 turns, without special training sessions. Here we describe the system and its performance when interacting with people in the role of an interviewer. A prior evaluation of the system included 10 interactions with a single artificial agent (a non-learning version of itself); the new data consists of 10 interaction sessions with 10 different humans. Results show performance to be close to a human's in natural, polite dialogue, with 20% of the turn transitions taking place in under 300 msecs and 60% under 500 msecs. The system works in real-world settings, achieving robust learning in spite of noisy data. The modularity of the architecture gives it significant potential for extensions beyond the interview scenario described here.

Keywords: Dialogue, Realtime, Turntaking, Human-Computer Interaction, Natural Communication, Machine Learning, Prosody.

1   Introduction

One of the challenges in giving computers the ability to participate in spoken dialogue is getting them to perform such activity at a natural pace. Although people can to some extent adapt to the often stilted interaction resulting from a system's lack of human-like turntaking, a system that adapts to human speaking style would be vastly preferable to one which requires its users to change their natural speaking style. In this paper we describe our work on building a flexible dialogue system, one that can adapt in realtime to a person's speaking style, based on prosodic features. As a framework for testing our theories we have created an artificial agent, *Askur*, that uses prosodic features to learn "polite" turntaking behaviors: minimizing silences and speech overlaps. Askur learns this on the fly, in natural, full-duplex (open-mic) dynamic interaction with humans.

Zs. Ruttkay et al. (Eds.): IVA 2009, LNAI 5773, pp. 446–459, 2009.

In natural interaction mid-sentence pauses are a frequent occurrence. Humans have little difficulty in recognizing these from proper end-of-utterance silences, and use these to reliably determine the time at which it is appropriate to take turn – even on the phone with no visual information. Temporal analysis of conversational behaviors in human discourse shows that turn transitions in natural conversation take on average 0-250 msecs [1,2,3] in face-to-face conversation. Silences in telephone conversations - when visual cues are not available - are at least 100 msecs longer on average [4]. In a study by Wilson and Wilson [1] response time is measured in a face-to-face scenario where both parties always had something to say. They found that 30% of between-speaker silences (turn-transitions) were shorter than 200 msecs and 70% shorter than 500 msecs. Within-turn silences, that is, silences where the same person speaks before and after the silence, are on average around 200 msecs but can be as long as 1 second, which has been reported to be the average "silence tolerance" for American-English speakers [5] (these are thus likely to be interpreted by a listener as a "turn-giving signal"). Tolerance for silences in dialogue varies greatly between individuals, ethnic groups and situations; participants in a political debate exhibit a considerably shorter silence tolerance than people in casual conversation – this can further be impacted by social norms (e.g. relationship of the conversants), information inferable from the interaction (type of conversation, semantics, etc.) and internal information (e.g. mood, sense of urgency, etc.). To be on par with humans in turntaking efficiency a system thus needs to be able to categorize these silences.

Artificial agents that can mactch humans in realtime turntaking behavior have been slow in coming. Part of this is due to poor collection of realtime behavioral data from interlocutors. A vast majority of current speech recognizers, for example, use silence detection as the *only* means for deciding when to reactively start interpreting the preceding speech. This leads to unnatural pauses, often one, two, or even three seconds in length, which may be acceptable for dictation but is ill-suited for realtime dialogue. Part of the challenge, therefore, is to get the system to behave quickly enough to match human-style interaction. However, achieving such low-latency turn transitions reliably cannot be done reactively [6]; to have any hope of achieving the 200-500 msec levels observed in human dialogue requires the system to *predict* what actions to take. This must be done using realtime perceptual data collected of interlocutor (unimodal or multimodal) behavior. As inter-subject and real-world scenario complexity puts practical limitations on the amount of hand-coding that can be brought to bear on the problem, the most sensible way to approach this problem is to engineer the system to automatically learn which features of speech can be used for this purpose.

We want to build a general learning mechanism that can automatically learn complex turntaking cues in realtime dialogue with human users. Our approach is based on the Ymir Turntaking Model (YTTM), which models turntaking as a negotiation process controlled jointly by the participants through loosely coupled perception-cognition-action loops [6], and proposes modular construction blocks for this purpose. The original implementation of this model has been expanded according to the Constructionist Design Methodology principle [7], to incorporate learning mechanisms. These allow the system to adjust to interlocutors in realtime and learn over time, achieving human-like performance characteristics in under 30 turns. To the best of our knowledge no system has so far been described in the literature that can adjust its turntaking style dynamically to individuals to achieve human-like performance characteristics, while continuing to improve its performance as it interacts with more people.

In Jonsdottir and Thórisson (2008) [8] we described the first version of the system and presented data on its learning ability when interacting with another artificial agent (a non-learning copy of itself), listening for features of the prosody of the Loquendo speech synthesizer to determine its turntaking predictions and behavior. The results, while promising, described interaction sessions between the system and a single synthesized voice, with negligible noise in the audio channel. Even though the learning in such a controlled artificial setup proved successful we did not consider this to be a guarantee that it would generalize to a real-life setting when conducting live interviews with people. To evaluate the learning mechanism in a more realistic scenario we configured the system to conduct realtime interviews with people over Skype. The interviews were designed to require no natural language processing[1], only prosodical features inform the behavior of the system as it learns to minimize its silences while trying to avoid overlaps.

After reviewing related work we describe the architecture of the learning system, the experimental setup, and then the results of the human subject study, showing how the system learns during the interaction.

2   Related Work

Sacks et al. [9] and Walker [10] were among the first to point out the possible role of prosody and intonation in enabling people to take smooth turns. Walker made a well-informed argument that conversants employ *relatime processing of prosodic information contained in the final few syllables of utterances* to determine when the appropriate moment is to give back-channel feedback, as well as take turn.

J.Jr. was an early computer agent demonstrating this ability [11]. Using realtime processing of a person's prosody, the system could analyze it fast and accurately enough to interject back-channel feedback and take turns in a highly human-like manner. The subsequent Gandalf agent [12] adopted key findings from J.Jr., based on the Ymir framework, an expandable granular AI architecture. Gandalf analyzed in realtime an interlocutor's gaze, gesture, body stance and prosody to determine appropriate turntaking and back-channel opportunities. This has been done more recently in the Rapport Agent [13], which uses

---

[1] The exclusion of speech recognition and language interpretation in this paper is a limitation of the current research focus, not a general limitation of the dialogue architecture we are developing.

gaze, posture and prosodic perception to, among other things, detect backchannel opportunities. While performing in realtime, approaching human-level pace in some cases, none of these systems were built to adapt their behavior to their interlocutors.

Although Reinforcement Learning and other learning methods have been used to some extent in dialogue systems, most of these attempts have been done via offline training of the system. Sato et. al [14] use a decision tree to enable a system learn when a silence signals a wish to give turn and Schlangen [15] has successfully used machine learning to categorize prosodic features from a corpus. Morency et al. [16] use Hidden Markov Model to learn feature selection for predicting back-channel feedback opportunities. However, by these studies, by and large, ignore the *active* element in dialogue – the need to test the quality of perceptual categorization by generating realtime behavior based on these, and monitoring the result. As dialogue is a realtime negotiation process [17] any such effort must include both parties in interaction in order to generalize to real-world situations. (A negotiation process of two parties cannot be simulated without including the effect that the behavior of one has on the other – in a realtime feedback loop.) Classifying perceptual features is certainly one step, but doing so in realtime is another, and generating behaviors based on these – behaviors that affect the other party in some way – yet a third one.

The Ymir Turntaking Model (YTTM, [6]) addresses realtime multimodal turntaking, taking both perception and action into account. YTTM specifies how perceptual data are integrated to derive *how and when* certain perceptual, turntaking and dialogue acts are appropriate, and how to behave according to such information. While the YTTM does not address learning it is based around a modular formalism that has enabled us to add such capabilities without restructuring its original model. We have based our approach and system on this model.

3   System Architecture

The goal of our work is to create a dialogue system that interacts at human speed and accuracy in natural conversation. With primary focus on incremental processing, adaptability and error recovery, our system autonomously learns to predict appropriate turntaking behaviors so as to minimize both awkward silences and overlapping speech in two-party realtime conversation with a human. Our speaking agent, Askur, performs this task by learning to appropriately adjust its silence tolerance during the dialogue (See Figure 1).

The architectural framework is described in more detail in [8] and [18]; a quick review of this work will aid in understanding what follows. The architecture, which is in continuous development, currently consists of 35 interacting modules in a publish-subscribe message passing framework. Its modularity and separation of topic knowledge and behavioral knowledge make it relatively easy to install and test specific "communication skill" components within the framework, compared to alternative approaches. The Ymir Turntaking Model

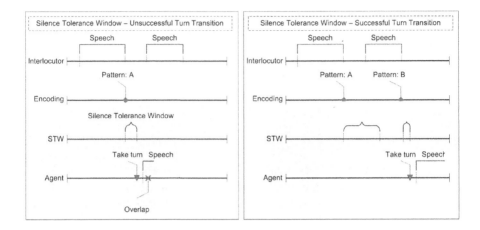

Fig. 1. The interlocutor's speech is analyzed in realtime; as soon as a silence is detected the prosody preceding the silence is decoded. The system makes a prediction by selecting a Silence Tolerance Window (STW), based on the prosody pattern perceived in the interlocutor. This window is a prediction of the shortest safe duration to wait before taking turn: a window that is too short will probably result in overlapping speech while a window that is too large may cause unnecessary/unwanted silence.

(YTTM) provides the backbone of the system [6]. Multi-modal deciders use information extracted from the external (perceptual) and internal environment, to synchronize the perceived and anticipated contexts, which in turn steer both perceptual and behavioral system events. Perception modules include speech and prosody analysis. Prosody analysis is generated as a stream, with an 80 msec fixed latency; speech interpretation can easily take up to a couple of seconds[2]. System responses are generated incrementally in a so-called content generation module where the topic knowledge lies. Speech is realized using the Loquendo text-to-speech synthesizer, which currently imparts a 200 msec latency from the decision to speak to the point when the sound of the first syllable of the first word reaches the audio speaker[3]. One way to compensate for this latency is to pre-start execution with the possibility of canceling it gracefully within 100 msecs, or the chosen Silence Tolerance Window (STW, see 1).

Our agent contains a learning framework that is separated from the decision-making through a service interface, with the benefit of thinner deciders and improved reusability of the learning functionality. The mechanism learns correlations between states and actions and is implemented with ϵ-greedy Q-learning algorithm. ϵ-greedy algorithms try to avoid getting stuck in a local maximum by

---

[2] While speech recognition does not matter to the present topic of learning turntaking, the system is built to include the full spectrum of speech events. Thus, speech recognition is an integral part of the system's architecture.

[3] 200 msecs is long in the context of human-like turntaking skills, but it is by far the best performance of any speech synthesizer we have achieved to date.

exploring less favorable actions in a certain percentage of trials. Q-learning was chosen partly because of this feature and partly because it is model-free, so the agent can start with no knowledge of possible states and actions. Modules that use the learning service contain their own action selection strategy and a general policy on what to do in unseen circumstances. This leaves action discovery solely in the hands of the service-recipient module. The recipient module encapsulates the state-action pair it wants evaluated into a decision for the learner to evaluate. The learner builds a policy of estimated returns for each state-action pair, which it publishes regularly. Each decider that wants to use learning information so published needs to reciprocally publish every decision it makes. A decision contains a state-action pair to be evaluated and a lifetime during which rewards can be assigned; rewards can also be assigned on timeout, representing scenarios where the lack of consequence should be rewarded.

3.1   Feature Selection and Extraction

Prior research has shown that the final part of speech preceding a silence can contain prosodic cues relevant to pragmatics [19]. Following [20] we use the last 300 msecs of speech preceding each silence. The incoming audio signal is handled in a 2-step process. We use the Prosodica prosody analyzer [21] to compute speech signal levels and speech activity. It analyzes prosody in steps of 16 msecs, producing a continuous stream of data from which high level features can be extracted.

Two distinct features are used to categorize all silences. The 300 msecs of the most recent tail of speech right before a silence is searched for the most recent local minimum/maximum pitch to identify the *starting point of the final slope*. Slope is split into three semantic categories: *Up*, *Straight* and *Down* according to formula 1; end-point is split into three groups for *relative value of pitch right before silence*: *Above*, *At* and *Below* the average pitch for the speaker (for the whole dialogue period), according to formula 2. This gives us 9 different combinations of features.

$$m = \frac{\Delta pitch}{\Delta msecs}, \begin{cases} \text{if } m > 0.05 \rightarrow slope = Up \\ \text{if } (-0.05 \leq m \leq 0.05) \rightarrow slope = Straight \\ \text{if } m < -0.05 \rightarrow slope = Down \end{cases} \quad (1)$$

$$d = pitch_{end} - pitch_{avg} \begin{cases} \text{if } d > Pt \rightarrow end = Above \\ \text{if } (-Pt \leq d \leq Pt) \rightarrow end = At \\ \text{if } d < Pt \rightarrow end = Below \end{cases} \quad (2)$$

where Pt is the average ± 10, i.e. pitch average with a bit of tolerance for deviation.

3.2   Formalizing the Learning Problem

The main goal of the learning task is to differentiate silences in realtime based on partial information of an interlocutor's behavior (prosody only) and predict the best reciprocal behavior. For best performance the system needs to find the right tradeoff between shorter silences and the risk of overlapping speech. To formulate this as a Reinforcement Learning problem we need to define states and actions for our scenario.

Using single-step Q-Learning the feature combination in the prosody preceding the current silence becomes the *state* and the length of the Silence Tolerance Window (STW) becomes the action to be learned. For efficiency we have split the continuous action space into discrete logarithmic values (see Table 1), starting with 10 msecs and doubling the value up to 1.28 seconds.

Table 1. Discrete actions representing STW size in msecs

Actions: 10 20 40 80 160 320 640 1280

The reward system used to support this learning problem needs to combine rewards from both length of silence and the occurrence of overlapping speech. We have come up with a reward scheme that encapsulates both. Rewards for decision that do not lead to overlapping speech are based on the size of the STW; a 10 msecs STW scores -10 while a STW of 1280 msecs scores -1280. This represents that shorter STW's are preferred over longer ones[4]. Overlapping speech is currently the only indicator that the agent made a mistake and decisions causing an overlap are rewarded -3000 points. To stimulate exploration of newly discovered actions all new actions start with estimated return at 0 points.

For accurate measurement of overlaps and silences the interviewing agent is equipped with 2 Prosody Trackers, one monitoring the interlocutor and the other monitoring its own voice. To reduce the number of actual generated overlaps due to erroneous trials, and to increase the available data that can be learned from, the agent gets a reward of -2000 for each canceled decision; this is used in situations where the selected STW turns out to be a tad too short. Another method of speeding up the learning is confining the learning space to only a few viable actions in the beginning, discovering new actions only as needed. This is assuming that there exists a single optimal STW for each pattern with degrading returns in relation to distance from that point; we do not need to explore a window of 40 msecs if a window of 80 msecs is considered worse than one of 160 msecs for a specific state. We start with only 2 available actions, 640 msec and 1280 msec, spawning new actions only as needed; spawning a smaller window only if the smallest available is considered the best and spawning a larger one if the largest tried so far is considered the best.

4   Experimental Setup

To evaluate the adaptability of our system we have conducted an experiment where the system, embodied as the agent Askur, automatically converses with

---

[4] We would like to thank Yngvi Björnsson for this insight.

10 human volunteers over Skype. Each subject is interviewed once, from start to finish, before the system goes on to the next subject. To eliminate variations in STW due to lack of something to say we have chosen an interview scenario, in which case the agent always has something to say until it runs out of questions and the interview is over. The agent is thus configured to ask 30 predefined questions, using silence tolerance window to control its turntaking behavior during the interlocutors' turn. Askur begins the first interview with no knowledge, and gradually adapts to its interlocutors throughout the 10 interview sessions.

A convenience sample of 10 Icelandic volunteers took part in the experiment, none of who had interacted with the system before. All subjects spoke English to the agent, with varying amounts of Icelandic prosody patters, which differ from native English-speaking subjects, and with noticable inter- and intra-subject variability. Each interview took around 5 minutes and the total data gathered is just over 300 turns of interaction (average 30 turns per subject). The study was done in a partially controlled setup; all subjects interacted with the system through Skype using the same hardware (computer, microphone, etc.) but the location was only semi-private and background noise was present in all cases.

The agent used the rewards, states and actions as described above, with expiration of STW decisions set to 1 second from the end of window; exploration was fixed at 10%.

5   Results

Given a group of people with a similar cultural background, can our agent learn to dynamically predict proper turn-transition silences during the dialogue. Can it adapt dynamically to each interlocutor during the interaction, while still improving as it interacts with more people? It can.

After having interacted with 8-9 people for about 30 turns each, our agent Askur achives human-level performance in minimizing pauses between turns: over 60% of turns are under 500 msecs and around 25% of turns are under 300 msecs. Furthermore, it learns to fine-adjust its turntaking behavior to a brand new person in under 30 turns. It does this while talking – no offline training trials are conducted. In our experiment the system achieves these levels in spite of interacting with non-native speakers of English. However, as our subjects' prosody patterns turned out to be significantly correlated, the agent keeps improving as more subjects interact with it.

Analysis of Askur's policy shows that out of 9 categories of prosody patterns one particular pattern has a much shorter Silence Tolerance Window (STW) than other patterns; only 38 msecs. This is for silences preceded with a final fall falling below average pitch (Down_Below) and is considerably shorter than the average length of Within-turn silence. Learned STW for all patterns can be seen in Table 2.

The data shows that Askur adapts relatively quickly in the very first 3 interviews, after which 50% of before-turn silences are shorter than 500 msecs (see Figure 2), compared to 70% in the human-human comparison data. 20% of silences are shorter than 300 msecs, compared to 30% within 200 msecs for the

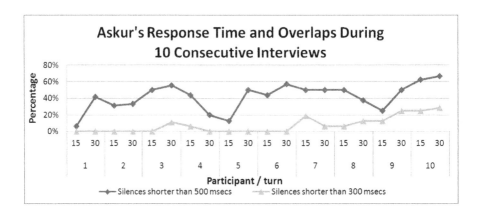

Fig. 2. Proportion of silences with human speed characteristics. The system interacts with each person for 30 turns, then switches to the next person for another 30, and so on for 10 sessions with 10 different people. For the first 3 interviews performance improves steadily, peaking at 60% of turn-transition silences under 500 msecs. Switching to a new person typcially does not impact the performance of the system. However, two obvious dips can be seen, for participant 4 and participant 8.

best-case human-human dialogue. Due to processing time in perception modules (73 msecs avg.) and "motor delay" in generating speech (206 msecs avg.) the agent never takes turn in shorter than 200 msecs (contrasted with 100 msecs for best-case human simple choice reaction time [22]). This performance in regards to response time is well acceptable and closely on par with human speed [1].

As can be seen in Figure 2 typically switching between people does not impair prior learning except for participants 4 and 8. We hypothesized that this might be due to interlocutor diversity, because of the unorthodox learning method of learning online while interacting with each subject sequentially. To investigate this hypothesis we analyzed the occurrences of the pattern Down_Below before silences in the speech of our 10 volunteers. The analysis shows that the occurrences vary between our volunteers from 2,7% to 41,03% of total occurrences at end of speech, and from 2,5% to 19,23% just before within-turn silences

Table 2. Learned Silence Tolerance Window (STW) based on prosody pattern

Prosody category	STW
Down_Below	38 msecs
Straight_At	160 msecs
Up_Below	320 msecs
Down_At	427 msecs
Straight_Below	440 msecs
Up_Above	480 msecs
Up_At	480 msecs
Straight_Above	640 msecs
Down_Above	640 msecs

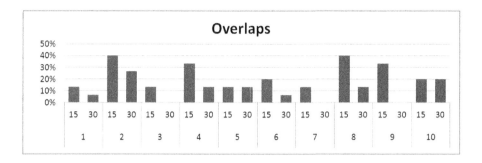

Fig. 3. Overlapped speech occurs on average in 26,3% of turns. Interestingly, overlaps periodically occur in 40% of turns without it permanently effecting performance and overlaps always decrease within each interview.

(see Table 3). This shows a considerable variation between subjects – even though subjects are all of same cultural background and speak the same (non-native) language in the sessions. Temporary lapses in performance are therefore to be expected. Yet the overall performance of the system keeps improving over the 10-person learning period. We can thus safely conclude that the subjects' diversity hypothesis is correct, and that the general trend shown by the data represent true learning on part of the system.

As can be expected in an open-mic conversation such as ours, overlaps were relatively frequent, with 26.3% of turns containing overlapping speech. This number, however, includes all simultaneous sound generated by each participant, regardless of whether it constituted actual speech, background noise or simply noise in the Skype channel. In the literature occurrence of overlapping speech has been found to vary considerably with type of conversation, observed to be as high as every 10th word in normal telephone conversations and telephone meetings [23] and 13% for normal conversation [24]. Interestingly, overlaps periodically occur in 40% of turns without it permanently effecting performance and overlaps always decrease within each interview (see Figure 3). 26.3% overlaps

Table 3. Usage of Down_Below per participant

Participant	turn-transitions	within-turn
1	7,69%	14,93%
2	14,81%	7,25%
3	34,78%	6,67%
4	6,25%	9,09%
5	2,70%	7,14%
6	27,27%	15,38%
7	41,03%	8,70%
8	18,75%	5,00%
9	11,11%	2,50%
10	25,00%	19,23%

when using prosody as the only information "channel" for determining turn transitions can thus be considered a success, especially given system's the continuous 10% exploration (we do not "train" the system and then turn learning off – learning is always on in our system).

5.1 Discussion

Research has shown that in casual conversation people adjust to the speaking style of their interlocutor, including the length of silences [4], producing a reasonably symmetric set of silences and overlaps for each participant. Our results show an asymmetry; Askur has in fact a noticably shorter duration for taking turn than the human subjects. This has a natural explanation, since in our dialogue Askur always has the role of an interviewer and the human are always in the role of the interviewee: The interviewer always knows what question to say next, whereas the human subject does not know what question comes next and has to think about what to answer. There is therefore typically a natural pause or hesitation while they think about what to answer to each question.

An important question that arises when learning on-the-fly against human subjects is whether the humans are actually participating in the learning performance of the system, essentially contributing to the learning by adapting their behavior to the system, consciously or unconsciously. If so this could conflate the results, reinforce "bad" behaviors of the system or otherwise bias the results. To answer this question we analyzed the data for cross-participant trends in modified behavior. While the use of filled pauses cannot be measured directly one way to detect them is to look at the duration of people's within-turn silences, which should be decreasing over time for each participant if the conflation hypothesis was correct. However, this was not the case: Average silence length stays constant throughout the interview for the participants (see Figure 4).

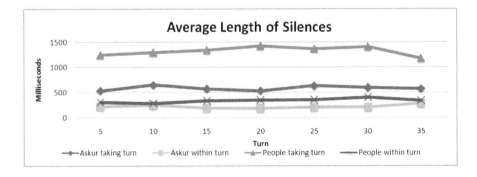

Fig. 4. Average silences when the agent interviews people. People's silences before taking turn are longer due to the fact that people have to think of what to say in response to the questions made by Askur. The length of silences within turn are constant throughout the interview verifying that people are not modifying their silences (by using filled pauses etc.) to accommodate the system.

In addressing this issue we also analyzed the use of final-fall preceding both within-turn and turn-transition silences. If people were learning to modify their use of final fall as a turn-giving signal we should see, towards the latter half of each interaction, a decrease in the occurrence of that pattern before within-turn silences and possibly increase before turn-transition silences. The data shows, however, that only 2 of the participants show this behavior while another 2 show the opposite behavior. The remaining 6 either decrease or increase the use at both within-turn and turn-transition silences (see Figure 5). No other common behaviors have been spotted that would suggest that the interlocutor is specifically aiding in the system's performance.

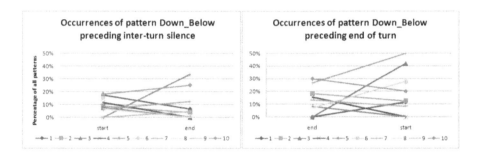

Fig. 5. Occurrences of Down_Below in people's speech has been measured for each interview. No trend in behavior is found that applies to majority of speakers.

6   Conclusions and Future Work

We have built a dialogue system that learns turntaking behaviors, minimizing silences and speech overlaps, using realtime prosody analysis. The system learns this on the fly, in full-duplex (open-mic) dynamic, natural interaction. The system can efficiently take turns with human-like timing in dialogues with people.

The system improves its performance by learning which prosodic information helps in determining appropriate turn transitions, combining features of pitch including final slope, average pitch and timed silences, as a evidence for predicting the desired turntaking behavior of interlocutors. As the system learns on-line it is able to adjust to the particulars of individual speaking styles.

We evaluated the system in realtime interaction with naive users. The system gets close to human-like speed when taking turns, with turn-transition silences as short as 235 msecs. 60% of turn-transition silences are shorter than 500 msecs after roughly 90 turns of learning, compared to 70% in human conversation.

In this evaluation all interlocutors were from the same cultural pool and thus had correlated intonation style, even though they were not speaking their native language. The learning system is embedded in a large expandable architecture, with significant potential for extensions beyond the interview scenario described here, including e.g. selecting dynamically between the goals of being polite (no gaps, no overlaps) and "rude" (always trying to interrupt if it has something to say). As the system is highly modular it can be broadened to include multimodal perception such as head movements, gaze, and more.

In the near future we expect to expand the learning system to handle more diversity in interactions and variation between individuals. We also plan to expand the system to show dynamic selection of dialogue styles/goals such as politeness, agression and passivity. Semantic analysis of speech content will be integrated seamlessly with the turntaking capability, with a hope of going well beyond present-day dialogue engines in flexibility and human-likeness.

Acknowledgments. This work was supported in part by a research grant from RANNIS, Iceland. The authors wish to thank Yngvi Björnsson for his contributions to the development of the reinforcement mechanisms and Eric Nivel for the Prosodica prosody analyzer.

References

1. Wilson, M., Wilson, T.P.: An oscillator model of the timing of turn-taking. Psychonomic Bulletin Review 38(12), 957–968 (2005)
2. Ford, C., Thompson, S.A.: Interactional units in conversation: Syntactic, intonational, and pragmatic resources for the management of turns. In: Ochs, E., Schegloff, E., Thompson, S.A. (eds.) Interaction and Grammar, pp. 134–184. Cambridge University Press, Cambridge (1996)
3. Goodwin, C.: Conversational Organization: Interaction Between Speakers and Hearers. Academic Press, London (1981)
4. ten Bosch, L., Oostdijk, N., Boves, L.: On temporal aspects of turn taking in conversational dialogues. Speech Communication 47(1-2), 80–86 (2005)
5. Jefferson, G.: Preliminary notes on a possible metric which provides for a standard maximum silence of approximately one second in conversation. Conversation: an Interdisciplinary Perspective, Multilingual Matters, 166–196 (1989)
6. Thórisson, K.R.: Natural turn-taking needs no manual: Computational theory and model, from perception to action, pp. 173–207 (2002)
7. Thórisson, K.R., Benko, H., Arnold, A., Abramov, D., Maskey, S., Vaseekaran, A.: Constructionist design methodology for interactive intelligences. A.I. Magazine 25, 77–90 (2004)
8. Jonsdottir, G.R., Thorisson, K.R., Nivel, E.: Learning smooth, human-like turntaking in realtime dialogue. In: Prendinger, H., Lester, J.C., Ishizuka, M. (eds.) IVA 2008. LNCS (LNAI), vol. 5208, pp. 162–175. Springer, Heidelberg (2008)
9. Sacks, H., Schegloff, E.A., Jefferson, G.A.: A simplest systematics for the organization of turn-taking in conversation. Language 50, 696–735 (1974)
10. Walker, M.B.: Smooth transitions in conversational turntaking: Implications for theory, vol. 110, pp. 31–37 (1982)
11. Thórisson, K.R.: Dialogue control in social interface agents. In: INTERCHI Adjunct Proceedings, pp. 139–140 (1993)
12. Thórisson, K.R.: Communicative humanoids: A computational model of psychosocial dialogue skills, Ph.D. thesis, Massachusetts Institute of Technology (1996)
13. Gratch, J., Okhmatovskaia, A., Lamothe, F., Marsella, S., Morales, M., van der Werf, R.J., Morency, L.P.: Virtual rapport. In: IVA, Marina Del Rey, California, pp. 14–27 (2006)

14. Sato, R., Higashinaka, R., Tamoto, M., Nakano, M., Aikawa, K.: Learning decision trees to determine turn-taking by spoken dialogue systems. In: ICSLP 2002, pp. 861–864 (2002)
15. Schlangen, D.: From reaction to prediction: Experiments with computational models of turn-taking. In: Proceedings of Interspeech 2006, Panel on Prosody of Dialogue Acts and Turn-Taking, Pittsburgh, USA (September (2006)
16. Morency, L.-P., de Kok, I., Gratch, J.: Predicting listener backchannels: A probabilistic multimodal approach. In: Prendinger, H., Lester, J.C., Ishizuka, M. (eds.) IVA 2008. LNCS (LNAI), vol. 5208, pp. 176–190. Springer, Heidelberg (2008)
17. Bonaiuto, J., Thórisson, K.R.: Towards a neurocognitive model of realtime turn-taking in face-to-face dialogue. In: Embodied Communication in Humans And Machines, pp. 451–483. Oxford University Press, Oxford (2008)
18. Thórisson, K.R., Jonsdottir, G.R.: A granular architecture for dynamic realtime dialogue. In: Intelligent Virtual Agents, IVA 2008, pp. 1–3 (2008)
19. Pierrehumbert, J., Hirschberg, J.: The meaning of intonational contours in the interpretation of discourse. In: Cohen, P.R., Morgan, J., Pollack, M. (eds.) Intentions in Communication, pp. 271–311. MIT Press, Cambridge (1990)
20. Thórisson, K.R.: Machine perception of multimodal natural dialogue. In: McKevitt, P., Nulláin, S.Ó., Mulvihill, C. (eds.) Language, Vision & Music, pp. 97–115. John Benjamins, Amsterdam (2002)
21. Nivel, E., Thórisson, K.R.: Prosodica: A realtime prosody tracker for dynamic dialogue. Technical report, Reykjavik University Department of Computer Science, Technical Report RUTR-CS08001 (2008)
22. Card, S.K., Moran, T.P., Newell, A.: The Model Human Processor: An Engineering Model of Human Performance, vol. II. John Wiley and Sons, New York (1986)
23. Andreas, E.S.: Observations on overlap: Findings and implications for automatic processing of multi-party conversation. In: Proceedings of Eurospeech 2001, pp. 1359–1362 (2001)
24. Markauskaite, L.: Towards an integrated analytical framework of information and communications technology literacy: from intended to implemented and achieved dimensions. Information Research 11 (2006), paper 252

Should Agents Speak Like, um, Humans?
The Use of Conversational Fillers by Virtual Agents

Laura M. Pfeifer and Timothy Bickmore

Northeastern University College of Computer and Information Science
202 WVH, 360 Huntington Avenue, Boston, MA 02115
{laurap,bickmore}@ccs.neu.edu

Abstract. We describe the design and evaluation of an agent that uses the fillers *um* and *uh* in its speech. We describe an empirical study of human-human dialogue, analyzing gaze behavior during the production of fillers and use this data to develop a model of agent-based gaze behavior. We find that speakers are significantly more likely to gaze away from their dialogue partner while uttering fillers, especially if the filler occurs at the beginning of a speaking turn. This model is evaluated in a preliminary experiment. Results indicate mixed attitudes towards an agent that uses conversational fillers in its speech.

Keywords: embodied conversational agent, fillers, filled pause, gaze.

1 Introduction

Embodied Conversational Agents (ECAs) have existed for over a decade and have been used for a variety of purposes, such as education, counseling and social engagement [1]. A goal of these agents is often to emulate human behavior through both verbal and non-verbal strategies. However, agents have traditionally used perfectly fluent language in their speech, despite the fact that human dialogue consistently contains disfluencies such as restarts, rephrases, and filled pauses [2].

While the use of filled pauses, or conversational fillers, such as *um*, *uh*, *like*, *you know*, etc., may be seen as a type of disfluency, many believe that fillers indeed carry linguistic signals, and are in the same class as English interjections, similar to *ah*, *well*, and *oh*, in which the speaker gives the listener cues about the dialogue structure [3]. For this paper, we will follow Clark and Fox Tree's definition of a conversational filler which, contrary to common belief, does not exist simply to "fill a pause" in speech. Rather, fillers are considered as actual words, and are used by speakers as collateral signals, in effect, to manage the on-going performance of the dialogue [4].

In this paper we explore verbal and non-verbal conversational strategies that agents can use to more closely match human-human dialogue. We present an empirical study of face-to-face dialogue by humans, which indicates a strong relationship between gaze patterns and conversational fillers in speech. We then evaluate this model in a preliminary randomized experiment with an ECA that uses fillers, and explore human reactions to the use of these fillers by agents.

Zs. Ruttkay et al. (Eds.): IVA 2009, LNAI 5773, pp. 460–466, 2009.
© Springer-Verlag Berlin Heidelberg 2009

2 Background and Related Work

Conversational fillers are a common form of grounding in dialogue and serve a variety of purposes. A speaker might use the fillers *um* and *uh* to indicate to the listener that they are searching their memory for a word [5], that they want to hold or cede their turn in the conversation [4], or to signal hesitation, doubt or uncertainty [6].

The fillers *um* and *uh* can also signal new, upcoming information. In one study, listeners were more successfully able to identify words from speech recordings if those words were preceded by the word *uh* [7]. In another study listeners selected a picture on a computer screen more quickly if the spoken description was preceded by the words "*theee, um*" [8].

Analysis of human-computer speech has found that people speak simply and directly when talking to a computer, and use significantly fewer disfluencies than normal [9]. However, no studies thus far have examined the use of fillers by an ECA, and the effects those fillers might have on a human dialogue partner.

3 The Use of Fillers and Gaze Behavior by Human Speakers

We conducted an empirical study to develop a model of behavior involving conversational fillers in face-to-face conversation. Since we planned to implement this behavior in an ECA, we also modeled some of the non-verbal behavior that accompanied the delivery of fillers. Preliminary analyses indicated that gaze behavior frequently co-occurred with the use of fillers, so we focused our initial non-verbal behavior modeling efforts on the gaze behavior of the speaker.

Five people participated in the study recruited via flyers posted around the Northeastern University campus, and were compensated for their time. Participants had to be at least 18 years of age, with English as their native language. Ages ranged from 19 to 57 years old (mean=32.6) and 60% were female. The study took place in the Human-Computer Interaction laboratory at Northeastern University. Participants were consented, completed a demographic questionnaire, and were then told they would be having a conversation with a professional exercise trainer about their exercise behavior. The trainer and her "client" were introduced, were seated facing each other, and the experimenter left the room. All conversations were videotaped for later analysis. The trainer and clients were blind to the purpose of the study.

3.1 Use of Fillers in Dialogue

Conversational fillers used by clients were coded throughout the entire conversation using Anvil [10]. Table 1 presents a summary of the conversations and use of fillers by the clients. The number of fillers within a dialogue turn was highly correlated with the number of words in the turn, $r=.81$, $p<.01$, and with the length (seconds) of the turn $r=.73$, $p<.01$. Throughout the conversations, *um* and *like* were the most commonly used fillers, with complete frequencies shown in Table 2. Use of fillers among clients showed near, but not significant differences by Friedman's Test, $\chi^2(6)=11.02$, $p=.088$, indicating a high amount of inter-subject variation regarding which fillers were commonly spoken, and how often they were used throughout the dialogue. Thirty percent of dialogue turns by clients contained a filler uttered as the first word. *Um* was the most common example (63%) of a filler used at the beginning of a turn, and 64% of all occurrences of *um* were located at the start of a dialogue turn.

Table 1. Client behavior in conversations analyzed

Client	Time Speaking (Seconds)	Num Turns	Time Uttering Fillers (Seconds)	% of Time Uttering Fillers	% of Turns with Fillers
1	238	36	29	12.33%	47.22%
2	491	88	41	8.33%	54.55%
3	642	82	35	5.39%	39.02%
4	895	64	72	8.07%	62.50%
5	535	56	104	19.40%	71.43%
Mean	560	65	56	10.70%	54.94%

Table 2. Number of fillers spoken by clients, per conversation turn

Client	um	uh	like	So	just	you know	kind of	Mean
1	0.81	0.03	1.25	0.25	0.47	0.08	0.11	0.43
2	0.76	0.00	0.26	0.18	0.41	0.11	0.00	0.25
3	0.16	0.28	0.16	0.16	0.10	0.28	0.04	0.17
4	2.02	0.31	0.25	0.38	0.23	0.58	0.11	0.55
5	0.29	0.05	5.52	1.04	1.45	0.07	0.13	1.22
Mean	0.81	0.13	1.49	0.40	0.53	0.23	0.08	0.52

3.2 Model of Gaze Behavior for Speech Containing Fillers

We coded client gaze patterns throughout the entire conversation. Gazes were divided into nine categories, according to the client's perspective: up, up and to the left, up and to the right, down, down and to the left, down and to the right, left, right, and at the trainer. Friedman's Test shows significant differences of gaze patterns among the clients both while speaking and uttering fillers, $\chi^2(8)=21.61$, $p<.01$, and while speaking without uttering fillers, $\chi^2(8)=21.71$, $p=.005$, indicating a high amount of inter-subject variation in gaze patterns.

Clients spent significantly more time looking *at* the trainer while speaking without using fillers (61%), and *away* from the trainer while uttering fillers (57%), *paired-t* (4) = -6.45, $p<.01$. We also analyzed client gaze patterns according to their location within a conversational turn (Table 3). When a conversational filler was uttered at the beginning of a turn, client gaze shifts were more likely to be directed *away* from the trainer, *paired-t* (4) = 3.33, $p<.05$. During the middle or end of a turn, clients were equally likely to shift their gaze *away* or *towards* the trainer.

Table 3. Percent of client gaze changes that are directed towards or away from the trainer, based on the location within a turn

Location Within a Turn	Speaking Filler		Not Speaking Filler	
	At Trainer	Away	At Trainer	Away
Beginning	30.69%	69.31%	63.59%	36.41%
Mid or End	49.53%	50.47%	49.53%	50.47%

4 Conversational Fillers and Gaze Model Implementation

An existing virtual agent framework was modified to provide appropriate co-occurring gaze and speech behavior during the presence of conversational fillers [11]. Co-verbal behavior is determined for each utterance using the BEAT text-to-embodied-speech system [12]. User contributions to the conversation are made by selecting an item from a multiple-choice menu of utterance options, updated at each turn of the conversation.

We observed gazing in the left direction to be the most common gaze-away pattern while uttering fillers, so we extended the agent animations to allow for speaking while gazing to the left (Fig. 1). We also extended the system to be able to speak while gazing at a document artifact held in the agent's hands. In previous work, we found that when explaining a document, humans gazed at the document between 65-83% of the time [11]. Upon re-analysis and consideration of fillers, we found that time gazing at the document was not affected by use of fillers.

Fig. 1. Co-occurring gaze and speech by the agent

5 Preliminary Evaluation

We conducted a preliminary evaluation to test the efficacy of an agent that uses conversational fillers in its speech. For this experiment, we used the fillers *um* and *uh*, as they have been shown to have comprehension effects [7]. In order to examine the effects of fillers in various conversational styles, each participant had two conversations with the agent: a social conversation and an educational conversation. The *social* conversation used a between-subjects (FILLERS vs. NO-FILLERS) experimental design and the *educational* conversation used a within-subjects (FILLER-PHRASE vs. NO-FILLER-PHRASE) experimental design. During the *educational* conversation, all participants interacted with an agent that used conversational fillers, with half of the key concepts preceded in speech by a filler. We hypothesize that ratings of satisfaction and naturalness will be higher for participants in the FILLERS condition of the *social* conversation, and that participants will perform better on test questions regarding content of the *educational* conversation, if the content was preceded in speech by a filler (FILLER-PHRASE).

The Loquendo text-to-speech engine was chosen for the experiment, and the intonation and timing of each filler was adjusted to sound as natural as possible. In most cases, this consisted of lowering the pitch, reducing the voice speed, and following the filler by a short pause (50-100 ms). The social script consisted of 14 turns of dialogue and lasted approximately one and a half minutes, and the educational script consisted of 34 turns of dialogue and lasted approximately four minutes. The educational dialogue contained a shortened, simplified version of an agent-based explanation of a hospital discharge pamphlet [11]. The participants talked to the agent using a Wizard-Of-Oz setup, and were instructed to say one of the allowed utterances displayed on a menu during each turn.

5.1 Measures

Along with basic demographics, we assessed computer attitudes with the question "How do you feel about using computers?" We also created a knowledge test based on the educational dialogue, containing eight questions on the content of the dialogue. Evaluation questionnaires were also developed, assessing satisfaction, trust, likability, perceived knowledge of the agent, along with naturalness of the dialogue and naturalness of the agent's eye-gaze behavior, all evaluated on 7-point scales. All measures were administered via paper-and-pencil.

5.2 Procedure

Twenty-three people participated in the evaluation study, aged 19-66 years, 70% female. Fifty-seven percent of participants indicated neutral attitudes towards computers, with the rest indicating positive attitudes towards computers. After informed consent was obtained, participants were randomized into conditions, and demographic questionnaires were administered. The experimenter left the room, the agent and participant conducted the social dialogue, and attitudinal measures on the agent and the conversation were administered. Participants were then asked to role-play that they were in the hospital, and the agent would explain a hospital discharge booklet to them. The experimenter left the room, and the agent and participant conducted the educational conversation. Afterwards, participants completed the knowledge test and attitudinal measures, followed by a semi-structured interview to obtain impressions of the experiment and agent.

5.3 Results

Attitudinal measures towards the agent after the social and educational conversations are shown in Table 4. There were no significant effects of study conditions on attitudes towards the agent. Trends indicate that participants in the NO-FILLERS condition *liked* the agent more than those in the FILLERS condition, $t(21)=1.69, p=.10$.

Table 4. Attitudinal measures towards the agent (mean (SD)). Measures are on a scale from 1 (not at all) to 7 (very much).

Question	Social Conversation			Educational Conversation
	Fillers	No Fillers	p	
How *satisfied* are you with the conversation experience?	6.00 (1.18)	5.58 (.996)	0.37	5.61 (1.20)
How much do you *trust* Elizabeth?	5.68 (1.10)	5.50 (.905)	0.67	5.72 (1.01)
How much do you *like* Elizabeth?	5.32 (.783)	5.92 (.900)	0.10	5.65 (1.03)
How *knowledgeable* was Elizabeth?	5.36 (.924)	5.17 (1.47)	0.76	5.96 (0.98)
How *natural* was the speaking style of Elizabeth?	4.09 (1.76)	4.33 (1.97)	0.71	4.22 (1.62)
How *natural* was the eye-gaze behavior of Elizabeth?	4.45 (1.80)	4.58 (1.50)	0.85	4.87 (1.66)

Knowledge test scores of the educational conversation were coded on the following scale: 0=incorrect, 0.5=partially correct, 1=correct. A comparison of the scores of test questions on dialogue content preceded in the conversation by a filler (FILLER-PHRASE), vs. questions on dialogue content not preceded by a filler (NO-FILLER-PHRASE) found no significant differences, *paired-t* (22) = .789, $p=.44$.

During semi-structured interviews, 22 of the participants were asked if they recognized whether or not the agent used the fillers *um* and *uh* during the dialogue (all participants heard fillers in at least one conversation). Eight participants (36%) thought that the agent did not use fillers, 4 (18%) were not sure, and 10 (46%) recognized the use of fillers.

Also during interviews, 15 participants volunteered an opinion, negative, positive or neutral, towards agents using fillers in their speech, or were asked by the interviewer, "How do you feel about a computer character using the words *um* and *uh* in its speech?" Participants with positive attitudes towards computers were significantly more likely to indicate that the usage of fillers by agents was a positive aspect of the conversation, compared to participants with neutral attitudes towards computers, $\chi^2(2)=8.89, p=.01$.

Overall, participants reported mixed feelings about interacting with an agent that uses fillers. Five participants indicated that the use of fillers by a conversational agent seemed inappropriate, given that computers have the ability to speak perfectly, and another five participants indicated that the usage of fillers by the agent was a positive aspect of the conversation and "humanized" the experience.

6 Discussion

Should agents speak like humans? It appears to be open for additional research. At this time we do not see significant differences on satisfaction and naturalness, and we did not observe the recall effects associated with fillers in human-human dialogue. Previous work showed these recall effects after participants listened to audio recordings, and it is possible that the addition of an ECA - providing an audio *and* visual signal - mitigates the effects. Another possible reason is that our agent's production of fillers and accompanying nonverbal behavior need further refinement in order to match human behavior. Although this preliminary evaluation is limited, it provides us with a good overview of attitudes towards the use of fillers by agents.

Our future work is focused on extending the evaluation study with a broader range of participants having various levels of computer attitudes, age, and personality. We also intend to evaluate a wider range of fillers by agents, such as *like*, *you know*, etc. Finally, we plan to evaluate the use of fillers by agents that speak with a text-to-speech engine to agents that speak with a human-recorded voice.

Acknowledgments. Many thanks to Jenna Zaffini and Donna Byron for their assistance with the study. This work was supported by NSF CAREER IIS-0545932.

References

1. Cassell, J.: Embodied Conversational Agents. MIT Press, Cambridge (2000)
2. Fox Tree, J.E.: The Effects of False Starts and Repetitions on the Processing of Subsequent Words in Spontaneous Speech. J. Mem. Lang. 34, 709–738 (1995)
3. Swerts, M.: Filled Pauses as Markers of Discourse Structure. J. Pragmat. 30, 485–496 (1998)
4. Clark, H., Fox Tree, J.E.: Using Uh and Um in Spontaneous Speaking. Cognition 84, 73–111 (2002)
5. Goodwin, C.: Forgetfulness as an Interactive Resource. Soc. Psychol. Q. 50, 115–130 (1987)
6. The American Heritage dictionary of the English language. Houghton Mifflin, Boston (2006)
7. Fox Tree, J.E.: Listeners' Uses of Um and Uh in Speech Comprehension. J. Mem. Cognit. 29, 320–326 (2001)
8. Arnold, J.E., Fagnano, M., Tanenhaus, M.K.: Disfluencies Signal theee, um, New Information. J. Psycholinguist Res. 32, 25–36 (2003)
9. Oviatt, S.: Predicting Spoken Disfluencies During Human-Computer Interaction. Comp. Speech Lang. 9, 19–35 (1995)
10. Kipp, M.: ANVIL – A Generic Annotation Tool for Multimodal Dialogue. In: 7th European Conference on Speech Communication and Technology, pp. 1367–1370 (2001)
11. Bickmore, T.W., Pfeifer, L.M., Paasche-Orlow, M.K.: Health document explanation by virtual agents. In: Pelachaud, C., Martin, J.-C., André, E., Chollet, G., Karpouzis, K., Pelé, D. (eds.) IVA 2007. LNCS (LNAI), vol. 4722, pp. 183–196. Springer, Heidelberg (2007)
12. Cassell, J., Vilhjalmsson, H., Bickmore, T.: BEAT: The Behavior Expression Animation Toolkit. In: SIGGRAPH 2001: Proceedings of the 28th annual conference on computer graphics and interactive techniques, pp. 477–486 (2001)

Turn Management or Impression Management?

Mark ter Maat and Dirk Heylen

Human Media Interaction, University of Twente
P.O. Box 217, 7500 AE Enschede, the Netherlands
{maatm,heylen}@ewi.utwente.nl

Abstract. We look at how some basic choices in the management of turns influence the impression that people get from an agent. We look at scales concerning personality, emotion and interpersonal stance. We do this by a person perception study, or rather an agent perception study, using simulated conversations that systematically vary basic turn-taking strategies. We show how we can create different impressions of friendliness, rudeness, arousal and several other dimensions by varying the timing of the start of a turn with respect to the ending of the interlocutor's turn and by varying the strategy of ending or not ending a turn when overlap is detected.

1 Introduction

It has been claimed that in conversations, speaker change occurs and that overwhelmingly one party talks at a time although the occurrences of more than one speaker at a time are common - but brief ([8]). These claims have been contested about as many times at they have been repeated ([2],[5],[6], for instance). However, in this paper we do not want to argue in favor nor against these claims. Instead, we will look at factors that influence this turn taking behaviour.

According to Goffman ([3]) conversation is expected to be effective transmission of talk, which means that it would be helpful to have "norms constraining interruption or simultaneous talk" (system constraints). But conversations are also social encounters, not only governed by requirements that regulate efficient information exchange, but also by what Goffman calls ritual constraints, regarding "how each individual ought to handle himself with respect to each of the others". These constraints should prevent a person from being rude or impolite. Another obvious factor that influences turn taking behaviour is emotions. "A clash of opinions also means a clash of turn-taking" ([6]). All these factors influence turn taking behaviour, which means that observing turn taking behaviour could be very informative about the kind of person one is, how one is feeling or how one wants to be perceived. Although turn taking has been studied widely, the connection with these ritual dimensions has been much less so, though investigations into the detection of some interpersonal variables in conversations have shown that turn taking behavior has an impact ([7]).

In the context of the Semaine project (http://www.semaine-project.eu), we are currently exploring how we can express personality, emotion and social attitudes of the agents that we are building through the implementation of their

Zs. Ruttkay et al. (Eds.): IVA 2009, LNAI 5773, pp. 467–473, 2009.

behaviors. In this paper, we focus on the way variations in turn-management strategies can be used as a resource to create different impressions of the characters. Our goal is therefore not so much to have our agents learn to take "smooth" turn transitions as in [4], for instance, in which the authors present a learning algorithm that tries to minimize the gap between two utterances and the periods in which both participants speak. We would not mind if an agent violates such rules. Violations like these happen constantly in every day conversations. What if an agent starts speaking before another has finished? What if the agent detects that the user starts speaking before it is finished? Should it stop speaking, continue speaking normally, or continue using elevated speech (that is speak louder) to try and win the battle for the floor[1]? Maybe it depends on the kind of character that we want to build.

In this paper, we look at how some basic choices in the management of turns influence the impression that people get from an agent. We look at scales concerning personality, emotion and interpersonal stance. We do this by a person perception study, or rather an agent perception study, using simulated conversations that systematically vary basic turn-taking strategies. We describe the study in the next section and discuss the results in Section 3.

2   Agent Perception Study

The goal of this study is to find out how variations in turn management strategies affects what people perceive the personality, emotional state and the interpersonal stance of an agent to be. We generated several conversations where one agent talks to another varying the ways in which one agent deals with overlap and when it starts speaking. These conversations were presented to human raters who judged the agent on various semantic scales. To generate the conversations we build a conversation simulator that allows one to define different turn management rules. Before we specify the turn management strategies and the impression measures that we examined, we will first say more about the conversation simulator.

Conversation Simulator. The conversation simulator allows one to program the behavior of two agents that can communicate with one another by sending each other information on their communicative actions. They indicate whether they are silent, speaking normally or using elevated speech. These signals, however, are subject to a small delay before they are recognized by the other agent.

Furthermore, to be able to define more refined rules for regulating turns, the agents can also send certain signals that indicate what they are about to do, for instance the intention to start or end the turn (also found in real human conversations, [1]). To simulate that turn taking signals can be ambiguous and misinterpreted by the recipient, a certain error margin is introduced. Signals that are sent can sometimes get lost or signals can be added or changed sometimes.

---

[1] These are some of the overlap resolution strategies that [9] presents.

The behavior of the two agents can be scripted. In these scripts one can define how an agent reacts to different situations. The core conversation simulator runs the scripts of the agents in parallel and takes care that the rules are executed and the variables are updated accordingly. The conversations of the agents can be visualized (Figure 1) and made audible.

For the speech rendition that was used in the experiment we wanted to output natural incomprehensible speech. To this end we extracted several sentences from the AMI corpus[2] with a clear start and end point. These fragments were then passed through a Pass Hann Band Filter, from 500Hz to 500Hz with a smoothing of 100Hz. With this method the fragments kept their prosodic information but lost their content.

Turn-management strategies/Stimuli. The procedures for turn management that we have considered in this study consist of *start-up* strategies and *overlap resolution* strategies. For each group we have defined three possible strategies, yielding nine different turn taking strategies in total by crossing them. A startup strategy determines when to start a new utterance. In our case, this can be exactly at the moment when the other agent is finished (**At**), with a certain delay (**After**) or before the other agent is finished (**Before**). The overlap resolution strategy determines the strategy to use when overlap is detected. In our case an agent can stop speaking (**Stop**), it can continue normally (**Normally**) or it can raise its voice (**Raised**). Of course in everyday conversations, real life people use a mixture of these strategies for different circumstances, but since the goal is to find out the effect of the single overlap resolution strategies only a single strategy was used in each conversation. The suggestion for these strategies comes from [9].

Fig. 1. Example conversations

Using the conversation simulator eight different agents were scripted using the turn taking strategies described. The strategy **Before+Stop** was discarded because it would start while the other person was speaking and immediately stop again, resulting in very unrealistic conversations. The other eight scripts resulted in very different conversations. In Figure 1 two examples of different conversations are shown. The contributions of the agent that varies its strategy (which we will refer to as the agent) are shown on the lower tier. The fixed system-agent (which we will also refer to as the system) was scripted to use different strategies based on chance and is shown on the top tier in each case. Note that the conversations are quite different. The question now is whether these interactions lead to different perceptions of the agent.

---

[2] http://www.amiproject.org

Experimental Set-Up. The variation in the turn management scripts results in completely different interaction patterns which might change the impression of how the agents relate to each other on an interpersonal scale, or they might change the impression of the personality of the agent. In our study we had ten people rate the eight conversations on each of the dimensions mentioned above. The raters were all between 20 and 30 years old, mainly students, 6 male, 4 female. We asked them to rate them on a five point scale as follows. We used the following scales in our study: *unfriendly-friendly, distant-pleasant, passive-active, cold-warm, negligent-conscientious, disagreeable-agreeable, rude-respectful, unpredictable-stable, unattentive-attentive, submissive-dominant, undependable-responsible, negative-positive, not aroused-aroused.* The last 2 scales were added because they are heavily used in the Semaine project.

The raters were seated in front of a PC which ran a powerpoint presentation. On each slide they could click on an audio file that would then play. The audio of the system agent came from the left speaker and the audio from the agent which they had to rate from the right speaker. We made sure that each rater knew which speaker they had to rate. To make the difference even clearer, the agent's speech was somewhat higher in pitch than that of the system agent.

These conversations were ordered such that conversations in which the system was more talkative than the agent alternated with conversations in which the agent was more talkative. We had five raters listen to this order (A) and five raters listened to an order in which the first four conversations of A changed position with the last four conversations of A. These results were combined for the analysis. The raters were asked to fill in the questionnaire on how they perceived the person from the right loudspeaker after each conversation.

3   Results

In this section we present the results of the ratings and a selection of our analyses.

To get a first impression of the results we give a summary of the ratings in Figure 2. In this table we show the means and the standard deviations for each of the scales and all the conversations. Using boldface we have marked the conversation that received the highest mean rate for a scale and using underlinings we marked the conversation with the lowest mean rate for the scale.

When one looks first at the bold face figures it is immediately obvious that the **AtStop** column, in which the agent will start speaking exactly when the system stops and stops when overlap is detected, attracts most of the high scores. It is the top highest rated version on positivity, friendliness, agreeability, respect, pleasantness, attentiveness, warmth and responsibility. On the other hand, **BeforeRaised**,where the agent starts before the system has ended and raises its voice in case of overlap is the top most rated version on negativity, un-friendliness, disagreeability, rudeness, distance, unpredictability, un-attentiveness, and coldness. It is also rated as the most "aroused" agent. These two strategies appear to be the most extreme.

What to think about the other highest/lowest scores? The **BeforeContinue** and **AfterRaised** agent show the lowest scores on the arousal and responsibility

Scale	Before & Continue		After & Stop		Before & Raised		At & Stop		At & Continue		After & Raised		At & Raised		After & Continue	
	Avg	Sd	Avg	Sd	Avg	Sd	Avg	Sd	Avg	Sd	Avg	Sd	Avg	Sd	Avg	Sd
Negative - Positive	2,6	1,1	2,6	0,5	2,1	0,9	3,7	0,7	2,8	0,9	2,4	0,5	2,3	0,7	3,1	0,9
Not aroused - Aroused	3,0	1,2	3,1	1,1	4,8	0,4	3,3	0,9	3,9	0,6	3,7	1,1	4,1	0,7	3,0	1,1
Unfriendly - Friendly	3,3	1,1	3,0	0,0	2,2	0,9	3,8	0,8	3,5	1,0	3,4	0,5	3,1	1,3	3,7	0,7
Disagreeable - Agreeable	2,4	1,2	3,1	1,5	1,7	0,8	3,5	1,1	2,3	0,7	2,2	0,6	2,4	1,1	3,3	0,8
Negligent - Conscientious	3,9	1,2	3,0	1,2	3,2	1,2	3,7	0,8	3,7	1,1	3,1	0,9	4,0	0,7	3,4	0,5
Rude - Respectful	3,2	1,2	3,7	0,8	2,0	1,2	4,2	0,8	3,0	1,1	2,9	0,7	2,9	0,9	4,1	0,6
Distant - Pleasant	2,6	0,8	2,5	0,7	2,5	0,8	4,2	0,8	2,7	0,8	2,6	1,0	3,0	1,1	3,1	1,0
Unpredictable - Stable	3,7	0,8	3,3	1,2	2,0	0,7	3,6	1,1	3,4	1,0	2,7	1,3	2,8	1,0	3,9	0,7
Unattentive - Attentive	3,4	1,2	3,3	0,5	3,0	1,3	4,3	0,5	3,5	1,1	3,5	0,7	3,7	0,9	3,6	0,5
Cold - Warm	2,5	1,2	2,9	0,6	2,4	0,5	3,9	0,6	2,9	0,9	2,7	0,7	2,7	0,9	3,2	0,8
Passive - Active	4,4	0,5	2,6	1,5	4,7	0,5	3,5	0,5	4,8	0,4	3,5	1,0	4,0	0,7	2,8	0,8
Submissive - Dominant	4,4	1,3	1,1	0,3	4,3	0,8	3,3	0,8	4,5	0,7	3,3	1,1	3,7	1,3	2,7	0,5
Undependable - Responsible	3,2	1,0	2,9	0,7	2,7	1,2	3,7	0,8	3,4	0,7	2,4	0,8	3,3	0,9	3,3	0,7

Fig. 2. Means and Standard Deviations of the ratings for each conversation

dimensions respectively. Interestingly though, the lowest score on arousal is 3,0 (which is shared between **BeforeContinue** and **AfterContinue**, which means that there is no agent that effectively performs low on arousal. Similarly, the current strategies do not yield an agent that is extremely negligent. The opposite, conscientiousness is rated highest when an agent does not wait (long) before the turn of the system has finished and continues (possibly speaking louder) when overlap is detected; i.e. the **BeforeContinue** and **AtRaised** score highest on conscientiousness. The impression of highest stability is reserved for the agent that starts speaking only after the system has finished but does not mind continuing when interrupted (without raising its voice), **AfterContinue**. An agent that waits before the other has finished but raises its voice when interrupted, **AfterRaised**, on the other hand, is not considered to be dependable.

Figure 3 contains the fragments grouped by startup strategy and overlap resolution strategy, with their mean and standard deviation. In these tables significance is indicated with one or more stars. The significance was calculated for every dimension scale by performing a two-paired t-test for all combinations (1+2, 2+3, 1+3). The type of t-test (equal variance or unequal variance) was determined by performing an f-test first. A group was said to be significantly different when both t-tests with the other groups scored an $p < 0.05$. So, for example, the negative value for raising the voice is significant because both the t-test with stop and the t-test with continue resulted in an $p < 0.05$. The left part of figure 3 shows that, for the startup strategy, most significant differences occur with the situation in which the agent starts before the system is finished. Starting before the end is seen as more unfriendly, disagreeable, rude, cold and more active, compared to starting at the end or after the end. The most pleasant person would be a speaker who starts directly at the end of the other person's speech, not sooner or later. The sooner a person starts to talk the more active

Scale	Startup Strategy						Overlap Resolution Strategy					
	Before		At		After		Stop		Continue		Raised	
	Avg	Sd	Avg	Sd	Avg	Sd	Avg	Sd	Avg	Sd	Avg	Sd
Negative - Positive	2,4	1,0	2,9	0,9	2,7	0,7	3,1	0,8	2,8	0,9	*2,3	0,7
Not aroused - Aroused	3,9	1,3	3,8	0,8	3,3	1,1	3,2	1,0	3,3	1,0	***4,2	0,9
Unfriendly - Friendly	*2,8	1,1	3,5	1,0	3,4	0,6	3,4	0,7	3,5	0,9	*2,9	1,1
Disagreeable - Agreeable	*2,1	1,1	2,7	1,1	2,9	1,1	3,3	1,3	2,7	1,0	*2,1	0,9
Negligent - Conscientious	3,6	1,2	3,8	0,9	3,2	0,9	3,4	1,1	3,7	1,0	3,4	1,0
Rude - Respectful	*2,6	1,3	3,4	1,1	3,6	0,9	4,0	0,8	3,4	1,1	*2,6	1,0
Distant - Pleasant	2,6	0,8	3,3	1,1	2,7	0,9	3,4	1,1	2,8	0,9	2,7	1,0
Unpredictable - Stable	2,9	1,1	*3,3	1,0	3,3	1,1	3,5	1,1	3,7	0,8	*2,5	1,0
Unattentive - Attentive	3,2	1,2	3,8	0,9	3,5	0,6	3,8	0,7	3,5	0,9	3,4	1,0
Cold - Warm	*2,5	0,9	3,2	0,9	2,9	0,7	*3,4	0,8	2,9	1,0	2,6	0,7
Passive - Active	*4,6	0,5	***4,1	0,8	*3,0	1,2	**3,1	1,2	4,0	1,1	4,1	0,9
Submissive - Dominant	4,4	1,0	3,8	1,1	***2,4	1,2	***2,2	1,3	3,9	1,2	3,8	1,1
Undependable - Responsible	3,0	1,1	3,5	0,8	2,9	0,8	3,3	0,9	3,3	0,8	2,8	1,0

Fig. 3. Strategies, * = $p < 0.05$, ** = $p < 0.01$, *** = $p < 0.001$

he is perceived one could say. This is pointed out by the highly significant result obtained. A final significant result is that the agent that starts after the system's end-of-turn (so with a pause between the utterances) is seen as more submissive.

In the right part of Figure 3 significantly different behaviors occur in the case where the agent stops as soon as overlap is detected and the case when it continues and raises its voice. Stopping when the agent detects overlap is perceived as warmer, more passive and more submissive than continuing. Continuing and talking louder is perceived as more negative, more aroused, less friendly, less agreeable, more rude and more unpredictable than stopping or continuing normally.

These findings to agree with our intuitions which, we think, shows the validity of this methodology. Turn-taking strategies do seem to have an effect on the perception of the agent and the conversations that were generated seem to reflect adequately the principles and parameters that we endow them with.

4   Discussion and Conclusions

In this paper we described a basic conversation simulator that can generate artificial conversations that closely resemble human face-to-face conversations. In particular, the conversation simulator allows one to manipulate several variables related to turn-management, abstracting away from the content of the talk.

We have used the simulator to generate a number of conversations where strategies for timing the beginning of a turn and the decision of continuation when overlap is detected were varied. We showed, through an "agent perception study", how these variations in turn-management changed the impressions that people received from the agent as they listened to the various conversations. The study shows that the manipulation of turn-taking strategies can lead to different perceptions of an agent on personality scales, interpersonal scales and emotional scales and that therefore these strategies can be used in the repertoire of expressive behaviors of agents reflecting these dimensions.

Future work will continue in several directions. The first concerns a methodological issue which involves the quality of the generated conversations. Another direction is to study other semantic scales than the ones presented here.

The result of this study will be used in actual interactive system, in which an agent will interact in real time with human interactants. This will also allow us to re-introduce contextual features such as topic and semantics that were ignored in this study that focused on the turn-taking tactics as such.

Acknowledgement. The research leading to these results has received funding from the European Community's Seventh Framework Programme (FP7/2007-2013) under grant agreement n° 211486 (SEMAINE).

References

1. Duncan, S., Niederehe, G.: On signalling that it's your turn to speak. Journal of Experimental Social Psychology 10(3), 234–247 (1974)
2. Edelsky, C.: Who's got the floor? Language in Society 10, 383–421 (1981)
3. Goffman, E.: Forms of Talk. Basil Blackwell, Oxford (1981)
4. Jonsdottir, G.R., Thorisson, K.R., Nivel, E.: Learning smooth, Human-Like turn-taking in realtime dialogue. In: Proceedings of the 8th international conference on Intelligent Virtual Agents, Tokyo, Japan, pp. 162–175. Springer, Heidelberg (2008)
5. O'Connell, D.C., Kowal, S., Kaltenbacher, E.: Turn-taking: A critical analysis of the research tradition. Journal of Psycholinguistic Research 19(6), 345–373 (1990)
6. Oreström, B.: Turn-taking in English Conversation. Liber, Lund, Sweden (1983)
7. Rienks, R.J., Heylen, D.K.J.: Automatic dominance detection in meetings using easily obtainable features. In: Bourlard, H., Renals, S. (eds.) MLMI 2005. LNCS, vol. 3869, pp. 76–86. Springer, Heidelberg (2006)
8. Sacks, H., Schegloff, E.A., Jefferson, G.: A simplest systematics for the organization of Turn-Taking for conversation. Language 50(4), 696–735 (1974)
9. Schegloff, E.A.: Overlapping talk and the organization of turn-taking for conversation. Language in Society 29(1), 1–63 (2000)

Human-Centered Distributed Conversational Modeling: Efficient Modeling of Robust Virtual Human Conversations

Brent Rossen[1], Scott Lind[2], and Benjamin Lok[1]

[1] CISE
University of Florida
Gainesville, FL 32611, USA
{brossen,lok}@cise.ufl.edu
[2] Dept of Surgery, Oncology
Medical College of Georgia
Augusta, GA 30912, USA
dlind@mail.mcg.edu

Abstract. Currently, applications that focus on providing conversations with virtual humans require extensive work to create robust conversational models. We present a new approach called Human-centered Distributed Conversational Modeling. Using this approach, users create conversational models in a distributed manner. To do this, end-users interact with virtual humans to provide new stimuli (questions and statements), and domain-specific experts (e.g. medical/psychology educators) provide new virtual human responses. Using this process, users become the primary developers of conversational models. We tested our approach by creating an example application, Virtual People Factory. Using Virtual People Factory, a pharmacy instructor and 186 pharmacy students were able to create a robust conversational model in 15 hours. This is approximately 10% of the time typical in current approaches and results in more comprehensive coverage of the conversational space. In addition, surveys demonstrate the acceptability of this approach by both educators and students.

Keywords: Virtual Humans, Agents and Intelligent Systems, Human-centered Computing, Distributed Knowledge Acquisition, End-user Programming.

1 Introduction

Preparing a Virtual Human (VH) to conduct a free-form conversation can take months. As an example, our research group recently created Vic, a VH who plays the role of a patient having stomach pain. Vic was created to be capable of a 10-minute free-form conversation about his symptoms with a pharmacy student. Vic's development took approximately 6 months and 200 hours of work to develop a conversational model with a 75% accuracy rate. This time requirement restricts the scalability of VH applications. This paper presents a distributed end-user approach, the use of which

Zs. Ruttkay et al. (Eds.): IVA 2009, LNAI 5773, pp. 474–481, 2009.

results in a more complete and accurate conversational model in a significantly shorter time.

Vic is one of the many VHs created in the last few years for domain-specific conversations. These VHs [1-3] conduct natural language conversations using unannotated corpus retrieval approaches [2, 4]. In order to function well, these models require VH developers to acquire a large conversation specific corpus [1-5]. The corpus consists of what the users will say to a VH (stimulus) and what the VH will say back (response). The current methods for acquiring these corpuses are logistically difficult and time-consuming [1-5].

We propose that VH users (as opposed to developers) generate the model using Human-centered Distributed Conversational Modeling (HDCM). HDCM applies ideas from Crowdsourcing [6] and Human-Computation [7] to the problem of enumerating the stimuli-response space of a conversation. HDCM acquires the knowledge from the people who have it, the domain novices and experts. Our evaluation results show that HDCM shortens the time to model the conversation (efficient) and the resulting VH conversational model is more comprehensive (robust).

2   Motivation and Related Work

VHs for natural language conversations are increasingly popular for communication skills training. Projects in military [1], psychology [3], and medicine [2, 8] have been created with significant collaborative effort from both domain experts and computer science experts. These publications report that it is logistically difficult and time consuming to create the necessary conversational corpora [1-3, 8].

Standard resources for creating conversational corpora include -- recordings of people in "natural" or staged interactions, asking experts, Wizard of Oz (WoZ) interactions, and automated spoken interactions [9]. From a survey of projects in this area [1-4], we see that the standard approach of VH developers creating these corpora is to:

1. *Gather Starting Stimuli:* VH Developers create a starting set of stimuli and responses by asking experts, and watching recordings of natural and/or staged interactions.
2. *Refine with Users:* To find additional stimuli, they bring end-users to the lab to use WoZ interactions, where users interact with a VH controlled by a human operator, or automated spoken interactions, where users interact with an automated VH.
3. *Validate with Experts:* VH Developers collaborate with experts to validate new stimuli and create responses to those stimuli.
4. *Repeat:* Iteratively repeat steps 2 and 3 until the domain expert and VH developers conclude that the accuracy of the conversational model is acceptable.

We will hereafter refer to this method as Centralized Conversational Modeling (CCM) because of the VH developer's role as the hub for transferring information from experts and novices to the conversation corpus. CCM is limited by the following three challenges:

Challenge 1: Corpus retrieval requires a corpus detailed enough for generalization. Recordings of "natural" or staged interactions and asking experts directly provide a good "starting point," but they are not detailed enough for generalization [5].

Unanticipated stimuli account for the majority of errors (51%) in a conversation modeled using CCM [2].

Challenge 2: There are logistical issues in the use of the corpora sources regarding legal use of existing material, monetary cost, required time, and end-user availability.

Challenge 3: VH developers may not know the domain, so time is needed with domain experts to validate new stimuli and create new responses via phone/email.

In practice, these three challenges result in few iterations of user testing, and each iteration having a limited number of users. Thus, the resulting conversation corpus has significant gaps in its stimuli coverage (many unanticipated stimuli). This causes increased response errors and a decreased ability for the VH interaction to achieve educational and training objectives. The HDCM method addresses these challenges by directly engaging end-users in the process of knowledge acquisition for conversational modeling.

The idea of directly engaging end-users for knowledge acquisition was explored in *Open Mind Common Sense* [6], the Open Directory Project, and Wikipedia. These projects fall under headings of crowdsourcing and community based-design, and they embody the idea of distributed collaborative work. Collaborative work implies that the contributors for these projects are motivated to *work* on the project itself. While these projects have found great success, their approach would not succeed for VH conversation training applications; novices (e.g. students) are not generally motivated to engage directly in the process of conversational modeling [8]. We find the solution to motivating users in Lois von Ahn's *ESP Game* [7]. Von Ahn pointed out that human-based computation can solve problems that are still untenable for computers to solve, e.g. searching images. Just as Von Ahn hid computer vision in the *ESP Game,* in HDCM we hide conversational modeling within interactions.

3   Human-Centered Distributed Conversational Modeling

HDCM applies the ideas of human-based computation and crowdsourcing to the challenge of conversational modeling. We saw in section 2 that the VH developer's role in creating the conversational model is collecting knowledge from the end-users and using that knowledge to "teach" the conversational model. Using HDCM, domain experts and novices collaborate to teach the VH how to converse. They collaborate asynchronously through a GUI that is useable without any knowledge of the technical details of conversational modeling, such as XML. End-users engage in the following iterative process to create a VH conversational model.

1. *Gather Starting Stimuli:* A domain expert primes the Conversational model with best guesses as to what will be said to the VH and what the VH should say back.
2. *Refine with Novice-Users:* Multiple novices have a typed conversation with the VH. The system collects new stimuli when the VH does not have a response, and when it responds incorrectly (details in section 3.1).

3. *Validate by Expert-User:* A domain expert asynchronously enters responses to which the VH could not respond, or to which the VH responded incorrectly.
4. *Repeat:* Phase 2 and 3 are repeated until an acceptable accuracy is reached as determined by the domain expert and VH developers.

Through interactions with a VH, the domain novices enumerate the space of what will be said to the VH; while domain experts enumerate the space of what the VH will say back. Compared to CCM, iterations of HDCM are completed faster, and can involve a greater number of end-users. This process generates a corpus that enumerates the space of a conversation. That corpus forms the basis of a VH conversational model for corpus retrieval conversations.

3.1 Virtual People Factory: An Implementation of HDCM

To evaluate HDCM we created Virtual People Factory (VPF). VPF is a web-application that implements the HDCM process described in section 3 and a web service that provides support for presentation in multiple display mediums (Fig. 1).

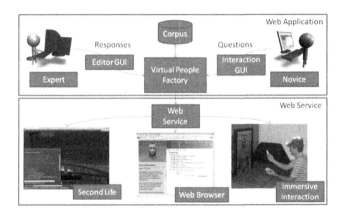

Fig. 1. Virtual People Factory System Overview[1]

We built VPF using open source software components: Apache Web Server, PHP Scripting Language, Javascript/JQuery, and MySQL Database. The system runs on a single server containing a Core2 Duo Quad-Core processor and 4GB of RAM. The application provides interfaces for both expert and novice users. Novice users perform interactions using the browser-based interview GUI. The interaction is similar to an instant messaging conversation[1].

To respond to user utterances, VPF uses an un-annotated corpus retrieval approach [2]. This approach uses keyword matching to find a list of corpus stimuli that are most similar to the current input stimulus[2]. During these interactions, VPF gathers three types of errors – *true negative, false negative*, and *false positive*. A *true negative* error

---

[1] Video Addendum: http://vpf.cise.ufl.edu/vpf_iva09/
[2] Details of our corpus retrieval approach found at: http://vpf.cise.ufl.edu/forum/

is when a user types a stimulus, and the system cannot find any response because there is no appropriate response. With a *false negative*, there is an appropriate response, but the corpus did not have a stimulus to locate that response. These errors are automatically logged in a list of new stimuli. However, VPF cannot reliably identify false positives. *False positives* result from a mismatched stimulus, where the VH did respond, but incorrectly. For example, the user asks, "Do you take *Tums* regularly?" and the character responds, "I take *Aspirin* all the time." Accordingly, when the VH responds incorrectly, the instructions ask users to press the "Mark Incorrect" button as seen in the video[1]. Pressing that button logs the false positive error as a new stimulus. After VPF gathers errors as new stimuli, the expert uses the resulting list of stimuli to add new stimuli and responses to the conversation corpus.

To validate new stimuli and create responses, experts use the Editor GUI[1]. In the Editor GUI, VPF shows the expert new stimuli one at a time. For each new stimulus, VPF provides its best guesses as to an existing correct response. VPF provides this list using the ordered list of responses from the corpus retrieval approach [2, 4]. The expert can choose one of those responses, or type in a new response. If they type in a new response, VPF provides a list of similar existing responses. The expert then selects an existing response, or uses their new response.

The resulting VPF conversational models are accessed in other applications using the VPF SOAP XML web-service. This web-service has been used to deploy VPF models in instant message interactions through a web-browser, spoken interactions through the *Interpersonal Simulator* [2], and typed interactions using *Second Life*. The web-service provides speech understanding, audio file serving, body and facial animations, and dialogue acts.

4   Evaluation Study: A Virtual Patient with a Stomach Ache

We used VPF to examine if the HDCM approach:

1. Enables an expert to create a conversational model,
2. Reduces conversational modeling time requirements,
3. Results in a conversational model with increased accuracy for spoken interactions.

To evaluate HDCM, a virtual patient named Vic was developed for an Introduction to Pharmacy Communications course taught by Dr. Carole Kimberlin in Spring of 2008. At minimum, Vic needed to discuss the following topics: his age, weight, gender, medical history (Hypertension, Hypothyroidism), and medication history (Zestril, Synthroid, Aspirin, Tums), and current stomach pain. To converse about these topics, Vic needed extensive domain specific knowledge. The pharmacy expert and pharmacy students provided this domain knowledge using the HDCM process.

The expert participant is the Pharmacy Instructor. She has computer experience on par with most medical professionals. The novice participants consisted of 12 teaching assistants (TAs) and 164 2nd year students from a Pharmacy Communication Skills course. Participant ages range from 20 to 60 with an average of 25.44.

Results

Conversational Modeling Time: There were three iterations of conversational modeling improvement. The first included the 12 TA interactions (group **TA**). The second included the first 44 student interactions (group **S1**). The last included the remaining 120 student interactions (group **S2**). Participants interacted for an average of 20 minutes, making the total student time 62 hours. These three rounds of user-testing required 15 hours of expert time over 2 weeks and created a conversational corpus consisting of 2655 stimuli and 595 responses.

Conversation Accuracy Improvements: We evaluated the interaction transcripts for accuracy by reviewing the response to each participant question. We marked the response as accurate if there was a semantic link between the stimuli and response[4]; meaning there was a response and it was correct according to Vic's symptoms and medical history. We analyzed the percentage of responses that were accurate for all of group TA, and a random 10 transcripts from groups S1 and S2. Results -- TA: *60.6%* (s.d. = 13.3%), S1: *71.2%* (s.d. = 6.7%), S2: *79.6%* (s.d. =5.3%). Thus, response accuracy improved with each cycle of testing/error correction.

Accuracy with Spoken Inputs: We examined the performance of the HDCM model with spoken transcripts and compared that to the performance of a conversational model created using CCM. To run the comparison, we analyzed Interpersonal Simulator [2] transcripts from 33 spoken interactions between pharmacy students and a VH patient. We removed inaccurate utterances due to speech recognition errors from the transcripts (16.7%), and analyzed the responses to the remaining utterances using both HDCM and CCM. Accuracy analysis revealed *74.5%* accuracy (s.d. = 11.1%) for the conversational model created with CCM while the one created with HDCM has *78.6%* accuracy (s.d. = 9.7%). Using a T-test on the raw accuracy numbers, we see a significant difference at p < .05 with t = 2.4.

Table 1. Results Overview: CCM vs HDCM

Method	Creators	Interactions	Expert Time	Novice Time	Stimuli	Responses
Centralized	VH Experts, Pharmacy Educators, 51 Students	Spoken Interactions	~200 Hrs	11 Hrs (13 Min Avg)	1418	303
Distributed	Pharmacy Educator, 186 Students	VPF Typed Interactions	15 Hrs	62 Hrs (20 Min Avg)	2655	595

Discussion

The results of this case study show that HDCM reduces the time needed to create the speech-understanding portion of a conversational model. Using HDCM, the Pharmacy Instructor was able to develop Vic in fifteen hours over 2 weeks, compared to the VH developers and experts creating Vic in ~200 hours over 6 months.

We see in Table 1 that there is a decrease in the required expert time by ~92.5% and increase in the total novice time by 545.5%. Given such a large amount of novice data and an effective method for processing this data, the pharmacy instructor was able to create a corpus of nearly double the size of the CCM method. This larger corpus yielded a significant 4.1% improvement in accuracy.

Feedback from both the pharmacy educator and pharmacy students stated that the experience was educationally beneficial. Surveys show that 32% of the students felt the experience was "very valuable" (ratings 8-10), with an average rating of 6.2/10. The Pharmacy Instructor expressed that "building this scenario was relatively easy with minimal training, and that the effort is worthwhile because the scenario can be used over and over."

5   Conclusions

The results of this study show that HDCM is an efficient method for generating VHs with the ability to recognize and respond to user speech. Since these studies, healthcare educators have begun using VPF to integrate VHs into the curricula of four medical schools in the United States. To accommodate curricular integration, they have created six additional medical scenarios for teaching interview skills.

In August 2008, we opened VPF to the public: http://vpf.cise.ufl.edu. VPF currently has 41 active users outside of our research group, including VH researchers, healthcare practitioners, psychologists, and high-school students. These users have explored creating characters outside of the healthcare domain including as educators and tour guides. From their work, as of March of 2009, VPF has facilitated 1600 interactions consisting of more than 35,000 utterances.

Acknowledgements. Special thanks go to Dr. Carole Kimberlin and Dr. Diane Beck for their participation in the pharmacy study. We also thank Dr. Andrew Raij, Aaron Kotranza, Joon Chauh and Dr. Kyle Johnsen for their advice and assistance during VPF's development. This work was made possible by a University of Florida Alumni Fellowship and National Science Foundation Grants.

References

1. Kenny, P., et al.: Building interactive virtual humans for training environments. In: ITSEC 2007, NTSA (2007)
2. Dickerson, R., et al.: Evaluating a Script-Based Approach for Simulating Patient-Doctor Interaction. In: SCS 2005 International Conference on Human-Computer Interface Advances for Modeling and Simulation, pp. 79–84 (2005)
3. Kenny, P., Parsons, T.D., Gratch, J., Rizzo, A.A.: Evaluation of justina: A virtual patient with PTSD. In: Prendinger, H., Lester, J.C., Ishizuka, M. (eds.) IVA 2008. LNCS (LNAI), vol. 5208, pp. 394–408. Springer, Heidelberg (2008)

4. Leuski, A., et al.: Building effective question answering characters. In: Proceedings of the 7th SIGdial Workshop on Discourse and Dialogue (2006)
5. Reiter, E., Sripada, S., Robertson, R.: Acquiring correct knowledge for natural language generation. Journal of Artificial Intelligence Research 18, 491–516 (2003)
6. Singh, P., et al.: Open Mind Common Sense: Knowledge Acquisition from the General Public. In: On the Move to Meaningful Internet Systems 2002: CoopIS, DOA, and ODBASE, pp. 1223–1237 (2002)
7. von Ahn, L., Dabbish, L.: Labeling images with a computer game. In: Proceedings of the SIGCHI conference on Human factors in computing systems, pp. 319–326 (2004)
8. Villaume, W.A., Berger, B.A., Barker, B.N.: Learning Motivational Interviewing: Scripting a Virtual Patient. American Journal of Pharmaceutical Education 70(2) (2006)
9. Ruttkay, Z., et al.: Evaluating Embodied Conversational Agents. Evaluating Embodied Conversational Agents 4121 (2004)

Issues in Dynamic Generation of Sign Language Utterances for a Web 2.0 Virtual Signer

Annelies Braffort, Jean-Paul Sansonnet, and Cyril Verrecchia

LIMSI-CNRS, Campus d'Orsay bat 508, BP 133,
F-91403 Orsay cx, France
{annelies.braffort,jps,cyril.verrecchia}@limsi.fr

1 Introduction

In this paper, we present our current study on the design of a virtual agent able to express sentences in Sign Language (SL), so-called 'Virtual Signer', in the context of interactive web-based applications.

Up now, little work has been carried out on web-based virtual signers. As for current research on virtual signers in standalone applications, it relies on two main approaches: Pre-synthesized animations based on motion capture [1] or rotoscoping [2], and generated animations [3], with very little interactivity. Our aim is to provide the virtual signer with richer interacting capabilities with the data contained in the web page.

2 DIVA, a Web 2.0 Platform Integrating Virtual Agents

To enhance interactivity, a solution is to use the Document Object Model (DOM). The DOM is a way to create, navigate into, modify or animated HTML documents. Our Web 2.0 platform, so-called 'DIVA', is based on this technology.

The animation engine is a JavaScript program that directly loads picture files in <div> DOM objects and then animates them, at the frame level. This makes it possible to compute animations movies and to compose them in JavaScript locally, i.e. on the client page, so that it is possible to mix them with DOM objects. In a web-based environment, we have to deal with tradeoffs such as the quality of the graphic display against the loading speed: We had to consider both the pixel size of the frames and the number of frames for one animation. For example, in our present experiments, the animations items are composed of 6, 15 or 30 frames with 500×500 pixels in .png format.

3 Issues for Dynamic Generation of SL Sentences

Sign language is a visual and gestural language. A SL utterance is composed of a sequence of gestural units involving the upper body, the arms and hands, the head, face and gaze. All these elements are articulated in the space located in front of the signer, so-called 'signing space'. Signs have variable realizations, highly depending

Zs. Ruttkay et al. (Eds.): IVA 2009, LNAI 5773, pp. 482–483, 2009.

on the context [4]. Thus, SL utterance synthesis implies to design specific spatiotemporal grammar rules [5]. Moreover, the coarticulation process influences both manual and non-manual features. This phenomenon is a complex process [6] that has not yet been modeled accurately so far.

In the context of the DIVA platform and its animation engine, we manage the generation of the SL utterances as follow: A SL utterance is built by concatenation of signs. Each sign is displayed as a predefined animation, built using rotoscoping, allowing a good realistic rendering. For all the signs the realization of which varies regarding to the context (e.g. pointing), we predefine several realizations (e.g. six for pointing); note that their combinatory is limited because we restrict to context-dependent utterances. For the coarticulation sign animations, we use one or more intermediary postures (chosen dynamically, according to the context): typically, hands are in front of the chest for signs.

4   Conclusion and Perspectives

At this moment, the implementation on the DIVA framework of a first SL page has been done, and our first prototype can be accessed at the DIVA SL Web page [7]. In a preliminary qualitative evaluation by a deaf person, animations are considered fluid, and intermediate postures do not disturb the clear understanding of the SL utterances. The actual evaluation with deaf subjects is currently in progress.

In further work, we will carry out three actions: first, include SL grammar processing in order to enhance the SL linguistic capabilities of the platform; then, develop a larger sign library; and finally, develop an e-learning platform for SL, in order to validate the Web-based approach to SL animation on a larger scale.

References

[1]   Adamo-Villani, N., Benes, B., Brisbin, M.: A natural interface for sign language mathematics. In: Bebis, G., Boyle, R., Parvin, B., Koracin, D., Remagnino, P., Nefian, A., Meenakshisundaram, G., Pascucci, V., Zara, J., Molineros, J., Theisel, H., Malzbender, T. (eds.) ISVC 2006. LNCS, vol. 4291, pp. 70–79. Springer, Heidelberg (2006)
[2]   VCom3D, http://www.vcom3d.com/vault_files/forest_asl/
[3]   Elliott, R., Glauert, J.R.W., Jennings, V., Kennaway, J.R.: An Overview of the SiGML Notation and SiGML Signing Software System. In: Streiter, O., Vettori, C. (eds.) Fourth International Conference on Language Resources and Evaluation, LREC 2004, Lisbon, Portugal, pp. 98–104 (2004)
[4]   Cuxac, C.: The Expression of Spatial Relations and the Spatialization of Semantic Relations in French Sign Language. In: Language Diversity and Cognitive Representations, pp. 123–142. Benjamins, Amsterdam (1999)
[5]   Braffort, A., Dalle, P.: Sign language applications: preliminary modeling. In: International journal on Universal Access in the Information Society, Special issue 6/4, Emerging Technologies for Deaf Accessibility in the Information Society. Springer, Heidelberg (2007)
[6]   Segouat, J.: A Study of Sign Language Coarticulation. In: 10th International ACM SIGACCESS Conf on Computers and Accessibility, ASSETS-2008, Halifax, CA (2008)
[7]   DIVA SL,
      http://www.limsi.fr/Individu/jps/online/diva/geste/
      geste.main.htm

Towards More Human-Like Episodic Memory
for More Human-Like Agents

Cyril Brom[1] and Jiří Lukavský[2]

[1] Charles University, Faculty of Mathematics and Physics, Prague, Czech Republic
[2] Institute of Psychology, Academy of Sciences, Prague, Czech Republic

1 Introduction

Episodic memory (EM) is an umbrella term for memory systems that operate with representations of personal history of an entity. The content of EM is related to particular places and moments, and connected to subjective feelings and current goals.

Recently, it has been argued that EM is one of the key components contributing to believability of intelligent virtual agents (IVAs), at least when agents interact with humans for more than a couple of minutes, because it allows the user to understand better the agent's history, personality, and internal state: both actual state and past state [e.g. 2, 5]. Technically, the EM is merely a data structure for loss compression of the flow of external events. The EM cannot be implemented as a pure log/video, because these are bad data structures (including human level). Why are they bad? First, they produce too large data. Second, they are not well organised with respect to future possible queries: neither a log nor a video have appropriate indexes in terms of database systems. A better approach is needed.

2 Overview of Our Model

We have started to pursue a systematic research on episodic memory for IVAs, beginning with investigating a single episodic memory module, what we now call the *core*, and continuing with widening the core by adding new subsystems that modulate the core and/or other subsystems. The core has been already presented [3]. It is a hierarchically organised memory for complex events (e.g. cooking a dinner) that can happen in large environments (house), and the IVA with the core can live in its world over long intervals (weeks). The memory features a gradual forgetting mechanism. For example, the IVA can originally remember that it was cooking a goulash yesterday morning, including all subtasks, but later forget the subtasks, keeping only the high-level information about the cooking. The forgetting is based on the age of episodes and their emotional salience. Thanks to the core, the agent can express itself, i.e. to answer questions such as: "What did you do yesterday between t_1 and t_2?".

The core has been extended with several memory appendages recently. First, the IVA can now express itself in a given number of sentences: "What did you do yesterday between t_1 and t_2? Summarise in 3 sentences." Second, instead of using exact time for dating episodes, which is not plausible, the memory now can learn human-like notions of time such as "after breakfast," "late afternoon," "when tired after lunch" etc. based on the history of the agent's interaction [4]. This part of the memory also

Zs. Ruttkay et al. (Eds.): IVA 2009, LNAI 5773, pp. 484–485, 2009.

allows the agent to adapt to temporal time shifts like a change of time zone. Additionally, thanks to this component, similar episodes can be blended in some situations; e.g., an agent who was watering a garden every evening cannot recall details of any particular watering episode when cued by time, but it can recall both that it was watering evenings last week and some detail of each watering when cued with time *plus* other details of the episode. Third, the memory has now a new module for representing long-term information about possible objects' locations in a familiar environment. This module is presented elsewhere [1], suffice it to say here that the module solves the issue of plausible estimation of possible objects locations, of those objects that are passive but can be moved by external forces beyond the agent's capabilities (e.g. a pen is moved by a fellow agent and put elsewhere). Finally, we have been implementing a module for plausible subjective representations of proximal space; basically intermediate-term allocentric and egocentric representations of locations of objects in the IVA's immediate surrounding. Our preliminary results suggest that our model will be able to organise some psychological data [e.g. 7, 6].

While the memory core and the timing module were investigated in a 3D world, other modules have been tested only in a 2D world. The most notable future works include porting all the modules to the 3D world, development a mechanism for emergence of false memories, and development a component for reconstructing high-level goals of a human user from the flow of the user's atomic actions. Without it, the memory is not able to represent efficiently what human users do in virtual worlds.

Acknowledgement. This work was partially supported by the Program "Information Society" under project 1ET100300517, by the Ministry of Education of the Czech Republic (Res. Project MSM0021620838), and by GA UK 21809. We thank to students working on this project: T. Soukup, J. Vyhnánek, J. Kotrla, and R. Kadlec.

References

1. Brom, C., Korenko, T., Lukavský, J.: How Place and Objects Combine? "What-Where" Memory for Human-like Agents. In: Ruttkay, Zs., et al. (eds.) IVA 2009. LNCS (LNAI), vol. 5773, Springer, Heidelberg (2009)
2. Brom, C., Lukavsky, J.: Towards Virtual Characters with a Full Episodic Memory II: The Episodic Memory Strikes Back. In: Proc. Empathic Agents, AAMAS workshop, pp. 1–9 (2009)
3. Brom, C., Pešková, K., Lukavský, J.: What does your actor remember? Towards characters with a full episodic memory. In: Cavazza, M., Donikian, S. (eds.) ICVS-VirtStory 2007. LNCS, vol. 4871, pp. 89–101. Springer, Heidelberg (2007)
4. Burkert, O.: Connectionist Model of Episodic Memory for Virtual Humans. Master thesis. Dept. Software & Comp. Sci. Education. Charles University in Prague (2009)
5. Castellano, G., Aylett, R., Dautenhahn, K., Paiva, A., McOwan, P.W., Ho, S.: Long-term affect sensitive and socially interactive companions. In: 4th Int. Workshop on Human-Computer Convers (2008)
6. Holmes, M.C., Sholl, M.J.: Allocentric coding of object-to-object relations in overlearned and novel environments. Jn. Exp. Psychol.: General 119, 1069–1087 (2005)
7. Waller, D., Hodgson, E.: Transient and Enduring Spatial Representations Under Disorientation and Self-Rotation. Jn. of Exp. Psychol.: Learning, Memory and Cognition 32(4), 867–882 (2006)

RealActor: Character Animation and Multimodal Behavior Realization System

Aleksandra Cerekovic, Tomislav Pejsa, and Igor S. Pandzic

University of Zagreb, Faculty of Electrical Engineering and Computing, Unska 3,
10000 Zagreb, Croatia
{aleksandra.cerekovic,tomislav.pejsa,igor.pandzic}@fer.hr

1 Overview

In this paper we present RealActor, a character behavior realization system for embodied conversational agents based on the Behavior Markup Language (BML). Developed several years ago as part of the SAIBA framework, BML is an XML dialect for describing physical realizations of multimodal human behaviors. It allows modeling of complex communicative utterances which include both verbal and non-verbal behavior. BML elements represent various primitive actions (e.g. speech, facial and body gestures) and multimodal behavior can be modeled by specifying temporal relationships between these elements. Our BML-based character animation system has the following features:

- specification of character behaviors using BML scripts
- start, stop, schedule or merge behaviors via high-level, BML-compliant API
- database of annotated animations shared between multiple characters
- motion playback system based on MPEG-4 FBA standard
- visual text-to-speech synthesis based on industry-standard Microsoft SAPI
- lip synchronization
- integration with any graphics engine via a minimal scene wrapper
- flexible art pipeline based on universal file formats (FBX, COLLADA, VRML) that includes tools for automated production of face models and morph targets for facial animation

The BML realizer (Fig. 1) is the core module of our system and consists of three central components: BML Parser, Behavior Planner and Behavior Scheduler. BML Parser parses BML scripts, generates appropriate behavior blocks and adds them to a list. Behavior Planner prepares each block for execution by adding timing information needed for multimodal behavior synchronization. For primitive animations this timing data is retrieved from the animation database, where each animation is annotated with time constraint and type information. Speech is handled using lip-sync or text-to-speech synthesis - if lip-sync is used, speech must be prerecorded and manually annotated with timing data, while timings for synthesized speech can be inferred at run-time. Finally, BML Scheduler is responsible for execution of prepared behaviors and uses timing information to decide which behaviors will execute and when.

Zs. Ruttkay et al. (Eds.): IVA 2009, LNAI 5773, pp. 486–487, 2009.

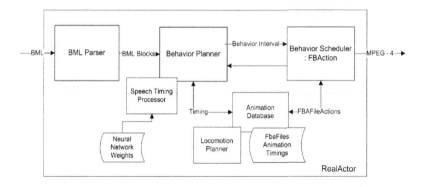

Fig. 1. Architecture of the BML realizer

Most TTS systems (including Microsoft SAPI used in RealActor) do not provide a priori phoneme and word timing information necessary for synchronization of synthesized text with non-verbal behavior. To address this issue, we utilize backpropagation neural networks (BNNs) to estimate word durations and align speech with animation in real-time. Our system is able to correctly align 92,26% of words for a short time interval (500 ms) and 73,26% of words for a long interval (1500 ms) with alignment error not exceeding the 80 ms threshold (which is the shortest discrepancy between audio and video perceptible to human beings). Furthermore, the system achieved 79,03% and 56,59% alignment rates with no measurable alignment error.

2   Results and Future Work

We have developed RealActor, an open-source character animation and multimodal behavior system based on Behavior Markup Language (BML). To our knowledge, it is one of only three BML-compliant animation systems in existence. We have developed a universal, language-independent solution to the issue of multimodal behavior synchronization that utilizes neural networks to estimate word durations. Furthermore, our system is designed in such a manner that it can be integrated with existing graphics engines and application frameworks with minimal effort, which we demonstrated by integrating RealActor with open-source engines such as OGRE, Horde3D and Irrlicht. While testing RealActor, we observed that manual authoring of BML scripts can be time-consuming and counter-intuitive and plan to address this by providing a graphical BML authoring tool or by deveping a higher-level component that would generate behaviors automatically. On lower level, we will introduce a new animation system that will utilize parametric motion graphs to synthesize long sequences of visually pleasing and interactively controllable motion.

Locomotion Animation by Using Riding Motion

Sung June Chang and Byung Tae Choi

Electronics and Telecommunications Research Institute(ETRI)
161 Gajeong-dong, Yuseong-gu,
Daejeon, Korea
dyad@etri.re.kr

1 Introduction

This paper provides a method to make locomotion animation using riding motion, which is synthesized by computer simulation. Our locomotion system uses riding motion to avoid collision between objects instead of traditional obstacle avoidance. The two-dimensional locomotion using obstacle avoidance has a problem in that positions that the agent move is limited if the number of agents is large. In game or film, user or artist should throw up natural movement to locate agents in the specific area to avoid obstacle. The major strengths of the algorithm is fast calculation and natural locomotion motion, the weakness is that the algorithm is not applied to various creatures

2 Riding Motion for Collision Avoidance

The traditional obstacle avoidance changes the original trajectory to avoid collision, which means that there is limitation for the trajectory. As the number of agents is larger, some agents should stop or move slowly because of that limitation. But in some cases, the stop or slow motion is not tolerable to show game or film's activeness. In those cases, there is no choice without giving up collision avoidance, which means that scene is not natural. But our riding motion does not restrict the original trajectory because it use upper trajectory. And it looks natural because the riding is real animal's behavior.

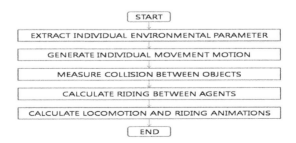

Fig. 1. Algorithm

Zs. Ruttkay et al. (Eds.): IVA 2009, LNAI 5773, pp. 488–489, 2009.
© Springer-Verlag Berlin Heidelberg 2009

We use two-phase method to make riding motion. In the first phase, simulation is generated without collision avoidance. If there is collision, then penetration between agents is occurred. No consideration of collision avoidance is necessary to calculate riding information correctly. There will be many collisions between agents. In the second phase, we firstly decide which agent is riding. There will be many strategies to choose, we choose the riding agent after comparing the angle between moving direction and collision direction. The agent with nearer angle is riding and the other is sat on. For the rider agent, we measure collision area between objects, and calculate the degree using the penetrate area by assuming the riding agent does not touch the floor or the most far part of the riding agent is touching. And calculate the agents' position using their property like height, then decide that the motion is "ride up"," ride down", or "ride on" by analyzing the first phase simulation. The detail algorithm is shown in Fig.1. For the ridee agent, there is nothing to do in the second phase.

As you see in the algorithm, it does not require many calculations. It is very fast, so we can apply locomotion animation using riding motion in the massive agents' simulation in Fig2. And the riding motion looks very natural in spite of simple calculation in turtle animation of Fig2 which use only our algorithm and simple foot skate solving algorithm.

Fig. 2. Massive locomotion agents and turtle animation using riding motion

Acknowledgments

This work was supported by the IT R&D program of MKE/IITA and MCST/KOCCA. [2007-S-051-02,Software Development for Digital Creature].

References

1. Park, S.I., Shin, H.J., Shin, S.: On-line locomotion generation based on motion blending. In: Proceedings of ACM SIGGRAPH Symposium on Computer Animation 2002, pp. 105–111 (2002)
2. Kwon, T., Shin, S.Y.: Motion modeling for on-line locomotion synthesis. In: Proceedings of the 2005 ACM SIGGRAPH/Eurographics symposium on Computer animation, Los Angeles, California, July 29-31 (2005)

Automated Generation of Emotive Virtual Humans

Joon Hao Chuah, Brent Rossen, and Benjamin Lok

CISE
University of Florida
Gainesville, FL 32611, USA
{jchuah,brossen,lok}@cise.ufl.edu

Keywords: Virtual Humans, Agents and Intelligent Systems, Virtual Reality, Affective sensing from text, Emotions.

1 Introduction

Emotive virtual humans (VHs) are important for affective interactions with embodied conversation agents [1]. However, emotive VHs require significant resources and time. As an example, the VHs in movies and video games require teams of animators and months of work. VHs can also be imbued with emotion using appraisal theory methods that use psychology based models to generate emotions by using the VH's goals and beliefs to evaluate external events. These external events require manual tagging or natural language understanding [2]. As an alternative approach, we propose tagging VH responses with emotions using textual affect sensing methods. The method developed by Neviarouskaya et al. [3] uses syntactic parses and a database of words and associated emotion intensities. We use this database, and because these emotions are associated with specific words, we can combine the emotions with audio timing information to generate lip-synched facial expressions. Our approach, AutoEmotion, allows us to automatically add basic emotions to VHs without the need for manual animation or tagging or natural language understanding.

2 Implementation

Our VH interaction system matches user inputs to a pre-defined set of VH text responses with recorded audio [4]. We combine the set of VH text responses with a database of words and associated emotion intensities [3] to create a list of emotion words for this particular VH. This list can be refined by the VH creator to modify intensities for specific words or remove scenario inappropriate words altogether. We then combine this list with word timing information generated by applying speech recognition to the recorded audio to create timings for each emotion based on the associated word. The result of this process is timed emotion intensities for each response. This emotion intensity information is used to mix facial expression and lip synch morph targets for use in the VH rendering system.

Zs. Ruttkay et al. (Eds.): IVA 2009, LNAI 5773, pp. 490–491, 2009.

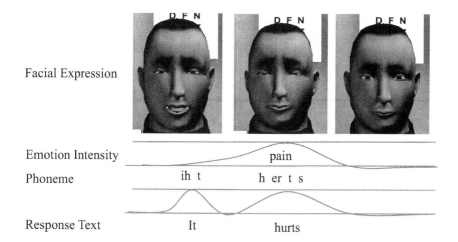

Facial Expression			
Emotion Intensity		pain	
Phoneme	ih t	h er t s	
Response Text	It	hurts	

Fig. 1. VH Facial expression changing to match phonemes and emotions

3   Conclusions and Future Work

AutoEmotion allows VH creators to add basic emotions to a character without the effort or complexity of pure manual animation or appraisal theory based approaches. These basic emotions can also be synced to specific moments in the VH response because they are associated with specific words. Beyond the basic emotions, VH creators can still manually add emotions and full body animation to increase expressiveness for key moments and responses.

We plan to conduct a user study to determine if AutoEmotion brings the VH's expressiveness and naturalness to an acceptable level. In this study we will use three conditions: AutoEmotion, no emotion, and random emotion. In the random emotion condition, the VH will randomly choose which emotion, if any, to display and with what intensity. From this study we will determine if AutoEmotion is a viable alternative to current approaches for emotions in VHs.

References

1. Raij, A., Johnsen, K., Dickerson, R., Lok, B., Cohen, M., Duerson, M., Pauly, R., Stevens, A., Wagner, P., Lind, D.S.: Comparing interpersonal interactions with a virtual human to those with a real human. IEEE Transactions on Visualization and Computer Graphics 13(3), 443 (2007)
2. Gratch, J., Marsella, S.: A domain-independent framework for modeling emotion. Cognitive Systems Research 5(4), 269–306 (2004)
3. Neviarouskaya, A., Prendinger, H., Ishizuka, M.: User study of affectIM, an emotionally intelligent instant messaging system. In: Prendinger, H., Lester, J.C., Ishizuka, M. (eds.) IVA 2008. LNCS (LNAI), vol. 5208, pp. 29–36. Springer, Heidelberg (2008)
4. Johnsen, K., Dickerson, R., Raij, A., Harrison, C., Lok, B., Stevens, A., Lind, D.S.: Evolving an immersive medical communication skills trainer. Presence: Teleoperators & Virtual Environments 15(1), 33–46 (2006)

Little Mozart: Establishing Long Term Relationships with (Virtual) Companions

Secundino Correia, Sandra Pedrosa, Juliana Costa, and Marco Estanqueiro

Urbanização Panorama, lote 2, loja 2, Monte Formoso, 3000-446 Coimbra, Portugal
{Secundino,Sandra.Pedrosa,Juliana.Costa,Marco}@Imagina.com

Abstract. This paper aims to present e the work developed at Cnotinfor within the LIREC project. We will present Little Mozart mind architecture and facial expressions. Our goal is to create a virtual e-learning agent capable of establishing meaningful interactions with children on how to compose and improve their knowledge of melodic composition and basics of musical language. In order to make our agent believable and engaging we resorted to facial and body 3D modeling techniques as a strategy for expressing emotion through multimodal communication.

Keywords: mind, emotion, expression, interaction.

1 Introduction

LIREC (LIving with Robots and interactivE Companions) it's a four year project conducted in a consortium led by Queen Mary University of London, in which Cnotinfor participates through its Centre for Technological Innovation.

Little Mozart is our pedagogical virtual agent and he aims to establish meaningful interactions with children on how to compose and improve their knowledge of melodic composition and basics of musical language. In order to teach melodic music basics Little Mozart uses Pedro Sousa's methodology, his methodology is based on a series of rules in what comes to the correct sequence of musical notes. The user's choices can result in more agreeable musical melodies, meaning that there are better combinations and harmonies to produce a composition. Another rule is the combination of tempi, the composition is made with 4 tempi, which results in combinations of 2 tempi plus 1 plus 1; 2 tempi notes plus 2; 3 tempi notes plus 1 or 4 tempi notes.

Little Mozart composition scenario is inside a house divided in several rooms each with one musical note and colour associated, so when the user chooses a room the associated note is added to the staff. The process continues until the melody is completed. Little Mozart has two other scenarios, one introductory, and another one where the user has the possibility to choose an instrument reproduce the created composition

2 Mind Architecture

The Little Mozart's mind implementing a model of emotions based on FLAME [2] (which is based on OCC theory [5]). The model reacts to world (game) events or

Zs. Ruttkay et al. (Eds.): IVA 2009, LNAI 5773, pp. 492–493, 2009.
© Springer-Verlag Berlin Heidelberg 2009

consequences of user actions. Those events are then conducted through a series of stages resulting in verbal, body and facial behaviours.

The stages are divided in two major components:

The Emotional Component starts evaluating the events against agent goals. The agent major goal is to improve user musical melodic composition. Then Appraises the previous evaluation influenced by the learning component (explained later). After this stage the emotion resulting from Appraisal state is Filtered according to mood. The behaviour selection is the last stage. This stage selects behaviours according to emotional state and influenced by information from the learning component.

The Learning Component learns from user previous actions and creates expectations about the next user actions. It also memorises some information about the user in two memory levels: the short term that stores n past emotional states and long term memory that stores statistical information about the user tendencies (musical melodic composition). The consequences of agent's actions on user are also memorised in order to better select behaviours.

3 Facial Expressions

Our prototype reflects our concern to increase Mozart's believability, through providing him with facial expressions. Therefore, based on Ekman's six basic emotions and his Facial Action Coding System, FACS [1], we developed 6 different facial expressions for happiness, sadness, fear, anger, disgust and surprise and supported the design process on previous studies on facial expression and emotion expression. We used a 3d manipulation software to model the muscles of Little Mozart's face using morphing technique, which allows modeling portions of the face which allows smooth transitions [3].

Fig. 1. Little Mozart's facial expressions

References

1. Donato, G., Bartlett, M.S., Hager, J.C., Ekman, P., Sejnowski, T.J.: Classifying Facial Actions. IEEE Transactions on pattern analysis and machine intelligence, 974–989 (1999)
2. El-Nasr, M.S., Yen, J., Ioerger, T.R.: FLAME: Fuzzy Logic Adaptive Model of Emotions. In: Autonomous Agents and Multi-Agent Systems, vol. 3, pp. 219–257 (2000)
3. Lerios, A., Garfinkle, Levoy: Feature-Based Volume Metamorphosis. Stanford University (2002)
4. Ortony, A., Clore, G., Collins, A.: The Cognitive Structure of Emotions. Cambridge University Press, Cambridge (1988)

Real-Time Backchannel Selection for ECAs According to User's Level of Interest

Etienne de Sevin and Catherine Pelachaud

CNRS - Telecom ParisTech
37/39, rue Dareau
75014 Paris, France
{etienne.de-sevin,catherine.pelachaud}@telecom-paristech.fr

1 Action Selection Algorithm for ECA Backchannels

A great challenge that is to be faced in the design of virtual agents is the issue of credibility, not only in the agent's aspect but also in its behavior [1]. To be believable, the agent has to decide what to do next according to the internal and external variables of the agent. Besides others, we have to deal with the problem of action selection which can be resumed to choose the most appropriate action among all possible (conflicting) ones [2]. In our case, actions are backchannels. This work is part of the STREP EU SEMAINE project[1] in which a real-time Embodied Conversational Agent (ECA) will be a Sensitive Artificial Listener (SAL) [3]. This project aims to build an autonomous talking agent able to exhibit autonomously appropriate verbal and non verbal behaviors in real-time when it plays the role of the listener in a conversation with a user.

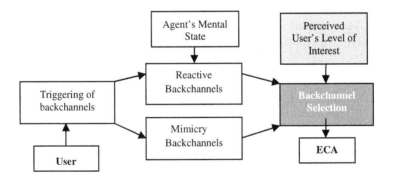

Fig. 1. Schematic view of the Backchannel architecture including a BC selection module

The proposed work is part of a pre-existing system for the generation of backchannels for an ECA listener [1][4] (see figure 1). Backchannel modules will generate potential conflicting actions and send them with their priorities to the backchannel

---

[1] http://www.semaine-project.eu

Zs. Ruttkay et al. (Eds.): IVA 2009, LNAI 5773, pp. 494–495, 2009.

selection algorithm. For example, the mimicry module could generate a head nod to mimic the user's head movement, whereas the reactive backchannel module could generate a head shake determined by the communicative function "disagree". There is a conflict between both head signals and as just one signal can be actually displayed, a choice has to be done.

The first step of our backchannel selection algorithm is to compute the probability of displaying backchannels (mimicry or reactive backchannels). Then the algorithm receives all potential reactive backchannels and mimicry. It calculates their updated priorities as a function of the user's interest level. These new priorities are the basis of selection because they allow us to compare different backchannels coming from the action proposer module. The priorities of backchannels can also be modified afterward according the contextual information of the interaction such as the estimated gaze of the user, the user's level of the disinterest and the phase of the interaction. The selection is event-based and in real-time. If backchannels are triggered, then a choice is made. Finally, the selection algorithm chooses the most appropriate backchannels based on the priority values according to the user's interest level and the context of the interaction.

2   Conclusion

The preliminary evaluation shows that our listener ECA behaves like we expected. The action selection chooses the appropriate action according to the user's interest level as perceived by the ECA. The user's estimated interest level is well-adapted to adjust the decisions of the ECA to choose which backchannel is the best to display in real-time. It is also a good indicator for inferring information about the user's intention to interact. As our action selection algorithm is generic, it can also be used in an application to select actions in a gaze-based sharing attention context [5].

Acknowledgments

This research was supported by the STREP SEMAINE IST-211486.

References

1. Bevacqua, E., Mancini, M., Pelachaud, C.: A listening agent exhibiting variable behaviour. In: Prendinger, H., Lester, J.C., Ishizuka, M. (eds.) IVA 2008. LNCS (LNAI), vol. 5208, pp. 262–269. Springer, Heidelberg (2008)
2. de Sevin, E., Thalmann, D.: A motivational Model of Action Selection for Virtual Humans. In: SocietyPress, I. (ed.) Computer Graphics International (CGI), pp. 213–220 (2005)
3. Douglas-Cowie, E., Cowie, R., Cox, C., Amir, N., Heylen, D.: The Sensitive Artificial Listener: an induction technique for generating emotionally coloured conversation (2008)
4. Peters, C., Pelachaud, C., Bevacqua, E., Poggi, I., Mancini, M., Chafai, N.: A Model of Attention and Interest Using Gaze Behavior. In: Panayiotopoulos, T., Gratch, J., Aylett, R.S., Ballin, D., Olivier, P., Rist, T. (eds.) IVA 2005. LNCS (LNAI), vol. 3661, pp. 229–240. Springer, Heidelberg (2005)
5. Peters, C., Asteriadis, S., Karpouzis, K., Sevin, E.: Towards a Real-time Gaze-based Shared Attention for a Virtual Agent. In: Workshop on Affective Interaction in Natural Environments in the Tenth International Conference on Multimodal Interfaces (2008)

Virtual Autonomous Agents in an Informed Environment for Risk Prevention

Lydie Edward, Domitile Lourdeaux, and Jean-Paul Barthès

Heudiasyc Laboratory, UMR CNRS 6599,
University of Technology of Compiègne

Abstract. This paper presents the work to enhance virtual agents with the abilities of interacting with the environment and planning based on goals and internal states. We describe how we designed intelligent virtual agents that are able to perform tasks on a high-risk plant and that respond to expected as well as unexpected events. We proposed an informed virtual environment where agents are able to interact with other agents or avatars. By enhancing their reasoning abilities with cognitive rules and the environment with knowledge the virtual agents are able to exhibit deviated behaviors.

1   Introduction

Our work concerns virtual humans evolving in a virtual environment dedicated for training and risk prevention. We aim at creating virtual intelligent agents that convey all accessible information and knowledge so as to emulate some interesting behaviors with a reasonable level of accuracy. We address the scientific interest to take into account human factors into complex decisional process and human variableness. In the field of training tools using virtual reality and human behavior modeling, we can cite Rickel and Johnson who designed STEVE, an autonomous animated agent that lives in a virtual world and interacts with students [1]. Based on a SOAR cognitive mono-agent architecture STEVE is able to know the state of the environment in real time and decide what actions to undertake. Gratch [2] also works on the domain of action selection with an emotional dimension. He shows that the emotional state of an agent influences his planning and selection of actions.

2   Our Approach

2.1   How to Represent Knowledge?

In order to perceive, take a decision, act in an autonomous way, agents need to access three kind of data : activity knowledge (which task to perform in the virtual environment), domain knowledge (actions, objects) and environmental knowledge (objects states, positions). We want our agent to answer the following questions : what are all the actions possible on an object ? What is the state of

Zs. Ruttkay et al. (Eds.): IVA 2009, LNAI 5773, pp. 496–497, 2009.

an object ? How to plan given high-level goal ? In what order to do the tasks ? We use an ontology to structure, organize and represent the environment and domain knowledge. To represent agent activity we propose a language HAWAI-DL that provides a hierarchical description of the activity [3].

2.2   How to Model Agent Cognitive States?

To let complex cognitive process become adaptable behaviors, contextual, erroneous and situated in good and constrained situations, we use two cognitive models in the domain of safety and human behavior in risky situations: CO-COM (Contextual Control Mode) and BTCU (Borderline Tolerated Conditions of Use) [4]. Hollnagel defines four types of control modes associated to time zones in which an agent can operate: strategic, tactical, opportunistic and scrambled. In addition we take into account physical, physiological and personality features for such models.

3   MASVERP: Multi-agent Agent Architecture

We propose a multi-agent system, MASVERP, for Multi-Agent System for Virtual Environment for Risk Prevention. Each cognitive agent has an architecture integrating a model of personality, a COCOM model and ontological models. Agents perceive their environment through a perceptive agent that sets up their representation. Once they take a decision, they communicate with an agent called COLOMBO[1] that decides if the action will succeed or not. According to their actions, their characteristics change as well as their control mode. We can visualize the evolution of such characteristics through a visualization agent.

4   Conclusion and Outlook

We developed a virtual human system, the major contribution of which is to use a cognitive model of human operators to generate deviated behaviors of virtual autonomous agents in a risky environment and presented the different needed bricks to build such a system.

References

1. Rickel, J., Johnson, L.: STEVE: A pedagogical agent for virtual reality. In: 2nd International Conference on Autonomous Agent, 9-13, pp. 332–333. ACM Press, New York (1998)
2. Gratch, J.: Emile: Marshalling Passions in Training and Education. In: 4th International Conference on Autonomous Agents (2003)
3. Edward, L., Lourdeaux, D., Lenne, D., Barthes, J.P.: Modelling autonomous virtual agent behaviours in a virtual environment for risk, IVEVA, Nanjing, China (2008)
4. Hollnagel, E.: Human Reliability Analysis: Context and Control. Academic Press, London (1993)

---

[1] French translation: Ontological Creation Linked to the MOdeling of OBjects.

An Immersive Approach to Evaluating Role Play

Lynne Hall[1], Ruth Aylett[2], and Ana Paiva[3]

[1] University of Sunderland, Sunderland, SR6 0DD, UK
[2] Heriot-Watt University, Edinburgh, EH14 4AS, UK
[3] INESC-ID, Porto Salvo, 2780-990, Portugal
lynne.hall@sunderland.ac.uk, ruth@macs.hw.ac.uk,
ana.paiva@inesc-id.pt

1 Evaluation Context: ORIENT

Games and Virtual Environments populated with virtual agents are usually tested and evaluated assessing the player's experience and flow outside the game experience. However, with player enjoyment related to their sense of immersion, there is clear potential for immersing evaluation into game play. We have developed an immersive in-role evaluation approach and applied it to ORIENT (*Overcoming Refugee Integration with Empathic Novel Technology*), a role-playing game designed for intercultural training for 13-14 year olds.

ORIENT is a synthetic character-based role play arising from work in developing models within which narrative engagement and empathy can be used to understand social, cognitive and emotional learning processes through role-play [1]. ORIENT is a 3D world projected onto a large screen with users interacting as a group of 3 Space Command personnel and is aimed at enhancing intercultural sensitivity. The ORIENT inhabitants (Sprytes) are driven by a modified version of the FAtiMA affective agent architecture [2] with these autonomous affective characters, designed to be able to carry out culturally-specific behaviour. Interacting with ORIENT should lead the learners to change their attitudes towards (cognition), their negative feelings about (emotion), and indifferent or pejorative behaviour towards members of other cultures.

2 Evaluation Approach: In-Role

In the in-role evaluation of ORIENT all participants (including the evaluation / technical team), artifacts, instruments, interactions and measurements were in-role. The ORIENT evaluation experience was designed to: be congruent with the narrative and context of ORIENT (a space command adventure); meet participant expectations and enhance role play; and provide the development team with essential information. 3 pre- and 5 post- interaction questionnaires (see figure 1) were developed through transforming well established data gathering instruments into "in role" counterparts and then embedding and reinforcing these with supporting artifacts. Pre-interaction instruments focused on participant information and cultural profile, providing the participant's base level of cultural intelligence. Post-interaction instruments focused on psychological measures related to cultural view; and on the user experience, with

Zs. Ruttkay et al. (Eds.): IVA 2009, LNAI 5773, pp. 498–499, 2009.

Fig. 1. Fragments from the Pre- and Post- Interaction Instruments

instruments focused at gaining the users' perspective on the interaction approach, storyline, characters and overall experience of the ORIENT software.

In early 2009, ORIENT was evaluated with 7 groups of teenage and 6 groups of adult users (students). Each evaluation session lasted around 90 minutes, with the entire session conducted in role, involving training, interaction and evaluation. The results were extremely positive, with the teenage users (21 participants) engaging wholeheartedly with the ORIENT experience. In the adult sessions, similar results were seen and in an additional post-evaluation debrief, the adults were directly asked about their experience of the evaluation. All participants rated the support material highly, with many commenting positively on the appearance of the artefacts and questionnaires. The key result from our evaluations was that users were unaware that they were participating in an evaluation, with the questionnaires enhancing rather than detracting from the in-role experience.

3 Successful Results... Next Steps

Results from the ORIENT evaluations revealed that participants reacted positively to this evaluation approach. The approach is both fun for the user and generates useful input for the design team. Current work focuses on further exploring the parameters of this immersive evaluation approach and the resultant impact on player experience.

Acknowledgments. This work was partially supported by European Community (EC) and is currently funded by the eCIRCUS project IST-4-027656-STP with university partners Heriot-Watt, Hertfordshire, Sunderland, Warwick, Bamberg, Augsburg, Wuerzburg plus INESC-ID and Interagens. The authors are solely responsible for the content of this publication. It does not represent the opinion of the EC, and the EC is not responsible for any use that might be made of data appearing therein.

References

1. Aylett, R., Paiva, A., Vannini, N., Enz, S., Andre, E., Hall, L.: But that was in another country: agents and intercultural empathy. In: AAMAS 2009, Budapest, Hungary (2009)
2. Dias, J., Paiva, A.: Feeling and Reasoning: a Computational Model. In: Bento, C., Cardoso, A., Dias, G. (eds.) EPIA 2005. LNCS (LNAI), vol. 3808, pp. 127–140. Springer, Heidelberg (2005)

At the Virtual Frontier: Introducing Gunslinger, a Multi-Character, Mixed-Reality, Story-Driven Experience

Arno Hartholt, Jonathan Gratch, Lori Weiss, and The Gunslinger Team[*]

University of Southern California, Institute for Creative Technologies, 13274 Fiji Way,
Marina del Rey, CA, USA
{hartholt,gratch,weiss}@ict.usc.edu

1 Introduction

Gunslinger is an interactive-entertainment application of virtual humans that transforms an iconic Wild West movie scene into a vivid semblance of reality. The project combines virtual humans technology with Hollywood storytelling and set building into an engaging, mixed-reality, story-driven experience, where a single participant can interact verbally and non-verbally with multiple virtual characters that are imbedded in a real, physical saloon. The Gunslinger project pushes the frontier of virtual humans research by combining question-answering dialogue techniques with explicit story representation. It incorporates speech recognition techniques and visual sensing to recognize multimodal user input. It further extends existing behavior generation methods such as SmartBody to drive tightly coupled dialogue amongst characters. These capabilities strive to seek a balance between open ended dialogue interaction and carefully crafted narrative.

Fig. 1. The Gunslinger set

2 System

Gunslinger is based on the Institute of Creative Technologies virtual humans architecture [1]. A speech recognizer is used to give hypothesized transcriptions of a raw speech signal [2]. A visual recognition module detects and tracks the participant's

---

[*] Anton Leuski, Louis-Philippe Morency, Matt Liewer, Marcus Thiebaux, Stacy Marsella, Prathibha Doraiswamy, Andreas Tsiartas, Kim LeMasters, Ed Fast, Ramy Sadek, Andrew Marshall, Jina Lee, Lance Pickens.

Zs. Ruttkay et al. (Eds.): IVA 2009, LNAI 5773, pp. 500–501, 2009.
© Springer-Verlag Berlin Heidelberg 2009

motion in the physical space over time while the visual understanding module infers higher level behaviors such as drawing a gun, facing a character, and movement with respect to a character. The NPCEditor is used for natural language processing and dialogue management [3]. It uses a statistical text classification algorithm that selects the character's responses based on the user's utterances. Gunslinger uses the Non-Verbal Behavior Generator (NVBG) [4] and SmartBody [5] to plan and realize the story's three characters, respectively. NVBG analyzes the speech text to propose non-verbal behaviors that are passed to SmartBody using the Behavior Markup Language. Sound is realized using ARIA, a real-time audio processing engine which leverages commodity computing hardware for high-quality audio processing [6].

3   Conclusions and Future Work

The Gunslinger project allowed us to advance the virtual humans work in such areas of multi-modal input, multi-party dialogue and story-driven interaction. The work advanced the state of these individual components and resulted in an architecture that could exploit synergies between them. We were able to advance the work being done in visual recognition and understanding by adapting efficient and reliable visual-sensing approaches to the problem of recognizing human nonverbal behaviors. The NPCEditor has been extended substantially with multiple characters support, scripting capabilities, story phases, vision integration and interruption. In the future we plan to extend Gunslinger in several directions. We will explore ways to increase the sensory fidelity of the system through the use of photorealistic characters, 3D motion parallax, and "4D" effects such as projected bullet holes. We are performing extensive user testing with the aim of extending the basic story line to allow a much richer range of user preferences. In summary, Gunslinger provides an exciting research sandbox to explore the limits of dramatic human-to-virtual-human interaction.

References

1. Kenny, P., Hartholt, A., Gratch, J., Swartout, W., Traum, D., Marsella, S., Piepol, D.: Building interactive virtual humans for training environments. In: Proceeding of I/ITSEC (2007)
2. Sethy, A., Narayanan, S., Ramabhadran, B.: Data-Driven Approach for Language Model Adaptation using Stepwise Relative Entropy Minimization. In: Proc. of ICASSP, vol. 4, pp. 177–180 (2007)
3. Leuski, A., Traum, D.: A statistical approach for text processing in virtual humans. In: 26th Army Science Conference, Orlando, Florida (2008)
4. Lee, J., Marsella, S.C.: Nonverbal behavior generator for embodied conversational agents. In: Gratch, J., Young, M., Aylett, R.S., Ballin, D., Olivier, P. (eds.) IVA 2006. LNCS (LNAI), vol. 4133, pp. 243–255. Springer, Heidelberg (2006)
5. Thiebaux, M., et al.: SmartBody: Behavior Realization for Embodied Conversational Agents. In: Proceedings of Autonomous Agents and Multi-Agent Systems (2008)
6. Sadek, R.: A Host-Based Real-Time Multichannel Immersive Sound Playback and Processing System. In: Proceedings of the Audio Engineering Society 117th Convention, New York (October 2004)

Designing an Educational Game Facilitating Children's Understanding of the Development of Social Relationships Using IVAs with Social Group Dynamics

Wan Ching Ho and Kerstin Dautenhahn

Adaptive Systems Research Group, School of Computer Science
University of Hertfordshire, Hatfield, Hertfordshire, AL10 9AB, UK
{w.c.ho,k.dautenhahn}@herts.ac.uk

Introduction. Social relationships are fundamentally important to humans. Children are born into a family social structure and gradually they become part of a wider social structure including peers, in which each individual's relationships are affected by other relationships. To most people expressing appropriate non-verbal social behaviours when interacting with others in a virtual environment (VE) is natural and effortless as they do so daily in the physical world. There is a minority group, such as people diagnosed with autistic spectrum disorder, who encounter difficulties when carrying out this task because of impairments of specific skills regarding social communication and communication [1]. In this paper, we study the design of a system using advanced VE and IVA technologies with the goal to help children with autism to explore and better understand social dynamics occurring in social networks involving groups of people.

Background. Synthetic agents have been widely employed to model so-called 'unconscious reactions' where agents can signal social availability and spatial awareness to others (e.g. in [2]). To achieve socially desired behaviour by agents in VE, researchers adopted models that concern the spatial distances, orientation and arrangement of agents in social situations. Specifically, the *F-formation system* defined by Kendon [3] and concepts on *proxemics* by Hall [4] are particularly challenging research topics for virtual learning environment (VLEs).

Modelling Social Relationships in IVAs. Based on our previous work [5], we enhanced a VLE populated by autonomous social agents aiming at facilitating the developments of social relationships among children. A play scenario, which is similar to the context of a group of children meeting in a school playground and a canteen, involves a small number of agents embodied in a VE (see Figure 1). A social structure that has emerged from the play represents the way in which peers are connected to each other and therefore reflects the dynamics of agents' social proxemics and group formation. Through the involvement of users in the scenario and the visualisation of individual relationships with others within the social structure, future testing with child users is hoped to show that the VLE

Zs. Ruttkay et al. (Eds.): IVA 2009, LNAI 5773, pp. 502–503, 2009.

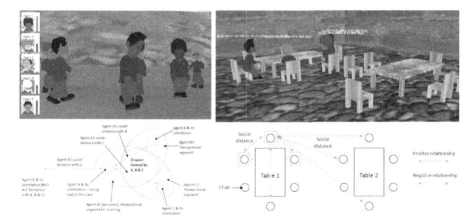

Fig. 1. Top-left: screenshot of the game interface visualising individual relationships from the user-controlled agent to others. Top-right: second part of the game scenario: Screenshot of a virtual 'canteen' with two tables. Bottom: design diagram showing the F-formation system and social proxemics (distances maintained by one agent while in proximity to others) applied to virtual agents when chatting to each other in the playground (left), and when sitting in the virtual canteen (right) – the agents' social relationships are demonstrated by their pre-defined sitting patterns.

will allow users to explicitly perceive and explore the social dynamics emerging from user-agent and agent-agent interactions. The improvement of children with autism's collaborative and social behaviour through the investigation of social relationships in the VE are the ultimate aim of this work.

Acknowledgments

This work was partially supported by European Community and was funded by the eCIRCUS project IST-4-027656-STP. We would like to thank Rafal Dawidowicz for the technical implementation of the VLE described in this paper.

References

[1] Frith, U.: Explaining the enigma. Blackwells (1989)
[2] Pedica, C., Vilhjálmsson, H.H.: Social perception and steering for online avatars. In: Prendinger, H., Lester, J.C., Ishizuka, M. (eds.) IVA 2008. LNCS (LNAI), vol. 5208, pp. 104–116. Springer, Heidelberg (2008)
[3] Kendon, A.: Spatial Organization in Social Encounters: the F-formation System. In: Studies in the behavior of social interaction, pp. 179–208. Indiana University, Bloomington and The Peter de Ridder Press, Lisse (1977)
[4] Hall, E.: The Hidden Dimension. Doubleday, New York (1966)
[5] Watson, S., Dautenhahn, K., Ho, W.C., Dawidowicz, R.: Developing relationship between autonomous agents: promoting pro-social behaviour through virtual learning environment. In: Trajkovski, G.P., Collins, S.G. (eds.) Handbook of Research on Agent-Based Societies: Social and Cultural Interactions. IGI Global (2009)

Real-Time Rendering of Skin Changes Caused by Emotions

Yvonne Jung, Christine Weber, Jens Keil, and Tobias Franke

Fraunhofer IGD
Fraunhoferstr. 5, 64283 Darmstadt, Germany
{yjung,cweber,jkeil,tofranke}@igd.fhg.de

1 Introduction and Related Work

For simulating communicative behavior, realistic appearance and plausible behavior is important. Postures and mimics also reflect emotional behavior. There exist various models of emotion, like the psycho-evolutionary theory developed by Plutchik [1], or Ekman's FACS. But most models are only suited for muscular expressions. A more unattended field however, also in graphics, is the change in color. Also, other physiological symptoms like crying are left unconsidered.

In contrast to the central nervous system, which is responsible for the conscious control of motor functions, the autonomic nervous system (ANS) controls unconscious inner functions that can result in physical reactions like blushing and pallor. Blushing [2,3] can occur when a sensation is very intense. Usually the cheeks are affected: there is a correlation between blushing and increase of temperature [3,4], especially in the forward facing upper regions. An average blushing takes $\Delta t = 35s$ with the strongest intensity after 15s. Face and ears also blush. Pallor is caused by a reduction of blood flow [2] e.g. due to fear. Regions that blush can also get pale. Other vegetative functions that are controlled by the ANS are weeping (sometimes accompanied by blushing) and sweat.

2 Concept, Emotional Model and Conclusions

Emotionally caused skin changes need to be customizable and consistent with existing animations. For realizing them, we need to know whether the face should blush or get pale, in which area the color should be changed, and the duration Δt. Therewith, the individual character data is generated, and can be used for animating facial color changes as outlined in [5]. Tears and beads of perspiration are integrated by specifying drop sizes and droplet sources in image space via texture coordinates and by starting an on-surface droplet flow simulation [6].

For creation and composition of emotions, we've developed an emotional model, which takes visually perceivable vegetative symptoms into account. It is based on Plutchik's model [1], but adopted to represent parameterizations of emotional states that result in different complexions as shown in Table 1. Thereby, emotions can be selected and further modified. When combining facial expressions with complexions (Fig. 1) the corresponding emotion is easier

Zs. Ruttkay et al. (Eds.): IVA 2009, LNAI 5773, pp. 504–505, 2009.

Table 1. Overview of visually distinguishable emotions incl. appearance

Neutral	Neutral face color, no changes
Joy	Rosy cheeks
Enthusiasm/ Ecstasy	Rosy cheeks, tears of joy
Surprise	Rosy cheeks
Disgust	Pale cheeks
Down	Low lacrimation
Sadness	Blushing cheeks, raised lacrimation
Grief	Blushing cheeks, red blotches, intensive lacrimation
Apprehension	Pale cheeks
Fear	Pale in the whole face
Panic	Pale face, low lacrimation, sweat on the forehead
Annoyance	Blushing cheeks
Anger	Blushing cheeks, red blotches in the face
Rage	Blushing cheeks, red blotches in face, red face

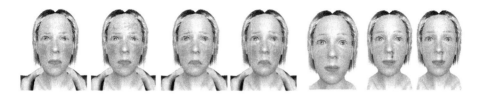

Fig. 1. Anger (left): cheeks blush and then red blotches appear. When sadly weeping, cheeks are blushing, too (middle). By changing color and/or positions, where droplets shall appear, effects like perspiration or nose bleeding can also be simulated (right).

perceivable and for strong emotions more plausible. Thus, skin changes can be controlled based on a parameterizable emotion model. To define this model, a classification of possible skin changes based on physiological and psychological knowledge was performed. Color changes and droplet flow simulation operate in real-time and can be combined with animations for convincing emotions.

References

1. Plutchik, R.: Emotion: Theory, Research and Experience. Acad. Pr., Sheffield (1980)
2. Kalra, P., Magnenat-Thalmann, N.: Modeling of vascular expressions. In: Computer Animation 1994, Geneva, pp. 50–58 (1994)
3. Mariauzouls, C.: Psychophysiologie von Scham und Erröten. PhD thesis, Ludwig-Maximilians-Universität München (July 1996)
4. Shearn, D., Bergman, E., Hill, K., Abel, A., Hinds, L.: Facial coloration and temperature responses in blushing. Psychophysiology 27(6), 687–693 (1990)
5. Jung, Y., Knöpfle, C.: Dynamic aspects of real-time face-rendering. In: Proceedings VRST Cyprus 2006, pp. 193–196. ACM, New York (2006)
6. Jung, Y., Behr, J.: GPU-based real-time on-surface droplet flow in X3D. In: Spencer, S. (ed.) Proceedings Web3D 2009, pp. 51–54. ACM Press, New York (2009)

Extensions and Applications of Pogamut 3 Platform

Rudolf Kadlec, Jakub Gemrot, Michal Bída, Ondřej Burkert, Jan Havlíček,
Lukáš Zemčák, Radek Pibil, Radim Vansa, and Cyril Brom

Charles University, Faculty of Mathematics and Physics,
Prague, Czech Republic
{rudolf.kadlec,jakub.gemrot,michal.bida}@gmail.com,
brom@ksvi.mff.cuni.cz

Keywords: storytelling, gestures, BML, ACT-R, emotions, education.

1 Introduction

We present recent extensions for the intelligent virtual agent development platform
Pogamut 3. These extensions are: the agent coordination language StorySpeak de-
signed for the purposes of storytelling applications, support for gestures based on
BML, the visual editor of reactive plans, connection of the cognitive architecture
ACT-R, an educational application aimed at orientation in urban areas and finally an
emotional model.

The Pogamut 3 platform is a tool for rapid prototyping of intelligent virtual agents'
(IVAs') behavior in the environment of the Unreal Tournament 2004 (UT04) computer game. So far the Pogamut was concerned mainly with behavior of a single agent
developed in Java or reactive planner POSH [3]. New extensions broaden the possible
use of the Pogamut platform and make it more usable in areas of storytelling, cognitive science and serious games. All described extensions will be available at the projects homepage [8]. A video[1] presentation showing these extensions in action is also
present on the homepage.

Following section will give a short overview of these extensions.

2 Extensions in Detail

StorySpeak is a language for behavior specification of IVAs. It is based on BDI [2]
and supports both goal-oriented and reactive plans specification. The language allows
a designer to coordinate behavior of multiple actors easily. The designer can write
plans for joint-intentions that are executed by multiple actors together.

Gestures module enables to describe poses and transitions between them in the
behaviour markup language BML [9]. The module provides a Java parser of the
BML, a MPEG-4 based transportation layer [4] and an execution engine written in

---

[1] The video is available on
http://artemis.ms.mff.cuni.cz/pogamut_files/IVA09-Pogamut.wmv,
other Pogamut related videos are on
http://artemis.ms.mff.cuni.cz/pogamut/
tiki-index.php? page=video+tutorials

Zs. Ruttkay et al. (Eds.): IVA 2009, LNAI 5773, pp. 506–507, 2009.
© Springer-Verlag Berlin Heidelberg 2009

Unreal Tournament's scripting language. This extension allows Pogamut to control an IVA's body on a fine level. In conjunction with the StorySpeak module, it provides support for storytelling applications.

POSH visual editor eases creation of reactive plans, making it possible to create simple IVAs even for non-programmers. POSH plans [3] visualized as tree structures can be edited by using drag-and-drop on basic behaviors from a palette of existing prototypes. The visual editor also eliminates syntactical errors that can discourage many newcomers.

ACT-R [1] to Pogamut binding called PojACT-R opens UT04 as a tool for cognitive modeling, allowing computational psychologists to test their models in highly dynamic virtual environments. These models have to be expressed in terms of the ACT-R architecture.

Educational scenarios aimed at enhancing orientation of children in urban areas are an example of the Pogamut platform application. The scenarios are scripted declaratively in the Drools rules engine [5].The extension provides a domain specific language for definition of orientation tasks. This enables users to make new scenarios without deep programming knowledge.

Emotions obtained by the integration of Gebhard's ALMA model [6] provide additional possibilities on how to make virtual agents in Pogamut more believable. ALMA is based on the OCC theory [7] – a widely used paradigm for modeling emotions for IVAs.

Acknowledgements

This work was supported by the GACR 201/09/H057 grant, by the Program "Information Society" under project 1ET100300517 and by GA UK no. 21809.

References

1. Anderson, J.R.: How can the human mind occur in the physical universe? Oxford University Press, Oxford (2007)
2. Bratman, M.: Intention, Plans, and Practical Reason. CSLI Publications ISBN 1-57586-192-5 (1999)
3. Bryson, J.J.: Inteligence by design: Principles of Modularity and Coordination for Engineering Complex AdaptiveAgent. PhD Thesis, MIT, Department of EECS, Cambridge, MA (2001)
4. Caoub, T., Petajan, E., Ostermann, J.: Very Low Bitrate Coding of Virtual Human Animation in MPEG-4 (2000)
5. Drool rules, http://www.jboss.org/drools/ (April 23, 2009)
6. Gebhard, P.: ALMA – A Layered Model of Affect,
   http://www.dfki.de/~gebhard/alma/index.html (April 23, 2009)
7. Ortony, A., Clore, G.L., Collins, A.: The cognitive structure of emotions. Cambridge University Press, Cambridge (1988)
8. Pogamut homepage, http://artemis.ms.mff.cuni.cz/pogamut (April 23, 2009)
9. Vilhjalmsson, H., Cantelmo, N., Cassell, J., Chafai, N., Kipp, M., Kopp, S., et al.: The behavior markup language: Recent developments and challenges. In: Pelachaud, C., Martin, J.-C., André, E., Chollet, G., Karpouzis, K., Pelé, D. (eds.) IVA 2007. LNCS (LNAI), vol. 4722, pp. 99–111. Springer, Heidelberg (2007)

Interactants' Most Intimate Self-disclosure in Interactions with Virtual Humans

Sin-Hwa Kang and Jonathan Gratch

University of Southern California
Institute for Creative Technologies
13274 Fiji Way, Marina del Rey, CA 90292, USA
{kang,gratch}@ict.usc.edu

1 Research Problem and Question

Recent studies have shown that virtual humans can facilitate social interactions among people who have difficulty in forming social bonds or help develop their social skills by interaction with virtual practice. Virtual human research tends to focus exclusively on appearance or behavior in assessing agent effectiveness, whereas other studies of human social interaction emphasize aspects of the social context, such as anticipated future interaction (AFI) which has been implicated as a key moderator of people's behavior in virtual interactions. It has been reported that anonymity [2] or interactants' AFI with their interaction partners [4,5] have a critical role in entailing greater self-disclosure. However, no studies of virtual humans have investigated the impact of the combination of interactants' visual appearance and AFI on their social responses, specifically revealing their intimate information. In this study, we examined the impact of different visual realism of virtual humans and interactants' AFI on interactants' self-disclosure, when their anonymity is secured and future interaction may be anticipated.

2 Experimental Design

The basic experimental design is a 2 (visual realism) x 2 (AFI versus No AFI) factorial between-subjects experiment involving two factors: i) two levels of visual realism of virtual humans – a human video and an animated drawing (Rapport Agent); ii) two conditions of future interaction – anticipation of future interaction and no anticipation of future interaction. One hundred and eight subjects (50% male, 50% female) from the general Los Angeles area participated in this study. The paired participants were randomly assigned to one of four experimental conditions in the 2 x 2 design. The interaction took place in two separate rooms where the paired participants (a subject with a confederate or the Rapport Agent in each interaction) were placed at different times, to avoid any initial face-to-face contact. Subjects were asked to complete a pre- and a post-questionnaire. In the interaction sessions, the subjects were given a hypothetical conversational scenario that could stimulate

Zs. Ruttkay et al. (Eds.): IVA 2009, LNAI 5773, pp. 508–510, 2009.

subjects' intimate self-disclosure. The confederate or the Rapport Agent was an interviewer who asked ten questions requiring self-disclosure of the subject [3]. The typical conversation was allowed to last about thirty minutes, but subjects were not informed of any specific time limitation.

To generate the avatar movement of the human video avatars, a web-cam (Logitech QuickCam Orbit MP) captured subjects' facial expressions. To allow video chat conversation, video conference software (Skype) was used. For the animated drawing avatars, we utilized the Rapport Agent, an embodied virtual agent, created by Gratch and his colleagues [1]. The subjects were informed that the Rapport Agent was an avatar controlled by another subject.

For the measurements, we videotaped subjects' verbal responses to answer their most common sexual fantasy[1] [3]. Two coders rated intimacy of interactants' verbal responses. Scales ranged from 1 (not intimate at all) to 5 (very intimate).

3   Preliminary Results and Conclusion

The results of Chi-Square Tests showed the proportion of interactants with AFI (No intimate information: 12.4%, Intimate information: 38.0%) was significantly different from the proportion of interactants with no AFI (No intimate information: 21.5%, Intimate information: 28.1%) in revealing their intimate "Common Sexual Fantasy" (Continuity Correction = 4.01, p < .05), whereas the results revealed no significant difference between the proportion of a human video avatar and the one of the Rapport Agent for interactants' intimate self-disclosure.

The results of Two-way between groups ANOVA showed no significant main effect of visual appearance of interaction partners [F(1,104) = .37, p > .05] or interactants' AFI [F(1,104) = 2.86, p > .05] on intimacy of interactants' responses which was rated by two coders, although the coders assigned slightly higher scores overall to the Rapport Agent condition compared to the other condition.

In conclusion, some of the outcomes support the conclusions of previous studies [4,5] and could provide a way of designing social interactions in which people need to reveal their personal information, such as psychotherapy or social skills training. However, data analysis of behavioral measures is in progress. Thus, we would like to hold our conclusion until we complete our data analysis of other behavioral measures that were designed to investigate people's verbal self-disclosure and nonverbal behaviors of rapport in this study.

Acknowledgements. This work was sponsored by the U.S. Army Research, Development, and Engineering Command and the National Science Foundation under grant # HS-0713603. The content does not necessarily reflect the position or the policy of the Government, and no official endorsement should be inferred.

---

[1] This question was one of ten intimate questions that were designed to stimulate people to reveal personal information and were asked to subjects in this study. The analysis of the other answers is in progress and not included in this paper.

References

[1] Gratch, J., Wang, N., Gerten, J., Fast, E., Duffy, R.: Creating rapport with virtual agents. In: Pelachaud, C., Martin, J.-C., André, E., Chollet, G., Karpouzis, K., Pelé, D. (eds.) IVA 2007. LNCS (LNAI), vol. 4722, pp. 125–138. Springer, Heidelberg (2007)
[2] Joinson, A.N.: Self-disclosure in computer-mediated communication: The role of self-awareness and visual anonymity. European Journal of Social Psychology 31, 177–192 (2001)
[3] Moon, Y.: Intimate exchanges: Using computers to elicit self-disclosure from consumers. Journal of Consumer Research 26(4), 323–339 (2000)
[4] Shaffer, D.R., Ogden, J.K.: On sex differences in self-disclosure during the acquaintance process: The role of anticipated future interaction. Journal of Personality and Social Psychology 51(1), 92–101 (1986)
[5] Walther, J.B.: Computer-mediated communication: Impersonal, interpersonal, and hyperpersonal interaction. Communication Research 23, 1–43 (1996)

Evaluation of Novice and Expert Interpersonal Interaction Skills with a Virtual Patient

Patrick G. Kenny, Thomas D. Parsons, Jonathan Gratch, and Albert A. Rizzo

Institute for Creative Technologies / USC
13274 Fiji Way Marina Del Rey, CA 90292, USA
{kenny,tparsons,gratch,rizzo}@ict.usc.edu

1 Introduction

Interactive Virtual Standardized Patients (VP) can provide meaningful training for clinicians. These VP's portray interactive embodied conversational characters with realistic representations of a mental or physical problem to be diagnosed or discussed. This research is a continuation of evaluating of our VP "Justina" [2] which suffers from Posttraumatic Stress Disorder (PTSD) from a sexual attack and presents the results of comparing novices, test subjects without medical training, and experts interacting with 'Justina' to find out if they could elicit the proper responses to make a diagnosis and to investigate the topics and questions the novices asked for coverage of the categories and criteria of PTSD as defined in the DSM-IV [1]. It is assumed that novices will perform better than experts, however the main investigation is to gather empirical data and understand why this is true and how this can be used to improve the system. There have not been, to the authors' knowledge, any studies in evaluating experts and non-experts with virtual human characters in the psychological domain.

The subject testing method consisted of recruiting novice participants from USC staff, students and interns. A total of 9 people took part in the study (3 females, 6 males). This was compared against the experts from the previous study, 15 subjects consisting of, medical students, psychiatry residents and fellows (6 females, 9 males). The subjects filled out pre and post questionnaires, the dialog exchange is transcribed and classified into the PTSD categories.

1.1 Data Analytics

For our analyses we focused on cohort (clinicians and novices) differences related to effective diagnostic interview skills. The keys aspects of the interview included differences between clinicians and novices on establishment and maintenance of rapport, attempts to gather information about the VP's problems and attempts at detailed inquiry to gain specific and detailed information from the VP. Question/response composites (VP_QR') were developed to reflect the shared relation existing between the responses of a VP and of DSM IV TR-specific Questions (from both cohorts) that are necessary for differential diagnosis. For the VP_QR' scores, we first calculated eigenvalues via least squares procedures and separate composite measures were created for each observation. The resulting weights were used in conjunction with the original variable values to calculate each observation's score. The VP_QR' scores were standardized according to a z-score. The data analysis was completed in three stages. First, the reference distribution is a correlation of each cluster of questions

Zs. Ruttkay et al. (Eds.): IVA 2009, LNAI 5773, pp. 511–512, 2009.
© Springer-Verlag Berlin Heidelberg 2009

(from the clinicians) making up a particular DSM PTSD Category with each (corresponding) cluster of responses from the VP representing the same DSM PTSD Category. The second was the same as the first but for novice questions and VP responses representing the same DSM PTSD Category. In the third stage, the differences between cohorts were assessed to see whether significant differences existed in each cohort's reference distribution of questions response pairs—from the VP representing the same DSM PTSD Category.

1.2 Results and Conclusion

The data for the 9 novices was compared to that of the 15 experts in the previous study. There were less questions asked in the communications (Novice questions: 24.13, VP responses 44.26; Expert: 34.00, VP responses 40.44), for the novices than for the experts. This implies that the novices were asking questions about general things and not specific criteria to help make a diagnosis and the clinicians were better able to maintain rapport then the novices. The novices kept revisiting the same topic and questions more than the experts, and spent a large amount of time on the incident rather than the diagnosis criteria. Additionally findings revealed a significant difference between cohorts on PTSD Categories A(Trauma Event), B(Re-experience event), C(Avoidance), E(Duration), and G(Rapport). No significant differences were found for categories D(Arousal) and F(Life Effects), Table 1.

Table 1. Ratios for 15 Experts and 9 Novices

Category	Mean Expert	Mean Novice	Std. Dev. Expert	Std. Dev. Novice	F-Value
PTSD_A_rto	9.03	0.18*	3.94	0.06	44.50
PTSD_B_rto	7.04	2.15*	3.33	1.42	17.23
PTSD_C_rto	6.21	-0.26*	1.64	0.10	136.45
PTSD_D_rto	1.08	1.66	0.50	2.43	0.82
PTSD_E_rto	-0.13	0.21*	0.08	0.14	57.61
PTSD_F_rto	0.69	1.20	0.42	1.18	2.34
PTSD_G_rto	38.30	-14.89*	10.72	1.80	214.05
PTSD_H_Q	3.67	2.44	3.66	2.07	0.83

*Significance at the .05 level.

The system could be improved by adding additional questions for Category D and since there was not a significant difference in F, the clinicians could use a bit more training here. It was anticipated that the novices would not do as well as the experts; however this was one of the first comparative analysis between novices and experts for VP's in the psychological domain.

References

1. DSM, American Psychiatric Association: Diagnostic and statistical manual of mental disorders, text revision (DSM-IV-TR), 4th edn. American Psychiatric Press, Inc., Washington (2000)
2. Kenny, P., Parsons, T.D., Gratch, J., Leuski, A., Rizzo, A.A.: Evaluation of Justina: A Virtual Patient with PTSD. In: Prendinger, H., Lester, J.C., Ishizuka, M. (eds.) IVA 2008. LNCS (LNAI), vol. 5208, pp. 394–408. Springer, Heidelberg (2008)

Voice Feed-Backing for Video Game Players by Real-Time Sequential Emotion Estimation from Facial Expression

Kiyhoshi Nosu, Tomoya Kurokawa, Hiroto Horita, Yoshitarou Ohhazama,
and Hiroki Takeda[1]

[1] School of High Technology for Human Welfare, Tokai University
317 Nishino, Numazu 410-0395, Japan
nosu@wing.ncc.u-tokai.ac.jp

Keywords: face, emotion, real-time estimation, video game.

1 Introduction

Video game technology now enables a new set of experiences for players in addition to conventional video games. Although the intensity of the technological research in this field is shifting from graphics to AI design and characters with embodied agents [1], there have been few studies involving the assessment of real-time sequential, emotional changes of video-game players. Research of this issue and the implications may assist in preventing game addiction and decreasing one's zest for learning. This paper proposes a novel interface to provide voice feedback to video-game players using real-time sequential emotion estimation from facial expressions.

2 System Configuration

A lot of research has been conducted on the estimation of emotion using facial expressions [2],[3] In this research, the time-sequential tracings of six facial feature points and emotion estimation, based on Maharanobis distance, are processed using a personal computer and utilized for real-time sequential emotion estimation of a video-game player [4]. The system configuration is shown as a schematic in Figure 1. Game controllers are connected to a game console, and a video camera (Video camera #1) records the facial expressions of the players as they engage in different gaming activities. Facial feature data is then extracted using a facial image processor. The differential sets of semantic words describing emotions used to classify the emotions exhibited by the video-game players are, 1) tired–absorbed, 2) painful–cheerful and 3) impatient–calm. A voice message corresponding to an emotion was generated every 30 sec, only when the system detected a strong emotion exhibited by the player.

Zs. Ruttkay et al. (Eds.): IVA 2009, LNAI 5773, pp. 513–514, 2009.
© Springer-Verlag Berlin Heidelberg 2009

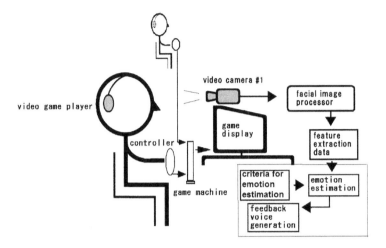

video camera #1

video game player

facial image processor

game display

controller

feature extraction data

criteria for emotion estimation

emotion estimation

game machine

feedback voice generation

Fig. 1. Schematic of real-time emotion estimation system using facial expressions of video-game players

3 Preliminary System Evaluation and Conclusion

Five pairs, comprised of 10 male university students from the Technology Department participated in the measurement as subjects/video-game players. The performance of emotion estimation from facial expressions was assessed using the coincidence ratio between the estimated emotions based on the real-time sequential emotion estimation and a subjective evaluation by the subjects. Since emotion is thought to be affected by voice feedback, the assessment was carried out both with and without the voice feedback. Although the overall coincidence ratios with and without voice feedback are similar, the coincidence ratios without voice feedback are better than those with voice feedback. For example, the overall coincidence ratios without voice feedback for "absorbed" and "cheerful" are 88 and 83%, while those with voice feedback for "absorbed" and "cheerful" are 80 and 56%, respectively.

Future studies will investigate the influence of voice stimulus and the game types/functions on the video-game player.

References

1. Callele, D., et al.: Emotional requirements in video games requirements engineering conference. In: 14th IEEE International Requirements Engineering Conference (RE 2006), pp. 292–295 (2006)
2. Lewis, M., et al.: Handbook of Emotions, ch. 13. Guilford Press, New York (2008)
3. Nosu, K., Kurokawa, T.: Facial Tracking for an Emotion-Diagnosis Robot to Support e-Learning. In: Proceedings of 2006 International Conference on Machine Learning and Cybernetics, pp. 3811–3816 (2006)

RMRSBot – Using Linguistic Information to Enrich a Chatbot

Tina Klüwer

German Research Center for Artificial Intelligence,
Alt-Moabit 91c, Berlin
tina.kluewer@dfki.de

1   Introduction and Motivation

Coming to open domain dialog it is still unrealistic to implement needed knowledge resources and dialog skills linguistically. Since the Non Player Characters (NPC) in our NPC Engine should be capable of open conversation we decided to use an Artificial Intelligence Markup Language (AIML) [1] chatbot as a first workaround. However AIML chatbots are not linguistically motivated, they use surface structures in tradition of Weizenbaums ELIZA [2], wherefore they do have too many shortcomings to use them in real dialog applications. One of the major problems is the handling of surface variation. To be able to process one sentence with different structures, they need as much patterns as there are syntactic alternatives, which leads to an exploding number of pattern template pairs. To reduce the costs of the manual development, AIML authors use simple regular expression operators, what in turn leads to the problem of being overly permissive. A possibility to abstract from the surface level and still be able to control the structure is to use information from syntactic and semantic analysis. In the presented system two scenarios were implemented: 1. Using part of speech information and 2. Using the results from a semantic analysis.

2   System

In the presented system the Heart of Gold (HoG) [3] a middleware for various linguistic components was integrated into a chatbot architecture. The HoG delivers results from different levels of parsing like Part-of-Speech, HPSG and Robust Minimal Recursion Semantics (RMRS) [4] a semantic formalism supporting underspecification, which is concerned with the representation of partial semantic information obtained from incomplete syntactic analysis.

After the preprocessing the input provided by an user via a webinterface is sent to the HoG which delivers a POS tagged annotation of the sentence as well as the belonging RMRS structure. If no complete semantic analysis was found, a flat underspecified RMRS structure is supplied. In the next step the results get transformed to the output form which is needed for the actual matching. While this is straightforward for the POS results, the RMRS structure needs to be reformulated to the desired AIML pattern form. The structural information

Zs. Ruttkay et al. (Eds.): IVA 2009, LNAI 5773, pp. 515–516, 2009.
© Springer-Verlag Berlin Heidelberg 2009

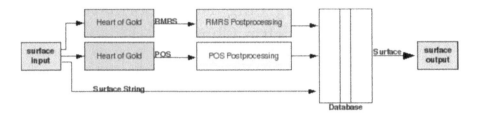

Fig. 1. System architecture

detected by the parser including the arguments of the found relations have to get resolved and linked to the identified elementary semantic predicates. The resulting string constitutes the basic pattern. As a last step a template matching the pattern is looked up in the database and returned to the user. Two test scenarios were implemented to match either the utterance plus POS or the utterance plus RMRS (including the POS information).

3   Conclusion and Future Work

In some tests with the original chatbot data it was found that the POS/RMRS baseline could efficiently reduce the number of necessary patterns. With the possibility to execute more control on the matching structures the shown method furthermore could apparently provide more adequate answers. In a first test with the ALICE data, we could successfully reduce the number of necessary patterns from 89 to 34 with the POS annotation and to 30 including the RMRS for the most used template. For the second most common template (87 patterns) we achieved 29 (POS) and 28 (RMRS). Since the examples didn't contain many structural variation, it can be assumed that the use of RMRS will conclude in still better results in the ongoing computer game work.

Acknowledgements. The work presented here was supported by the project KomParse funded by the ProFIT programme of the Federal State of Berlin and the EFRE programme of the European Union. Many thanks go to the project members.

References

1. Wallace, R., Bush, N.: Artificial Intelligence Markup Language (AIML) Version 1.0.1 (2001)
2. Weizenbaum, J.: ELIZA - A computer program for the study of natural language communication between man and machine. Communications of the ACM 9(1), 36–45 (1966)
3. Schaefer, U.: Integrating Deep and Shallow Natural Language Processing Components - Representations and Hybrid Architectures. Saarbrücken Dissertation Series in Computational Linguistics and Language Technology 22 (2007)
4. Copestake, A.: Report on the design of RMRS, Technical Report D1.1a, University of Cambridge, UK (2003)

Cultural Differences in Using Facial Parts as Cues to Recognize Emotions in Avatars

Tomoko Koda[1] and Zsofia Ruttkay[2]

[1] Faculty of Information Science and Technology, Osaka Institute of Technology
1-79-1 Kitayama, Hirakata City, Osaka, 573-0196, Japan
[2] Human Media Interaction, Dept. of Electrical Engineering,
Mathematics and Computer Science, University of Twente, The Netherlands
koda@is.oit.ac.jp, zsofi@cs.utwente.nl

Keywords: avatar, character, facial expression, cross-culture.

1 Introduction

Avatars are frequently used in virtual worlds and online games to convey emotions across cultures. However, our previous study suggested there are cultural differences in recognizing avatar's facial expressions [1]. Yuki et al.'s study using emoticons and photorealistic human face images suggests Americans tend to interpret emotions based on the mouth, while Japanese tend to focus on the eyes [2]. Inspired by Yuki's study, this study uses cartoonish avatar faces to find cultural differences in using facial parts as cues to recognize avatar emotions. This paper reports the preliminary result of an experiment conducted between Japanese and European subjects.

2 Experiment

The purpose of the experiment is to find cultural differences in using eyes and mouth as cues to recognize facial expressions of a cartoonish avatar. We designed three facial expressions, namely, happy, sad, and disgust, using CharToon [3], a design tool for 2D cartoon faces. The three facial expressions designed followed FACS [4], and were pre-evaluated to make sure they convey the intended emotions. We created 6 static expressions by combining the eyes and mouths of the three expressions, i.e., happy eyes and sad mouth, happy eyes and disgusted mouth, sad eyes and happy mouth, etc. Fig.1 shows an example of a combined expression that uses sad eyes and happy mouth.

Subjects were asked to evaluate perceived emotions of each combined expression using 7-point scales of valenced emotions (7: happiest to 1: saddest). Thirty three Japanese and 34 European (18 from the Netherlands, 16 from other European countries) participated in the survey.

Zs. Ruttkay et al. (Eds.): IVA 2009, LNAI 5773, pp. 517–518, 2009.
© Springer-Verlag Berlin Heidelberg 2009

Fig. 1. An example of a combined facial expression (sad eyes and happy mouth)

3   Results and Discussion

The subjects' answers of perceived emotions (happy-sad) showed the following results. Japanese rated the expressions with happy eyes as significantly happier than Europeans regardless of the shape of the mouth (average rating of happiness as 7 is the happiest was EU=2.75, JP=3.21, $p<0.01$). While Europeans rated the expressions with a sad mouth as significantly sadder than Japanese regardless of the shape of the eyes (EU=2.77, JP=3.12, $p<0.01$). When focusing on the ranges of the ratings of perceived emotions, Japanese responded to the differences in the eyes more dynamically, while the European subjects responded to the differences in the mouth more dynamically ($p<0.05$).

These results imply overall tendencies of Japanese concentrating on the shapes of the eyes, while Europeans concentrating on the shapes of the mouth when recognizing facial expressions of an avatar. Thus, we can assume Yuki's finding with emoticons and photorealistic images [2] are also applicable to cartoonish avatars. Further study should use wide variety of designs and animated expressions.

Acknowledgements. This research is supported by a Grant-in-Aid for Scientific Research (C) 20500196, 2008-2010) from the Japan Society for the Promotion of Science. Genta Kameyama created the avatar expressions and conducted the survey.

References

1. Koda, T., Ishida, T., Rehm, M., Andre, E.: Avatar culture: cross-cultural evaluations of avatar facial expressions. AI & Society Journal of Knowledge, Culture and Communication (2009) DOI: 10.1007/s00146-009-0214-5
2. Yuki, M., Maddux, W.W., Masuda, T.: Are the windows to the soul the same in the East and West? Journal of Experimental Social Psychology 43, 30–311 (2007)
3. Ruttkay, Z., Noot, H.: Animated CharToon faces. In: 1st international symposium on Non-photorealistic animation and rendering, pp. 91–100 (2000)
4. Ekman, P., Friesen, W.V.: Facial action coding system: A technique for the measurement of facial movement. Consulting Psychologists Press, Palo Alto (1978)

Adaptive Mind Agent

Brigitte Krenn, Marcin Skowron, Gregor Sieber, Erich Gstrein, and Jörg Irran

Austrian Research Institute for Artificial Intelligence,
Freyung 6, 1010 Vienna, Austria
Research Studios Austria - Studio Smart Agent Technologies,
Thurngasse 8, 1090 Vienna, Austria
{brigitte.krenn,marcin.skowron,gregor.sieber}@ofai.at,
erich.gstrein@researchstudio.at, joerg.irran@reflexagenz.net
http://www.ofai.at, http://sat.researchstudio.at

1 Introduction

We present the Adaptive Mind Agent, an intelligent virtual agent that is able to actively participate in a real-time, dynamic environment. The agent is equipped with a collection of processing tools that form the basis of its perception from and action on the environment consisting of web documents, URLs, RRS feeds, domain-specific knowledgebases, other accessible virtual agents and the user. How these predispositions are finally shaped into unique agent behaviour depends on the agent's abilities to learn through actual interactions, in particular the abilities: (i) to memorize and evaluate episodes comprising the actions the agent had performed on its environment in the past depending on its perceptions of the user requests and its interpretation of the user's feedback reinforcing or inhibiting a certain action; (ii) to dynamically develop user-driven interest and preference profiles through memorizing and evaluating the user clicks on selected web pages.

The agents reside in a JAVA-/OSGi-based platform realizing a component-based development and execution model that allows for modular composition of different kinds of agents from a set of building blocks [1]. The source code of the platform including the Adaptive Mind implementation is available under gpl from http://rascalli.sourceforge.net/. The running system, an Adaptive Mind Agent in the popular music domain, is accessible via http://www2.ofai.at:8180/rascalli where one creates the own agent, shapes and monitors its interests and preferences, and via a 3D interactive ECA client for windows downloadable from http://www.ofai.at/rascalli/demonstrators/ECA.html.

2 Adaptive Mind

At the core of the Adaptive Mind stand the components for episode-based action selection and for user-driven agent profiling. The former is wrapped by action selection rules, and a dialogue and interaction model. The latter influences what is in the agent's focus. All together this determines which agent actions are triggered by a certain user utterance. In the following, we briefly address the two components.

Zs. Ruttkay et al. (Eds.): IVA 2009, LNAI 5773, pp. 519–520, 2009.

Episode-Based Learning of Action Selection: To model the action capabilities of the agent, we have adapted an action-based model for learning affordances in robots [2] leading to tool-specific application spaces containing all the episodes experienced with the individual actuator tools including the agent's perception of the input and outcome situations. The appropriate new action to be selected and executed by the agent is determined based on the similarity of only a small number of features in the input situation (utterance and question class, utterance interest and focus), and on the evaluation of positive and negative user feedback on the outcome of the agent's action. This allows rapid prototyping and eases integration with new tools. The following methods are applied in the given order: 1. recent positive feedback given the same input situation; 2. majority positive feedback given the same input situation; 3. positive feedback given a similar input situation (vector space based similarity calculation); 4. random selection with exclusion of the action with the recent negative feedback received from the user applied to the same input situation.

Learning of User Interests and Preferences: By navigating through a music browser from within the agent application, the user provides the agent with a growing episode base of user actions (e.g. view, listen to, rate positive, rate negative) on items (e.g. artist, song) at certain times. This information is stored and aggregated into the agent's interest profile using standard machine learning approaches and an adaptation strategy supporting neglect, where the agent's preference profile is split into a short-time preference profile refined by the user actions within a session, and a long-term profile based on the short-term profiles. For details see [3], the section on "Agent Modelling Server". As far as we are aware of, we have for the first time combined the mind implementation of virtual information processing and communication agents with personalization technology usually employed in e- and m-commerce, and at the same time we have introduced a cognitive notion of memory into personalization technology.

Acknowledgments. The work has been supported by EU FP6-IST-027596 RASCALLI and by the Austrian Federal Ministry for Transport, Innovation and Technology. The authors also would like to acknowledge the work of numerous colleagues from the RASCALLI project for the development and implementation of (sub)components the Adaptive Mind Agent interfaces with.

References

1. Eis, Ch.: RASCALLI Platform: A Dynamic Modular Runtime Environment for Agent Modeling. Master's Thesis. Vienna University of Technology, Vienna, Austria (2008)
2. Irran, J., Kintzler, F., Pölz, P.: Grounding Affordances. In: Cybernetics and Systems. Austrian Society for Cybernetic Studies, Vienna (2006)
3. Krenn, B., et al.: Responsive Artificial Situated Cognitive Agents Living and Learning on the Internet. Final Activity Report FP6-IST-027596. Austrian Research Institute for Artificial Intelligence, Vienna, Austria (2009)

Study on Sensitivity to ECA Behavior Parameters

Ladislav Kunc and Pavel Slavík

Faculty of Electrical Engineering,
Czech Technical University in Prague, Czech Republic
{kuncl1,slavik}@fel.cvut.cz

1 Introduction

Embodied conversational agents (ECAs) provide one possible way of incorporating nonverbal portion of speech into voice based user interfaces. Part of agent's visual behavior and its appearance is often solved "statically." There is another possibility to change appearance – *dynamically* (for example head or eye movements, mouth opening, etc.). Our hypothesis is that some "dynamic" parameters are more important for the user than the other ones. In this paper we present the pilot user study and statistical evaluation of four parameters. Eye blinking is one of the parameter we investigate. The importance of agent's gaze (blinking as part of it) was discussed several times for example by Raidt [1].

2 Experiment

During our evaluation we performed four experiments in order to evaluate four behavioral parameters. The experiment was a test of human preference (and sensitivity). Participants saw pair of video files in one trial and chose the preferred one.

ECA application. Our pairwise comparisons required application that is capable of generating ECA sequences and allows modification of some parameters. We used ECAF toolkit [2]. This toolkit is capable of displaying 3D talking head and could produce video sequences of animated head from English text. The visual and audio output is lip-synchronized. Audio is synthesized by means of state of the art concatenative speech synthesis. We evaluated following parameters: *eye's blinking* – no blinking ($p = 0.0$), default ($p = 0.0085$), fast blinking ($p = 0.1$), *teeth color (static)* – pure white (default), grey-yellow, darker grey-yellow, *vertical mouth opening (speech)* – less (80%), default (100%), more (110%), *head movements (pseudo-random)* – no movement, default, faster movements.

Evaluation videos. We used 15 videos generated by ECAF toolkit for the test. One video had length 19 seconds. The talking head was looking at the listener all the time. In every video the talking head said the same sentence not to bias the results by choice of sentence.

Zs. Ruttkay et al. (Eds.): IVA 2009, LNAI 5773, pp. 521–522, 2009.

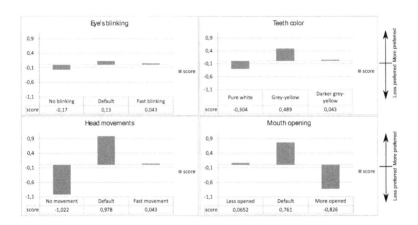

Fig. 1. Graphs of standard score of four evaluated parameters

3   Results and Discussion

In total 93 participants carried out 1380 pair comparisons in our experiment. For each comparison the video chosen by participant was given score 1 and the second video (not the chosen one) was given score 0. These data were filled in 3×3 matrix for each parameter separately. The Thurstone's Law of Comparative Judgment – Case V [3] will be used to convert the scores into standard scores that are comparable (see Fig. 1). The experiments were statistically significant (ANOVA test – $F > F_{critical}$ and $p < 0.05$, $F_{critical} = 3.028$).

Figure 1 shows that our test participants seem to be less sensitive to eye's blinking frequency than to the other parameters (the scores are very similar). The other three parameters (teeth color, head movements and mouth opening) indicate some form of human sensitivity to them – the preference scores of parameter values are different. The teeth color parameter shows more similar score in comparison to the both movement parameters. In future work, we would like to perform regular usability test of such an personalized ECA application to collect the users reactions.

Acknowledgement. This work was funded by EU 6th FP under grant FP6-033502 and has been partially supported by MSMT under research program MSM 6840770014.

References

1. Raidt, S., et al.: Gaze Patterns during Face-to-Face Interaction. In: The Int. Conf. on Web Intelligence and Intelligent Agent Technology, pp. 338–341 (2007)
2. Kunc, L., Kleindienst, J.: ECAF: Authoring Language for Embodied Conversational Agents. In: Text, Speech and Dialogue, pp. 206–213 (2007)
3. Thurstone, L.L.: A law of comparative judgment. Psychological Review 34, 273–286 (1927)

Influence of Music and Sounds in an Agent-Based Storytelling Environment

António Leonardo, António Brisson, and Ana Paiva

Instituto Superior Técnico and INESC-ID, Av. Prof. Cavaco Silva,
IST, Taguspark
Porto Salvo
ajml@ist.utl.pt, antonio.brisson@gaips.inesc-id.pt,
ana.paiva@inesc-id.pt

1 Introduction

The importance of sound and music in movies (Film Scoring) is undeniable. Film Scoring is used as a complement to the visual content helping to better understand it. The use of these artistic elements can be extended to interactive storytelling (IS) environments where stories are also told in a dynamic and interactive way. Because of IS particularities, such as the unpredictability of user actions and story development, this extension is not straightforward, and presents a problem that needs to be addressed. Further, the presence of autonomous virtual agents makes the creation of these stories more emergent, making difficult the process of creating sounds and music that is adequate. This paper presents a framework that proposes a possible solution to score a story created in these environments by intelligent virtual agents. Additionally, we studied the influence of some particular elements of sound and music (such as tempo, use of different instruments, etc) on the viewers and their perception of the actions of the characters and thus, on the consequent understanding of the story.

2 D3S Framework

The D3S (Dynamic Story Shadows and Sounds) framework was built with the main objective of increasing the understanding and enjoyment of a viewer of an interactive story generated in a virtual environment with autonomous virtual agents. It follows two parallel layers when considering music execution: *event sounds* and *background music*.

Event sounds are used to underscore actions of the virtual characters that occur in the scene. Differently, background music, offers some of the film score functions, with a special focus on enhancing the understanding of the story. In D3S, this type of music is classified in four different categories: character themes, background music that emphasizes emotions, background music for key moments and background music as filler.

Certain musical features can dynamically change according to the evolution of the environment. In D3S we considered: *volume*, *instrumentation*, and *tempo*.

Zs. Ruttkay et al. (Eds.): IVA 2009, LNAI 5773, pp. 523–524, 2009.

Volume is associated with emotions intensity. Different instruments are associated with different characters so that the audience has a better perception of what is happening in the story and who is doing what. The third parameter manipulated was music *tempo* which is associated with environment's arousal.

This framework was successfully integrated with two storytelling environments: *I-Shadows* [1] and *FearNot!* [2].

3   Results and Conclusions

Pursuing the goal of enriching virtual with artistic features that lead to better perception of the story is one of the goals of the D3S framework that intended to be a contribution to both the fields of Interactive Storytelling and Automatic Scoring. With it, we intended to explore a different approach on how to produce sound and music to accompany a story and help the viewer to understand it better while offering a more entertaining experience.

The results obtained showed that, with the help of music and sounds, viewers could understand better the story being created and have a more enjoyable experience while watching it.

More specifically, the association between instruments and characters is a good way of hinting which actions a certain character is doing, helping the audience to identify them. Changes in volume of sounds associated to actions between characters have an influence on the perception of the strength of the relation between them. Background music helps to emphasize the emotions felt by the hero by changing the nature of its theme: Themes with features associated to happiness (such as major mode and faster tempo) might suggest that the character is happy, while themes with features associated to sadness (such as minor mode and slower tempo) might suggest that he is sad. Background music can also have a big impact about what is happening in scene - If we have two characters acting with a type of music, the audience might think they are doing something. If we change the type of music radically, they might think they are doing something completely different. Finally, we also concluded that it helps the viewer to perceive the intensity of the environment through changes in tempo.

From the results obtained, we can draw some conclusions about the importance of music associated with virtual characters, emphasizing the importance that sound and music has in these characters perception, and eventually in their believability.

References

1. Brisson, A.: I-Shadows. Using Affect in an Emergent Interactive Drama. MSc Thesis, Instituto Superior Técnico, Portugal (2007)
2. Aylett, R., Vala, M., Sequeira, P., Paiva, A.: FearNot! – an emergent narrative approach to virtual dramas for anti-bullying education. In: Cavazza, M., Donikian, S. (eds.) ICVS-VirtStory 2007. LNCS, vol. 4871, pp. 202–205. Springer, Heidelberg (2007)

Widening the Evaluation Net

Brian Mac Namee and Mark Dunne

DIT AI Group, Dublin Institute of Technology, Dublin, Ireland
`firstname.lastname@dit.ie`

Abstract. Intelligent Virtual Agent (IVA) systems are notoriously difficult to evaluate, particularly due to the subjectivity involved. From the various efforts to develop standard evaluation schemes for IVA systems the scheme proposed by Isbister & Doyle, which evaluates systems across five categories, seems particularly appropriate. To examine how these categories are being used, the evaluations presented in the proceedings of IVA '07 and IVA '08 are summarised and the extent to which the five categories in the Isbister & Doyle scheme are used is highlighted.

1 IVA Evaluations and IVA '08 and IVA '09

As Intelligent Virtual Agent (IVA) research has matured, evaluation has become more important. However, evaluation of IVA systems is notoriously difficult as there are a whole range of issues that must be considered (e.g. *are the behaviours of agents believable?*, *are agents socially capable?*, *does the system run efficiently in real-time?*), and that these issues tend to be quite subjective. However, without good evaluations it is very difficult to compare competing systems and track the development of the field as a whole.

Fortunately, there are a number of proposed standard evaluation schemes for IVA research. One scheme that seems particularly useful was proposed by Isbister & Doyle [1] for evaluating pedagogical conversational agents which evaluates systems under five categories: *Believability*, *Social Interface*, *Application Domains*, *Agency & Computational Issues*, and *Production*.

To examine the state-of-the-art in evaluation in IVA research, the evaluations described in the proceedings of IVA '07 [2] and IVA '08 [3] were summarised. Each full paper published (31 and 45 in IVA '07 and IVA '08 respectively) was examined, and the evaluations described were categorised under the 5 categories in the Isbister & Doyle scheme. Papers for which evaluation is simply inappropriate are placed under the category *N/A*. Finally, those papers that do not describe any evaluations are placed in the category *None*. Figure 1 shows first how many of the papers in each year evaluate under each of the categories in the scheme, and the *N/A* and *None* categories; together with histograms of how many of the categories are covered in the evaluations presented each year.

2 Conclusions and Future Work

The points to notice from the graphs in figure 1 are: there are a large number of papers in which no evaluation is described; it is clear that some of the evaluation

Zs. Ruttkay et al. (Eds.): IVA 2009, LNAI 5773, pp. 525–526, 2009.

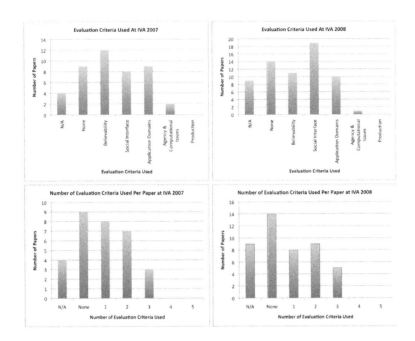

Fig. 1. The number of full papers which evaluated under each of the categories and a histogram of the number of evaluation categories from the Isbister & Doyle scheme used in evaluations reported in full papers at IVA '07 and IVA '08

categories feature more frequently than others; and in most cases evaluation is performed in only one or two categories. The purpose of this work, so, is to hold a mirror to the evaluations performed within the IVA research community and show that, although there are some example of very fine evaluations reported in the literature, there is still a considerable amount of work to do as the field matures. We would suggest that expanding evaluations to cover better breadth of the Isbister & Doyle scheme would be a good way to move in this direction.

References

1. Isbister, K., Doyle, P.: Design and evaluation of embodied conversational agents: A proposed taxonomy. In: Proceedings of the 1st International Conference on Autonomous Agents and Multi-Agent Systems (AAMAS 2002) -Conference Workshop: Embodied Conversational Agents -Let's Specify and Evaluate Them (2002)
2. Pelachaud, C., Martin, J., André, E., Chollet, G., Karpouzis, K., Pelé, D. (eds.): 7th International Conference on Intelligent Virtual Agents. LNCS (LNAI), vol. 4722. Springer, Heidelberg (2007)
3. Prendinger, H., Lester, J., Ishizuka, M. (eds.): 8th International Conference on Intelligent Virtual Agents. LNCS (LNAI), vol. 5208. Springer, Heidelberg (2008)

Are ECAs More Persuasive than Textual Messages?

Irene Mazzotta, Nicole Novielli, and Berardina De Carolis

Department of Informatics, University of Bari
via Orabona 4, 70125 Bari, Italy
{mazzotta,novielli,decarolis}@di.uniba.it

1 Introduction

Embodied Conversational Agents (ECAs) are commonly accepted as a new metaphor of Human Computer Interaction in several application domains. They are also used with the roles of influence and behavior change. We present an empirical evaluation study to compare the motivational impact of a persuasive message when conveyed by Valentina (a female young character [1]) and when presented through a text. The believability of our agent has been successfully evaluated in our previous research.

2 The Experimental Study: The Method

Participants. Sixty Italian students aged between 16 and 25, equally distributed by gender and background.

Study Design. A 2x2 between subject study where the variables involved were background (computer science vs. humanities) and output modality (ECA vs. text).

Preparation of Material. The message was produced according to the strategies applied by PORTIA [2], a user-adapted persuasion system that selects the most promising strategy to induce a behavioral change, in the Healthy Eating domain. In this study we refer to a hypothetical user profile: we made some assumptions about our subjects' presumed goal's value, consistently with their gender and age. To conduct the evaluation, we prepared an electronic-based *pre-test questionnaire* and a paper-based *post-test questionnaire*. The main purpose of the pre-test was to exclude that possible differences obtained in the post-test were due to difference in the healthy eating knowledge. The post-test enabled to evaluate how the persuasion message was percept as effective. It was divided in three main parts, each of them investigated on a specific aspect of the message: self-report about *information quality* (questions about degree of satisfaction, helpfulness, and easiness) and *perception of the persuasion strength* (questions about persuasiveness, reliableness, and validity), and objective measures of *degree of recalling* (single choice questions on the informative content).

Procedure. Participants were invited to individually enter the room, sit down in front of a computer and follow the instruction on the monitor. After receiving a short explanation describing the purpose of the experiment, they filled out the pre-test and received the persuasive message: in the text-based experiment, subjects read the message on the monitor, while in the ECA condition, they listened to the message conveyed by Valentina. Finally, they filled out the post-test questionnaire.

Zs. Ruttkay et al. (Eds.): IVA 2009, LNAI 5773, pp. 527–528, 2009.
© Springer-Verlag Berlin Heidelberg 2009

3 Results and Discussion

The analysis of the pre-test questionnaires confirmed our assumptions about the hypothetical user and ensured that differences in the post-text were not due to differences in the healthy eating knowledge of the participants.

To compare the motivational impact of the persuasion message in the two output conditions, we analyzed post-test questionnaire data using a t-test. Results (Table 1) show that the message conveyed through Valentina received an overall better evaluation. In particular, no significant differences occurred in terms of *Satisfaction* and *Helpfulness*, but the textual message is easier to understand (*Easiness*). On the contrary, the message conveyed by the ECA is perceived as significantly more persuasive and reliable (*Persuasiveness* and *Reliability*).

Table 1. Results of t-test with $\alpha=0.01$. Ratings are on a Likert scale from 1 to 5

			Text	Valentina	t value	One-sided p
Information Quality	Satisfaction	avg	3.9	4.1	1.05	0.30
		std.dev	0.66	0.80		
	Helpfulness	avg	3.6	3.9	1.40	0.17
		std.dev	0.81	0.84		
	Easiness	avg	4.0	3.3	2.77	0.008
		std.dev	0.85	0.92		
Perception of the Persuasion Strength	Persuasiveness	avg	3.9	4.4	2.67	0.01
		std.dev	0.89	0.67		
	Reliability	avg	3.5	4.2	2.77	0.008
		std.dev	1.22	0.77		
	Validity	avg	3.9	4.1	1.09	0.28
		std.dev	0.90	0.76		

However, the recalling degree (in terms of proportion of correct answers given by subjects) is higher for participants in the text-based experiment. This is coherent with findings of some previous research [3] which show how the presence of the face may distract participants and consequently lead them to poorer memory for target information. To conclude, we could make the hypothesis that textual messages are more appropriate for simple 'information giving' tasks, while the persuasion part of the message (reflecting the social and emotional intelligence of the reasoner) could be conveyed by an ECA [4] to increase the effectiveness of the persuasion strategy.

References

1. de Rosis, F., Novielli, N., Carofiglio, V., Cavalluzzi, A., De Carolis, B.: User Modeling And Adaptation In Health Promotion Dialogs With An Animated Character. International Journal of Biomedical Informatics, 514–531 (2006)
2. Mazzotta, I., de Rosis, F., Carofiglio, V.: PORTIA: A user-adapted persuasion system in the healthy eating domain. IEEE Intelligent Systems 22(6), 42–51 (2007)
3. Berry, D.C., Butler, L.T., de Rosis, F.: Evaluating a realistic agent in an advice-giving task. International Journal of Human-Computer Studies 63, 304–327 (2005)
4. Georg, G., Cavazza, M., Pelachaud, C.: Visualizing the Importance of Medical Recommendations with Conversational Agents. Intelligent Virtual Agents, 380–393 (2008)

Adapting a Virtual Agent
to Users' Vocabulary and Needs

Ana Cristina Mendes, Rui Prada, and Luísa Coheur

Instituto Superior Técnico, Technical University of Lisbon/INESC-ID
ana.mendes@l2f.inesc-id.pt

1 Introduction

DuARTE Digital is an agent that engages in inquiry-oriented conversations about an art artifact. Since it was build for a Museum, interactions are supposed to be directed to different types of audience: an interaction with an art expert should be carried out in a different way than an interaction with a child; likewise, interactions with users interested in learning should be distinct from interactions with users having only entertainment goals. Being so, an agent needs to undergo two tasks: it must understand the user's knowledge about the topic, and his/her learning goals; it should adapt its vocabulary and dialogue strategy to cope with the user's characteristics and expectations.

This paper presents a simple and straighforward model of interaction that allows a virtual agent to understand its interlocutors based on their vocabulary and to adapt to their expertise and needs.

2 Interaction Model

The model of interaction is described in terms of a two dimensions graph (Fig. 1): the X axis corresponds to the level of the user's expertise on the topic; the Y axis relates with the degree of the interaction's orientation towards a sub-topic.

DuARTE Digital holds a knowledge base (KB) with the possible users' questions and the answers the agent can provide to users. The agent's lexicon is weighted based on its difficulty level and clustered according to sub-topics. Every answer in DuARTE's KB is tagged with: easy, neutral or complex, based on the difficulty level of its compounding words; and, as concise, neutral or detailed, depending on their informative content.

The user's expertise is calculated by: $E_m = E_{(m-1)} + D_q$, where: E_m is the perceived expertise in a moment m given a question q, and $D_{(q)}$ is the difficulty level of the uttered question q. Answers are provided according to (α is a threshold): if $E_{(m)} > \alpha$ the user is an *expert* and give a complex answer; if $E_{(m)} < -\alpha$ the user is *unacquainted* and give an easy answer; otherwise give a neutral answer (X axis). The orientation of an interaction on a moment m towards a topic t is defined as $I_{t(m)}$ and calculated based on the history of questions the user has formulated and their proximity with the sub-topics. Answers are given according to (β is a threshold): if $I_{t(m)} > \beta$ the interaction is *directed*, therefore utter a detailed answer; if $I_{t(m)} < -\beta$ the interaction is *stray*, therefore utter a concise answer and guide the dialogue; otherwise utter a neutral answer (Y axis).

Zs. Ruttkay et al. (Eds.): IVA 2009, LNAI 5773, pp. 529–530, 2009.
© Springer-Verlag Berlin Heidelberg 2009

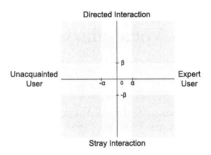

Fig. 1. The interaction model

3   Evaluation

Two experiments were carried out to evaluate the model: *a)* simulated interactions; and, *b)* interactions with human subjects in a controled environment.

Virtual users were created by picking 10 random questions from KB. These questions were presented to DuARTE, emulating real interations. To evaluate the X axis, virtual users were classified according to their expertise (as *expert, neutral* or *unacquainted*). When DuARTE used the model of interaction, in 87% of the questions it gave an answer adequated to the virtual user's expertise (against 53%). To evaluate the Y axis, interactions were classified as being oriented or not. When the model was used, 9 questions were answered by DuARTE that a real user would not need to ask if he would be interested in a particular sub-topic

Human subjects were also manually classified as *expert, neutral* or *unacquainted*, depending on their age, academic background and familiarity with the artifact. After the interaction with the agent, most of the users (11/12) reported having understood every word. We believe this situation occurred because no *complex* answers were given. One user revealed a non-understanding about the words employed: DuARTE classified him as *neutral* (instead of *unacquainted*), suggesting the applicability of a model that differenciates users based on their expertise. Some users did not formulate questions as expected: the manually classified *expert* users did not fully explore the agent's capabilities by employing complex terms. No user was oriented towards a sub-topic; like expected, users did not know what to ask about the artifact. The agent's guidance was here of great use: in nearly 60% of the situations, the user's next question was based on a hint provided by the agent. They found it interesting and useful that the agent provide them with directions. Nearly 88% of the users were satisfied or very satisfied with the interaction, and they get more frustrated when DuARTE provides a wrong answer than when it gives an answer which they might not understand.

Information State Based Multimodal Dialogue Management: Estimating Conversational Engagement from Gaze Information

Yukiko Nakano[1] and Yuji Yamaoka[2]

[1] Dept. of Computer and Information Science, Seikei University, Japan
y.nakano@st.seikei.ac.jp
[2] Dept. of Computer and Information Sciences, Tokyo University of Agriculture
and Technology, Japan

1 Motivation

Thanks to the progress of computer vision technologies and human sensing technologies, human behaviors, such as gaze and head poses, can be accurately measured in real time. Previous studies in multimodal user interfaces and intelligent virtual agents presented many interesting applications by exploiting such sensing technologies [1, 2]. However, little has been studied how to extract communication signals from a huge amount of data, and how to use such data in dialogue management in conversational agents.

On the basis of the motivation above, this paper presents a conversational agent that has the following functionalities;

1. Engagement estimation mechanism that judges whether the user is engaged in the conversation or not by combining the gaze point data and the discourse focus information.
2. Information State based dialogue model that can maintain multiple heterogeneous verbal/nonverbal information in multimodal conversations.
3. Conversation management mechanism that can consider the user's conversational engagement in deciding the agent's next action.

2 Architecture of an Engagement Sensitive Conversational Agent

The system architecture is shown in Fig. 1. First, the Input Controller receives the recognition results from input devices: julius-4.0.2 for Windows speech recognition system and Tobii X-120 eye tracker. It also takes interpretation results from the understanding modules, such as language understanding and conversational engagement estimation.

The Engagement Estimation Module is implemented based on our previous study [3]. This component receives eye-gaze information from an eye tracker, and it judges whether the user is engaged in the conversation according to the gaze movement patterns defined as gaze 3-grams. The results of the judgment are sent to the Input Controller.

Zs. Ruttkay et al. (Eds.): IVA 2009, LNAI 5773, pp. 531–532, 2009.

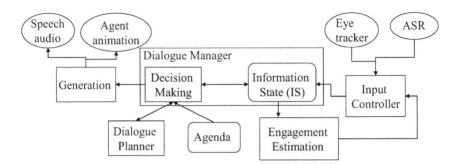

Fig. 1. System architecture

Then, the heterogeneous information coming through the Input Controller is integrated and maintained in the Dialogue Manager implemented based on the idea of Information State (IS) [4, 5]. In addition to the verbal information obtained from the speech input, the Dialogue Manager can process nonverbal information represented as a large amount of numerical data sent from the eye tracking system. To synchronize different kinds of information with different grain sizes, a unique time stamp is assigned to each piece of information. This allows us to access any type of information by specifying the time and the module name. Moreover, the IS configuration is defined in XML format, and the developers can design their own IS by registering the information to be stored and the modules subscribing the information.

The Dialogue Planner determines the agent's next action by referring to the communicative goals in the Agenda as well as the user's engagement status stored in the IS. Finally, the agent's speech and animations are generated in a synchronized way.

We have already built a prototype system of a sales agent in a virtual cell phone shop. The sales agent explains new models of cell phones to a user, and the user can interact with the agent through a speech recognition system. When the system detects the user's disengagement, the agent generates a probe questions like "Would you like to move on to the next cell phone?", and "Do you have any question?" We have already found that the engagement estimation mechanism works well, now we are conducting an evaluation experiment for our fully automatic conversational agent.

References

1. Qvarfordt, P., Zhai, S.: Conversing with the user based on eye-gaze patterns. In: CHI 2005 (2005)
2. Nakano, Y.I., et al.: Towards a Model of Face-to-Face Grounding. In: The 41st Annual Meeting of the Association for Computational Linguistics (ACL 2003), Sapporo, Japan (2003)
3. Ishii, R., Nakano, Y.: Estimating User's Conversational Engagement based on Gaze Behaviors. In: Prendinger, H., Lester, J.C., Ishizuka, M. (eds.) IVA 2008. LNCS (LNAI), vol. 5208, pp. 200–207. Springer, Heidelberg (2008)
4. Matheson, C., Poesio, M., Traum, D.: Modelling Grounding and Discourse Obligations Using Update Rules. In: 1st Annual Meeting of the North American Chapter of the Association for Computational Linguistics, NAACL 2000 (2000)
5. MIDIKI, http://midiki.sourceforge.net/

Synthetic Characters with Personality and Emotion

Ary Fagundes Bressane Neto and Flávio Soares Corrêa da Silva

Laboratory of Interactivity and Digital Entertainment
University of São Paulo
Rua do Matão, 1010, São Paulo, Brazil
{bressane,fcs}@ime.usp.br

1 Introduction

Researchers of systems for Digital Entertainment have resorted to Artificial Intelligence to create characters that are more adaptable to new situations, less predictable, with fast learning capabilities, memory of past situations and a variety of convincing and consistent behaviors.

Recent studies in cognitive psychology and neuroscience analyze the fundamental role of personality and emotions in human cognition, based on the notions of perception, attention, planning, reasoning, learning, memory and decision making. These notions can be characterized as modules in a formal model to describe the personality and emotions of autonomous agents, whose manifestations can be directly dependent upon personality and emotional states. Future research in affective computing must explore how emotions interact with other modules in agent architectures (such as memory and decision making), as well as how emotions influence the interactions with other agents [1].

In this paper we introduce an architecture for the construction of synthetic characters with personality and emotions. This architecture is based on the BDI model, extended with an Affective Module composed by three submodules: Personality, Mood and Emotion, which influences the cognitive activities of perception, memory and decision making of agents.

2 The Architecture

Our architecture has been implemented using Jason [2]. Jason is an open source interpreter of an extension of the agent-oriented programming language AgentSpeak, which in turn is an extension of logic programming for the BDI agent architecture.

We have extended the architecture defined by AgentSpeak to include the Affective Module. The Affective Module is used to influence the other modules, turning the actions of the agent more believable. It is founded on the notions of personality, mood and emotion. Personality is what individuates human beings. It is assumed to be stable, and influential on behavior as well as on the intensity of emotions. In our model we have adopted the model of The Big Five Personality

Zs. Ruttkay et al. (Eds.): IVA 2009, LNAI 5773, pp. 533–534, 2009.

Factors [3], whose focus is on description rather than on the understanding of personality. Mood is a state that results from the cumulative effect of emotions and which strongly influences human cognitive functions [4]. Similarly, in our work we use the model defined by Mehabian [5], which divides mood in pleasure, excitement and dominance. Emotion is a state of immediate effect and short duration. It is activated by events, actions or specific objects, and normally influence manifestations like facial expressions, gestures and voice intonation. The model of emotions that we have adopted in our experiments is the OCC model [6].

The influence of personality and emotions in cognitive processes in our model is implemented as relations between these factors and three functions: selection of events of interest, selection of plans and beliefs and selection of intentions.

3   Proof of Concept

In order to evaluate the architecture, we are working on two proofs of concept. The first one is the construction of an agent for the computer game Robocode [7], which is a battle simulation game. With this proof of concept, it will be possible to observe the behavior of each agent and verify whether the personality, the mood and the emotional states influence the way they get information from the environment and in their adaptative choice of actions and strategies.

The second proof of concept will explore the construction of synthetic characters for virtual environments. In this proof of concept, the user will interact with a character in a controlled virtual environment, as proposed in the JamSession project [8]. It shall be possible to evaluate in detail the evolution of affective states and how they affect the cognitive state of agents.

Acknowledgments. This research has been supported by FAPESP and Microsoft Research, grants 08/53977-3 and 08/08632-8.

References

1. Laird, J.E.: Extending the Soar Cognitive Architecture Frontiers in Artificial Intelligence and Applications, 224–235 (2008)
2. Jason, http://jason.sourceforge.net/
3. McCrae, R.R., Oliver, P.J.: An Introduction to the five-Factor model and its applications. Journal Of Personality, 175–215 (1992)
4. Ekman, P., Davidson, R.J.: On emotion, mood, and related affective constructs. The nature of emotion. Oxford University Press, New York (1994)
5. Mehrabian, A.: Pleasure-arousal-dominance: A general framework for describing and measuring individual differences in Temperament. Current Psychology, 261–292 (1995)
6. Ortony, A., Clore, G.L., Collins, A.: The Cognitive Structure of Emotion. Cambridge University Press, Cambridge (1988)
7. Robocode, http://robocode.sourceforge.net/
8. JamSession, http://lidet.ime.usp.br/JamSession/

Modelling and Implementing Irrational and Subconscious Interpersonal and Intra-personal Processes

Andrew Nicolson

School of Education, University of the West of England, Bristol BS16 1QY, UK
andrew.nicolson@uwe.ac.uk

Keywords: affective computing, artificial conversational entities, cognitive architecture, emotion models, non-player characters, process modeling, psychodynamics, social robotics, transactional analysis, virtual humans.

1 A 'Psychodynamics Engine' for Affective Architectures

Although there is progress in modeling and implementing affective phenomena – computation of emotion – the new direction proposed here is to model and represent irrational and subconscious processes, the hidden aspects of the human psyche as analysed by Freud and his successors, and by other disciplines in psychotherapy.

The outcome will be a 'psychodynamics engine' that does not simply respond emotionally to context and interaction, but is driven by its own convoluted patterns, triggers and processes. This can potentially be used in an affective architecture for games, companioniable robotics, online virtual entities etc., interacting with humans.

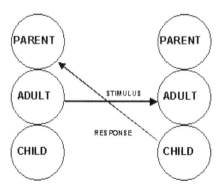

Fig. 1. A crossed transaction in Transactional Analysis. Available ego states *(circles)* of two entities result in characteristic patterns of stereotyped stimulus/response *(arrows)*. From Lapworth, Sills and Fish (1993) Transactional Analysis Counselling. Winslow, Bicester, Oxon.

There are some sub-disciplines of psychotherapy that, regardless of truth-value, can provide well-defined and plausible models of the functioning of the unconscious mind. These may include Eric Berne's Transactional Analysis, Harvey Jackins' Co-counselling theory, Neuro-Linguistic Programming, and even Freud's psychoanalysis.

Zs. Ruttkay et al. (Eds.): IVA 2009, LNAI 5773, pp. 535–536, 2009.

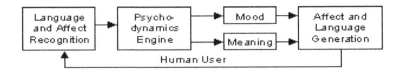

Fig. 2. Skeleton Architecture for deployment of psychodynamics engine in games, robots, etc.

2 Related Work

The unexpected potency of Weizenbaum's ELIZA [1] set a precedent. Tamagotchi toys appear to have personal feelings, and elicit bonding. Breazeal's Kismet robot [2] responds to a person's mood. In The Sims™ 3 game [3], players will "Create realistic Sims with distinctive personalities" (but not, apparently, the power of speech).

Sloman et al. [4] have elaborated the CogAff schema. They challenge the present approach by asserting, "the more human-like robot emotions will emerge, as they do in humans, from the interaction of many mechanisms serving different purposes, not from a particular, dedicated emotion mechanism." Working at DFKI, Gebhard [5] has developed ALMA, a durationally layered model of affect that covers emotion, mood and personality. Similarly, the Dynamic Emotional Representation of Tanguy et al. [6] integrates 3-layered emotional responses in a virtual actor.

Bryson's [7] BOD development methodology for AI, together with her POSH dynamic plans for action selection, offer appropriate development tools, as does ACT-R's cognitive modeling architecture [8].

Acknowledgments. Thanks are due to Dr Rosalind Picard, MIT Media Lab, and Dr Ian Beeson, Bristol Institute of Technology, University of West of England. Their brief remarks at different times inspired the development of this research programme.

References

1. Weizenbaum, J.: ELIZA – A Computer Program for the Study of Natural Language Communication Between Man and Machine. Communications of ACM 9(1), 36–45 (1966)
2. Breazeal, C.: Designing Sociable Robots. MIT Press, MA (2002)
3. Electronic Arts Inc. (2009), http://www.thesims3.com
4. Sloman, A., Chrisley, R., Scheutz, M.: The Architectural Basis of Affective States and Processes. In: Fellous, Arbib (eds.) Who Needs Emotions? OUP, Oxford (2003)
5. Gebhard, P.: ALMA – A Layered Model of Affect. In: Proc. AAMAS 2005, Utrecht (2005)
6. Tanguy, E., Willis, P., Bryson, J.: Emotions as Durative Dynamic State for Action Selection. In: 20th International Joint Conf. on AI, Hyderabad (2007)
7. Bryson, J.: Behavior-Oriented Design of Modular Agent Intelligence. In: Kowalszyk, et al. (eds.) Agent Technologies, Infrastructures & Applications for e-Services. Springer, Heidelberg (2003)
8. Anderson, J., Matessa, M., Lebiere, C.: ACT-R: A theory of higher level cognition and its relation to visual attention. Human Computer Interaction 12(4), 439–462 (1997)

A Method to Detect an Atmosphere of "Involvement, Enjoyment, and/or Excitement" in Multi-user Interaction

Yoshimasa Ohmoto, Takashi Miyake, and Toyoaki Nishida

Kyoto University, Graduate School of Informatics,
Yoshidahonmachi, Sakyo-ku, Kyoto-shi, Kyoto-hu, Japan
{ohmoto@,miyake@ii.ist.,nishida@}i.kyoto-u.ac.jp

Keywords: multi-user interaction, affective interaction, physiological indices.

1   Introduction

In multi-user interaction, Embodied Conversational Agents (ECAs) have to detect mental states of each user to interact smoothly and naturally. In addition, mental states of a person may be affected by extrinsic factors, such as states of people around. Physiological indices was useful to understand mental states of a person. However, it was impractical that ECAs measure physiological indices of users. The purpose of this study was whether we could detect intrinsic "involvement, enjoyment, and/or excitement" ("IEE") of a person and extrinsic "IEE"of an atmosphere, by using visual information. In other words, the purpose is to develop a method to detect an atmosphere of "IEE" in multi-user interaction.

In some researches, a state of a user was detected by a context of a speech, prosodic features, or a direct use of physiological indices (e.g. [1], [2], [3], [4]). It is, however, difficult to implement to an agent which is used in real-world interaction because they constrain conditions of a measuring environment and a users' interaction. In addition, few researches, however, investigated an agent's behavior and/or a way to detect states of users in multi-user interaction. We experimentally investigated not only intrinsic "IEE" of an individual but also extrinsic "IEE" by an atmosphere in multi-user interaction. We used physiological indices for reliable evaluations. In this study, we define "IEE" as "mental states when people are activated by a mood in the interaction, such as involvement, enjoyment, excitement and so on."

2   Experiment and Analyses

We investigated three issues; 1) whether a person's "IEE" could be detected by using visual information, 2) whether the atmosphere of "IEE" could affect members who did not directly involve in the "IEE," 3) whether the affected "IEE" could be detected by using visual information. For the investigation, we

Zs. Ruttkay et al. (Eds.): IVA 2009, LNAI 5773, pp. 537–538, 2009.

conducted an experiment to record responses of participants in "IEE" situation on videos and physiological indices. Four participants formed a group. A total of three pairs, 12 students, participated. The participants asked to answer quizzes by a quiz agent. They answered 30 quizzes.

We analyzed data, which was videos and physiological indices.

First, the average concordance rates between judgements by visual information and ones by physiological indices were 67%. Therefore, people could detect others' "IEE" states by using visual information in some degree. On the other hand, judgements by visual information were non-"IEE" states though judgements by physiological indices were "IEE" states. We expect that the reason is that small "IEE" which it was difficult to detect by visual information could be detected by using physiological indices.

Second, in all the cases, the average concordance rates were highest when the threshold was a most sensitive value. Therefore, we could confirm that small "IEE" which it was difficult to detect by visual information could be detected by using physiological indices. On the other hand, we suggest that the small "IEE" could be detected by using visual information with a small threshold.

Third, the affected "IEE" could be detected by using visual information with a low threshold. Judgements of "IEE" by physiological indices in the scenes were decreasing as the threshold was decreasing; the threshold two minimized the difference of determinations between by visual information and by physiological indices. Therefore, we confirmed that the atmosphere could affect members who do not directly involve in the "IEE."

3   Conclusion

As will be appreciated from the foregoing description, both intrinsic and extrinsic "IEE" could be detected by moving distances and speeds of user's body motions. Each threshold to detect motions was different, the threshold to detect extrinsic "IEE" was lower than that of intrinsic "IEE." We could suggest that one method to detect "IEE" of a person and an atmosphere of "IEE" by using visual information in multi-user interaction.

References

1. Eichner, T., Prendinger, H., André, E., Ishizuka, M.: Attentive presentation agents. In: Pelachaud, C., Martin, J.-C., André, E., Chollet, G., Karpouzis, K., Pelé, D. (eds.) IVA 2007. LNCS (LNAI), vol. 4722, pp. 283–295. Springer, Heidelberg (2007)
2. Gebhard, P., Kipp, K.H.: Are computer-generated emotions and moods plausible to humans? In: Gratch, J., Young, M., Aylett, R.S., Ballin, D., Olivier, P. (eds.) IVA 2006. LNCS (LNAI), vol. 4133, pp. 343–356. Springer, Heidelberg (2006)
3. Mandryk, R.L., Inkpen, K.M.: Physiological Indicators for the Evaluation of Co-located Collaborative Play. In: Proceedings of the 2004 ACM conference on Computer supported cooperative work, pp. 102–111 (2004)
4. Prendinger, H., Ishizuka, M.: The empathic companion: a character-based interface that addresses users' affective states. Applied Artificial Intelligence 19(3/4), 267–285 (2005)

Want to Know How to Play the Game? Ask the ORACLE!

Paola Rizzo[1], Michael Kriegel[2], Rui Figueiredo[3], MeiYii Lim[2], and Ruth Aylett[2]

[1] Interagens s.r.l., c/o ITech, Via G. Peroni 444, 00133 Rome, Italy
p.rizzo@interagens.com
[2] Heriot-Watt University, Riccarton, Edinburgh, EH144AS, UK
{michael,myl,ruth}@macs.hw.ac.uk
[3] INESC-ID, Av. Prof. Dr. Cavaco Silva, 2780-990 Porto Salvo, Portugal
rui.figueiredo@gaips.inesc-id.pt

Keywords: Agents in games, applications of virtual agents, architectures for virtual agents.

1 The ORACLE Agent

This paper describes the ORACLE, an embodied intelligent virtual agent designed and built for helping players of a serious game named ORIENT [1]. The game challenges players at the socio-cultural level, because it requires them to learn how to interact smoothly with alien characters in order to save their planet. The ORACLE is a virtual agent on a mobile phone, whose goal is to enhance the users' learning in the game. The agent can both react to the players' questions, and proactively intervene for suggesting things to users or for commenting on their performance.

The players can interact with the ORACLE by pressing at any time the "Help!" button on the user interface: the ORACLE analyzes the game situation and displays on the phone a set of disambiguation questions; when the user selects one of them, the ORACLE plays a predefined answer corresponding to that question. The ORACLE can also proactively intervene in specific situations: in such cases, the phone rings for attracting the user's attention, and then the ORACLE talks (see demo video[1]).

The ORACLE mind mainly consists of a production system containing "reactive" rules, that fire when the user presses the "Help!" button, and "proactive" rules, that fire according to the occurrence of specific events in ORIENT. The ORACLE body consists in a 2D Adobe Flash™ character animated in real time by a patent-pending software developed by Interagens. The ORACLE architecture is made up of a Java socket server that connects ORIENT, Drools[2], a forward-chaining production system, and the Flash client, installed on a phone that supports socket connections.

A preliminary evaluation of a Wizard-of-Oz version of the ORACLE has been carried out in Germany, based on 10 subjects filling 14 Likert-scale questions and providing a written comment. The results were quite promising: users liked the ORACLE

---

[1] http://www.macs.hw.ac.uk/EcircusWeb/Videos/oracle.avi
[2] http://www.jboss.org/drools/

Zs. Ruttkay et al. (Eds.): IVA 2009, LNAI 5773, pp. 539–540, 2009.
© Springer-Verlag Berlin Heidelberg 2009

design, voice and clarity, although they found it a bit distracting; 7 out of 9 comments showed that the subjects found the ORACLE quite helpful. We now aim at evaluating the autonomous version of the ORACLE with users.

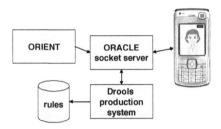

Fig. 1. The ORACLE software architecture

2   Related Work

An "intercultural game" similar to ORIENT is [2], but here the virtual assistant's role is confined to help trainees practice a foreign language. Conati (e.g. [3]) applies a probabilistic learner model to control a pedagogical agent in a computer game that teaches number factorization: here the agent only relies on the probabilistic learner model for guessing what the student needs, while in our work disambiguation questions are deemed useful in providing more relevant interventions.

Acknowledgments

This work was partially supported by European Community (EC) through its funding for the eCIRCUS project IST-4-027656-STP with university partners Heriot-Watt, Hertfordshire, Sunderland, Warwick, Bamberg, Augsburg, Wuerzburg plus INESC-ID and Interagens. The authors are solely responsible for the content of this publication. It does not represent the opinion of the EC, and the EC is not responsible for any use that might be made of data appearing therein.

References

1. Aylett, R., Lim, M., Kriegel, M., Leichtenstern, K., Rizzo, P.: ORIENT: interactive agents for stage-based role-play. In: AAMAS 2009, Budapest, Hungary (2009)
2. Johnson, W.L., Wang, N., Wu, S.: Experience with serious games for learning foreign languages and cultures. In: Proceedings of the SimTecT Conference, Australia (2007)
3. Conati, C., Maclaren, H.: Empirically Building and Evaluating a Probabilistic Model of User Affect. User Modeling and User-Adapted Interaction (to appear)

Varying Personality in Spoken Dialogue with a Virtual Human*

Michael Rushforth, Sudeep Gandhe, Ron Artstein,
Antonio Roque, Sarrah Ali, Nicolle Whitman, and David Traum

Institute for Creative Technologies
13274 Fiji way, Marina Del Rey, CA 90292
lastname@ict.usc.edu

This poster reports the results of two experiments to test a personality framework for virtual characters. We use the Tactical Questioning dialogue system architecture (TACQ) [1] as a testbed for this effort. Characters built using the TACQ architecture can be used by trainees to practice their questioning skills by engaging in a role-play with a virtual human. The architecture supports advanced behavior in a questioning setting, including deceptive behavior, simple negotiations about whether to answer, tracking subdialogues for offers/threats, grounding behavior, and maintenance of the affective state of the virtual human. Trainees can use different questioning tactics in their sessions. In order for the questioning training to be effective, trainees should have experience of interacting with virtual humans with different personalities, who react in different ways to the same questioning tactics.

We extend the existing architecture by allowing the domain designer to author different personalities for the same character. To model the personality, we use the well known five factor model, where each factor can be further decomposed into 6 facets [2]. Here, we choose to model facets that are relevant for a tactical questioning dialogue character. The personality model is implemented by manipulating two aspects of the dialogue manager, the affect model and subdialogue networks used for responses. The **affect model** governs the choice of whether to be compliant with the questioner. It is composed of several affective variables that are updated when relevant dialogue moves are made. We model some aspects of personality as changes to these updates. For example, the facet of *Vulnerability (Neuroticism)* is modeled as the factor by which the social bonding variable decreases for face-threatening dialogue moves such as insults. The **response generation subdialogue networks** decide the appropriate response for a given dialogue state. For example, the facet of *Honesty (Agreeableness)* is modeled as a 4-category variable, which determines the frequency and conditions under which the virtual human will lie or refuse to answer questions about sensitive information.

In our first experiment, we evaluate whether the trainees can perceive the intended personality of a virtual human through a single interaction. We have

---

* This work was sponsored by the U.S. Army Research, Development, and Engineering Command (RDECOM), and the content does not necessarily reflect the position or the policy of the Government, and no official endorsement should be inferred.

Zs. Ruttkay et al. (Eds.): IVA 2009, LNAI 5773, pp. 541–542, 2009.

implemented two personalities that differ in the traits of assertiveness, modesty, honesty, trust, positive emotion, activity, compliance and conscientiousness. 12 participants interacted in text-only modality with a virtual character twice; once with each personality. After each interaction, the participants scored the character's personality facets on a 5-point Likert scale. Results show that our model produced significant results for trust, conscientiousness and compliance; and some trends in the right direction for modesty, honesty and positive emotion. This suggests that our personality model can generate perceptible differences. This does not answer the question of which parameter changes produce differences in which perceived personality facets.

To begin addressing this, our second experiment focuses more narrowly on one of the personality facets that is most salient for tactical questioning, *Assertiveness*. Two different personality conditions were tested, one being more assertive than the other. Each of the 16 participants in the experiment completed two dialogues; one for each personality condition. The interactions used speech and non-verbal interaction with an animated virtual human. After completing each dialogue, the participants filled out a survey, which consisted of a modified version of test items associated with *assertiveness* in the International Personality Item Pool (IPIP) [3]. The scores for the 10-item survey are in the range of 10–50, with a larger number indicating the greater amount of assertiveness. The assertive condition was perceived as more assertive than the nonassertive condition (Assertive: mean 37.4, SD 4.73; Nonassertive: mean 34.7, SD 8.77). The difference between the two conditions was significant on a one-tailed paired (within subjects) t-test ($t(15) = 1.77$, $p = 0.049$).

Subjective feedback from the participants suggested that the non-verbal behavior may have been a confounding factor. In focus more clearly on the role of the textual dialogue aspects, we asked two judges to evaluate the transcripts of these dialogues for assertiveness. The results showed a much larger significant difference with one-tailed t-test (Judge 1: Assertive: mean 36.25, Nonassertive:mean $27.25, t(7) = 2.415, p = 0.023$; Judge 2: Assertive: mean 42.63, Nonassertive: mean 32.38, $t(7) = 4.012$, $p = 0.003$). More detailed descriptions of the personality models and the experiments can be found in [4].Future work will look at incorporating gesture and facial expressiveness as part of the model.

References

1. Gandhe, S., DeVault, D., Roque, A., Martinovski, B., Artstein, R., Leuski, A., Gerten, J., Traum, D.: From domain specification to virtual humans: An integrated approach to authoring tactical questioning characters. In: Interspeech (2008)
2. McCrae, R.R., Costa Jr., P.T.: A five-factor theory of personality. In: Handbook of Personality: Theory and Research, pp. 139–153 (1999)
3. Goldberg, L.R., Johnson, J.A., Eber, H.W., Hogan, R., Ashton, M.C., Cloninger, C.R., Gough, H.G.: The international personality item pool and the future of public-domain personality measures. Journal of Research in Personality 40(1), 84–96 (2006)
4. Rushforth, M., Gandhe, S., Roque, A., Artstein, R., Whitman, N., Ali, S., Traum, D.: Varying personality in spoken dialogue with a virtual human. Technical Report ICT-TR-03-2009, Institute for Creative Technologies (May 2009)

Agent-Assisted Navigation for Virtual Worlds

Fahad Shah, Philip Bell, and Gita Sukthankar

University of Central Florida
sfahad@cs.ucf.edu, ph.bell@knights.ucf.edu, gitars@eecs.ucf.edu

1 Introduction and Background

This paper describes the design and training of an agent that helps users navigate in Second Life (SL), a massively multi-player online game environment.SL allows users to create a virtual avatar and explore areas constructed by other users. With the increasing number of places to visit it is difficult for a user to explore all the places.The built-in keyword search mechanism is fairly limited and users typically find new places through personal exploration or tips from their friends.This motivates the need for a recommendation system that can suggest places to visit, personalized with the user's destination preferences.

In this paper, we present a framework for 1) learning a mapping between users' activities and locations in the virtual world and 2) predicting their future destinations from prior travel patterns. By learning a map of the virtual world, our agent can make recommendations about other locations to visit in the virtual world.This paper builds upon our experience from previous implementation of a similar system [1] to include multi-label learning and explicit user requests.

2 Application

The basic dataflow for our destination prediction application is summarized in Figure 1. We use the Waikato Environment for Knowledge Analysis (Weka) [2] to learn models of the users' activities in Second Life.For multi-label learning and prediction we used MULAN (Multi-label classification) [3], a software extension to Weka that contains several methods for multi-label classification.

3 Results and Conclusion

To evaluate our system, we conducted a small pilot study examining the perceived utility of the navigational agent at assisting users' with searches in the SL virtual world. Additionally we evaluated the classification performance of the supervised learning algorithms used by our navigational agent.

The purpose of user study was to evaluate the performance of the navigational agent by having the agent assist users' with a scavenger hunt task where the users were given a list of objects to find (with and without) using our HUD.The feedback suggested that our agent does not seem to significantly speed the time required to do the scavenger hunt (20 mins) but still users reported a positive user experience while interacting with

Zs. Ruttkay et al. (Eds.): IVA 2009, LNAI 5773, pp. 543–544, 2009.

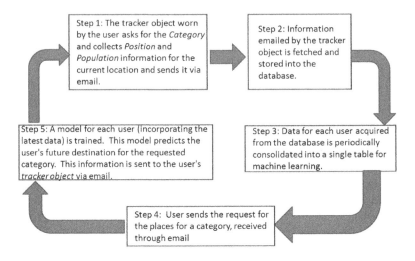

Fig. 1. Application workflow

the agent and said that they liked the idea and plan to use it after the study and also have their friends try it.

The goals of classification performance evaluation task were to: (1) predict the user destination (x, y, z) ; and (2) predict the region for a given category. The results for destination prediction using the M5P and KNN (K=10 here) algorithms give a 0.94 or above correlation coefficient for x,y an z. This shows excellent correlation between predicted and ground-truth values in all dimensions. We evaluated the prediction for region name using Decision Tree, KNN and Bayes Net with similar classification accuracies of around 76%.Since there are thirty six regions in our database, the baseline (chance) performance on this task is only 0.03%. All of the algorithms perform much better than this baseline, confirming our belief that there is significant spatial structure for user-created attractions in Second Life.

Predictions of the user's activity patterns could be used as a basis for creating per-user experiences and user- targeted advertising. Many people use the internet to create a social presence,this presents an opportunity for researchers to collect rich user data from these interactions to create a more personalized and user-friendly experience.

References

1. Shah, F., Bell, P., Sukthankar, G.: Identifying user destinations in virtual worlds. In: Florida Artificial Intelligence Research Society (2009)
2. Weka, http://www.cs.waikato.ac.nz/ml/weka/
3. MULAN, http://sourceforge.net/projects/mulan/

A Real-Time Transfer and Adaptive Learning Approach for Game Agents in a Layered Architecture

Yingying She and Peter Grogono

Department of Computer Science and Software Engineering
Concordia University, Montreal, Quebec, Canada
{yy_she,grogono}@cse.concordia.ca

1 Approach

Game agents(NPCs) should have the ability to react in cooperate, and have the ability to learn from mistakes and build up their own experience. In this paper, we describe a general approach for transfer learning and adaptive mechanism for game agents' real-time planning and learning system in which agents modify their behavior in response to changes of the PCs.

The agents' behavior is processed in a layered architecture as in Figure 1(a). The lower layer focuses on the individual game agents' behavior planning. The upper layer focuses on the team behavior coordinating. The knowledge planned in the planning layer feeds into the learning layer. The planning layer is a redesign PRS(Procedural Reasoning system). Each game agent is modeled as BDI(Belief Desire Intention) agent which can be represented as a tuple of four elements $\{B, D, I, P\}$: *Belief*, *Desire*, *Intention* and *Plan*. The interpreter for each agent exchanges information with these four components, and can be represented as a function $G : B \times D \times I \times P \mapsto I$.

The learning layer extends individual game agent's planning to a multi-agent learning, especially the team cooperation in real-time. Game agents interact with their opponent by observing opponents' action which is the external knowledge B_e sensed by them in real-time. The coordinator for all game agents in the same team revises the planning outcome by processing it in transfer learning and adaptation mechanism. Behavior creation for AI game agents typically involves generating behaviors and then debugging and adapting them through experimentation [1]. For game AI, the use of transfer learning means that less time is spent in the design, coding and debugging in multi-agent behaviors; instead, more time is spent in "teaching" game agents to behave from previous or related experience. In addition, it is not reasonable to provide game agents explicit relation mapping from a source task to a target task as general transfer learning mechanisms do. The adaptive mechanism has to be used in order to optimize the transfer learning process in real-time since the uncertainty of PCs. In detail, the adaptive mechanism defines a number of strategies(production rules) to steer the team of agents' behavior. These strategies treat the team as a whole; and the opponent of the team is the cause of the whole team behavior's change.

We assume there are N game agents in the team. At each learning cycle, the coordinator groups game agents' planning result together as $\prod I_k$ ($k \in [1, N]$). *Experience E* is the training data source which is a combination of a series of successful

Zs. Ruttkay et al. (Eds.): IVA 2009, LNAI 5773, pp. 545–546, 2009.
© Springer-Verlag Berlin Heidelberg 2009

team performance. It is a small database of experienced records which are represented as a tuple of three objects $E_j = \{\gamma_j, B_e, \prod I_k\}$, where j is the record ID of *Experience*. The coordinator updates E when it gets a better experience record than a existing record. The reward value γ is used in the transfer learning which makes effort to maximize the team performance of game agents. The reward function can be described as $R : B \times \prod I_k \mapsto \gamma$. The transfer learning function can be represented as $T : \prod I_k \times B \times \prod E_j \to \prod I'_k$.

As the process in Figure 1(b), the learning layer processes game agent's intention I_k as these steps. **1.** The $\prod I_k$ sent from the planning layer; the $\gamma_{current}$ is calculated. **2.** The $\gamma_{current}$ is compared with γ_j in E_j which has the same B_e. If $\gamma_j > \gamma_{current}$, $\prod I'_k$ is retrieved from E_j, and replaced the current $\prod I_k$. Else, the current $\prod I_k$ is assigned to $\prod I'_k$. **3.** The $\prod I'_k$ is revised based on team strategies. Some game agents' I'_k might have to change in order to match the whole team behavior. **4.** If the second revised process requires change in the $\prod I'_k$, related intentions is retrieved from knowledge modules and replace the existing I_k. **5.** The second revised $\prod I''_k$ is output from the learning layer.

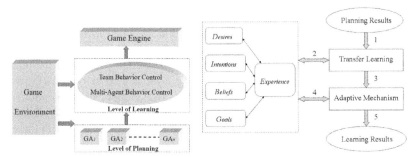

(a) The Multi-layer Agent Architecture   (b) The Transfer and Adaptive Learning

Fig. 1. The Agent's Planning and Learning Process

2   Conclusion

We have presented an approach of transfer and adaptive learning for game agents in a multilayer architecture. Intelligent game agents can efficient reason based on different PCs in dynamic game environment by using this approach. Our test showed that game agents' capability to improve their performance when they face unpredictable PCs. Furthermore, we plan to refine the transfer learning for complicated learning tasks.

Reference

1. Ontanon, S., Ram, A.: Adaptive computer games: Easing the authorial burden. In: AI Game Programming Wisdom 4, Course Technology Cengage Learning, pp. 617–631 (2008)

Intelligent Tutoring Games with Agent Modeling

D.W.F. van Krevelen*

Section Systems Engineering — Faculty of Technology, Policy and Management
Delft University of Technology, Jaffalaan 5, 2628 BX Delft, The Netherlands
d.w.f.vankrevelen@tudelft.nl
www.tudelft.nl/dwfvankrevelen

Abstract. Business strategy educators increasingly rely on simulation games to provide students with experience in strategic decision making. Business games however often limit interaction to operational decision making so discovering the value of alternative strategies in different situations may take a lot of time. Furthermore, to ensure students can grasp the system complexity at this operational level, game scenarios remain relatively simple. We hypothesize that business game effectiveness for strategy education can increase if players instead create teams of delegate agents to appropriately handle operations in more complex settings. To test this we are working on an intelligent learning environment that will help players create successful teams of agents to handle operations.

Introduction. In the web-based *Distributor Game*[1] students play wholesalers and explore various inventory and trade strategies in a highly competitive multi-player simulation [1]. These sessions however are time consuming and focus much on the operational level of supply chain management. Yet custom agents could much more quickly handle operations and show the effects of various procurement or bidding strategies. Creating successful agents still requires students to know the domain but potentially reduces the feedback and learning times. In addition the agents will carry out their strategy transparently and consistently, so the validity of an agent's success or failure due to the player's choice of strategy may be even higher than if students perform operations manually as well.

Agent Modeling Approaches. We aim to investigate whether users learn about various business strategies more effectively if they design delegate agent teams that manage operations transparently, consistently and intelligently. To test this hypothesis we are developing an intelligent tutoring game based on the Distributor Game that supports players as they model a successful team of agents to handle infrastructure logistics. In earlier work [2] we suggest four agent modeling approaches from literature with increasing difficulty for the player: (a) select predefined behaviors as in the Trading Agent Competition [3], (b) imitate behavior enacted by the player [4], (c) shape behavior as it evolves to optimize user-defined rewards [5] and (d) visually programming the behavior directly [6].

---

* This research is funded in part by the Next Generation Infrastructures Foundation and in part by the Delft University of Technology.
[1] http://www.gscg.org/

Zs. Ruttkay et al. (Eds.): IVA 2009, LNAI 5773, pp. 547–548, 2009.
© Springer-Verlag Berlin Heidelberg 2009

Intelligent Tutoring Games. If players want to quickly master any of these agent modeling approaches and focus on the domain itself, some intelligent tutoring may be useful. We will therefore also look at relevant techniques used in intelligent tutoring systems [7]. Still, our approach is quite different from recent intelligent tutoring games used for instance to teach programming concepts [8] or robot control skills [9] since we focus on agent team strategy. More related are the *teachable agents* used in Betty's Brain [10] where players teach, query and quiz an agent based on a concept map. Rather than concept maps however, in our agent modeling game players will evaluate autonomous agent behavior in simulations of complex multi-actor systems such as infrastructures and markets.

Conclusion. Using an intelligent business simulation game, we intend to show that intelligent tutoring games can support strategy education more effectively if students learn to design delegate agent teams to handle operations for them. In future work we hope to compare the effect of various agent modeling techniques on student performance in learning about business and logistics strategy.

References

1. Van Houten, S.P.A., Verbraeck, A., Boyson, S., Corsi, T.: Training for today's supply chains: An introduction to the Distributor Game. In: Kuhl, M., Steiger, N., Armstrong, F., Joines, J. (eds.) WSC 2005: Proc. 37th Winter Simulation Conference, Orlando, FL, USA, December 4-7, pp. 2338–2345. IEEE Press, Los Alamitos (2005)
2. Van Krevelen, D.W.F.: Intelligent agent modeling as serious game. In: Dignum, F., Bradshaw, J., Silverman, B., van Doesburg, W. (eds.) AGS 2009: Proc. AAMAS 2009 Workshop on Agents for Games and Simulations, Budapest, Hungary, May 10. LNCS. Springer, Heidelberg (Forthcoming, 2009)
3. Sadeh, N., Arunachalam, R., Eriksson, J., Finne, N., Janson, S.: TAC-2003: A supply-chain trading competition. AI Magazine 24(1), 92–94 (2003)
4. Priesterjahn, S.: Online imitation and adaptation in modern computer games. PhD thesis, University of Paderborn, Paderborn, Germany (March 11, 2008)
5. Stanley, K.O., Bryant, B.D., Miikkulainen, R.P.: Real-time neuro-evolution in the NERO video game. IEEE Trans. Evolutionary Computation 9(6), 653–668 (2005)
6. Roque, R.V.: OpenBlocks: An extendable framework for graphical block programming systems. Master's thesis, MIT Dept. of Electrical Engineering and Computer Science, Cambridge, MA, USA (May 2007)
7. Wenger, E.: Artificial intelligence and tutoring systems: Computational and cognitive approaches to the communication of knowledge. Morgan Kaufmann Publishers Inc., San Francisco (1987)
8. Gómez-Martín, M.A., Gómez-Martín, P.P., González-Calero, P.A.: Game-driven intelligent tutoring systems. In: Rauterberg, M. (ed.) ICEC 2004. LNCS, vol. 3166, pp. 108–113. Springer, Heidelberg (2004)
9. Craighead, J.: Distributed, game-based, intelligent tutoring systems—the next step in computer based training? In: Smari, W.W., McQuay, W.K. (eds.) CTS 2008: Int'l Sym. on Collaborative Technologies and Systems, Irvine, CA, USA, May 19-23, pp. 247–256. IEEE Press, Los Alamitos (2008)
10. Leelawong, K., Biswas, G.: Designing learning by teaching agents: The Betty's Brain system. Int. J. of Artificial Intelligence in Education 18(3), 181–208 (2008)

The Impact of Different Embodied Agent-Feedback on Users´ Behavior

Astrid von der Pütten[1], Christian Reipen[1], Antje Wiedmann[1],
Stefan Kopp[2], and Nicole C. Krämer[1]

[1] University Duisburg-Essen, Forsthausweg 2, 47057 Duisburg, Germany
[2] University of Bielefeld, Sociable Agents Group, 33549 Bielefeld, Germany
astrid.von-der-puetten@uni-due.de,
christian.reipen@stud.uni-due.de,
antje.wiedmann@stud.uni-due.de, skopp@techfak.uni-bielefeld.de,
nicole.kraemer@uni-due.de

Abstract. This study investigated whether emotional expressions of an ECA influence the participants´ nonverbal and verbal behavior. 70 participants took part in a small talk (10 min.) situation with the ECA MAX who was presented with two different types of feedback: emotional feedback (EMO), which provided a feedback about the emotional state of MAX (including smiles and compliments) and envelope feedback (ENV), which provided a feedback about the comprehension of the participants´ contributions. In general we found that participants showed frequent behavior known from human-human-communication, such as proactive greetings or waving goodbye. Additionally, with regard to some behaviors, the agent´s behavior had an impact: Participants in EMO significantly gave more compliments and exhibited more phrases of politeness ("Thank you!") than in ENV.

Keywords: evaluation study, nonverbal behavior, emotional feedback, envelope feedback, social effects of ECAs, behavioral data.

That the behavior of ECAs has an impact on humans has been shown in numerous studies, for a review see [1]. However, most evaluation studies concentrate on subjective measurements such as *self-reported acceptance* and *self-reported social effects* or objective measurements like *efficiency* and *performance,* but there is a lack of studies which use *nonverbal behavior* for objective measurements [1]. In the present study (based on [2], for previous results see [3]) we were interested in whether behavior emerges that is usually observed when interacting with fellow humans and whether this behavior is affected by the ECA´s behavior. With regard to the latter aspect our research questions were: What are the effects of different types of feedback on (1) the participant´s nonverbal behavior (smiling and laughing) and (2) the qualitative verbal behavior (e.g. greeting, bidding farewell, etc.)?

The study was conducted with the ECA MAX [4]. MAX can express himself multimodal, and is able to respond to natural language input (via a "Wizard of Oz"

Zs. Ruttkay et al. (Eds.): IVA 2009, LNAI 5773, pp. 549–551, 2009.
© Springer-Verlag Berlin Heidelberg 2009

procedure [5]). To test our research questions, we tested versions of MAX with and without envelope feedback (including vocal backchannels (e.g "Ja" (yes), "mhm") and nonverbal signals (head tilt, nod, frown)), as well as with and without emotional feedback (MAX consistently showed a smile in the beginning and the end of the conversation and gave a compliment ("Your clothes are cool!")). As independent variables we thus varied the existence of emotional and envelope feedback in a 2 x 2 between subjects design. As dependent variables we (1) counted the number of smiles and laughs, did a qualitative analysis of the conversations with regard to (2) politeness, (3) how leave-taking was processed, (4) whether or not the participants proactively began the conversation and (5) what kind of conversation style the participant chose. Seventy persons, ranging from 17 to 48 years age (m=24.09; sd=5.717), participated in the study. Participants on average laughed 8.76 times (sd=7.696), the of smiling were on average 15.44 (sd=7.600). 54% of the participants said "Thanks" and 26% said "You're welcome" to MAX at least once and 59% made or returned a compliment to MAX. By means of a MANOVA we identified a main effect for emotional feedback: Participants who had experienced emotional feedback were more polite and significantly thanked MAX more ($F(1;69)= 15.523$; p= .000; partial eta^2= .190; mean values: EMO= 1.374 (sd=1,060), ENV= 0.861 (sd=1,046)) and more often made or returned a compliment to him ($F(1;69)= 9,580$; p= .003; partial eta2= .127; mean values: EMO= 1.317 (sd=1,207), ENV= 0.861 (sd=1,094)). 24.3% said good bye to MAX, in addition to this 15.7% waved to MAX. Most of the participants (63%) behaved proactively (greet MAX first and/or asked him a question), whereas 27% waited for MAX to speak up first. After the greeting phase 60% chose to chat with MAX, whereas 21.4% instructed Max to give an explanation. The rest did not make a choice and quietly waited for what would happen next.

We found that participants displayed several behaviors that are common in face-to-face interactions among humans. The combination of human-like appearance and non-verbal behavior of MAX seems to have an affordance character: two third of the participants started the conversation with MAX proactively by greeting him. Participants chose to have a chat with MAX rather than getting an explanation about specific topics. With regard to the different kinds of feedback we demonstrated that participants in EMO significantly gave more compliments and thanked the agent more often than participants in ENV. These results tie in nicely with previous results for emotional feedback (participants experienced more feelings of interest [3]) and supports the assumption that emotional feedback leads to larger social effects in the user. In conclusion, we demonstrated that objective measurements like observing participants´ nonverbal behavior or analyzing qualitative verbal behavior can give some new insights into ECA evaluation and provide more evidence for validity and reliability of subjective measures.

References

1. Krämer, N.C.: Soziale Wirkungen virtueller Helfer: Gestaltung und Evaluation von Mensch-Computer-Interaktion. Kohlhammer, Stuttgart (2008)
2. Cassell, J., Thórisson, K.R.: The Power of a Nod and a Glance: Envelope vs. Emotional Feedback. In: Animated Conversational Agents. Applied Artificial Intelligence 13, pp. 519–538 (1999)

3. Von der Pütten, A., Reipen, C., Wiedmann, A., Kopp, S., Krämer, N.C.: Comparing emotional vs. envelope feedback for ECAs. In: Prendinger, H., Lester, J.C., Ishizuka, M. (eds.) IVA 2008. LNCS (LNAI), vol. 5208, pp. 550–551. Springer, Heidelberg (2008)
4. Kopp, S., Gesellensetter, L., Krämer, N.C., Wachsmuth, I.: A conversational agent as museum guide – design and evaluation of a real-world application. In: Panayiotopoulos, T., Gratch, J., Aylett, R.S., Ballin, D., Olivier, P., Rist, T. (eds.) IVA 2005. LNCS (LNAI), vol. 3661, pp. 329–343. Springer, Heidelberg (2005)
5. Dahlbäck, N., Jönsson, A., Ahrenberg, L.: Wizard of Oz studies – why and how. In: Proceedings of the ACM International Workshop on Intelligent User Interfaces (1993)

Web-Based Evaluation of Talking Heads: How Valid Is It?

Benjamin Weiss[1], Christine Kühnel[1], Ina Wechsung[1], Sebastian Möller[1], and Sascha Fagel[2]

[1] Quality & Usability Lab, Dt. Telekom Laboratories, TU Berlin, Germany
Benjamin.Weiss@tu-berlin.de
[2] Institut für Sprache und Kommunikation, TU Berlin, Germany

1 Introduction and Material

Web-based tests are an established method for the evaluation (e.g. [1]). However, the validity of web-experiments has not yet been evaluated for the field of embodied conversation agents (ECAs). In this paper, evaluation results obtained in a non-interactive scenario in our lab [2] are compared to a similar web-based experiment. 3 different talking head components and 2 freely available speech synthesis systems (TTS) are combined. The head components used are the thinking head (TH), MASSY (MS), and a speaker cloning system (CL). The TTS include Mary ('hmm-bits3') and Mbrola ('de2'). We recorded videos of the talking heads speaking sentences related to the smart home domain like: *The following devices can be turned on or off: the TV, the lamps and the fan.'*

2 Procedure

The laboratory experiment consists of two parts, which are separately used as two versions for the web-experiment. In the per-set part a whole set of ten stimuli is presented for every head-voice combination to induce a strong impression of the different conditions. Each set is followed by a questionnaire, assessing overall quality. The per-sentence part consists of single stimuli presented in randomized order. Each stimulus had to be rated concerning speech quality, visual quality, and overall quality. A five point scale was used for quality assessment (from 'very good' to 'very bad'). To achieve a maximum duration of 15 min for each version of the web-experiment CL was excluded in the per-sentence version and the per-set version was reduced to those six sentences rated most similar in the laboratory.

3 Results

For the web-experiment, data from 36 participants (per-set) and 42 participants (per-sentence), and for the laboratory condition, data from 12 participants is analysed. For the overall quality assessed per-set, the ranking of the six

Zs. Ruttkay et al. (Eds.): IVA 2009, LNAI 5773, pp. 552–553, 2009.

Table 1. ANOVA results for overall quality for the variables 'setting' (lab, web) 'head component' (MS, TH), 'voice component' (Mbrola, Mary)

variable	F	p
SETTING	(1,275)=0.26	= .61
VOICE	(1,275)=15.65	< **.001**
HEAD	(2,275)=47.63	< **.001**
SETTING:VOICE	(1,275)=0.85	= .36
SETTING:HEAD	(2,275)=2.41	= .09
VOICE:HEAD	(2,275)=0.84	= .43
SETTING:HEAD:VOICE	(2,275)=0.22	= .80

conditions is similar for both settings (TH>MS>CL, Mary>Mbrola). ANOVA shows no significant difference between web and laboratory setting (cf. Table 1): Posthoc test reveal that the difference between TH and MS is not significant. Due to the exclusion of CL in the per-sentence version, this data is not directly comparable for both settings as it is for the per-set data. Results of the former show similar rankings for the web and laboratory condition (TH>MS, Mary>Mbrola). However, the significant differences are only identical for speech quality. In the per-sentence version of the web-experiment the impact of the head component on overall quality is absent, whereas a significant result for 'voice' on visual quality is found. One might argue that less distinction of the head components concerning overall quality might be more representative, as the participants' setting is more realistic for real applications in the web-based than in the laboratory experiment. However, this has yet to be proven. Therefore, the validity of the web-experiment results is only confirmed for the per-set version.

4 Conclusion

The results presented here show that a short web-experiment is in principle suitable to replace laboratory tests for a non-interactive evaluation concerning overall quality of talking heads. This is encouraging for further usage of the per-set methodology for talking head quality assessment in short interactions to also test conversational aspects.

References

1. Koda, T., Ishida, T.: Cross-cultural study of avatar expression interpretation. In: International Symposium on Applications and the Internet, SAINT 2006 (2006)
2. Kühnel, C., Weiss, B., Wechsung, I., Fagel, S., Möller, S.: Evaluating talking heads for smart home systems. In: Proc. International Conference on Multimodal Interfaces (ICMI) (2008)

Gérard

Interacting with Users of French Sign Language

Charly Awad, Kyle Duarte, and Thibaut Le Naour

Université de Bretagne Sud, Laboratoire VALORIA, Bâtiment Yves Coppens,
F-56017 Vannes, France

Abstract. Our aim is to implement a motion capture database for the synthesis of virtual agents signing in French Sign Language (LSF), taking into account the semantic information implicitly contained in language data. The Gérard system is a first iteration along the path toward efficient and convincing animations of an LSF signer.

1 Introduction

Designing virtual humans that use signed languages has been a challenge for the virtual agent animation community. Our Gérard system embodies the easy and efficient generation of French Sign Language sequences from a database of annotated motion-capture signs, utilizing advances in the field of computational linguistics to bring virtual accessibility to a Deaf audience.

2 Data Storage, Indexing, and Query

Gérard's supporting architecture sits at the crossroads of computer science and linguistics by considering both annotated semantic data and raw motion data during sequence synthesis. Sign-component access is optimized by multiple indexation patterns, following both the semantic structures of the stored signs, as well as the spatial and kinematic features of the motion-capture data. These storage and retrieval approaches allow simultaneously for increased dynamics in composed sign sequences, and for more efficient data processing times.

In order to prepare for the animation process, previously captured motion data is manually annotated per French Sign Language signs. These annotations are stored in XML files in one database in the Gérard system; a second database stores the raw motion data[1]. On recall, the semantic database is queried for signs or sign streams to enter the concatenation process, followed by their corresponding streams of motion capture data. Concatenation seams are interpolated across the signs' transitions, and the resulting motion stream is fed to the renderer.

---

[1] Both databases run Oracle Berkeley Database, [1].

Zs. Ruttkay et al. (Eds.): IVA 2009, LNAI 5773, pp. 554–555, 2009.

3   Language (i.e., Motion) Synthesis

The render engine, inspired by the GPUMesh library [2], efficiently and flexibly uses vertex buffer streams during the rendering process. Model animation is achieved with Gérard's skeletal structure being computed on the CPU, while skinning calculations are deported to a vertex shader on the GPU, a technique that improves the performances of both processes. For our application, bump mapping and shadow mapping techniques were carried out on the GPU, to render light and shadow, respectively.

Where other animation engines require extensive computational investment to produce choppy language segments, the Gérard engine manipulates language data with ease, producing convincing French Sign Language conversations quickly. The system's unique database structure considers the equal importance of computational and linguistic concerns for sign language generation, and gracefully achieves a product currently unrivaled in its field.

4   Conclusion

In application, we expect Gérard to provide accessible services to the Deaf regarding weather, train, and other announcements, as well as aide in teaching new signers the vocabulary and grammar of a rich language through interactive dialogues.

Preliminary qualitative assessments of Gérard's signing skills have been positive: users of French Sign Language have been able to understand Gérard during a synthesized LSF stream, an important early achievement. Quantitatively, the Gérard engine performs animations in impressive time, but our continued goal is real-time interaction with human agents. Gérard will thus have to become even more efficient to attain this strict standard.

References

1. Oracle Corporation: Oracle berkeley db,
   http://www.oracle.com/database/berkeley-db
2. Lefebvre, S.: Gpumesh library,
   http://www-evasion.imag.fr/Members/Sylvain.Lefebvre/GPUmesh/

Method for Custom Facial Animation and Lip-Sync in an Unsupported Environment, Second Life™

Eric Chance and Jacki Morie

USC Institute for Creative Technologies, 13274 Fiji Way,
Los Angeles, California, USA 90292
{chance,morie}@ict.usc.edu

Abstract. The virtual world of Second Life™ does not offer support for complex facial animations, such as those needed for an intelligent virtual agent to lip sync to audio clips. However, it is possible to access a limited range of default facial animations through the native scripting language, LSL. Our solution to produce lip sync in this environment is to rapidly trigger and stop these default animations in custom sequences to produce the illusion that the intelligent virtual agent is speaking the phrases being heard.

Keywords: lip-sync, Second Life™, virtual world.

1 Introduction

Our current project is an intelligent virtual agent that identifies and greets users, and instructs them how to interact with a game-like environment constructed in the virtual world of Second Life™ (SL). Our intelligent agent can easily print text to screen, but we decided that we could offer greater immersion if we could make the intelligent agent's avatar lip-sync to voice recordings that conveyed strong affective content. This is a problem because SL does not offer support for lip-sync. While SL does allow for many custom avatar animations (in bvh format), the hands and the face of the avatar, specifically, do not allow for customized animations. The user can access a limited range of about 18 default facial animations such as "surprised," "afraid," and "kiss," but there is no supported way to do complex facial animations, such as those needed for lip-sync.

SL has implemented some experimental architecture to accommodate a basic "mouth-flap" animation that moves the avatar's mouth open and closed if a user is streaming sound (voice) through their microphone. The agent could use this feature and stream our recorded audio phrases through the mic channel, but this has disadvantages. It requires the user to have voice enabled in their client program, and the simplistic result does not provide any emotional range, nor does it attempt to match appropriate mouth movements to the rhythm of the speech.

2 Solution

Our solution is to trigger the default facial animations in rapid succession using the native scripting language, LSL. If two facial animations are put together back to back, in

Zs. Ruttkay et al. (Eds.): IVA 2009, LNAI 5773, pp. 556–557, 2009.
© Springer-Verlag Berlin Heidelberg 2009

rapid succession, we can suggest various morphemes or their constituents. For instance, the puckered lips of avatar_express_kiss can lead into avatar_express_open_mouth, to suggest the sound "bo."

Animations in SL all have an assigned priority, and most of the facial animations have the same priority. This means that the facial animations cannot simply be stacked against each other back-to-back because each subsequent animation will not interrupt the previous one. An animation must be triggered, allowed to play for the appropriate duration, and then that animation must be disabled before the next one is immediately triggered.

This does not cause animations to appear excessively choppy. Most animations in SL, have ease-in and ease-out times, and the facial animations appear to be no exception. What this means is that if an animation is interrupted, the avatar will slowly ease back into the default animation, or the next animation that is triggered, rather than snap back in a jarring manner.

2.1 Example Code

```
float w=0.1; //seconds to delay before starting next
animation

llPlaySound( "SoundFile" , 1.0);
llStartAnimation( "express_anger_emote" );
llSleep(w);
llStopAnimation( "express_anger_emote" );
llStartAnimation( "express_repulsed_emote" );
llSleep(w*2);
llStopAnimation( "express_anger_emote");
   //continue until end of audio
```

It is not an elegant solution, but it is far more effective than anything normally possible within the limitations of the platform.

2.2 Other Concerns

Two additional concerns should be considered when using this method: script time dilation (the server dynamically allocates processor time to scripts based on overall simulator performance), and the loading time for each sound. Script time dilation isn't a major concern in most locations, but it could be very minimally improved in certain situations if the value "w" from the example above is altered in response to the value returned by llGetRegionTimeDilation().

The major concern of the two is sound loading time. Most content in SL is streamed to the user, so the sound will play after a brief lag time when the animation sequence is first played. This can be mitigated if the intelligent agent tracks new users and triggers llPreloadSound() for each new user that approaches.

Spectators, a Joy to Watch

Ionut Damian, Kathrin Janowski, and Dominik Sollfrank

Institute of Computer Science, Univeristy of Augsburg,
86135 Augsburg, Germany

1 The Scene

The tennis game that is described in the xml is a double, thus there are four
tennis players on the court. There is a handful of spectators that are really
excited about the game. The spectators have different preferences about the
teams that they favor or are neutral. To vary the mood-states, each spectator
has an euphoria factor that determines how much a change in the mood-state
will affect it. The mood-state of a spectator is shown with expressive facial
expressions and some typical animations. Additionally to the animations and
expressions the mood-state is expressed by speech as well.

The moods that are expressed are
euphoric, happy, slightly happy, neutral, slightly sad, sad and disappointed. The division of these fields
is not uniformly distributed. The neutral field is bigger than others so that
not every score will result in a change
of the mood-state if it is currently
neutral. The fields for the extreme values euphoric and disappointed is quite
small so that even a simple point may
result in a change. Another factor that
results the mood-state is the importance of the scene. The effect of a

Fig. 1. The scene with some spectators

score in a match ball is much higher than a 15-15. From time to time, a spectator will not just look at the ball, but look at a specific player. This results in a
behavior variant in the spectator crowd and thus in a more natural appearance
of the scene. To make the scene more convincing, a referee is integrated that
comments the current score via text-to-speech as you know it from TV.

2 The System

Parsing and simulating events The given XML file offers rich information about
the tennis game. It is split into information about the four players, the ball
and the score. The entries consist of an index and a start and end value. In
the beginning, all the information from the XML file is read into vectors. The
information about the ball is only given by actions and vague positions with

Zs. Ruttkay et al. (Eds.): IVA 2009, LNAI 5773, pp. 558–559, 2009.

height and side. A major part of this work is to interpolate the position values of the ball between the given positions. This interpolation is necessary because otherwise the spectators would not be able to follow the ball.

Inverse kinematics. The gaze behavior of the spectators is done via inverse kinematics. Inverse kinematics is the process of determining the parameters of a jointed flexible object (a kinematic chain) in order to achieve a desired pose. The GameIKComponent, which was developed for the Horde3D GameEngine [1], the so called Cyclic-Coordinate Descent (CCD) method. This method has many advantages, one of them being the ease with which one can extend its range of use beyond simple IK [4]. Another functionality of the GameIKComponent, called IK_Gaze, allows moving the eyes and head of a character. It is based on an adjusted version of the CCD algorithm. The gaze problematic can be viewed as a more specific case of inverse kinematics, and therefor treated in a similar way by manipulating a predefined kinematic chain until the last node of the chain (called end effector) points towards the target, in this case, until the eyes look at the target. The fact that it uses an iterative algorithm with simple loops makes IK_Gaze a reliable, real-time method of animating characters. IK_Gaze gives us a realistic way of porting the human gaze action on virtual characters. Emotions, conversations and other social behaviors become more human-like.

The spectators. As our Tennis Spectator, we chose a cartoon character called Ritchie, of whom an older version has already been used for various projects. The new model uses the Facial Action Coding System (FACS) for facial animation, which was developed by Ekman and Friesen [3]. In FACS, expressions are split into Action Units (AU) which mostly correspond to the movement of a particular face muscle. By recombining these Action Units, complex emotional and conversational signals are created. This method allows for more flexible and predictable animation than blending between basic emotions of the whole face, since all parts are assigned individual deformations. Consequently, possible conflicts between contrary movements (such as a smiling mouth speaking an O) can be avoided by choosing either of them or fine-tuning their respective intensity. An even more important benefit is that new, more specific facial expressions can be easily composed based on parameters. The Ritchie model was created using Autodesk's 3ds Max, with Biped animations for gestures and Morph Targets for the required AUs. These were created consulting mainly the Facial Expression Repertoire [2], which provides video examples for almost all AUs, as well as a library showing how to combine them to produce a wide range of emotional expressions.

References

1. Augsburg University. Horde3D GameEngine (2008),
   http://mm-werkstatt.informatik.uni-augsburg.de/projects/GameEngine/
2. Filmakademie Baden-Wuerttemberg,
   http://research.animationsinstitut.de/
3. Ekman, P., Friesen, W.: Facial Action Coding System: A Technique for the Measurement of Facial Movement (1978)
4. Lander, J.: Oh my god, i inverted kine! (1998)

IVAN – Intelligent Interactive Virtual Agent Narrators

Ivan Gregor, Michael Kipp, and Jan Miksatko

DFKI, Embodied Agents Research Group, Campus D3.2,
66123 Saarbrücken, Germany
{Ivan.Gregor,Michael.Kipp,Jan.Miksatko}@dfki.de

1 Motivation

Multimodal user interfaces are becoming more and more important in human–machine communication. Essential representatives of such interfaces are virtual agents that aim to act like humans in the way they employ gestures, facial expression, posture and prosody to convey their emotions in face-to-face communication. Furthermore, if we employ a presentation team [1] to convey facts, the performance becomes more entertaining for the audience. Distinct characters should have different roles and personality profiles. Moreover if we integrate interaction capabilities for the user, the system becomes more personalized and enjoyable.

The GALA challenge is to provide behaviourally complex, affective commentary on a continuous event in real-time. Two approaches for implementing such a commentary agent are: plan-based and rule-based. An example of a rule-based agent is ERIC [2], developed at DFKI. While ERIC was a monologic system, we integrate two commentators, therefore dialogue planning offers itself as the best strategy.

2 System Description

We employ two virtual agents with varying "roles" that simultaneously comment on a tennis match. Roles can be e.g. "sports reporter" and "former tennis professional". Both agents are furthermore endowed with personality, emotions, have preferences for a particular tennis player or team and individual background knowledge about players and previous matches.

The system consists of several components: simulator, knowledge manager, dialogue planner, virtual character engine (commercial). The simulator reads an ANVIL [3] file and, when started, sends timestamped events via socket to the knowledge manager. To add interactivity, the user can fire a question using buttons on the simulator GUI at any time.

The knowledge manager takes the low-level events (e.g. player A serves) and infers higher level events (e.g. ralley finished, player B is about to win, etc.). These facts are passed to ALMA [4] which maintains the affective state of the agents and to the dialogue planner, implemented in JSHOP [5], to generate context-dependent surface utterances including gesture and facial expressions. For output, XML commands are generated from the plan and sent to the Charamel virtual character engine.

Zs. Ruttkay et al. (Eds.): IVA 2009, LNAI 5773, pp. 560–561, 2009.
© Springer-Verlag Berlin Heidelberg 2009

An example of a plan operator.

```
name: "winning return"
goal: comment_on_ralley
preconditions:
    (Commentator ?A),(FormerPlayer ?B),(WinReturnBy ?P1),
    (LostBy ?P2),(Pref ?A ?P1 pos),(Pref ?B ?P1 pos)
body:
    positiveWinReturn ?A ?P1 ?P2
    positiveCommentOnWinReturn ?B ?P1 ?P2
```

Generated dialogue move:

```
    Commentator: "Beautiful drop by ?P1."
    FormerPlayer: "?P1 completely outfoxed ?P2."
```

The IVAN system is able to automatically generate affective dialogue based on real-time low-level events. The dialogue planner takes speaker roles, personality, emotions, and attitudes into account. It can smoothly integrate pre-defined background knowledge and react to interactive user events (questions). IVAN's output is presented by two embodied agents with speech, gesture and facial expressions.

References

1. André, E., Rist, T., van Mulken, S., Klesen, M., Baldes, S.: The Automated Design of Believable Dialogues for Animated Presentation Teams
2. Strauss, M., Kipp, M.: ERIC: A Generic Rule-based Framework for an Affective Embodied Commentary Agent. In: Proceedings of the 7th International Conference on Autonomous Agents and Multiagent Systems, AAMAS-2007 (2007)
3. Kipp, M.: ANVIL – A Generic Annotation Tool for Multimodal Dialogue. In: Proceedings of the 7th European Conference on Speech Communication and Technology (Eurospeech 2001), Aalborg, pp. 1367–1370 (2001)
4. Gebhard, P.: ALMA – A Layered Model of Affect. In: Proceedings of the Fourth International Joint Conference on Autonomous Agents and Multiagent Systems (AAMAS-2005), Utrecht, pp. 29–36 (2005)
5. JSHOP - Simple Hierarchical Ordered Planner,
   http://www.cs.umd.edu/projects/shop/

CREACTOR – An Authoring Framework for Virtual Actors

Ido A. Iurgel[1], Rogério E. da Silva[1,2], Pedro R. Ribeiro[3], Abel B. Soares[1], and Manuel Filipe dos Santos[1]

[1] DSI (Information Systems Dep.), University of Minho, Guimarães, Portugal
[2] UDESC (Santa Catarina State University), Joinville-SC, Brazil
[3] CCG (Computer Graphics Center), University of Minho, Guimarães, Portugal
idoiurgel@gmail.com, rsilva@joinville.udesc.br,
pedroribeir@gmail.com, abelbarbosasoares@gmail.com,
mfs@dsi.uminho.pt

Abstract. We present ongoing work on *CREACTOR*, a research oriented authoring system for virtual actors. CREACTOR will provide a framework for experimenting with different authoring processes and AI-technologies. The main goal is the creation of virtual actors that can be employed for the development of 3D movies, following the analogy of a real director who can issue a variety of commands to real actors. Here, we present a concept called AI-tweening: employing AI to create in-between behaviors.

Keywords: Virtual Actors, Authoring, Interactive Storytelling, Artificial Intelligence, Virtual Character Animation.

1 Introduction

This work is part of the ongoing VirtualActor-project[1]. The project is devising an authoring framework for interactive, adaptable, situation aware, partly autonomous virtual actors (cf. also [1]). The animator/director shall direct virtual actors by providing them with the text to speak, explaining the dramatic situation (using concepts of an ontology and GUIs for this); the actors will try to infer the appropriate expressions, animations, and the timing (our work is related to [2] and [3], though Perlin focuses on scripting methods and Matheas on maintaining a plot structure). CREACTOR, the authoring framework, is an experimentation platform for exploring different solutions and processes. The actors are implemented as talking heads. CREACTOR focuses on providing a broad number of features and modules that are at first implemented in a shallow way. Future steps shall then identify the most important dependencies and possible enhanced solutions on the level of the modules.

---

[1] VirtualActor is a two years project supported by the Portuguese Foundation for Science and Technology (FCT), reference PTDC/EIA/69236/2006, that has started in summer 2008.

Zs. Ruttkay et al. (Eds.): IVA 2009, LNAI 5773, pp. 562–563, 2009.

2 Example: AI-Tweening

CREACTOR shall enable the author to define the performance at various levels of abstraction, the definitions ranging from abstract commands of a director to specific changes on the level of the body of the virtual actors. The authoring process shall be iterative, because of the necessity of constant visual feedback of the creative work; assisted, because of the manifold alternative steps that the author can take at every moment; and, in a later step, dialogic, in the sense that the system shall be able to urge the author to provide additional information about his intentions, in order to enable the system to complete underspecified animations autonomously.

As an example of our current work, we present here the concept of "AI-tweening", that serves also to illustrate the intended authoring process: CREACTOR assists the author by indicating that the user first needs to define the main plot points, and then to specify the desired behavior of the virtual actors for these plot-points. The system then produces an estimation, based on AI-knowledge, of intermediate behaviors. This is the process of "AI-tweening". For instance, between an angry and a calm behavior, the system inserts a "cool down"-transition. The autonomous generation of "AI-tweens" serves as basis for the author to further enhance the animation. Currently, an initial implementation with conceptual graphs [4] as knowledge representation serves to demonstrate the concepts. In a future step, the system shall be able to actively gather additional required information, asking for instance whether there is a turning point that causes the anger to disappear, or whether it is a gradual fading away.

3 Conclusion

CREACTOR is ongoing work on an authoring platform for virtual actors. It shall facilitate the understanding of and experimentation with the most complex features that are required for employing virtual actors for the creation of 3D movies. Our next steps will encompass a deepening of the concept and implementation of AI-tweening, and implementation of additional experimental authoring concepts to the platform.

References

1. Iurgel, I.A., Marcos, A.F.: Employing Personality-Rich Virtual Persons – New Tools Required. Computers & Graphics 31, 827–836 (2007)
2. Perlin, K.: Building virtual actors who can really act. In: Balet, O., Subsol, G., Torguet, P. (eds.) ICVS 2003. LNCS, vol. 2897, pp. 127–134. Springer, Heidelberg (2003)
3. Mateas, M., Stern, A.: Façade, an Experiment in Building a Fully-realized Interactive Drama. In: Game Developers Conference, San Jose, CA, March 4-8 (2003)
4. Sowa, J.F.: Conceptual Graphs. In: Van Harmelen, F. (ed.) Handbook of Knowledge Representation, pp. 213–237. Elsevier, Amsterdam (2008)

The Multi-modal Rock-Paper-Scissors Game

György Kovács, Csaba Makara, and Attila Fazekas

University of Debrecen
Egyetem tér 1., 4032 Debrecen, Hungary
{gykovacs,csmakara,attila.fazekas}@inf.unideb.hu
http://ipgd.inf.unideb.hu

Abstract. The multi-modal rock-paper-scissors game is an interactive computer game where the opponent of the human player is a virtual agent appearing on the computer screen. The game is similar to the game between humans, the communication takes place by the tools of image and sound processing.

Keywords: Virtual Agents, Multi-modal Human-computer Interfaces.

1 Introduction

The evaluation and testing of interfaces in the field of multi-modal human-computer interaction is a challenging problem, because the efficiency of the interfaces usually cannot be measured in numbers. The prejudice of people make the testing even more difficult, because people usually do not behave regularly if they know that their behaviour will be analysed. However if the interfaces are tested in an environment where the tester people do not think about the situation in which they are - because they concentrate on how to win a game - the results will contain fewer false data. At the University of Debrecen, we are developing information systems using as many modalities of communication as possible to make the testing of individually developed components easier: feeding back the recognized issues to the human player the efficiency of the input components can be measured by analysing the reactions of the human player. Earlier we have developed the multi-modal chess player Turk 2[1] which uses several modalities of human-computer interaction like face detection, gesture recognition and speech recognition. The multi-modal rock-paper-scissors game provides more facial gestures and verbal communication in shorter time then the chess game.

2 The System

The system consists of several individually developed interface components. The facial gestures, hand gestures and the speech of the human player are used as input modalities. The output modalities are the generated hand gesture and generated speech, facial gestures and emotions appearing on the face of the virtual agent.

Zs. Ruttkay et al. (Eds.): IVA 2009, LNAI 5773, pp. 564–565, 2009.

Face analysis. The face plays very important role in human-human communication because the facial expressions can change the meaning of the speech totally. This component localizes the face of the human player and classifies the emotional state in the happy, sad, natural and bored classes. On the implementation level Viola and Jones's classification technique is used which is implemented as part of the OpenCV library.

Hand gesture recognition. The most important part of the application is the recognition of hand gestures. For this purpose an own component is developed. The hand is detected on the frames of the video stream by skin color and the shape of the hand is compared to the shape of the hands in the database.

Speech recognition. Due to the structure of the game complex speech processing is not needed. For the recognition of the 'yes', 'no', 'rock', 'paper' and 'scissors' words the HTK software system is used.

Talking Head. The output channels are grouped together in the first Hungarian talking head expressing emotions (developed at the University of Debrecen) [2]. The input of this component is the output text and emotion of the virtual agent. The speech is generated by the Profivox text-to-speech system. The lips of the virtual agent move according to the generated speech. In the development of this component the aim was the human-like behaviour instead of the photo-realistic visualization. Due to the MPEG4 standard we used in the talking head component, 3D photo realistic head models could also be driven by our system.

3   Summary

We have developed the multi-modal rock-paper-scissors game. Recording the game lots of information can be acquired about the efficiency of the individual components because the system feeds back the recognized emotional state of the human player through the emotion of the virtual agent by mirroring or expressing the opposite emotion.

The system recognizes if human player is sitting in front of the virtual agent and asks the player to play. If the answer is 'yes', the virtual player waits for the human player to move his hands two times rhythmically. The time of the third movements is estimated from the prosody of the movements and the virtual agent shows one of the 'rock', 'paper' or 'scissors' gestures while recognizes the hand gesture of the human player. If the human player is late, the agent utterances he is cheating. The agent states who is the winner and asks for a new game.

References

1. Sajó, L., Kovács, G., Fazekas, A.: An application of Multi-Modal Human-Computer Interaction - The Chess Player Turk. In: Proc. of AQTR 2008, vol. 2, pp. 316–319 (2008)
2. Kovács, G., Ruttkay, Z., Fazekas, A.: Virtual Chess Player with Emotions. In: Proc. of Fourth Hungarian Conference on Computer Graphics and Geometry, pp. 182–188 (2007)

A Gesture Analysis and Modeling Tool for Interactive Embodied Agents

Quan Nguyen and Michael Kipp

DFKI, Saarbrücken, Germany
{quan.nguyen,michael.kipp}@dfki.de

Abstract. In conjunction with Anvil and suitable annotation schemes, *GAnTooL* (A Gesture Annotation And Modeling Tool for Anvil) is a tool to annotate human nonverbal behavior like gestures and poses efficiently with the help of a skeleton. Using intuitive controls the user can quickly mirror the observed speaker's poses. The results can be used to build gesture descriptions and whole lexicons that transfer human behavior to interactive embodied agents. These agents can then be animated realtime with a character animation engine like *EMBR*. *GAnTooL* can also be used to create rough animations for games or movies: an export option in the *Collada* standard allows further editing in standard 3D modeling tools.

1 Introduction and Motivation

Virtual characters are useful in many application fields like computer games, movies or human-computer interaction where it is essential to generate nonverbal behavior (gestures, body poses etc.). An important technique for reproducing human-like gestures is to analyze real human behavior. The underlying motion data can be simple TV videos, manually animated characters or motion capture data. Motion capture data is very precise but requires special equipment and needs to be post-processed manually. Traditional keyframe animation is very time-consuming. Animation/movie studios often use a combination of motion capture and traditional animation, motion capture for providing raw data, then to be refined by human artists. However, the drawback of both techniques is that the data is without meaning (e.g. temporal structure, meaningful shapes). Motion data can also be acquired by manual annotation in a tool like Anvil[1,2]. However, the encoded information is only imprecise approximation of the original movement. For instance, the annotation scheme by [2] classifies movements and positions. The scheme divides gestures into basic movement phases (preparation, hold, stroke, etc.) and encodes the approximate hand position but not the exact position and orientation of the joints and hands.

GAnTooL fuses the advantages of 3D animation software and annotation schemes: On the one hand, it allow to encode poses with the precision of 3D animation tools and, on the other hand, temporal information and semantic meaning can be added, all in a single tool. Thus annotated data contains exact position and orientation of joints and hands and the exact time of the pose. This

Zs. Ruttkay et al. (Eds.): IVA 2009, LNAI 5773, pp. 566–568, 2009.

tool assists the coder by offering easy-to-handle and intuitive skeleton and camera controls, interpolation of gestures and realtime animation of the skeleton. With these data and in conjunction with the *EMBR* character animation engine virtual characters can be naturally animated using procedural animation [3].

2   GAnTooL

With *GAnTooL* (A Gesture Annotation And Modeling Tool for Anvil) the coder is able to directly annotate gestures and poses with the help of a skeleton, in direct comparison with the relevant video frame. The tool implements intuitive controls to allow the user to quickly mirror the original speaker's pose. Various export formats allow to reuse the annotated data in 3D modeling tools or realtime animation engines like *EMBR*.

Skeletal posing: 3D posing is difficult because it necessitates manipulation of multiple joints with multiple degrees of freedom. The two methods of skeleton manipulation are forward kinematics (FK) and inverse kinematics (IK). Pose creation with FK, i.e. rotating single joints, is slow. IK allows the positioning of the end effector (usually the hand) and all joint angles are then computed. Since IK allows much faster posing, it is the method offered in *GAnTooL*. The coder can pose the skeleton by moving the end effector to the desired position. To adjust the final pose the coder can correct the single joints individually using FK. This is important because IK can result in unnatural poses. For IK it is necessary to define kinematic chains which can be done in the running system. By default, both arms are defined as kinematic chains. The underlying skeleton can be freely defined using the standard *Collada*[1] format.

Pose Matching: For every new pose edit, *GAnTooL* takes the current frame from the video and places it as a background image behind the skeleton. This screenshot serves as reference for the to be annotated pose. By marking the shoulders the screenshot will be put in correct position and matched to skeleton size. Therefore the coder can directly copy the pictured pose in the screenshot. To check up on the result of the current pose annotation, our tool provides the Side-View-Window which offers three different adjustable views (different camera position + angle) on the skeleton. The user can also move the scene camera in the main editor window to get a better view of the skeleton.

Animation by Interpolation: Poses between key poses are interpolated automatically, thus the skeleton can be animated. With this animation the coder is able to compare directly, how this movement matches the original motion. If there are differences between the generated gesture and the original movement, the coder can improve the animation by adding new key poses. Thumbnails of the key poses are shown in the edit interface to allow intuitive navigation and editing.

---

[1] https://collada.org

Data Export: The annotated data can be used by many applications because *GAnTooL* can export to two standard formats: *Collada* and *BML* (Behavior Markup Language)[2]. BML is a description language for human nonverbal and verbal behavior. *Collada* is a standard to exchange data between 3D applications, supported by many 3D modeling tools like Maya, 3D Studio MAX or Blender. The animation data of *GAnTooL* can be used to animate own skeletons in these tools or for realtime animation with animation engines like *EMBR*.

References

1. Kipp, M.: Anvil – a Generic Annotation Tool for Multimodal Dialogue. In: Proceedings of Eurospeech, pp. 1367–1370 (2001)
2. Kipp, M., Neff, M., Albrecht, I.: An Annotation Scheme for Conversational Gestures: How to economically capture timing and form. Journal on Language Resources and Evaluation - Special Issue on Multimodal Corpora 41(3-4), 325–339 (2007)
3. Neff, M., Kipp, M., Albrecht, I., Seidel, H.-P.: Gesture Modeling and Animation Based on a Probabilistic Recreation of Speaker Style. ACM Transactions on Graphics 27(1), 1–24 (2008)

---

[2] http://wiki.mindmakers.org/projects:bml:main

Author Index